GEORGINA CAMPBELL'S
Ireland

The Best of Irish Food & Hospitality

Independently Assessed & Personally Selected

Georgina Campbell Guides

Editor: Georgina Campbell
Production Editor: Bob Nixon

Epicure Press, PO Box 6173, Dublin 13, Ireland

website: www.ireland-guide.com
email: info@ireland-guide.com

12th Edition, published autumn 2013.
Updates available from www.ireland-guide.com at all times

Front cover photograph: The Red Door Tea Room, Ballintoy, Co. Antrim
                           Image courtesy of David Wallace

City and county introductions © W.M. Nixon
Design and Artwork by Brian Darling
Printed and bound in Spain
First published 2013 by Georgina Campbell Guides Ltd.

ISBN: 978-1-903164-334

GEORGINA CAMPBELL'S ireland

Editor's Introduction	4
Route Maps / Route Planner	540

ENTRIES: REPUBLIC OF IRELAND

Dublin City	5
County Dublin	73
County Carlow	94
County Cavan	102
County Clare	107
Cork City	128
County Cork	143
County Donegal	197
County Galway	214
County Kerry	252
County Kildare	288
County Kilkenny	299
County Laois	312
County Leitrim	317
County Limerick	323
County Longford	335
County Louth	337
County Mayo	348
County Meath	367
County Monaghan	377
County Offaly	380
County Roscommon	388
County Sligo	393
County Tipperary	404
County Waterford	419
County Westmeath	436
County Wexford	445
County Wicklow	461

ENTRIES: NORTHERN IRELAND

Belfast City	473
County Antrim	487
County Armagh	496
County Down	501
County Fermanagh	521
County Londonderry	527
County Tyrone	537

Editor's Introduction

There has never been a better time to explore Ireland. It's easier and more enjoyable to get around this beautiful country than it ever has been, and it is enhanced by a constantly changing range of experiences to enrich the traveller, whether visitor or resident - while the good value offered makes it accessible to all.

Since its origins in the 1980s, this guide has seen major changes in Irish food and hospitality and that is reflected in the guide itself. Now in a handy, easily used format which will be especially useful when you have no access to a computer or in areas that are out of coverage for access on mobile phones, this new compact edition is intended as a companion to our website. It brings together all of the key strands of food and accommodation that feature on our website, ireland-guide. com, and which aim to lead a varied readership to the best choices that will enhance any journey, holiday, business trip or outing. It includes information on the producers and speciality foods that appear on menus around the country, and highlights some of the places where they may be bought - which should be especially helpful to self catering visitors.

The sheer beauty of the country and its coastline is always reason enough to travel here and a constant source of joy. And that beauty is far from being skin deep. The food produced by our land and sea is among the best in the world and it is heartening to see how producers are emphasising their stewardship of the land and sea, and engaging with consumers about the provenance and sustainability of the foods they provide - something which Bord Bia's "Just Ask!" campaign is encouraging, among others.

Dining trends see foraging, raw foods and a welcome new interest in vegetables (often 'home' grown) showing strongly on leading menus, balanced by 'big meat' experiences in the new wave of grills and BBQ restaurants. There's a focus on 'healthy' meats like wagyu, Piemontese beef and game, especially venison, and free range pork - while fish and seafood are hugely popular when dining out. Highly refined cooking remains a feature in some top restaurants, but good mainstream food reflects the demand for a more relaxed dining experience, with bistro and rustic styles to the fore - along with modern versions of timeless Irish themes.

Old traditions meet new in many cases - a surge of renewed interest in baking has introduced traditions previously untypical of Ireland, for example, especially yeast and sourdough breads. But it has also seen the revival of many old Irish favourites and the proliferation of quaint tea rooms, which is very good news for travellers who would have been hard pushed to get a cup of tea and a bun in many places ten years ago.

Whatever the reason for your outing, we hope this book will lead you to many memorable experiences - enjoy Ireland!

Georgina Campbell.

Georgina Campbell
Editor.

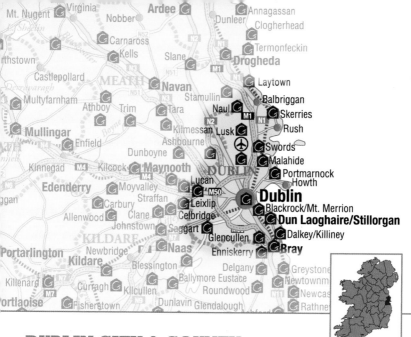

DUBLIN CITY & COUNTY

Dublin - A Town for our Times

Dublin's commercial and creative energy is matched by the vibrancy of its everyday life and hospitality. It's an old town whose many meandering stories have interacted and combined to create today's busy riverside and coastal metropolis. Through a wide variety of circumstances, it has become an entertaining place well suited to the civilised enjoyment of life in the 21st Century.

Located beside a wide bay with some extraordinarily handsome hills and mountains near at hand, the city has long had the dictates of stylish living as an important part of its makeup. From time to time the facade has been maintained through periods of impoverishment, but even in the earliest Mediaeval period this was already a major centre of craftsmanship and innovative shop-keeping.

With so much of it about, most Dubliners wear their city's history lightly in an environment where the past lives with the present in ancient monuments, historic buildings, gracious squares and a fine old urban style that still manages to be gloriously alive. This if anything is emphasised by the city's modern architecture, seen particularly in the area around the Liffey in the former docklands in the International Financial Services Centre north of the river, and across the river around Grand Canal Dock.

Dubliners may seem to take the dynamic interaction of ancient, classic and modern for granted, but then they have to get on with life. They've a vigorous appetite for it. So they'll quickly deflate any visitor's excessive enthusiasm about their city's cultural significance with some throwaway line of Dublin wit, or sweep aside some highfalutin notions about legendary figures of supposed cultural importance by recalling how their grandfathers had the measure of that same character when he was still no more than a pup making a nuisance of himself in the neighbourhood pub.

The origins of the city's name are in keeping with this downbeat approach. From the ancient Irish there came something which derived from a makeshift solution to local inconvenience. Baile Atha Cliath - the official name in recent times - means nothing more exciting than "the townland of the hurdle ford". Ancient Ireland being an open-plan sort of place without towns, the site of the future city was no more than a river crossing between the territories of several comfortable monasteries.

GEORGINA CAMPBELL'S IRELAND

But where the residents saw some inconvenience in the river, the Vikings sensed an opportunity. When they first brought their longships up the River Liffey around 837AD, they knew of a sheltered berth in a place which the locals of the hurdle ford called Dubh Linn - "the black pool". The Vikings settled along Wood Quay and around what is now Dublin Castle, created a massive trading centre - and eventually went native.

The name of the port was to go through mutations as the Vikings were succeeded in management by the Normans, who in turn were in the business of becoming English, and then more Irish than the Irish themselves. Today's name of Dublin is the one the Vikings came upon - though the pre-Viking Irish would have pronounced it as something more like "doo-lin". With the Normans putting manners about the place, the descendants of Vikings and their Irish kinsfolk tended to move north of the Liffey where Oxmantown was Eastmantown – the Danes were the Eastmen, while the Norwegians were the Northmen or Norsemen or Normans, and sometimes all three.

It was confusing for those who wanted to get on with day-to-day life in Dublin, but some sense of it was made with the Liffey divide which still prevails today in Dublin's northside-southside interface, though analysts suggest that it is now becoming more east-west, with the M50 and the exclusivity of Dublin's coastal regions providing a barrier which the Normans knew as The Pale, a name which in itself has survived through various permutations of English power.

As for the great seaport, it is still very much part of the city, and has never been busier. With forty major ship movements every day, sea and city are closely intertwined. However, Dublin Port is becoming a people-oriented transit focus, a giant ferry and cruise-liner port in the midst of residential, hospitality, administrative, business, service, entertainment and cultural centres.

Dublin virtually shunned the heavier side of the Industrial Revolution, or at least took some care to ensure that it happened elsewhere. More recently, the growth of computer-related industries was a very Dublin thing – what better way to deal with the vagaries of the Irish weather than in a workplace which has to be climate-controlled? And in times past, the city's few large enterprises tended to be aimed at personal needs and the consumer market, rather than some aspiration towards heavy industry. Typical of them was Guinness's Brewery, founded in 1759. Today, its work-force may be much slimmed in every sense, but it still creates the black nectar, and if a new mash is under way up at the brewery and the wind is coming damply across Ireland from the west, the aroma of Guinness in the making will be wafted right into the city centre, the moist evocative essence of Anna Livia herself, while the imaginatively renovated Guinness Storehouse - with its interactive museums, restaurants and bars - provides Ireland's premier visitor centre.

Although some of the vitality of the city faded in the periods when the focus of power had been moved elsewhere, today Dublin thrives as one of Europe's more entertaining capitals. While it may be trite to suggest that her history has been a fortuitous preparation for the needs of modern urban life in all its variety of work and relaxation, there is no denying Dublin's remarkable capacity to provide the ideal circumstances for fast-moving people-orientated modern industries. Nevertheless it's a civilised city where the importance of education is a central theme of the strong family ethos, this high level of education making it a place of potent attraction in the age of information technology.

Such a city naturally has much of interest for historians of all kinds, and a vibrant cultural life is available for visitors and Dubliners alike. You can immerse yourself in it all as much or as little as you prefer, for today's Dublin is a city for all times and all tastes, and if you're someone who hopes to enjoy Dublin as we know Dubliners enjoy it, we know you'll find much of value here.

LOCAL ATTRACTIONS & INFORMATION

▶ **Botanic Gardens**
Glasnevin, D9
01 8374388

▶ **Christchurch Cathedral**
Christchurch Place, D8
01 6778099

▶ **Dublinia** (living history)
Christchurch 01 4758137

▶ **Guinness Storehouse**
01 4084800

▶ **National Museum of Ireland**
Collins Barracks 01 6777444

▶ **Jameson Distillery**
Smithfield, Dublin 7
01 8072355

▶ **Kilmainham Gaol**
Kilmainham 01 4535984

DUBLIN 1

101 Talbot Restaurant

100-102 Talbot Street Dublin 1 ☎ *01 874 5011 www.101talbot.ie*

Popular with the theatre set and perfect for a quick feed or group get-together, this modest Talbot Street favourite may be casual, but it delivers with a winning formula of tasty, affordable food, relaxed surroundings and a lively atmosphere. **Seats 80**. *Open L&D, Tue-Sat. Closed Sun & Mon, Christmas. CC.*

Bar Italia

26 Lr. Ormond Quay Dublin 1 ☎ *01 874 1000 www.baritalia.ie*

Centrally located, this café-style branch of Stefano Crescenzi and Davide Izzo's popular Italian chain focuses on authentic recipes, great flavours and value for money. Attentive Italian waiters, colourful, flavoursome food – including Venetian speciality 'ciccetti', a type of Italian tapas – and superb espressos make it a charming choice. **Seats 80** *(outdoors, 12). Food served daily 8am-11pm. Closed 25-26 Dec, 1 Jan. CC.*

Bar Italia IFSC

Custom House Square Lower Mayor Street IFSC Dublin 1 ☎ *01 670 2887 www.baritalia.ie*

Another branch of Stefano Crescenzi and Davide Izzo's popular chain, this no-frills Italian café-style restaurant is renowned for authentic Italian food, superb espressos, extensive wine list and modest prices. Outdoor tables allow customers to survey the comings and goings of Customs House Square while offering an affordable Italian experience. **Seats 100** *(outdoors, 25); Open Mon-Sun, 8am-10pm (from 12 noon Sun). Closed Sun, 24 Dec - 5 Jan. CC.*

Best Western Plus Academy Plaza Hotel

Findlater Place Off O'Connell Street Dublin 1 ☎ *01 878 0666 www.academyplazahotel.ie*

Recently refurbished, this comfortable, well-appointed hotel is conveniently tucked off O'Connell Street. The contemporary bar, guest rooms and suites are finished to a high standard and housekeeping is pristine throughout the hotel. Well-trained hotel staff take pride in the hotel and business guests are especially well catered for. **Rooms 304** *(225 shower only). Closed Dec 23-28. CC.*

Boojum

Millenium Walkway Dublin 1 ☎ *01 872 9499 www.boojummex.com/dublin.html*

If you've had enough of the usual 'tex mex' offering and want a more genuine Mexican experience then look no further than Boojum. This friendly, no-frills cantina-style Mexican serves up tasty custom-built burritos with counter service on Dublin's Millennium Walkway. The modestly priced menu is simple and easy to follow and the sleek decor includes a small collection of tables and chairs outdoors. *Open Mon-Sat, 11.30am-9pm (from 12 Sat). Closed Sun.*

Chapter One Restaurant

18/19 Parnell Square Dublin 1 ☎ *01 873 2266 www.chapteronerestaurant.com*

Set in the arched basement beneath the Irish Writers' Museum this atmospheric restaurant offers one of the country's finest dining experiences, focusing on Irish artisan produce and innovative techniques. Chef-patron Ross Lewis and front of house manager and co-owner Martin Corbett, together with an exceptional team, have earned an enviable reputation for outstanding modern Irish cooking and superb service. The cooking is classic French, lightly tempered by modern influences, and showcasing specialist Irish produce whenever possible. From a leisurely lunch to the rightly renowned pre-theatre menu or an evening of culinary theatre at the Chef's Table, a meal here is always delicious and memorable. *Seats 85*. *L Tue-Fri, D Tue-Sat. Closed L Sat, all Sun & Mon, 2 weeks Christmas, 2 weeks August. CC.*

 **Clarion Hotel Dublin IFSC**

Excise Walk IFSC Dublin 1 ✆ *01 433 8800 www.clariondublincity.com*

A stylish, contemporary hotel with clean lines, Asian food and top-notch facilities. High standards and the central location have proved very popular with leisure guests, as well as business guests and the financial community, especially at weekends. *Rooms 179*. *Kudos Bar & Restaurant: Mon-Fri,12-8. Kudos closed L Sun. CC.*

 Dublin Wine Rooms

1 Burton Hall Mayor Square IFSC Dublin 1 ✆ *01 605 4912 www.dublinwinerooms.com*

Boasting a great location and outdoor seating, this unusual wine bar and deli offers over 300 wines – and, uniquely, the 50+ by the glass are all available to taste before buying. *Deli Mon-Fri 12-5, Restaurant L Mon-Fri, D Sat, Wine Bar D Sat. Closed Sun.*

 **ely bar & brasserie**

CHQ IFSC Dublin 1 ✆ *01 672 0010 www.elywinebar.ie*

Offering almost 100 wines by the glass, top-notch organic food, great coffee and relaxed service this contemporary space is a winner day or night. A younger sister in this small chain of Dublin restaurants, the décor is dashing, and includes a lovely outdoor terrace. The wine list runs to over 500 bottles and there's also a carefully selected beer list. *Seats 350* (outdoors, 120). *Food served Mon-Sat 12-11pm (to 10pm Mon-Wed). Closed Christmas week. CC.*

 Enoteca delle Langhe

Blooms Lane Dublin 1. ✆ *01 888 0834*

A buzzy little shop-cum-winebar in Dublin's 'Italian quarter' specialising in rustic fare. *Seats 50 (+outdoor). Open Mon-Sat all day 12.30-11; closed Sun.*

 EPICUREAN FOOD HALL

Lr Liffey Street Dublin 1 ✆ *01 2836077*

A popular place for international foods, sold at very reasonable prices, the hall is a collective of small units with shared seating - open during the day every day (opens later on Sunday, remains open for late shoppers on Thursday evening); it's an enjoyable place to browse.

 The Gibson Hotel

Point Village Dublin 1 ✆ *01 681 5000 www.gibsonhotel.ie*

Ideally located beside the O2 The Gibson is one of Dublin's newest hotels. Expect hip décor, and plenty of modern touches. There's a Luas stop right outside the door, and the spacious heated terrace and leafy internal courtyard make perfect spots for summer evenings or dining at pan-Asian Coda Eatery. Bedrooms are chic and luxurious and the buffet breakfast is a high point. *Rooms 252. CC.*

The Gresham

23 Upper O'Connell Street Dublin 1 ✆ *01 874 6881 www.gresham-hotels.com*

At the centre of Dublin society since the early nineteenth century, this historic Dublin hotel is constantly busy thanks to a modern makeover, comfortable surrounds, welcoming service and the traditional Toddy's Bar & Brasserie - which is a popular meeting place and one of several dining options.The Writers' Lounge is a favourite for Afternoon Tea. *Rooms 288. D daily 5.30-10pm. Hotel open all year. CC.*

The Hot Stove Restaurant

38/39 Parnell Square West Dublin 1 ✆ *01 874 7778 www.thehotstoverestaurant.com*

Ex-Four Seasons sommelier Simon Keegan and chef Joy Beattie make an impressive team at this bastion of civilised dining on Parnell Square, and their take on modern Irish hospitality is both refreshing and welcome. The great wine list has no tasting notes:diners are encouraged to chat to Simon and take advantage of his encyclopaedic knowledge. Offering quality with value and close to The Gate Theatre, this is the new hot spot for savvy pre-theatregoers. *L Tue-Fri; D Tue-Sat.* **Directions:** *West Parnell Square, opposite car exit from Rotunda Hospital.*

Jurys Custom House Inn

Custom House Quay Dublin 1 ✆ *01 607 5000*

Close to train, Luas and bus stations, this well-located hotel beside the IFSC is a good value business hotel. Large bedrooms have all the expected facilities, but with a higher standard of finish than most of its sister hotels. As well as a large bar, there is a restaurant on site, plus conference facilities and a staffed business centre. *Rooms 239. Closed 24-26 Dec. CC.*

Jurys Inn Parnell Street

Parnell Street Dublin 1 ✆ *01 878 4900 www.jurysinns.com*

A useful addition to the choice of city centre accommodation north of the Liffey, this modern budget hotel offers the value expected of Jurys Inns - no frills (and, specifically, no room service) but rooms are spacious and comfortably furnished. *CC.*

Kimchi Restaurant @ The Hop House

160 Parnell Street Dublin 1 ✆ *01 872 8318 www.hophouse.ie*

One of the most successful of the 'new-Irish' restaurants the authentic Korean and Japanese cooking has earned a loyal ethnic and Irish clientele at this lively restaurant-within-a-bar. Close to theatres, cinemas and music venues, Kimchi makes for a very affordable and tasty pre-show dining option. The Hop House bar, in which the restaurant is contained, has a boisterous beer garden to retire to. *Mon–Thu 12pm–11pm, Sat 12pm–11.30pm, Sun 5pm–10.30.*

Le Bon Crubeen

81-82 Talbot Street Dublin 1 📞 *01 704 0126 www.leboncrubeen.ie*

Generous portions, accomplished cooking and incredible value define the success of this friendly city-centre bistro, close to Connolly Station. The décor may stray into traditional pub territory but the food at Le Bon Crubeen is very much brasserie fare. Portions are generous and an all-afternoon lunch is handy to know about. The daily set dinner menu offers great value, as does Le Jazz Supper late night menu (Sat). **Seats 75** *(outdoors, 12). L&D daily. CC.*

 ## Mitchell & Son

CHQ Building IFSC Dublin 1 📞 *01 612 5540 www.mitchellandson.com*

One of this famous wine retailer's two Dublin outlets (the other is in Terenure). They are responsible for the survival of the unique Green Spot whiskey, which was formerly matured in sherry casks by Irish Distillers.

 ## Mitsuba

154 Parnell Street Dublin 1 📞 *01 814 6888 www.mitsuba.ie*

Great value Japanese restaurant offering authentic sushi, bento boxes, noodle ramen and teppanyaki specials. *L & D Mon-Fri. D Sat & Sun.*

 ## The Morrison Hotel

Lower Ormond Quay Dublin 1 📞 *01 887 2400 www.morrisonhotel.ie*

Following a lengthy closure and complete refurbishment, this quayside boutique hotel recently re-opened and is now operated by Doubletree by Hilton. **Rooms 138.** *Closed 24-27 Dec. CC.*

  ## MV Cill Airne - Blue River Bar & Bistro and Quay 16

Quay 16 North Wall Quay Dublin 1 📞 *01 817 8760 www.mvcillairne.com*

Popular for after work drinks in summer, you can enjoy casual food or fine dining aboard this beautifully restored ship, formerly tender to a 1960s liner, is now docked on the Liffey. The restaurant offers a promising menu, albeit at a premium, while the upstairs bistro is a great location for a drink and a quick bite to eat. Near O2; Grand Canal Theatre 5 min walk over bridge. *Sat & Sun open 3pm subject to local events. Blue River Bistro Bar: food served Mon-Fri 12-10; Quay 16 Restaurant:D Mon-Sat.*

Panem

Ha'penny Bridge House 21 Lower Ormond Quay Dublin 1 📞 *01 872 8510*

A hidden gem on the North Quays, this tiny bakery and café serves some of the best pastries, coffee and Belgian hot chocolate in Dublin. Ann Murphy and Raffaele Cavallo's little bakery has been delighting discerning Dubliners since 1996 and no cost is spared in sourcing the finest ingredients: Panem bread is baked freshly each day using organic flour and they import their own 100% arabica torrisi coffee from Sicily. *Open Mon-Sat, 9-5pm. Closed Sun, 24 Dec-4/5 Jan. No CC.*

Paris Bakery & Pastry

18-19 Moore Street Dublin 1 ✆*01 804 4112; www.parisbakery.ie*

Yannick Forel and his team produce a full range of those wonderful typically French artisan breads and gorgeous pastries here every day - and they also have an extensive deli and speciality food area, wine sales and a restaurant with that pared back French chic that works equally well whether tucking into a (somewhat Frenchified) Full Irish at opening time or salmon en croute for a very reasonably priced dinner. *Mon-Wed 8am-9pm, Thu-Sat 8am-10pm, Sun 10am-9pm.*

 Ristorante Romano

12 Capel Street Dublin 1 ✆*01 872 6868*

An old-fashioned Italian with simple décor, honest cooking, huge portions and old school service. Friendly and generous-spirited, this is a simple cafe-style restaurant that delivers great home cooking with a little extra oomph - and good value wines too. *Open 7 days.*

 Soup Dragon

168 Capel Street Dublin 1 ✆*01 872 3277 www.soupdragon.com*

A stylish way to have a hot meal on a budget, this tiny but charming café offers an imaginative selection of tasty soups and stews homemade daily. Some change daily, while others stay on the menu for a week or a season. Served with complimentary fruit and bread there's also lovely house-baked goodies, fresh juices and good coffee. *Mon-Fri 8-5.30. Closed Sat & Sun. No CC.*

 Terra Madre

13A Bachelor's Walk Dublin 1 ✆*01 873 5300*

The signage is so low key that you may well walk past this bijou basement Italian without noticing it – look out for the two tiny wrought iron tables outside the door for smokers. But once you find it there'll be no forgetting it. A little slice of Italia right on Dublin's quays: simplicity is the key and each ingredient is chosen for its quality and authenticity. *L Tue-Sat. D daily.*

 **The Winding Stair**

40 Lower Ormond Quay Dublin 1 ✆*01 872 7320 www.winding-stair.com*

Cosy, hip and bustling, this little Dublin restaurant beside the Ha'penny Bridge serves lip-smacking modern Irish food with wonderful views over the Liffey. Wooden floorboards, bentwood chairs and simple tables keep it cosy and relaxed and the menu sings with 'the organic and real', from signature dishes to outstanding renditions of classics. Aided by nostalgia, it also has loads of personality and has earned a loyal following. **Seats 60**; L&D served daily. Closed 25/26 Dec, 31 Dec, 1 Jan, Good Friday, 17 Mar. CC.

WJ Kavanagh's

4-5 Dorset Street Dublin 1 ✆ *01 873 0990 www@wjkavanaghs.com*

The smart team behind WJ Kavanagh (see entry) have done it again here, retaining all the best elements of an old fashioned bar - plus a serious menu of comfort food favourites, with craft bewery drinks pairings. Dining mainly takes place up front, where enthusiastic staff nip between bar and kitchen; not all dishes are equal but there's plenty of great cooking taking place, with lovely artisan ingredients. *Mon-Thu 4-11.30, Fri 4-12.30, Sat 4-12.30, Sun 12.30-11pm.*

 Wynns Hotel

35/39 Lower Abbey Street Dublin 1 ✆ *01 874 5131 www.wynnshotel.ie*

Traditionally a country people's hotel in Dublin city centre, this affordable, three-star hotel is just off O'Connell Street, with the Luas stopping outside its door. Recently refurbished, it provides all the modern comforts at a keen price with a lovely, traditional welcome. **Rooms 65**. *Closed 25 Dec. CC.*

DUBLIN 2 - TEMPLE BAR

The hub of the action for many visitors, the area others may wish to avoid. Whatever your feelings for the tourist centre of Dublin, everybody should visit it once during daytime to judge it for themselves. Street performers and buskers ply their trade in and around Temple Bar Square which can be a great place to sit down and enjoy the atmosphere on a sunny day. There are many interesting places to visit, including the Irish Film Centre that hosts ever changing exhibitions and free weekly outdoor cinema screenings at Meeting House Square in the summer The whole area is full of bars and restaurants, and one of Ireland's best Farmers Markets is held here every Saturday (10am-4.30pm).

 777 Restaurant

7 Castle House South Great Georges Street Dublin 2 ✆ *01 425 4052 www.777.ie*

Part Mexican cantina, part New York cool, 777 serves up authentic Mexican cooking alongside a dazzling array of over 80 tequilas and mescals. The rustic south-of-the-border Mexican fare includes tasty dishes prepared on a wood-burning grill. Tables come with a selection of fiery sauces to up the heat and savvy owner John Farrell (proprietor of Dillingers and Butcher Grill in Ranelagh) has created a stylish and cool dining experience, even if it is a little pricy. *L Sat & Sun; D daily.*

 Alexander Hotel

Merrion Square Dublin 2 ✆ *01 607 3700 www.ocallaghanhotels.com*

Close to Merrion Square this busy hotel is well appointed, offering stylish accommodation, professional service and a warm welcome. In contrast to its subdued public face, the interior is strikingly contemporary and colourful, both in public areas and bedrooms, all of which are furnished to a very high standard. Meals are offered at the hotel's Caravaggio's Restaurant and a bar menu at Winners contemporary cocktail bar. **Rooms 102**. *Open all year. CC.*

 **Avoca Café**

11-13 Suffolk St. Dublin 2 ✆ *01 672 6019 www.avoca.ie*

Expect lunchtime queues at this centrally located outpost of the craft shop empire that majors in meticulously sourced ingredients, home cooking and irresistible baked goods – much of which can be bought in the basement in their extensive delicatessen. A favourite daytime dining venue, the restaurant has low-key style and an emphasis on creative, healthy cooking that is common to all the Avoca establishments. **Seats 100**; *all day Mon-Sat 10-5.30 (hot food served until 4.30pm Mon-Fri), 11am-5pm Sun. Reservations accepted. Closed 25/26 December, 1 Jan. CC.*

 The Bailey

1-4 Duke Street Dublin 2 ✆ *01 670 4939*

The famous Victorian pub has a special place in the history of Dublin life – literary, social, political; now styled bar-café, it is favoured as a comfortable spot for lunch or after-work drinks in convivial surrounds. *Coffees and scones 9-11.30; food menu 12-9. Closed 25 Dec & Good Friday.*

 Bang Restaurant

11 Merrion Row Dublin 2 ✆ *01 400 4229 www.bangrestaurant.com*

Situated over three floors, this smart restaurant is classy and sophisticated while still being relaxed and informal. Confident, inventive and seasonal cooking uses the finest Irish produce, all name checked on the menu. The impeccable service and lively atmosphere make Bang an excellent choice for everything from a midweek meal to a special occasion. **Seats 90**. *L Mon-Fri, D Mon-Sat. Closed Sun. CC.*

 Bar Pintxo

12 Eustace Street Temple Bar Dublin 2 ✆ *01 672 8590 www.porthouse.ie*

Younger sister of The Port House on South William Street this friendly tapas wine bar boasts exposed brick walls, sanded wooden floors, an outdoor terrace and racks of wine bottles. Expect simple, well-cooked hearty Iberian tapas served in atmospheric surroundings, with lashings of Spanish and Portuguese wine. **Seats 120** *(outdoors, 30); open daily 11am-11pm. No reservations. Closed 25 Dec. CC.*

 Bear

34-35 South William Street Dublin 2 www.bear.joburger.ie

Bear is a hip steakhouse offering industrial-style décor, low lighting and a no-reservations policy to a trendy clientele. Owned by Joe Macken (of Crackbird, Skinflint and Jo'Burger) and Ireland rugby captain Jamie Heaslip, its main offerings are unusual steak cuts served alongside interesting sides and tasting plates. Service is brisk and friendly with paper napkins and cutlery served in tin cans and homemade lemonade in glass jars. **Seats 80**. *Food 12-9 daily.*

  Bewley's Café

Bewley's Building Grafton St Dublin 2 ✆ *01 672 7720 www.bewleys.com*

Grafton Street's quintessential meeting place since 1840, Bewley's is still well loved for its coffee, scones and bustle; also serves full meals, although menus are surprisingly international

13

for such a venerable Dublin institution. It changed hands amid much public debate in 2005 but, despite renovations, has somehow retained its unique atmosphere together with some outstanding architectural features, notably the Harry Clarke stained glass windows. *Seats 370. Open daily early until late. Closed 25 Dec, Bank Hols. CC.*

 ## Bison Bar

11 Wellington Quay Dublin 2 📞 *086 056 3144 www.bisonbar.ie*

Serving succulent and smoky melt-in-the-mouth meat alongside 150 whiskies and 50 tequilas, this on-trend bar and Texan barbecue is fresh, exciting and fun. With just five cuts of meat and five great sides you can expect delicious no-frills food in a cool and comfy traditional pub environment. And it's fantastic value too. *Mon-Sun 12-9pm.*

 ## Bite

29 South Frederick Street Dublin 2 📞 *01 679 7000 www.bitedublin.com*

An unusual and much-hyped fish and chips and cocktails joint, this funky little venue looks welcoming from the outside and you'll be greeted warmly by charming staff. Offering fish lovers a gourmet twist on traditional fast food favourites, cooking can be inconsistent but ingredients are well sourced and there is some good value to be had. *Seats 100. L&D daily.*

The Blackboard Bistro

4 Clare Street Dublin 2 📞 *01 676 6839*

 Tucked away in a tiny basement near Trinity College, this boho bistro offers simple French dining served with a personal touch. Run by people who take their food, wine and service seriously it's much like a small Parisian neighbourhood restaurant, full of character and chic bistro charm. Short menus of simple rustic cooking are written on the large blackboard and change daily. *L & D Tue–Sat. Closed Sun, Mon, 25-30 Dec. CC.*

  ## Blazing Salads

42 Drury Street Dublin 2 📞 *01 671 9552 www.blazingsalads.com*

The energetic and focused Fitzmaurice family are behind one of Dublin's greatest food success stories - what began as one of the city's first wholefood restaurants, in 1982, is now a thriving deli business. With an enviable reputation for their deliciously healthy creations, this is a place for everyone who loves good food - and especially those who have a food intolerance, or simply prefer to eat 'free-from' foods, including superb breads from Joe Fitzmaurice's organic Cloughjordan Wood-Fired Bakery in Co Tipperary. *Open Mon-Fri 9-6, Sat 9-5.30. Closed Sun.*

Bloom Brasserie

11 Upper Baggot Street Dublin 2 📞 *01 668 7170 www.bloombrasserie.ie*

Pol O hEannraich, former head chef at Dax, runs this basement premises, with the aim of offering 'quality food at reasonable prices' along with a broad choice of wines. Accomplished cooking, modern décor, a great terrace, value menus and a dedicated chef-proprietor make it a crowd-pleaser day or night. **Seats 75**. *L Mon-Fri, D Mon-Sat. Closed Sat L, Sun, bank hols. CC.*

 ## Brasserie Le Pont

25 Fitzwilliam Place Dublin 2 ☎ *01 669 4600 www.brasserielepont.ie*

Everything about Brasserie Le Pont is elegant, polished and chic - and any visit here is sure to be a special treat thanks to the impeccably trained staff. Excellent cooking is informed by French traditions and (sometimes name checked) Irish ingredients, with particular dedication to serving good seafood; signature dishes include Le Pont Dublin Bay prawn cocktail, Le Pont fish pie and Le Pont bouillabaisse, and you may expect great renditions of these classics. *Mon-Fri from 10am (morning tea/coffee/pastries); L from12 noon; D Tue-Sat from 5.30pm. CC.*

 ## Brasserie Sixty6

66-67 South Great Georges Street Dublin 2 ☎ *01 400 5878 www.brasseriesixty6.com*

Aside from a statement chandelier and some unusual artwork, the main decorative theme of this deceptively large restaurant is a wall of mismatched plates, echoing the traditional kitchen dresser; it adds up to a comfortably stylish setting for a place offering something different from the standard fare - food from the rotisserie is the main speciality, also sociable sharing plates - and coeliac friendly food is highlighted. **Seats 180**. *Open all day 12-11.30pm, L 12-5, D 5-11.30. Closed 25-26 Dec, 1 Jan, Good Fri. CC.*

 ## Bridge Bar & Bistro

The Malting Tower Grand Canal Quay Dublin 2 ☎ *01 639 4941 www.bridgebarandgrill.ie*

Close to the Bord Gáis Energy Theatre this intimate, laidback bistro serves up seriously good modern cooking at great prices. Tucked beneath a railway bridge off a cobbled street it's an atmospheric restaurant in a historic setting with outdoor seating. Service is attentive and warm, headed up by the glamorous Martina Fox, while the excellent cooking uses seasonal ingredients in creative ways. **Seats 70** *(outdoors, 20). L Mon - Fri; D Mon-Sat. Closed Sat L, Sun, bank hols, 23 Dec - 5 Jan, Good Fri. CC.*

Brioche ce Soir

65 Aungier Street Dublin 2 ☎ *01 475 8536 www.brioche.ie*

By day it's a jaunty little café with great coffee and attitude; by night it turns into a cheeky bistro affair serving tasting plates, the French equivalent of tapas. The short menu may be limited by the tiny kitchen but this hasn't stymied chef Gavin McDonagh's creativity. A good balance of meat, seafood and vegetarian dishes, plus a few charcuterie offerings, are created and served as they are ready. Rustic and relaxing, Brioche ce Soir is hitting all the right notes. *D Thu-Sat, 6-10.30pm. Cafe Mon-Sat from 7am. Closed Sun. CC.*

 ## Brooks Hotel & Francescas Restaurant

Drury Street Dublin 2 ☎ *01 670 4000 www.brookshotel.ie*

Minutes from Grafton Street this discreetly luxurious hotel offers excellent accommodation, good breakfasts and an oasis of calm in the city centre. The style is a pleasing combination of traditional with contemporary touché and the elegant Francesca's restaurant is especially good. Overseen by head chef Patrick McLarnon, who sources mainly local ingredients with great care, his cooking is imaginative and there's a strong emphasis on fish and seafood. **Rooms 98**. *Restaurant seats 30. D daily. Closed to non-residents 24/25th December. Hotel open all year. CC*

 ## Bull and Castle - Gastro Pub and Beer Hall

5/7 Lord Edward Street Dublin 2 ☎ *01 475 1122 www.bullandcastle.ie*

Popular with tourists this medieval-styled pub and 'beer hall' serves better-than-average pub fare and an outstanding selection of beers, including cask conditioned, Irish micro brews and an interesting international selection. Easily spotted opposite Christchurch cathedral by its colourful facade, there is something for everyone on the wide-ranging menu and service is friendly and informal. **Seats 90** *(outdoors, 20). L&D daily. Closed Good Fri, 25/26 Dec. CC.*

 ## Buswells Hotel

23 Molesworth Street Dublin 2 ☎ *01 614 6500 www.buswells.ie*

A home-from-home for Irish politicians, this row of 18th century townhouses near the Dáil (Irish Parliament) is a traditional hotel of character. Reasonably priced for the area, it has excellent business facilities and a popular bar menu, while the elegant Truman's restaurant offers a pleasing ambience, extensive menus and a good wine list. **Rooms 67** *(7 shower only). Restaurant seats 60. L & D Wed-Sat. Closed 25-26 Dec. CC.*

 ## Butlers Chocolate Café

24 Wicklow Street Dublin 2 ☎ *01 671 0591 www.butlerschocolates.com*

Good coffee, delicious hot chocolate and a complimentary handmade chocolate on the side make Butlers a favourite café. Boxed or personally selected loose chocolates, caramels, fudges and fondants are also available for sale. One of a small chain, with the Butlers Chocolate Experience, Dublin 17, heading up the group. *Open Mon-Fri 8am-7pm, Sat 9am-7pm, Sun 11am-6pm. Closed 25-26 Dec, Easter Sun & Mon.*

 ## Cafe Bar H

Grand Canal Plaza Dublin 2 ☎ *01 899 2216*

Owned by property developer Harry Crosbie, this contemporary tapas bar on Grand Canal Square is close to the Bord Gais Energy Theatre, making it especially lively pre- and post-show. Outdoor tables fill up fast on warmer evenings, musicians provide upbeat evening entertainment and the place really comes to life after the theatre closes; well known chef Johnny Cooke's menu features all the Spanish favourites and an all-European wine list. *Seats 40. Mon-Sat 12-11. Sun (show days only) 4-9.*

 ## Café en Seine

40 Dawson Street Dublin 2 ☎ *01 677 4567 www.cafeenseine.ie*

Still one of Dublin's trendiest spots, the magnificent Art Deco interior and soaring ceilings create wow factor in this continental style café bar serving food and drinks. Not so much a bar as a series of bars, informal food is a feature too and there's a popular Sunday Jazz Brunch. *Open from 12 daily. Bar to 3am Wed-Sat. Light food from noon; Bar Menu from 5pm. Sun Brunch 12-5pm. Closed 25-26 Dec & Good Fri. CC.*

Café Mao Chatham Row

2-3 Chatham Row Dublin 2 📞 *01 670 4899 www.cafemao.com*

Bright, spacious and popular, Mao majors in good value flavoursome Asian fusion food alongside a good selection of Asian beers and cocktails. Colourful décor, a convivial atmosphere and broad menu ensure a loyal clientèle. ***Seats 110*** *(outdoors, 20).. Open Mon-Tue, 12-10pm; Wed-Sat, 12–11pm; Sunday 1.30-9pm. CC.*

 Camden Court Hotel

Camden Street Dublin 2 📞 *01 475 9666 www.camdencourthotel.com*

The central location, swimming pool, relatively reasonable rates and complimentary secure parking make this reliable and friendly hotel a city option to consider. ***Rooms 246****. Closed 23-28 Dec.*

 Carluccio's Caffe

52 Dawson Street Dublin 2 📞 *01 633 3957 www.carluccios.com*

Prices are reasonable at this sleek Italian restaurant, café and deli, serving breakfast through to light lunches, four-course evening meals and popular take-out coffee and pastries. Décor is bright and breezy and menus change with the seasons, featuring exciting regional favourites that your local Italian probably doesn't offer. ***Seats 120****. Open: Mon-Fri 7.30am-10.30pm; Sat 8am-10.30pm; Sun 9am-10pm. CC.*

 The Cedar Tree

11A South Andrew Street Dublin 2 📞 *01 677 2121 www.cedartree.ie*

Dublin's oldest Lebanese restaurant serves up tasty Middle Eastern classics in a relaxed and welcoming environment. The basement restaurant doesn't have an eye-catching exterior but is cosy and atmospheric with an extensive menu of good value, aromatic dishes. ***Seats 50****: D daily, phone to check lunch opening.*

  Celtic Whiskey Shop

27-28 Dawson Street Dublin 2 📞 *01 675 9744 www.winesonthegreen.com*

The shop for serious whiskey lovers. Offers Ireland's most comprehensive range of Irish whiskey and international whiskies and spirits, served by helpful, knowledgeable staff; exclusive whiskeys (including special releases from independently owned distilleries), whiskey launches, tasting evenings and distillery trips are often arranged. *Mon-Sat 10.30-9 (Thu to 9). Sun & bank hols 12.30-7.*

 Chez Max

1 Palace St Dublin 2 📞 *01 633 7215 www.chezmax.ie*

There are now two choices of venue: the original Chez Max café by Dublin Castle and newer 'bistrot' on Baggot Street. The latter boasts a more elaborate range, but both offer bistro staples such as French onion soup, escargots, boeuf bourguignon and moules frites. Cooking is generally competent, and the atmospheric setting and French wine list should always work their charm. ***Seats 66*** *(outdoors, 25). Open B, L & D daily; B from 8am Mon-Fri, 10am Sat and 11am Sun. Closed 25 Dec, 1 Jan. CC. Also at: 133 Lr Baggot St D2, (01) 661 8899.*

Chili Club

1 Anne's Lane South Anne Street Dublin 2 ✆*01 677 3721 www.chiliclub.ie*

Serving authentic Thai cuisine, Dublin's original Thai restaurant is still a cosy, well-run spot tucked in a laneway off Grafton St. Small and intimate, with beautiful crockery and genuine Thai art and furniture set lunch and early evening menus offer especially good value. **Seats 40**. *L Wed-Fri, D Tue-Sun. Closed L Sat&Sun, all Mon, 25 Dec-1 Jan. CC.*

The Clarence & Tea Room

6-8 Wellington Quay Dublin 2 ✆*01 407 0800 www.theclarence.ie*

On the edge of Temple Bar, this is one of Dublin's most iconic hotels. The Arts & Crafts interior on the edge of Temple Bar is elegantly hip, with accommodation offering a combination of contemporary comfort and period style. Guests love the clubby Octagon Bar with its impressive cocktail menu, while the magnificent Tea Room restaurant, with its own Essex Street entrance, serves up inventive cooking. **Rooms 49**. *Restaurant seats 90. L&D daily. Octagon Bar open from 5pm Tue-Sat. Restaurant closed 24 Dec-27 Dec. CC.*

The Cliff Town House

22 St Stephen's Green Dublin 2 ✆*01 638 3939 www.theclifftownhouse.com*

Sister-property to the celebrated Cliff House Hotel in Waterford this elegant Georgian townhouse hotel, overlooking St Stephen's Green, focuses on creative Irish cooking in its handsome dining room. The lively restaurant's firm emphasis is on seafood and the cooking has flair. Upstairs there's a smart bar, and this boutique hotel also has a private dining room overlooking the Green as well as ten stylish bedrooms. **Seats 75**. *L&D Mon-daily. Closed 25 & 31 Dec, 1 Jan, Good Fri. CC.*

Cocoa Atelier

30 Drury Street Dublin 2 ✆*01 675 3616 www.cocoaatelier.ie*

Superb continental chocolates and related indulgences handmade in Ireland by chocolatier Marc Amand. Made with the very best of chocolate (up to 85%) and in dozens of flavours, whatever you choose is sure to delight. This exquisite shop is the place to head for when you're looking for the very best of all things chocolate - especially for gifts, as the packaging is as special as the chocolates themselves - also a stunning range of oher items, including ingredients. *Open: Tue-Sat 10.30-6 (Thu to 7pm).*

Conrad Dublin & Alex Restaurant

Earlsfort Terrace Dublin 2 ✆*01 602 8900 www.conraddublin.com*

Nicely refurbished, this comfortable big-brand hotel is especially pleasing to business guests and has real heart thanks to warm service, thoughtful details and the pleasantly contemporary guestrooms. Specialising in steak and seafood, the reliable Alex restaurant is bright and spacious, with impeccably professional staff serving well presented contemporary dishes. A well-chosen wine list reflects the restaurant's demand for quality. **Rooms 191**. *Restaurant seats 92. D daily; L Sun only. Restaurant closed D 25 Dec, L 26 Dec. Hotel open all year. CC.*

Cooks Academy Cookery School

19 South William Street Dublin 2 ✆ *01 611 1666* *www.cooksacademy.com*

Justifiably styling themselves 'Dublin's Premier Cookery School', Vanessa and Tim Greenwood's stylish purpose-built city centre cookery school offers a wide range of cookery and wine lessons for both the amateur enthusiast and the professional cook. The facilities are outstanding - and they are matched by an expert team of tutors and guest chefs.

 ## Coppinger Row

Coppinger Row off South William St Dublin 2 ✆ *01 672 9884* *www.coppingerrow.com*

A hip, casual dining spot with cool décor, chilled music and great cocktails, Coppinger Row brings laid-back affordable dining to the heart of the town. Simple modern cooking is fresh and flavoursome and the efficient, knowledgeable and friendly staff make it well worth a visit. *Seats 80 (outdoors, 3). Open Tue-Sat 12-11pm & Sun 12-10pm. Closed Mon. CC.*

Cornucopia

19 Wicklow Street Dublin 2 ✆ *01 677 7583* *www.cornucopia.ie*

Beloved of students, alternative diners and mainstream diners who never expected to enjoy vegetarian food so much, this well-established wholefood restaurant caters for all kinds of restrictive diets (gluten-free, dairy-free etc) with its home cooked vegetarian offerings. It's very informal, especially during the day (when window seats are well placed for people watching), and regulars like it for its simple wholesomeness. Vegetarian breakfasts are a speciality and ingredients are organic, as far as possible. *Seats 48. Mon-Sat 8.30am-9pm (to 8pm Sat), Sun 12-7. Closed 25-27 Dec, 1 Jan, Easter Sun/Mon, Oct Bank Hol Sun/Mon. CC.*

Dada

44-45 South William Street Dublin 2 ✆ *01 617 0777* *www.dadarestaurant.com*

Step into Dada Restaurant and you'll find yourself transported to a little corner of Morocco. The moody interior, earthy colours and ornate mosaics set the tone for a broad collection of Morocco's vast and colourful cuisine. Service is knowledgeable and friendly and the keenly priced wine list presents a great opportunity to sample some Moroccan wine. *Seats 140. Open daily for L & D. Closed 25 Dec.*

 ## Damson Diner

52 South William Street Dublin 2 ✆ *01 677 7007* *www.damsondiner.com*

Marc and Conor Bereen, of nearby Coppinger Row restaurant, and Oisín Davis, the talented mixologist from the Sugar Club nightclub, are the trio behind this hip restaurant and cocktail bar; the mix of Asian and American style food, and clever and innovative cocktails, in a very trendy setting, is a sure-fire recipe for success. Buty it's not just a really hip, buzzy place - the food in Damson Diner is seriously good. *Seats 60. Open 'lunchtime 'til late'. CC.*

Darwins

80 Aungier Street Dublin 2 ✆ *01 475 7511 www.darwins.ie*

Meats for Michael Smith's friendly and comfortable restaurant are supplied by the family butchers, and carnivores relish the certified Irish Angus steaks, aged for 28 days, and good lamb dishes. There's an international flavour to the eclectic menu, which also offers a seafood selection and full vegetarian menu. Service is friendly, though restraint may be needed with side orders, as prices can creep up quickly. **Seats 50**. *D Mon-Sat. Closed Sun, 25-26 Dec & Bank Hols. CC.*

 The Davenport Hotel

Merrion Square Dublin 2 ✆ *01 607 3900 www.ocallaghenhotels.com*

This Merrion Square classic offers the best of location, Irish hospitality and well-equipped bedrooms to both business and leisure travellers. Guestrooms are furnished to a high standard with orthopaedic beds and the warm and helpful staff make it a very comfortable base within walking distance of shops and galleries. **Rooms 115**. *Open all year. CC.*

 Davy Byrnes

21 Duke Street Dublin 2 ✆ *01 677 5217 www.davybyrnes.com*

Pints of Guinness, Irish stew and oysters top the bill at one of Dublin's most famous and atmospheric pubs, beloved by Dubliners as much as tourists. Despite the fame from its appearance in James Joyce's Ulysses it remains a genuine, well-run place, just off Grafton Street, with tasty traditional bar food at reasonable prices. *Bar food served daily, 12-9 (winter to 5). Closed 25 Dec & Good Fri. CC.*

 Dax Restaurant & Dax Café Bar

23 Upper Pembroke Street Dublin 2 ✆ *01 676 1494 www.dax.ie*

Exciting food, charming service, a superb (and unapologetically French) wine list and lots of atmosphere make this reliable French restaurant and bar a popular spot. Regularly packed, despite being off the main thoroughfare, Dax manages to feel delightfully exclusive, like a secret club. Juxtaposing rustic decor with fine dining essentials it's a comfortable, intimate space with a menu that's studded with luxurious ingredients. Above the restaurant, Dax Café Bar is ideal for smart-casual lunch, tapas or a glass of wine. *Dax Café Bar: Mon 7.30-5; Tue-Fri 7.30-late; Sat 4.30-late. Closed Sun. Restaurant* **seats 65**; *Open L Tue-Fri; D Tue-Sat. Closed Sat L, Sun, Mon, 25 Dec-4 Jan, 1 or 2 weeks in Aug. CC.*

 Diep Le Shaker

55 Pembroke Lane Dublin 2 ✆ *01 661 1829 www.diep.net*

Matthew Farrell's eternally fashionable and popular Diep serves up expertly cooked Thai classics in a lively and comfortable dining room. The smart two-storey restaurant is elegantly appointed and buzzy, and the authentic cooking is excellent. Interesting regional evening menus offered to groups of 6+ include A Taste of Bangkok, A Taste of Chiang Mai and A Taste of Phuket. **Seats 100**. *L Teu-Fri, D Tue-Sat. Closed Sun & Mon.*

Dobbins Wine Bistro

15 Stephens Lane Dublin 2 ☎*01 661 9536 www.dobbins.ie*

Those in the know enjoy long lunches and lively dinners in this stylish restaurant where ingredients are sourced and cooked with care. Hidden away near Merrion Square and something of a Dublin institution, a major revamp transformed the décor without compromising the reputation for great hospitality, consistently delicious food and a love of wine. Although often described as 'expensive', Dobbins offers great value on their early dinner and lunch menus. *Seats 120; L Mon-Fri, D Tue-Sat; Sun L only. Closed L Sat, D Sun, Mon, bank hols, 24 Dec-2 Jan. CC.*

 Doheny & Nesbitt

5 Lower Baggot Street Dublin 2 ☎*01 676 2945*

Grab a pint in this celebrated Victorian bar and sit back to witness the tapestry of Irish society unfold. Relaxing, lively and fun, it has been greatly extended recently and is now in essence a superpub, though it has at its heart the original, very professionally run bar and a traditional emphasis on drinking and conversation. *Closed 25 Dec & Good Fri.*

 Domini & Peaches Kemp at the Restaurant

Level 3 Brown Thomas 88-95 Grafton Street Dublin 2
☎*01 677 8262 www.itsa.ie/restaurants—cafes/restaurants/restaurant@bt*

Tucked into Dublin's chicest department store, this stylish restaurant serves scrumptious breakfasts, brunches, lunches and desserts. A delightful retail pick-me-up, it's operated by the well known catering sisters, Peaches and Domini Kemp. There are tempting cakes and pastries available all day, and a nice little Children's Menu too. *Open shop hours - last orders for hot food 5.50pm (Thu 8pm; Sat 6.15pm); beverages, pastries & desserts served until the store closes each day.*

 Dunne & Crescenzi

14 & 16 South Frederick Street Dublin 2 ☎*01 677 3815 www.dunneandcrescenzi.com*

A glass of wine, plate of antipasti and great coffee will transport you to Italy in this bustling and unpretentious spot where well-sourced food is a priority and Irish ingredients are used where appropriate. Serving simple rustic food at reasonable prices, this is the original branch of the hugely successful husband-and-wife-run chain. There are even some little tables on the pavement though expect to queue: this place has a loyal following. *Seats 60 (outdoors, 20). Open Mon-Sat 8-11, Sun 10am-10pm. CC.*

 Eden Bar & Grill

7 South William Street Dublin 2 ☎*01 670 6887 www.edenbarandgrill.ie*

Younger sister to the popular Eden (now NEDE) in Temple Bar, this is a cool city centre bistro with casual dining and killer cocktails. *Seats 100. L&D daily. CC.*

Elephant & Castle

18 Temple Bar Dublin 2 ✆ *01 679 3121*

A buzzy Temple Bar favourite, this casual spot is known for its trademark chicken wings and also serves great home made burgers, generous salads and tasty brunch options. Service can be a little slow but the lively atmosphere ensures the time passes agreeably. *Seats 85. Open daily 8am-11.30pm. Closed Christmas & Good Fri. CC.*

ely gastropub

Grand Canal Square Hanover Quay Dublin 2 ✆ *01 633 9986 www.elywinebar.ie*

The third and most recent of Erik and Michelle Robson's wine bar/cafés, this hip waterside haunt serves seasonal, meticulously-sourced smart-casual food (some from the family farm) alongside the outstanding wine list and cocktail offerings that are the trademark of the group. It has a young, stylish atmosphere, large dining areas on two levels and a fully heated covered terrace area. Good service is also a strong point. *Seats 200 (outdoors, 80); Food served all day, Mon-Sun 12-10pm (to 11pm Fri & Sat). Closed Christmas week, bank hols. CC.*

ely winebar

22 Ely Place Dublin 2 ✆ *01 676 8986 www.elywinebar.ie*

Diners and drinkers love the chic and atmospheric old Georgian townhouse, which became the first of Erik and Michelle Robson's 'series' of Ely wine bar/ cafés in 1999. The exceptional wine list is backed up by other specialities including a list of premium beers, and appealing menus offer tasty, well-sourced food, including organic meat from the family farm in County Clare. *Seats 90. Open Mon-Sat 12 noon-12.30 am. Food served Mon-Sat 12-10.30pm (to 11pm Fri/Sat). Closed Sun, Christmas week, bank hols. CC.*

The Exchequer

3-5 Exchequer Street Dublin 2 ✆ *01 670 6787 www.theexchequer.ie*

With its a smarter than average interior and decidedly clubby feel this genuine gastro-pub serves up tasty roasts, casseroles, seafood and pies at affordable prices. A broad drinks menu includes European micro beers and cool cocktails, and there's smooth tunes and chic décor to guarantee a stylish and good value experience. *Seats 85 (outdoors, 8); Open all day for food 12-10pm (to 8pm Sun). Closed public holidays. CC.*

Fade Street Social

Fade Street Dublin 2 ✆ *01 604 0066 www.fadestreetsocial.com*

'The full social event' - accomplished cooking with huge emphasis on flavour ensures that Dylan McGrath's latest exciting venture offers some of the best mid-priced food in Dublin. Many of the ingredients are Irish, but influences range from Mediterranean to American and Asian. The cooking is clever and quite different from anything else in Dublin: return visits will be a must, as diners will be hungry to try more dishes from this exciting chef's menu. *Seats 120. Gastro bar: L & D Fri-Sun 2-10.30 & D Mon-Thu 5-10.30. Gastro bar closed L Mon-Thu. Restaurant: L Mon-Fri 12.30-2.30, D Mon-Sun 5-10.30. Restaurant closed L Sat & Sun.*

 **Fallon & Byrne**

11-17 Exchequer Street Dublin 2 ✆ *01 472 1000 www.fallonandbyrne.com*

Upstairs above Dublin's favourite food store, a bright and airy dining space serves classic French food with flair and panache. Simple menus feature authentic French cooking that's great tasting, good value and well presented. Professional staff and a lively buzz complete the picture, and there's an atmospheric basement wine bar, if you'd prefer a light bite surrounded by bottles of tempting wine. *Restaurant: **Seats 100**. Open L Mon-Sun; D Mon-Sat. Wine Cellar open Mon-Sat 11am-10pm (Thu-Sat to 11pm), Sun & Bank hols, 12.30-9pm. Closed Sun D, 25/26 Dec, Good Friday. CC.*

 The Farm

3 Dawson Street Dublin 2 ✆ *01 671 8654 www.thefarmrestaurant.ie*

Funky and lively, this good value restaurant serves simple and tasty organic and mainly local food, although often with international inspiration. The bright design and pavement tables attract passers by, and it has a local following too, so there may be a queue; but, once seated, service is prompt and informative and there's something to suit all tastes and budgets. Children are made very welcome. ***Seats 90** (outdoors, 10); open 11am-10pm (from noon Sun). Closed 25/26 Dec. CC. Also at: 133 Upper Leeson Street, Dublin 4.*

 Fire

The Mansion House Dawson Street Dublin 2 ✆ *01 676 7200 www.mansionhouse.ie*

With its dramatic dining room in the historic Mansion House, diners can expect slick service and good food at this popular spot. Affordable and unpretentious European food is cooked to a high standard and the cosmopolitan outdoor seating area, sophisticated style and impressive interior explain this restaurant's well-earned reputation. ***Seats 200**; L Thu-Sat; D Mon-Sat. Closed Sun, Bank hols; 25/26 Dec. CC.*

 **The Fitzwilliam Hotel**

St Stephens Green Dublin 2 ✆ *01 478 7000 www.fitzwilliamhotel.com*

Luxurious, discreet and contemporary, The Fitzwilliam is an intimate and stylish five-star. A complete refurbishment has refreshed the hotel's sleek good looks with smart guestrooms, some overlooking St Stephen's Green. In addition to the hotel's destination restaurant, Thornton's (see entry), breakfast, lunch and dinner are served daily in the attractive informal restaurant, Citron. And not only does the Fitzwilliam have a chic little bar, a gym that's open around the clock and in-house hair and beauty salon - but also Ireland's largest roof garden. ***Rooms 139**. Open all year. CC.*

 Good World Chinese Restaurant

18 South Great Georges Street Dublin 2 ✆ *01 677 5373*

Long-running and popular with the local Chinese community, diners can expect excellent dim sum and authentic dishes not often found on European menus. A more interesting and authentic Chinese menu is available as well as the standard one and service is both friendly and efficient. ***Seats 95**. Open 12.30pm-midnight daily. Closed 25-26 Dec. CC.*

Gotham Café

8 South Anne Street Dublin 2 ✆ *01 679 5266 www.gothamcafe.ie*

A lively casual dining spot, just off Grafton Street, this family-friendly place is popular for its specialities, including gourmet pizzas, home made burgers, pasta and salads. Offering consistent quality at fair prices, including light breakfasts from 10.30am, it's no wonder this great café is such a longstanding success. *Seats 65 (outdoors, 10). Food served Mon & Tue, 10.30am-10pm; Wed-Sat 10.30am-11pm; Sun & Bank Hols 11.30am-10pm. Closed 25-26 Dec & Good Fri. CC. Also at: Gotham South, Stillorgan.*

 Green 19

19 Camden Street Lower Dublin 2 ✆ *01 478 9626 www.green19.ie*

Serving tasty home-style cooking from well-sourced ingredients at fair prices, this bright and buzzy Camden Street hang-out is a real crowd pleaser. Menus offer the kind of food many of us could rustle up at home ourselves, were we so inclined to do, including bacon & cabbage. Desserts are smart takes on nostalgic classics and it's nice to see in-house soft drinks offered - while imaginative cocktails make it a good place to start off your night. *Seats 50 (outdoors, 10). Open daily L & D. CC.*

 The Green Hen

33 Exchequer Street Dublin 2 ✆ *01 670 7238 www.thegreenhen.com*

All-day dining close to Grafton Street, this relaxed brasserie serves everything from brunch to an all-day bar menu and more intimate dinners. The bar beckons passersby in with cocktails of the day while the restaurant extends its menu from keenly-priced lunch into dinner with hearty plat du jour offerings. French influenced bistro fare is generally well executed.

 The GreenHouse

Dawson St. Dublin 2 ✆ *01 676 7015 www.thegreenhouserestaurant.ie*

Expect culinary fireworks when you dine at this Dawson Street standout, where the food almost looks too good to eat. Each dish is a visual thrill, with dramatic colours, unusual ingredients and quirky details. The work of Finnish chef Mickael Viljanen, enticed to Dublin from Gregan's Castle by Greenhouse owner Eamonn O'Reilly, the canny chef-proprietor of, amongst other successes, One Pico. The small and chic dining room sets the tone for a culinary extravaganza while the excellent front of house team enhances the sense of occasion. Dinner is offered as 3-, 5- or 7-course tasting menus while a two-course lunch, normally offered at €25, gives diners the chance to enjoy this outstanding food in a more affordable way. (Restaurant of the Year 2013). *L & D Tue-Sat.*

 Harrington Hall

69/70 Harcourt Street Dublin 2 ✆ *01 475 3497 www.harringtonhall.com*

This former guesthouse near St. Stephens Green is now an hotel, and offers comfortable, affordable accommodation in well-preserved Georgian surroundings - and private parking. Once home to a Lord Mayor of Dublin, it has been sympathetically and elegantly refurbished. Housekeeping is to a high standard and breakfast in the lovely basement room is good. Street noise can affect front rooms on Saturday nights. *Rooms 28 (4 shower only). Open all year. CC.*

Hatch & Sons

Basement 15 St Stephen's Green Dublin 2 📞 *01 661 0075 www.hatchandsons.co*

Set in the basement of Dublin's Little Museum (customers get a 10% discount on entry to the museum) this wonderful city centre flagship for Ireland's artisan produce, Hatch & Sons is run by food writer and caterer Domini Kemp, her sister Peaches and food consultant Hugo Arnold. A stylish modern take on traditional pleasures, rustic fare is complemented by tempting baking - their carrot cake may just be Dublin's finest. *Open all day, with late opening to 8pm on Thu.*

 Herbstreet

Hanover Quay Grand Canal Dock Dublin 2 📞 *01 675 3875 www.herbstreet.ie*

A cool café with soul, Herbstreet serves delicious contemporary food including great brunches and casual early dinners. Overlooking Hanover Quay the deceptively spacious spot includes 1950s chairs, eco-friendly lighting design and an intriguing drinks list. The menu is quirky too and they're keeping a low carbon footprint! *Open daily, B&L Mon-Fri, Brunch Sat-Sun 10am-4pm, D Thu-Sat. Closed D Sun-Wed.*

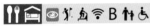 **Hilton Dublin**

Charlemont Place Dublin 2 📞 *01 402 9988 www.hilton.com/dublin*

An attractive, modern hotel in a serene setting overlooking the Grand Canal, and minutes from the city centre (Luas stop outside the door), it caters well for both leisure and business guests. Public facilities include the Stil Bar and Lounge and a coffee shop and, although some rooms may be a little dated, guests can expect comfort and lovely service. Uisce Restaurant offers modern menus and the cooking is sound. *Underground carpark.* **Rooms 193**. *Restaurant seats 78. D daily. Hotel closed 25 Dec. CC.*

 Hugo's

6 Merrion Row Dublin 2 📞 *01 676 5955 www.hugos.ie*

Gina Murphy's welcoming wine bar and restaurant is easily recognised by its bright turquoise facade. Although the main appeal of Hugo's is as a wine bar, there's a growing emphasis on food, all of which is made fresh daily. The buzzy vibe, comfy décor and friendly staff make it a convivial and busy spot. **Seats 70**; *open noon-11pm daily (from 11am Sun). Closed 25-27 Dec, Good Fri, 1 Jan. CC.*

 Il Posto

10 St. Stephen's Green Dublin 2 📞 *01 679 4769 www.ilpostorestaurant.com*

The classy dining room and hearty cooking make this up-market Stephen's Green Italian a well-loved choice. Written in Italian (with detailed translations in English), the menu is promising, offering a full range of imaginative antipasti, pasta, fish and meat dishes. The wine list is exclusively Italian, with plenty of choice in the mid range, though this stylish restaurant is not a budget outing. **Seats 60** *(outdoors, 10); L&D Mon-Sat. Closed Sun; bank hols; 25, 26, 31 Dec. CC.*

Il Primo Restaurant

16 Montague Street Dublin 2 ✆ *01 478 3373 www.ilprimo.ie*

With its cult following Il Primo offers rustic Italian food and specially imported wines in a lively and informally stylish atmosphere. This long established Italian restaurant, now owned by chef Anita Thoma, majors in flavoursome, no-nonsense cooking served up by friendly front of house staff - and with an impressive wine list strong on Tuscany to match the stylish food. Risotto is a speciality. **Seats 70**. *L & D Mon-Sat. Closed Sun, Bank Hols. CC.*

 Il Valentino Continental Bakery

5 Gallery Quay Grand Canal Harbour Dublin 2 ✆ *01 633 1100 www.ilvalentino.ie*

Husband-and-wife team Valentina and Owen Doorly are the duo behind this terrific Grand Canal Basin bakery and they're passionate about Italian food. Modern décor belies the traditional values at play in this top class Italian cafe where artisan breads, authentic pizzas and delicious treats draw a loyal fan base. **Seats 26**. *Open Mon-Fri 7am-7pm; Sat, Sun & Bank Hols 9am-5pm. Closed 25 & 26 Dec. CC.*

 Indie Dhaba

21-26 Anne's Lane Anne Street South Dublin 2 ✆ *01 707 9898 www.dhaba.ie*

The latest in the small chain of stylish Indie restaurants, and bringing "tapas style dining to Indian food", the setting here is hipster-stylish, with a flashy cocktail bar, music pumping, and a Bollywood movie playing at the back. With an open kitchen with an enviable line-up of kit-like tandoors and grills, and stylish, funky décor it's emphatically modern Indian. **Seats 80**. *Wed-Sun 12-12, Tue-Sat 12-1am.*

 The International Bar

23 Wicklow Street Dublin 2 ✆ *01 677 9250*

Just a minute's walk from Grafton Street, this unspoilt Victorian bar makes a great meeting place. It's not a food spot, but good for chat and music. *Closed 25 Dec. & Good Friday.*

 Isabels

112 Lower Baggot St Dublin 2 ✆ *01 661 9000 www.isabels.ie*

From gourmet sandwiches and salads by day to tasty bistro fare by night, this chic and cosy basement spot doubles up as an atmospheric and intimate wine bar. Daytime and evening menus are similarly pitched, food is beautifully presented and the short menu includes plenty of seasonal produce. Wine plays a key role, whether it's a bottle of something rare and stellar, or one of 18 interesting wines by the glass. **Seats 60** *(outdoors, 24). B daily. L Mon-Fri; D Tue-Sat; Sun 9am-11pm. Closed Sun L & D, 25 Dec, 1 Jan. CC.*

Jaipur

41 South Great Georges Street Dublin 2 ✆ *01 677 0999 www.jaipur.ie*

The original branch of the celebrated Jaipur group, this trailblazing Indian restaurant serves delicious regional food in a smart and contemporary environment. The sophisticated dining room is a comfortable backdrop to head chef Mahipal Roma's fragrant cooking, which uses mostly Irish ingredients alongside imported spices. Service is attentive and discreet and Jaipur's carefully selected wine list is especially suited to the spicy fare. **Seats 100**. *L Thu-Sun, D daily. Closed 25-26 Dec. CC.*

 John Mulligan

8 Poolbeg Street Dublin 2 ✆ *01 677 5582*

One of Dublin's oldest and best-loved pubs, Mulligan's 'wine & spirit merchant' is mercifully un-renovated and likely to stay that way - dark, with no decor (as such) and no music, it's just the way so many pubs used to be.

 Kehoe's

9 South Anne Street Dublin 2 ✆ *01 677 8312*

One of Dublin's best, unspoilt traditional pubs, Kehoe's changed hands relatively recently and added another floor upstairs, but without damaging the character of the original bar. Very busy in the evening – try it for a quieter daytime pint instead. *Closed 25 Dec and Good Friday.*

  Kilkenny

5-6 Nassau Street Dublin 2 ✆ *01 677 7075 www.kilkennyshop.com*

A pleasant spot to have a casual bite to eat: ingredients are fresh and additive-free (as are all the products on sale in the shop's Food Hall) and everything has a home-cooked flavour. Salads, quiches, casseroles, home-baked breads and cakes are the specialities, and they are reliably good - and you will also find Irish craft beers and cider on the Café menu. Breakfast offers outstanding value. **Seats 190**; *Open Mon-Sat, 8.30-5 (Thu to 7), Sun & bank hols 10-5. Licensed. Closed 25-26 Dec, 1 Jan, Easter Sun. CC.*

 Kitchen Complements

South Anne Street Dublin 2 ✆ *01 677 0734 www.kitchencomplements.ie*

Recently relocated to South Anne Street, this is the first (and usually only) port of call for keen cooks looking for the right gear for the job. Bakeware is a speciality and cookery classes and demonstrations are frequently held here. *Open Mon-Sat 10-6 (Thu to 7), Sun 12.30-5.30. Online shop.*

 **L'Ecrivain**

109a Lower Baggot Street Dublin 2 ✆ *01 661 1919 www.lecrivain.com*

One of Dublin's top restaurants, this destination dining room promises to please with its combination of Derry Clarke's multi-starred cooking and Sallyanne's front of house hospitality. Classic French techniques meet the best of Irish produce in the kitchen to create a menu of imaginative and elegant dishes. Renowned sommelier Martina Delaney presides over an impressive cellar, and her knowledge and passion of the broad wine list guarantees a perfect match for your food. The convivial vibe has always been a trademark of L'Ecrivain, and the good value lunch menus mean it's an affordable option for a smart business lunch too. **Seats 104** *(outdoors, 22). L Mon, Thu, Fri. D Mon-Sat. Closed L Sat, Sun, Bank Hols, Christmas, New Year, Easter. CC.*

L'Gueuleton

1 Fade Street Dublin 2 ✆ *01 675 3708 www.LGueuleton.com*

This no-frills French restaurant took Dublin by storm when it opened in 2004 – so much so that, in a very short time, it became necessary to extend. The atmospheric hipster hangout offers a combination of rustic French dishes from the classic to the more unusual. Throw in cramped tables, a little bar and snappy service, and you've one lively and fun bistro experience. **Seats 75** *(outdoors, 20). L&D daily. Closed Good Fri, 25-27 Dec, 1 Jan. CC.*

 La Cave Wine Bar & Restaurant

28 South Anne Street Dublin 2 ✆ *01 679 4409 www.lacavewinebar.com*

Margaret and Akim Beskri have run this characterful place just off Grafton Street since 1989 and it's well-known for its cosmopolitan atmosphere, late night opening and lots of chat. There's an excellent wine list of over 350 bins (predominantly French) and the food is classic French too. The La Cave Wine School offers both fun evenings and Wine & Spirit Education Trust approved certificate courses. **Seats 28**. *Open Mon-Sat 12-11pm, Sun 5-11pm. Closed L Sun, L Bank Hols, 25/26 Dec, Good Fri. CC.*

 La Mère Zou

22 St Stephen's Green Dublin 2 ✆ *01 661 6669 www.lamerezou.ie*

Skilful bistro cooking is served with flair in this intimate little basement dining room on St Stephen's Green. A Dublin favourite for two decades, menus feature rustic French and Belgian cooking delivered with real skill and panache. Bistro favourites like bouillabaisse, foie gras and duck confit sit alongside traditional casseroles and the warm service and convivial space make this a lovely spot to linger with wine or a Belgian beer. **Seats 55** *(outdoors, 6). L Mon-Sat. Closed Sun, Bank Hols, 25 Dec - 5th Jan. CC.*

 The Larder

8 Parliament Street Dublin 2 ✆ *01 633 3581*

The name says it all, this casual dining spot off Dame Street works hard to deliver no-nonsense, flavoursome cooking based on the best of local ingredients. Breakfast brings lip-smacking choices, lunch a deli lover's delight of gourmet sandwiches and evenings a modest menu of charcuterie, salads, enticing mains delicious and desserts. An unpretentious place that punches above its weight. **Seats 20**; *B daily; L Mon-Fri; D Tue-Sun. CC*

 Las Tapas de Lola

12 Wexford St Dublin 2 ✆ *01 4244100 www.lastapasdelola.com*

Fun, lively and serving great food, the authentic Spanish tapas here will transport you to sunny Spain no matter what the Dublin weather. Relive your holiday memories, from the excellent sangria to piquant patatas bravas it's serving some of the best tapas this side of Barcelona. *Mon-Wed: 5-10.30, Thu-Sat 5-11, Sun 5- 10.30.*

Le Petit Parisien

17 Wicklow Street Dublin 2 ✆ *01 671 7331 www.lepetitparisien.ie*

For a slice of 1920's Paris hit this charming French café where the counters are loaded with delicious house-baked treats. Relax in the intimate and dimly lit historic looking surroundings while nibbling on a flaky croissant and early morning coffee or perhaps a lunchtime croque monsiuer followed by tarte au citron. (Accessible from The Mercantile, 25 Dame Street.) *Mon-Sat B'fast 8-12; L12-4, Aft Tea & Supper 5pm till late Mon-Sat; Sun Brunch 10-6pm.*

 ## Les Frères Jacques

74 Dame Street Dublin 2 ✆ *01 679 4555 www.lesfreresjacques.com*

A long-running fine dining restaurant where the staff, wonderful cooking and atmosphere are inimitably Gallic. The cooking may be classic French but they do it with a light touch that Irish diners especially appreciate. Lunch at Les Frères Jacques is a treat (and good value) but dinner is a feast; seafood is a speciality, including lobster. On the wine list, which naturally favours France, reductions of as much as 50% per bottle are often offered on Mondays and Tuesdays. **Seats 65**. *L Mon-Fri; D Mon-Sat. Closed L Sat, all Sun, 24 Dec-3 Jan. CC.*

  ## Listons

25/26 Lower Camden Street Dublin 2 ✆ *01 405 4779 www.listonsfoodstore.ie*

Boasting "a product range of over 4,000 lines with many organic products in all categories", this highly regarded food store believes in choice and offers carefully sourced deli and grocery ranges; also wines sourced from small independent importers, and a great seasonal fresh food menu to download from their website. *Open: Mon – Fri 9am - 6.30pm. Sat 10am - 6pm.*

 ## The Long Hall Bar

51 South Great George's St. Dublin 2 ✆ *01 475 1590*

A wonderful old pub with magnificent plasterwork ceilings, traditional mahogany bar and Victorian lighting. One of Dublin's finest bars and well worth a visit. *Closed 25 Dec & Good Fri.*

 ## Maldron Hotel Cardiff Lane

Cardiff Lane Sir John Rogerson's Quay Dublin 2 ✆ *01 643 9500 www.maldronhotels.com*

This centrally-located 4* hotel on the south bank of the Liffey is close to the Grand Canal Basin and Bord Gais Energy Theatre. It's an attractive waterside position and - across the Sean O'Casey pedestrian bridge - has easy access to the north quays, IFSC (financial services centre), the National Convention Centre and the O2. Equally attractive to business and leisure guests, with excellent amenities including a 22m pool, and good value. **Rooms** *304. CC .*

 ## Marco Pierre White Steakhouse and Grill

51 Dawson Street Dublin 2 ✆ *01 677 1155 www.marcopierrewhite.ie*

Linen-clad tables hint at fine dining, but simple steaks are the order du jour at Marco Pierre White's smart and buzzy steakhouse. Individual lamps on each table add to the speakeasy ambience, as do the unusually late opening hours. Several cuts of steak are offered at reasonable prices with a choice of classic sauces; the early dinner menu offers special value. **Seats 90** *(outdoors, 28). Open daily 12-11pm. Closed Dec 25 & Good Fri. CC.*

 **The Marker Hotel**

Grand Canal Square Dublin 2 ☎ *01 687 5100 www.themarkerhoteldublin.com*

Overlooking the Grand Canal Basin, Dublin city's most striking modern hotel opened in April 2013. Predictably impressive public spaces include a ground floor cocktail bar and brasserie among other dining and socialising areas - and, very unusually for a city hotel, the Spa includes a 23 metre infinity pool. Views from the upper floors are magnificent and used to full advantage; among other persuasive selling points, this luxurious hotel lays claim to Dublin's most appealing Presidential Suite. *Rooms 187*.

 Market Bar & Tapas

Fade Street Dublin 2 ☎ *01 613 9094*

Soak up the atmosphere of one of Dublin's buzziest pubs while chowing down on tasty, if not always authentic, tapas. Located in the Victorian redbrick block best known for the George's Street Market Arcade, this attractive, noisy, bar is a great place for a group of friends. *Food Mon-Sat 12-10; Sun 4-10. Closed 25-26 Dec, Good Fri. CC.*

Matt the Thresher

31-32 Lower Pembroke Street Dublin 2 ☎ *01 676 2980 www.mattthethresher.ie*

Chef Stephen Caviston, of the celebrated fishmonger family, is the man at the stove in this lively city centre bar and grill where exciting seafood cooking is the star attraction - and choices for non-fish eaters star Tipperary beef. It's bright and stylish although, with double height ceilings, a tiled floor and bare tables it gets noisy when busy. *Lunch, Mon-Sat 12-5pm, Dinner, 5-9.45pm; Sun, 1-8pm. CC.*

 McDaids

3 Harry Street Dublin 2 ☎ *01 679 4395*

Established in 1779, McDaids more recently achieved fame as one of the great literary pubs, and its association with Brendan Behan brings a steady trail of pilgrims from all over the world to this traditional premises just beside the Westbury Hotel, but it is popular with Dubliners too. History and character are generally of more interest than food here, although limited food is available. *Closed 25 Dec & Good Fri.*

 **Merrion Hotel**

Upper Merrion Street Dublin 2 ☎ *01 603 0600 www.merrionhotel.com*

Comprising four meticulously renovated Georgian townhouses, The Merrion Hotel is a luxurious retreat in the heart of historic Dublin. A warm Irish welcome, historic décor, plush bedrooms and classy service make it five-star all the way. Luxurious public areas, perfect for business meetings or afternoon tea, and an attractive cocktail bar for evening time are matched by beautifully furnished guest rooms and the sumptuous Tethra Spa. Dining options include Restaurant Patrick Guilbaud (see separate entry), the elegant vaulted *Cellar Restaurant* and atmospheric Cellar Bar. In a world of indentikit hotels with bland service, The Merrion feels incredibly special. *Rooms 142. Cellar Restaurant seats 86. L Mon-Fri; D daily. Sun Brunch 12.30-2.30. Cellar Bar: open 11am-11pm Mon-Sat, food served 12-9.30pm. Hotel open all year. CC.*

Milano

38 Dawson Street Dublin 2 📞 *01 670 7744*

A stylish pizzeria serving quality food that's both family-friendly and good for big groups. Although best known for its wide range of excellent pizzas (it's owned by the UK company Pizza Express) it's more of a restaurant than the description implies and families are made especially welcome.

Mont Clare Hotel

Merrion Square Dublin 2 📞 *01 607 3800 www.ocallaghanhotels.com*

A few doors away from the National Gallery this central and relatively well-priced hotel is slightly old-fashioned but ideal for city breaks and for business guests staying in executive rooms.The old stained glass and mahogany Gallery Bar has retained its original pubby atmosphere and makes a good meeting place. *Rooms 74. Closed 23-28 Dec. CC.*

Montys of Kathmandu

28 Eustace Street Temple Bar Dublin 2 📞 *01 670 4911 www.montys.ie*

A graphic window illustration of Buddha's eyes, that enduring symbol of Nepal, has been drawing diners into this cosy Nepalese restaurant for over fifteen years. Owner Shiva Gautum set the bar high when it opened and standards continue to this day with wonderful Nepalese food cooked and served by Nepalese staff in this chilled and buzzy Temple Bar favourite. *Seats 65. L Mon-Sat; D daily 5-11pm. Closed L Sun, 25-26 Dec. CC.*

Morgan Hotel

10 Fleet Street Temple Bar Dublin 2 📞 *01 643 7000 www.themorgan.com*

A boutique bolthole in the heart of Temple Bar, expect clean lines, luxurious beds, cool cocktails and an oasis of calm. Décor is cool and minimal, staff are very helpful and the breakfast buffet is excellent. Casual dining is available in the Morgan Bar, where an excellent (and extensive) tapas menu is served all day. It offers relaxation by day, and a stylish party spot by night. *Rooms 121. Closed 25 & 26 Dec. CC.*

Murphys Ice Cream

27 Wicklow Street Dublin 2 📞 *086 031 0726 www.murphysicecream.ie*

Kerry's finest ice cream is also in Dublin, ready to be scooped, slurped in situ with coffee and cake, or taken away in the distinctive blue livery. The range of flavours is growing all the time –unusual ones include sea salt, and also balsamic vinegar, but most are a little more familiar. *Open daily 12-9 in winter, 11-10 in summer.*

Neary's

1 Chatham Street Dublin 2 📞 *01 677 8596*

Gleaming brass and mahogany form the backdrop to this charming timeless Edwardian pub which has been in the present ownership for over half a century. A stone's throw from Grafton Street, it's handy for lunch, as a meeting place or for an evening of banter. *Closed 25 Dec & Good Fri. CC.*

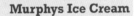

NEDE

Meeting House Square Temple Bar Dublin 2 ✆ *01 670 5372 www.nede.ie*

NEDE, the reincarnation of EDEN (a Temple Bar hot spot during Ireland's boom) is now home to Irish chef Louise Bannon and her Belgian partner Yannick van Aeken. Former pastry chef and sous chef, respectively, at Copenhagen's celebrated Noma, the pair aim to bring some of Noma's natural food wizardry to Dublin's diners. Quality and restraint in the kitchen allows their carefully chosen ingredients and sophisticated techniques to wow. *Seats 96 (outdoors 32). Closed 25 Dec-2 Jan. L Tue-Sat 12-3; D Tue-Sat 5.30-10; Brunch Sun 12-4.*

Number 31

31 Leeson Close Lr Leeson Street Dublin 2 ✆ *01 676 5011 www.number31.ie*

Beloved by design buffs, Noel and Deirdre Comer's architectural gem marries cool guesthouse accommodation with a homely welcome and luxurious little extras. Formerly the home of leading architect, the late Sam Stephenson, the elegant bedrooms have exceptionally comfortable beds and breakfasts, served at communal tables are a treat. There's a lovely homely feel and with its stay-in-all-day atmosphere, you might find it hard to leave. *Rooms 21. Open all year. CC.*

O'Donoghue's

15 Merrion Row Dublin 2 ✆ *01 660 7194 www.odonoghues.ie*

O'Donoghues has long been the Dublin mecca for visitors in search of a lively evening with traditional music – live music every night is a major claim to fame – but a visit to this famous pub near The Shelbourne Hotel at quieter times can be rewarding too. *Closed 25 Dec & Good Fri.*

O'Neill's Pub & Townhouse

37 Pearse Steet Dublin 2 ✆ *01 671 4074 www.oneillsdublin.com*

Established in 1885 this cosy Victorian bar has plenty of snugs and alcoves and serves reasonably priced home-cooked food. It's run in a quirky, laid-back manner that seems to be straight out of James Joyce and, depending on your outlook, will amuse or infuriate. The simple, comfortable accommodation would have particular appeal for a fairly youthful clientèle. *Bar meals daily. Closed Christmas & Good Fri. CC.*

Odessa Lounge & Grill

13/14 Dame Court Dublin 2 ✆ *01 670 7634 www.odessa.ie*

The brunch spot of choice for hung-over hipsters for over 15 years, the retro décor and cool tunes - and attractive special offers - in this funky lounge-restaurant make up for sometimes unreliable cooking. You can also dine upstairs in the spacious Odessa Club, where the same lounge-vibes, sharp cocktails and casual eating are on offer. Cool and relaxed, the building becomes a chilled out, stylish club by night. *Seats 190. Sat & Sun open brunch 11.30-4; D Tue-Sun. Closed Mon, Bank Hols, 25/26 Dec. CC.*

Olesyas Wine Bar

18 Exchequer Street Dublin 2 ✆ *01 672 4087 www.olesyaswinebar.com*

Olesya's is a bright and modern wine bar that's a cosy spot for a casual meal or drinks. Serving over 400 wines from a simple-to-follow wine list, diners can enjoy Russian-influenced food and a casual European vibe. It's a relaxed and buzzy space with something to suit every budget and palate. **Seats 50** *(outdoors, 6). Open daily 12.30 – 11pm. CC.*

One Pico Restaurant

5-6 Molesworth Place Schoolhouse Lane Dublin 2 ✆ *01 676 0300 www.onepico.com*

Quietly located in a laneway near St. Stephen's Green, Eamonn O'Reilly's stylish One Pico is one of Dublin's most popular fine dining restaurants. The surroundings are elegant, as is the exceptionally good cooking. Sophisticated, technically demanding dishes, starring first class ingredients, are executed with confidence and flair. Service is professional and friendly and a well-chosen wine list offers some 80 bottles. This is a fine restaurant and has earned its place among the city's best. **Seats 65.** *Open daily noon-11.30pm. Closed bank hols, 24 Dec-5 Jan. CC.*

The Palace Bar

21 Fleet Street Dublin 2 ✆ *01 671 7388*

With strong connections with writers and journalists for many a decade The Palace Bar's unspoilt frosted glass and mahogany are impressive enough but the special feature is the famous sky-lighted snug, which is really more of a back room. *Closed 25 Dec & Good Fri.*

Pearl Brasserie

20 Merrion Street Upper Dublin 2 ✆ *01 661 3572 www.pearl-brasserie.com*

Just a few doors away from The Merrion Hotel, Sebastien Masi and Kirsten Batt's stylish brasserie serves some of the cleverest food in town. Chic, classy and fashionable, the basement room has been beautifully styled and there's an unmistakably Gallic air, from the predominantly French staff to the extensive wine list and menu. Exquisite flavour combinations, beautiful presentation and attentive service make this a gem of a restaurant in every way possible. **Seats 80.** *L Mon-Fri, D Mon-Sat. Closed Sun, bank hols. CC.*

Peploe's Wine Bistro

16 St Stephen's Green Dublin 2 ✆ *01 676 3144 www.peploes.com*

A chic basement bistro on St Stephen's Green where classy food and interesting wines are served by smart staff. The décor is reminiscent of a 1950s New York brasserie and, although the dining room appears cramped, it is comfortable with pleasant, professional service. Quality bistro cooking benefits from a fair sprinkling of luxurious ingredients and the extensive wine list and convivial atmosphere enhance the experience. **Seats 90**. *Open 12.30-3.30pm & 6-10.30pm daily. Closed 24-29 Dec, Good Fri. CC.*

The Pepper Pot

First Floor Powerscourt Townhouse Centre South William Street Dublin 2 ✆ *087 790 3204 www.thepepperpot.ie*

All the tables at this first floor café in Powerscourt Town House overlook the central area, allowing excellent views. The Pepper Pot takes pride in the fact that they make and bake everything daily so, although the savoury basics may simply be soup, sandwiches and salads, it's all good homemade fare. But, of course, it's the mid-morning or afternoon tea that brings a lot of custom, thanks to the superb homebaked treats at this lovely café. **Seats 60**. *Mon-Fri 10-6 (Thu to 8), Sat 9-6, Sun 12-6.*

Pichet

14-15 Trinity Street Dublin 2 ✆ *01 677 1060 www.pichetrestaurant.com*

With the dashing Masterchef presenter Nick Munier front of house, and chef Stephen Gibson from L'Ecrivain in the kitchen, Pichet has impressive credentials. The classy, light-filled bistro is part Gallic flair, part Irish charm, with keenly priced menus featuring simple, good food with plenty for the curious foodie as well as more conventional diners. In addition to the restaurant, Pichet coffee shop is open during the day for breakfast, light lunches and snacks. *Mon-Fri 8am-10.30pm, Sat 10am-11pm, Sun 12-9pm.*

The Pig's Ear

4 Nassau Street Dublin 2 ✆ *01 670 3865 www.thepigsear.ie*

The relaxed décor and views of Trinity College's grounds make a perfect setting for Stephen McAllister's fabulous and affordable comfort food. Champion of Ireland's finest produce, he revels in taking traditional Irish favourites and presenting them in fresh and imaginative ways. Modestly billed as 'no frills' food, this understatement belies the wonderful cooking using world-class ingredients - and this pleasing restaurant is now taking its well-earned place among Dublin's fines. **Seats 80**. *L&D Mon-Sat. Closed Sun & Bank Hols. CC.*

The Port House

64a South William St. Dublin 2 ✆ *01 677 0298 www.porthouse.ie*

Gorgeously dark and atmospheric this hip little tapas bar is lit by candlelight. Bringing a taste of Spain to South William Street menus offer a couple of dozen tapas-size items. Cooking is good, there are some value wines, and it's a fun, relaxed spot. **Seats 100** *(outdoors, 6); Tapas served daily, all day 11-1am (Sun to 11pm). Closed 25-26 Dec. CC.*

The Porterhouse

16-18 Parliament Street Temple Bar Dublin 2 *℃ 01 679 8847*
www.theporterhouse.ie / www.porterhousebrewco.com

The Porterhouse opened Dublin's first microbrewery pub in 1996, a pioneer in what has become Ireland's booming craft beer movement. They are now Ireland's largest independent brewery, but you don't even have to like beer to love it here. Imaginative décor, better than average bar food and an upbeat atmosphere are part of the attraction too. ***Seats 50****. Open 11.30 - 12 daily (Thu-Sat to 2/2.30). Bar food served 12-9 daily (Sun 12.30-9.30). Closed 25 Dec & Good Fri. CC.*

 Queen of Tarts

4 Cork Hill Dame Street Dublin 2 *℃ 01 670 7499 www.queenoftarts.ie*

This little tearoom is constantly abuzz with happy customers tucking into the delicious baked goods, both sweet and savoury, that are the stock in trade of sisters Yvonne and Regina Fallon. Most people pop in for a snack, but you could just as easily have a 3-course lunch. Inexpensive, consistently excellent food, lovely atmosphere and great service. [*Also around the corner at: 3-4 Cow's Lane, Temple Bar, tel 01 633 4681]. ***Seats 25****. Open daily: Mon-Fri 8am - 7pm (L12-7); Sat, 9am-7pm; Sun 10am - 6pm. Closed 24-28 Dec, bank hols. CC.*

 **Residence - Restaurant Forty One**

41 Saint Stephen's Green Dublin 2 *℃ 01 662 0000 www.residence.ie*

 Stylish, elegant and hip, fine food aficionados flock to Residence to savour Graham Neville's luxurious and magical cuisine at Restaurant Forty One (The Guide's Restaurant of the Year 2012). Housed on the top floor of the private members club (and, thankfully open to non-members) three elegant dining rooms showcase Graham Neville's exquisite cooking featuring a thrilling roll call of seasonal Irish produce. A special occasion destination, the perfectly pitched service ensures it's still a relaxed, impressive and contemporary affair. *D Tue-Sat; L Tue-Sun. Closed Sun, Mon, bank hols, 24-30 Dec. CC.*

 **Restaurant Patrick Guilbaud**

21 Upper Merrion Street Dublin 2 *℃ 01 676 4192 www.restaurantpatrickguilbaud.net*

 Every capital city has its great restaurant and Guilbaud's is Dublin's gastronomic heaven. Elegant and luxurious, this special dining room is part of a Georgian townhouse adjoining the Merrion Hotel. Head chef Guillaume Lebrun has presided over this fine kitchen since the restaurant opened in its original premises in 1981, and is renowned for exceptional modern classic cuisine, based on the best Irish produce in season, with menus changed daily. His

luxurious, wide-ranging menus include a wonderfully creative 8-course Dégustation Menu at €130, with a shorter midweek alternative offered at €90; at the other end of the spectrum, a daily table d'hote lunch menu has long offered the best value fine dining in Ireland. Each dish is a masterpiece of flavour and beautiful presentation matched by faultless service under the relaxed supervision of Restaurant Manager Stéphane Robin with Patrick Guilbaud often present to greet guests personally. Contemporary French cooking at its best. *A handsome book, 'Restaurant Patrick Guilbaud The First Thirty Years', is available from the restaurant and can be purchased online through their website; all profits go to the Irish Hospice Foundation. **Seats 80**. *L & D Tue-Sat. Closed Sun & Mon, bank hols, Christmas week. CC.*

Ristorante Terrazzo Italia

Second Floor Powerscourt Townhouse Centre South William Street Dublin 2
☎ *01 670 8577 www.terrazzoitalia.com*

A lively daytime haunt on the second floor balcony of Powerscourt Townhouse, diners can expect unpretentious top-notch Italian food from chef-proprietor Gianfranco Locci who is the Director of the Professional Association of Italian Chefs in Ireland. But Terrazzo Italia is much more than just great Italian food; it's also all about ambience and warm, friendly service. *Tue, Wed, Fri & Sun 12-6pm, Thu & Sat 12–8pm. Closed Mon.*

Rustic Stone

17 South Great George's St Dublin 2 ☎ *01 707 9596 www.rusticstone.ie*

Run by Dylan McGrath, one of Ireland's most talented and creative chefs (and Masterchef presenter), the menu at this fashionable and buzzy restaurant offers healthy food in flavour combinations destined to wow. Dylan may have left his fine dining roots behind but his creative genius is put to good use in everything from the stunning salads to light bites, creative burgers, pasta and hot stone dishes you cook yourself at the table on volcanic rock. An icon-laden menu denotes whether the delicious dishes are wheat-, gluten-, dairy-, and sugar-free, low in saturated fat, vegetarian, or contain a superfood. *Mon-Fri L&D, Sat & Sun all day from 1pm.*

Saagar Indian Restaurant

16 Harcourt Street Dublin 2 ☎ *01 475 5060 www.saagarindianrestaurants.com*

Run by Meera and Sunil Kumar, Saagar is in the basement of a house where Bram Stoker, author of Dracula, once lived; it is one of Dublin's oldest Indian restaurants and, although a little dated, has enduring appeal. The food is authentic, with menus offering a wide range of regional speciality dishes, all prepared from fresh ingredients and coded with a range of one to four stars to indicate the heat level. Service is knowledgeable and attentive. **Seats 60**. *L Mon-Fri; D daily 5.30-11. Closed L Sat, L Sun & Christmas week. CC.*

Saba

26 -28 Clarendon Street Dublin 2 ☎ *01 679 2000 www.sabadublin.com*

Pushing the boundaries of familiar Thai cuisine, the chic and stylish Saba serves up delicious food and super cocktails in a vibrant atmosphere. The décor is black, modern and sophisticated, and there's some real culinary adventure alongside old favourites. There are now plenty of other places to get authentic cheap and cheerful Vietnamese and Thai food, but this is the smart version and well worth the culinary detour. Cookery classes are offered too, and Saba The Cookbook is available from their website, with proceeds to charity. **Seats 130**. *Open daily noon-10pm (to 12 Fri/Sat). Closed 25-26 Dec. CC.*

Salamanca

1 St Andrew's Street Dublin 2 ☎ *01 677 4799 www.salamanca.ie*

A relaxed bar and Spanish restaurant that serves up well-priced, tasty tapas. The menu – which is in Spanish with English explanations – is flexible enough to suit anything from a light lunch to a full dinner and there's plenty of delicious choices. Spanish staples are generally well handled, and the handy location, delightful staff and good value make this place busy at peak times. ***Seats 120***. *Mon-Thu, 12 noon-11 pm, Fri & Sat to midnight, Sun 1-10pm. Closed 25/26 Dec. CC.*

 San Lorenzos

Unit 9 Castle House South Great Georges Street Dublin 2 ☎ *01 478 9383 www.sanlorenzos.ie*

Temple Garner's signature style of Italian-American cooking has a loyal following and his latest venture showcases his gutsy cooking at its best. Add in a cool pared back dining room and impressive front-of-house team and you'll see why it's hard to get a table in this hip lunch, brunch and dinner spot. *L Thu-Sun; D daily. CC.*

 Seagrass

30 South Richmond Street Portobello Dublin 2 ☎ *01 478 9595 www.seagrassdublin.com*

Seagrass is smart, stylish and serious about food. Chef-proprietor Séan Drugan's delicious creations show real skill and his menu is packed with original and creative dishes, many with European influences. There's a short wine list but you may prefer to bring your favourite tipple, as they operate a Bring Your Own policy. There's no corkage charged either, making a meal at Seagrass real value. ***Seats 95*** *(outdoors, 4). Open daily for L&D. CC.*

Shanahan's on the Green

119 St. Stephen's Green Dublin 2 ☎ *01 407 0939 www.shanahans.ie*

This opulent restaurant on St Stephen's Green was Dublin's first dedicated American-style steakhouse. Their wide-ranging menu also offers plenty of other meats, poultry and seafood but the big attraction for hungry diners with deep pockets is their certified Irish Angus beef. The wine list includes many special bottles with a strong presence from the best of Californian producers. ***Seats 100***. *L Fri only (except for groups). D Mon-Sat. Closed Sun, Christmas period. CC.*

 **The Shelbourne Dublin**

27 St Stephen's Green Dublin 2 ☎ *01 663 4500 www.theshelbourne.ie*

Beautifully renovated, this 19th century hotel is still the heart and soul of Georgian Dublin. Famed for its bars, afternoon tea and sense of old world luxury, the modern facelift has done little compromise its iconic feel. From uniformed doormen to sparkling chandeliers the accommodation is equally luxurious, especially rooms overlooking St Stephen's Green. The famous Horseshoe Bar and larger No. 27 Bar & Lounge remain Dublin institutions, while dining can be enjoyed in the stylish Saddle Room or Lord Mayor's Lounge. The new Spa at The Shelbourne is a luxurious, high spec addition to the hotel and service everywhere is superb. ***Rooms 265***. *Restaurant* ***seats 120***; *L&D daily. Bar food served 11-9pm daily. Open all year. CC.*

Sheridans Cheesemongers

11 South Anne Street Dublin 2 ☎ *01 679 3143 www.sheridanscheesemongers.com*

Just as the pioneering West Cork cheesemakers revived artisan cheesemaking in Ireland, the Sheridan brothers transformed attitudes to maturing it, buying it and caring for it. Stocks reflect the seasons and are mainly Irish, but other equally carefully sourced European foods are also available. Synonymous with good cheese in Ireland, this is Sheridans' most famous shop, although the business originated in Galway, where it still prospers. *Open daily & cheeses sold at selected farmers' markets; shops also at: Galway, Waterford (Ardkeen Quality Food Store) & Carnaross, Co Meath.*

 Silk Road Café

Chester Beatty Library Dublin Castle Dublin 2 ☎ *01 407 0770 www.silkroadcafe.ie*

The waft of fresh spices on the air will lead you to this casual café on the ground floor of the Chester Beatty Library at Dublin Castle. Majoring on tasty Middle-Eastern dishes at excellent prices, Abraham Phelan and his dedicated team bring together Middle Eastern, Mediterranean, vegetarian and organic options. Relaxed, informal and great value, it has a loyal following. **Seats 65**. *Open Mon-Fri, 10-5. Closed Mon (Oct-May), Good Friday, 24-26 Dec, Bank Hols. CC. [Also at: Little Jerusalem, Rathmines, Dublin 6. Tue-Sun, 3-10.30; T: 01 412 6912]*

 Skinflint

19 Crane Lane Dublin 2 ☎ *01 670 9719 www.joburger.ie/skinflint*

Quirky and aptly named this is an urban pizza joint for the 21st century from the team behind Jo'Burger and Crackbird, using the same winning formula of focusing on one speciality and doing it well. It's the place to dip into sharing bites, or enjoy a unique spin on super thin and crispy 'flat bread' style pizzas with gourmet toppings using artisan ingredients, and Irish craft beers are offered too. *Sun-Mon 12-9, Tue-Thu 12-10, Fri Sat 12-10.30. CC.*

 SoHo

17 South Great Georges Street Dublin 2 ☎ *01 707 9596 www.sohodublin.com*

The look is reminiscent of a 1960s caff, conveying a clear message that your money won't be wasted here - a nice thought underlined by friendly, efficient staff who demonstrate that your time is valued too. Everything is home-made on the premises, all the meat is Irish and vegetarian dishes are highlighted on the menu – and if you don't need dessert, you can have chocolate truffles with your coffee instead.

 The Stag's Head

1 Dame Court Dublin 2 ☎ *01 679 3687*

In Dame Court, just behind the Adams Trinity Hotel, this impressive establishment has retained its original late-Victorian decor and is one of the city's finest pubs. It can get very busy at times but this lovely pub is still worth a visit.

Stauntons on the Green

83 St Stephen's Green Dublin 2 📞*01 478 2300 www.stauntonsonthegreen.ie*

Well-located with views over St Stephen's Green this comfortable guesthouse with period reception rooms and private gardens offers moderately priced accommodation, with all the necessary amenities and private parking. **Rooms 57** *(24 shower only). Closed 24-27 Dec. CC.*

 ## Stephen's Green Hotel

St Stephen's Green Dublin 2 📞*01 607 3600 www.ocallaghanhotels.com*

Superbly located, this hotel on the south-west corner of St Stephen's Green incorporates two refurbished Georgian house but also boasts a four-storey atrium, and contemporary décor. The very comfortable air-conditioned bedrooms have exceptionally good facilities, particularly for business travellers, and there's a bar and restaurant on site. **Rooms 99**. *Open all year. CC.*

 ## Steps of Rome

1 Chatham Street Dublin 2 📞*01 670 5630 www.stepsofrome.ie*

An inexpensive little Italian place specialising in pizza, this authentic one-room café just beside Neary's pub is a favourite lunch spot or meeting place for many discerning Dubliners. **Seats 18**. *Open Mon-Sat 12 noon-11pm (to 11.30pm Thu-Sat), Sun 12-10pm. No CC.*

 🏃 📶 B ## Temple Bar Hotel

Fleet Street Temple Bar Dublin 2 📞*01 677 3333 www.templebarhotel.com*

In the heart of the city and handy for both sides of the river this pleasant hotel has good-sized bedrooms and decent amenities at relatively reasonably prices. **Rooms 129**. *Closed Christmas. CC.*

 ## The Dining Room at La Stampa

35 Dawson Street Dublin 2 📞*01 612 7911 www.lastampa.ie*

Recently re-launched as The Dawson, this beautiful dining room has lost none of its renowned glamour and panache - although now open all day, it is likely to remain a fashionable evening destination for a celebration or romantic date. **Seats 200**. *Open 7am-11pm daily. Closed 25 Dec. CC.*

 ## Thornton's Restaurant

128 St Stephen's Green Dublin 2 📞*01 478 7008 www.thorntonsrestaurant.com*

With views overlooking St Stephen's Green, Kevin and Muriel Thornton's renowned fine dining restaurant enjoys a central location on the top floor of the Fitzwilliam Hotel. One of Ireland's most gifted chefs, Kevin uses impeccably sourced ingredients to create hugely imaginative culinary delights that please the eye as much as the taste buds. The set lunch menu offers outstanding value, with dinner menus from €76 for three-courses. Whether you're seeking the ultimate culinary experience of Thornton's legendary 8-course surprise menus or simply dropping by for casual canapés in the lounge, you're guaranteed a sensational experience. With charming staff and a stellar wine list this is Irish dining at its finest. **Seats 80**. *D Tue-Sat; L Thu-Sat. Closed 24 Dec - 2 Jan. CC.*

Toners

139 Lower Baggot Street Dublin 2 *01 676 3090* *www.tonerspub.ie*

One of the few authentic old pubs left in Dublin, Toners is definitely worth a visit. Among many other claims to fame, it is said to be the only pub ever visited by the poet W.B. Yeats.

Toscana

3 Cork Hill Dame Street Dublin 2 *01 670 9785* *www.toscanarestaurant.ie*

Just across the road from Dublin Castle, PJ and Dee Butuci's pleasing Italian restaurant has an unusual USP - many of the ingredients used in the kitchen come from their own Co Wicklow farm. There are menus for every part of the day, with quite a selection of seasonal dishes - and children are well looked after, with healthy choices available. *Open 7 Days from 12 noon till Late.*

Town Kildare Street

21 Kildare Street Dublin 2 *01 662 4800*

Formerly Town Bar & Grill, the rebranded Town Kildare Street has repositioned itself as a 'high-end casual' brasserie - and the kitchen is now headed up by Cathal Leonard, former Head Chef at Chapter One. The stylish subterranean décor hasn't changed, so fans will feel right at home. An appealing selection of brasserie dishes uses carefully sourced seasonal Irish ingredients with lots of cheffy touches and the high level of creativity and skill provides plenty of potential for a memorable experience. *Seats 80. Tue-Sat: L from 12.30pm, D from 5.30pm. Closed Sun & Mon. CC.*

Trinity Capital Hotel

Pearse Street Dublin 2 *01 648 1000* *www.trinitycapitalhotel.com*

The clash of jewel colours make this bright, modern and comfortable hotel stand out from the pack. Centrally located for business and leisure, the lobby wine and coffee bar make handy meeting places. Rooms are comfortable and Café Cairo offers an above-average experience for a hotel restaurant, providing an appealing alternative for guests who prefer to dine in. *Rooms 172 (10 shower only). Closed 24-26 Dec. CC.*

Trinity Lodge

12 South Frederick Street Dublin 2 *01 617 0900* *www.trinitylodge.com*

An attractively maintained guesthouse just yards away from Trinity College, guests can expect a high standard of accommodation at a reasonable price. As is the way with Georgian buildings, rooms get smaller towards the top so the most spacious accommodation is on lower floors. There are numerous good restaurants nearby. *Rooms 23 (16 shower only). Open all year. CC.*

Trocadero Restaurant

3/4 St Andrew Street Dublin 2 *01 677 5545* *www.trocadero.ie*

An institution with thespians and theatregoers since 1956, the long-running Troc serves retro food in suitably theatrical surrounds. Although recently refurbished, the ambience remains intact with photos of the celebrities who've passed through the place and cosy, and intimate seating. Greatly updated dishes reminiscent of the '70s are served up by lovely, friendly staff in this unapologetically old school haunt. *Seats 110*. D Mon-Sat. Closed Sun, 25 Dec - 2 Jan, Good Fri. CC.

 Unicorn Restaurant

12B Merrion Court off Merrion Row Dublin 2 ✆*01 662 4757* *www.unicornrestaurant.com*

Perennially fashionable, this long-standing Italian is known for good regional and modern Italian food, in a wonderfully convivial space. Famous for its antipasto buffet, piano bar, directly imported wines and exceptionally friendly staff it's particularly charming in summer, as the doors open out onto a terrace. The entire team from sister restaurant Il Segreto has recently taken over this restaurant and will no doubt ensure its continued success. *Seats 80* (outdoors, 30). Open Mon-Sat, 12.30-11pm. Closed Sun, bank hols, 25 Dec-2 Jan. CC.

 The Vintage Kitchen

7 Poolbeg St Dublin 2 ✆*01 6798 705* *www.thevintagekitchen.ie*

Sister restaurant to Portobello's popular Seagrass, The Vintage Kitchen follows the same appealing MO of wonderful cooking, superb value and a no-corkage BYO policy. Short but appealing menus brim with the best of Irish ingredients and, despite the casual setting, there's some seriously stylish cooking going on. L Tue-Sat 11.30-3, D Tue -Sat 5-10. CC.

 Wagamama

Unit 4B South King Street Dublin 2 ✆*01 478 2152* *www.wagamama.ie*

Part of the UK chain, this large Japanese noodle canteen majors in tasty Asian staples and no-nonsense service. In a huge basement canteen that's simple, functional (and noisy) diners share long tables. Staff are friendly and efficient, delivering generous noodle dishes and Japanese classics as they're ready. Informal, tasty food at a good price. *Seats 136*. Open Sun-Wed noon- 10pm, Thu-Sat noon-11pm. Closed 25-26 Dec. CC.

 **The Westbury Hotel**

Grafton Street Dublin 2 ✆*01 679 1122* *www.doylecollection.com/westbury*

Possibly the most conveniently situated of all Dublin's luxury hotels, The Westbury Hotel is seconds from Grafton Street (and with underground parking). Unashamedly sumptuous, the hotel's public areas drip with chandeliers although the bedrooms are more contemporary. Fashionable for afternoon tea, the hotel is also popular with business and corporate guests. Wilde, the beautiful Art Deco-influenced restaurant offers modern in-house dining while there's casual brasserie and bar fare Cafe at Novo. *Rooms 205*. Wilde Restaurant seats 120. L&D Tue-Sat. Wilde closed Sun & Mon. Hotel open all year. CC.

 **The Westin Dublin**

Westmoreland Street Dublin 2 ✆*01 645 1000* *www.thewestindublin.com*

Comprising two Victorian landmark buildings The Westin oozes character and style. The old bank's features have been beautifully incorporated: the magnificent Banking Hall makes a stunning conference and banqueting room, while the vaults serve as the stylish Mint bar. Luxuriously appointed, the service and facilities are superb and include the elegant Exchange Restaurant and Cocktail Bar. Carefully compiled me nus offer quality cooking, with an emphasis on seafood, and offer surprisingly good value. Sunday Brunch is quite an institution. **Rooms 163**. Restaurant **seats 60**. L Tue-Fri, D Tue-Sat, Sun Brunch only, 12-4.30pm. Restaurant closed Mon, L Sat, D Sun. Hotel open all year. CC.

Whitefriar Grill

16 Aungier Street Dublin 2 ✆ 01 475 9003 www.whitefriargrill.ie

You could almost miss this cosy spot on a dash up Aungier Street, but it's worth seeking out, especially for a relaxed weekend brunch. Chunky tables, chilled tunes, flickering nightlights, and a neat little bar create a laidback vibe for the delightfully original menus. The cooking is precise, presentation pretty, portions generous and flavours superb, making this a great asset to the area. Reasonably priced too, including the short but well considered wine list. D Tue-Sun; Brunch Sat & Sun, 12-4pm. Closed Mon. CC.

Yamamori Noodles

71 South Great George's Street Dublin 2 ✆ 01 475 5001 www.yamamorinoodles.ie

Affordable, speedy cooking with lots of flavour is the secret of Yamamori's success. The lively Japanese noodle joint, with long bench seating, is especially popular with students and large groups. Buzzy and fun, specialities include ramen, sushi and sashimi served in generous portions that give great value. [Also at: Yamamori Izakaya, 12/13 South Great Georges St, Dublin 2 (www.yamamoriizakaya.ie); Yamamori Sushi, 38/39 Lower Ormond Quay, Dublin 1 (www.yamamorisushi.ie)] **Seats 130**. Open daily, 12.30-11.30. Closed Christmas, 1 Jan, Good Fri.

DUBLIN 3 - CLONTARF / FAIRVIEW

Fairview and its more fashionable shoreside neighbour, Clontarf, are a few miles from central Dublin and convenient to attractions such as the Croke Park stadium; championship golf at the Royal Dublin Golf Club, walking, bird watching, kite surfing and many other activities on Bull Island, a large sand island in Dublin Bay. St Anne's Park is lovely, with its leafy walks, rose garden and weekly farmers' market at the Red Stables (Sat). There are also sites of historical significance such as the Casino at Marino and Fairview Crescent, a former home of Bram Stoker, author of Dracula.

Clontarf Castle Hotel

Castle Avenue Clontarf Dublin 3 ✆ 01 833 2321 www.clontarfcastle.ie

This 17th century castle has been cleverly renovated to combine the charm of the old with the comfort of the new. Popular with the business community, the luxurious, warmly decorated bedrooms and excellent staff ensure it's a comfortable spot for a leisure break too. The striking Fahrenheit Grill majors in steaks and seafood. **Rooms 111**. Fahrenheit Grill: D daily; L Sun only. Bar food in Knights Bar all day. Hotel open all year. CC.

The Croke Park Hotel

Jones's Road Dublin 3 ✆ 01 871 4444 www.doylecollection.com

The first major hotel to be built in this area, the well-designed Croke Park Hotel brings much-needed facilities and is very useful for business visitors, and fans attending events at Croke Park stadium just across the road. Food in the hotel's Sideline Bistro is a step above the standard hotel fare. **Rooms 232** (10 shower only). Closed 24-27 Dec. CC.

Downstairs Restaurant

Hollybrook Park Clontarf Dublin 3 📞*01 833 8883 www.downstairs.ie*

Tucked away from Clontarf's main drag this smart and comfortable basement restaurant has become something of a culinary hot spot. Proprietor-chef Brian Walsh (whose CV includes time with Dylan McGrath) offers stylish and tasty seasonal cooking of well-sourced food at reasonable prices in a relaxing atmosphere. The quirky décor and handsome cocktail bar add to the appeal of this lively bar-cum-restaurant. *Seats 85. D Tue-Sat, Sun 1–9. Closed Mon. CC.*

 The Food Room

48 Clontarf Road Clontarf Dublin 3 📞*01 833 2259 www.thefoodroom.ie*

Putting a former car showroom to good use, Alison and Barry Stephens' deli, grocers and café always hits the spot. *Open 7 days. Mon-Fri 8-7, Sat & Sun 9-6 (bank hol weekends Sun 10-5. Mon 10-4).*

 Hemmingways

2B Vernon Avenue Clontarf Dublin 3 📞*01 833 3338*

A charming neighbourhood favourite, serving up fabulously fresh seafood, expect a hearty welcome from the owner, Brian Creedon. The kitchen's strengths lie in its choice of ingredients and skilled seasoning – seafood is the star but everything is cooked to perfection with deliciously fresh and clean flavours and rustic bistro style presentation. A shortish wine list is fairly priced and Hemmingways' Irish coffees are legendary. *Seats 28; D Tue-Sat, Sun Tapas, 5-8pm. Closed Mon, 25 Dec. CC.*

 Kennedys Food Store & Bistro

5 Fairview Strand Fairview Dublin 3 📞*01 833 1400 www.kennedysfoodstore.com*

A successful deli, bakery, takeaway, daytime café and evening bistro. Outside tables are a hit, despite the busy road, and the bustling ground floor café serves up quality cooked breakfasts, good coffee and delicious home-baked treats. Lunchtime offers creative salads, sandwiches on Bretzel Bakery bread and hot specials. Desserts are a highlight of the evening bistro menu. *Bistro open D Tue-Sat. Shop open all day, daily.*

 Kinara Restaurant

318 Clontarf Road Dublin 3 📞*01 833 6759 www.kinara.ie*

Serving delicious Pakistani and North Indian cuisine with views overlooking Bull Island, there's little to fault at this smart and elegant Clontarf restaurant. Firmly established as the area's leading ethnic restaurant (and one of the best in Dublin) there's a declared commitment to local produce on the exciting menu and each dish is clearly described. The quality of cooking is exemplary and fine food is backed up by attentive, professional service and fair prices. *Seats 77. L Thu-Sun, D daily (early D menu Mon-Thu). Closed 25-26 Dec, 1 Jan. CC.*

 Moloughney's

9 Vernon Avenue Clontarf Dublin 3 📞*01 833 0002 www.moloughneys.ie*

The best kind of neighbourhood restaurant: a fun and relaxed place that's great for coffee, breakfast, lunch or a serious dinner. Kind, attentive staff work quickly and efficiently, and children are not only welcome but have proper daytime and evening menus. Food is seasonally influenced and everything is home made and delicious. *Seats 105 (outdoors, 8). Open all day, daily, B, L & D. Closed 25/26 Dec, 1st week Jan. CC.*

Nolans Supermarket

49 Vernon Avenue Clontarf Dublin 3 ✆ *01 833 8361 www.nolans.ie*

A supermarket with a difference, this excellent well-stocked independent grocers and speciality food store is the place northsiders head for when they want a good range of artisan foods from all around Ireland. It's a fantastic shop, managing to be both a broad-range supermarket for the local community and a speciality store - and nothing is too much trouble for the brilliant staff. *Open Mon-Sat 8.30-7 Thurs & Fri to 9pm). Closed Sunday.*

Restaurant Ten Fourteen

324 Clontarf Road Clontarf Dublin 3 ✆ *01 805 4877 www.restaurant1014.com*

With clear views across to Bull Island it's easy see why Restaurant Ten Fourteen's outdoor tables are always busy. Indoors this bustling bistro (named for the famous Battle of Clontarf) serves up a mouth-watering selection of crowd pleasers in a comfortable, stylish room. Portions are generous, service efficient and prices reasonable, with all profits going directly to CASA, the Caring and Sharing Association, which owns the restaurant. *Seats 60 (outdoors, 12). Open from 10am-"late" daily L&D Mon-Sat. Closed 25/26 Dec. CC.*

Tibors Bistro

11b Vernon Avenue Clontarf Dublin 3 ✆ *01 833 3989 www.tibors.ie*

Tibors is the quintessential bistro, with cheerful staff, classy décor (which works equally well in the day or night), convivial atmosphere, charming service and good food. Portions are generous and quality ingredients are evident across all dishes. The layout of the room means parties, families and couples can all be catered for in real comfort, which is a smart move in a neighbourhood restaurant. *Seats 75 (outdoors, 30). Open Mon-Sat, 12-11.30pm. Sun 11am-10.30pm. Closed Christmas. CC.*

Wrights of Marino

21 Marino Mart Dublin 3 ✆ *01 833 3636 www.wrightsofmarino.com*

"If it swims we have it!" is the well chosen motto at this third-generation fish shop. Oak smoked salmon is the speciality they're best known for, but they carry a wide range of other fish and seafood too. They also have a special reputation as a quality wholesaler, and you'll see them credited on many of the top menus around Ireland. *Closed Sun.*

DUBLIN 4

Aberdeen Lodge

53 Park Avenue Ballsbridge Dublin 4 ✆ *01 283 8155 www.aberdeen-lodge.com*

Centrally located (close to the Sydney Parade DART station) this handsome period house is in a pleasant leafy street and offers all the advantages of a hotel at guesthouse prices. Elegantly furnished guestrooms, pleasant staff, immaculate housekeeping and a particularly good breakfast with views of the beautiful garden are a real draw. **Rooms 17**. *Residents' meals available. Open all year. CC.*

Alix Gardners Cookery School

71 Waterloo Road Dublin 4 ✆ *01 668 1553 www.dublincookery.com*

Alix Gardener offers practical, fun, and informal cookery classes in Ballsbridge, in central Dublin. Trained at The Cordon Bleu and Leith's in London, Alix Gardner is a founder member of Euro-Toques Ireland (est. 1986) and was the first to set up a practical cookery school in this country; she offers a wide range of practical and demonstration classes at all levels, and also operates a catering service.

Ariel House

50-54 Lansdowne Road Ballsbridge Dublin 4 ✆ *01 668 5512 www.ariel-house.net*

In the shadows of Aviva stadium this impressive family-run guesthouse offers luxurious accommodation, warmly professional service and immaculate house keeping. Breakfast, served in an extended conservatory overlooking the garden, is especially lavish, catering for diverse appetites. Not surprisingly it's a favourite port of call for many returning guests. **Rooms 37** *(1 shower only). Closed 21 Dec - 4 Jan. CC.*

Asador

1 Victoria House Haddington Road Dublin 4 ✆ *01 254 5353 www.asador.ie*

With its flavoursome food and great service, the stylish Asador has brought something different to Dublin dining. The stainless steel firepit that gives the super cool Asador restaurant its name is modelled on the rustic asados of local meats cooked over vine cuttings in the Castilla-Leon region. Beef steaks are the speciality, ranging from rib-eye and fillet to 10-ounce sirloin and cotes-de-boeuf for two, but there is plenty else to choose from too. *Open from 12 noon daily; [L Mon-Fri;Brunch Sat & Sun; D daily]*

Baan Thai

16 Merrion Road Ballsbridge Dublin 4 ✆ *01 660 8833*

Delicious aromas and oriental music greet you as you climb the stairs to Lek and Eamon Lancaster's well-appointed first floor restaurant opposite the RDS. Thai furnishings and music make a comfortable setting for the range of tasty Thai dishes on offer. [*Also at: Leopardstown, 01 293 6996; Central Park Luas Station]. **Seats 64**. *L Wed-Fri. D daily. Closed 24-26 Dec. CC.*

Bella Cuba Restaurant

11 Ballsbridge Terrace Dublin 4 ✆ *01 660 5539 www.bella-cuba.com*

Colourful décor, lively music and good mojitos set the tone for a flavour-packed Caribbean experience at this Cuban restaurant. Juan Carlos's cooking demonstrates the Spanish,

Caribbean and South American influences on Cuba's food and there are no cheffy tricks, just good honest cooking. Service is professional and friendly, adding to the appeal of this cheerful restaurant. *Seats 33. L Wed-Fri; D daily. Closed 25-28 Dec, Good Fri. CC.*

Berman & Wallace

Belfield Office Park Beaver Row Clonskeagh Dublin 4 ✆ *01 219 6252 www.bermanandwallace.com*

Berman & Wallace is now one of Dublin's best-known caterers but here, in an unusual location surrounded by offices, local workers are well served with tasty and honest daytime cooking from this popular brasserie-style restaurant. Alongside a wide-ranging menu of crowd-pleasing dishes there are juices and smoothies for the diet conscious, and wines by the glass or bottle. *Seats 80 (outdoors, 20). Open Mon-Fri, 7.30-2.30. Closed Sat/Sun, Christmas, Easter, bank hols. CC.*

Bewleys Hotel

Merrion Road Ballsbridge Dublin 4 ✆ *01 647 3300 www.bewleyshotels.com*

This modern hotel's clever design incorporates a handsome landmark period building right beside the RDS. Bedrooms are spacious and well-equipped and you get a lot of comfort at a very reasonable cost. *Rooms 304. Closed 24-26 Dec. CC.*

 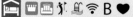

Blakes Hotel & Spa

50 Merrion Road Ballsbridge Dublin 4 ✆ *01 668 8324 www.blakeshotelandspa.com*

A boutique bolt-hole in the Embassy Belt, the handsome period exterior belies the ultra modern accommodation, private spa and outdoor pool at this chic address. Handily situated for anyone attending exhibitions in Dublin, as it's directly opposite the RDS, it offers great breakfasts and an attractive alternative to hotel accommodation. *Rooms 34. Open all year. CC.*

Brownes

18 Sandymount Green Sandymount Dublin 4 ✆ *01 269 7316*

By day it's gourmet sandwiches and baked goods; by night classical French fare at this popular BYO neighbourhood spot. *Seats 22. D 6-10pm.*

The Burlington Hotel Dublin

Upper Leeson Street Dublin 4 ✆ *01 618 5600 www.doubletree3.hilton.com*

One of Dublin's largest and most famous hotels, the Burlington hotel came into the ownership of Hilton Hotels in 2012 and has recently been re-branded the DT Dublin Hotel.

Butlers Town House

44 Lansdowne Road Ballsbridge Dublin 4 ✆ *01 667 4022 www.butlers-hotel.com*

On a corner site in Dublin's 'embassy belt' and close to the Aviva stadium, this large townhouse/guesthouse has been extensively refurbished and luxuriously decorated in a Victorian country house style. A small hotel in all but name it offers attractive public rooms, individually decorated bedrooms (some with four-posters) and good breakfasts. *Rooms 19. Closed 21 Dec-5 Jan. CC.*

Canal Bank Café

146 Upper Leeson Street Dublin 4 ✆ *01 664 2135*
http://www.tribeca.ie/cbc_pages/cbc_index.html

Trevor Browne and Gerard Foote's well-known almost-canalside Dublin restaurant majors in quality informal food or 'everyday dining', but the philosophy has always been to use only the best ingredients - organic beef and lamb, free-range chicken and a wide variety of fresh fish daily. The broad menu is user-friendly and backed up by a lively daily specials board and their tasty, modern fare is served up in a relaxed and low key dining space. *Seats 65. Open 10am-11pm daily. Closed 25-26 Dec. CC.*

The Chop House

2 Shelbourne Road Dublin 4 ✆ *087 299 4176 www.thechophouse.ie*

Imaginative, well-judged cooking is the calling card of this busy gastro-pub, run by Euro-Toques chef Kevin Arundel. Good value menus are short, but nicely varied and interesting, with steaks, notably Hereford 32-day aged steaks, the speciality. Just as the ingredients are excellent so too is the cooking, with everything attractively presented. The warm, buzzy atmosphere makes this a relaxed and informal spot. *Seats 45 (outdoors, 14). Open L Mon-Fri, Sat brunch, D Mon-Sat. Sun traditional roast & à la carte 1-8. CC.*

Clynes Bros

12 Fitzwilliam Street Ringsend Dublin 4 ✆ *01 668 0456 www.otoolesbutchers.com*

Ringsend Branch of O'Toole Master Butchers, Terenure, Dublin 6W (see entry). Specialists in top quality meats, including organic. *Open Mon-Sat, 8.30-6. Closed Sun.*

Dunne & Crescenzi

11 Seafort Avenue Sandymount Dublin 4 ✆ *01 667 3252 www.dunneandcrescenzi.com*

Offering the same lively experience as its popular city centre big sister, this atmospheric neighbourhood café, restaurant and wine shop serves delicious ingredients-led Italian food, including excellent antipasti, directly sourced Italian wines and good coffee. Convenient to the RDS and Aviva Stadium, this is a good spot for a meal before or after an event. *Seats 50; Open all day, Mon-Fri 7.30am-late; Sat & Sun 9am-late. CC.*

 **Dylan Hotel Dublin**

Eastmoreland Place Dublin 4 ☎ *01 660 3000 www.dylan.ie*

 A haven of tranquillity just yards from one of Dublin's busiest city roads, this attractive boutique hotel is in a splendid Victorian building yet noted for its edgy design, with luxurious, individually designed bedrooms fitted to a very high specification. The hotel's Dylan Restaurant is expensive, but boasts a commitment to traceability, seasonality and high quality ingredients in its modern Irish cooking. The stylishly furnished bar, with a chic outdoor terrace, attracts a good buzz of customers with an all-day menu as well as their vast list of speciality cocktails. **Rooms 44**. *Restaurant seats 60 (outdoors, 20); L&D daily. Hotel closed 25-26 Dec. CC.*

 **Four Seasons Hotel**

Simmonscourt Road Dublin 4 ☎ *01 665 4000 www.fourseasons.com/dublin*

Set in its own gardens on a section of the Royal Dublin Society's show grounds, this large five star hotel offers opulent facilities; air-conditioned rooms appeal equally to leisure and business guests and there's a wonderful spa and lap pool. The grand foyer is flanked by three bars - the traditional Lobby Bar, Lounge bar with its extensive whiskey collection, and contemporary ICE, which is popular with Dubliners. Executive Chef Terry White's contemporary international menus at Seasons Restaurant combine best local ingredients with classical French cooking and offer a wide-ranging choice of luxurious dishes. Outstanding conference and meeting facilities make the hotel ideal for corporate events. **Rooms 196**. *Restaurant seats 75. L&D daily. Open all year. CC.*

 **The French Paradox**

53 Shelbourne Road Ballsbridge Dublin 4 ☎ *01 660 4068 www.thefrenchparadox.com*

The French Paradox combines a wine shop, a large and atmospheric ground floor wine bar and a dining room on the first floor. Pierre and Tanya Chapeau are renowned for their directly imported wines and food is, in theory, secondary here; but, although the choice is deliberately limited the quality is exceptional and includes great nibbles to enjoy with wine. An original and atmospheric destination. **Seats 55** *(outdoors, 12). L&D Mon-Fri; open all day Sat, 12-10; 'French Tapas' Mon-Sat 3-5. Closed Sun (except for "Rugby Match" Sundays & throughout December), Christmas, Bank Hols. CC.*

 Furama Restaurant

G/F Eirepage House Donnybrook Dublin 4 ☎ *01 283 0522 www.furama.ie*

In the sleek black interior of Rodney Mak's long-established restaurant, Freddy Lee, who has been head chef since the restaurant opened in 1989, produces terrific Chinese food with an authenticity which has been unusual in Ireland until recently. The comfortable dining room and relaxed hospitality are the perfect backdrop to the expertly cooked and beautifully presented authentic dishes. **Seats 70**. *L Thu-Fri, D Mon-Sat, Sun 1.30pm-10pm .Closed L Mon-Wed & Sat, 24-26 Dec & Good Fri. CC.*

Glenogra House

64 Merrion Road Ballsbridge Dublin 4 ✆ *01 668 3661 www.glenogra.com*

Minutes from the RDS, Peter and Veronica Donohoe's comfortable guesthouse offers wonderful service, old-school décor and really great breakfasts. The public areas have all been refurbished and, from the minute you arrive there is a great sense of welcome and hospitality. **Rooms 13** *(2 shower only). Closed 22 Dec - 10 Jan. CC.*

 Grand Canal Hotel

Grand Canal Street Dublin 4 ✆ *01 646 1000 www.grandcanalhotel.com*

Smartly maintained and with a secure car park, this well priced three star hotel is within walking distance of Dublin city centre and the Ballsbridge area and ideal for events at Grand Canal Theatre or Aviva Stadium, or for business. Rooms are spacious, there's a fine gym and a fairly standard but well-presented buffet breakfast is served in a pleasant breakfast room. **Rooms 1422.** *Closed 22-28 Dec. CC.*

 **Herbert Park Hotel**

Ballsbridge Dublin 4 ✆ *01 667 2200 www.herbertparkhotel.ie*

With lovely views over leafy Herbert Park this large, privately-owned contemporary hotel is bright, modern and comfortable. Public areas on the ground floor make a popular meeting place with excellent light meals and drinks provided by efficient waiting staff. The bright and modern style is also repeated in the very comfortable bedrooms and a good breakfast is served in the Pavilion Restaurant. **Rooms 153.** *Open all year. CC.*

 Indie Spice Sandymount

23-24 Sandymount Green Sandymount Dublin 4
✆ *01 232 0220 www.indiespice.com/sandymount/*

With restaurants in Belfast, Naas, Swords and Dublin city centre, experienced restaurateur Tariq Salahuddin knows better than most how to create a successful Indian restaurant in Ireland. Like its sisters, the stylish Sandymount Indie Spice not only serves good food - with a Bengali bent, including authentic thali - but also majors on atmosphere and great service. *Open 7 days. Mon-Fri L & D; Sat all day 12-11.30; Sun all day 1-11. CC.*

 Itsa Café

6a Sandymount Green Sandymount Dublin 4 01 219 4676 www.itsa.ie

Formerly Itsa4 and now rebranded as a café, this branch of sisters Domini and Peaches Kemp's small chain of Itsa outlets serves everything that they are famous for - notably the iconic bagels and good home baking. Open Wed-Sun 9am-5pm.

Juniors

2 Bath Avene Dublin 4 ✆ *01 664 3648*

Squashed into a row of red brick shopfronts, Juniors is a laidback Dublin restaurant of the type more often seen in the side streets of Paris or Naples. By day it's a cramped New York style deli serving really good sambos and salads, by night a hip Italian joint dishing up fresh, flavour-packed cooking. No bookings, but you can wait in the pub next door. **Seats 26.** *Open all day.*

Keshk Cafe

71 Mespil Road Dublin 4 📞*01 667 3002 www.keshkcafe.ie*

The no-frills decor at Moustafa Keshk's cheap and cheerful restaurant is compensated for by really tasty Mediterranean food, with an Egyptian leaning. Generous portions and BYO (nearby suppliers include Spar next door) make it great value - and no corkage is charged. Vegetarians are well served, the service is charming and the honest cooking is both satisfying and delicious. A little gem. *Seats 32. Open daily, 12-"late". CC.*

 Kites Restaurant

15-17 Ballsbridge Terrace Ballsbridge Dublin 4 📞*01 660 7415*

Renowned for its quality Chinese cooking, with a smattering of other styles, this bright Ballsbridge dining room always offers warm and friendly service. The cuisine is a combination of Cantonese, Szechuan, Peking and Thai – predominantly Cantonese – and menus range from the standard set meals to a list of specials. Courteous, good humoured and charming service adds to the experience. *Seats 100. L&D daily. Closed 25-26 Dec. Good Fri. CC.*

 La Péniche

Grand Canal Mespil Road Dublin 4 📞*087 790 0077 www.lapeniche.ie*

Experience French bistro fare aboard a prettily tricked out barge moored on Dublin's leafy canal. The barge is smartly got up with red velvet couches and seat covers, and gleaming varnished tables. It's quite a squeeze when fully booked, but that's all part of the fun. Thursdays dinner is even more fun, eaten under way as La Péniche cruises the canal. *Seats 45 (outdoors, 40). Open: D Wed-Sun Closed Mon & Tue (except group bookings), 1-15 Jan. CC.*

 **The Lobster Pot**

9 Ballsbridge Terrace Ballsbridge Dublin 4 📞*01 660 9170 www.thelobsterpot.ie*

Serving classic seafood dishes for over 30 impressive years, this lovely old-school restaurant prides itself on good food and wonderfully old-fashioned service. Owner Tommy Crean, restaurant manager (and sommelier) John Rigby and head chef Don McGuinness have been working here together since 1980 and their philosophy of offering the freshest of fish and seafood and 'tampering as little as possible with the product' has stood the test of time. Retro dining at its best. *D Mon-Sat. Closed Sun, 24 Dec-4 Jan, bank hols. CC.*

 Merrion Hall

54 Merrion Road Ballsbridge Dublin 4 📞*01 668 1426 www.halpinsprivatehotels.com*

A luxurious guest house opposite the RDS, the ivy-clad and atmospheric building boasts period-style décor and lovely reception areas. New rooms have almost doubled the original accommodation and there's a well-stocked library and, spacious dining room. In common with other Halpin establishments, good breakfasts are served here. *Rooms 34. Open all year. CC.*

 Mespil Hotel

Mespil Road Dublin 4 📞*01 488 4600 www.mespil.com*

Overlooking the Grand Canal and within walking distance of St Stephen's Green and all the city centre attractions in fine weather, this is an attractive, modern hotel, with nicely appointed rooms, excellent service and good value breaks. Public areas are spacious and elegant in an easy contemporary style, and the comfortable lobby makes a good meeting place. *Rooms 255*. *Closed 24-26 Dec. CC.*

 Mulberry Garden

Mulberry Lane Donnybrook Dublin 4 ☎*01 269 3300 www.mulberrygarden.ie*

Hidden down a mews lane behind a row of shops in Donnybrook, this stylish little gem opens just three nights and offers just six dishes on its weekly-changing menu. Despite the limitations foodies flock to the contemporary and novel courtyard restaurant thanks to head chef John Wyer's accomplished cooking, seasonally driven menus that showcase Irish foods and excellent service. A separate vegetarian menu is available alongside a large wine list. D only, Thu-Sat.

 **O'Connells Restaurant in Donnybrook**

135 Morehampton Road Donnybrook Dublin 4 ☎*01 269 6116 www.oconnellsdonnybrook.com*

O'Connell's restaurant has been part of the Dublin dining scene for over ten years, having begun life in Bewley's Hotel in Ballsbridge. Run by Tom O'Connell, a brother of Darina Allen of Ballymaloe Cookery School, this casual brasserie's philosophy is to use only the very best Irish ingredients – local, artisan, free-range and organic where possible – all cooked with great care. The menu sings of freshness and each dish is flavoursome and well conceived. Value for money has always been a key feature right down to the exceptionally informative wine list. *Seats 170 (outdoors, 20). Open Mon 5-10pm; Tue-Sat, 12-10.30pm & Sun L 12.30-3.30 & Supper 4.30-7.30pm). Closed Mon L, 25 Dec - 5 Jan. CC.*

🏠🎫🅴🍴🛜🅱🚻♿ **Pembroke Townhouse**

90 Pembroke Road Ballsbridge Dublin 4 ☎*01 660 0277 www.pembroketownhouse.ie*

A handsome Georgian townhouse with comfortable bedrooms, nice public areas and delicious breakfast with good home baking. Guests will enjoy hands-on manager Fiona Teehan's thoughtful touches like the invitation to 'raid the larder in the middle of the night for home baked cookies.' It's all pretty luxurious and you'll find the amenities usually expected of a hotel, including an elegant drawing room and study for residents' use, and secure private parking. *Rooms 48 (3 shower only). Closed 22 Dec - 5 Jan. CC.*

 PinkGinger

4 Serpentine Road Sandymount Dublin 4 ☎*087 986 4964 www.pinkginger.ie*

Well known for her involvement with the Avoca restaurants, Ballymaloe graduate Eimer Rainsford now runs her own 'boutique cookery school'. Students attend Supperclubs, which are classes for private groups of eight who choose the theme for the evening, watch the demonstrations and then, as Eimer puts it "sit back, feast and enjoy the wonderful food prepared with a glass of wine." A tasty little number. *Classes usually begin at 7pm.*

🍴🏠🎫🍴🛜🚻♿ **Radisson Blu St Helen's Hotel**

Stillorgan Road Dublin 4 ☎*01 218 6000 www.radissonblu.ie/sthelenshotel-dublin*

Set in formal gardens just south of Dublin's city centre, with views across Dublin Bay, there's a fine 18th century house at the heart of this impressive hotel. Careful restoration and imaginative modernisation have created interesting public areas, while bedrooms, in a modern block, are comfortably furnished to a high standard in contemporary style. Talavera, the hotel's informal Italian restaurant, has a good atmosphere and serves a well-balanced menu - and you can expect the trademark Radisson breakfast buffet too. *Rooms 151. Restaurant seats 140. D daily. Hotel open all year. CC.*

 The Restaurant at Donnybrook Fair

1st Floor 89 Morehampton Road Donnybrook Dublin 4
☎ *01 614 4849 www.donnybrookfair.ie/restaurant*

Above the shop floor of Dublin's chicest supermarket you'll find the restaurant, a bright and airy space with a relaxed modern vibe. Open all day, it offers seasonally influenced menus and is a popular place to meet for a bite. Cookery classes and courses also offered. *Seats 100. Mon-Sat, 8am - 9.30pm (L 12-4, D 5-9.30); Sun brunch only, 9-4pm. Closed Sun eve, 25 Dec, 1 Jan. CC.*

 Rigbys

126 Upper Leeson Street Dublin 4 ☎ *087 793 9195*

A café and New York style deli by day, Rigby's turns into a maverick no-menu restaurant three nights a week. James Rigby's background is in fine dining and he cooks in plain view behind the small deli counter; the limited menu keeps costs low, as there's minimal wastage. Well-stocked wine shop next door. An offbeat, lively and entertaining experience. *Deli open daily Mon-Sat, 'restaurant' Thu-Sat D. BYOB.*

 Rock Lobster

Above Kiely's Pub 22-24 Donnybrook Road Dublin 4 ☎ *01 202 8585 www.rocklobster.ie*

Fun, tasty and confident. Lobster and steak dishes are the undeniable stars but, overall, the imaginative menu here is a breath of fresh air. Both Canadian and Irish lobsters are sourced and daily specials usually include Irish fish; five cuts of beef, including a 1 kilo 55-day porterhouse, are prime Irish too, and bursting with flavour. Live music at weekends. *Open: L&D Mon-Fri; Sat & Sun all day from 1pm. CC.*

Roly's Bistro, Cafe & Bakery

7 Ballsbridge Terrace Ballsbridge Dublin 4 ☎ *01 668 2611 www.rolysbistro.ie*

This bustling Ballsbridge bistro has been a hit since the day it opened over 20 years ago. Today, head chef Paul Cartwright's lively interpretation of classical French cooking gives more than a passing nod to Irish traditions, world cuisines and contemporary styles, and carefully sourced ingredients are the sound foundation for cooking that rarely disappoints. Quality with good value has been the philosophy of the restaurant from the outset. *Roly's Cafe & Bakery also open on the ground floor, 7.30am-10.30pm is ideal for a casual bite and also sells breads from their own bakery. Restaurant seats 150. L&D daily. Roly's Cafe & Bakery, 7.30am-10.30pm. Closed 25-27 Dec inc. CC.*

Sandymount Hotel

Herbert Road Sandymount Dublin 4 ✆ *01 668 4321 www.mountherberthotel.ie*

Close to the Aviva stadium this sprawling three star hotel offers well-priced accommodation (with free parking) within walking distance of the city centre and close to DART station. Friendly service, simple but comfortable (if rather small) rooms, nice gardens with seating and good value make it useful to know about. *Rooms 172. CC.*

Schoolhouse Hotel

2-8 Northumberland Road Ballsbridge Dublin 4
✆ *01 667 5014 www.schoolhousehotel.com*

Full of personality, this former schoolhouse, with its pleasant canalside location, offers boutique accommodation in spacious and comfortable rooms. The lively bar and beer garden are popular with locals and it is generally a comfortable and calm place to stay. It has a reputation for good food too, in both bar and restaurant. *Rooms 31. Bar meals daily. Restaurant L Mon-Fri, D daily. Closed 24-26 Dec. CC.*

The Sussex

8-9 Sussex Terrace Upper Leeson Street Dublin 4 ✆ *01 676 2851 www.thesussex.ie*

David Coffey's smart brasserie-style restaurant above O'Brien's pub is attractively fitted out with brass fixtures, warm lighting and a real fire. The Sussex offers an inviting menu, with a strong emphasis on impeccably-sourced, modern Irish cuisine. Whatever you choose, it will be perfectly crafted: unfussy yet full of flavour and attractively presented. If you're looking for great casual Irish dining without the 'diddly-eye', this is it. *Seats 70. Open 12-11pm daily. Closed Sat pm, Good Fri, 24-26 Dec. CC.*

Terroirs

103 Morehampton Road Donnybrook Dublin 4 ✆ *01 667 1311 www.terroirs.ie*

Francophiles will thrill to the choices on offer at Seán and Francoise Gilley's wine and food shop in Donnybrook. First port of call for covetable gifts for foodies, it's a feast for the eyes as well as the palate, and fun too; the best seller is 'les champignons' - caramel mushrooms.

Waterloo House

8-10 Waterloo Road Ballsbridge Dublin 4 ✆ *01 660 1888 www.waterloohouse.ie*

Evelyn Corcoran's pair of Georgian townhouses make a luxurious and reasonably priced base in a quiet location, which is very convenient to the city centre and also Lansdowne Road, RDS and some of the city's most famous restaurants. Equally attractive to the business or leisure traveller, excellent breakfasts are a high point of any stay. *Rooms 17. Closed Christmas. CC.*

GEORGINA CAMPBELL'S IRELAND

DUBLIN 5 - RAHENY AREA

Raheny is a pleasant suburb with some excellent amenities including St. Anne's Park, once home to the Guinness family; this is one of the finest parks in North Dublin - stretching from Raheny village down to the coast at Bull Island, and then along to the edges of Clontarf, it has extensive parkland walks, famous rose gardens and playing fields. A protected Victorian red brick stable yard (1885) has been renovated and converted, offering artists' studios, a gallery, and a café. A farmers' market is held here (Sat 10-5), and a monthly arts & crafts market (Sun).

Il Fornaio

55 Kilbarrack Road Dublin 5 ✆ *01 832 0277 www.ilfornaio.ie*

Il Fornaio is a great little restaurant/bakery serving simple, ingredients-led authentic Italian food in casual surroundings; their pizzas are renowned and it's a handy place to pick up the makings of a picnic. **Seats 40**. *Mon-Fri 8.30am-10pm, Sat & Sun 10am-11.30pm.*

McHughs Wine & Dine

59 Saint Assam's Park Raheny Dublin 5 ✆ *01 832 7435 www.mchughs.ie/dine*

Tasty, good value cooking in a relaxed dining room are the staples of this pleasant neighbourhood bistro. **Seats 60**. *L&D Mon-Sat; Sun: 12–9pm. Closed 25/26 Dec, 1 Jan, Good Fri. CC.*

DUBLIN 6

Antica Venezia

97 Ashfield Road Ranelagh Dublin 6 ✆ *01 497 4112*

A real throw-back in time and refreshingly so: this entirely Italian-run restaurant has a classic Italian 70's interior complete with candlewax-dripped Chianti bottles on every table. Cooking is also traditional Italian, with a menu that could easily date back to the Seventies too. Consistently good food is matched by great service that is laid back but attentive. **Seats 45**. *D daily, L Fri only. CC.*

Bijou Bistro

47 Highfiield Road Rathgar Dublin 6 ✆ *01 496 1518 www.bijourathgar.ie*

A distinctly French atmosphere prevails at this neighbourhood restaurant where care and attention to detail have gone into every aspect of this modern bistro. Cooking is accurate and stylish – and presented on plates decorated with a colourful art deco flourish. **Seats 100** *(outdoors, 24). Bistro open 7 days 10am-11pm. Restaurant D Wed-Sun; Sun L 12-5pm. Restaurant closed Sun D, Mon, Tue. House closed 25/26 Dec. CC.*

The Butcher Grill

92 Ranelagh Village Dublin 6 ✆ *01 498 1805 www.thebutchergrill.ie*

Steaks and all manner of meat are the order du jour at this compact and cool carnivore heaven, which is also strong on seafood. Sister restaurant to neighbouring Dillingers, this busy joint is pitched at a similar clientèle – Ranelagh locals and hungry young professionals. Service in this popular place remains brisk and informed even when staff come under pressure at peak times. **Seats 35**. *D daily. Brunch/Roasts: Sat & Sun 1–4.*

The Corner Bakery

17 Terenure Road North Dublin 6 *01 490 6210 www.cornerbakeryterenure.com*

Husband-and-wife-team Dave Brown and Cara Lloyd's brilliant little family-run craft bakery's particular claim to fame is cupcakes - but it's equally strong on bread (brown soda, country sourdough), pastry and cakes (try the '5* chocolate cake'), and much more... the range expands to meet demand for their quality products - and a show window allows you to watch them being made. *Open: Mon-Fri 8.30-6,Sat 8-6,Sun 9-2. Closed Public Holidays. CC*

Dillinger's

47 Ranelagh Village Dublin 6 *01 497 8010 www.dillingers.ie*

A complete revamp has turned John Farrell's edgy modern grill into a retro diner, all black and green décor - but still with the trademark quirky menu, fun atmosphere and excellent staff. Serving up a slice of New York cool in downtown Ranelagh Dillngers attracts a buzzy crowd with its laidback cooking. Expect US classics like corndogs, ribs and macaroni cheese - and a great value midweek seafood sharing platter - served with cocktails and wine. **Seats 45**. *Brunch Sat/Sun 12-4pm; D daily. Closed L Mon-Fri. CC.*

Eatery 120

120 Ranelagh Dublin 6 *01 470 4120 www.eatery120.ie*

A lively restaurant serving tasty, seasonal food in casual but stylish surroundings, this is a neighbourhood restaurant with a difference. Long opening hours and its 'where haute-cuisine meets home cooking' policy endear it to local followers, who love the seasonality of menus proudly based on local ingredients, the friendly atmosphere and brilliant, accurately cooked food. **Seats 100** *(outdoors 16). L Fri only; Sun Brunch 11am-4pm; D daily. Closed L Mon-Thu, 25-26 Dec, Good Fri. CC.*

Fothergills Deli

141 Upper Rathmines Road Dublin 6 *01 289 3190 www.fothergillsdeli.com*

Quality catering company and deli offering irresistible freshly baked cakes, pastries and desserts - alongside excellent savoury fare including ready meals, great salads and sandwiches. *Open 9.30-6 daily.*

Jo'Burger

137 Rathmines Road Dublin 6 *01 491 3731 www.joburger.ie*

Burgers cooked to order with dozens of dressings make Joe Macken's cool, good value burger joint opposite the Travelodge a firm favourite. Noisy, loudly decorated, and busy – it's perfect for those looking for a fun atmosphere and excellent reasonably priced food. Salads are also available (but no desserts), and several foreign beers, ciders and wine. **Seats 58**. *Mon-Sun, 12 noon -11pm. Closed 25-26 Dec. CC.*

John Downey & Son

97 Terenure Road East Dublin 6 *01 490 9239 www.organicfoodsireland.com*

These legendary butchers are suppliers of many exceptionally good things such as organic meats, poultry and eggs - also game and exotics, including Irish wild boar, Irish buffalo and

Irish ostrich. John and Mark Downey and team's many awards include recognition from the Great Taste Awards and the Irish Food Writers' Guild - who both picked out their traditional spiced beef for special praise; although normally a Christmas speciality, it is now sold all year. *Open Mon-Sat 8.30-5.30 (half day Wed to 1pm).*

 ## Kiernans SuperValu

27 The Rise Mount Merrion Dublin 6 ✆ *01 288 1014*

SuperValu supermarkets are renowned for their individuality, hands-on service and commitment to supporting local producers and Irish artisan products. 'Real Food, Real People' is the slogan and it is especially apt at Damien Kiernan's excellent Mount Merrion store, which stocks an exemplary range of artisan foods and has become a magnet for food lovers shopping in the area. *Open: Mon-Fri 7.30am-8pm, Sat 8-6, Sun 10-5. CC.*

 ## Kinara Kitchen

17 Ranelagh Village Ranelagh Dublin 6 ✆ *01 406 0066 www.kinarakitchen.ie*

A hipper version of its Clontarf sister, this stylish restaurant offers outstanding, flavour-packed Pakistani food and thoughtful service. The long narrow space feels more like a cool nightclub though the food follows Kinara's tried and trusted formula and offers the same exciting (and easy to follow) menu as its Clontarf sister. *Open daily 11am-11pm. CC.*

 ## La Réserve

53 Ranelagh Village Dublin 6 ✆ *01 496 8825 www.lareserve.ie*

La Réserve may be small but there's no limit to the capabilities of Burgundian chef-proprietor Jerome Fernandes, who champions the best of Gallic cooking. This chic and charming little French brasserie serves wonderful regional dishes cooked with real flair, service is great - and lunchtime specials offer outstanding value. **Seats 28**. *L Tue-Fri; Brunch Sat-Sun 11-4; D Tue-Sun. Closed Mon*

  ## Lawlors Butchers

143 Upper Rathmines Road Dublin 6 ✆ *01 497 3313 www.lawlorsbutchers.com*

James Lawlor's highly regarded butchers shop is famous for its well aged steaks, free range poultry and pork - and great service. Also in Ranelagh, at: Mortons@Beechwood (www.mortons.ie/beechwood). *Open: Mon-Fri 9-7, Sat 8-6. Closed Sun.*

 ## Michie Sushi

11 Chelmsford Lane Ranelagh Dublin 6 ✆ *01 497 6438 www.michiesushi.com*

Off the beaten track, Michel Piare's tiny Japanese restaurant is worth seeking out for its commitment to serving exceptional food. Down a narrow laneway the tiny 17-seater creates simply stunning Japanese dishes to eat in the modest dining room or take home. While most Japanese places are still serving pre-made sushi to varying standards, Michie Sushi has raised the bar, delivering the finest Japanese food in the country, made with real flair and talent. *Tue-Sun 12-10pm. Also at: 64a, George's Street Upper, Dun Laoghaire, Co. Dublin; T: 01 538 9990.*

Mortons

15-17 Dunville Avenue Ranelagh Dublin 6 ✆ *01 497 1254 www.mortons.ie*

Since 1934 Mortons has been supplying provisions to discerning Dubliners and, in the caring hands of Gary Morton, this third generation store continues to hold its place as one of the great Dublin food stores. Stocks the best of everything - fresh fruit, veg, meat and fish; Irish organic produce; farmhouses cheeses; deli products and wines - it really is the one stop shop. *Open: Mon-Fri 8-8, Sat 8-6.30, Sun 11-4. [Branches at: Hatch Street (near St Stephen's Green) and Beechwood, Ranelagh.]*

Peperina Garden Bistro

25 Dunville Avenue Ranelagh Dublin 6 ✆ *01 543 0018 www.peperina.ie*

Diego Cabrera's bright and lively neighbourhood café aims to please with its fresh baking, tasty breakfast and lunch menus and rustic weekend dinners offering simple, home style cooking with Mediterranean leanings. Friendly service and a relaxed vibe complete this good value experience. *Mon-Wed 8.30-6, Thu-Fri 8.30am-10pm, Sat 9am-10pm, Sun 10-5.*

Pinocchio Restaurant

Luas Kiosk Ranelagh Dublin 6 ✆ *01 497 0111 www.pinocchio.ie*

Italians Marco Giannantonio and Maurizio Mastrangelo teamed up to open this authentic restaurant and winebar beneath the Ranelagh Luas station in 2008. It's a pleasant, casual spot serving thoughtful Italian fare and excellent coffee. *Seats 35. Open: Mon-Fri 7.30am-midnight, Sat & Sun 12 noon-midnight. Closed 24 Dec - 2 Jan. CC.*

TriBeCa

65 Ranelagh Village Dublin 6 ✆ *01 497 4174 www.tribeca.ie*

An outpost of the Canal Bank Café, Ger Foote and Trevor Browne's Ranelagh classic serves tasty, casual fare to hungry locals who enjoy the upbeat, high-energy environment. The bright and airy NY style restaurant isn't cheap, but its wholesome, tasty food and generous portions make it good value for money. *Seats 80 (outdoors, 12). Open daily, 12-11 (from 11am Sun). Closed Dec 25-26. CC.*

The Wild Goose Grill

1st Floor 1 Sandford Road Ranelagh Dublin 6 ✆ *01 491 2377*

Another of the growing number of Dublin restaurants that start with wine and make food a secondary element, this stylish first floor restaurant above McSorleys pub is the brainchild of former Ely manager, Kevin McMahon. A superb wine list is matched by eclectic cooking, all served up in an elegant dining room. Something sophisticated for D6 denizens. *Seats 90. D Tue-Sat. Sun 1-8. Closed Mon, also Sun in Aug; 25-26 Dec. CC.*

Bellagio

92 Terenure Road North Terenure Dublin 6W ☎ *01 492 7625 www.bellagiorestaurant.ie*

Inside this smartly glass-fronted restaurant you'll find a definite Italian atmosphere, from the music, food and waiters, right down to the large bottle of extra-virgin olive oil on every table. Bellagio delivers deliciously authentic food, good value and great Italian service – perfect for a girlie lunch, informal business meeting, tasty dinner, or simply people watching through that big glass frontage. All round, a great asset to Terenure. *L&D daily.*

O'Toole Master Butchers

138 Terenure Road North Dublin 6W ☎ *01 490 5457 www.otoolesbutchers.com*

Quality-led fourth generation butchers; known for their forward-looking philosophy, they are always ahead of the trend. They were the first Irish butchers to stock the world famous Wagyu/Kobe Beef and also have a special reputation for high quality poultry - particularly bronze turkeys. Meats are bought directly from farmers and their on-carcass beef is naturally aged for 21 days. *Open: Mon-Sat 8.30-6. Also at: Clynes Butchers, 12 Fitzwilliam Street, Ringsend, D4.*

The Lovely Food Co

14 Terenure Road West Terenure Dublin 6W ☎ *01 492 7717 www.lovelyfood.ie*

A gourmet café with real passion, foodies come for the warm welcome, relaxed service and tempting fare. There's something special about this little place – the buzz of customers enjoying the excellent food and friendly, efficient service is part of the charm but, more than that, Paul Breen's well-named café has brought vitality to the whole area. Once hooked, customers go back time and again. Cookery classes too. **Seats 24**. *Opening Hours: Mon, 8.30am-5pm; Tue-Fri 8.30-9.30pm; Sat 10-9.30pm; Sun 10-5pm.*

Vermilion

94-96 Terenure Road North Terenure Dublin 6W ☎ *01 499 1400 www.vermilion.ie*

A purpose-built restaurant on the first floor above the Terenure Inn pub, the smart, contemporary decor reflects an innovative food philosophy, which offers colourful, beautifully presented and updated versions of many Indian favourites. **Seats 90**. *D Tue-Sun. Closed Mon, 25-26 Dec, Good Fri. CC.*

DUBLIN 7

Dublin 7 is in the north inner city on the banks of the River Liffey, and is within walking distance of all of the major sites and attractions in Dublin. It includes the well known city centre neighbourhoods of Smithfield and the Four Courts, which are both alongside the River Liffey. Tourist attractions include the Four Courts, the superb Collins Barracks museum and the Old Jameson Distillery (01 807 2355; www.whiskeytours.com), where the whiskey tour is a 'must visit' while in the city.

Fresh - The Good Food Market

Smithfield Village Dublin 7 ☎ *01 485 0271 www.freshthegoodfoodmarket.com*

Irish owned independent Dublin supermarkets, with emphasis on fresh and speciality produce; butchers, fish counter, café, sushi, wok counter (hot meals); premium brands like Blazing

Salads organic breads and Janet's Country Fayre chutneys and relishes are stocked. Also at: Grand Canal Square, Dublin 2; Camden Street, Dublin 2. *Open: Mon-Fri 7am-10pm, Sat 8am-10pm, Sun & banks hols 9am-10pm.Underground Car Park Off Queen Street (7am-11pm).* [*Also at: Grand Canal Square, Dublin 2; Camden Street, Dublin 2.*]

Hanley at the Bar

The Distillery Building May Lane Dublin 7 ✆ *01 878 0104*

Offering good contemporary cooking in very chic surroundings, well known caterer Claire Hanley's smart daytime restaurant near the Jameson Distillery is perennially popular with local business lunchers and lawyers from the nearby Law Library and Four Courts. High stools at the bar provide a comfortable perch if waiting (it gets very busy at lunch time); delivery service offered too. *Open Mon-Tue 8am-5pm, Wed-Fri 8am-8pm.*

Kish Fish

40 - 42 Bow Street Smithfield Dublin 7 ✆ *01 854 3940 www.kishfish.ie*

Established in 1966 by Tadgh O'Meara, Kish Fish is now under the stewardship of his three sons Bill, Tadgh and Damien, ably assisted by their mother Fidelma, who looks after the shop with Jimmy Smith; attached to the processing plant, it offers a wide range of fresh fish and shellfish. *Open Tue-Fri 9-5.30, Sat 9-2. Closed Sun & Mon. Also at: Malahide Industrial Park, Coolock, Dublin 17.*

Kooky Dough

The Spade Enterprise Centre 112-115 King Street North Smithfield Dublin 7 ✆ *01 617 4849 www.kookydough.ie*

Sophie Morris and Graham Clarke's convenience product Kooky Dough may not be baking in the usual sense, with all its weighing and measuring and other ritual preparations, but their cookies are made with natural ingredients and certainly taste homemade. A very handy item to keep in the fridge or freezer ready to slice up and pop into the oven at any time. *Widely available.*

L Mulligan Grocer

18 Stoneybatter Dublin 7 ✆ *01 670 9889 www.lmulligangrocer.com*

An old Stoneybatter grocers that's been converted by owners Michael Fogarty, Colin Hession and Seaneen Sullivan into a quirky gastropub with lovely character. Over 150 whisk(e)ys and a selection of Irish craft beers complement the artisan-inspired food, so even if you don't have so much as a bite to eat, a visit here would be well worth a small detour just to absorb the atmosphere and enjoy a drink. Friendly staff know their food and drink and this big-hearted place is hugely popular. *Open 4pm Mon-Fri, food from 5pm. 2pm Sat & Sun, food from 3pm.*

Lilliput Stores

5 Rosemount Terrace Stoneybatter Dublin 7 ✆ *01 672 9516*

Small but perfectly formed, this tiny shop just off Arbour Hill brings many a treat to a recently gentrified area; run by Brendan O'Mahony (the Dublin face of the Real Olive Co - well known at markets), it stocks artisan products (the gorgeous Chez Emily chocolates list them as suppliers) and quality everyday foods. *Closed Sun.*

The Old Jameson Distillery

Bow Street Smithfield Dublin 7 ✆ *01 807 2355*
www.tours.jamesonwhiskey.com/Home/The-Old-Jameson-Distillery-Dublin/bars-restaurant.aspx

While most tourists in Dublin will visit the restored Old Jameson Distillery to do the tour (which is fascinating) it can also be a handy spot for a drink in one of the bars or a bite to eat/lunch at the Third Still restaurant. The standard of cooking is generally higher than might be expected at a popular tourist attraction - although it would be nice to see Irish food culture showcased as enthusiastically as the drinks. *Restaurant **Seats 55**. Open Mon-Fri 9am-5pm. Distillery open daily all year. Closed 24-26 Dec, Good Fri. CC.*

Plan B

56 Manor Street Stoneybatter Dublin 7 ✆ *01 670 6431*

Just north of the River Liffey and close to the Phoenix Park, this appealing Italian is a consistently popular neighbourhood restaurant. Whether for a quick and tasty bowl of soup at lunchtime or a relaxing evening meal, its reputation for reliably good food at reasonable prices is well earned. ***Seats 34**. Open Tue-Sat 12-10pm & Sun from 5pm. Closed Mon. CC.*

Seven

73 Manor Street Dublin 7 ✆ *01 633 4092*

It's decidely small, so the well balanced cooking at this charming and compact restaurant means tables are hard to come by. Carefully sourced quality ingredients and well-cooked unfussy food has made Seven a great hit with local residents. ***Seats 38**. L Mon-Fri; D daily.*

Soulful Bistro

46 Manor St Stoneybatter Dublin 7 ✆ *01 86 88 400 www.soulful.ie*

Moira Gray's modest Stoneybatter bistro strives to deliver nutritious, great value food at breakfast, lunch and dinner. Comfort food is the MO of this casual spot, with everything made in house, from the granola to the tomato ketchup. *Mon, Wed-Fri 8.30am-10pm, Sat-Sun, 9am-9pm. Closed Tue.*

DUBLIN 8

Dublin 8 is the only postcode that crosses the River Liffey and is made up of areas on both sides of the river, at the western edges of the city centre. The best known areas/attractions in Dublin 8 for the visitor to Dublin are the Guinness Brewery, Kilmainham Gaol, The Irish Museum of Modern Art, Christchurch Cathedral, St. Patrick's Cathedral and the Phoenix Park. Heuston Station (serving the West and South West of Ireland) is also in Dublin 8. The Guinness Brewery (St. James Gate; 01 471 4261) is home to the modern glass-walled Gravity Bar which serves the most spectacular pint of Guinness in Dublin - indeed, in all Ireland from its unique position atop the impressive Guinness Storehouse, a handsome 1904 building. The Guinness Museum tells the story - using fascinating high tech exhibits - of the famous company's 250-plus years in business. It also includes (on Level 5) the traditional Brewery Bar, serving nourishing Irish fare (seafood chowder, beef & Guinness stew). NB: you have to pay in to use these bars. Down the road is Royal Hospital Kilmainham and the Irish Museum of Modern Art, which has good parking facilities and a café.

 **Ashling Hotel**

Parkgate Street Dublin 8 ✆ *01 677 2324 www.ashlinghotel.ie*

Well-managed, busy and relatively well priced, this recently refurbished Dublin hotel is conveniently situated within walking distance of Heuston Intercity rail station, Guinness Brewery, Phoenix Park and Dublin Zoo, historic Kilmainham Gaol, the Old Jameson Distillery and The National Museum of Ireland at Collins Barracks. Bus and light rail transport to O'Connell Street (ten minutes away) is on the doorstep. **Rooms 225**. *Closed 25/26 Dec. CC.*

 Brazen Head

20 Lower Bridge Street Dublin 8 ✆ *01 677 9549 www.brazenhead.com*

Possibly Ireland's oldest pub, the hospitality and craic at this atmospheric pub are still much in demand. Built on the site of a tavern dating back to the 12th century, it's full of genuine character and serves wholesome food at reasonable prices. There's live music nightly in the Music Lounge.

  Bretzel Bakery

1a Lennox Street Portobello Dublin 8 ✆ *01 475 2724 www.bretzel.ie*

William Despard and Cormac Keenan's famous Jewish bakery dates back to 1870 and they're still reckoned to sell the best bagels in Dublin. Specialising in proper handmade bread, including sourdough and rye bread made the old-fashioned way and baked in the original brick-lined ovens, they also produce delicious confectionery, seasonal specialities and tray bakes and cakes for parties. As well as selling from their two bakeries, Bretzel supply a number of speciality food stores. *Open: Mon 8.30-3, Tue-Fri 8.30-6, Sat 9-5, Sun 9-1.Also at: 8 Upper Rathmines Road, beside the Post Office.*

 **The Cake Café**

The Daintree Building Pleasants Place (behind Camden Street) Dublin 8
✆ *01478 9394 www.thecakecafe.ie*

A love of traditional food and recognition of the environmental impact of their business are the driving forces behind Michelle Darmody's paradise for cake lovers. We can't figure out if it's the wonderful baking, the delightful savoury courses, the homely décor or delicious beverages that make this café so fabulous. Pleasant by name and pleasant by nature. **Seats 16** *inside and 25 outside. Open 8.30am to 5.30pm Mon Fri, Sat 9-6. Closed Sun, Bank Hols, 2-3 weeks at Christmas, 3 days at Easter. CC.*

 **Camden Kitchen**

3 Camden Market Grantham Street Dublin 8 ✆ *01 476 0125 www.camdenkitchen.ie*

Though the name suggests something a little more rough and ready than the rather finessed fare on offer, this bistro offers well-sourced ingredients with a cheffy leaning. Chef-proprietor

Padraic Hayden applies the skills he acquired in the likes of One Pico and The Dylan and there's superb value to be had at this cool and elegant neighbourhood spot. **Seats 50**. *Open L Tue-Fri; D Tue-Sat. Closed Sat L, Sun & Mon, 25-26 Dec; 1-7 Jan. CC.*

  ## Ennis Butchers

463 South Circular Road Rialto Dublin 8 📞 *01 454 9282 www.ennisbutchers.com*

Derek Bolger has built up a great reputation for his craft butchers shop, which stocks a wealth of good things. Great meats include dry-aged beef and carefully sourced produce from small suppliers, such as Thomas Salter's rare breed free range pigs from Co Carlow, and there's also plenty of other quality fare, including fresh fish, organic vegetables and wines. Note the catchy shopping bags too. *Open Mon-Sat 8-7. Closed Sun.*

 ## Enoteca Torino

Grattan Crescent Inchicore Dublin 8 📞 *01 453 7791*

A pleasant walk away from Kilmainham Gaol, this good value Italian restaurant serves favourite dishes with flair. The atmosphere is cosy and the restaurant has an immediate feel of authenticity. **Seats 40**; *Mon-Sun, 10-am-11pm (from 12 Sun).*

  ## Hilton Dublin Kilmainham

Inchicore Road Kilmainham Dublin 8 📞 *01 420 1800 www.hilton.com/dublinkilmainham*

Attractively located minutes from Heuston Station and many attractions, this comfortable modern hotel a short distance from the city centre offers spacious bedrooms and good amenities. Designed to have equal appeal for leisure and business guests, rooms are well-appointed and there are contemporary in-house bar and restaurant options. **Rooms 120**. *Closed 24-27 Dec. CC.*

 ## itsa@IMMA

Irish Museum of Modern Art Royal Hospital Kilmainham Dublin 8 📞 *01 612 9666 www.itsa.ie*

While not a destination restaurant, itsa@IMMA can be a pleasant pitstop for visitors to this world-class gallery who are in need of rest and refreshment. Good baking is a strength. **Seats 50**. *Open Monday 10-3pm, Tue-Sat (& Bank Hol Mon) 10-5pm, Sun 12-5pm. Closed 25 Dec. CC.*

 ## Junos Cafe

26 Parkgate Street Dublin 8 📞 *01 670 9820 www.junoscafe.com*

Well chosen seasonal ingredients are used in the creative cooking at this relaxed and casual restaurant. Talented Finnish chef Juha Salo delivers imaginative cooking, including home-smoked food and unusual vegetarian dishes, across many menus offered at this old-school caff cum new-school bistro. The décor is diner-esque, the staff cheerfully competent, and the mood casually upbeat: very enjoyable. **Seats 35**. *B & L Mon-Fri, Afternoons Thu & Fri, D Thu-Sat, Brunch Sat & Sun 10am-4pm. Closed D Sun-Weds, Bank Hols. CC.*

Jurys Inn Christchurch

Christchurch Dublin 8 ✆ *01 454 0000*

For good budget accommodation which is with walking distance of the main city centre areas on both sides of the Liffey and close to Dublin Castle and events in Temple Bar; large multi-story car part at the rear has direct access to the hotel. **Rooms 182.** *Closed 24-26 Dec. CC.*

Konkan Indian Restaurant

46 Upper Clanbrassil Street Nr Harolds Cross Bridge Dublin 8 ✆ *01 473 8252 www.konkan.ie*

Talented chefs whip up quality Indian fare at this modest-looking restaurant with charming service. Located just before the Harold's Cross Bridge, the small welcoming dining room delivers delicious Indian cooking in a relaxed setting that's full of character - and for a great price. **Seats 32**; *Mon–Sun 5-11pm. Closed 24-25 Dec. CC. [Also at:1 Upper Kilmacud Road Dundrum D14].*

Lennox Cafe Bistro

31 Lennox Street Portobello Dublin 8 ✆ *01 478 9966 www.lennoxcafe.ie*

This appealing all-day neighbourhood restaurant in a quiet location near Portobello Bridge has a few tables outside for fine weather. Serving no-fuss contemporary food it's popular with discerning locals for its relaxed atmosphere, fair prices and smart interior. Weekend brunch is a speciality. *Open daily, 9.30am-6pm. CC. [Also at:The Table Restaurant and Wine Bar, 1-2 Portobello Road, Dublin 8 (01) 4736727]*

Locks Brasserie

Number 1 Windsor Terrace Portobello Dublin 8 ✆ *01 420 0555 www.locksbrasserie.com*

One of Dublin's nicest dining rooms, this canalside favourite continues to woo diners with its classic French cooking with a luxe bistro twist. Run by Sebastien Masi and Kirsten Batt, whose excellent Pearl Brasserie is one of Dublin's finest restaurants, the dream team of Keelan Higgs (ex Chapter One) in the kitchen and Pearl stalwart Thomas Pinoncely as manager, ensures diners experience wonderful seasonal cooking and charming service. Glamorous, hip and fashionable. **Seats 70.** D *Mon-Wed; Thu-Sun from 12-late. Closed L Mon-Wed, Christmas week. CC.*

The Lord Edward

23 Christchurch Place Dublin 8 ✆ *01 454 2420 www.lordedward.ie*

Old-fashioned cooking and retro style seafood dishes are the order du jour at Dublin's oldest seafood restaurant spanning three floors. The Lord Edward provides a complete contrast to the current wave of trendy restaurants. Caught in a time warp, the range of fish and seafood dishes offered is second to none, and the fish cookery is excellent, with simplest choices almost invariably the best. **Seats 40.** *L Wed-Fri, D Wed-Sat. Also Bar Food Mon-Fri, 12-2.30. Closed L Sat and all Sun-Tue, 24 Dec-2 Jan, bank hols. CC.*

Lovin Catering

49 Francis Street Dublin 8 📞 *01 454 4912 www.facebook.com/lovincatering*

Kevin Doyle, former manager of The Gallic Kitchen (relocated to Abbeyleix, Co Laois) now owns this business renowned for baked goods with his wife Natasha. They renamed it Lovin Catering and it continues the quality - and many of the favourite products - which established its reputation. *Open from 7am Mon-Sat. Wed-Fri to 6pm, Sat to 5pm. Buy also at Dun Laoghaire, Marlay Park and Stillorgan farmers' markets.*

 The Phoenix Café

Ashtown Castle The Phoenix Park Visitors Centre Dublin 8 📞 *01 677 0090*

Hidden away next to the Aras an Uachtaráin Visitor Centre, you'll find Helen Cunningham's Phoenix Café. The lovely sylvan setting and carefully prepared food make this delightful café a hidden gem, where the vast majority of ingredients are organic. *Seats 80 inside, 70 outside. open daily 9.30am-5pm (to 4pm Dec-Jan). Closed 10 days over Christmas. No SC. No CC.*

 **Radisson Blu Royal Hotel**

Golden Lane Dublin 8 📞 *01 898 2900 www.radissonblu.ie/royalhotel-dublin*

A smart hotel close to the commercial heart of the city and many attractions; with predictably well-appointed accommodation, it caters especially well for business guests. The famous Radisson breakfast buffet is served in Verre en Vers, a stylish dining room which operates as a brasserie style restaurant for other meals. As well as the main bar ('SURE'), The Vintage Room offers somewhere for a quieter drink. *Rooms 150. CC.*

 Ryan's of Parkgate Street

28 Parkgate Street Dublin 8 📞 *01 677 6097 www.fxbrestaurants.com*

A true Victorian pub with wonderful history and character, Ryan's is one of Ireland's finest and best-loved pubs. Bar food is available every day except Sunday and, upstairs, there's a small restaurant, FXB at Ryans, serving food which is a step up from bar meals. *Pub food: Mon-Fri, 3-11. Restaurant: D daily. Closed 25-26 Dec, 1 Jan, Good Fri. CC.*

DUBLIN 9

The Botanic Gardens (Botanic Road; 01 804 0300; www.botanicgardens.ie; open 9am daily) are in Glasnevin and provide a great (free!) morning or afternoon out for visitors to Dublin. They are only a few minutes bus or taxi ride from the city centre and guided tours are available at various times of the day. Further out from the city is DCU (Dublin College University) which is home to one of Ireland's most exciting multi-venue performance spaces - The Helix (Collins Avenue, Glasnevin; 01 700 7000; www.thehelix.ie). The Helix comprises three auditoria serving a mixture of high quality music, drama and entertainment. Since its opening in 2002 by President Mary McAleese, The Helix has generated an impressive reputation for staging cutting edge and diverse theatre and music.

 Andersons Creperie

1a Carlingford Road Drumcondra Dublin 9 📞 *01 830 5171 www.andersons.ie*

A little piece of France tucked off the busy main road, the younger sibling of Noel Delany / Patricia Van der Velde's Anderson's Food Hall & Cafe is a retro-styled café serving up an appetising selection of sweet and savoury gourmet crêpes and, like its sister in Glasnevin, well sourced deli fare from Ireland and abroad. A choice of wines and Breton cider make this a pleasant choice for an early evening meal too. **Seats 45**. *Open daily, 9am-7pm (to 8pm Fri; from 10am Sun). Closed 24 Dec-2 Jan, Good Fri, Easter Sun. CC.*

 ## Andersons Food Hall & Café

3 The Rise Glasnevin Dublin 9 ☎*01 837 8394 www.andersons.ie*

Previously a butchers shop, this popular deli, wine shop and continental-style café off Griffith Avenue offers a wonderful selection of charcuterie and cheese from Ireland and the continent, a short blackboard menu of hot dishes and specials, and lovely cakes. The wine list changes regularly - or, at a very modest corkage charge, you can choose any bottle on sale to have with your food. **Seats 43** *(outdoors, 18); Open Mon-Sat, 9-7 (to 8.30 Thu-Sat), Sun 10-7. Closed 1 week over Christmas, Good Fri & Easter Sun. CC.*

 ## The Brian Boru

5 Prospect Road Glasnevin Dublin 9 ☎*01 830 4527 www.thebrianboru.ie*

Handy to the nearby Botanic Gardens this extended traditional pub strays into gastro-pub territory with its extensive and well-executed menu. Food is served daily and Sunday lunch is especially popular when locals come for the tasty roasts, generous portions, and the relaxed ambience.

 ## The Cheese Pantry

104 Upper Drumcondra Road Drumcondra Dublin 9
☎*01 797 8936 www.thecheesepantry.com*

With its custom-built cheese room, 'foodie' pantry items and an impressive selection of wines, Aidan and Karen McNeice's popular business looks like a deli and wine shop - but very good food is served here too.

 ## Egans House

7-9 Iona Park Glasnevin Dublin 9 ☎*01 830 5283 www.eganshouse.com*

Traditional hospitality, comfortable rooms and a warm welcome set Pat and Monica Finn's pleasant Glasnevin guesthouse apart. Near the Botanic Gardens, it offers well-maintained accommodation at a reasonable price. **Rooms 23** *(22 shower only). Open all year. CC.*

 ## John Kavanagh (Grave Diggers)

1 Prospect Square Glasnevin Dublin 9 ☎*01 830 7978*

Adjacent to the Glasnevin cemetery, John Kavanagh's is a genuine Victorian bar (1833), totally unspoilt - and it has a reputation for serving one of the best pints in Dublin. Food is now also served. Theme pub owners eat your hearts out.

 ## The Maples House Hotel

79-81 Iona Road Glasnevin Dublin 9 ☎*01 830 4227 www.mapleshotel.com*

Simplicity and comfort reign at this modest and reliable hotel conveniently located near the Botanic Gardens and Dublin City University. The neat double-fronted Victorian redbrick has an attractive hotel bar and bistro too. *CC.*

Porterhouse North

Cross Guns Bridge Glasnevin Dublin 9 ✆ *01 830 9922*

Originally the Iona Garage, this trendy canalside pub building retains some of the original art deco features. Youthful, with a pizza oven and outdoor seating. Sister business to Dublin's original craft brewery, The Porterhouse (see entry). *Food served daily from 12 noon. CC.*

 Honest2Goodness

136a Slaney Close Dublin Industrial Estate Glasnevin Dublin 11 ✆ *087 629 4713 www.honest2goodness.ie*

More like the ideal supermarket than a famers' market really... you can get just about everything you need for your weekly shop here, all under one roof. Artisan bread, fresh fruit and veg (Irish wherever possible), meat, fish, preserves, baked treats, everyday essentials, wine, even cut flowers are all here - and hot food too, from H2G Ready2Go Café. Worth a detour. *Saturdays only, 9.30 – 4.00.*

DUBLIN 12

 J L Fitzsimons Fresh Fish Shop

183A Kimmage Road West Crumlin Cross Dublin 12 ✆ *01 455 4832*

This second generation family-run shop began life in the old Fish Market (Smithfield); it offers a wide range of fresh whitefish and shellfish with live lobster, crab and oysters available from a tank in-store. Closed Sun & Mon.

  Natasha's Living Foods

79 Parkwest Enterprise Centre Lavery Avenue Parkwest Dublin 12 ✆ *01 620 5711 www.natashaslivingfood.ie*

Natasha Czopor's passion for 'raw and living food' has led to the production of some very unusual cakes, confectionery, savouries and salads. Look out for her homemade crackers, perhaps flavoured with carrot and thyme, nibbles like sprouted flax ginger snaps - or, the one that really stands out from the crowd, her Kale Crunchies, an award winning alternative to crisps.

DUBLIN 14

 The Arch Bistro

Above Glenside Pub 20 Landscape Road Churchtown Dublin 14 ✆ *01 296 6340 www.thearchbistro.com*

The traditional exterior of The Glenside pub belies the modern restaurant that's nestling under its thatched roof. Run independently by a friendly team who clearly love good food, it offers accomplished cooking, thoughtful service, a comfortable dining room and superb value. It may be tucked off the beaten track, but this neighbourhood gem is definitely worth a detour. *Seats 75. L&D Tue-Sun. Closed Mon. CC.*

DUBLIN 15

 The Anglers Rest

Lower Road, Strawberry Beds Castleknock Dublin 15 ☎ *01 820 4351* *www.theanglersrest.ie*

Quirky decor, buckets of atmosphere and carefully considered food make this traditional favourite a great spot for Sunday lunch or a trad session by night. Owned by well known fishmongers, the Wright family of Howth, it boasts a popular seafood restaurant as well as the cosy Salmon Bar, where live traditional music is played five nights a week by the turf fire. A good spot for an outing with friends or visitors. *Bar food served 12-9pm. CC.*

 Carlton Hotel Blanchardstown

Church Road Tyrrelstown Dublin 15 ☎ *01 827 5600* *www.carltonhotelblanchardstown.com*

Less than twenty minutes from the airport (the hotel will arrange collection and drop off), this modern four-star hotel in a fast-developing suburb in north-west Dublin is comfortable and stylishly decorated, with excellent facilities including ample conference rooms, a guest library, and a gym. Good for business. *Rooms 155. Closed 24-25 Dec. CC.*

 **Castleknock Hotel & Country Club**

Porterstown Road Castleknock Dublin 15 ☎ *01 640 6300* *www.castleknockhotel.com*

With its own golf course, extensive conference facilities and countryside views, this large modern hotel makes a pleasant base for both business and leisure guests. Located just outside Castleknock Village it offers spacious, comfortably furnished bedrooms. There's formal dining in The Park restaurant, and an informal option in The Brasserie, where breakfast is also served. *Rooms 138. Closed 24-26 Dec. CC.*

 Crowne Plaza Blanchardstown

The Blanchardstown Centre Navan Road Blanchardstown Dublin 15 ☎ *01 897 7777* *www.cpireland.crowneplaza.com/Crowne-Plaza-Blanchardstown.html*

In an excellent location right next to the Blanchardstown Shopping Centre this four-star hotel offers good facilities, attractive public spaces and stylish bedrooms. Most obvious as a business hotel, but there's a lot to attract leisure guests to this area – Ikea is only up the road, but with Dublin Zoo, Phoenix Park and the National Aquatic Centre all nearby it's a good spot for families too. *Rooms 188.*

 Jaipur Restaurant Ongar

Unit 35 & 39 Ongar Village Dublin 15 ☎ *01 640 2611* *www.jaipur.ie*

This branch of the highly regarded Jaipur chain of Indian restaurants is a real asset to the area. The sleek modern dining room and magical cooking bring all the flavours of India to Ongar with panache. Friendly staff provide a prompt welcome and offer enticing menus of traditional Indian fare alongside dishes with a more unusual twist. *Seats 45; D Tue-Sun. Closed Mon, 25-26 Dec. CC. [* Also at: Jaipur Dalkey, Co.Dublin; Jaipur Malahide, Co.Dublin; Jaipur Dublin 2; Chakra by Jaipur, Greystones & Ananda Restaurant Dundrum.]*

The Twelfth Lock

Castleknock Marina The Royal Canal Castleknock Dublin 15
☎ *01 860 7400 www.twelfthlock.com*

A picturesque location beside the Royal Canal is key to the appeal of this small hotel. Guest rooms are on the lower ground floor and a little dark, but it has a lively bar, modern food and people like the warm, friendly atmosphere. The main bar is light and airy, with a heated terrace overlooking the lock. **Rooms 10** *(1 disabled). Bar Meals daily. Bistro D Wed-Sat. CC.*

DUBLIN 16

Ananda

2-4 Sandyford Road Dundrum Town Centre Dublin 16
☎ *01 296 0099 www.anandarestaurant.ie*

A partnership between Asheesh Dewan, owner of the outstanding Jaipur restaurants, and Atul Kochhar, the first Indian chef to receive a Michelin star for his renowned London restaurant Benares, this glamorous wow factor dining room sets the scene for cutting-edge Indian cuisine. Executive chef Sunil Ghai creates the culinary treats that challenge the broadest perceptions of Indian cooking. The purity of flavours, wonderfully presented dishes, smart service and beautiful dining room make Ananda appealing on so many levels. **Seats 85**. *L Fri-Sun; D daily. Closed L Mon-Thu; 25-26 Dec. CC.[* Also at: Jaipur Dalkey, Co.Dublin; Jaipur Malahide, Co.Dublin; Jaipur Dublin 2; Jaipur Ongar & Chakra by Jaipur, Greystones.]*

Café Mao

The Mill Pond Civic Square Dundrum Town Centre Dublin 16
☎ *01 296 2802 www.cafemao.com*

This modern, airy two-storey Asian fusion restaurant is a younger sister of the well-known Café Mao restaurants in Dublin. Conveniently located in a restaurant piazza to the rear of the shopping centre, it's a bright and buzzy spot offering interesting, simple and tasty food that is served quickly and at a reasonable price. Popular for its healthy food, good value and friendly efficient service. **Seats 130** *(outdoors, 50). Food daily 12-10pm (to 10.30pm Fri/Sat). Closed 25/26 Dec. CC.*

Harvey Nichol's First Floor Restaurant

Dundrum Town Centre Sandyford Road Dublin 16 ☎ *01 291 0488*
www.harveynichols.com/restaurants/first-floor-dublin/first-floor-dublin-restaurant

It may seem strange to go for dinner in a department store, but Harvey Nichols has long been associated with fine food. Its Irish outpost at Dundrum Town Centre is no different and the First Floor brasserie has its own entrance. The dramatic and comfortable dining room offers imaginatively interpreted modern cooking, served with flair and precision. **Seats 80**. *L Tue-Sun, D Tue-Sat. Closed Sun D, all day Mon and 25/26 Dec. CC.*

IMI Residence

Sandyford Road Dublin 16 📞 *01 207 5900*
www.imi.ie/TNS/info_article/accommodation.aspx

Within easy access of the M50, (Sandyford Industrial Estate exit), this campus-like residence with self-service breakfast is ideally suited to the cost-conscious business traveller but may also appeal to other visitors on restricted budgets. It is a residence rather than a hotel, quite like upmarket university campus accommodation. **Rooms 50** *(all shower only)*.

 Jamie's Italian

Unit 1 Pembroke District Dundrum Town Centre Dublin 16 📞 *01 298 0600*
www.jamieoliver.com/italian/ireland/dundrum-dublin

The buzz and energy at Jamie's Italian is everything you'd expect from an outpost of the cheeky Essex TV chef's expanding empire: vivacious, eager staff, contemporary urban décor and a broad ranging menu crammed with quality ingredients. Pasta is hand made, and most dishes sing with flavour and beautifully fresh ingredients. Children are made feel very welcome and it's good value too. **Seats 120**. Open Mon & Tue 12-10.30pm; Wed-Fri 12-11pm; Sat 11.30-11pm & Sun 12-10pm. CC.

 L'Officina by Dunne & Crescenzi

Dundrum Shopping Centre Dundrum Dublin 16 📞 *01 216 6764 www.officina.ie*

Understated décor lets the wonderful food and service do the talking at this quality Italian restaurant. Younger sister to the well-known Dunne & Crescenzi restaurants, it's decorated in tune with the style of food service – simple, no-fuss, efficient. Impeccably sourced ingredients form the backbone of the healthy menus, where the use of artisan products is proudly highlighted. L'Officina offers great quality at a fair price and the staff are terrific. **Seats 60**. Open Mon-Sat, 10.30am-10pm; Sun 12-10pm. CC.

  The Merry Ploughboy

Rockbrook Edmondstown Road Rathfarnham Dublin 16 📞 *01 493 1495 www.mpbpub.com*

Formerly known as Doherty's, the business was bought in 2006 by a band of traditional musicians known as The Merry Ploughboys, who have since developed this popular drinking hole into a leading live music and entertainment venue. The food in no way plays second fiddle to the music at The Merry Ploughboy, with its well thought out menu and quality suppliers listed. Popular with tourists but also locals.

DUBLIN 17

  Butlers Chocolate Experience

Clonshaugh Business Park Oscar Traynor Road Dublin 17
📞 *01 671 0599 www.butlerschocolates.com*

Butlers chocolates are a favourite Irish indulgence and the Butlers Chocolate Experience allows visitors to go behind the scenes and see how they're made. Tours, family day's out, demonstrations etc are all available; booking is required. Both the chocolates and the more recently introduced ice creams are also widely available from the Butlers Chocolate Cafés in

Dublin and elsewhere and other retail outlets. *See website for details of the Chocolate Experience, café locations and opening times, also retail outlets. Online shop.*

DUBLIN 18

Bordering onto Stillorgan (sometimes Dublin 4, or Co Dublin) and Blackrock (Co Dublin), Dublin 18 is a chameleon area, with edges a little blurred and, it seems, sometimes shifting... But one thing is certain, and it's that the burgeoning business parks have ensured the choice of interesting places to eat and comfortable places to lay your head are on the increase.

The Beacon Hotel

Beacon Court Sandyford Business Region Dublin 18 ☎ *01 291 5000*

In prosperous south county Dublin, Sandyford has become the focus for extensive development, and this sister hotel to The Morgan in Temple Bar (see entry) is a welcome facility and popular with business travellers. Within sight of the M50 motorway, close to the Luas tramline, (15 minutes to the city centre), it looks no different to the neighbouring glass/concrete exteriors of a private hospital and office block, but internally the hotel is a model of cutting edge design. *Rooms 88.*

Bewleys Hotel Leopardstown

Central Park Leopardstown Dublin 18 ☎ *01 293 5000 www.bewleyshotels.com/*

One of the Bewleys trademark large modern hotels, near Sandyford Industrial Estate, it offers simple, well-designed accommodation at a very reasonable price. There's a restaurant, The Brasserie, and a bright, open lounge with a south facing sun deck looking towards the mountains.

Bistro One

3 Brighton Road Foxrock Village Dublin 18 ☎ *01 289 7711 www.bistro-one.ie*

Consistency and a food philosophy that embraces the seasons are key to the success of Mark Shannon's perennially popular neighbourhood restaurant. Ingredients are carefully sourced, with suppliers credited on seasonally-driven menus. Main courses are mainly excellent renditions of the classics, and desserts include homemade ice cream. Expect genuine hospitality, good cooking and no gimmicks. *Seats 75; L&D Tue-Sat. Closed Sun, Mon & 25 Dec - 2 Jan. CC.*

The Box Tree

Stepaside Village Stepaside Dublin 18 ☎ *01 205 2025 www.theboxtree.ie*

Hungry guests can head straight in to their table in the restaurant or call in to the attractive modern pub next door, The Wild Boar, which is in common ownership with The Box Tree and offers a more casual setting to enjoy food from the same kitchen, or for drinks before and after your meal. A good buzz, stylish surroundings and value for money make this a popular place. *Seats 70 (outdoors, 18). L&D daily. Closed 25 Dec.CC.*

China Sichuan Restaurant

The Forum Ballymoss Road Sandyford Industrial Estate Dublin 18
☎ *01 293 5100 www.china-sichuan.ie*

The modern interpretations of classic Sichuan cuisine offered by David Hui and his team are rightly renowned. A wide-ranging à la carte is complemented by value menus at lunchtime and in the evening. "Chef's Recommendations" highlight the kitchen's authentic Sichuan dishes based on centuries old recipes, and well-versed servers explain dishes and their ingredients. Sunday lunches are especially popular with families. **Seats 90** *(outdoors, 20). L Sun-Fri; D daily. Closed L Sat, 25 Dec & Good Fri. CC.*

 ## The Gables Restaurant

The Gables Foxrock Village Dublin 18 ☎ *01 289 2174 www.mccabeswines.ie*

Choose one of the 800 wines on offer at this Foxrock wine shop before opening it in the smart adjoining dining room. This imaginative venture by McCabes Wines, whose shop is part of the restaurant, offers a great wine experience in addition to brunches and stylish contemporary food. **Seats 70** *(outdoors, 20). Open 8am-10pm daily (Sun 1-4pm & 5-8). Closed 25 Dec, Good Fri. CC.*

 ## La Rouge Wine & Grill

Unit 1 St Gabriels Court Bray Road Cabinteely Dublin 18 ☎ *01 275 0127 www.larougegrill.ie*

The brainchild of well known restaurateur Ann Marie Nohl formerly of Expresso Bar Café, in Ballsbridge, this compact grill and wine bar is a different animal altogether, with its sumptuous Parisian ambience. Here too, however, quality ingredients are at the heart of every meal served and, although not long, menus offer something a little different - as does Ann Marie's interesting drinks list. **Seats 28**. *D daily 5-10.30pm.*

 ## Pielows Restaurant

4 Village Centre Cabinteely Dublin 18 ☎ *01 284 0914 www.pielows.com*

It can be tricky to get a table at this classy Cabinteely outfit, run by experienced restaurateurs who know the value of simple. That's because the Pielow's focus on quality, from the smart décor to food that's outstanding for its simplicity, freshness and flavour. The wine list is very interesting and anyone who has had enough of cheffy extravagances should add Pielow's to their list of must-visit restaurants. **Seats 32**. *D Tue-Sat. CC.*

  ## Thomas's

Brighton Road Foxrock Village Dublin 18 ☎ *01 289 4101 www.thomasoffoxrock.ie*

Slow Food member Thomas Murphy's shop is a hard place to pass by, with its appealing balance of artisan, organic and other quality foods from Ireland and abroad - and well-chosen wines too.

DUBLIN 20

 ## The Baking Academy of Ireland

20 Lucan Road Old Palmerstown Village Dublin 20 ✆ *01 845 1214 www.bakingacademyireland.ie*

It was a good day for Ireland's aspiring bakers when former head of the National Bakery School in Dublin, Master Baker Derek O'Brien, decided to start his baking academy a few years ago, offering hands-on courses in bread and cake baking, chocolate making and sugar craft cake decoration. Any student fortunate enough to undertake a course here could not be in better hands, as uniquely experienced and enthusiastic tutors will guide and inspire beginners and seasoned enthusiasts alike. "We will teach you the craft and skills to do it successfully - every time."

DUBLIN 22

Dublin 22, on the western edges of the city, is a busy commercial area known mainly for its industrial estates and business parks - and the huge Liffey Valley Shopping Centre.

 ## Bewleys Hotel Newlands Cross

Newlands Cross Naas Road Dublin 22 ✆ *01 464 0140*

Large, comfortable bedrooms and good business facilities set the standard at this family friendly budget hotel. Free parking and the adjacent Bewley's Restaurant provides very acceptable food. ***Rooms 299*** *(5 shower only). Closed 24-26 Dec. CC.*

 ## Mooreen House

Belgard Road Newlands Cross Dublin 22 ✆ *01 459 2682 www.mooreen.ie*

Set in 20 peaceful acres next to Newlands Cross, Nuala Price's remarkable Art Deco house is a genuine hidden gem and oozes 1930's elegance with its original furnishings and luxurious rooms. No dinner is offered but there is a beautiful drawing room with an open fire and drinks available for guests to help themselves. Breakfast is served in an amazing dining room overlooking the croquet lawn. Magical! ***Rooms 3***.

DUBLIN 24

Tallaght is one of the fastest developing areas of western Dublin and lies at the foot of the Dublin - Wicklow mountains. Particularly well known for its shopping centre and its Luas (tram) line, making travelling to the city centre very easy.

McConnells Fish

Unit 2 Whitestown Industrial Estate Dublin 24 ✆ *01 4524 100 www.mcconnellsgsf.ie*

Established in 1928, McConnells was once a fond fixture on Grafton Street; known especially for salmon, including smoked organic and speciality long-sliced salmon, also gravadlax and barbecue salmon; other smoked products include mackerel, trout and poultry. *Online shop.*

COUNTY DUBLIN

Dublin County is divided into the three administrative "sub-counties" of Dun Laoghaire-Rathdown to the southeast, South Dublin to the southwest, and the large territory of Fingal to the north. But although these regions are among the most populous and economically active in all Ireland, the notion of Greater Dublin being in four administrative parts is only slowly taking root - for instance, all postal addresses still either have a Dublin city numbered code, or else they're simply County Dublin. So if you feel that the frenetic pace of Dublin city is overpowering, you'll very quickly find that nearby, in what for many folk still is County Dublin, there continue to be oases of a much more easy-going way of life waiting to be discovered.

Admittedly, the fact that the handsome Dublin Mountains overlook the city in spectacular style means that, even up in the nearby hills, you can be well aware of the city's buzz. But if you want to find a vigorous contrast between modern style and classical elegance, it can be found in an unusual form at Dun Laoghaire's remarkable harbour, where one of the world's most modern ferryports is in interesting synergy with one of the world's largest Victorian artificial harbours.

A showcase marina within the haven, expensively built so that its style matches the harbour's classic elegance, has steadily developed, while the harbour area of Dun Laoghaire town beside it continues to be improve in quality and vitality.

Northward beyond the city into Fingal, despite the proximity of the airport you'll quickly discover an away from-it-all sort of place of estuary towns, extensive farming, pleasant parkland, fishing and sailing ports, and offshore islands alive with seabirds, while South Dublin balances the other regions with its a pleasant mixture of the urban and the intensely rural.

LOCAL ATTRACTIONS & INFORMATION

▸ **Ardgillan Castle**
Balbriggan/Skerries
01 849 2212
▸ **Newbridge House, Park &**
Traditional Farm Donabate
01 843 6534

▸ **National Maritime Museum,**
Dun Laoghaire Haigh Terrace
01 280 0969
▸ **Malahide Castle, Demesne &**
Botanic Gardens Malahide
01 846 2184

▸ **Marlay Demesne Gardens**
Rathfarnham
01 493 7372
▸ **Working Windmills**
Skerries
01 849 5208

 Gourmet Food Parlour

Grange Gallery Oldtown Road Ballyboughal Co Dublin
☏ *086 603 6235 www.gourmetfoodparlour.com*

One of a small Dublin chain of quality café/wine bars, this casual and spacious venue in The Grange Gallery serves light Mediterranean fare and homemade desserts in a family-friendly setting. An interesting destination for a day out; the intriguing Gallery garden is designed by acclaimed landscape architect Jane McCorkell. *Cafe open Mon-Fri 09.30-5.30, Sat-Sun 10-6.* **Directions:** *Centre of Ballyboughal.*

The Butlers Pantry

1a Montpellier Place Temple Hill Blackrock *Co Dublin* ✆ *01 284 3933 www.thebutlerspantry.ie*

Part of Eileen Bergin's much-loved chain, this benchmark deli, bakery and caterer offers quality home style cooking, fresh ready meals and great breads and cakes to take away. *Open 7 days. Mon-Fri 8.30am-9pm, Sat 8.30-8, Sun 9-7. CC*

  Cakes & Co

Jane Cottage Newtownpark Avenue Blackrock *Co Dublin* ✆ *01 283 6544 www.cakesandco.com*

Leaders in producing celebration cakes for all occasions, this dynamic team offers a variety of fillings and can even ice your own homemade cake for you. Suppliers of sugar craft equipment.

  Dublin Cookery School

2 Brookfield Terrace Blackrock *Co Dublin* ✆ *01 210 0555 www.dublincookeryschool.ie*

Lynda Booth's modern, purpose-built cookery school offers 100 different classes a year for individuals and groups. All levels are catered for with single day sessions through to one-week courses and fulltime one- and three-month professional certificates. **Directions:** *Off Carysfort Avenue: turn off into Brookfield Avenue (Clarks shoes on corner) then right into Brookfield Terrace; cookery school is on the left.*

  The Organic Supermarket

2c Main Street Blackrock *Co Dublin* ✆ *01 278 1111 www.organicsupermarket.ie*

Ireland's first dedicated organic supermarket, Darren Grant's stylish shop is audited by The Organic Trust and offers thousands of products, including a wide range of ethically traded ingredients. *Open Mon-Fri 8-8, Sat 10-8, Sun 11-6. Also online sales.*

  Ouzos Bar & Grill

Main Street Blackrock *Co Dublin* ✆ *01 210 1000 www.ouzos.ie*

Sibling to its popular Dalkey namesake, this lively contemporary restaurant and bar showcases the freshest local fish and seafood, notably lobster, along with excellent steaks. Good cooking, informed service and warm hospitality make an excellent formula. *Open L& D daily. Closed 25-27 Dec, Good Fri. CC.* **Directions:** *Main Street.*

 Tonic

5 Temple Road Blackrock Village *Co Dublin* ✆ *01 288 7671 www.tonic.ie*

A contemporary bar with comfy couches, stylish fittings and a heated terrace offering drinks and relaxed dining to a younger, cooler suburban crowd. Perhaps mainly a place to drop into for a drink in stylish surroundings; the nightclub upstairs is popular at weekends too. **Seats 100.** *Open 12am-12pm; food served all day 12-9pm. Closed 25 Dec & Good Fri. CC.* **Directions:** *Centre of Blackrock village.*

DALKEY

Dalkey is named after its neighbouring island and grew up as a medieval port. Following the construction of the railway it thrived as a seaside suburb from the 19th century onwards until the present day when it has become a popular spot for the rich and famous to reside. It is well served by the DART and buses, with spectacular views of Killiney Bay and Dalkey Island, with many interesting shops, art galleries and restaurants. Dalkey Hill provides a pleasant wooded park to walk in and Dalkey Castle and Heritage Centre (+353 (0) 12 858 366, open all year) are a must see for any visitor. Dalkey Island provides the opportunity for an interesting boat trip, and once on the island visitors can explore the ruins of a 17th century church, or try a spot of fishing or seal watching.

The Dalkey Food Company

Dalkey Co Dublin ✆ *01 235 2657 www.thedalkeyfoodcompany.com*

Producing an interesting range of artisan soups this dynamic Dalkey couple, Ballymaloe-trained chef Ivan Varian and partner Ellie Balfe, supply local shops, cafés and pubs, as well as offering cookery lessons and private catering.

Daniel Finnegan

2 Sorrento Road Dalkey Co Dublin ✆ *01 285 8505 www.finnegans*

A much-loved Dalkey institution for over 40 years, the cosy wood-panelled interior and traditional Irish 'snugs' is flooded by natutral light. Great for pints and and chat, and with an extensive whiskey selection, its traditional fare (including fresh fish from the nearby harbour) makes it a popular lunchtime spot, even with Michelle Obama and her daughters who chose to have lunch here on their visit to Ireland in 2013. *Bar food 12.30-3pm Mon-Sun. Closed 25 Dec, Good Fri & & New Year. CC.* **Directions:** *Near Dalkey DART station.*

Hicks of Dalkey

18 Castle Street Dalkey Co Dublin ✆ *01 285 9568*

Quality butchery from a branch of the celebrated Hicks family. Donal Hick, like his brothers, mastered his craft in Germany; he produces quality pork products, including several specialities, which he offers at his neat shop in Dalkey.

Jaipur Restaurant

20 Castle Street Dalkey Co Dublin ✆ *01 285 0552 www.jaipur.ie*

A stylish branch of the small chain of highly regarded progressive Indian restaurants, this neighbourhood favourite boasts trademark contemporary interiors and menus that are an attractive combination of traditional and more creative dishes. Fresh and dried spices are directly imported and proprietor Asheesh Dewan and head chef Kuldip Kumar also make the most of beautiful Irish ingredients. **Seats 70**; *L Sun only. D daily. Closed 25 Dec. CC.* **Directions:** *On Dalkey's main street.*

Ouzos

22 Castle St Dalkey Co Dublin ✆ *01 285 1890 www.ouzos.ie*

Flying the flag for Irish seafood, this buzzy neighbourhood restaurant serves up locally caught fish, with the fishing vessel proudly named on the menu. Carnivores are well catered for too with a range of prime dry-aged steaks from Co Carlow, hand-cut to order in-house. Among its other attractions are cosy décor, a value wine list, engaging service and an imaginative children's menu. *Open daily noon-10pm (to 9.30pm Sun & Bank Hols). Closed 25-27 Dec, Good Fri. CC.* **Directions:** *Main Street Dalkey, 100m past the church.*

The Queen's Bar & Restaurant

12 Castle Street Dalkey Co Dublin ☎ *01 285 4569*

Dating back to 1745 The Queen's is the oldest pub in Dalkey, and is an atmospheric spot. Traditional bar fare is available alongside the more contemporary offerings at Queen's Restaurant upstairs. Cosy and welcoming, service can come under pressure at busy periods. *Restaurant* **seats 70**. *D daily. Bar menu Mon-Fri, 12-4 & 5-7.30; Sat 12-4; Sun 12.30-3.45. Closed 25 Dec & Good Fri. CC.* **Directions:** *Centre of town, beside Heritage Centre.*

Ragazzi

109 Coliemore Road Dalkey Co Dublin ☎ *01 284 7280*

Renowned for its theatrical Italian waiters and great value, this lively Italian bistro keeps the locals coming back for more with its upbeat atmosphere and tasty food. Lovely pastas, luscious bruschettas and crisp-based pizzas with scrumptious toppings make it a wonderful neighbourhood restaurant. *D daily.*

Roberts of Dalkey

24 Castle Street Dalkey Co Dublin ☎ *01 608 9193 www.robertsofdalkey.com*

While it is mainly a fishmongers, offering a wide choice of fresh seafood, this stylish shop also sells organic meats and vegetables, Irish artisan foods and deli products including ready meals prepared by Roly's of Ballsbridge. Innovative and engaging, they provide recipes and Saturday morning cooking demonstrations - and have an online shop.

Select Stores

1 Railway Road Dalkey Co Dublin ☎ *01 285 9611 www.selectstores.ie*

The store at this landmark corner building has been in the McCabe family since 1959. Today, run by the enthusiastic Oliver McCabe, it is part juice bar, part health store, part greengrocers, part deli, and this unique local shop offers a selection of organic, natural and wholefood products.

Thai House Restaurant

21 Railway Road Dalkey Co Dublin ☎ *01 284 7304 www.thaihouse.ie*

Established in 1997, Tony Ecock's bustling restaurant draws loyal customers who enjoy the authentic Thai cooking that doesn't pander too much to the western palate. Set menus are popular in the cosy dining room and there is also an extensive à la carte, a warm welcome and good value to be had. **Seats 42**. *L Sun only. D Tue-Sun. Closed Mon. CC.* **Directions:** *100 metres from Dalkey DART Station.*

Thyme Out

2a Castle Street Dalkey Co Dublin ☎ *01 285 1999 www.thymeout.ie*

"Fresh, wholesome, tasty and always gone at the end of the day", that's the philosophy at this lovely shop and deli, where evening meals are ready in the fridge and everything is made on site. Ingredients are top notch and you can drop by to stock up on deli favourites, and baked treats (including gluten free) or simply take out a tasty sandwich and coffee. Catering offered too. *Open Mon-Sat 8.30-7, Sun 10-5.*

The Waterside House Hotel

Balcarrick Road Donabate Co Dublin ✆ *01 843 6153 www.watersidehousehotel.ie*

Owner-managed by the Slattery family, of Co Meath's Station House Hotel, this mid-range beachside hotel has much to recommend it - notably its fine dining restaurant, Samphire, where Head Chef Tom Walsh cooks outstanding 'classical French cuisine with a modern Irish twist'. While not luxurious it's a comfortable base for business and leisure, near the airport and with miles of golden beach on the doorstep; unsurprisingly, it's also a popular wedding venue. **Rooms 35**. Open all year. Tower Bistro, food daily 8am-9pm. **Samphire Restaurant:** L&D daily, 12-3.30 & 5-9.45. Early D 5-7. **Directions:** North of Dublin airport, 5 minutes off M1.

DUBLIN AIRPORT

 Carlton Hotel Dublin Airport

Parkway House Old Airport Road Dublin Airport Co Dublin ✆ *01 866 7500 www.carlton.ie*

This comfortable and well appointed purpose-built four-star hotel offers excellent amenities, especially for the business traveller, and good sound proofing. Staff are invariably cheerful, there's secure parking and a convenient complimentary shuttle bus to the airport terminals. **Rooms 100**. *Closed 24-26 Dec. CC.* **Directions:** *Close to Dublin airport on the Swords/Santry road.*

 Clarion Hotel Dublin Airport

Dublin Airport Co Dublin ✆ *01 808 0500 www.clarionhoteldublinairport.com*

Amenities at this modern hotel include business/conference facilities, reliable (Asian/European) food and 24-hour shuttle bus to the terminals - although it is possible to walk. Departure and arrival screens in the bar allow travellers to keep an eye on flights. Guests may use the nearby ALSAA Leisure Complex, with gym and swimming pool. **Rooms 248**. Closed 24-25 Dec. CC. **Directions:** *In airport complex, on right when entering airport.*

 **Crowne Plaza Dublin Airport Hotel**

Airport Area Northwood Park Santry Dublin 9
✆ *01 862 8888 www.cpireland.crowneplaza.com*

An impressive and very attractively located new hotel in a leafy setting with spacious rooms, complimentary parking and 24-hour shuttle to the airport. State-of-the-art conference facilities and meeting rooms make it a good choice for business meetings. **Rooms 204**. Open all year. CC. **Directions:** *In Santry Demesne (off the old airport road and beside Morton Athletic Stadium).*

 **Hilton Dublin Airport Hotel**

Airport Area Northern Cross Malahide Road Dublin 17
✆ *01 866 1800 www.hilton.co.uk/dublinairport*

Ten minutes from the airport terminals, this large international hotel provides very comfortable accommodations and good facilities including a shuttle bus, making it a solid choice for travellers - and also for conferences and business meetings. **Rooms 166**. Closed 23-26 Dec. CC. **Directions:** At junction of N32 and Malahide Road.

Radisson Blu Hotel Dublin Airport

Dublin Airport Co Dublin ✆ *01 844 6000 www.radissonblu.ie/hotel-dublinairport*

A spacious modern hotel with attractive bar and restaurant, just two minutes drive from the main terminal (shuttle service available). Double-glazed rooms include a high proportion of executive rooms (12 designated lady executive). Business and conference facilities are in high demand. **Rooms 229.** *Closed 24-25 Dec. CC.* **Directions:** *In airport complex, on left when entering airport.*

 Travelodge Dublin Airport

Pinnock Hill Roundabout Swords Dublin Airport Co Dublin

Offers comfortable, inexpensive, pet-friendly accommodation and complimentary parking near Dublin Airport. Spacious bedrooms with king size beds and comfy duvets can accommodate up to two adults and two children. No frills (bring your own toiletries), but there's tea & coffee making and multi-channel TV.

DUN LAOGHAIRE

Dún Laoghaire is a seaside town and ferry port situated some 12km southeast of Dublin city centre. The name derives from its founder, Laoghaire, a 5th century High King of Ireland, who chose the site as a sea base from which to carry out raids on Britain and France. The harbour is notable for its two granite piers - one of which is the busiest pier for leisure walking in Ireland - and is home to four yacht clubs.

There are two farmers markets in Dun Laoghaire (Peoples Park, Sunday 11-4; Marine Road, Friday 10-5). Gardens to visit in the area include Carysfort Lodge (Blackrock; 01 288 9273) and Shirley Beatty's Garden (18 Waltham Terrace, Blackrock 01 283 2934. The best golf is found a little further south in County Wicklow - Powerscourt Golf Club (Enniskerry, 01 204 6033) and Druids Glen Golf Club (Newtownmountkennedy, 01 287 3600). Both piers are popular for fishing and there are also charter boats available (Dun Laoghaire Boat Charter, Tel: 01 282 3426).

 Café Mao

The Pavilion Dun Laoghaire Co Dublin ✆ *01 2148090 www.cafemao.com*

Relaxed, casual Asian-fusion food is the USP of this bright and spacious seafront restaurant. Quick and healthy dishes are good value and the outdoor tables make it a popular brunch spot on fine days. **Seats 120.** *Open daily 12 - 11 (to 10 Sun). Closed 25 Dec, Good Fri. CC.*

  Cavistons Seafood Restaurant & Emporium

59 Glasthule Road Dun Laoghaire Co Dublin ✆ *01 280 9245 www.cavistons.com*

One of Dublin's top foodie destinations since opening in 1996, the Caviston family are long-standing fishmongers-turned-restaurateurs. Their gourmet food store complements the celebrated little seafood restaurant next door where spanking fresh seafood dishes delight food lovers across three packed sittings and early weekend dinners. Pricy but wonderful. **Seats 28**; *L Tue-Sat, 3 sittings. D Fri & Sat night only. Closed D Tue-Thu, all Sun, Mon & Christmas/New Year. CC.* **Directions:** *Between Dun Laoghaire and Dalkey, 5 mins. walk from Glasthule DART station.*

Eagle House

18 Glasthule Road Dun Laoghaire *Co Dublin* ☎ *01 280 4740*

A lovely traditional pub with nautical memorabilia and bric-a-brac, you'll find a cosy and welcoming interior and reliably tasty bar meals.

  Georges Fish Shop

Monkstown Court Monkstown Farm Dun Laoghaire *Co Dublin*
☎ *01 230 3011 www.georgesfishshop.com*

A modern fish shop in Monkstown, run by the Rogerson family for over 30 years, George's sells fresh fish and shellfish alongside a selection of homemade ready-to-cook seafood dishes. *Closed Sun & Mon.*

 Gourmet Food Parlour

7 Cumberland Street Dun Laoghaire *Co Dublin* ☎ *01 280 5670 www.gourmetfoodparlour.com*

From breakfast and brunch through to lunch, coffees and evening tapas this appealing modern deli and café has an emphasis on quality at an affordable price. Live music on weekend nights enhances the whole tapas bar experience.

 Hartley's

1 Harbour Road Dun Laoghaire *Co Dublin* ☎ *01 280 6767 www.hartleys.ie*

A neoclassical railway station-turned-handsome restaurant, this harbour-front landmark makes an elegant and relaxed dining spot. The contemporary cooking is well priced and, on sunny days or warm evenings the generous terrace is lovely for dining or enjoying a well-made cocktail. **Seats 100** *(outdoors, 60); L&D Tue-Sun. Closed Mon, 25-26 Dec. CC.* **Directions:** *Coast road, beside DART, opposite the Pavilion.*

  J Hick & Sons Gourmet Foods Ltd

Rear 15A Georges St Upper Dun Laoghaire *Co Dublin* ☎ *01 284 2700 www.hicks.ie*

Outstanding pork butchers, with four generations of experience behind them. The German-trained Hick brothers, Ed and Brendan, offer a wide range of traditional and innovative products, including the kassler that the late Jack Hick was responsible for introducing to Ireland, their superb speciality sausages - and their sensational new bacon jam. *Sell at Temple Bar Food Market (Sat), Farmleigh Market Phoenix Park (Sun), Kilruddery in Bray(Sat, from Easter); their products are also sold in their factory shop (at wholesale prices), and available at premium retail outlets eg Avoca Handweavers, Cavistons and BrookLodge, Co Wicklow. Factory shop: Wed-Fri 10-2.*

 P. McCormack & Sons

67 Lr Mounttown Rd Dun Laoghaire *Co Dublin* ☎ *01 280 5519*

A traditional family run pub since 1960, this neatly presented Mounttown local is full of character and boasts a lovely conservatory and attractive outdoor space for eating or drinking. There's a popular lunchtime carvery but evening menus offer more interesting food. *Bar food daily, 12-3 & 4-10. Closed 25 Dec, Good Fri. CC.* **Directions:** *Near Dun Laoghaire at Monkstown end.*

Rasam

18-19 Glasthule Road Dun Laoghaire Co Dublin ☎ *01 230 0600 www.rasam.ie*

Nisheeth Tak's impressively decorated restaurant is a stylish and comfortable setting for top quality, varied Indian fare. Menus focus on lighter Indian cuisine, with many special ingredients, including rare herbs and spices unique to the restaurant, all ground freshly each day. The extensive wine menu is thoughtfully selected for compatibility with the cuisine and the delightful service ensures a standout dining experience. *Seats 75; D daily. Closed 25-26 Dec, Good Fri. CC.* **Directions:** *Over The Eagle pub.*

Royal Marine Hotel

Marine Road Dun Laoghaire Co Dublin ☎ *01 280 1911 www.royalmarine.ie*

Dun Laoghaire's handsome Victorian landmark enjoyed a major transformation in 2007, with the addition of a lovely spa, conference centre, and contemporary rooms and suites. Many of the rooms have wonderful views over the harbour and Dublin Bay and the hotel has a restaurant and two bars – including the Hardy, with a good cocktail menu. *Rooms 228. CC.* **Directions:** *Town centre, 200m from ferry terminal.*

Tribes

57a Glasthule Road Glasthule Dun Laoghaire Co Dublin ☎ *01 236 5971 www.tribes.ie*

Glasthule's smart family-friendly restaurant serves modern French-influenced bistro fare with panache. Contemporary décor and cheerful staff contribute to the relaxed vibe while lovely seasonal cooking is the real star. Value menus run all evening long, with plenty of choice ensuring a quality dining experience. *Seats 60 (outdoors, 10). D daily, L Sun only. Closed 25-26 Dec, 1 Jan, Good Fri. CC.* **Directions:** *Just past Dun Laoghaire heading South.*

Weafer & Cooper

71-73 Glasthule Road Glasthule Dun Laoghaire Co Dublin ☎ *01 231 1971 www.weaferandcooper.com*

With a distinctly European vibe this chilled-out neighbourhood bistro offers appealing breakfast, lunch and dinner menus that balance classic dishes with imaginative contemporary options. Edgy industrial décor and the sliding glass front all add to the casual style and appeal, while the weekend brunch and wood-fired pizza big draws. *Mon-Fri from 9am - Sat & Sun from 12pm.*

White Tea at Brian S Nolan

1st Floor 102 Upper George's Street Dun Laoghaire Co Dublin ☎ *087 361 5600*

Walk through the portals of one of Dun Laoghaire high street's most elegant old buildings, make your way past colourful bolts of furnishing fabric and take the lift, to tea and cake lover's bliss. The White Tea rooms span the first floor frontage of what was once the Northern Bank manager's drawing room, now dispensing the comforts of fresh baked lemon drizzle cake and deep layered coffee and walnut gateau. *Seats 30. Open Mon-Sat, 9am-4pm.* **Directions:** *Dun Laoghaire High Street.*

Johnnie Fox's Pub

Glencullen Co Dublin 📞 *01 295 5647 www.jfp.ie*

This iconic traditional pub in the Dublin Mountains – claiming to be the highest in the country – serves an all-day menu accompanied by traditional music at night. With welcoming log fires, rickety old furniture and "Famous Hooley Nights" this warm and friendly pub is as popular with tourists as it is with hill walkers. An amusing place to take visitors from abroad. *Seats 352 (outdoors, 60). Open daily, L&D; soup/snacks available 2.30pm-5pm. Full menu Fri-Sun, 12.30-9.30. Closed 24-25 Dec & Good Fri. CC. **Directions:** 5 mins from junction 15 of M50.*

HOWTH

The fishing and sailing port of Howth is easily accessible by DART from Dublin, and is an interesting place to wander around. The seafood restaurants and fish shops along the west pier attract a loyal clientéle, and for many a year it's been a tradition to come out from town after work on a Thursday to buy fish for the fast day on Friday - while that is largely a thing of the past, the shops still stay open later on Thursday evenings, which gives the place a special buzz in summer, when people stay on for a walk around the harbour or a bite to eat before going home. There is a lengthy beach that stretches as far as Sutton and there is also a spectacular cliff top walk around the peninsula that overlooks Dublin Bay - this should not be missed on a fine day. Ireland's largest public golfing complex is at Deer Park; this is also home to a Howth Castle (with cookery school). There's a lovely hill walk amongst the famous Rhodendron gardens, the spectacular sea and coastal views from the top are breathtaking and, on a clear day, you can see as far as the Mountains of Mourne in Northern Ireland, or even the Isle of Man.

Abbey Tavern

Abbey Street Howth Co Dublin 📞 *01 839 0307 www.abbeytavern.ie*

A historic Howth stalwart, part of this famous pub dates back to the 15th century, and the immaculately maintained premises retain authentic features like open turf fires, original stone walls, flagged floors and gaslights. Its long-running dinner-and-trad music nights are popular with visitors. While not a dining destination, the atmospheric dining room, is one of Dublin's longest-established restaurants. *Bar food served daily. Restaurant **seats** 70, D Fri-Sat. Restaurant closed Sun, Mon & possibly other evenings; establishment closed 25 Dec & Good Fri. CC. **Directions:** Centre of Howth.*

Aqua Restaurant

1 West Pier Howth Co Dublin 📞 *01 832 0690 www.aqua.ie*

Sea views and modern cooking make this contemporary seafood restaurant a favourite. Formerly a yacht club, it has a cosy bar with an open fire while the stylish dining room has floor-to-ceiling windows. A la carte menus are influenced by local seafood (and sometimes beef from nearby Lambay island), while the restaurant's allotment supplies seasonal herbs and vegetables. The value of the set menus keeps people going back. *Seats 80. L & D Wed-Sun. Closed Mon (& Tue in winter), 25-26 Dec, Good Fri. CC. **Directions:** End of the West Pier*

Beshoffs the Market

17-18 West Pier Howth Co Dublin 📞 *01 839 7555 www.beshoffs.ie*

Howth Pier's original fishmonger is now a stylish fish shop, with a deli and grill bar serving up oysters and seafood-based tapas. Attached to its more formal sister restaurant, Ivans, the

Market's Grill Bar offers a casual setting. Tuck into a tasty snack accompanied by a glass of wine or good coffee before picking up the makings of your evening meal.

 The Brass Monkey

12 West Pier Howth Co Dublin ✆ *01 806 3746 www.brassmonkey.ie*

A jaunty little restaurant-cum-wine bar, this cosy West Pier spot is a Howth favourite. Serving up tasty local seafood in the guise of tapas or larger plates the menu is largely European, with a few Asian influences. A large bar and the charming, chatty staff lend real character to this casual and fun restaurant. **Directions:** *Mid-way down the West pier*

 Casa Pasta

12 Harbour Road Howth Co Dublin ✆ *01 839 3823*

Howth's quintessential family restaurant, the newly revamped space still offers diners all the old favourites of pizza, pasta and salads. An affordable crowd-pleaser, with a relaxed maritime theme, the ambience is now a little more grown up but children are still especially well accommodated. *Open daily D 6-11, (Sun 12-10). Closed 25 Dec, Good Fri.* **Directions:** *Harbour front, overlooking Howth Yacht Club.*

  The Country Market

16 Main Street Howth Co Dublin ✆ *01 832 2033 www.countrymarket.ie*

Visitors tend to stay around the harbour, but 'up in the village', just above the church and past the flower shop, this prettily presented independent food store, deli and café is where food-loving locals go for their top quality ingredients, wines and treats - and the upstairs café is a pleasant meeting place serving deliciously simple freshly prepared food and drinks in a friendly atmosphere.

  Dorans on the Pier

West Pier Howth Co Dublin ✆ *01 839 2419 www.dorans.ie*

Long-established fishmongers Sean Doran (owner of the neighbouring The Oar House and Octopussys restaurants) sells a particularly good selection of fresh whitefish and shellfish with live lobster and oysters available from a tank in-store. Smart, well-informed staff are very helpful.

  Ella

7 Main Street Howth Co Dublin ✆ *01 839 6264 www.ellawinebar.com*

At Aoife Healy's chic little restaurant and wine bar in the centre of Howth village, local fans enjoy the relaxed, intimate atmosphere, consistently good cooking and obliging staff. Flavourful dishes are pleasingly simple and there's an emphasis on fresh local foods and great selection of wines by the glass. **Seats 45**. *Open L&D Mon-Sat. Closed Sun. CC.* **Directions:** *Centre of Howth village, opposite church*

  The House

4 Main Street Howth Co Dublin ✆ *01 839 6388 www.thehouse-howth.ie*

Karl Dillon's chilled out bistro in one of Howth's nicest buildings is committed to local, organic and artisan produce. Quietly stylish, creative cooking of moderately priced bistro-style dishes is served with flair, including a class brunch menu. Innovative specials at this hip and casual neighbourhood spot include 'Midweek Surprise Dinner for a Tenner' and Wednesday Jazz. *Seats 60 (outdoors, 50). Food served Mon 9am-5pm, Tue-Sat, 9am-10pm, Sun 10am-9.30pm. Closed Mon D, 25/26 Dec. CC.* **Directions:** *In the centre of Howth village, before the church.*

Ivans Oyster Bar & Grill

17-18 West Pier Howth Co Dublin 📞 *01 839 0285 www.ivans.ie*

The first in a line of restaurants on Howth's West Pier, this contemporary dining room is named for Ivan Beshoff, who founded the famous fishmonger dynasty almost a century ago. Serving exciting seafood dishes (including peerless fish and chips) and speciailsing in oysters, the bright space is especially popular for summertime dining. *Seats 100 (outdoors, 20). Restaurant/Tapas Bar L&D daily. Closed D 24 Dec, 25 Dec, D 31 Dec, 1 Jan, Good Fri. CC.* **Directions:** *Beginning of West pier.*

King Sitric Fish Restaurant & Accommodation

East Pier Howth Co Dublin 📞 *01 832 5235 www.kingsitric.ie*

Over 40 years in business, Aidan and Joan MacManus' elegant seafood restaurant with rooms is one of Dublin's longest established fine dining establishments. This destination dining room takes full advantage of the harbour views while menus demonstrate Aidan's commitment to showcasing the best of seasonal local produce. Alongside outstanding mainly seafood dishes for every budget and occasion, his wine list is one of the country's finest. *On the ground floor, the contemporary smart-casual *East Café Bar* is run by son of the house, Declan MacManus, with his girlfriend Susan McKiernan. Offering a limited menu, Aidan's fantastic food and great value, it is proving a real winner. *Rooms 8. Restaurant seats 70. D Wed-Sat (also Mon in summer). Sun all day, 1-7pm. Restaurant closed Tue (& Mon in winter), bank hols, Christmas. East Café Bar closed Tue. CC.* **Directions:** *Far end of the harbour front, facing the east pier.*

The Kitchen in the Castle

Howth Castle Howth Co Dublin 📞 *01 839 6182 www.thekitcheninthecastle.com*

An atmospheric cookery school in the restored Georgian kitchens of Howth Castle, offering a wide range of cookery classes and demonstrations. Whatever the theme, the aim is the same: "...to reconnect you with food. We want to nurture your creativity, give you a good grounding in the basics and the confidence to cook delicious food, at any time."

Mulloys

West Pier Howth Co Dublin 📞 *01 661 1222 www.mulloys.ie*

Third generation fishmongers, well known on Dublin's Lower Baggot Street for many years, are now located in Howth, where they have a processing plant, smokery and retail shop. They specialise in prime fish and their own premium smoked salmon.

Nickys Plaice

West Pier Howth Co Dublin 📞 *01 832 6415 www.nickysplaice.ie*

Despite being the last fish shop on the pier, many regulars make a beeline for this family-run concern with a long tradition in the fish business in Howth. Alongside fresh whitefish and shellfish all smoked fish is processed on the premises in their smokery - one of the last of its kind – using a very traditional process that ensures a unique product.

The Oar House

8 West Pier Howth Co Dublin 📞 *01 839 4562 www.oarhouse.ie*

Relaxed and atmospheric, the nautically themed Oar House is a family favourite majoring in deliciously fresh seafood and a crowd-pleasing menu, including daily specials. Generous portions, caring service and good value ensure this casual West Pier staple is popular year-round. *Seats 50 (outdoors, 20). Open all day 12.30-10.30 (to 10pm Sun). Closed Good Fri, 25 Dec. CC.* **Directions:** *Half way down West pier.*

Oceanpath Seafood

Claremont Industrial Estate 9a West Pier Howth Co Dublin 📞 *01 839 8900 www.dunns.ie*

Dating back to 1822, Dunns of Dublin is Ireland's oldest fish company and remained in the family until it was sold to another family-run company, Oceanpath, in 2006. Specialising in smoked seafood their West Pier shop offers wild when available, Irish Organic, and farmed salmon as well as other smoked and ready to eat seafood products.

Octopussys Seafood Tapas

West Pier Howth Co Dublin 📞 *01 839 0822*

Specialising in seafood tapas this casual and colourful West Pier tapas bar – owned by neighbouring fish shop, Doran's on the Pier – pleases with its fresh and simple dishes. Compact and relaxed restaurant, staff are helpful and it's a pleasant spot to spend a sunny afternoon. *Seats 30, open daily. CC.* **Directions:** *Half way down the West pier.*

Okra Green

1 Island View Harbour Road Howth Co Dublin 📞 *01 832 6038 www.okragreen.ie*

When something different is called for, this attractive and reliable Pakistani restaurant on the harbour front could be just the ticket. The welcome is warm and courteous, and helpful staff are quick to make customers comfortable and explain menus which offer variations on familiar styles - tandoori, jalfrezi, biryani - with good vegetarian choices. Long opening hours and good value make this an appealing restaurant to call into without a reservation. *Seats 65. D daily 5-11pm, L Fri-Sun 12-3pm; Sun open all day.* **Directions:** *On Howth sea front.*

Ray Collier

3 Main Street Howth Co Dublin ✆ *01 832 2002*

Highly regarded Associated Craft Butchers of Ireland member known for quality meats and customer care. This is the place to find the local Baily beef (finished on Howth peninsula), and Lambay Island beef which is available for a short season in autumn.

 Marine Hotel

Howth Area Sutton Cross Co Dublin ✆ *01 839 0000   www.marinehotel.ie*

Located on the seaside of busy Sutton Cross this attractive and well-run neighbourhood hotel is popular for social occasions. Bedrooms, some of which have sea views, have recently been refurbished and it's the best option in the area for business guests. *Rooms 48 (6 shower only). Closed 25-26 Dec. CC.*

 Fitzpatrick Castle Hotel Dublin

Killiney Co Dublin ✆ *01 230 5400   www.fitzpatrickhotels.com*

Located in the fashionable suburb of Killiney, this imposing castellated mansion overlooking Dublin Bay dates back to 1741 and attracts a diverse clientele, being a popular local meeting place and equally suited to business and leisure guests. Surrounded by landscaped gardens, it's an old-world hotel with modern facilities including spacious bedrooms, business and conference amenities and a fitness centre with swimming pool and spa. *Rooms 113. Closed 24-26 Dec. CC. Directions: On Killiney road.*

 Finnstown Country House Hotel

Newcastle Road Lucan Co Dublin ✆ *01 601 0700   www.finnstown.com*

This likable manor house may have dated décor, but lovely staff and afternoon teas are a plus. Bar food and evening meals also served. hotel with old world décor serving bar food, afternoon tea and evening meals. *Rooms 82. Restaurant seats 100. L Sun-Fri; D Mon-Sat. House closed Christmas. CC. Directions: Off main Dublin-Galway Road (N4), Adamstown exit.*

 McAllister's Quality Fishmonger

11 Village Centre Lucan Co Dublin ✆ *01 628 0062   www.mcallistersfish.com*

The McAllister family's inviting fishmongers not only offers an impressive variety of appealingly displayed fresh fish and shellfish, but also a high level of customer service. Always delighted to encourage customers to try something new, they have plenty of suggestions ('Bill's Recommended Recipes') and also take pride in reassuring customers that the produce they sell is sustainably sourced from responsibly managed stocks. *Open Tue-Fri 9-5.30, Sat 9-4.30. Closed Sun.*

  Superquinn

Newcastle Road Lucan Co Dublin ✆ *01 624 0277   www.superquinn.ie*

A chain of 23 Irish-owned supermarkets, founded in 1960. Specialising in fresh food it demonstrates a serious commitment to local producers ("4 out of every 5 euro we spend is on fresh produce from local suppliers") and, while competitively priced, products offered are not exclusively price-led.

La Banca

Main Street Lucan Village Co Dublin ☎ *01 628 2400 www.labanca.ie*

A welcoming neighbourhood restaurant off Lucan's main street, this bright and modern dining room offers a comprehensive selection of mainly Italian fare, from pasta favourites to more unusual regional specialities. There's an excellent choice of chicken, lamb, steak and fish dishes and the friendly Italian staff are always helpful. *Open D Tue-Thu, Fri & Sat 1-10.30, Sun 1-9.30pm Closed Mon.*

  Llewellyns Orchard

Quickpenny Road Lusk Co Dublin ☎ *087 284 3879 www.llewellynsorchard.ie*

When David Llewellyn started out a decade or so ago, he was just growing apples and selling them; deciding to add value to his crop, he developed the well known range of natural apple juices, cider and vinegar. Double L Irish Cider is made from Irish apples only, in Bone Dry and Medium Dry versions. Cider making courses offered in autumn. *Llewellyn juices are widely available from selected outlets; some also stock the vinegar. Buy Double LL Irish Cider at farmers' markets, the Drink Store and Wines on the Green in Dublin. Contact David directly for current list of stockists.*

MALAHIDE

The attractive coastal town of Malahide offers quality shopping and an abundance of things to do. The town is alive with bars, cafés and restaurants. Malahide Castle & Gardens, surrounded by 250 acres of parkland, is a must-visit destination.

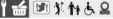 **Avoca Malahide**

Malahide Castle & Gardens Malahide Co Dublin ☎ *01 893 1900 www.avoca.ie*

In an old stone courtyard beside the castle, a large L-shaped room overlooking two gardens has a blackboard along one end wall detailing the day's main offerings. The food is up to their usual high standards, all home cooked and based as much as possible on local and artisan produce - although a table service option along the lines of the lovely Fern House Café (at their flagship Kilmacanogue store) would be very welcome here. *Open 7 days. Café: Mon-Fri, 9.30-5, Sat, Sun & Bank Hols 9.30-5.30. CC.* **Directions:** *In grounds of Malahide Castle*

 Bon Appetit

9 St James Terrace Malahide Co Dublin ☎ *01 845 0314 www.bonappetit.ie*

In a four-storey Georgian building, talented chef-patron Oliver Dunne offers diners a choice of venues: sophisticated fine dining on the first floor, where luxury ingredients are served as delicious works of art in *Le Restaurant*. The entrance level offers 'Le Bon Vin,' a smart wine and 'taster plates' bar; and the lower ground floor is an informal but equally stylish restaurant *'La Brasserie'*, where head chef Aaron Carroll turns out seasonal bistro cooking with an original twist. An impressive operation. *Le Restaurant* **seats 100**: *L Thu-Sat. D Wed-Sat; Sun 1pm-8pm. La Brasserie: D Tue-Sat, L Sun. Closed Mon, 1st week Jan, 1st two weeks Aug. CC.* **Directions:** *Centre of Malahide, overlooking Tennis club.*

Cape Greko

Unit 1 First Floor New Street Malahide Co Dublin ☎ *01 845 6288 www.capegreko.ie*

This friendly first floor restaurant offers a genuinely relaxed Greek Cypriot experience and is a fun, good value place for a group outing. Simple decor and friendly staff complement the classic selection, from tzatziki, hummus and grilled haloumi to lamb kleftiko and couscous, and there's live music on Friday nights. **Seats 54**. L Sat & Sun. D daily. CC. **Directions:** At the corner of New Street above Marios Pizzas.

FoodWare Store

19 Old Street Malahide Co Dublin 📞01 845 1830 www.foodwarestore.com

Aisling Boyle and Jill Sloan are both Ballymaloe trained, and it shows in both the homecooked foods that they prepare for customers, and in the carefully selected items they offer for sale, whether it be dry goods, artisan cheeses or wines. They love to give credit to their valued suppliers - and catering menus and cookery classes are also offered. Open Mon-Sat 9.30- 6. Closed Sun.

Gourmet Food Parlour

Gannon Park Coast Road Malahide Co Dublin 📞01 828 3661 www.gourmetfoodparlour.com

An appealing modern deli and café with an emphasis on quality at an affordable price. Located on the coastal outskirts of Malahide, it's a bright spot for a tasty lunch or coffee and home baked treat. Very family-friendly, with play area. Open Mon-Sun, 9-6. **Directions:** At Malahide United Football Club overlooking the beach and Malahide-Portmarnock coastal walk.

Grand Hotel

Malahide Co Dublin 📞01 845 0000 www.thegrand.ie

A traditional, old style hotel set in six acres of gardens with lovely views over Malahide estuary. The original building dates back to 1835 while recent additions include an excellent leisure centre and extensive conference and banqueting facilities. Its best feature is the friendly and helpful staff and, while bedrooms may seem a little dated, they are good-sized and comfortably furnished. **Rooms 203**. Closed 24-26 Dec. CC. **Directions:** Centre of Malahide.

Jaipur Restaurant

St James Terrace Malahide Co Dublin 📞01 845 5455 www.jaipur.ie

One of six in the impressive Jaipur group, this chic new-wave Indian restaurant was completely refurbished recently and the Georgian basement room feels calm and exclusive. Offering a modern take on traditional Indian food, head chef Anughau Srivastava creates colourful, well-flavoured dishes; selected wine complement the subtle spicing, and well-trained staff enhance the experience. **Seats 45**; D daily. Closed 25-26 Dec. CC. **Directions:** In Georgian terrace facing the tennis club in Malahide.

Kajjal - Pakistani & Eastern Cuisine

Unit 7 The Green Malahide Co Dublin 📞01 806 1960 www.kajjal.ie

Sister restaurant of Clontarf's highly regarded Kinara, diners can expect the same qualities of style, delicious food and friendly, attentive staff. Serving 'Pakistani and Eastern cuisine', the menu offers an exciting mix of regional cooking, expert spicing and attractive presentation. Stylish décor and an interesting wine list complete the offering. CC. **Directions:** Opposite the bottom of Old Street.

Seabank Bistro

Coast Road Malahide Co Dublin 📞 *01 845 1988 www.seabankbistro.ie*

Successfully combining the charm of a seaside café with the cosiness of a neighbourhood restaurant, this nautically themed dining room and little terrace has year round appeal. Seafood plays a large part in the repertoire although non-fish eaters can expect plenty of choice too. Consistent cooking, generous portions and a lively atmosphere all make this a popular choice. **Seats 42** *(outdoors, 20); Open D daily. CC.* **Directions:** *Just outside the East side of Malahide village, a couple of minutes walk from the village centre.*

Siam Thai Restaurant

1 The Green Malahide Co Dublin 📞 *01 845 4698 www.siamthai.ie*

One of Dublin's longest-established Thai restaurants, the popular Siam Thai overlooks Malahide village green. A covered heated terrace and full bar make it an appealing choice with menus offering many of the Thai classics. Friendly staff are knowledgeable and efficient. **Seats 120** *(outdoors, 30). L&D daily. Closed 25-26 Dec. CC.* **Directions:** *near marina overlooking the green.*

The Purty Kitchen

3-5 Old Dunleary Road Monkstown Co Dublin 📞 *01 284 3576 www.purtykitchen.com*

One of Dublin's oldest pubs, dating back to 1728, this characterful Dun Laoghaire spot has been sensitively renovated by owner Ashley Sheridan to preserve its historic feel. It offers over 40 craft beers, including many Irish brews, and they also offer a BYOB policy Monday to Thursday. Tasty, good value cooking features stand-out Irish produce, which is used to good effect and name checked on the menu. *Food Mon-Fri 12-9.45, Sat-Sun, 12.30-9.45. Closed 25 Dec, Good Friday. CC.* **Directions:** *On left approaching Dun Laoghaire from Dublin by the coast road.*

Salt Café

The Crescent Monkstown Co Dublin 📞 *01 202 0230 www.avoca.ie*

Part of Avoca's only dedicated food market, this lovely café doubles up as a popular lunchtime and dinner spot too. Décor is a blend of shabby chic and vintage styling; by day it's bright and open, by night candlelit and intimate. Chef Marc McGillycuddy uses plenty of great Irish products in his fresh, clean cooking and there's an amicable buzz in this charmingly chic neighbourhood restaurant. *B&L Mon-Sat; D Wed-Sat; Sun 12.15-7pm. CC.* **Directions:** *Centre of Monkstown.*

Seapoint Fish & Grill

4 The Crescent Monkstown Co Dublin 📞 *01 663 8480 www.seapointrestaurant.com*

A bright and breezy dining room, this Monkstown favourite draws locals in with a range of offerings from morning coffee, light lunches and a dinner menu with clean flavours and impressively affordable choices. A strong team includes accomplished chef Nick Clapham and proprietor Shane Kenny whose wine knowledge informs the well-priced, comprehensive wine list. **Seats 70** *(outdoors, 12). L&D Tue-Thu; Fri & Sat all day 12-10.30pm. Sun L 12-8.30pm. Closed Mon. CC.* **Directions:** *Centre of Monkstown.*

Michael's Food & Wine

57 Deerpark Road Mount Merrion Co Dublin ✆*01 278 0377*

Michael and Mary Lowe's low-key wine shop and deli doubles up as a relaxed Italian trattoria. Pavement tables, simple regional dishes and quality antipasti ensure a brisk local trade. *Seats 24; Open Mon-Sat from 11.30. D Thu-Fri, L Sat only. CC. Directions: Situated off Fosters Avenue on Deerpark Road just past Kiely's.*

  The Herb Garden

Forde-de-Fyne Naul Co Dublin ✆*01 841 3907 www.theherbgarden.ie*

A certified organic herb nursery, Denise Dunne grows herbs of many kinds, and specialises in herb garden design. Visitors by appointment only.

  The Cake Stand

Newcastle Co Dublin ✆*086 040 7676 www.thecakestand.ie*

Producing what she modestly refers to as 'quality cakes and desserts', French trained patissier Iseult Janssens takes pride in using local ingredients - organic where possible, including her own free range eggs. Classic French pastries and desserts, authentic macarons, cupcakes with a difference and glamorous special occasion and wedding cakes are all offered. Variations of her exquisite creations can be made to meet special dietary needs, eg dairy-free or gluten-free.

  Letts Craft Butchers

Main Street Newcastle Co Dublin ✆*01 458 0156 www.lettscraftbutchers.com*

A member of the Irish Craft Butchers Association, meats at this interesting shop include beef from a single farm, Fitzpatrick's of Castledermot, Co Kildare, game in season, fresh vegetables, fish from Kish Fish in Coolock and Traditional Cheese Company cheeses. *Open Mon-Sat 9-6.30.*

  Keogh's Potatoes

Peter Keogh & Sons Ltd Westpalstown Oldtown Co Dublin ✆*01 843 3175 www.keoghs.ie*

Aside from growing various types of spuds (including organic and Selenium high anti-oxidant) these enterprising farmers are famous for developing the brilliant Keogh's Hand Cooked Crisps, with flavours like Dubliner cheese, Irish Atlantic Sea Salt and Irish Cider Vinegar. National Potato Day, in August, was their idea too, inviting the public to 'do your bit for the Irish spud!

  **Portmarnock Hotel & Golf Links**

Strand Road Portmarnock Co Dublin ✆*01 846 0611 www.portmarnock.com*

Originally owned by the Jameson family of whiskey fame, this recently refurbished golf hotel is in a wonderful beach side position, enjoyed to advantage from the front bedrooms and Seaview Lounge - an ideal meeting place for Afternoon Tea. The Jameson Bar has character and Osborne Brasserie offers imaginative semi-formal dining on weekends. *Rooms 138. Restaurant seats 80. D only Fri-Sat, 7-10. Bar menu daily. Open all year. CC. Directions: On the coast in Portmarnock.*

Avoca Cafe Rathcoole

Naas Road Saggart Co Dublin *01 257 1800 www.avoca.ie*

Scrumptious home cooking and delicious baking are part of the draw at this large purpose-built lifestyle store's restaurant and café. Both share a large outdoor terrace, which is very popular when the weather allows and a large enticing food hall looks out onto newly landscaped gardens. **Seats 100**; *Open daily 9.30-5pm (to 8pm Thu).* **Directions:** *By edge of Naas Road, just west of Citywest campus.*

SKERRIES

So far remarkably unspoilt, Skerries is not completely undeveloped but its essential atmosphere has remained unchanged for decades (perhaps because it does not yet have marina and all its attendant development) and it makes a refreshing break from the hurly-burly of Dublin city. The harbour is renowned for its fishing, notably Dublin Bay prawns, and the surrounding area is famous for market gardening, so it has always been a good place for a very subtstantial bite to eat - and there are several pubs of character along the harbour front to enjoy a pint before your meal. While in the area, allow time to visit Skerries Mills (working windmills (Tel: 01 849 5208)) and Ardgillan Castle and Victorian Gardens (Tel: 01 849 2212) nearby at Balbriggan.

The Blue Bar

Harbour Road Skerries Co. Dublin 01 849 0900 www.bluebar.ie

A fun, casual, harbourside spot with good food, with an extensive menu offering a great range of gourmet burgers plus plenty of seafood and locally sourced fruits and vegetables. The drinks menu includes Irish and world craft beers, both on tap and bottled, and cocktails. A great family-friendly choice for a day out by the sea - and also an evening venue. *Open 12.30-9.30; late night bar on Saturdays.*

Egans Ocean Fresh

84a Strand Street Skerries Co Dublin *01 849 5224 www.egansfreshfish.com*

With over 80 years in business Tony Gunnery's fourth generation family fishmongers opened their Skerries store in 2008. Friendly and helpful, they stock a wide variety of fresh, locally caught fish.

Olive

86a Strand Street Skerries Co Dublin *01 849 0310 www.olive.ie*

Peter and Deirdre Dorrity's charming specialist food shop and café in the centre of Skerries has a wide pavement with an outside seating area - a very pleasant place to enjoy a bite to eat while people-watching in fine weather. Good coffee, tasty home made deli food and a carefully selected range of artisan produce make this cosy café a foodie favourite. **Seats 30** *(outdoors, 30).* *Open daily 8.30-6pm (Sun from 9am). Closed Christmas. CC.* **Directions:** *Turn right at monument in town, on the right.*

 **Red Bank House & Restaurant**

5-7 Church Street Skerries Co Dublin ☏ 01 849 1005 www.redbank.ie

This converted bank building with guestrooms promises a fine dining experience focusing on Irish ingredients, old-style service and a good wine list. Renowned chef-proprietor, Terry McCoy's, is an avid supporter of local produce, with fresh seafood from Skerries harbour providing the backbone of his menu, supported by many other foods from the surrounding area. The dessert trolley is legendary, as is great value Sunday lunch. *Seats 60. D Mon-Sat; L Sun only. Rooms 18. Restaurant closed 24-28 Dec. Accommodation open all year. CC. Directions: On Church Street pposite AIB Bank in Skerries*

 **Stoop Your Head**

Harbour Road Skerries Co Dublin ☏ 01 849 2085 www.stoopyourhead.ie

Serving up fresh, simple seafood at great prices this lively harbourside pub and restaurant is always popular. Chef Andy Davies' majors in 'fresh, simple and wholesome' cooking which can be enjoyed in the simple and comfortable surroundings. There's a shortish but appropriate wine list and non-fish eaters are well catered for. *Seats 50 (outdoors, 20). Food served June-Aug, 12-9.30pm. Otherwise L & D daily. Closed 25 Dec & Good Fri. CC. Directions: On the harbour front in Skerries.*

 **The White Cottages**

Balbriggan Road Skerries Co Dublin ☏ 01 849 2231 www.thewhitecottages.com

A stylish bed and breakfast on the Skerries shore, with unbroken sea views, this boutique hideaway is owned by Jackie and Joe O'Connors who offer guests the warmest hospitality. With just 4 bedrooms, decorated in Scandinavian seaside tones, this unusual B&B serves up delicious breakfasts and even lobster lunches and afternoon tea by arrangement. *Rooms 4 (2 shower only). Open all year. No CC. Directions: On coast road to Balbriggan.*

  Donnelly Fresh Foods

Roslin Food Park St Margarets Co Dublin ☏ 01 890 8100

Irish produced bagged salads, from field to shop in 24 hours – a welcome replacement for imported salads. Available in in Superquinn stores nationwide, Donnybrook Fair, Spar, Londis and local Costcutters.

  Keelings

FoodCentral St Margarets Co Dublin ☏ 01 813 5600 www.keelings.com

Growers in north Co Dublin since the 1930s, this remains a family-run company, albeit a very large one. Both growers and distributors, Keelings are among Ireland's most forward-looking producers, growing a very wide and constantly evolving range of soft fruits, top fruits - notably Bramley apples and, from 2013, cherries - salad leaves and other vegetables, including protected crops like peppers and aubergines. Look out for the 'Keelings - Taste the Passion' labels.

Beaufield Mews Restaurant & Gardens

Woodlands Avenue Stillorgan Co Dublin ☎ *01 288 0375 www.beaufieldmews.com*

In sensitively modernised 18th century coach house and stables, Dublin city's oldest restaurant is in the Cox family for over 50 years and full of character. Upstairs the Loft Brasserie offers evening dining, while The Coachhouse restaurant downstairs is open for weekend lunches and groups. Surrounded by beautiful mature gardens it feels like a lovely country retreat; a summer Sunday lunch here is a special treat, with the outdoor patio wonderful for drinks. **Seats 200** *(outdoors, 20). Loft Brasseries D only, Wed-Sun; Coach House L Sat & Sun only). Closed Mon & Tue except for groups, 24-26 Dec, Good Fri. CC. Directions: off Stillorgan dual carriageway/N11.*

Stillorgan Park Hotel

Stillorgan Road Stillorgan Co Dublin ☎ *01 200 1800 www.stillorganpark.com*

Sister to the famous Talbot Hotel in Wexford this well-run property offers good facilities and frequently refurbished rooms. Regular renovations over the years ensure a lively modern style throughout and ample free parking is an attraction. Contemporary cooking well above the standard expected of hotels is served in the attractive, informal Purple Sage Restaurant. **Rooms 150**. *Restaurant* **seats 120**. *L Mon-Fri; D daily. CC.* **Directions:** *Situated on main N11.*

Essence Bistro

75 Main Street Swords Co Dublin ☎ *www.essencebistro.com*

This inviting bistro's welcoming exterior draws in hungry passers-by, who find a modest, informal restaurant with friendly local staff and an emphasis on genuine value. Menus offered by owner-chef Robbie Burns and his brother, Owen, are inspired mainly by the seasonal produce of north Co Dublin (suppliers listed) and their policy of sourcing quality ingredients and cooking them with skill and simplicity is a winner with loyal regulars. **Directions:** *Swords town centre. Times: L&D Tue-Sat, all day Sun (D-9). Closed Mon.*

Gourmet Food Parlour

Unit 2-3 St Fintans North Street Swords Co Dublin ☎ *01 897 1496 www.gourmetfoodparlour.com*

Part of the popular Dublin chain this bright and spacious modern deli and informal restaurant serves breakfast, baked goods and lunch, alongside a selection of antipasti and well chosen list of wines by the glass. Tapas evenings take place on Thursday, Friday and Saturday nights and there's a nice outdoor seating area. **Seats 72**; *open Mon-Sat 8am-5.30pm (from 10am Sat); Sun 12-6pm & D Thu, Fri & Sat only (Tapas). CC.* **Directions:** *North Street is at the Castle end of Swords Town.*

Indie Spice

Burgundy House Forster Way Swords Co Dublin ☎ *01 807 7999 www.indiespice.com/swords/*

One of a small chain of popular restaurants offering quality Indian cuisine and good value, this Swords' restaurant has a warm and stylish interior that sets the tone for some interesting Indian cooking, with courteous service. The long menu offers a real taste of exotic India, from familiar styles to more unusual chef specials. **Seats 130**. *L&D Mon-Fri; Sun 1-11pm. Closed 25/26 Dec. CC.* **Directions:** *Behind the Plaza shopping centre, on the first floor.*

La Boulangerie Francaise

Unit 77 Applewood Village Swords Co Dublin ☎ *086 102 2786 www.laboulangeriefrancaise.ie*

Husband and wife team Damian and Florence Cusack have been operating this speciality bakery and café since 2006 - and while it is Florence, who looks after front of house, who is French and her Irish husband Damian looks after production, it's a very French operation with continental breads dainty little tartlets, gorgeous desserts and immaculately decorated cakes on offer. *Mon-Sat 9-5. CC.* **Directions:** *Centre of Applewood Village.*

 The Old Boro

Main Street Swords Co Dublin ☎ *01 895 7445 www.thesmithgroup.ie*

A school for over 90 years this historic building has an interesting architectural pedigree been handsomely renovated and refurbished as a smart pub. Operated by the Smith Group it maintains the traditional feel of the building with a lovely contemporary aspect.

The Old Schoolhouse Bar & Restaurant

Coolbanagher Church Road Swords Co Dublin ☎ *01 840 4160 www.theoldschoolhouse.ie*

Offering assured bistro style cooking in a cosy pub setting, with an unashamed focus on their signature steaks and seafood - and with lovely service from friendly and efficient staff - this very fairly priced dining destination is understandably popular with locals, but also well worth remembering whenever a meal in the airport area is needed. *Open Mon-Sun, 11am-11pm. CC.* **Directions:** *Behind Main Street (West side).*

Tartine Organic Bakery

Unit 16 Seatown Business Park Seatown Road Swords Co Dublin ☎ *01 890 3301 www.tartine.ie*

Renowned for their finesse and flavour, artisan baker Thibault Peigne's continental breads are made by traditional methods, using the finest organic ingredients. Sourdough breads, French pastries and cakes are among the treats you can buy from the bakery - and look out for them in quality-led speciality stores and restaurants too, as he is also a wholesale supplier. *Open: Mon-Fri, 8am-5pm.* **Directions:** *Off the dual carriageway, behind Woodies.*

Roganstown Hotel & Country Club

Swords Area The Naul Road Co Dublin ☎ *01 843 3118 www.roganstown.com*

A handsome country estate in north county Dublin this golf hotel, with its Christy O'Connor Junior-designed course, offers much to non-golfing guests too. Good food, warm hospitality, comfortable modern rooms and a smart leisure centre make it a pleasant place to stay - and useful to consider as an alternative to standard airport hotels. **Rooms 52** *(3 shower only). Closed 24-26 Dec. CC.* **Directions:** *From Swords village, take Ashbourne road. Turn right Naul.*

 Chez Emily

Cool Quay The Ward Co Dublin ☎ *01 835 2252 www.chezemily.ie*

Exquisite artisan chocolates by Belgian-trained chocolatiers Ferdinand Vandaele and Helena Hemeryck, with 30 varieties available year round alongside seasonal specialties. *Open Mon-Fri 8-4, Sat 10-4. Closed Sun. Also at: Chocolate Boutique Ashbourne, Mon-Sat, 10-6. Also available at selected retail outlets, in north Dublin and nationwide.* **Directions:** *Near Mabestown.*

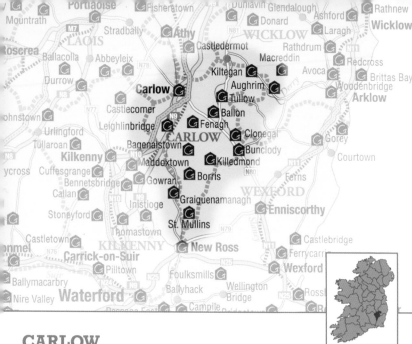

CARLOW

Carlow's character and charm is within easy reach of Dublin, and the metropolitan commuter spread is present, yet also kept at bay with a lively sense of place. Although it is Ireland's second smallest county, it confidently incorporates such wonderful varieties of scenery that it has been memorably commented that the Creator was in fine form when He made Carlow. Whether you're lingering along the gentle meanderings of the waterway of the River Barrow, or enjoying the upper valley of the River Slaney while savouring the soaring outlines of the Blackstairs Mountains as they sweep upwards to the 793m peak of Mount Leinster, this gallant little area will soon have you in thrall.

There's history a-plenty if you wish to seek it out. But for those who prefer to live in the present, the county town of Carlow itself fairly buzzes with student life and is also home to the impressive VISUAL Centre for Contemporary Art & The George Bernard Shaw Theatre. A more leisurely pace can be enjoyed at riverside villages such as Leighlinbridge and Bagenalstown. Leighlinbridge - pronounced "Lochlinbridge" - has for many years been Carlow's most community-conscious riverside village, the holder of a Tidy Towns Gold Medal and an Entente Floriale winner. There are also welcome improvements taking place to fulfill Bagenalstown's potential as a proper miniature river port, while the hidden hillside village of Borris is an enchantment in itself.

LOCAL ATTRACTIONS & INFORMATION

▸ **VISUAL Centre for Contemporary Arts & George Bernard Shaw Theatre**
Old Dublin Rd., Carlow,
www.visualcarlow.ie
059 917 2400

▸ **Tourist Information**
Carlow town
059 9170776

▸ **Carlow Rural Touris**
Carlow county
059 913 0411 / 9130446

▸ **Carlow Craft Brewing**
Bagenstown
059 972 0509

▸ **Altamont Gardens**
Tullow
059 915 9444

BAGENALSTOWN

 ## Carlow Brewing Company

Muine Bheag Business Park Royal Oak Road Bagenalstown Co Carlow
📞 *059 972 0509 www.carlowbrewing.com*

Carlow Brewing Company, aka O'Hara's, was established in 1996 and is one of Ireland's most successful new wave craft breweries. Brewed with natural ingredients and no artificial additives these aromatic beers are full of flavour and available in both bottle and cask. Tours give Ireland's indigenous brewing history and include tastings.

 ## Kilgraney House

Borris Road Bagenalstown Co Carlow 📞 *059 977 5283 www.kilgraneyhouse.com*

Set in wooded grounds and gardens on a lovely site overlooking the Barrow Valley, Bryan Leech and Martin Marley's stylish Georgian house near Altamont gardens is tranquil and restorative. Their monastic herb gardens and kitchen garden provide an abundance of good things for Bryan to transform into delicious dinners. Showcasing local and artisan produce, they offer a true taste of the area, both in the holistic overall experience and in Bryan's creative cooking. **Rooms 8** *(3 shower only); Set D open to non-residents, must book (8 pm). Closed Mon-Tue and Dec-Feb incl. CC.* **Directions:** *Just off the R705, halfway between Bagenalstown and Borris.*

 ## Lorum Old Rectory

Kilgraney Bagenalstown Co Carlow 📞 *059 977 5282 www.lorum.com*

Everybody loves Bobbie Smith's welcoming mid-Victorian cut stone granite rectory near Altamont gardens, which now makes an elegant and homely place to stay. Repeat guests travel specially for her easy hospitality and delicious home cooking using mainly organic and home-grown ingredients; rack of local lamb is a speciality. **Rooms 4** *(all shower only); residents' D (must book; 8pm). Closed Dec-Feb incl. CC.* **Directions:** *Midway between Borris & Bagenalstown on the R705.*

BALLON

Ballon boasts a rich history of stone masonry, one of Ireland's oldest crafts, whilst Ballon Hill provides excellent views of the surrounding countryside. A guided tour of Malone's 12 acre fruit farm (see entry) is well worthwhile. Nearby is Altamont Gardens, Tullow (059 915 1769); set in a small and uniquely beautiful estate, the 'most romantic gardens in Ireland' are among County Carlow's premier tourist attractions.

 ## Ballykealey Manor Hotel

Ballon Co Carlow 📞 *059 915 9288 www.ballykealeymanorhotel.com*

Gothic arches and Tudor chimney stacks add quirky character to this 1830s building; set in well-maintained grounds and recently refurbished, it's a romantic spot and a popular wedding venue. The Oak Room: This aptly-named restaurant retains original features; with a welcome open fire on chilly days, it makes a handsome setting for enjoyable food. **Rooms 12** *(4 shower only). Restaurant* **seats 32**. *D daily; L Sun only; also daily bar menu. Closed 24 Dec. CC.* **Directions:** *16km from Carlow on the N80.*

The Forge Restaurant

Kilbride Cross Ballon Co Carlow 📞*059 915 9939*

'The Forge for home baking and local produce' is their motto and it sums up nicely the appeal of Mary Jordan's unpretentious daytime restaurant. The granite building dates back to the 1700s and, off the road and with ample parking, it's a great place to break a journey or when visiting nearby Altamont. **Seats 60** *(outdoors, 30). Open 9.30-5 daily (Sun 12-5.30). Closed 10 days Christmas. CC.* **Directions:** *Off the N80, between Ballon and Bunclody.*

Malones Fruit Farm

Closh Ballon Co Carlow 📞*059 915 9477*

The Malone family grow a wide variety of fruit on their 12 acre farm near Altamont Gardens. Fresh fruit is sold at the farm shop in season; frozen fruit and a full range of homemade products are available all year. Many products are also sold in retail outlets and markets, including Carlow Farmers' Market. *Open May-Oct, daily; Nov-Apr, Wed-Sat.* **Directions:** *1 km outside Ballon on N80, near N81 junction.*

Sherwood Park House

Kilbride Ballon Co Carlow 📞*059 915 9117 www.sherwoodparkhouse.ie*

Built around 1700, Patrick and Maureen Owens' delightful Georgian farmhouse next to Altamont Gardens (and with lovely gardens itself) is beautifully located, with sweeping views over the countryside. Antique-laden rooms boast brass and canopy beds, and candlelit dinners offer real home cooking of local produce. **Rooms 5.** *D by reservation. No CC.* **Directions:** *Signed from the junction of the N80 and N81.*

BORRIS

This captivating village is located in the shadow of the Blackstairs Mountains and offers beautiful scenery, excellent for either walking and scenic drives, or perhaps a visit to one of the many local craft workers. Interesting local sites include the fine old Borris House, the historic Macmurrough Kavanagh estate (059 977 1884; borrishouse.com), with gardens, nature trails and self-catering cottages. Anglers are well catered for on both the River Barrow and the Brandon lake and, for more active pursuits, Borris offers cycling, canoeing, quad biking, clay pigeon shooting - and, for the really adventurous, Mount Leinster is a great spot for hang gliding.

M O'Shea

Borris Co Carlow 📞*059 97 73106*

Halfway up the steep main street of Borris, the old grocery of this unspoilt old-world grocery-pub links into a modern-day shop next door - a practical arrangement that brings past and present together in a delightful way. Conversions and extensions provide more space for music sessions and there's a patio at the back for fine weather. Charming. Sandwiches, snacks all day. Music every fortnight or so: "it's a bit random". *Closed 25 Dec & Good Fri.*

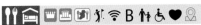 **The Step House Hotel**

66 Main Street Borris Co Carlow ☎*059 977 3209 www.stephousehotel.ie*

James and Cait Coady redeveloped their lovely property - former dower house of the Macmurrough Kavanaghs (Borris House) and the pub next door (in the Coady family for 5 generations) - and their stylish boutique hotel has made this pretty heritage village a destination for short breaks and weddings. Plush accommodation even includes a room with two bathrooms, one of them suitable for wheelchairs. Cellar Restaurant: This atmospheric restaurant with archways and vaulted ceilings is in the kitchens of the old house. Head Chef Alan Foley's pride in the food of the area is palpable: a special experience. *Rooms 20. Restaurant seats 50. D only, Thu-Sun. Also bar meals daily & Sun L. Closed 25 Dec, 3 wks Jan. CC.* **Directions:** *From main Carlow-Kilkenny road, take turning to Bagenalstown. 16km to Borris.*

CARLOW

Situated on the banks of the river Barrow about 80km from Dublin, Carlow (www.carlowtourism.com) is a friendly, bustling youthful town, with a large student population attending the local Institute of Technology and good amenities. The name Carlow is derived from the old Irish place name Ceatharloch, meaning 'four lakes' and the countryside around the town is attractive, with many pretty towns and villages, scenic routes and places of historic interest to visit. There is plenty of good food to be found, and garden lovers visiting the area are spoilt for choice with four superb gardens all within 30km of Carlow town; Hardymount (Tullow; 059 915 1769); Ballon Garden (Ballon; 059 915 9144); Altamont (Tullow; 059 915 9444) and Heywood Gardens, Ballinakill, Co Laois; (057 873 3563). Golfers will be happy too, with three championship courses within 30km [Carlow Golf Club (059 913 1695); Mount Wolseley Golf Club (Tullow; 059 915 1674) and Rathsallagh Golf Club (Dunlavin; 045 403 316)].

 **Barrowville Townhouse**

Kilkenny Road Carlow Co Carlow ☎*059 914 3324 www.barrowville.com*

Just a short walk from the town centre, Dermot and Anna Smyth's exceptionally comfortable and immaculately maintained period guesthouse is set in lovely gardens. There's a pleasant and relaxing residents' drawing room with an open fire, grand piano and plenty to read, and very good breakfasts are served in a handsome conservatory (complete with a large vine) overlooking the riverside back garden. *Rooms 7 (2 shower only). Closed 24-26 Dec. CC.* **Directions:** *South side of Carlow town on the N9.*

 Brasserie 15

114-115 Tullow Street Carlow Co Carlow ☎*059 914 3455 www.brasseriefifteen.com*

Next door to his bar, The Met, and sharing the entrance, Laurence Murray's smart-casual restaurant is in a very attractive building with appealing dining areas on two levels. Philip Hutton's varied menus include 21-day dry-aged steaks, impressively cooked fish dishes and some unusual accompaniments; all this plus good value and great staff make it an evening destination of choice. *Open Mon-Sat from 5 pm, Sunday lunch only.*

Lennons @ VISUAL

Visual Centre for Contemporary Art Old Dublin Road Carlow Co Carlow
☎ *059 917 9245 www.lennons.ie*

Well known restaurateur Sinead Byrne and her son Ross run the restaurant at this stunning amenity in the heart of Carlow Town. There's a spacious terrace and floor to ceiling windows allow views of Carlow Cathedral and Carlow College across the grass. Local artists' paintings are displayed for sale and there's great pride of place - a perfect spot to enjoy simple, homely food based on the best local and regional artisan produce. **Seats 68**. *Open daytime daily. Closed Bank Hols, Good Fri, 25 Dec. CC.* **Directions:** *Centre of Carlow Town (Old Dublin Road).*

Mimosa Wine & Tapas Bar

College Street Carlow Co Carlow ☎ *059 917 0888 www.mimosawinebar.com*

In the centre of Carlow town, directly opposite the Cathedral, this stylish and sociable venue has everything that makes a good night out with friends. Like a little piece of Spain, the atmosphere is authentic with good music, wine racks around the bar and a hand-written blackboard tapas menu that delivers with tasty well cooked food. *D Wed-Sun. Closed Mon & Tue. CC.* **Directions:** *Centre of town, opposite the Cathedral.*

Rattlebag Café

202 Barrack Street Carlow Co Carlow ☎ *059 913 9568*

This popular and attractively presented cafe on the way in to Carlow Town (Dublin Waterford road) is pretty enough to make you stop the car when passing. A friendly place to drop into for good home baking and tasty light meals. **Seats 36** *(outdoors, 4); Open 9-5 Mon-Sat; closed Sun. Closed Easter, 25-26 Dec, 1 Jan. CC.*

Coolanowle Country House

Carlow area Ballickmoyler Carlow Co Carlow ☎ *059 862 5176 www.coolanowle.com*

Organic farm, lovely B&B accommodation, home cooking with their own meats, fruit and vegetables, online produce sales, self-catering, holistic treatments and even weddings/events - Bernadine and Jimmy Mulhall have thought of everything. Set on three acres of natural woodland with three lakes - with lots for children to do, it's an ideal destination for family holidays, and for people of any age who enjoy rural life. Farm shop. **Rooms 9** *(two in annexe). D & Sun L by reservation. CC.* **Directions:** *Well signed off N80, between Carlow and Portlaoise.*

Sha-Roe Bistro

Main Street Clonegal Co Carlow ☎ *053 937 5636*

On the borders of Wexford, Carlow and Wicklow, Henry and Stephanie Stone's small but beautifully appointed and atmospheric restaurant is in a fine 18th century building in the riverside village of Clonegal. Friendly and professional, with welcoming fires for chilly days and a pretty courtyard for sunny ones, it has become a destination for the growing number of diners who appreciate Henry's outstanding, and beautifully simple, seasonal cooking. *Seats 28. D Wed-Sat, L Sun only. Closed Sun D, Mon, Tue and Jan. CC. **Directions:** Off N80 Enniscorthy-Carlow road.*

Carlow Farmhouse Cheese

Ballybrommell Fenagh Co Carlow ✆*059 972 7382*

Elizabeth Bradley produces a mild, semi-hard Edam style raw milk cheese, which she sells at Carlow Farmers' Market and may be spotted on menus in the area. Available both plain and flavoured - black pepper (a favourite); chilli; cumin; also more complex variations including sundried tomato with basil and 'a hint of garlic' and nettle with dried onion - it's sold both young (three months) and when matured to give deeper flavours (six months).

Blackstairs Eco Trails

Mary White Killedmond Co Carlow ✆*059 977 3849 www.blackstairsecotrails.ie*

With foraging all the rage, urbanites hankering after the country life will love these eco trails run by former Green Party Minister, Mary White, and her husband Robert. Aimed at all age groups, the 2 hour walks are easy ('low hills or no hills') and relaxed. Learn all about the bio-diversity of the area as you go along - and, if your foraging is successful, you will take something home for dinner. Walks begin at 12.30.

 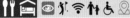
The Lord Bagenal Hotel

Main Street Leighlinbridge Co Carlow ✆*059 977 4000 www.lordbagenal.com*

Beautifully situated on the River Barrow, James and Mary Kehoe's large modern hotel retains some of the best features of the original inn. A popular lunchtime carvery/buffet draws local diners, but it is the restaurant that will be of interest to visitors; James Keogh's art collection (and notable wine list) set the scene for head chef George Keogh's cooking, which has finesse. *Rooms 39. Restaurant seats 80. D Wed-Sat, L Sun only. Bar meals daily. Closed 25 & 26 Dec. CC. **Directions:** Signed off main N9 Dublin/Waterford Road.*

Rachels Garden Café

Arboretum Garden Centre Kilkenny Road Leighlinbridge Co Carlow
✆*059 972 1558 www.arboretum.ie*

This pleasant restaurant at Frank and Rachel Doyle's impressive Arboretum offers an attractive selection of wholesome food. A self-service counter presents an appetising display of salads and quick-serve dishes - everything is fresh and home-made with good ingredients, and the friendly and helpful staff are always happy to assist. Licensed. Open Mon-Sat 9-5.30pm (until 8pm Thur), Sun 11-5pm. *Closed 25 Dec & 1 Jan. CC. **Directions:** Well signed off N9 Dublin/Waterford Road.*

Mullichain Café

The Old Grainstore St Mullins Co Carlow ✆*051 424 440 www.oldgrainstorecottages.ie*

"Great coffee, fantastic atmosphere and chat to beat the band" are the promise at the café in this fine restored grain house, where owners Martin & Emer O'Brien also offer "fresh scones with the morning coffee and a read of the paper, smoked salmon and a glass of wine for the lunch." All this and a good riverside walk in a beautiful and tranquil setting. What more could anyone ask for? *Open: Tue-Sun 11-6, closed Mon except bank hols (but then closes the following Tue). Winter closure Nov-Mar. Directions: On the quayside in St Mullins village.*

 Mulvarra House

St Mullins Graiguenamanagh Co Carlow ✆*051 424 936 www.mulvarra.com*

Noreen Ardill's friendly and well-maintained modern house is in a stunning location overlooking the River Barrow above the ancient and picturesque little harbour of St Mullins and, although it may seem unremarkable from the road, this relaxing place is full of surprises. *Rooms 5. D by reservation; licensed. Closed Mid Dec-Mid Jan. CC. Directions: Take R702 from Borris, turn right in Glynn; signposted from Glynn.*

 Ballyderrin House & Cookery School

Shillelagh Road Tullow Co Carlow ✆*059 915 2742 www.ballyderrin.com*

The Holligan family offer comfortable B&B accommodation at their home near the market town of Tullow and, with Pamela Holligan's well known cookery school on site, good food is sure to be part of the experience. (Contact Ballyderrin for details of courses.) Pamela also produces baked goods and preserves and, in the pre-Christmas period, sells these in her on-site shop along with other local artisan products. *Rooms 4 (all shower only). Closed 25-26 Dec. CC. Directions: From Tullow take Shillelagh road, R725; signed, on left.*

The Chocolate Garden

Rath Tullow Co Carlow ✆*059 648 1999 www.chocolategarden.ie*

Aka Wicklow Fine Foods, Jim and Mary Healy's innovative family-run business is alongside Rathwood Home & Garden World and Rath woodlands. A quality product range includes handmade chocolates, biscuits, fudge, chocolate spreads, and their own Tipperary Organic Ice Cream, previously made in Clonmel; also chocolate workshops, a café and ice cream parlour, and online sales. *Open daytime Mon-Sun. Closed 3 wks Jan. CC. Directions: 5km outside Tullow on the Shillelagh/Gorey road (R725).*

  Coolattin Cheddar

Knockeen Tullow Co Carlow ✆*086 389 4482 www.coolattincheddar.com*

Tom Burgess makes Coolattin Cheddar in summer using the fresh (unpasteurised) milk from the farm's own herd of pasture-fed Friesian-Jersey cows. Matured for at least a year before sale to allow the nutty flavour to mature, Coolattin is easily recognised by its distinctive red wax and the contrasting hard, pale yellow interior. Sold at at Farmleigh, Carlow and Kildavin markets, and some independent stores.

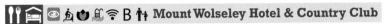 **Mount Wolseley Hotel & Country Club**

Tullow Co Carlow 📞 *059 918 0100 www.mountwolseley.ie*

In a lovely area of rolling hills and river valleys, this immaculately presented modern hotel and Christy O'Connor-designed championship course creates a good impression on arrival - as do the friendly, helpful staff. It's a popular short break destination and guests have the choice of dining in the smartly appointed Frederick's Restaurant or eating more casually in the lounge. *Rooms 143. Restaurant seats 180 (outdoors, 30). D daily; lounge menu all day. Hotel closed 25-26 Dec. CC. Directions: N7 from Dublin, left in Castledermot for Tullow. Take left at bridge, then right.*

 Murphy's Butchers

Church Street Tullow Co Carlow 📞 *059 915 1316 www.murphysbutchers.com*

Quality comes first at the Murphy family's third generation butchers shop, which continues proud traditions, including respect for animal husbandry and welfare, careful choice of breed, knowledgeable selection of individual animals, and dry ageing of beef - each of which makes a valuable contribution to the flavour and texture of their acclaimed meats. *Open Mon-Sat, 8-6.*

 Rathwood

Rath Tullow Co Carlow 📞 *059 915 6285 www.rathwood.com*

With country walks, an outdoor play area, and even an on site train, this award-winning garden centre and shopping emporium is ideal for a journey break (or even a day out).The tellingly named Fresh Approach restaurant offers good wholesome food all day (special diets catered for). There's a also a heated patio, a smoothie/juice bar, and even a function room. A useful place to know about. *Seats 130 (+ conservatory & outdoors). Open daytime daily, incl bank hols; licensed. Closed 25/26 Dec, 1 Jan. CC. Directions: Well signed on R725 to Shillelagh.*

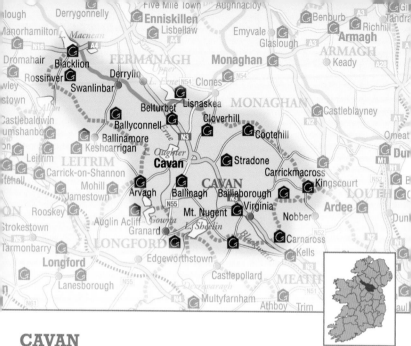

CAVAN

This is one of Ireland's most watery counties. It's classic drumlin country, interwoven with more lakes than they know what to do with. But the very fact that the meandering waterways dictate the way of the roads means that much of Cavan is hidden. In today's intrusive world, this is a virtue. It is a place best discovered by the discerning visitor. Much of it has quiet and utterly rural charm, seemingly remote. But it isn't so very far from Belfast or Dublin, and modern Cavan can surprise with its entrepreneurial flair.

Yet if you take your time wandering through this green and silver land - particularly if travelling at the leisurely pace of the deservedly renowned Shannon-Erne Waterway which has joined Ireland's two greatest lake and river systems - then you'll become aware that this is a place of rewardingly gentle pleasures. And you'll have time to discover that it does have its own mountain, or at least it shares the 667 m peak of Cuilcagh with neighbouring Fermanagh.

No ordinary mountain, this - it has underground streams which eventually become the headwaters of the lordly River Shannon, while 47 kms to the southeast is the source of the River Erne near Bellanagh - it eventually flows northwest, so Ireland's greatest rivers are closely interwined, yet only connected by canal.

Cavan is much more extensive than is popularly imagined, for in the northeast it has Shercock with its own miniature lake district, while in its southeast it takes in all of Lough Ramor at the charming lakeside village of Virginia. It also shares Lough Sheelin, that place of legend for the angler, with Westmeath and Meath, while in the far northwest its rugged scenery hints at Donegal. And always throughout its drumlin heartlands you can find many little Cavan lakes which, should the fancy take you, can be called your own at least for the day that's in it.

LOCAL ATTRACTIONS & INFORMATION

▸ **Cavan County Museum**
Ballyjamesduff
049 854 4070

▸ **Cavan Crystal** Cavan town
049 433 1800

▸ **International Pork Festival
(June)** Ballyjamesduff
049 854 4242

▸ **Maudabawn Cultural Centre**
Cootehill *049 555 9504*

▸ **Cavan Equestrian Centre**
Cavan *049 4332017*

▸ **Lakeview Gardens** Mullagh
046 9242480

Polo D Restaurant

Main Street Ballyconnell Co Cavan ✆*049 952 6228*

Paul and Geraldine's O'Dowd's cottagey restaurant offers atmosphere and a warm welcome from Geraldine and her team as well as Paul's wholesome cooking. Country generosity is the name of the game here - you get a good selection of side vegetables as well as a big portion of the main dish - and don't skip on dessert as it may well be the highlight of your meal. *Seats 50. D Wed-Sat. Closed Sun-Tue, may also close Wed in winter. CC. **Directions:** Main Street.*

Slieve Russell Hotel & Country Club

Ballyconnell Co Cavan ✆*049 952 6444 www.quinnhotels.com*

Close to the attractive canal-side town of Ballyconnell and set in landscaped grounds, this very large hotel has outstanding conference and leisure facilities and is a popular golfing and spa-break destination. With marble colonnades and a grand central staircase, its flamboyance may take first-time visitors by surprise, but it is very much the centre of the local community. *Rooms 222. Open all year. CC. **Directions:** Take N3 from Dublin to Cavan, proceed to Belturbet then Ballyconnell.*

BELTURBET

Belturbet is a bustling, unspoilt little town on the River Erne. An excellent base for exploring the river and the Shannon-Erne Canal, cruisers can be hired in Belturbet and the area attracts anglers for the variety of catch to be had in the local waters. Golfers will appreciate the challenge that the nearby championship standard Slieve Russell Golf Club (Ballyconnell; 049 952 5090) provides; while garden lovers can visit the restored Victorian gardens at Hilton Park (Clones, 047 56007) by appointment.

 Corleggy Farmhouse Cheese

Corleggy Belturbet Co Cavan ✆*049 952 2930 www.corleggy.com*

In rich pasture land beside the River Erne, Silke Cropp makes her wonderful range of goat, sheep and cows' milk cheeses. Silke is one of Ireland's longest-practising cheesemakers, and the original, Corleggy, is a natural rind hard goats' cheese with complex flavours. Others - Quivvy (soft, goat)l; Drumlin, (hard, cow, in several flavours); and Creeny (semi hard, sheep) - have since joined the range. Cheese-making lessons sometimes offered.

 International Fishing Centre

Loughdooley Belturbet Co Cavan ✆*049 952 2616 www.brochet-irlande.com*

At a lovely waterside location, the Neuville family offers residential fishing holidays; the restaurant is not open to the public in the usual way, but people on boating holidays may come in off the river when there is room. It's like a little corner of France, with all signage in French, including the menus which are clearly displayed and offer a range of traditional dishes, many of them from Alsace - and great value. *Rooms 18. Restaurant **seats 35**. D daily (residents & river guests only). Closed 15 Nov-15 Mar. CC.*

Seven Horseshoes

Belturbet Co Cavan ✆ *049 952 2166*

Although officially an hotel, the heart of this friendly place is the bar, which is full of character, with an unusual wattle hurdle ceiling, plenty of local history, an open fire for cold days and the pleasingly dim atmosphere that makes Irish pubs so relaxing. Hearty home cooking is served in the bar at reasonable prices and accommodation is offered in simple, comfortably appointed modern en-suite rooms. *Restaurant D daily, L Sun only. Bar food available daily.* **Rooms 10.** **Directions:** *at the centre of town.*

MacNean House & Restaurant

Main Street Blacklion Co Cavan ✆ *071 985 3022 www.macneanrestaurant.com*

Neven Maguire's position as one of Ireland's leading chefs is well earned, and the prospect of a meal at the restaurant that he and his wife Amelda run in this little border town has long attracted devotees from all over Ireland, and beyond. Once a modest restaurant with rooms, they have made it a spacious place of sumptuous comfort, providing the setting that is deserved by Neven's exceptional cooking of the local foods that he has always championed with such passion. **Seats 50.** *D Thu-Sun (high season Wed-Sun); L Sun only, two sittings.* **Rooms 19.** *Restaurant closed Mon, Tue (& Wed off season); establishment closed 1 Jan-8 Feb. CC.* **Directions:** *On N17, main Belfast-Sligo road.*

BJ Crowe Quality Meats

2 Connolly Street Cavan Co Cavan ✆ *049 436 2671*

An award winning member of the Associated Craft Butchers of Ireland (ACBI), Barry John Crowe's loyal customers (and the ACBI judges) especially like his sausages. Traditional with a modern twist, they have the high meat content that is essential for a good sausage that will cook well without shrinkage - and they taste as good as they look and smell.

Cavan Crystal Hotel

Dublin Road Cavan Co Cavan ✆ *049 436 0600 www.cavancrystalhotel.com*

In common ownership with the adjacent Cavan Crystal Showroom and Visitor Centre, this modern hotel has good facilities - a health and fitness club, conference and banqueting - making it a focal point for local activities. The smart first floor restaurant offers wholesome, hearty lunches and fine dining at night, when long-serving head chef Dave Fitzgibbon's creative cooking makes the most of his carefully sourced seasonal ingredients. **Rooms 85.** Restaurant **seats 100** L& D daily. CC. Hotel closed 24 & 25 Dec. **Directions:** On N3, on Dublin side of town.

The Oak Room Bistro

Main Street Cavan Co Cavan ✆ *049 437 1414 www.theoakroom.ie*

The focus at is Norbert Neylon's popular town centre restaurant is (very sensibly) on offering value for money, but his background is in fine dining and he is a talented chef. An inviting, spacious first floor room makes a pleasant setting to enjoy his good cooking of a varied menu, which is always plentiful and tasty, with 'real food' options for children especially notable. **Seats 70.** *D Tue-Sun. Closed Mon, 24-26 Dec. CC. Directions: next door to Ladbrokes on the first floor.*

The Side Door

Drumalee Cross Cootehill Road Cavan Co Cavan 📞*049 433 1819*

A younger sister restaurant to the successful and admirably consistent restaurant in Navan (The Loft), The Side Door is based on the same principles of accessibility, offering good quality international food at a fair price. Suppliers are credited, so customers can enjoy the likes of spicy buffalo wings and homemade burgers with confidence. **Seats 90**. *D Wed-Sun, L Sun only. Closed Mon & Tue; Good Fri, 25 Dec. CC.* **Directions:** *On the Cootehill Road, edge of Cavan town, above the Orchard Bar.*

Radisson Blu Farnham Estate Hotel

Farnham Estate Cavan Area Co Cavan 📞*049 437 7700 www.farnhamestate.com*

A winding driveway through lush parkland and golf course brings you to the dramatic entrance of this mainly modern hotel, with a giant glass atrium linking the classical building dating from 1810 to the striking 21st century extension. A popular destination for short breaks - golf, spa and, more recently, foraging. Low impact design entails long corridors to many rooms. Head Chef Philippe Farineau ("French Heart, Irish Produce") offers good cooking in the attractively situated smart-casual Botanica Restaurant. **Rooms 158**. *Restaurant* **seats 180**. *L&D daily. Open all year. CC.* **Directions:** *N3 to Cavan town; signed, on Killeshandra Road (3km).*

The Olde Post Inn

Cloverhill Co Cavan 📞*047 55555 www.theoldepostinn.com*

Gearoid and Tara Lynch's restaurant is in an old stone building in a neatly landscaped garden which served as a post office until the 1970s. Gearoid, a former Commissioner General of Euro-Toques Ireland, is a talented chef and committed to supporting local producers and showing respect for regional and seasonal foods, so a meal at this atmospheric restaurant promises to be a true be a taste of Ireland - and indeed of the region. Tara manages front of house with quiet efficiency and, after dinner, residents relish the fact that the rooms are only yards from the fire in the cosy bar. **Seats 120**. *D Tue-Sun, L Sun only. Closed Mon.* **Rooms 6** *(2 shower only). Closed 24-27 Dec. CC.* **Directions:** *9km north of Cavan town: take N54 at Butlersbridge, 2.5km on right in Cloverhill village.*

O'Leary's

14 Bridge Street Cootehill Co Cavan 📞*049 555 2142*

A gem worth seeking out in this charming little planned town - a small and friendly grocery-deli, jam-packed with good things including local foods (eg Govender's and Aines chocolates, Mossfield cheeses) and with a tiny café serving Illy coffee. *Open Mon-Sat, 9-6.30.*

KINGSCOURT

An active market town, in the south east corner of Cavan, visitors can enjoy exploring the beautiful countryside of nearby Lough an Leagh Mountain or the Dun na Ri forest park. Kingscourt offers good coarse fishing at the local lakes such as Evrey and Greaghlone or the golfer can play 9 holes at Cabra Golf Course (+353 (0) 28 966 7714). Nearby at Muff Rock, an annual horse fair is held on the 12th of August - it is the oldest horse fair in Ireland.

 **Cabra Castle Hotel & Golf Club**

Kingscourt Co Cavan ☎*042 966 7030 www.cabracastle.com*

Set amidst extensive grounds and with lovely countryside views, the Corscadden family's imposing hotel is a sister property to Ballyseede Castle Tralee (see entry) and the recently acquired Bellingham Castle, Co Louth (undergoing renovation). It has large public rooms, antique furnishings and even suits of armour in the foyer, but the atmosphere is relaxing (perhaps surprisingly, as Cabra Castle is believed to be haunted...) Popular locally for family occasions, also a destination for golf breaks, conferences and functions. ***Rooms 107***. *Closed at Christmas. CC.*

 Aine Hand Made Chocolates

Stradone Village Co Cavan ☎*049 432 3744 www.chocolates.ie*

Master Chocolatier Ann Rudden's handmade Irish chocolates are based entirely on natural ingredients. The range is wide, covering sugar free chocolates and hot chocolate, bars and truffles, gift bags and hampers, wedding favours and special occasions. Widely distributed within Ireland and internationally. *Online shop.*

VIRGINIA ♀

This attractive town is on the the northern side of beautiful Lough Ramor, which has wooded shores and a great reputation for coarse fishing. It makes a good base for a fishing holiday, or simply exploring an attractive and unspoilt part of the country. For travellers between Northern Ireland and Dublin it's the ideal spot to take a break.

 St Kyrans Country House & Restaurant

Dublin Road Virginia Co Cavan ☎*049 854 7087 www.stkyrans.com*

In a stunning shoreside location, Patrick and Helena Keenan's smart-casual restaurant with rooms (registration pending) looks right up Lough Ramor - where little fishing boats and wildlife activity around pretty wooded islets are a constant source of interest. Even before you eat a mouthful, it's easy to see why this has become a destination restaurant, drawing diners from a wide area. ***Seats 45***. *L Wed-Sun, D Mon-Sun.* ***Rooms 8*** *(registration pending). CC.* **Directions:** *Signed on left when approaching Virginia from Dublin direction.*

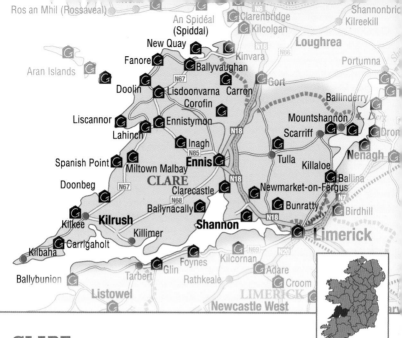

CLARE

Clare is impressive, a larger-than-life county which is bounded by the Atlantic to the west, Galway Bay to the north, the River Shannon with Lough Derg to the east, and the Shannon Estuary to the south. Yet it's typical of Clare that, even with its boundaries marked on such a grand scale, there is always something extra added.

Thus the Atlantic coasts includes the astonishing and majestic Cliffs of Moher. Close under them in dangerous water is the majestic breaker known as Aileens, the surfer's Nirvana. Less challenging nearby, but still at the top of world standards, is one of Ireland's greatest surfing beaches at Lahinch, which is also a golfer's Nirvana. As for that Galway Bay coastline, it is where The Burren, the fantastical North Clare moonscape of limestone which is home to so much unexpectedly exotic flora, comes plunging spectacularly towards the sea around the attractive village of Ballyvaughan.

To the eastward, Lough Derg is one of Ireland's most handsome lakes, but even amidst its generous beauty, we find that Clare has claimed one of the most scenic lake coastlines of all. As for the Shannon Estuary, well, Ireland may have many estuaries, but needless to say the lordly Shannon has far and away the biggest estuary of all. It is the port of call for the largest freight ships visiting Ireland, and on its northern shore is Shannon Airport. Yet the Estuary is also home to a numerous and remarkable friendly dolphin population, with Kilrush the most popular port for dolphin-watching, all just down the road from the busy county town of Ennis.

LOCAL ATTRACTIONS & INFORMATION

› **Aillwee Cave** Ballyvaughan
  065 707 7036
› **Bunratty Castle & Folk Park
  c/o Shannon Heritage Centre**
  Bunratty *061 360788*
› **Clare Heritage Centre** Corofin
  065 683 7955

› **Killimer-Tarbert Ferry**
  Killimer *065 905 3124*
› **Kilrush Heritage Centre**
  Kilrush *065 905 1577*
› **Scattery Island Interpretive
  Centre** Kilrush
  065 9052139

› **Vandeleur Walled Garden**
  Kilrush *065 905 1760*
› **Craggaunowen (Celts &
  Living Past)** Quin
  061 360 788
› **Knappogue Castle** Quin
  061 360 788

BALLYVAUGHAN

This attractive little port is best known for its major attraction, the Aillwee Cave, but its seafood comes a close second - and, as it is in a leafy valley with a wide range of amenities close at hand, it makes a comfortable base for exploring the Burren.

 Aillwee Cave

Ballyvaughan Co Clare ✆*065 707 7036 www.aillweecave.ie*

There is a much of interest to food lovers for visitors to this 2-million-year-old cave. While the cave's café is not a destination in itself, cheese-making demonstrations show how Burren Gold cheese is made, and there is a well-stocked food shop; free tastings of the cheeses and home-made fudge are available here, and other goodies to take home, including local honey. The Burren Birds of Prey Centre shares the site. *Café **seats 60**. Open daily 10-5.30. Shop closed mornings in Dec; Christmas. CC. **Directions:** 4.5 km south of Ballyvaughan.*

 An Fear Gorta (Tea & Garden Rooms)

Ballyvaughan Co Clare ✆*065 707 7157 www.tearoomsballyvaughan.com*

In a pretty stone building dating back to 1790, Jane O'Donoghue's charming harbourside tea room is full of character. A tempting display of home-baked fare is laid out on an old cast-iron range, to be enjoyed in the delightful back garden or the homely dining room, or to take away. Licensed. ***Seats 40** (outdoors, 15). Open mid Apr-Oct, daily Jul & Aug 11am-6pm. Closed Tue & Wed early season; Tue in June & all Nov-mid Apr. CC. **Directions:** On the harbour front.*

 An Fulacht Fia

Coast Road Ballyvaughan Co Clare ✆*065 707 7300 www.anfulachtfia.com*

On the coast road between the Cliffs of Moher and nearby Ballyvaughan village, John and Mairin Connole's purpose-built restaurant An Fulacht Fia ('Cooking Pit') commands views over Galway Bay. Appealing cooking by Head chef Irmantus Bagocius uses locally supplied ingredients from the Burren area, which are sustainable, traceable and organic. ***Seats 80** (outdoors, 8). D daily, L Sun. May also be light lunches in summer. Closed Jan-Feb, but call to check days/times of opening off season. CC. **Directions:** On the coast road.*

  Burren Fine Wine & Food

Corkscrewhill Road Ballyvaughan Co Clare ✆*065 707 7046 www.burrenwine.ie*

Although primarily a charming spot for a daytime bite to eat (including traditional Afternoon Tea), Cathleen Connole's restaurant just off the Burren Waymarked Walk also offers packed lunches for walkers and they sell hampers. Everything served is delicious, with good home baking a particular strength. ***Seats 35** (outdoors, 20). Open daytime, daily. Closed Oct-Apr. **Directions:** Corkscrew Hill road.*

Gregans Castle Hotel

Ballyvaughan The Burren Co Clare ✆*065 707 7005 www.gregans.ie*

While offering simple West of Ireland joys like warming turf fires and unparalleled views across the Burren landscape, Simon and Freddie Haden's quietly luxurious and restorative country house hotel has also earned a reputation as one of Ireland's top food destinations. Cooking in a style that is 'modern European but distinctively Irish and unpretentious', and with an emphasis on food provenance, talented chef David Hurley, takes enormous pride in showcasing the wonderful foods of the locality. *Rooms 21. Restaurant seats 50. D daily, Tasting Menu. L (Corkscrew Bar) Afternoon Tea, daily. Hotel closed Late Nov-mid Feb. CC. **Directions:** On N67, 5km south of Ballyvaughan.*

 Hylands Burren Hotel

Ballyvaughan Co Clare ✆*065 707 7037 http://www.hylandsburren.com/*

Open fires in public areas create the welcoming atmosphere for which this hotel is famous - and a modern bedroom wing at the back offers comfortable accommodation with good amenities. Restaurant meals are available in the evening and an extensive bar menu, which includes a range of dishes based on local seafood, is offered all day. *Rooms 30. Closed Nov-Apr.*

 L'Arco Italian Restaurant

Main Street Ballyvaughan Co Clare ✆*065 708 3900 www.burrenrestaurant.com*

Behind the Quinn family's craft shop in the centre of Ballyvaughan they also run L'Arco, with Italian chefs from Sardinia. Offering an authentic and affordable Italian dining experience, it would suit families and diners seeking well-made pizza and pasta at reasonable prices and in comfortable surroundings. *Seats 80. D Mon-Sat, also Sun in summer. Off-season restricted opening - check for details. CC. **Directions:** Main Street of Ballyvaughan.*

O'Loclainn

Ballyvaughan Co Clare ✆*065 707 7006 www.discoverballyvaughan.com*

Aka "O'Loclainn's Irish Whiskey Bar", Peter and Margaret O'Loughlen's little harbourside bar is the quintessential traditional Irish pub. Except for a couple of hours over the middle of the day on Sunday it's very much an evening place and, in addition to the charm of its dimly characterful interior and friendly owners, the O'Loughlens' vast whiskey collection is a particular claim to fame. Ttraditional Irish music too. Open Mon-Sun 8pm-12.30am, also Sun 12-3. *Open Mon-Sun 8pm-12.30am, also Sun 12-3.*

Bunratty Cookery School

Manderley House Deerpark Bunratty Co Clare ☎*061 713 500 www.bunrattycookeryschool.ie*

Donnagh Gregson offers a wide variety of courses catering for every level, ranging from one-day and transition year classes to cooking for special diets and team building courses. Also ' Gregson & Co', offering speciality ingredients and hampers. 1-day courses, €130.

 Bunratty Manor Hotel

Bunratty Village Bunratty Co Clare ☎*061 707 984 www.bunrattymanor.ie*

Noel and Fiona Wallace's small family-run hotel is a homely place to stay close to Shannon airport. **Rooms 20** (most shower only). CC. **Directions:** Adjacent to Bunratty Castle.

 Durty Nelly's

Bunratty Co Clare ☎*061 364 861 www.dirtynellys.ie*

Although often seriously over-crowded with tourists in summer, this famous and genuinely characterful old pub in the shadow of Bunratty Castle somehow manages to provide cheerful service and consistently above-average food to the great numbers who pass through its doors. *L&D daily. Closed 25 Dec & Good Fri. CC.* **Directions:** *Beside Bunratty Castle.*

 Gallagher's Seafood Restaurant

Bunratty Co Clare ☎*061 363 363 www.gallaghersofbunratty.com*

A pretty thatched house with a history dating back to the 17th century, Gallagher's is an atmospheric restaurant, with its rustic interior candlelit at night. Having a well earned reputation for good food as well as atmosphere, it's a destination for a good meal out and much enjoyed by visitors. A well cooked range of both traditional and innovative fish and seafood dishes is the speciality, plus a scattering of other choices, including ever-popular popular surf and turf, served by pleasant and efficient staff. Extensive wine list. *D daily, L Sun only.* **Directions:** *Just off N18 Limerick-Shannon road near Bunratty Castle.*

 **The Long Dock**

West Street Carrigaholt Co Clare ☎*065 905 8106 www.thelongdock.com*

Tony and Imelda Lynch's classic 19th century pub has earned a well-deserved reputation for its friendly atmosphere and good food, especially local seafood. Well cooked, hot and tasty, great seasonal local produce and nothing too fussy: what more could you want? Traditional 'Dish' food is given its due respect and, if you visit on a Friday, you'll find a display of Imelda's good home baking laid out for sale too. **Seats 45** *(outdoors, 30). Food 11am-10pm summer (to 9pm winter).* *Closed Mon-Wed off-season (Nov-Mar), except Christmas. CC.* **Directions:** *Signed from Kilkee (10 minutes).*

 **Burren Perfumery Tea Rooms**

Carron Co Clare ✆*065 708 9102 www.burrenperfumery.com*

When touring Clare you will be pleased to find this charming spot. Although small and simple, the tea rooms at Sadie Chowen-Doyle's perfumery are pretty, with floral oilcloths, fresh flowers and mismatched crockery creating a happy riot of pastels - and everything they do is of high quality, made freshly on the premises, and uses local and organic produce. *Seats 20; open daily 11-4.15 (to 5 on Sun), Apr-Sep (Perfumery open all year except Christmas.) CC.* **Directions:** *In the Burren, east of Gort - off R480 & N67.*

  Fergus View

Kilnaboy Corofin Co Clare ✆*065 683 7606 www.fergusview.com*

Mary Kelleher's neat farmhouse enjoys a lovely view of the Clare countryside and regular visitors will always notice the changes and improvements that are made each winter. Rooms are compact but have many thoughtful touches and this would make an hospitable and inexpensive base for exploring this fascinating area. A bery good breakfast showcases local and home-grown foods. *Rooms 5* (1 shower only; 1 not en-suite, with private bathroom). Closed Nov - end Feb. No CC. **Directions:** 3km north of Corofin, on Kilfenora Road (R476).

 Cratloe Hills Sheeps' Cheese

Brickhill House Cratloe Co Clare ✆*061 357 185 www.cratloehillscheese.com*

Ireland's original sheep's milk cheese, Cratloe Hills cheese has been made by Sean and Deirdre Fitzgerald since 1988.

 Aran View House Hotel

Coast Road Doolin Co Clare ✆*+353 65 707 4061*

The Linnane's family-run hotel makes a good base for a family holiday - it is only a mile to a good beach, there is sea-angling and golf nearby and, of course, there is the traditional music for which Doolin is world famous. *Rooms 19. (9 shower only). CC Closed Nov-1 May.*

  **Ballinalacken Castle & Restaurant**

Doolin Co Clare ✆*065 707 4025 www.ballinalackencastle.com*

Away from the bustle of Doolin and Lisdoonvarna, with wonderful views of the Atlantic and the West coast, Declan O'Callaghan's unusual property is easily identified from afar by the 15th century castle standing on it - and it offers welcoming fire, refurbished rooms (many with sea views) and good food in the restaurant. *Rooms 12 (1 shower only). Restaurant seats 32; open to non-residents; D Wed-Mon Establishment closed Nov-mid Apr. CC.* **Directions:** *Coast road, R477. North of Doolin Village.*

The Chocolate Shop

Fisher Street Doolin *Co Clare* ✆*061 922 080 www.wildeirishchocolates.com*

Next door to Doolin's most famous pub, O'Connors, The Chocolate Shop is a seasonal outlet for Wilde's artisan chocolates, handmade in East Clare at Tuamgraney.

  The Clare Jam Company

Luogh North Off Coast Road Doolin *Co Clare* ✆*065 707 4778*

In an idyllic location just 1.5km south of Doolin (and with stunning views in fine weather), you'll find David and Vera Muir's little cottage shop offering over two dozen homemade preserves, some traditional others less so. Strawberry champagne jam and Connemara whiskey marmalade are keenly sought out, as is their tomato chutney. ***Directions:*** *Signed on Doolin-Cliffs of Moher road.*

  Cullinan's Seafood Restaurant & Guesthouse

Doolin Co Clare ✆*065 707 4183 www.cullinansdoolin.com*

James and Carol Cullinan have earned a loyal following at their stylish and comfortable little restaurant with accommodation overlooking the Aille river - you may even be entertained by fishermen fly fishing while you enjoy your meal. And the speciality here is seafood, all of which is caught off the West coast and delivered daily. ***Seats 25****; D Thu-Sat & Mon-Tue. Closed Sun & Wed, Nov-Easter.* ***Rooms 8*** *(3 shower only). Closed mid Dec-mid Feb. CC.* ***Directions:*** *Centre of Doolin.*

   Fabiolas Patisserie

Ballyvoe Doolin *Co Clare* ✆*086 660 2582*

Just up the hill from Doolin village, keep an eye out for the Brian Hackett Jewellery sign on the former Doolin Crafts Gallery, as there are plenty of treats in store here - not only Brian's beautiful hand-crafted jewellery, but also some seriously delicious things to eat, as his partner Fabiola's fabulous little bakery and café is next door. ***Seats 16*** *(outdoors, 20). Open Thu-Sun, 10.30am-6pm. Closed Tue & Wed. No CC.* ***Directions:*** *Just up the hill from Doolin village.*

 The Riverside Bistro

Roadford Doolin *Co Clare* ✆*065 707 5604*

With a welcoming turf fire in the restaurant for chilly days and seating in the lovely garden for lunch and early evening meals in fine weather, this welcoming village restaurant offers simple, well-cooked food at very pocket-friendly prices served by friendly and helpful staff. ***Seats 32*** *(+outdoors). L&D Wed-Sat, Sun 12-6pm (times may vary in high season, Jun-Aug). Closed Mon, Tue.* ***Directions:*** *Top of Doolin village.*

 **Roadford House Restaurant**

Killagh Doolin *Co Clare* ✆*065 707 5050 www.roadfordrestaurant.com*

Located on the edge of the buzzy village of Doolin, Frank and Marion Sheedy's smart contemporary restaurant is an oasis of calm - a place where everything is operated in a personal and highly professional manner. A favoured destination for the many regulars who appreciate

Frank's stylish cooking of local fare. **Seats 34**; D Tue-Sun (high season, call to check low season). Accommodation also available. Closed Mon, end Oct - 1 Apr. CC. **Directions:** In centre of village take slip road opposite Mc Dermotts pub, 50m up on right hand side.

Stone Cutters Kitchen

Luogh North Doolin Co Clare ✆ 065 707 5962 www.stonecutterskitchen.com

Karen Courtney and Myles Duffy's traditional thatched cottage between Doolin and the Cliffs of Moher is well-signed and it's very family-friendly. With outdoor playground, indoor toys, quirky furnishings and Myles's good home cooking it's just what families want when they're out and about in the area. **Seats 50** (outdoors, 24). Open daily Easter & May-Sept 12.30-9.30pm, open weekends only Easter-May. CC. **Directions:** Opposite Doolin Pottery on the Doolin-Cliffs of Moher road (R478) 1.6km north of the cliffs.

DOONBEG

The historic village of Doonbeg grew up around Doonbeg Castle which was built by Philip Macsheeda Mor Mac Con in the 16th century for the Earl of Thomond. The village is an excellent base for the water sport enthusiast as there is surfing at Doughmore strand and Spanish Point, scuba diving nearby in Kilkee and sailing at Kilrush Marina. Anglers are well catered for with excellent shore angling and chartered deep sea angling, whilst the equestrian enthusiast can take a pony trekking trip. There are also scenic coast walks - and you might even be lucky enough to spot a dolphin.

Lodge at Doonbeg

Doonbeg Co Clare ✆ 065 905 5600 www.doonbeglodge.com

Although Doonbeg Golf Club is a private club, both golf and accommodation are welcome to visitors when available. The Lodge has an Irish 'great house' feel with an American opulence - accommodation is not just very luxurious, but downright gorgeous. And the food is also very good; cooking showcases local foods and small producers with style, notably in The Long Room fine dining restaurant, overlooking the ocean. **Rooms 76**. The Long Room seats 70, D daily, L Sun only. Darby's bar menu daily. CC. **Directions:** On N67, 16km north of Kilkee.

Morrissey's Seafood Bar & Grill

Doonbeg Co Clare ✆ 065 905 5304 www.morrisseysdoonbeg.com

This attractive family-owned bar/restaurant beside the River Cree in Doonbeg village is currently run by the energetic Hugh McNally, who has skilfully extended and re-styled it in recent years, giving it a lovely riverside decking area and youthful appeal. Seafood is the speciality and everything is very fresh, with a good selection offered in season. Accommodation is also offered. Restaurant **seats 70** (outdoors, 30); L&D Tue-Sun. No reservations. Closed Mon and Nov, Jan, Feb. CC. **Directions:** Beside the bridge.

GEORGINA CAMPBELL'S IRELAND

ENNIS

The county town - and the main road junction of County Clare - Ennis has a venerable history, dating back to 1241 when Ennis Abbey was founded by Donough Cairbeach O'Brien for the Franciscans. It became a famous seat of learning so it is appropriate that this characterful old town with winding streets is equally notable for its progressiveness in some areas of enterprise. Famous for traditional music, sessions are held regularly at many venues in the town. Weekly farmers' market (Fri 8-2, Upper Market Street car park).

Bluebell Falls Goat Cheese

Ballynacally Ennis Co Clare ✆*065 683 8024 www.bluebellfalls.ie*

The Keane family's delicious Bluebell Falls Goats Cheese is made daily; their goats' diet is mainly freshly cut grass, so the cheese takes its flavour from their grassland in the hills overlooking the Shannon Estuary. Their range of beautiful cheeses (plain and flavoured, soft and hard) is constantly evolving. Excellent online range includes products from other artisan producers.

Café Noir @ Glór

Glor Causeway Link Ennis Co Clare ✆*065 684 3103 www.cafenoir.ie*

This excellent Limerick based group of French-inspired coffee houses has three outlets in the city (see entries), and this newer one in Ennis. *Open Mon-Sat, 10-4.*

Ennis Gourmet Store

1 Barrack Street Ennis Co Clare ✆*065 684 3314 www.ennisgourmetstore.com*

Founder Anne Leyden and wine expert David Lasbleye run this well known shop and bistro/café, which stocks a wide range of speciality foods from Ireland and the continent, with local artisan products taking pride of place. *Open all day (to 8.30 Thu-Sat). Sometimes closes Sun.*

Food Heaven

21 Market Street Ennis Co Clare ✆*065 682 2722 www.foodheaven.eu*

Everybody loves Noirin Furey's home bakery, café & deli for its friendliness and buzz - and for her delicious, fresh-flavoured food. The secret to this success is her commitment to using only the very best ingredients so, whether you're eating in or buying to take away, you'll never be disappointed. Home baking is the speciality, but there's much more to it than that with delicious meals served frm breakfast onwards. A great spot, and very useful to know about if you're self-catering in the area. *Open Mon-Sat 8.30-6.* **Directions:** *Centre of Ennis.*

Newpark House

Ennis Co Clare ✆065 682 1233 www.newparkhouse.com

Strange as it may seem to find an authentic farmhouse in an unspoilt country setting within easy walking distance of Ennis town centre, the Barron family home is a genuine exception. Of historical interest, it's run by Declan Barron, who is constantly busy with the small improvements that make for a comfortable stay - and who can give advice on researching your roots. **Rooms 6** *(1 shower only). Closed 1 Nov-Easter. CC.* **Directions:** *1.5km outside Ennis on R352; turn right at Roslevan Shopping Centre.*

   **Old Ground Hotel**

O'Connell Street Ennis Co Clare ✆065 682 8127 www.flynnhotels.com

The Flynn family's iconic ivy-clad hotel is a former manor house dating back to the 18th century and, set in its own gardens, it is an oasis of calm in the bustling centre of Ennis. It offers the quirky charm of the traditional Irish hotel and good food in the bar (Poet's Corner) and elegant old-fashioned dining room (Brendan O'Regan Room Restaurant), also the Town Hall Café next door (see entry). **Rooms 105**. *Restaurant seats 60, L&D daily. Closed 25-26 Dec. CC.* **Directions:** *Town centre.*

 Rene Cusack Fish

Market Street Ennis Co Clare ✆065 689 2712 www.renecusack.ie

A branch of the excellent Limerick family fishmongers business, founded by the late Rene Cusack and now run by his son Paul. (See Limerick entry.)

 **Rowan Tree Café Bar**

Harmony Row Ennis Co Clare ✆065 686 8669 www.rowantreecafebar.ie

Beside Harmony Bridge, the Rowan Tree is a hostel as well as a café and bar, and has some outside tables overlooking the water in this attractive market town. Its menu declares its ethics – local food where possible, properly sourced food, the best ingredients and something for vegetarians and vegans, too. **Seats 100** *(outdoors, 20). Open daily, 10am-10pm. Closed 25 & 26 Dec. CC.* **Directions:** *Access via Harmony Bridge (Abbey St carpark).*

 **Temple Gate Hotel**

The Square Ennis Co Clare ✆065 682 3300 www.templegatehotel.com

This privately-owned hotel has successfully blended existing Gothic themes into the newer build, and it provides comfort and convenience at a reasonable price. There's traditional music every weekend - and the shops and many famous music pubs of Ennis town centre are just across a cobble-stone courtyard. Legends Restaurant is a popular destination for local diners as well as residents. **Rooms 70**. *Restaurant* **seats 120**. *Legends D daily, L Sun only. Bar meals L&D daily. Closed 25-26 Dec. CC.* **Directions:** *Town centre.*

 Town Hall Café

O'Connell Street Ennis Co Clare ✆065 682 8127 www.flynnhotels.com

Adjacent to (and part of) The Old Ground Hotel, the Town Hall Café has a separate street entrance and a contemporary feel. Well restored, it's an impressive high-ceilinged room with sensitively spare decor. A quality operation, it's atmospheric at night (à la carte), while daytime menus offer a mixture of modern bistro-style dishes and tea-room fare. *Seats 60*. *Open daily B,L&D. Closed 25 Dec. CC.* **Directions:** *Town centre.*

 Tulsi

Carmody Street Ennis Co Clare ✆*065 684 8065.*

Although smartly decorated, there is little about the decor of this friendly restaurant to give it an Indian atmosphere. However, it has a well-earned reputation for authentic Indian cooking and helpful, professional service, and is a useful place to know about. *Seats 70. D daily, L Sun only. CC.* **Directions:** *Next to ESB.*

 Byrnes Restaurant

Main Street Ennistymon Co Clare ✆*065 707 1080 www.byrnes-ennistymon.ie*

In a fine period house at the top of the main street in this old market town, Richard and Mary Byrnes' stylish, high-ceilinged restaurant has views of Ennistymon's famous cascading river from the restaurant and an extensive outdoor dining area at the back. Accomplished contemporary Irish cooking, with an emphasis on local seafood and meats, plus interesting vegetarian options too. Accommodation is offered. *Seats 55. D daily. L daily in summer only. Closed Christmas. Phone to check opening times Nov-Feb. CC:* **Directions:** *On Main Street.*

 Mount Callan Farmhouse Cheese

Drinagh Ennistymon Co Clare ✆*065 707 2008 www.irishcheese.ie*

Michael & Lucy Hayes' excellent traditional cheddar style cheese is made near Ennistymon, using raw milk from a single herd. Look out for it on menus and in local food shops.

 Unglerts Bakery

New Road Ennistymon Co Clare ✆*065 707 1217*

Continental and Irish traditions meet at this popular bakery. It's easy to spot thanks to the mural of Ennistymon town by artist Kevin Mulligan that adorns the gable wall and here, behind an otherwise traditional shopfront, lies the genial Stephan Unglert's little shop - a destination for people who care about real bread and other baked goods since the mid-80s.

 **Vasco**

Craggagh Fanore Co Clare ✆*065 707 6020 www.vasco.ie*

Situated in the heart of the Burren in 'Ireland's longest village', Karen and Ross Quinn's eye-catching business is an all-day café-restaurant and deli - and many other things besides. The much travelled multi-lingual pair offer eclectic menus, but their delicious food is firmly rooted in the produce of the area. Well worth a visit - and you can pick up a picnic from the adjacent deli too. *Seats 45 (outdoors, 22). Restaurant May-Sep: Tue–Sun, 11-9; otherwise: Thu-Sun, 12-8.30. Closed Mon (except bank hols), Nov-mid Mar. CC.* **Directions:** *On the coast road between Doolin and Ballyvaughan, opposite O'Donoghue's pub.*

St Tola Organic Goat Cheese

Inagh Farmhouse Cheese Maurice's Mills Inagh Co Clare ✆*065 683 6633 www.st-tola.ie*

A familiar product on many of the country's best menus, Siobhan Ni Ghairbhith's multi-award-winning St Tola is made just south of the Burren, and visitors are welcome. The goats are lovely and children, especially, will love them. The tour includes a cheese making demonstration and tasting - visitors may be surprised by the extent of the range, currently comprising about eight equally excellent but quite different cheeses. *Farm open: Easter-to end Oct, Mon & Thu, tours 2pm and 3pm. Closed bank hol Mondays.*

KILFENORA

One of the most famous music centres in the west of Ireland. The Visitor Centre is worth visiting (and offers good home baking). The area is a rambler's dream while golfers and surfers will be tested to the utmost by the nearby Lahinch Golf Clubs (065 708 1003) famous links and the challenging waves of Lahinch strand.

  ## Burren Free Range Pork

Kilfenora Co Clare ✆*086 881 5974 www.burrenfreerangepork.com*

Whey from the Kilshanny cheese-making process nearby is one of the natural products used to feed the happy Burren pigs - Saddlebacks and Saddleback/Tamworth cross - that Eva Harald and her husband Stephen Hegarty raise for the Burren Free Range Pork that she sells at local markets (Ennis & Ennistymon). Look out for it on menus, and you can buy from the farm (by appointment).

  ## Vaughan's Pub

Kilfenora Co Clare 065 708 8004 www.vaughanspub.com

This famous pub has been in the family since about 1800, and serves traditional Irish food (seafood chowder, bacon and cabbage, beef and Guinness stew) based on local ingredients. Renowned for its music and dancing, held in the (previously thatched) barn, which attracts visitors from all over the world. ***Directions:*** *In the centre of Kilfenora.*

 ## Diamond Rocks Cafe

West End Kilkee Co Clare ✆*065 908 3812 www.diamondrockscafe.com*

Margaret and Kevin Haugh's friendly café sits atop a hill at the base of a stunning cliff walk to The Diamond Rocks. The views alone will tempt you to go there, but the food should too: two huge blackboards list out the day's chowders, sandwiches, salads, pizzas, panini, homemade cakes and desserts; everything is homemade and the staff are wonderful. *Open 9am-7pm daily, Jun 1-Sep 15. Also weekends all year, bank hols, Easter, Christmas-New Year (27 Dec-3 Jan).* ***Directions:*** *West end of Kilkee.*

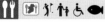 ## Murphy Blacks

The Square Kilkee Co Clare ✆*065 905 6854*

Cillian is an ex-fishing skipper who ensures the freshest fish possible and the effort that goes into ensuring the best from suppliers shows, in succulent, well-flavoured food. He is in charge of front of house, and Mary is the chef - a winning combination that has earned Murphy Blacks a reputation well beyond the immediate area. **Seats 42** *(outdoors, 12) D Mon-Sat (weekends only October-May). Closed Sun. CC.* **Directions:** *Centre of town.*

Naughton's Bar

46 O'Curry Street **Kilkee Co Clare** ✆*065 905 6597 www.naughtonsbar.com*

Styled a Fish and Steak Bar, the accent at Elaine Haugh and Robert Hayes' smartly presented and very popular pub is on seafood and simplicity; a well balanced menu offered plus extra seafood specials each night, and good accompaniments like home cut real chips or baked potato and seasonal vegetables. **Seats 60** *(outdoors, 35). D daily in season. CC.* **Directions:** *Down O'Connell Street towards the sea, left on to O'Curry Street before beach.*

The Pantry

O'Curry Street **Kilkee Co Clare** ✆*065 905 6576 www.thepantrykilkee.com*

Owned and operated by Imelda Bourke and her husband, Pat, baking starts at The Pantry at 5.30 each morning, and they produce the most amazing selection of breads, cakes and desserts. Later Imelda and her kitchen team create wonders for lunch... There is a marvellous and somewhat chaotic buzz here. *Open daily 8am-6.30pm in season. Closed Oct-Easter. CC.* **Directions:** *Down O'Connell Street towards the bay, take a left into O'Curry Street just before the sea.*

Stella Maris Hotel

O'Connell Sreet **Kilkee Co Clare** ✆*065 905 6455 www.stellamarishotel.com*

There's a real 'sense of Clare' at Ann and Martin Haugh's long established family-run hotel, which is well located in the centre of Kilkee, overlooking the bay and only yards from the beach. Child- and pet-friendly, it's a place of of traditional old-fashioned comfort and generous, wholesome food. **Rooms 19** *(7 shower only). Closed 25 Dec.*

The Strand Restaurant & Guesthouse

Strand Line **Kilkee Co Clare** ✆*065 905 6177 www.thestrandkilkee.com*

In the family for 130 years, this seafront restaurant with rooms is run by Johnny Redmond (the chef), and his wife Caroline. Outside seating under a neat awning overlooks the bay and the restaurant has floor to ceiling windows, so all tables can enjoy the view along with Johnny's (mainly) local seafood menus. *Restaurant* **Seats 46** *(outdoors, 12) D daily in summer, check opening times off season.* **Rooms 6** *(5 shower only). Closed Jan & Feb. CC.* **Directions:** *On the waterfront.*

KILLALOE / BALLINA

At the southern end of Lough Derg - a handsome inland sea set in an attractive blend of mountain and hillside, woodland and farm - Killaloe straddles the Shannon with two townships - Ballina in Tipperary on the east bank, and Killaloe in Clare, with the ancient cathedral across the river to the west. However, while it's all usually known as Killaloe (Co Clare), establishments of interest to the guide happen to be mainly on the east (Tipperary) side of the river. On Sundays the farmers market (Between the Waters, 11am-3pm) makes a lovely place to wander around while sampling and buying the finest local produce.

Brasserie Mark Anderson

Anna Carriga Killaloe Co Clare ✆*061 620 710 www.annacarriga.com*

A holiday village is an unlikely location for one of the country's most interesting smart-casual restaurants, perhaps, but Mark Anderson's eponymous brasserie on the western shore of Lough Derg is worth seeking out. The best of ingredients (many of them free-range, organic or wild) are showcased in even the simplest dishes. *D Wed-Sun, L Sun only.* **Directions:** *5km north of Killaloe, on the Scarriff road (R463). On the left as you enter the Anna Carriga Estate.*

 ## Cherry Tree Restaurant

Lakeside Ballina Killaloe Co Clare ✆*061 375 688 www.cherrytreerestaurant.ie*

The area's leading fine dining restaurant enjoys a lovely waterside location and a reputation for consistently excellent contemporary cooking. Owner-chef Harry McKeogh's pleasing trademark is a direct cooking style, without too many cheffy twirls - allowing the great ingredients he sources with such care to take centre stage. *Seats 60. D Tue-Sat (Thu-Sat in winter), L Sun only (check opening off season). Closed Mon, Tue (also Wed in winter), 24-26 Dec, last week Jan, 1st week Feb. CC.* **Directions:** *At Ballina side of bridge, turn down towards the Lakeside Hotel; just before the hotel, on the left.*

 ## Flanagans On The Lake

Ballina Killaloe Co Clare ✆*061 622 790 www.flanagansonthelake.com*

Also known as Flanagans Prime Steakhouse, this large contemporary bar and restaurant is attractively located right on the banks of the River Shannon. With plenty of space, a wide ranging menu and a friendly, relaxed atmosphere, Flanagans offers something for everybody. *Seats 220. Food 12-10pm daily, closed Mondays in winter.* **Directions:** *Centre of town.*

 ## Goosers

Ballina Killalloe Co Clare ✆*061 376 791 www.goosers.ie*

This famous almost-riverside pub has welcoming open fires in the cosy bars for chilly days and also plenty of tables and benches outside for fine weather. Visitors will find some traditional dishes - oysters, mussels, Irish stew, beef & Guinness casserole, bacon and cabbage - among the wide choice offered in both the bar and restaurant. *Seats 80. Food daily 12-10pm. Closed 25 Dec & Good Fri. CC.* **Directions:** *By the river.*

 ## Kingfisher Lodge

Lower Ryninch Ballina Killaloe Co Clare ✆*061 376 911 www.kingfisherlodge-ireland.com*

Right on the shores of Lough Derg, Barry and Mary Holloway's B&B just outside Ballina/Killaloe has two acres of lakeside gardens. Quiet and relaxing, and with a private harbour, it's an ideal base for a fishing holiday, or to explore the area (Limerick is nearby and Co Clare is just across the bridge linking the twin towns.) *Rooms 3.* **Directions:** *Near Ballina on R494.*

Lakeside Hotel

Killaloe Co Clare ✆061 376 122 *www.lakesidehotel.ie*

This friendly and beautifully located hotel overlooks the River Shannon, with lovely views from many of the rooms. Handy to the town yet quietly located, it has good facilities and has long been the hub of the local community. **Rooms 46** *(some shower only). Closed 21-27 Dec. CC.* **Directions:** *Well signposted in Ballina.*

 Liam O'Riain's

Killaloe Co Clare ✆061 376 722

Robert Bradwell's charming pub is the oldest in Ballina. Not a food place, it's a real old atmospheric bar with a cosy open fire, where people meet to chat and, perhaps, play cards (Thursday nights in winter).Traditional music on Tuesday nights, wider range last Friday of the month; sometimes impromptu. *Open Mon-Fri from 4pm; Sat/Sun from 1pm. Directions: Main Street beside church.*

 Tuscany Bistro

Main Street Ballina/Killaloe Co Clare ✆061 376 888 *www.tuscany.ie*

Smartly presented and welcoming, this authentic Italian is an appealing addition to the dining options in Killaloe/Ballina, and good value too. *Open Tue-Sun 12.30-9pm (to 10pm Thu-Sun). Closed Mon. CC. Also at: Annacotty, Co Limerick.*

 The Wooden Spoon

Bridge Street Killaloe Co Clare ✆061 622 415

Formerly a pub, Laura Kilkenny's café, bakery & deli still has that special character – and a welcome open fire - and she has earned a following for local seasonal ingredients and good simple cooking (notably the delicious baking), served with a generous dash of real hospitality. Tue-Thu 9.30am-6pm, Fri & Sat 12-9pm, Sun 12-6pm. Bakery open Tue-Sat. CC. **Directions:** Street on hill overlooking the bridge between Killaloe and Ballina.

KILRUSH

Formerly a significant Shannon port, Kilrush town is built around a square with a large Market House in the centre. A wide street runs from the square towards the harbour, where there is now an impressive marina facility. Boat trips are available to watch the Shannon bottlenose dolphins, and also to see the early Christian ruins on Scattery Island, now uninhabited but an interesting place for an outing. The town was planned by the local landlords, the Vandeleurs, whose most obvious legacy is the beautiful Vandeleur Walled Garden (065 905 1760, with café), once the forgotten garden of Kilrush House, and now an oasis of tender and tropical plants that thrive in the area's unique climate. For Irish traditional music enthusiasts, there is an unusual music festival, Eigse Mrs Crotty, which focuses on concertina-playing.

The Buttermarket Café

Burton Street Kilrush Co Clare ✆ *065 905 6854*

Just off the Square, Cillian Murphy and Mary Redmond (of the well known Kilkee seafood restaurant Murphy Blacks) run this delightful daytime café in the former Buttermarket Gallery. Its old-meets-new atmosphere is charming and relaxing – and suits the down-to-earth good home cooking very well. Baking is a special strength. *Seats 36* (outdoors, 12). Mon-Sat, 9.30-5pm. Closed Sun. No CC. *Directions:* Opposite Brew's Car Park off the town square.

 **Crottys**

Market Square Kilrush Co Clare ✆ *065 905 2470 www.crottyspubkilrush.com*

Its corner location on the town square gives a clue to the historic importance of Rebecca Brew and Kevin Clancy's imposing 19th century pub with accommodation. It's a wonderful place, with all the features that make Victorian Irish pubs so special, and a first port of call for many visitors. Good food is important too, ranging from light daytime bites to more substantial evening meals. **Rooms 5**. Food daily (L&D). **Directions:** Centre of Kilrush. Parking on the square.

LAHINCH

This bustling seaside resort is especially popular with lovers of the great outdoors - one of Ireland's greatest surfing beaches is here, on Liscannor Bay, and it is equally renowned for golf (Lahinch Golf Club; 065 708 1003); Doonbeg Golf Club (065 905 5600) is also just a short drive away. Non golfers will also find plenty to do in the area, and a long sandy beach and Seaworld, a leisure complex, also attract family holidaymakers to Lahinch.

 **Barrtra Seafood Restaurant**

Lahinch Co Clare ✆ *065 708 1280 www.barrtra.com*

Views of Liscannor Bay take centre stage from Paul and Theresa O'Brien's traditional, whitewashed cottage; aside from the stunning location, local seafood is the star attraction, notably lobster. Theresa's excellent, unfussy cooking makes the most of a wide range of fish, while also offering a choice for those with other preferences (including vegetarian/special diets), at customer-friendly prices. **Seats 40**. *Food all day 1-10pm. Open Fri & Sat Mar-May, Fri-Wed in Jun, 7 days Jul & Aug. Weekend only Oct-Dec. Phone to check opening hours off season. Closed Jan-Feb. CC.* **Directions:** *Signed off N67, 6km south of Lahinch.*

  Kilshanny Cheese

Derry House Kilshanny Lahinch Co Clare ✆ *065 707 1228*

Peter Nibbering's gouda style cheeses are made with the milk from neighbouring farms and quickly become familiar to visitors to Clare, as they feature on menus and in food shops and markets in the area; all six varieties are also sold at the Milk Market (Saturday) in Limerick.

Moy House

Lahinch Co Clare ☎ *065 708 2800 www.moyhouse.com*

This stunning house just outside Lahinch is one of Ireland's most appealing (and luxurious) country houses and is run with warmth and efficiency by General Manager Brid O'Meara. Like most of the gorgeous bedrooms, the large antique-furnished drawing room has wonderful sea views - a favourite spot to enjoy aperitifs from the honesty bar before dining, or to relax in front of the fire with coffee and petits fours after dinner. **Rooms 9** *(3 shower only). Residents' D Mon-Sat; restaurant closed Sun.* Closed Nov-end Mar. CC. **Directions:** *On the sea side of the Miltown Malbay road, outside Lahinch.*

O'Looney's Bar & Restaurant

The Promenade Lahinch Co Clare ☎ *065 708 1414 www.olooneys.ie*

The West Coast surf bar par excellence, this smart modern split-level bar/restaurant enjoys a great location, overlooking one of Ireland's best surfing beaches. While more bar than restaurant, it's a pleasant spot to enjoy the view (perhaps watching surfers doing what they do best) and have a bite to eat. **Seats 140.** *Closed Mon-Fri off season (Nov-Mar), 25-28 Dec, Good Fri. CC.* **Directions:** *On the promenade, overlooking the beach.*

Vaughan Lodge

Ennistymon Road Lahinch Co Clare ☎ *065 708 1111 www.vaughanlodge.ie*

Michael and Maria Vaughan's hotel - purpose-built to high specifications, mainly with the comfort of golfers in mind - offers peace and relaxation within easy walking distance of the town centre. Also an excellent restaurant featuring interesting artisan foods from area and beautifully cooked local seafood (over half of the à la carte menu in summer). **Rooms 22** *(1 shower only). Restaurant* **seats 60.** *D Tue-Sun. Closed Mon, Nov-Mar. CC.* **Directions:** *On N85 just at the edge of Lahinch on the left.*

Vaughans Anchor Inn

Main Street Liscannor Co Clare ☎ *065 708 1548 www.vaughans.ie*

The Vaughan family's traditional bar has great character, with open fires and lots of memorabilia. Although famed for their seafood platters (and they are fantastic - and great value too), there's much more to the menu than that: Denis Vaughan is an exceptionally talented and creative chef and uses as much local produce as possible. And everything really is fresh - the menu may even be changed in mid-stream because there's something new coming up off the boats. **Seats 106.** *Food 12-9.30 daily. Closed 25 Dec. (Open Good Fri for food, but bar closed.) CC.* **Directions:** *4km from Lahinch on Cliffs of Moher route.*

The Burren Smokehouse

Lisdoonvarna Co Clare 📞*065 707 4432 www.burrensmokehouse.ie*

Established in 1989, Birgitta and Peter Curtin's Burren Smokehouse is most famous for their salmon; mainly produced using the renowned Clare Island organic salmon, it is among Ireland's finest. You can taste it at their Burren Smokehouse Visitor Centre, where they sell their own products (including their own cheese, made in Kilshanny) and other artisan foods and crafts. *Also online shop. Smokehouse Visitor Centre open all year, times vary.*

 ## The Roadside Tavern

Lisdoonvarna Co Clare 📞*065 707 4084 www.roadsidetavern.ie*

Easily spotted by the mural on the gable wall, Peter Curtin's historic and hospitable hostelry oozes character and, famous for music for over a century, many legendary musicians have played here. More recent attractions are beer from their own micro-brewery, and good food – notably smoked fish from the family's other equally famous business, the nearby Burren Smokehouse. *Opening times are subject to change; L&D available daily in summer.*

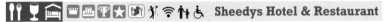 ## Sheedys Hotel & Restaurant

Lisdoonvarna Co Clare 📞*065 707 4026 www.sheedys.com*

John and Martina Sheedy run one of the west of Ireland's best-loved small hotels - it offers some of the most luxurious accommodation and the best food in the area, yet still has the warm ambience and friendly hands-on management which make a hotel special. John showcases local produce with style (and makes everything from scratch - breads, biscuits, jams and preserves, ice creams...) and, while relaxed and informal, the sheer quality has made it a destination for food lovers. **Rooms 11**. *Restaurant* **seats 25**. *D daily. Bar menu also offered. Hotel closed Oct-Easter. CC.* **Directions:** *200m from town square on road to Sulphur Wells.*

 **Wild Honey Inn**

Kincora Road Lisdoonvarna Co Clare ☎ *065 707 4300 www.wildhoneyinn.com*

Aidan and Kate McGrath's Wild Honey is a true inn, offering rest, relaxation, refreshment and good company. But Aidan's good food is the main focus and deciding against opening a formal restaurant was a key decision, reflecting a wish to be seen as a pub offering high quality food in an informal setting. *Seats 45-50*. *L Thu-Sun, D Thu-Mon*. *Rooms 14 (10 shower only). Accommodation closed mid Jan-mid Feb. CC. Directions: From town centre take Ennistymon road; 300m on left.*

 **Berry Lodge & Cookery School**

Annagh Miltown Malbay Co Clare ☎ *065 708 7022 www.berrylodge.com*

Rita Meade's attractive and hospitable Victorian country house near the coast is well-established as a restaurant with comfortable (and stylish) accommodation, specialising in golf breaks. She showcases the great seafood and meats of the area in both the restaurant and her popular cookery school, which offers a range of courses throughout the year. *Seats 40*. *D Mon-Sat in season (must book). Closed Sun*. *Rooms 5 (all shower only); House Closed 1 Dec-Easter. CC. Directions: N67 south from Milltown Malbay, over Annagh Bridge, second left, first right to Berry Lodge.*

 Black Oak Restaurant

Rineen Miltown Malbay Co Clare ☎ *065 708 4403*

Set prominently on a hillside – and well-signed off the main Miltown Malbay to Lahinch Road - Aidan and Emily Feeney's well known restaurant enjoys uninterrupted views over Liscannor Bay towards The Cliffs of Moher. Generous cooking of local produce; house special is Seafood Pot with Saffron Bouillabaisse. *Seats 65*. *D Tue-Sat. Closed Sun & Mon (except Sun of bank hol weekends); end Oct (after bank hol) to Easter. CC. Directions: 7km outside Lahinch village on the Miltown road.*

MOUNTSHANNON

The lakeside village of Mountshannon prospers in a sunny south-facing position. It is an attractive, relaxed village with plenty to recommend it including a nice traditional pub-grocery shop and a friendly hotel. Mountshannon is a favourite haunt of anglers for the mayfly season on Lough Derg, with fishing boats available for hire. Mountshannon is also well placed for exploring the lake's western shores, with plenty of scope for walks and bicycle rides. The harbour offers a bathing area that is popular with families, and the area is a popular sailing centre.

 An Cupán Caifé

Main Street Mountshannon Co Clare ☎ *087 294 3620 www.ancupan.ie*

Although the surroundings may be simple at Dagmar Hilty's welcoming café, there is an obvious commitment to quality. Locally sourced ingredients are a point of pride, with suppliers credited on the menus - and sauces are not only home-made, but also gluten-free. *Seats 24. Open D Wed-Sat, Sun 1-8pm (incl Afternoon Tea). Closed Mon (except bank hols), Tue, all Nov-Feb. Advisable to check opening times, especially off season. CC.* **Directions:** *Main street Mountshannon.*

 ## Mountshannon Hotel

Main Street Mountshannon Co Clare ✆*061 927162 www.mountshannon-hotel.ie*

When you visit a traditional country hotel you find the real Ireland and Mountshannon is a particularly attractive spot. It's one of very few south-facing waterside villages in the area - and the harbour is just a short stroll from this modest and friendly family-run hotel with welcoming fire in the bar. **Rooms 14.** *Bar meals daily. Restaurant late week/weekends. CC.*

  ## Linnalla Ice Cream

New Quay Co Clare ✆*065 707 8167 www.linnallaicecream.ie*

Made using the milk from their shorthorn cows, which are native to the Burren, the name of Brid and Roger Fahy's delicious ice cream is inspired by the farm's waterside location, Linnalla' meaning 'swan lake'. Well signed from the coast road. It may seem a long way to this little shop/ice cream parlour but it's an interesting detour. *Open daily in summer (May–Sep); weekends only in winter (Oct –May).* **Directions:** *signed from the shore road, New Quay.*

 ## Linnanes Lobster Bar

New Quay Co Clare ✆*065 707 8120 www.linnanesbar.com*

Eileen and Vincent Graham's cottagey pub-restaurant on the edge of the Burren is right on the rocks at New Quay, with wonderful views across Galway Bay and a traditional bar with an open fire for chilly days. There are other options, but local fish is the draw: try the impressive Seafood Platter, big enough to share between two. *Bar open daily in summer; food served lunchtime onwards. Off season, bar open daily, check times. CC.* **Directions:** *On the coast road, midway between Kinvara and Ballyvaughan*

       ## Mount Vernon

Flaggy Shore New Quay Co Clare ✆*065 707 8126 www.mountvernon.ie*

Set back from the shore with views to the cliffs of Aughinish, you enter another place at Mount Vernon, a magical and historic country house whose owners, Mark Helmore and Aly Raftery, seem to have a special empathy with it. There's a leisurely feel and an emphasis on organic and local foods, including Aly's wild Burren house preserves, which guests can purchase as gifts. **Rooms 5** *(4 en-suite, 1 with private bathroom). Residents D nightly, must book. Closed 1 Jan-1 Apr. CC.* **Directions:** *Signed off N67, between Kinvara and Ballyvaughan.*

 ## The Russell Gallery

New Quay The Burren Co Clare ✆*065 707 8185 www.russellgallery.net*

Factor in a call to Andy and Stefania Russell's impressive yet visitor-friendly gallery when exploring this beautiful coastline - they have a stylish little wine bar/café too, offering tasty light food and interesting wines. *Open all year: Tue-Sat 10-6pm, Sun 12-6pm. Closed Mon. CC.*

 **Carrygerry Country House**

Newmarket-on-Fergus Co Clare ☎*061 360500 www.carrygerryhouse.com*

It's only 10 minutes from Shannon airport, yet Niall and Gillian Ennis's lovely 18th century residence is a world away, in a beautiful rural setting. The ambience is very pleasant, with spacious, comfortable reception rooms, open fires and an hospitable atmosphere. The conservatory restaurant showcases local ingredients, especially seasonal herbs and vegetable, and Niall changes his menus monthly. **Rooms 11** *(3 shower-only). Restaurant* **seats 54**. *D Tue-Sat. House closed 23-26 Dec.* CC. **Directions:** *Very close to Shannon airport, on the old Newmarket-on-Fergus road.*

 **Dromoland Castle**

Newmarket-on-Fergus Co Clare ☎*061 368 144 www.dromoland.ie*

The ancestral home of the O'Briens, barons of Inchiquin and direct descendants of Brian Boru, High King of Ireland, this is one of the few Irish estates tracing its history back to Gaelic royal families. It is now one of Ireland's grandest hotels and, in the the warm and watchful care of General Manager Mark Nolan and his team, one of the best-loved. Outstanding service and Head Chef David McCann's wonderful food invariably match the surroundings. **Rooms 98**. *Restaurant* **seats 84**. *D daily. Also The Gallery all-day menu, including Afternoon Tea. The Fig Tree Restaurant at Dromoland Golf and Country Club, open all day. Closed 25 Dec. CC.* **Directions:** *26km from Limerick, 11km from Shannon. Take N18 to Dromoland interchange; exit & follow signage.*

 The Inn at Dromoland

Newmarket-on-Fergus Co Clare ☎*061 368 161 www.theinnatdromoland.ie*

Formerly The Clare Inn, this modern hotel overlooking the Shannon estuary was recently reunited with the Dromoland estate and is now a sister hotel to Dromoland Castle. Moderately priced, and with good conference, business leisure and family facilities, this well located hotel has wide appeal. **Rooms 183**. *Appealing packages offered. CC.*

  Irish Seed Savers Association

Capparoe Scarriff Co Clare ☎*061 921 866 www.irishseedsavers.ie*

A registered charity, the Irish Seed Savers Association is a large environmental non-governmental organisation. They research, locate, preserve and use traditional varieties, cultivars of fruit, vegetables, potatoes and grains. Visitors to this fascinating place are advised: "Wet weather gear and good walking shoes are advisable so that you can walk around the gardens and orchards in comfort". *Open daily Mon-Sat all day, Sun pm.*

Oakwood Arms Hotel

Shannon Airport Co Clare ✆*061 361500 www.oakwood arms.com*

A neat owner-managed hotel with an aviation theme and good facilities, including conference facilities. Although slightly dates it is friendly and reasonably priced. **Rooms 100.** Children welcome.

Rezidor Park Inn

Shannon Airport Co Clare ✆*061 471 122; www.rezidorparkinn.com*

Formerly a Great Southern, this hotel's USP today is that it is directly accessible from the main terminal building at Shannon Airport. It's in an unexpectedly lovely location overlooking the estuary and - although the room décor will not be to everyone's taste - with its views and rather gracious atmosphere in some parts of the hotel, it retains a little of the old romance of flight. **Rooms 114.** Closed 24-27 Dec. CC.

Red Cliff Lodge

Spanish Point Co Clare ✆*065 708 5756 www.redclifflodge.ie*

Now one of the top destinations in West Clare, John O'Meara's attractive thatched restaurant with accommodation overlooks Spanish Point Beach and offers both delicious food and spacious, luxuriously appointed suites with kitchenettes. Although informality and pocket-friendly pricing is emphasised, it's an impressive set-up, and sumptuously decorated. *Restaurant **seats 60**. L&D daily in summer (call to check hours advised, especially off season).* **Rooms 6** (3 shower only). CC. Closed Nov & Jan. **Directions:** Southwest of Miltown Malbay.

Wilde Irish Chocolates

Unit 6, Enterprise Centre Tuamgraney Co Clare ✆*061 922 080 www.wildeirishchocolates.com*

Inspired by Oscar Wilde's most famous quote 'I can resist anything but temptation', Patricia Farrell's business is well and truly artisan, as all the chocolates are made, decorated and packaged by hand in East Clare on the shores of Lough Derg. *Widely distributed and sold at markets; factory shop at Tuamgraney (weekdays); online sales.*

Flappers Restaurant

Main Street Tulla Co Clare ✆*065 683 5711*

The most remarkable thing about Jim and Patricia McInerney's small split-level restaurant in the village of Tulla is that it has been consistently enjoyable over such a long period. The dishes Patricia sends out from the kitchen are a daily testament to her imagination, insistence on good ingredients and attention to detail. **Seats 40**. Open all day Mon-Fri, L Sat, D Fri-Sat. Closed Sun, bank hols; 2 weeks Nov & Jan. CC. **Directions:** Main Street.

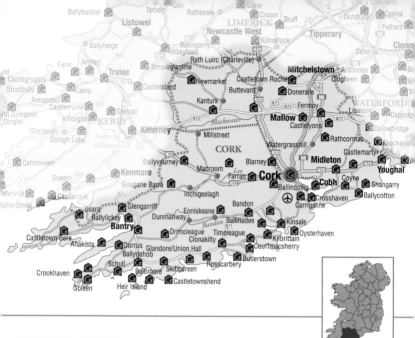

CORK CITY

It is Cork, of all Ireland's cities, which seems most warmly at comfort with itself, the heart of a land flowing in milk and honey. Cork is all about the good things in life. At its best, the southern capital has a Mediterranean atmosphere, and there's no doubting its Continental and cosmopolitan flavour, and Cork people's relaxed enjoyment of it all.

The central thoroughfare of St Patrick's Street was a river channel until 1783, as the earliest parts of Cork city were built on islands where the River Lee meets the sea. But for more two centuries now, it has been Cork's main street, affectionately known to generations of Corkonians as "Pana". Oliver Plunkett Street and Grand Parade have received sympathetic improvement to create a city centre with attractive pedestrian priorities. And the potential of the Port of Cork area in the city for sensitive re-development is being progressed, while the vigour of business life is matched by an active arts scene.

Cork's unique qualities, and its people's appreciation of natural produce, make it a favoured destination for connoisseurs. Trading in life's more agreeable commodities has always been what Cork and its legendary merchant princes were all about. At one time, the city was known as the butter capital of Europe, and it continues to be unrivalled for the ready availability of superbly fresh produce, seen at its best in the famous English Market where Grand Parade meets Patrick Street.

The way in which sea and land intertwine throughout the wonderfully sheltered natural harbour, and through the lively old city itself, has encouraged waterborne trade and a sea-minded outlook. Thus today Cork is at the heart of Ireland's most dynamically nautical area, a place world-renowned for its energetic interaction with the sea, whether for business or pleasure.

LOCAL ATTRACTIONS & INFORMATION

▸ **Guinness Cork Jazz Festival**
(late Oct) *021 421 5170*
▸ **Cork International Film Festival** (October)
021 4271711

▸ **Glucksman Gallery, UCC**
021 4901844
▸ **Triskel Arts Centre**
www.triskelartscentre.ie
Tobin St *021 4272022*

▸ **Cork City Gaol**
021 430 5022
▸ **Cork Tourist Information**
021 425 5100

Cork International Airport Hotel

Cork Airport Cork 📞*021 454 9800 www.corkinternationalairporthotel.com*

Linked by a covered walkway leading to the door of the new Cork Airport terminal, this hotel could not be handier for the time-pressed traveller. Accommodation is designed to please and this, together with free parking and a shuttle service into the city centre, make it an option for short breaks too. **Rooms 150**. CC.

  ## Park Inn by Radisson

Cork Airport Kinsale Road Cork 📞*021 494 7500 www.parkinn.ie*

Formerly the Radisson Blu, this stylish modern hotel is very handily located, close to the terminal. Well equipped for business guests, it aims to provide a tranquil haven for travellers amid the hustle and bustle of a busy airport. **Rooms 81**, *all executive*. **Directions:** *Off Cork-Kinsale road; situated within Airport complex.*

  ## Travelodge Cork

Near Cork Airport Blackash Frankfield Road Cork
📞*021 431 0722 www.travelodge.ie/cork-hotel*

Well situated for family, corporate or short break travellers looking for a comfortable budget base near Cork city and airport with free parking (regular bus service to city centre). Spacious rooms with king size beds can sleep a family of four. No service (except 24hr reception). Tea/coffee making and multi channel TV, but bring your own toiletries. Pets allowed by arrangement (in bedroom, small fee). Useful to know. **Directions:** *At Kinsale Road Roundabout.*

 ## Amicus

23 Paul Street Plaza Cork City 📞*021 427 6455 www.amicusrestaurant.ie*

Ursula and Robert Hales' centrally located restaurant is a lot bigger than its original location around the corner (where its more intimate sister, 'Restaurant 14A', is today), but this lively place is still a very popular destination. Real, uncomplicated food, fair pricing and a youthful atmosphere add up to an attractive package which clearly pleases locals and visitors alike. *Reservations suggested.* **Seats 165** *(outdoors, 24). Open Mon-Sat 8am-11pm, Sun 12-9.30pm. Closed 25-26 Dec. CC.*

  ## Arbutus Breads

Unit 2B Mayfield Industrial Estate Mayfield Cork City 📞*021 450 5820*

Named after the legendary Cork hotel, Arbutus Lodge, that the Ryan family ran until 1999, Declan Ryan's iconic bakery started in classic style in his garage. Today, with am international team of bakers, he produces over two dozen speciality breads. many young bakers have taken up the 'real bread' challenge recently, but Declan was a decade ahead of the current trend and there is still nobody to beat the Arbutus team. *Sells at markets (Midleton & Douglas, Sat; Mahon Point, Thu; Macroom, Tue) and distributed to selected outlets nationwise. Baking courses offered.*

Arthur Mayne's Pharmacy

7 Pembroke Street Cork City ☎*021 427 9449* www.corkheritagepubs.com

Probably Cork's most unusual licensed premises - visitors to publican Benny McCabe's 120 year old former pharmacy are amazed to find many original fittings (and their contents) still in place. By contrast a state-of-the-art enomatic system allows customers to sample two dozen wines at little cost, an dan impressive range is offered at the bar. Head Chef Darren Connolly's ingredients are "from the English Market"; try a lunchtime Cork spiced beef sandwich stack, perhaps, or charcuterie and cheese boards in the evening. *Open daily 10-'late' (Sun from noon).*

Barry's Tea

Kinsale Road Cork City ☎*021 491 5000* www.barrystea.ie

No nation has embraced tea drinking more enthusiastically than the Irish, and this iconic brand is invariably listed by ex-pats among the things they miss most about Ireland when away. As well as the famous core products - Gold Blend, Classic Blend and Original Blend - their range of ethically sourced teas includes a growing number of fruit infusions, herbal and other speciality teas. Widely stocked and also available to purchase online.

The Boardwalk Bar & Grill

The Boardwalk Lapps Quay Cork City ☎*021 427 9990* www.theboardwalkbarandgrill.com

Owned by businessmen Neil Prendiville of Cork Local Radio and hotelier John Gately, this stylish venture in the centre of Cork was always bound to be a hit. And so it is: both the quality bar food and the evening steakhouse, The Grill Room, consistently please Corkonians and visitors to the city alike - including plenty of visiting stars. *Grill Room* **seats 140**. *Open Mon-Sat, 10am-11.30pm (Fri & Sat to 12.30pm). Closed Sun. CC.*

Café Gusto

3 Washington Street Cork City ☎*021 425 4446* www.cafegusto.com

A smart frontage hints at the big ideas at work in this little designer wine bar & café near Singer's Corner. Marianne Delaney, former manager of The Exchange on George's Quay, and her Ballymaloe-trained partner Denis O'Mullane, take pride in sourcing the very best quality ingredients, and specialise in great coffee, gourmet rolls, wraps and salads, either to go or to eat on the premises, and Mediterranean-inspired evening menus. *Also at Lapp's Quay.* **Seats 20**. *Open Mon-Sat, 7.45am-5pm and D Thu-Sat, 5-10pm (Fri & Sat to 11). Closed Sun, D Mon-Wed, bank hols. CC.*

Café Paradiso

16 Lancaster Quay Western Road Cork City ☎*021 427 7939* www.cafeparadiso.ie

Denis Cotter's ground-breaking vegetarian restaurant produces such exciting mainstream cooking that even the most committed of carnivores admit to relishing every mouthful and it attracts devotees from all over Ireland - and beyond. Innovative, strongly seasonal menus are based on the best organic produce available and the cooking is nothing less then stunning. **Seats 45** *(outdoor seating, 6). L Fri & Sat only. D Tue-Sat. Closed L Tue-Thur, Sun, Mon, Christmas week. CC.*

The Castle Café

Blackrock Castle Observatory Blackrock Cork City ☎*021 435 7911 www.castlecafe.ie*

A sister to the popular Market Lane Restaurant in Cork (see entry), this scenically located café has earned a reputation for tasty Mediterranean-influenced family-friendly food and good value. Quality ingredients (locally sourced where possible) are a point of pride, everything is homemade and vegetarian and coeliac-friendly dishes are available. *Seats 60 in main café + outdoor tables. Open daily, all day from 9.30am (to 9pm Tue-Sat). Closed bank hols, Good Fri & 25 Dec. CC. **Directions:** About 3km east of Cork city centre; very close to Mahon Point SC.*

The Chocolate Shop

English Market Cork City ☎*021 425 4448 www.chocolate.ie*

Niall & Rosemary Daly's small but immaculately stocked specialist shop is not affiliated to any manufacturer and sells an exceptional range of artisan chocolates, both Irish names and international brands. Ranges stocked include the very best of organic, diabetic and gluten-free chocolate, cooking and drinking chocolates and other speciality confectionery, like Pandora Bell lollipops - and the famous Hadji Bey's Turkish Delight (www.hadjibey.ie), which is the pride of Cork. Mon-Sat, 9-5. Also online sales.

Cinnamon Cottage

Monastery Road Rochestown Cork City ☎*021 489 4922 www.cinnamoncottage.ie*

Carol and Kieran Murphy's charming bakery and deli was one of the early trailblazers in the new wave of 'real' food in Ireland. They offer a wide range of delicious things to go and every kind of gorgeous baked goods from the everyday (soda breads, scones) to irresistible cakes for every occasion - and there's a carefully selected range of wines, and a catering service too. *Open Tue-Thu 9.30-6, Fri 9.30-6.45, Sat 9.30-6, Sun 12-5.30. Closed Mon. **Directions:** On Rochestown Road/R610, next to the Rochestown Inn.*

Clarion Hotel Cork

Lapps Quay Cork City ☎*021 422 4900 www.clarionhotelcorkcity.com*

Those who like contemporary hotels and enjoy the buzz of the city centre will love this centrally located hotel with its wide terrace and boardwalk along the River Lee. Well-appointed accommodation includes riverside suites and a penthouse suite, and excellent amenities include a spa, swimming pool, and gym. A choice of dining is offered, between Kudos (Asian, informal and *Oysters Restaurant* (see separate entry). *Rooms 191. Closed 24-27 Dec. CC.*

The Club Brasserie

Lapps Quay Cork City ☎*021 427 3987*

In a new building on a pedestrianised riverside site, this well-located and atmospheric restaurant is run by respected local restaurateurs Harold Lynch and Beth Haughton. Known for their commitment to quality ingredients - sourced locally where possible - and for cooking unfussy food with style, it's always a pleasing dining experience. Harold Lynch and Beth Haughton also provide the excellent catering at *The Woodford Pub* (see entry). *Seats 85. B 8-11am; L Mon-Sat; D daily. CC.*

 **The Cornstore Winebar & Grill**

40a Cornmarket Street Cork City ☎*021 427 4777 www.cornstorecork.com*

In the buzzy Coal Quay renewal area, this sister establishment to Padraig Frawley's highly regarded Cornstore in Limerick (see entry) is in a stylishly converted two-storey granite mill building. Menus are varied, but the pièce de résistance is The Cornstore's range of premium steaks and their unique in-house steak ageing unit ensures exceptionally tender meat. Appealing food, value for money and sharp service that manages to be both friendly and efficient make this a popular venue. **Seats 180.** *L & D Mon-Sat, Sun all day 12-9pm. Closed 25 Dec. CC.*

 Crawford Gallery Café

Emmet Place Cork City ☎*021 427 4415 www.crawfordartgallery.ie/Cafe.html*

One of Cork city's favourite informal eating places, this is an outpost of Ballymaloe House, Shanagarry, and currently run by Jean Manning. The frequently changed menus in this striking room reflect the Ballymaloe philosophy that food is precious and should be handled carefully, so freshly prepared dishes are made from natural local ingredients and a meal here can be a real treat. **Seats 65**. *Open Mon-Sat, 9.30-3pm. Closed Sun, bank hols, 10 days over Christmas. CC.*

Dan Lowrey's Tavern

13 Mc Curtain Street Cork City ☎*021 4505071*

This characterful pub beside the Everyman Palace Theatre was established in 1875 and is named after its founder. Long before the arrival of the "theme pub", Lowrey's was famous for having windows which originated from Kilkenny Cathedral. Run by Anthony and Catherine O'Riordan since 1995, Catherine oversees the kitchen herself and it's a good place for a fairly priced home-cooked meal. **Seats 30** *(outdoors, 10). L & D daily (Sandwiches available all day). Closed 25 Dec & Good Fri. No CC.*

  Delicious

Unit 1 Innishmore Industrial Estate Cork City ☎*021 487 5780 www.delicious.ie*

Denise and Michael O'Callaghan's well-named enterprise produces handmade gluten- and wheat-free breads and cakes. Reflecting the philosophy that "being on a restricted diet should not mean a restricted food experience", the production process begins, as with all good baking, with sourcing the best ingredients Approved by the Irish Coeliac Society, many of their products are also dairy and yeast free. *Available in selected outlets; online shop.*

  Elbow Lane Craft Beer

Elbow Lane Brewhouse Ltd 5-6 Oliver Plunkett Street Cork City www.elbowlane.ie

Named after streets and alleyways of Cork city - Angel Lane, Elbow Lane and Wisdom Lane - Elbow Lane beers are all-natural craft beers produced by the team behind the Market Lane and Castle Café restaurants in Cork, who wanted to create beers that could be paired with their food. First on the market, in August 2012, was their Angel Stout, followed by Elbow Lager and Wisdom Ale (a red ale). Check their website for updates. Stockists initially limited to a select few places in Cork including Castle Café, Market Lane Restaurant and Bradley's Supermarket and Off Licence.

 ## Electric

41 South Mall Cork City ☎*021 422 2990 www.electriccork.com*

In a dream riverside location, this restored Art Deco building is owned by Tastefest Cork founder Ernest Cantillon and Denis O'Mullane, of the excellent Café Gusto and Liberty Grill (see entries). A Fish Bar inspired by the simple seafood cookery of Spain and Portugal opened in 2013 - a great addition to an already great food offering. Main ingredients are from the English Market, keeping the menus seasonal, and stylishly good cooking is in the modern bistro style, with simple, un-cheffy presentation - and it's not just 'the usual' menu. With cocktails and craft beers on offer and a great buzz, it appeals to all ages. *Seats 70 (+30 outdoors on balcony). Times (food): Mon-Wed 5.30-10pm, Thu-Sat 12.30-10pm, Sun 12-9pm. Bar menu also available. CC.*

 ## Eves Chocolate Shop

8 College Commercial Park Magazine Road (near Dennehy's Cross) Cork City
☎*021 434 7781 www.evechocolates.ie*

The exquisite artisan treats at Eve St Leger's very special factory shop make it 'worth a detour' for chocoholics. Using traditional hand-made methods and only the best ingredients - including top quality dark, milk and white chocolate and fresh Irish cream - Eve's skilfully crafted range is known for its great flavour and texture. The distinctive black and white boxes are also easy to spot in other shops. *Open Mon-Fri 9.30-6, Sat 9.30-1.Extra hours at Christmas and Easter, contact for details. Directions: Near UCC, beside Dennehy's Cross.*

ENGLISH MARKET

Visitors to Cork City with an interest in food and fresh produce have a treat in store at the famous English Market (open daily), and should also visit Coal Quay Market, which is held in Cornmarket Street every Saturday. It is hard to imagine a visit to Cork without at the very least a quick browse through the English Market and - although it is most famous for its huge range of fresh food stalls selling everything from wet fish, and almost forgotten meats and vegetables to cheeses, freshly baked breads and speciality, imported produce, notably olives - there's a growing choice of places to top up the browser's energy levels along the way, noteable Farmgate Café on the first floor (see entry).

 ## Farmgate Café

English Market Cork City ☎*021 427 8134 www.farmgate.ie*

A sister restaurant to the Farmgate Country Store and Restaurant in Midleton (see entry), Kay Harte's Farmgate Café shares the same commitment to serving fresh, local food - and, as it is located in the gallery above the English Market, where ingredients are purchased daily, it doesn't come much fresher or more local than this. Everything they do, from breakfast to afternoon tea, is outstanding, and some offerings are unique. They make almost forgotten regional dishes using the food they buy in the market, for example, and have introduced lesser known foods such as corned mutton to their menus alongside famous old Cork ones with a special market connection, like tripe & drisheen and corned beef & champ with green cabbage. A real treat. *Seats 110. Meals Mon-Sat, 9am - 5pm. Closed Sun, bank hols, Dec 25-3 Jan. CC.*

 **Fenns Quay Restaurant**

5 Sheares Street Cork City ☎*021 427 9527 www.fennsquay.ie*

Owned by Kate Lawlor (the head chef) and front of house manager Pennapa (Pen) Wongsuwan, this busy restaurant is in a 250-year old listed building, but it is bright and welcoming with striking modern paintings. Kate's passion for careful sourcing of ingredients permeates her pleasing bistro-style cooking; everything possible is local and seasonal, providing the freshest possible foundation for Mediterranean-influenced food with an emphasis on flavour. *Seats 60 (outdoors, 10); Open all day Mon-Sat 8am-10pm. Closed Sun, 25 Dec, bank hols. CC.*

 Flemings Restaurant

Silver Grange House Tivoli Cork City ☎*021 482 1621 www.flemingsrestaurant.ie*

A large Georgian family house with a productive garden is home to Michael and Eileen Fleming's classical French restaurant with rooms. Michael's cooking is invariably excellent, presentation elegant, and service both attentive and knowledgeable. A great antidote to the sameness of modern multicultural restaurants - a visit to a classic restaurant like this is a treat to treasure. *Seats 80 (outdoors, 30). L Tue-Sun, D Tue-Sat. Closed Sun D, Mon, 24-27 Dec. Accommodation: four spacious, comfortably furnished en-suite rooms CC. Directions: Signed off main Cork-Dublin route, 4km from city centre.*

 Franciscan Well Brewery & Brewpub

North Mall Cork City ☎*021 421 0130 www.franciscanwellbrewery.com*

The Franciscan Well Brewery, founded in 1998 and acquired by Coors Molson in 2013, is now one of the oldest craft brewers still operating in Ireland. Molson Coors plans to build an additional brewery elsewhere in Cork city, with a view to exporting the beer to the UK, Canada and the US. However Shane Long, the brewery founder and current chairman of the Irish Craft Brewers Association, will retain control of product development. The brewery also has its own brew pub, boasting one of the best beer gardens in Cork city.

 Fresco

Lewis Gluckman Gallery UCC Campus Cork City ☎*021 490 1848 www.glucksman.org/cafe*

Well known for their fusion dishes and a favourite destination for Sunday Brunch with the family, the café at the Glucksman Gallery has earned a following. Large windows flood the minimalist room with natural light, and simple but delicious food is presented with Asian flair. It can be very enjoyable, especially when sitting outside on fine summer evenings. *Open Mon-Fri 8.15am-5pm, Sat 10-5, Sun 12-5. CC.*

 Gallo & Galetti

Unit 7/8 High Street Centre Wilton Cork City ☎*021 434 1095 www.galloandgaletti.ie*

Cork's answer to Jamie's Italian, acclaimed Cork chef-restaurateur Brendan Cashman's new venture in Wilton is bright and spacious, with an eager to please team - and the food is excellent. Given its wide appeal, high standards and good value for money, Gallo & Galetti should please a lot of people and very handy for visitors to the hospital. It's another interesting change of direction for a fine dining chef - and having a top chef at the helm is a big bonus for customers at this very accessible restaurant. *Tue -Sun 12-10. CC.*

Gresham Metropole Hotel

MacCurtain Street Cork City ✆*021 4508122 www.gresham-hotels.com*

This imposing city-centre hotel next door to the Everyman Palace Theatre and backing on to the River Lee, celebrated its centenary in 1998. Long associated with the arts and entertainment industry, public areas and the atmospheric Met Tavern feature mementos of stars past and present. ***Rooms 112*** *(10 shower only). Open all year. CC.*

Hayfield Manor Hotel

Perrott Avenue College Road Cork City ✆*021 484 5900 www.hayfieldmanor.ie*

Set in gardens near University College Cork, the city's premier hotel has the feel of a large period house. Managed with warmth and discreet efficiency, it provides every comfort and a remarkable level of privacy and seclusion, just a mile from the city centre. It also offers two destination dining choices: stylish bistro cooking in Perotts Garden Bistro; or the elegant evening restaurant Orchids for fine dining. ***Rooms 88***. *Orchids: Seats 90. L Sun only. D Mon-Sat. Perrotts Restaurant, L&D daily. CC.*

Hotel Isaacs & Greenes Restaurant

48 MacCurtain Street Cork City ✆*021 450 0011 www.isaacscork.com*

Opposite the Everyman Palace Theatre and approached through a cobbled courtyard, this attractive hotel has comfortable spacious rooms at a fairly reasonable price. Some rooms at the back have a charming outlook onto a waterfall, which is floodlit at night and makes an unusual feature when seen from the restaurant. ***Rooms 47*** *(4 shower only). Restaurant seats 100 (outdoors, 30). L Mon-Sat; D daily. Restaurant closed Sun L & Mon in winter, hotel closed 24-27 Dec. CC.*

 ## House Café

Cork Opera House Emmet Place Cork City ✆*021 490 5277*

A "fresh and exciting twist on modern culinary classics" is the promise from the team behind this café, Victor Murphy, Stephen McGlynn and chef Eoin O' Reilly - and their friendly staff make all welcome, whether for a full meal from the eclectic menu or just coffee and a home baked treat. Great locally sourced seasonal produce and skilful cooking make this a useful place to know about. Mon-Sat 10-5.30 & show nights to 9pm. No CC.

 ## Idaho Café

19 Caroline Street Cork City ✆*021 427 6376*

"Real food for real people" was the original motto of Richard and Mairead Jacob's 'small but perfectly formed' cafe, just behond Brown Thomas - and you could now make that real local food. They try to source all primary ingredients from within a 100km radius of this place which - bright and bubbly like the owners themselves - has been providing a restorative treat in the city centre since 2001. Deliciously simple fare, especially great baking. ***Seats 30*** *(outdoors, 10). Open Mon-Sat, 8.30-5pm. Closed Sun, Bank Hols, 24-26 Dec. No CC.*

Imperial Hotel

South Mall Cork City 📞*021 427 4040 www.flynnhotels.com*

This thriving hotel in Cork's main commercial and banking centre dates back to 1813 and has a colourful history - Michael Collins spent his last night here, and that suite now bears his name. Recent renovations have brought new life to its fine old public areas and transformed the accommodation - and the stylish contemporary **Pembroke Seafood Bar & Grill** has become a destination restaurant. **Rooms 126** (8 shower-only). Closed 24-26 Dec. CC.

Isaacs Restaurant

48 MacCurtain Street Cork City 📞*021 450 3805 www.isaacsrestaurant.ie*

In 1992 Michael and Catherine Ryan, together with partner/head chef Canice Sharkey, opened this large, atmospheric modern restaurant in an 18th-century warehouse and it immediately struck a chord with people tired of having to choose between fine dining and fast food, a trend-setter in the modern Irish food movement. Ingredients are carefully sourced, the cooking is consistently accomplished and menus are freshened by occasional inspired introductions - and a visit here is always great fun. **Seats 120**. L Mon-Sat, D daily. Closed - L Sun, Christmas week, L Bank Holidays. CC.

Jacobs On The Mall

30A South Mall Cork City 📞*021 425 1530 www.jacobsonthemall.com*

Its location in the former Turkish baths creates a highly unusual and atmospheric contemporary dining space for one of Cork's most popular restaurants. Modern European cooking is the promise and this restaurant bases its reputation on close attention to sourcing the best ingredients allied to skilful cooking. The results are commendably simple and pleasing. **Seats 130**. D Mon-Sat; L Thu & Fri only. Closed Sun, 25/26 Dec, L on bank hols. CC.

Jacques Restaurant

Phoenix Street Cork City 📞*021 427 7387 www.jacquesrestaurant.ie*

An integral part of Cork life since 1982, sisters Eithne and Jacqueline Barry's delightful restaurant has changed with the years, evolving from quite a traditional place to a smart and - since 2013 - much larger contemporary space. But the fundamentals of warm hospitality and great food never waver and that is the reason why many would cite Jacques as their favourite Cork restaurant. Menus are based on carefully sourced ingredients from a network of suppliers built up over many years and often include unusual ingredients which, in this creative kitchen, make for magical meals. *D only Mon-Sat. Closed Sun, Bank Hols, 24-27 Dec. CC.*

Kathleen Noonan Pork & Bacon

Unit 21 Grand Parade Market Grand Parade Cork City 📞*087 297 1895*

Kathleen Noonan first took a stall in the English Market in 1955 and is now semi-retired, so her daughter Pauline Mulcahy has taken up the baton, selling traditional pork products. It is now the only stall dealing exclusively in pig meat – crubeens (trotters or pigs feet), pig's tails, bodice, skirts, kidneys, loin bones, knuckles, hocks as well as more familiar cuts like rashers and collar bacon. *Open 9.30-5.30.*

Kay O'Connell Fishmongers

13-20 Grand Parade Market Grand Parade Cork City ☎*021 427 6380*

O'Connell's renowned fish stall began life over 40 years ago, started by the late Kay O'Connell, mother of Paul and Pat, who run it today. The stall stretches to an impressive eighty feet in length offering a vast range of fresh whitefish and shellfish with live lobster, crab and oysters available from a tank in-store. They also sell smoked and frozen fish, and have recently added a seafood delicatessen, which brings a contemporary dimension to the business. *Open 8-5.30.*

 L'Atitude 51

1 Union Quay Cork City ☎*021 239 0219 www.latitude51.ie*

Billing itself as a wine café this quirky riverside venue is part tapas bar, part wine bar with a distinctly continental flair. Open for quality coffee (Fermoy-roasted Badger & Dodo) and pastries in the morning, a short weekday lunch menu comprises imaginative soup, sandwiches on Arbutus bread and a daily hot dish. But the evening tapas menu is the real draw, with a selection of European and artisan ingredients served up as delicious taster plates. *L Mon-Fri 12.30-3pm, D daily 6-10pm, Sat brunch 12.30-3pm.*

 **Lancaster Lodge**

Lancaster Quay Western Road Cork City ☎*021 425 1125 www.lancasterlodge.com*

Robert White's large, modern purpose-built guesthouse beside the River Lee Hotel has secure parking in the grounds and offers hotel quality accommodation at a moderate price. Public areas are not grand but reception is prompt and friendly, there is bottled water on each floor, newspapers in the bright contemporary dining room (where a good breakfast is served) and generally pleasing surroundings throughout, including original art works. ***Rooms 48*** *(5 shower only). Closed 23-28 Dec. CC.*

 Les Gourmandises Restaurant

17 Cook Street Cork City ☎*021 425 1959 www.lesgourmandises.ie*

Just off South Mall, this little restaurant feels like an outpost of France - the menu at the entrance will draw you in, and you'll be glad you noticed it. It's run by Patrick and Soizic Kiely - both formerly of Restaurant Patrick Guilbaud but, although that says a lot about the key standards, there's nothing flash about the quiet style of this restaurant which offers stylish cooking with great flavour, based on the day's market and with local suppliers listed. ***Seats 30***. L Sun only; D Tue-Sat (& bank hol Sun). Closed Sun D, Mon (except bank hols); 1 week in August. CC.

 Liberty Grill

32 Washington Street Cork City ☎*021 427 1049 www.libertygrillcork.com*

Liberty Grill is a sister restaurant to Café Gusto (Washington Street & Lapps Quay), so you may expect the same food philosophy based on quality ingredients, where possible organic and locally sourced. It offers real, tasty all day food and good value in pleasant surroundings; a youthful clientèle creates a buzz - sometimes it can be very noisy. ***Seats 50***. *Open Mon-Thu 8am-9pm, Fri-Sat 8-10. Closed Sun, Bank Hols. CC.*

Maldron Hotel Cork

John Redmond Street Cork City ☎*021 452 9200*

Formerly the Shandon Hotel, the Maldron offers budget accommodation just a short walk from the city centre and, with good business and leisure facilities, including a swimming pool, it is well worth considering for a family visit to Cork or for meetings and conferences. Arrangement with nearby carpark. **Rooms 101**. *Closed 24-26 Dec. CC*

Market Lane Restaurant & Bar

5 & 6 Oliver Plunkett Street Cork City ☎*021 427 4710 www.marketlane.ie*

Judy Howard, Tracy Corbett and Conrad Howard own this bustling two-storey restaurant and bar near the English Market. A sister to the Castle Café at Blackrock Castle (see entry) it is a friendly and welcoming place with a lively atmosphere; fresh and artisan produce from the English Market is used as much as possible and they offer good quality food – and real value for money. **Seats 136** *(outdoor seating available). Food: Mon-Sat 12–9pm (to 10.30pm Sat), Sun 1-9pm (except bank hols). Closed Good Fri, 25/26 Dec. CC.*

Maryborough Hotel & Spa

Maryborough Hill Douglas Cork City ☎*021 436 5555 www.maryborough.com*

Quietly situated on the south of the city and very convenient to Cork airport and the Jack Lynch Tunnel, this very family-friendly privately owned hotel has a fine country house at its heart. A popular meeting place, with spacious public areas overlooking gardens and good food, it has well designed modern rooms and excellent leisure facilities. **Rooms 93**. *Restaurant* **seats 120**. *L&D daily.Closed 24-26 Dec. CC.*

The Meat Centre

Stall 16 Aisle 1 English Market Cork City

One of the great characters of the Market, Ken Barrett has held a stall since 1980 and he farms the cattle, sheep and pigs that are butchered here, so the food chain is as short as it gets. As well as all the regular cuts, you'll find the old traditional ones such as bodice, sheeps' tongue and pickled pigs head – maybe also mutton, which is hard to find these days. *Open 8-5.30*

The Montenotte Hotel

Montenotte Cork City ☎*021 453 0050 www.themontenottehotel.com*

Previously the Country Club Hotel, the 'new' Montenotte is perched high over the city in a select residential area. The trump card is the view, and it offers a pleasant budget-conscious alternative to city centre accommodation with good leisure faciities. **Rooms 108**. *CC.*

Nash 19 Restaurant

19 Princes Street Cork City ☎*021 427 0880 www.nash19.com*

Home from home for its many loyal customers for two decades, Claire Nash's bustling city centre restaurant is just a stone's throw from the English Market – the source of much of the local and indigenous produce they are known for, including vegetables, fresh sustainable catches and meats. 'Simple food cooked honestly' is their mantra, and it's a very child friendly place too. **Seats 130**. *Open Mon-Fri, 7.30am-5pm. (Shop open to 6pm). Closed Sat, Sun, Bank Hols, 10 days over Christmas/New Year. CC.*

O'Conaills Chocolates

16 French Church Street Cork City ✆*021 437 3407*

This chocolate bar and shop is the main retail outlet for these well known artisan chocolates, which include diabetic chocolate and they're made by third generation chocolatier Casey O'Conaill in Carrigaline (+353 21 437 3407), south of Cork city. Only the highest quality ingredients are used, and it shows. The premium hot chocolate has developed cult status and fans are prepared to queue for it. *Mon-Sat 10-6, Sun 11-5. Also at:13 Princes Street.*

O'Flynns Butchers

36 Marlborough Street Cork City ✆*021 427 5685*

Although it is a block away from the English Market, where there are a dozen or so excellent butchers to choose from, many loyal customers make this legendary butchers shop a destination. Run by brothers Simon and Patrick O'Flynn, it is a very traditional outfit, known for the exceptional quality of its meats and skilled butchering, good advice - and a bit of banter too. Kassler and spiced beef are among their specialities. *Open Mon-Thu 9-5, Fri 8-5, Sat 8-4.*

O'Keeffes Shop

2/3 Wellington Road St Lukes Cross Cork City ✆*021 450 2010 www.okeeffes-shop.ie*

Cork food-lovers head to Donal O'Keeffe's long-established store just a short distance from the city centre for its treasure trove of local artisan foods including Arbutus breads (and Granny Ryan's Soda Bread Mix), Belvelly Smokehouse fish, Caherbeg free range pork, Glenilen dairy products and cheeses (supplied by On The Pig's Back); excellent deli, and wines too. Take a moment to browse their product range online – then build a visit into your itinerary when visiting Cork. *Open Mon-Sun, 7.30am-10pm (hours on Bank Holidays may be shorter). Closed 25 Dec.*

On The Pig's Back

Unit 26 St Patrick's Woollen Mills Douglas Cork City

French woman Isabelle Sheridan's reputation in Cork was already established at her brilliant shop in the English Market (see below), long before she opened up this branch in Douglas. Here she has a lovely, lively deli and café, in a quirky room with a large tree as its centrepiece, where you may sit down and enjoy some great food after doing your shopping. *Mon-Sat 9-5.30 (lunch 12-3).*

On The Pigs Back

Stall 11 English Market Cork City ✆*021 427 0232 www.onthepigsback.ie*

Isabelle Sheridan has been a key figure at the English Market for many years – and she has earned a national reputation, both for the quality of her own charcuterie – notably her patés and terrines - and for the range of Irish and French artisan foods that she has collected to sell alongside them, including Declan Ryan's Arbutus breads, the best farmhouse cheeses, Caherbeg free range pork products, Rosscarbery sausages, Krawczyk's products, Gubbeen Smokehouse products and many more. *Open Mon-Sat, 8-5.30. Also at: Unit 26 St Patrick's Mill Douglas Co Cork; +353 (0)21 4617832 (with café)].*

ORSO Kitchen & Bar

8 Pembroke Street Cork City ✆ *021 243 8000 www.ORSO.ie*

Opened in September 2012 by husband and wife team Conrad and Judy Howard and Tracey Corbett (Market Lane; Castle Café, Blackrock), ORSO Kitchen and Bar brings welcome Mediterranean sunshine to Cork city centre. Informal and inviting with a lively buzz, it's open from early until late - and, as well as great food, there's an impressive wine list offering taster glasses (75ml) and craft beers. **Seats 40**. *Mon-Wed 8-6, Thu 8-10, Fri & Sat 8-10.30.*

 Oysters

The Clarion Hotel Lapps Quay Cork City ✆ *021 427 3777 www.oysters.ie*

Head Chef Alex Petit and the team at Oysters make the very best of the fresh and tasty seafood caught only a few hours earlier off the Cork coast. An impressive room and friendly reception set the tone for a very enjoyable meal. The cooking has finesse and prices are generally fair for the standard offered - it's easy to see why this pleasing place has become one of Cork city's most popular restaurants. **Seats 160**. *D only Tue-Sat, 5.30-10 Set D €35.00 (5.30-7), also à la carte. Closed Sun & Mon.*

  The Pavilion Garden Centre & Earthly Delights Café

Myrtle Hill Ballygarvan Cork City ✆ *021 488 8134 www.thepavilion.ie*

The O'Leary family's well run garden centre has a good lifestyle section, offering tempting homewares and cookbooks, and good food too. An attractive café focuses on wholesome homemade food based on seasonal local ingedients - and delicious home bakes (eat in or take home). *Open Mon-Sat, 9-6, Sun 1-6.*

  Quay Co-op

24 Sullivan's Quay Cork City ✆ *021 431 7026 www.quaycoop.com*

Founded as a radical alternative community project in 1982, Cork's original organic food store, in-house bakery and vegetarian restaurant is more rounded now but has retained its character and - far from being a dated concept- continues to gain new fans. *Shop open Mon-Sat, 9-5. Café Mon-Sat, 10-9, Sun 12-9.*

 Radisson Blu Hotel & Spa Cork

Ditchley House Little Island Cork City ✆ *021 429 7000 www.radissonblu.ie/hotel-cork*

On the eastern edge of Cork city, adjacent to an industrial estate, the location of this hotel is not attractive but it is near the Jack Lynch Tunnel, which gives easy access to the airport, and it is set in landscaped gardens. Designed to appeal to both leisure and business guests, accommodation is to the expected high standard, as are leisure facilities. **Rooms 129** *(15 shower only). Open all year. CC.*

  The Real Olive Company

Unit 33 Grand Parade Market Grand Parade Cork City www.therealoliveco.com

Since 1994 the legendary Toby Simmonds has offered discerning shoppers the best in olives, oils, and Mediterranean fare - and is a popular fixture at farmers' markets around the country too. The range has grown a lot - and now includes their own Toonsbridge Buffalo Mozzarella, which won an Irish Food Writers' Guild Good Food Award (2013), but there has been no change to the underlying principles of choice and quality. *Open 8.30-5.30 Also at: Toons Bridge Dairy (see entry) near Macroom, with café.*

 **The River Lee Hotel**

Western Road Cork City 📞*021 425 2700 www.doylecollection.com*

In a riverside site on Western Road, this impressive establishment is one of Cork's most popular hotels, especially perhaps for business guests. Imaginatively designed to make the very most of its attractive location, all of the main public areas have balconies, including the aptly named the Weir Bistro where local produce is showcased in classic modern cooking and served in a waterside setting. The very comfortable bedrooms are designed and finished to an unusually high specification, and leisure facilities are also excellent. *Rooms 182. Weir Bistro: B'fast daily & D Tue-Sat; D Sun & Mon served in the Weir Bar (also offers bar menu daily). Open all year. CC.*

 **Rochestown Park Hotel**

Rochestown Road Douglas Cork City 📞*021 489 0800 www.rochestownpark.com*

Once home to the Lord Mayors of Cork, the original parts of this mainly modern 4* hotel feature gracious, well-proportioned public rooms and it is set in lovely grounds. It has a special reputation for business and conferences, and is convenient to the airport and the Jack Lynch Tunnel. Excellent leisure facilities include a thalassotherapy centre; the first in an Irish hotel it predated the current fashion for spas by many years. *Rooms 150. Open all year except Christmas. CC.*

 Star Anise

4 Bridge Street Cork City 📞*021 455 1635*

Virginie Sarrazin's chic contemporary restaurant offers imaginative food, sassy service, and an interesting wine list too. Seasonal foods are at the heart of the cooking, with local specialities name checked on menus. *Seats 40; L & D Tue-Sat. Open all year. CC.*

 Table

Brown Thomas Dept. Store 18-21 Patrick Street Cork City 📞*021 427 5106 www.itsa.ie*

A cousin of sisters Peaches and Domini Kemp's highly regarded Dublin operation The Restaurant at Brown Thomas, this is a stylish daytime restaurant at the chicest store in town. Fresh, colourful and tasty, it is classic Kemp fare with quality suppliers credited - and their fans will find many familiar dishes, including great salads. *Seats 52. Food served Mon-Sat, 9am-6.30pm (to 7.30pm Thurs). Open same hours as BT. CC.*

Tom Durcan

The English Market Cork City ✆*021 427 9141 www.tomdurcanmeats.ie*

Tom Durcan Meats is far from being one of Ireland's longest-established butchers - but it is one of the most highly-regarded and, being right next to the fountain at The English Market, very easy to find. Tom takes pride in local sourcing and his meat, especially dry-aged beef, is sought after by many discerning chefs. But the product he's most famous for is a Christmas speciality, Cork Traditional Spiced Beef; the ritual spicing begins in October and they sell over a ton of spiced beef every December.

                                                          Vikki's

The Old Post Office 85a Sundays Well Road Cork City ✆*021 439 6575*

Vikki's charming café and deli in the Cork City Gaol area offers a limited menu, but is well done with tasty home bakes made freshly every day. Eat cosily indoors beside the fire in winter, or find a seat in the the garden or at a pavement table in summer. The deli is impressive, a who's who of local producers, and you'll find everyday essentials here too. *Tue-Fri 10-7, Sat 10-6. Closed Sun & Mon.*

                                                    Wagamama Cork

4-5 South Main Streer Cork City ✆*021 427 8874 www.wagamama.ie*

A Cork branch of the popular Japanese chain (see Wagamama Dublin), Wagamama noodle bar offers healthy, tasty and inexpensive meals, including an extensive choice of meat, seafood and vegetarian pan Asian dishes, all cooked to order and promptly served. *Seats 120. Open 12-11 daily. CC.*

                                            The Woodford

19-20 Paul Street Cork City ✆*021 425 3931 www.thewoodford.ie*

This atmospherically located bar is in the old Woodford Bourne wine merchants premises, with catering by Harold Lynch and Beth Haughton of the Club Brasserie (see entry). Quality ingredients sourced from the best local artisan food producers and the nearby English Market provide the delicious foundation for flavoursome food that goes far beyond the standard expected of bar meals in Ireland. Friday and Saturday nights are aimed at a young crowd, with a late bar. *L Mon-Sat: 12-4; D Tue-Sat 5.30-8.30. No food Sun or D Mon.*

COUNTY CORK

Cork is Ireland's largest county, and its individualistic people take pride in this distinction as they savour the variety of their territory, which ranges from the rich farmlands of the east to the handsome coastline of West Cork, where the light of the famous Fastnet Rock swings across tumbling ocean and spray-tossed headland.

In this extensive county, the towns and villages have their own distinctive character. In the west, their spirit is preserved in the vigour of the landscape. By contrast, East Cork's impressive farming country, radiating towards the ancient estuary port of Youghal, is invitingly prosperous.

The spectacularly located township of Cobh - facing south over Cork Harbour - asserts its own identity, with a renewed sense of its remarkable maritime heritage being expressed in events such as a Sea Shanty Festival, while the town's direct link with the Titanic - Cobh was the ill-fated liner's last port of call - is also commemorated in many ways.

Different again in character is Kinsale, a bustling sailing/fishing port which is home to many intriguing old buildings, yet is a place which is vibrantly modern in outlook, and it has long been seen as Ireland's gourmet capital.

The county is a repository of the good things of life, a treasure chest of the finest farm produce, and the very best of seafood, brought to market by skilled specialists. As Ireland's most southerly county, Cork enjoys the mildest climate of all, and it's a place where they work to live, rather than live to work. So the arts of living are seen at their most skilled in County Cork, and they are practised in a huge territory of such variety that it is difficult to grasp it all, even if you devote your entire vacation to this one county.

LOCAL ATTRACTIONS & INFORMATION

- **Bantry House** Bantry
  027 50047
- **Tourism Information** Bantry
  027 50229
- **Blarney Castle** Blarney
  021 438 5252
- **Fota Estate (Wildlife Park, Arboretum)** Carrigtwohill
  021 481 2728
- **Mill Cove Gallery** (May to Sept.) Castletownbere
  027 70393
- **Annes Grove** (gardens)
  Castletownroche *022 26145*

- **Lisselan Estate Gardens**
  Clonakilty *023 33249*
- **The Queenstown Story** Cobh
  021 4813591
- **Sirius Arts Centre** Cobh
  021 4813790
- **Garinish Island** Glengarriff
  027 63040
- **Charles Fort** Kinsale
  021 4772263
- **Desmond Castle** Kinsale
  021 4774855
- **Cork Racecourse** Mallow
  022 50207

- **Jameson Heritage Centre**
  Midleton *021 4613594*
- **Mizen Vision Signal Station**
  Mizen Head
  028 35115 / 35225
- **Ferries to Sherkin, Cape Clear and Fastnet** Schull
  028 28278
- **West Cork Arts Centre**
  Skibbereen *028 22090*
- **Myrtle Grove** Youghal
  024 92274

AHAKISTA

The small village of Ahakista is near Bantry, on the Sheep's Head Way between Kilcrohane and Durrus villages. The nearest long sandy beaches are a short drive away, but there are small quiet beaches around Bantry Bay, where you will often have the beach to yourself and it is an ideal base for touring the Bantry Bay area. The area offers enjoyable cycling routes and scenic walks, including the Sheep's Head Way and Beara Way, and angling opportunities. The West Cork Garden Trail is of particular interest, also the many historical sites.

Arundels by the Pier

Kitchen Cove Ahakista Co Cork ☎027 67033

This delightful harbourside pub has been in the Arundel family for over 100 years; current owners, Shane and Fiona Arundel, have modernised it without losing the the spirit of the old bar, which remains a popular meeting place for locals. Their delicious simple food has a pleasing local accent and it's served in the bar, in a newer first floor dining room and outdoor dining areas which include very family friendly options. *Seats 18. (10 tables outside). Open daily in summer, food served 12.30-8.30. Call to check opening times off season. CC.* **Directions:** *At Ahakista pier.*

Hillcrest House

Ahakista Durrus Bantry Co Cork ☎027 67045 *www.ahakista.com*

Hospitality comes first at this comfortable, family-friendly working farm overlooking Dunmanus Bay, where Agnes Hegarty's guests - including walkers, who revel in the 88km "Sheep's Head Way" - are welcomed with a cup of tea and home-baked scones on arrival. Self catering also available all year. *Rooms 4 (3 shower only). Closed 1 Nov - 1 Apr. CC.* **Directions:** *3 km from Bantry, take N71 and turn off for Durrus, then Ahakista - 0.25km to Hillcrest.*

The Tin Pub

Ahakista Durrus Bantry Co Cork ☎027 67203

Margaret Whooley runs one of the most relaxed bars in the country: known affectionately as "the tin pub" after its corrugated iron roof, it has a lovely rambling country garden going down to the water, where children are welcome to burn off excess energy. Not really a food place, but they sometimes set up a DIY barbecue. *Open from about 1pm in summer, closed Oct-May.* **Directions:** *Sheeps Head direction, from Durrus.*

Healys Honey

Maglin Ballincollig Cork ☎021 487 1258 *www.healyshoney.ie*

A keen beekeeper, Patrick Healy, developed a business from his hobby when he established this company in the 1970s. It is now a successful family-run enterprise producing, purchasing and distributing honey, which is widely available from independent stores and supermarkets.They blend honey from Ireland and other countries (sources stated on the labels), and also offer a premium product, Pure Irish Honey, when available.

Ó'Crualaoí Butchers

Main Street Ballincollig Co Cork ☎021 487 1205 *www.ocrualaoi.com*

A philosophy based on offering top quality, traceable local meat, and great customer service from friendly and knowledgeable staff are at the heart of the O'Crualaoí Butchers success. They combine the traditional values of the family butchers with the forward looking mindset that has enabled them to develop a very successful modern shopping experience - including impressive deli counters. *Hours: Open Mon-Thu 7am-6.30pm, Fri 7am-7pm, Sat 7am-6pm. Closed Sun. Ballincollig Deli Open:Mon-Fri 8am-7pm, Sat 8am-6.30pm, Sun 10am-3pm.*

Taste a Memory Foods

Ballincollig Co Cork ✆*021 466 6000 www.tasteamemory.ie*

Anne Bradfield's evocatively named 'Taste A Memory' pies and ready meals have earned a huge fan club, thanks to the fresh local ingredients used and real homemade flavours. No additives or preservatives are used, just quality meats, vegetables and spices. In addition, these tasty meals are low in fat and low in salt, and most of them are gluten free. Available at major supermarkets and some independent food stores.

  ## Úna's Pies

4 Innishmore Industrial Estate Ballincollig Co Cork ✆*087 285 9957*

Quality - "the finest Irish ingredients and using suppliers we know and trust" - and real homemade flavour is the secret of Una Martin's success with her delicious pies. The range of products is not huge - eight pie varieties of which five are chicken (try the one with Gubbeen chorizo and red pepper), one beef (steak & Murphys, of course) and two vegetarian - but each one has a loyal following. Sold at farmers' markets and selected retail outlets in Munster.

 ## The Spinning Wheel

Ballincollig Area Griffin's Garden Centre Agharinagh Dripsey Co Cork
✆*021 733 4286 www.griffinsgardencentre.ie*

The bright and airy restaurant in Margaret Griffin's prize winning Garden Centre is famous for (at least) two things: Granny and glass. The glass allows views of the colourful gardens, but you may not get to see Granny – she's usually very busy with the baking... Local ingredients are carefully sourced and well prepared, so the simple meals served are really lovely. If you don't have time for a meal, do at least try to enjoy some of that traditional baking.

  ## Diva Boutique Bakery, Café & Deli

Main Street Ballinspittle Co Cork ✆*021 477 8465*

Whatever the time, Ballinspittle is the perfect place for a journey break to visit Shannen Keane's brilliant daytime bakery, café & deli. Everything here is down to earth real, with meat coming from local butcher, Lordans, greens from nearby Horizon Farm and free range eggs from Beechwood Farm - and, of course, all the breads and baked goods are made here in their own bakery. And they sell all sorts of other gorgeous things in the shop too... Deelish! *Open Thu-Sat: 9.30am-5pm; Sun 11am-5pm.*

BALLYCOTTON

This hilly fishing village on the Atlantic coastline 40km from Cork has a vibrant fishing fleet, fantastic views over the harbour, scenic cliff walks and rich birdlife - it is one of Europe's top bird watching sites. Attractions nearby include The Old Midleton Distillery (+353 (0) 21 461 3594, open all year, guided tours available); golfers can choose between 10 courses within a 16km radius of Ballycotton, including the Fota Island Golf Club (+353 (0) 21 4883700). Chartered deep sea angling is also easily available.

 **Bayview Hotel**

Ballycotton Co Cork ✆*021 464 6746 www.thebayviewhotel.com*

John and Carmel O'Briens' fine hotel overlooking Ballycotton Harbour enjoys a magnificent location on the sea side of the road, with a path down through its own gardens to the beach. Head chef Ciaran Scully has been at the Bayview since 1996 and his creative cooking has earned a following and at its best a visit to this fine restaurant can be memorable. The beachside Garryvoe Hotel nearby is a sister property popular for family holidays and is one of Ireland's top wedding venues. **Rooms 35**. *Restaurant* **seats 45**. *D daily, L Sun only. Closed Nov-Apr. CC.* **Directions:** *At Castlemartyr, on the N25, turn onto the R632 in the direction of Garryvoe - Shanagarry - Ballycotton.*

 The Herring Gull

The Pier Ballycotton Co Cork ✆*021 464 6768*

Talented local chef Colm Falvey operates this pleasing restaurant above the pier in Ballycotton. Seafood is of course the speciality and it is simply and carefully cooked by Colm, as is usual with this excellent chef. *Open Tue-Sun in summer, weekends only off season (D Fri & Sat, all afternoon Sun). CC.* **Directions:** *At The Inn by the Harbour.*

 Rory O'Connell Cookery School

Ballybraher Ballycotton Co Cork ✆*086 851 6917 www.rgoconnell.com*

Chef and teacher Rory O'Connell is a master in the art of beautiful, stunningly simple food, and has quietly earned a place as one of Ireland's most highly regarded chefs. He teaches at Ballymaloe Cookery School and also offers a wide range of bespoke cookery classes, catering for all levels and both groups and individuals, at his 18th century farmhouse near Shanagarry.

 Sunville House

Ballycotton Co Cork ✆*021 464 6271 www.sunvillebb.com*

Bright, spacious and welcoming, Patrick and Anna Casey's well-named B&B would be a comfortable and relaxing place to stay, with a taste of Anna's home baking to welcome you on arrival (freshly baked scones and homemade jam perhaps) and plenty of lounging space - including a a sunny conservatory and pleasant gardens to enjoy on fine days, and siting room with a log fire for chilly ones. **Rooms 6**. *CC.* **Directions:** *North-west of Ballycotton, off R629.*

  Willie Scannell

Ballytrasna Ballycotton Co Cork ✆*021 464 6924*

The growers of beautiful vegetables and fruit get too little recognition in Ireland, but the observant diner eating out around East Cork could hardly fail to notice that many of the flavoursome vegetables - and, especially, the 'Ballycotton potatoes' that give so much pleasure - are produced by Willie Scannell. A good traditional low chemical grower, he produces both early and main crop potatoes along with carrots, swedes and white turnips, summer cabbage, lettuce and parsley. Available from: local farmers' markets, local shops and direct.

Jam Cork

Hanley's of Cork Frankfield Road Ballycurreen Co Cork ☎*021 4323 018 www.jam.ie*

Offering James Mulchrone's trademark deliciously simple fresh food, the warm friendliness and casual chic of Jam works especially well here in the first Cork operation. It's a great family-friendly destination for an outing, with plenty of parking and outdoor seating for fine weather as well as the smart and comfortable café. *Open 7 days; Mon-Sat 9-5.30, Sun 12-5.30.* **Directions:** *On the Frankfield Road, near the Kinsale road roundabout in Hanley's of Cork Garden and Home Centre. [Also in Cork City at:* **Little Jam/Mam's Kitchen** *(T:021 4272 227), 38 Princes Street, Cork - shop only, no café .]*

BALLYDEHOB

Ballydehob - which, apparently, means 'where the sun always shines' - is said to be a microcosm of Irish local history, and legends and folklore certainly abound in the locality. The village is a pretty patchwork of pastel-painted buildings, and very typical of the area.

 Antonio's Ristorante & Pizzeria

Main Street Ballydehob Co Cork ☎*028 37139*

Antonio and Julie Pisani's reasonably priced and authentic Italian restaurant is an atmospheric place, complete with traditional red and white checked tablecloths and a big fireplace. Whether popping in for a quick bite or a pizza (they also do takeaway, including pizzas), or for a relaxed evening out from the full menu, this popular restaurant is a great place to know about. Open Mon-Sat, all day into evening & Sun afternoon. **Directions:** Main Street

 **Hudsons**

Main Street Ballydehob Co Cork ☎*028 37565*

The Hudsons' long established store offers a good range of organic wholefoods, home baking and carefully selected local produce; also a nice little vegetarian café. Open Mon-Sat, 9.30-6.

 Levis' Bar

Corner House Main Street Ballydehob Co Cork ☎*028 37118*

This 150-year-old bar and grocery is a characterful and delightfully friendly place, whether you are just in for a casual drink or a relaxed evening out. Opening times vary. Closed 25 Dec & Good Fri.

 Skeaghanore West Cork Duck

Skeaghanore East Ballydehob Co Cork ☎*028 37428 www.skeaghanoreduck.ie*

Since the mid 1990s Eugene and Helena Hickey's delicious Skeaghanore Duck has been delighting visitors to West Cork - hand-reared on their farm overlooking Roaring Water Bay, it has the great texture and fullness of flavour that you only find in well-fed free range poultry and is proudly featured on menus in all the area's best restaurants. Sold in selective shops in the area.

West Cork Gourmet Store

Staboll Hill Ballydehob Co Cork ✆ *028 25991*

Joanne Cassidy stocks an eclectic range of food and food/wine related items in this delightful store, and offers tempting daytime food, including cream teas. Garden. Open all day Mon-Sat, some evenings in summer.

 Ballyhoura Mountain Mushrooms

Ballyhoura Co Cork ✆ *086 810 0808* *www.ballyhouramushrooms.ie*

Lucy Deegan and Mark Cribbin's enterprising north Cork company grows a unique range of speciality mushrooms and also supplies a wide range of wild and foraged foods including plants like wild garlic, sorrel and wild strawberries in season. They offer dried mushrooms too, and an interesting range of mushroom products. *Sold at Farmers' markets: Mahon Point (Thur, 10-2) Cornmarket Street (Sat 9-3) Midleton (Sat 9-1)*

BALLYLICKEY

Midway between Bantry town and Glengarriff, Ballylickey is at the head of the stunning Bantry Bay, known for its magnificent scenery and gentle climate. The West Cork Garden Trail lists many beautiful private and public gardens, including Garinish Island which is accessible by ferry. There are also many local archaeological sites to visit, family attractions and outdoor activities including cycling, golf, angling and sailing.

 Ballylickey House

Ballylickey Bantry Bay Co Cork ✆ *027 50071* *www.ballylickeymanorhouse.com*

Built some 300 years ago by Lord Kenmare as a shooting lodge, and home to the Franco-Irish Graves family for five generations, this fine house enjoys a romantic setting overlooking Bantry Bay. Current owner Paco Graves offers bed and breakfast in both the main house and a number of cottages and chalets in the wonderful gardens. **Rooms 6**. Closed end Sept-Easter. CC. **Directions:** On N71 between Bantry & Glengarriff.

 **Seaview House Hotel**

Ballylickey Bantry Co Cork ✆ *027 50462* *www.seaviewhousehotel.com*

A warm welcome and personal supervision are the hallmarks of Kathleen O'Sullivan's restful country house hotel close to Ballylickey Bridge. Many of the rooms have sea views, and family furniture and antiques add warmth and character. With the emphasis firmly on local produce, especially seafood, country house cooking is the style in the elegant restaurant, which overlooks the garden and has views over Bantry Bay. **Rooms 25** (1 shower only). Restaurant: **Seats 50**; D daily. Hotel closed mid Nov-mid Mar. CC. **Directions:** On N71 between Bantry and Glengarriff.

Folláin Teo

Ballyvourney Industrial Estate Ballyvourney Co Cork ☎ *026 45288 www.follain.ie*

A familiar brand to two generations, Peadar and Mairin O'Lionaird's preserving company Folláin ('Wholesome') was established in 1983 and is still a family concern. The range includes some seasonal specialities and, uniquely, the blackberry jam is made with wild berries picked from the West Cork hedgerows; it's a popular way to earn a few bob while having a day out - you can join the picking team by applying through their website. Widely available.

  The Mills Inn

Ballyvourney Co Cork ☎ *026 45237 www.millsinn.ie*

One of Ireland's oldest inns, The Mills Inn is in a Gaeltacht (Irish-speaking) area and dates back to 1755. It was traditionally used to break the journey from Cork to Killarney and still makes a useful stopping place, offering all day food. A large gift shop includes artisan food and drink among many other items. ***Rooms 16*** *(some shower only). CC.* ***Directions:*** *On N22, 20 minutes from Killarney.*

  Putóg de Róiste

Putog Teoranta Unit 6 Udaras na Gaeltacht Industrial Estate Ballyvourney Co Cork ☎ *026 45680 www.deroiste.ie*

Unlike most black puddings, which are made with dried (usually imported) blood, the De Róiste and Allen families of Ballyvourney were determined that their puddings would be made in the traditional way with fresh pork - and fresh blood. You'll find them at the Toonsbridge Dairy shop (see entry), and The Real Olive Company also distributes them to independent shops in Dublin. You may spot them on menus at good restaurants too.

BALTIMORE AREA

Baltimore village has strong associations with the sea, and sailing, diving, angling and kayaking are among the most popular activities here. It's a place with a unique laid-back holiday atmosphere. For its size Baltimore offers a good choice of eating places, although the seasonal nature of west Cork means that opening times can be very variable and leases change from year to year. Just a 10-minute trip ferry from Baltimore harbour, Sherkin Island is a small island 5.5 km long and 2.5 km wide, with a population of only a hundred or so and three lovely safe beaches. There are some lovely walks in the Baltimore area, and beautiful gardens to visit, as well as golf, horseriding and much more. Nearby Skibbereen hosts a farmers' market in the Old Market Square (opposite AIB Bank) on Saturday mornings.

Bushe's Bar

The Square Baltimore Co Cork ✆ *028 20125 www.bushesbar.com*

Everyone feels at home in this famous old bar, especially visiting and local sailors. It's choc-a-bloc with genuine maritime artefacts such as charts, tide tables, ships' clocks, compasses, lanterns, pennants et al but it's the Bushe family's hospitality that makes it really special. And Marion Bushe's simple, deliciously homely bar food of course. *Bar food served daily, all day (from L on Sun). Closed 25 Dec & Good Fri. CC* **Directions:** *In the middle of Baltimore, on the square overlooking the harbour.*

Casey's of Baltimore

Baltimore Co Cork ✆ *028 20197 www.caseysofbaltimore.com*

Michael and Ann Casey's hotel just outside Baltimore enjoys dramatic views over Roaring Water Bay to the islands beyond, notably from the restaurant, and also many of the comfortable rooms. Specialising in seafood - as does the friendly and cosy old-world bar - the restaurant is well-placed for the view. **Rooms 14** *(1 shower only); self catering also offered. Restaurant* **Seats 80***: L & D daily. Closed 21-27 Dec. CC.* **Directions:** *On right entering the village (R595 from Skibbereen).*

Glebe House Gardens

Glebe Gardens Baltimore Co Cork ✆ *028 20232 www.glebegardens.com*

Jean and Peter Perry's wonderful gardens just outside Baltimore attract a growing number of visitors each year and they have a delightful café for those in need of a restorative bite; it's all very wholesome - and they generously allow you to bring your own picnic too, if preferred. Small shop; plants, preserves etc for sale. *Café open Easter-Sep. Wed-Sun all day, also D Wed-Sun in summer. Closed Mon (except bank hols) & Tue. No CC.* **Directions:** *Off Skibbereen-Baltimore road: entrance directly opposite 'Baltimore' sign as you enter the village.*

Inish Beg House Cookery School

Inish Beg Baltimore Co Cork ✆ *028 21745 www.inishbeg.com*

Paul and Georgiana Keane's beautiful island estate makes a lovely setting for interesting cookery classes, perhaps showcasing produce from their organic farm. Bespoke classes can be arranged for guests staying on the estate, including children, and groups (family gatherings, hen parties etc). Courses by guest chefs have included John Desmond of nearby Heir Island and the Kenmare chocolatier, Benoit Lorge, among others. **Directions:** *Signed off Skibbereen-Baltimore road.*

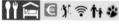

La Jolie Brise Pizza & Grill

The Square Baltimore Co Cork ✆ *028 20600 www.waterfrontbaltimore.ie*

This cheerful mainly outdoor spot is run by Youen Jacob Jnr, and is part of The Waterfront Hotel complex which neatly frames a corner of the square. Generous, handmade-made pizzas (also to take away) and pastas; well-priced local seafood and timeless favourites like char-grilled sirloin steaks: all youthful, accessible use of local ingredients. **Seats 40** *(outdoors 40). Open 8.30am-11pm daily. Closed 25 Dec. CC.* **Directions:** *The Square, Baltimore.*

Rolf's

Baltimore Co Cork ✆*028 20289 www.rolfscountryhouse.com*

The Haffner family's delightful complex - which began as a holiday hostel and is now styled 'country house' - has been extensively upgraded over 25 years. Euro-Toques chef-owner Johannes Haffner uses home-grown, organic and local produce in both the daytime café and evening restaurant; menus offer more meat than others in the area, also some classics and retro dishes. **Rooms 14** *(all shower only).* Restaurant: **Seats 60** *(outdoors, 50). B 8.30-11, L 12-2.30, D 6-9. Open all week. Closed 24-26 Dec. CC. * Self catering cottages also available.* **Directions:** *On Baltimore Hill, 10 minute walk from village.*

The Waterfront

The Square Baltimore Co Cork ✆*028 20600 www.waterfrontbaltimore.ie*

This stylish development is marked by Youen Jacob's commitment to quality - it doesn't merely fit into the square, it completes it. This new hotel has generous big rooms, style and vibrancy - and some of the long-established Chez Youen dishes are still on the menu at the first floor Lookout restaurant, overlooking the harbour, while the cheerful continental-style café La Jolie Brise Pizza & Grill (see entry) also still spills out on to the pavement alongside. **Rooms 13** *(3 shower only). Bar meals 12.30-9pm daily. Lookout Restaurant:* **Seats 80***. Seasonal; open daily from 6.30pm after Easter. Chez Youen:now used as an photograhic gallery but available for groups of 40+. Closed 24/25 Dec. CC.* **Directions:** *On the waterfront, overlooking the harbour.*

Island Cottage

Baltimore Area Heir Island Skibbereen Co Cork ✆*028 38102 www.islandcottage.com*

John Desmond and Ellmary Fenton's Island Cottage Restaurant is extraordinary by any standards. John Desmond's single-handed cooking of the freshest ingredients is that of a consummate professional and, while some may find the primacy of order – advance booking only with deposit, no credit cards, do's and don'ts – a bit off-putting, most are won over by the singular dining experience, unchanging and successful for over twenty years. **Seats 24** *(max table size 10; be prepared to share a table). Restaurant open 15 Jun-15 Sep, Wed-Sat in Jul & Aug. 8.15-11.45 pm; one sitting served at group pace. Closed Sun-Tue, and mid Sep-May (phone to check off season opening days/times). No CC. *Off season cookery courses available.* **Directions:** *Ferry from Cunnamore pier.*

The Islanders Rest

Baltimore Area Sherkin Island Skibbereen Co Cork ✆*028 20116 wwww.islandersrest.ie*

This, the island's only hotel, would make a comfortable base for a break and is understandably popular for weddings, as the island location has romantic appeal. It is quite basic but the rooms are clean and the bar offers a fair choice of dishes, including good steaks. Pleasant service by staff and owner. ***Rooms 21***. *Food daily. Check opening off season.*

BANDON

Bandon, set deep in the valley of the Argideen River is an historic town, and home to West Cork Heritage Centre (023 41677); housed in the former Christ Church in Bandon's main street, it features a unique exhibition in which visitors are transported through time to experience Bandon town in years gone by. Food and agriculture have always been important to Bandon town as products from the area such as meat, butter and corn were mainly exported through the nearby port of Kinsale and merchants imported wines, spices, sugar and tobacco. Today, the town hosts a farmers' market every Saturday, and has a growing number of restaurants, cafés and specialist food shops.

  Chapel Steps

Patrick's Place Bandon Co Cork ✆*023 885 2581 www.chapelsteps.ie*

Siobhan and Sean O'Reilly's church theme may be atmospheric, but this West Cork success story is a thoroughly modern restaurant providing warm and efficient service, focused contemporary cooking and good value. Formerly Siobhan's family's butchers shop famed for excellence, the ethos lives on through their aged Black Irish Angus Steaks and use of local produce. *Wed-Sun 10am till late CC.* **Directions:** *Patrick's Place is at the junction of Market Street and St Patricks Quay.*

 Duchess Tea Rooms

14 Bridge Street Bandon Co Cork ✆*087 418 8887 www.duchesstearooms.ie*

Sophie Atkinson-Hall's comfortably decadent tea rooms are an oasis in this busy town, where you may enjoy your tea or coffee with a tempting pastry or a well-baked scone with lashings of cream and jam. Although afternoon tea is a feature here, you may also indulge in breakfast, brunch and lunch, and there's always a great soup. *Open Mon-Sat, 10-5. Closed Sun. No CC.* **Directions:** *Just off McSwiney Quay to the south of the bridge in the centre of Bandon.*

  Kilbrogan House

Bandon Co Cork ✆*023 884 4935 www.kilbrogan.com*

This elegant three-storey Georgian townhouse, built in 1818, faces out onto Kilbrogan Hill, a quiet, mostly residential street in Bandon town. It is a lovely place to stay and siblings Catherine and David Fitzmaurice are great hosts, keen to ensure that their guests find all the best places to visit (and eat) during their stay in Bandon. ***Rooms 4***. *Closed Dec, Jan. *Self catering also available, rates on application. CC.* **Directions:** *Turn right at Methodist church, follow signs for Macroom, bear left at statue. Take 1st right 200m up hill on right.*

 **The Poachers Inn**

Clonakilty Road Bandon Co Cork 📞*023 884 1159 www.poachersinnbandon.com*

Seafood is the speciality at Barry and Catherine McLoughlin's smart blue and white painted bar and restaurant just outside Bandon. Fresh local produce is central to this kitchen and Barry's wonderfully flavourful dishes are based on freshest seafood from Castletownbere and other nearby ports; everything is cooked to order and the focus is on pleasing the customer. *Restaurant:* **Seats 50** *(outdoors, 10); D Thur-Sat (+bank hol Sun) only. Bar food served daily. Restaurant closed Sun night & Mon-Wed, house closed 25 Dec. CC.* **Directions:** *On the main West Cork road heading out of Bandon, right hand side.*

  Seymour's Fine Foods

2 Cloughmacsimon Business Park Bandon Co Cork 📞*086 330 9378 www.seymours.ie*

Best known for their delicious handmade shortbread - purists may like the plain Bandon butter shortbread best, but the cranberry & almond variety is exceptionally more-ish too. Together with Pat and Ann O'Farrell of Carrigaline Cheese, they produce a savoury range and they also make some seasonal specialities, such as shamrock shortbread for St Patrick's Day. Available in good local shops and selected speciality outlets nationwide.

   URRU Culinary Store

The Mill McSwiney Quay Bandon Co Cork 📞*023 885 4731 www.urru.ie*

People come from afar (and a stop en route to holiday in West Cork has become de rigeur) to shop at Ruth Healy's stylish, modern culinary store on the river: a kitchen shop, deli, foodstore and café, it offers a unique combination of quality products hand-picked because they're special - also great coffees and teas too, to sip with your artisan snack. And you can stock up on fresh produce, including local honey, farm milk and country garden flowers. **Seats 16.** *Open Mon-Sat 8.45am-5.30pm. Wine from shop plus €5 corkage. Closed Sun, Bank Hols, 25-28 Dec. CC.* **Directions:** *Entering Bandon from Cork, turn right at Methodist church, then immediate left. River on right, shop on left at end of quay.*

BANTRY

Delightfully situated at the head of Bantry Bay, this historic town has much to offer the visitor - notably the mid-18th century Bantry House (027 50047; www.bantryhouse.com), which is still a family home; set in lovely grounds and gardens, it houses the French Armada Museum. The Beara peninsula is to the northwest, with Sheep's Head also nearby, on the peninsula south of Bantry Bay and all have many spectacular walks. Rowing, sailing and golf are popular pastimes for visitors to the area. There are many superb gardens in the area - too many to name.

Central Fish Market

New Street Bantry Co Cork ☎*027 53714 www.thefishkitchen.ie/centralfishmarket.htm*

Colman Keohane's well stocked shop offers a large range of whitefish and shellfish both fresh and frozen, with live lobster available from a tank in-store; above it, The Fish Kitchen restaurant puts the produce to good use for hungry customers. ***Directions:*** *Bantry town centre.*

  ## Durrus Farmhouse Cheese

Coomkeen Durrus Bantry Co Cork ☎*027 61100 www.durruscheese.com*

One of the earliest of the 'new wave' of farmhouse cheesemakers, Jeffa Gill has been producing her beautiful washed-rind semi-soft cheese in her dairy in the quiet Coomkeen Valley on the Sheeps Head Peninsula since 1979. It is widely recognised as one of the great Irish cheeses, and two other varieties, Durrus Óg and Dunmanus are now produced. Widely available and may be purchased, by arrangement, at the farm where cheesemaking may also be observed through a viewing panel. *Open 'nearly every day', 9am to 3pm, but please call ahead.* ***Directions:*** *A little north-west of Durrus, off the minor road between Durrus and Bantry.*

 ## Fish Kitchen

New Street Bantry Co Cork ☎*027 56651 www.thefishkitchen.ie*

This agreeable little restaurant is above the Central Fish Market - and the location is no coincidence, as Colman Keohane and Anne Marie Murphy, owners of the fish shop and restaurant respectively, are siblings. Much of the simply cooked fish and seafood comes from Bantry Bay, and the real story at The Fish Kitchen is told o n the blackboard daily special's list. ***Seats 28***. *Open Tue-Sat (& Mon Jul/Aug), 12-9pm. Closed Sun (except Bank Hols), Mon (except Jul & Aug). Open all year. CC.* ***Directions:*** *Town centre – above the Central Fish Market.*

  ## Fruit Hill Farm

Trawlebawn Bantry Co Cork ☎*027 50710 www.fruithillfarm.com*

Manfred Wandel's online organic and environmentally friendly garden supply shop is not only a favourite port of call for organic gardeners nationwide, but also a useful source of quality products for all gardeners. Seed potatoes offered include the red maincrop variety Axona, with natural blight resistance and the floury texture that is generally preferred by Irish gardeners (and cooks). Online shop - personal visits by appointment only.

  ## Mannings Emporium

Ballylickey Bantry Co Cork ☎*027 50456 www.manningsemporium.ie*

A supporter of local West Cork artisan produce for many years, Val Manning is rightly credited with playing an important part in making the Irish food revolution happen and has recently been joined in the mission by his equally enthusiastic niece, Laura Manning, and her husband Andrew Heath. Once a classic country post office and shop, this famous roadside gourmet food store, deli and and café is now an Aladdin's cave of good things - and not a place to pass by. *Open Mon-Sat 9-6.30, Sun 9-5. Online shop (hampers).* ***Directions:*** *On N71 at Ballylickey.*

 **Maritime Hotel**

The Quay Bantry Co Cork ☎*027 54700 www.themaritime.ie*

Smart and contemporary, this almost waterside hotel is welcoming and colourful with some funky features and a linear design following the shoreline that allows most areas to take advantage of the view. Menus at the Ocean restaurant are international in style but feature locally sourced foods, including Bantry lamb and the famous Bantry Bay mussels. **Rooms 110**. *Restaurant* **seats 90**. *L&D daily. Closed 1 wk Christmas. CC.* **Directions:** *Below Bantry House on the quay.*

 **O'Connor's Seafood Restaurant**

The Square Bantry Co Cork ☎*027 55664 www.oconnorsbantry.com*

Sporting elegant model yachts in the front window, this long-established seafood restaurant has a welcoming interior mingling chic décor with maritime artefacts. The owner, former head chef Patrick Kiely, now heads the courteous service team. Seafood sourced mainly from West Cork and Kerry stars on menus offering both Irish and internationally inspired dishes; the renowned Bantry Bay mussels, cooked several ways, are a speciality. **Seats 50**. *L&D daily. Closed L Bank hols, Good Fri, 25 Dec, 2 weeks Jan, Sun Oct-May, but call to confirm opening times off-season. CC.* **Directions:** *Town centre; prominent location on square.*

 Organico Cafe Shop Bakery

2 Glengarriff Road Bantry Co Cork ☎*027 51391 www.organico.ie*

Sisters Hannah and Rachel Dare run this bakery, food shop and vegetarian café near the centre of town. Spelt loaves are a particular speciality at the bakery, which produces a delicious range of breads, cakes, pizza etc, which are also offered at the café, where Rachel, a Ballymaloe-trained cook, is the force behind the menu. **Seats 50**; *Open Mon-Sat, 9.30-5.30pm. L 12-3.30pm. Closed Sun, Bank Hols, 24 Dec - 15 Jan. CC.* **Directions:** *On road from Main Square to Glengarriff, 3 mins walk from tourist office.*

  Rory Conner Knives

Ballylickey Bantry Co Cork ☎*027 50032 www.roryconnerknives.com*

Bespoke knives and associated services from a master craftsman: West Cork cutler Rory Conner is one of Ireland's most sought-after manufacturers of specialist hand made knives for numerous purposes. He crafts beautiful domestic knives - table cutlery, kitchen knives, carving sets, cheese knives - and also special tools for activities ranging from hunting, fishing and sailing to gardening and hand crafts. A superb resource for anyone with special requirements, and a wonderful, long lasting gift.

  The Snug

The Quay Bantry Co Cork ☎*027 50057 www.thesnugbantry.com*

Maurice and Colette O'Donovans' well-named bar in Bantry is a cosy and welcoming place, bustling with life and ideal for a wholesome bite at moderate prices. Maurice is the chef and takes pride in using local produce and giving value for money; his menus feature a wide range of popular dishes - including Bantry Bay mussels, of course. *Food served daily, 11am-9pm (Sun 12.30-9). Closed 25 Dec & Good Fri. CC.* **Directions:** *Beside Garda Station, on the quay as you enter Bantry.*

The Stuffed Olive

New Street Bantry Co Cork ✆*027 55883*

Welcoming aromas of coffee introduce the customer to a cornucopia of fine fare: excellent coffee, cakes and a range of smoothies, filled baguettes and salads from the blackboard menu. Patricia Messom & Margi Kelly's delightful little shop/deli is crammed with specialist foods and wines, with a few stools by the window for on-site eaters. *Open Mon-Fri from 9am. Open all year. Closed Sun. No CC. **Directions:** Opposite SuperValu.*

The Tea Room

Bantry House & Garden Bantry Co Cork ✆*027 50047 www.bantryhouse.com*

Whether as destination, or for refreshment when visiting the the house and garden at the Shelswell-White family's 18th century mansion overlooking Bantry Bay, (both open to the public), a visit to their Tea Room is highly recommended. Once you have seen the mouthwatering food laid out for display you will be very glad you chose to come here - and the elegant surroundings and wooded walks are a bonus. ***Seats 110**. Food daily 10am-5.30pm. Set lunches can also be booked for groups of up to 35. Shop. Closed Nov-Feb. CC. **Directions:** Main car park located off N71 on the way into Bantry Town.*

The Westlodge Hotel

Bantry Co Cork ✆*027 50360 www.westlodgehotel.ie*

This hotel's USP is its weather proofed offering for successful family holidays. A wide range of outdoor activities can be organised, and - this is its greatest strength - there's also a good leisure centre to keep energetic youngsters happy if the weather should disappoint. Although quite dated, bedrooms have been fairly recently refurbished (book a front one if possible) and the staff are friendly and helpful. ***Rooms 90**. Closed 21-28 Dec. CC. **Directions:** N71 to Bandon, R586 from Bandon.*

BEARA PENINSULA

The scenic Beara Penninsula has a very away from it all atmosphere and makes a great destination if even for a day out with, perhaps, a stop in Castletownbere (see entry). There is a farmers market in Castletownbere on the first Thursday of each month.

Milleens

Eyeries Beara Co Cork ✆*027 74079*

Here on their farm in a remote and beautiful location, Norman, Veronica and Quinlan Steele produce the iconic Milleens cheese – the first of the new wave of Irish farmhouse cheeses, which they first introduced to the market in 1978. Very much a product of its area it is made with pasteurised whole milk and has a complex creamy flavour reminiscent of both the farmyard and the herby fields. It is made in traditional rounds (1.2kg) and now also in an innovative doughnut shape and miniature cheeses - known as Milleens 'O' (1kg), and the Milleens Dote (200g); usually sold between 4 and 12 weeks old. Well distributed.

Mossies at Ulusker House

Beara Area Trafrask Adrigole Beara Co Cork ✆ *027 60606 www.mossiesrestaurant.com*

Mossies is situated in lovely gardens just outside the village of Ardrigole and, having been lovingly restored by former owners David and Lorna Ramshaw, this old house now makes a wonderful place to stay. It came into new ownership in 2013 but David and Laura live nearby and Lorna remains involved with Mossies. **Rooms 4** *(all shower only); No CC.* **Directions:** *Well signed on Glengarriff to Castletownbere road.*

BLARNEY

Blarney, 5 miles (8km) north of Cork city, is world famous for its castle and the Blarney Stone, with its traditional power of conferring eloquence on those who kiss it... Although it attracts a lot of tourists, its convenience to the city also also make it a good base for business visitors.

Ashlee Lodge

Tower Blarney Co Cork ✆ *021 438 5346 www.ashleelodge.com*

Anne and John O'Leary's luxurious purpose-built guesthouse is just a couple of miles outside Blarney and handy to Cork city and many golf courses. Everything is immaculate, the spacious hotel standard bedrooms are exceptionally comfortable, breakfast is impressive - but the most outstanding feature is the O'Learys themselves, who are exceptionally helpful hosts and keen to share their local knowledge. **Rooms 10** *(1 shower only). D by arrangement only. Closed 20 Dec - 31 Jan. CC.* **Directions:** *Located on R 617 Blarney-Killarney road.*

Blairs Inn

Cloghroe Blarney Co Cork ✆ *021 438 1470 www.blairsinn.ie*

In a quiet, wooded setting near Blarney, this pretty riverside pub is run by John and Anne Blair and their sons Duncan and Richie, a warmly hospitable family who take real pride in welcoming visitors. Skilfully cooked meals feature local Cork and Kerry produce, notably local Angus beef and seafood, in wholesome dishes, and an impressive range of craft beers and ciders is offered. **Seats 45** *(restaurant/bar) & 100 in garden. Bar menu daily. Restaurant L&D. Closed 25 Dec & Good Fri. CC.* **Directions:** *5 minutes from Blarney village, on the R579.*

Blarney Castle Hotel

Village Green Blarney Co Cork ✆ *021 438 5116 www.blarneycastlehotel.com*

Offering a lovely combination of old and new, the Forrest family's attractive hotel dates back to 1837 and overlooks the village green in the centre of Blarney, beside the castle. The heart of the hotel is the original Victorian bar, which is full of character, the spacious, bright bedrooms have pleasing views, and staff are very hospitable. **Rooms 13** *(1 shower only). Restaurant D and bar meals daily. Closed 24-25 Dec. CC.* **Directions:** *Centre of Blarney, on village green (next to Blarney castle entrance).*

Muskerry Arms

Blarney Co Cork ✆ *021 438 5200 www.muskerryarms.com*

Those who enjoy a small and lively establishment may like the Muskerry Arms which is a traditional pub and guesthouse, offering clean, inexpensive accommodation and warm hospitality, with live music in the bar each evening. **Rooms 11** *(all shower only). Bar meals daily 8am-9pm,*

BUTLERSTOWN

Butlerstown is a pretty pastel-painted village, with lovely views across farmland to Dunworley and the sea beyond. Nearby Clonakilty hosts a farmers market on Thursdays (mostly food) and Saturdays (both food and crafts), 10am - 2pm, while in Clonakilty a visit to Lisselan Gardens (023 33249) is a must.

  O'Neill's

Butlerstown Bandon Co Cork ✆*023 884 0228*

Dermot and Mary O'Neill's unspoilt pub is as pleasant and hospitable a place as could be found to enjoy the view and admire the traditional mahogany bar and pictures. The anchor from the S.S. Cardiff Hall is displayed outside and it is a popular stopping off point for the "Seven Heads Millennium Coastal Walk", with children (and well-behaved pets) welcome. *Closed 25 Dec & Good Fri. No CC.* **Directions:** *On the Courtmacsherry - Clonakilty coast road.*

  Carrigaline Court Hotel & Leisure Centre

Main Street Carrigaline Co Cork ✆*021 485 2100 www.carrigcourt.com*

This conveniently-located modern hotel is very much at the heart of the local community, and is known for hands-on management and attentive staff. Bedrooms are comfortable and well equipped for business guests. The pleasing Collins Bar features big screens for matches and traditional Irish music sessions (Monday nights, local players). **Rooms 88**. *Closed 22-26 Dec. CC.* **Directions:** *Follow South Link Road and then follow signs for Carrigaline.*

  Carrigaline Farmhouse Cheese

The Rock Carrigaline Co Cork ✆*021 437 2856 www.carrigalinecheese.com*

Produced at their farm southwest of Cork city, Ann and Pat O'Farrell's versatile semi-soft Carrigaline Farmhouse Cheese is handmade in three flavours (natural, garlic & herbs and smoked) and widely available.The milk from their pasture-fed Friesian cows is pasteurised on site, and the cheese is made with vegetarian rennet without the use of any artificial preservatives or additives. Available in major supermarkets and many speciality food stores.

  Delicious

Unit 6 Carrigaline Industrial Park Carrigaline Co Cork ✆*021 491 9583 www.delicious.ie*

Working on the philosophy that "Being on a restrictive diet should not mean a restricted food experience", Denise & Michael O'Callaghan's well-named artisan bakery produces many of the treats normally out of bounds for coeliacs, including gluten free versions of special occasion cakes and the traditional Christmas fare (Christmas cake, pudding and mince pies). Widely available in good grocers and supermarkets, and also from their online shop.

  Glenwood House

Ballinrea Road Carrigaline Co Cork ✆*021 437 3878 www.glenwoodguesthouse.com*

Very conveniently located for Cork Airport and the ferry terminal, Adrian Sheedy's purpose-built guesthouse offers hotel standard accommodation with a homely atmosphere - an open fire to relax beside on chilly evenings, and gardens to enjoy in fine weather. A good breakfast includes home-made breads and preserves. *Rooms 15 (5 shower only). Breakfast 7-10. Closed mid Dec-mid Jan. CC. Directions: Entering Carrigaline from Cork, turn right at Ballinrea roundabout, 150m on the left.*

  ## The Good Fish Company

Carrigaline Industrial Estate Crosshaven Road Carrigaline Co Cork
☎021 437 3917 www.goodfish.ie

Denis Good has been processing and wholesaling seafood in Carrigaline for many years. This modern outlet offers a wide range of fresh whitefish and shellfish products with live lobster and crab available from a tank in-store. Also at: Ballincollig, Cork, Douglas and Kinsale.

 ## Ó'Crualaoí Butchers & Delicatessen

Main Street Carrigaline Co Cork ☎021 437 6716 www.ocrualaoi.com

Founded in Ballincollig in 1957, O'Crualaoi Butchers has since spread its wings to places such as Fermoy, Wilton and Carrigaline. The Carrigaline branch is much more than a butchers shop. It is a state-of-the-art 'food retail hub' comprising a butchers counter, an excellent deli counter and a popular café serving excellent food at very competitive prices. Seating is quite basic, but there's also an outdoor area with a large play-house. *Open: Mon-Fri 8am-7pm, Sat 8am-6.30pm, Sun 10am-5pm.*

  ## Roberts Cove Inn

Carrigaline area Roberts Cove Minane Bridge Nr Carrigaline Co Cork
☎021 488 7100 www.robertscoveinn.com

Scenically located in a bay with views of the famous Daunt Rock beacon, Roberts Cove Inn is built on the site of an old mill. Owned since 1988 by Denis Quinn, this warm and friendly place has character – and a well-earned reputation for atmosphere and good food, in both the bar and restaurant. *Seats 80 (outdoors, 14); L Mon-Sat; D daily 6-10pm. Bar food served all day Sun & Bank Hols. Open all year. CC. Directions: From Carrigaline take R611 Kinsale road, left at Ballyfeard for Minane Bridge, follow signs to Roberts Cove.*

  ## Ardsallagh Goats Products

Woodstock Carrigtwohill Co Cork ☎021 488 2336 www.ardsallaghgoats.com

The Murphy family have run Ardsallagh Goats Farm since 1996 - beginning with one goat to provide milk for the children, who suffered from eczema, it is now the largest producer of goat's milk in Ireland.They produce goat's milk and yogurt from a mixed herd on their own farm, and an excellent range of cheeses that is made with their own and extra milk, bought in from neighbouring farms. Available from supermarkets and independent stores nationwide.

  ## Bramley Lodge

Tullagreine Carrigtwohill Co Cork ☎021 488 2499 www.bramleylodge.ie

On the junction to Cobh just off the N25, Bramley Lodge is well located - but Gillian Kearney's restaurant-cum-food store has more going for her than location: the food is top notch and well priced. There's proper food for children, a large outdoor seating area and the menu changes daily so that too helps draw the regulars back time after time.The foodstore offers many of the foods produced for the cafe and other classy food items, many of them sourced from local suppliers. *Mon-Thu 8-7, Fri & Sat 8-9, Sun 9-7.*

The Café @ Ballyseedy

Ballyseedy Garden Centre Fota Retail Park Carrigtwohill Co Cork
☎ *021 247 696 www.ballyseedy.ie*

With outdoor seating on a patio area that mingles into the colourful plants displayed for sale, this cheerful café is set amidst the lifestyle section of an impressive East Cork garden centre. Everything is home made and delicious: using the best of fresh seasonal food is the philosophy, with lots of tempting deli and café fare to choose from. Mon-Sat: 9am-6pm; Sun & Bank Hols: 10am-6pm. CC. **Directions:** N25 Cork-Youghal road, before Midleton, take the Fota Island turn off; left at roundabout, signed Fota Retail Park.

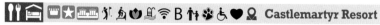 **Castlemartyr Resort**

Castlemartyr Co Cork ☎ *021 421 9000 www.castlemartyrresort.ie*

 Built around a 17th century manor house and the ruins of an adjacent castle that belonged to the Knights Templar and dates back to 1210, this is an impressive property by any standards. Accommodation is predictably luxurious, as are amenities that include a stunning leisure centre and spa. But other equally impressive high points of a stay here include delicious, mainly local food (choice of dining options from casual to fine dining) and, above all, the genuine hospitality of a mainly Irish team under the management of Andrew Phelan (formerly of Mount Juliet). **Rooms 103**. *Self catering also available. Restaurants: Bell Tower (fine dining)* **Seats 50**; *D Tue-Sat. Knight's Bar, à la carte daily, 12-9.30. Golf Clubhouse (informal): daily in summer, 7.30-9.30. Hotel closed Sun-Thu Nov-Apr & 20-27 Dec. CC.* **Directions:** *On main N25 from Cork between Midleton and Youghal.*

 Pat Shortt's Bar

Castlemartyr Co Cork ☎ *021 462 3230 www.patshorttsbar.com*

Owned by the popular entertainer Pat Shortt, this great old bar on the main street of Castlemartyr is full of traditional Irish pub character with an open fire and friendly staff. Ballymaloe trained musician-turned-chef, Mike Hanrahan, makes sure there's always plenty of wholesome fresh local food to tempt customers - and there's plenty of good music to be enjoyed at the weekends too. Food: Mon-Thu 12-5, Fri-Sat 12-8, Sun 12.30-5.

CASTLETOWNBERE

Although parts of it could be described as a "place that time forgot", there is some regeneration in the fishing port of Castletownbere and it is a natural place to take a break when exploring the Beara peninsula. South-west of the town, the partially completed development that was to have become the 5* Capella Dunboy Castle Hotel is a curiosity, on the 40-acre waterside site of the original castle. Berehaven is a safe anchorage for yachts and is ideal for watersports, from sea angling to windsurfing. The area is also ideal for land-based outdoor activities with golfing, hiking, biking and hill walking all available nearby.

MacCarthy's

The Square Castletownbere Co Cork ☎ *027 70014*

Dating back to the 1870s, Adrienne MacCarthy's famous old pub and grocery store really is the genuine article. Atmosphere and live traditional music are the most obvious attractions, but the grocery is real and provisions the local fishing boats. You can also get a very good, simple bite to eat here - a superb freshly-made crab sandwich perhaps, bulging with spanking fresh crabmeat, and a big pot of tea - for amazingly little. One to savour. Simple bar food is available. *Mon-Sat, 10.30am-6pm. Closed 25 Dec & Good Fri. No CC.* **Directions:** *In town square.*

Taste

Unit 1 Bank Place Castletownbere Co Cork ☎ *027 71943*

In a scenic area without many places to stop for a bite, Sheila Power's lovely shop meets visitors' needs perfectly, offering delicious artisan deli and picnic fare among a wide range of carefully selected foods, and wines. Sandwiches and wraps are made ready to go - although not a café, there are a few seats outside the shop where you can sit on a fine day. *Open Mon-Sat.*

Irish Atlantic Sea Salt

Castletownbere Area Lickbarrahan Cahermore Beara Co Cork
☎ *027 73222 www.irishatlanticsalt.ie*

Michael and Aileen O'Neill established Irish Atlantic Sea Salt in 2009. The first natural sea salt to be commercially produced in Ireland, it has unique characteristics due to the purity and high salinity of the Atlantic seawater on the remote Beara Peninsula. Saltier than other similar products and with a genuine sea-fresh flavour, very little is needed as it tastes so pure. On sale in speciality food shops and from some supermarkets and independent stores.

CASTLETOWNSHEND

A uniquely charming fishing village with an unusual number of 18th century stone built houses and the impressive Townshend Castle (+353 (0) 283 6100). The castle was built between 1650 and 1750, on its own grounds on the water's edge of Castlehaven Harbour. Activities include walking, golf, horse riding, fishing, sailing, tennis, cycling and canoeing.

Mary Ann's Bar & Restaurant

Castletownshend Skibbereen Co Cork ☎ *028 36146*

Dating back to 1846, this famous pub has been in the energetic and hospitable ownership of Fergus and Patricia O'Mahony since 1988; they have loved it and maintained it well - and have built up a great reputation for food in both the bar and the restaurant. Seafood is the star, of course, with house specialities including a magnificent Platter of Castlehaven Bay Shellfish and Seafood and lovely home-baked brown bread. *Restaurant* **Seats 30** *(outside, 100). L&D daily in summer. Bar food daily. Closed Mon Nov-Mar, 25 Dec, Good Fri & 3 weeks Jan. CC.* **Directions:** *8km from Skibbereen, on lower main street.*

Woodcock Smokery

Gortbrack Castletownshend Skibbereen Co Cork ☎ *028 36232 www.woodcocksmokery.com*

Ireland has many excellent smokehouses, and some outstanding ones, but few would disagree that the benchmark has been set by Sally Barnes whose iconic Woodcock Smokery dates back to 1981. Uncompromising regarding the quality of her raw material, her traditionally smoked range of 'Wild and Sustainable Fish Products', notably smoked salmon, has earned every conceivable accolade. Woodcock Smokery products are available from selected outlets throughout Ireland, especially in Co Cork; also mail order.

    ## Clonmore Goats Cheese

Clonmore Newtownshandrum Charleville Co Cork ✆ *063 70490*

Tom and Lena Biggane's highly regarded hard gouda-style goats cheese, Clonmore, was developed from recipes passed on to them by a Dutch neighbour. It is made only from the heat-treated milk of their own herd of 'spoilt' goats, who have access to unusually lush pasture. A small quantity of a hard, mild cows' milk cheese, Shandrum, is also made. Available locally and also sold by some speciality suppliers, including Sheridans.

CLONAKILTY

Clonakilty is a quaint town of narrow streets, brightly coloured houses and hanging baskets. For visitors to the area there are several safe beaches nearby, walks in the countryside and local attractions such as The West Cork Model Railway Village, Lisselan Estate Gardens (023 33249) and Lios-na-gCon Ringfort. Clonakilty hosts a farmers' market on Thursdays (mostly food) and Saturdays (both food and crafts), 10am - 2pm. The product that Clonakilty is most famous for today is black pudding (see entry for Edward Twomey). You will, of course, find local black pudding on every breakfast menu in the area.

    ## An Sugan

41 Wolfe Tone Street Clonakilty Co Cork ✆ *023 883 3498* *www.ansugan.com*

The O'Crowley family has owned this characterful bar and restaurant since 1979: it has always been a friendly, well-run place and, although it can be very busy at times, their reputation for good food is generally well-deserved. Local food, especially seafood, is the focus and menus include some excellent sharing plates offering a range of seafood; artisan meats; and cheeses. Charming accommodation of a very high standard is also offered, and a new Wine Bar, Aris, is nearby in Asna Square. **Seats 42**; *Food 12-9.30 daily.* **Rooms 7** *(all shower only).* *Closed 25/26 Dec & Good Fri. CC.* **Directions:** *From Cork, on the left hand side as you enter Clonakilty.*

 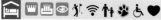   ## Dunmore House Hotel

Muckross Clonakilty Co Cork ✆ *023 883 3352* *www.dunmorehousehotel.ie*

 The magnificent coastal location of the O'Donovan family's immaculately maintained hotel has been used to advantage to provide sea views for all bedrooms and to allow guests access to their own stretch of foreshore. Hands-on owner-management, appealing public areas, well-appointed bedrooms - and, most of all, the professional, friendly staff make this an exceptionally pleasing hotel. **Rooms 29** *(6 shower only).* *Closed Christmas; 15 Jan-8 Mar. CC.* **Directions:** *4 km from Clonakilty town, well signed.*

Edward Twomey

16 Pearse Street Clonakilty Co Cork ✆*023 883 4835 www.clonakiltyblackpudding.ie*

Thanks to that great butcher, the late Eddie Twomey, Clonakilty is known internationally for the deliciously grainy black pudding that he made to an old recipe. Since Edward's untimely death in 2005, Colette Twomey has taken up the reins with great enthusiasm and business acumen, having moved the production to a new level, without sacrificing the essential quality and character of the original handmade product. They do everything else well here too, offering a full range of fresh meats and meat products, all of a very high standard. *Open Mon-Sat, 9-6.* **Directions:** *Town centre.*

 Fernhill House Hotel & Gardens

Clonakilty Co Cork ✆*023 883 3258 www.fernhillhousehotel.com*

The house at the heart of this family-run hotel dates back 200 years and it has been an hotel since the 1950s which probably explains the easy hospitality which is its greatest asset. Popular for weekend weddings and midweek business guests, it's a pleasant, comfortable hotel set in gardens, and you can be sure of a good breakfast. But, pleasing as the hotel and its surroundings are, its USP is the friendly and efficient staff whose genuine warmth makes people want to return. **Rooms 27**. CC

 Harts Coffee Shop

8 Ashe Street Clonakilty Co Cork ✆*023 883 5583*

 For over a decade, good home cooking has been the attraction at Aileen Hart and Tony O'Mahoney's friendly coffee shop, and the consistently high standard they have maintained over that time has regulars making a beeline for this welcoming spot as soon as they hit town. A nifty little menu offers all kinds of deliciously healthy meals, ranging from breakfast and lunch specials (if you're lucky the special might be Ummera smoked chicken Caesar) to gorgeous cakes and home-baked scones just like your granny used to make, served with cream.... **Seats 30**; Open Mon-Sat, 9.30-5. Closed Sun, 3 weeks Christmas. No CC. **Directions:** Clonakilty town centre.

 **Inchydoney Island Lodge & Spa**

Inchydoney Island Clonakilty Co Cork ✆*023 883 3143 www.inchydoneyisland.com*

One of Ireland's first seawater spa destinations, this famous hotel enjoys views over Inchydoney's two 'Blue Flag' beaches - which bring crowds to the area in summer. Special breaks are a major attraction - fishing, equestrian, golf, therapies and, more recently, kayaking - and the hotel has introduced some imaginative initiatives for families. Several dining options are offered, withe the 7-course tasting menu A Taste of West Cork a nightly feature in the Gulfstream Restaurant. **Rooms 67**. Restaurant **seats 70** (outdoors, 30); D daily; L Sun only. Informal/ bar meals 11-9 daily. Closed Christmas. CC. **Directions:** N71 from Cork to Clonakilty, then causeway to Inchydoney.

The Malthouse Granary

30 Ashe Street Clonakilty Co Cork ✆*023 883 4355 www.malthousegranary.ie*

Originally built in 1772 as part of an adjoining brewery, Irene Collins' smartly presented restaurant in the heart of Clonakilty town has lost none of its character and charm. Together with local artwork (for sale), original features create an atmospheric setting for Irene's good cooking. Menus mainly showcase the area's best seasonal produce, although imports like the ubiquitous tiger prawn may make an appearance too. **Seats 50**. *D daily in summer. Closed Sun & Mon off season. CC.* **Directions:** *Town centre, on main street.*

 Mella's Fudge

Lisavaird Co-Op Clonakilty Co Cork ✆*086 159 5949 www.mellasfudge.com*

Mella McAuley started making her real butter fudge and selling it to local shops when she was only a schoolgirl - fast forward about 15 years and it's still made the same way and has been winning accolades a-plenty. The four flavours include classic vanilla of course, also rum & raisin, walnut, and chocolate. Everyone has their favourite, but the starring role in every bar goes to West Cork butter. Sells in speciality shops in Ireland, also some in the UK, including Selfridge's.

 O'Keeffe's of Clonakilty

Emmet Square Clonakilty Co Cork ✆*023 883 3394 www.emmethotel.com*

Known for Marie O'Keeffe's terrific cooking, this popular weekend bistro is hidden away in the centre of Clonakilty, on a lovely serene Georgian square - a most attractive location. O'Keeffe's has direct access from the Emmet Hotel (www.emmethotelcom) and bookings are made through the hotel. Marie's creative modern cooking has a loyal following, and seafood tends to take the starring role. **Seats 50** *(outdoors, 40); D usually Sat only. Bar L daily, in Emmet Hotel. Restaurant closed Sun-Fri. 25 Dec. CC.* **Directions:** *In the centre of Clonakilty - turn left into Emmet Square at the Catholic Church.*

 Quality Hotel & Leisure Club Clonakilty

Clogheen Clonakilty Co Cork ✆*023 883 6400 www.qualityclonakiltyhotel.com*

This exceptionally family-friendly hotel on the edge of Clonakilty town is an ideal place to holiday with kids, and a former winner of our Family Friendly Hotel Award. As well as large family and interconnecting rooms, there are 20 two-bedroom suites and five holiday homes. Fantastic on-site facilities have always been a big attraction here and they continue to improve - fun for kids and relaxing for parents. **Rooms 96**. *Closed 25/26 Dec. CC.* **Directions:** *N71 to Clonakilty from Cork.*

  Richy's Restaurant & The R Café

Wolfe Tone Street Clonakilty Co Cork ✆*023 882 1852 www.richysbarandbistro.com*

Richy Virahsawmy's centrally located restaurant and its cool daytime sister, the R Café, are the kind of relaxed places that attract a real cross-section of people. The broadly Mediterranean food style has a leaning towards Spain - and proudly features locally sourced ingredients that often include less usual foods, like samphire. Superb thin-based pizzas and foccacia breads are a speciiality since the recent acquisition of a pizza oven. **Seats 80** *(outdoors, 16). Open daily 9am-late for B,L&D. Closed 25 Dec. CC.* **Directions:** *Next to tourist office.*

Scallys SuperValu

Fax Bridge Cork Road Clonakilty Co Cork ✆*023 883 3088 www.supervaluclon.ie*

Scallys is one of Ireland's best-known family-run supermarkets. There's a strong focus on regional speciality foods, including a great range of fresh fish and shellfish landed by West Cork fishermen.

 **Deasy's Harbour Bar & Seafood Restaurant**

Clonakilty Area Ring Village Clonakilty Co Cork ✆*023 883 5741*

Just across the road from the water in the pretty village of Ring, this friendly traditional pub has a decking area and views of Clonakilty Bay and the boats moored nearby. Renowned for its atmosphere and chef Caitlin Ruth's great seafood cooking, this has become a popular spot so book well ahead, especially in high season. *Seats 50; D Wed-Sat. L Sun only ('light L' Sat). Closed Sun D, Mon, Tue and 24-26 Dec. CC. **Directions:** At Ring, 2km outside Clonakilty.*

COBH

Seated on the historical island of Barrymore, Cobh is built on a hill so the town is shaped in an appealing pyramid style, with the town houses rising on top of one another, with great views of the harbour and the surrounding hills. Cobh's extensive maritime history is exhibited in the Cobh Museum (+353 (0) 21 481 4240), open April to October it is in a former Scots Presbyterian church on the main road into Cobh from Cork. At the Cobh Heritage Centre (+353 (0)21 481 3591), The Queenstown Story tells the history of emigration from the port - which is now an important port of call for cruise liners - and The Titanic Experience (+353 (0)21 481 4412) is housed in the original White Star Line offices. The Sirius Arts Centre (+353 (0) 21 481 3790), founded in 1988 includes galleries and exhibitions by local artists and the artist in residence.

 Belvelly Smokehouse

Belvelly Cobh Co Cork ✆*021 481 1089 www.frankhederman.com*

This is Ireland's oldest smokery and Frank Hederman's produce is internationally renowned. Although most famous for his smoked salmon, which has won acclaim from many top chefs, the product range includes smoked mackerel (whole and in fillets, also offered with various dressings); smoked mussels in oil of vinaigrette; and baked salmon. *Sold at markets, notably Midleton Farmers' Market (Sat, 9-1) and the English Market in Cork city; also available by mail order and from the smokehouse shop (phone for opening hours). **Directions:** Well signed on the main Cobh road.*

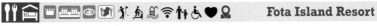 **Fota Island Resort**

Fota Island Cobh Co Cork ✆*021 488 3700 www.fotaisland.ie*

Accommodation is luxurious at this beautifully located resort, with panoramic views over woodlands or golf course - and the kitchen showcases wonderful Irish ingredients. The Fota Spa is a big attraction, and the resort offers many activities in addition to the three championship golf courses. Children are made very welcome, with a dedicated kids programme offered in school holidays. *Rooms 131. Fota Restaurant: Seats 80 (outdoors, 30). D daily; Bar food daily 12-8pm. Hotel closed 25-26 Dec. CC. **Directions:** N25 east from Cork 8km then take a left and follow signs for Fota Island.*

Gilberts Restaurant & Townhouse

11 Pearse Square Cobh Co Cork ✆*021 481 1300 www.gilbertsincobh.com*

Named after the laneway that links Pearse Square with nearby Casement Square, the Bird and Daly families' restaurant with rooms in a corner property has the name writ large on the gable end. Inside, the layout is unusual and overnight guests need to present themselves at the restaurant on arrival; there is no lift but, once comfortably installed, the rooms are spacious, smartly decorated, and thoughtfully furnished (back rooms are quieter at weekends). Long restaurant opening hours entail offering a wide range of menus; the tone is generally modern, but old favourites like steak and oyster pie feature too, and there may be special 'Titanic' dinner menus on some evenings. *Restaurant open daily Easter to end Oct, all day from 9am-late (Sun from 11am).* **Rooms 4** *(all shower only; one self catering suite). CC. Rest closed Sun & Mon off season.* **Directions:** *At the top of Pearse Square.*

  Knockeven House

Rushbrooke Cobh Co Cork ✆*021 481 1778 www.knockevenhouse.com*

John and Pam Mulhaire's large and peacefully situated 1840s house is an exceptionally comfortable place to stay, offering guests the best of every world: lavish decor and facilities worthy of a top-class hotel, along with great hospitality, and reasonable prices. And Pam is a natural hostess who enjoys treating her guests to delicious breakfasts, and snacks at any time. **Rooms 4.** *Closed 15-26 Dec. CC.* **Directions:** *Signed, on the outskirts of Cobh.*

 WatersEdge Hotel

Yacht Club Quay Cobh Co Cork ✆*021 481 5566 www.watersedgehotel.ie*

The name says it all at this attractive hotel, which is neatly slotted between the road and the harbour, taking full advantage of its unique waterside setting. Most of the spacious bedrooms have a sea view and some have French windows opening onto a verandah. It's just a couple of minutes walk from the train station (and Heritage Centre) and special rates are available to guests using local amenities. **Rooms 19.** *(Special offers listed on website.)*

 Radisson Blu Hotel Cork Airport

Cork Airport Cork ✆*021 494 7500*

This stylish modern hotel is very handily located, close to the terminal. Ideal for a first or last night's stay, it's also a useful meeting place. Although well equipped for business guests it attracts a short break market too. **Rooms 81.** *CC.* **Directions:** *Off Cork-Kinsale road; situated within airport complex.*

CROOKHAVEN

The small village of Crookhaven is almost at the end of Mizen Head, tucked snugly on the sheltered side of a narrow neck of land which creates a deep inlet - the 'crooked haven' which may have given the little settlement its name. Known for the excellent sandy beaches at nearby Barleycove and a laid-back holiday atmosphere, this away-from-it-all village somehow offers not just one but a choice of good pubs and eating places that open each summer for the families on holiday locally, and the many visitors who make a point of exploring the peninsula.

  ## The Crookhaven Inn

Crookhaven Skibbereen Co Cork *028 35309 www.thecrookhaveninn.com*

Emma and Freddy Olsson run this popular pub cum restaurant and chef Freddy is serious about his food. The evening menu of a couple of soups and about a dozen main courses is supplemented by daily blackboard specials, emphasising the ready availability of locally caught fish and seafood. For above average fare and great atmosphere,it is worth seeking out, particularly in summer. *L&D daily, 11-9 (to 8pm low season weekdays). Closed Tue & Wed in April only; mid Oct-1 April. CC.* **Directions:** *Mizen Peninsula.*

 ## O'Sullivans Bar

Crookhaven Skibbereen Co Cork *028 35319*

Right on the harbour at Crookhaven, with tables beside the water, the O'Sullivans' long-established bar can be heaven on a sunny day. All the food served in the bar is freshly prepared: homemade soups and chowders, baskets of shrimps (in summer) with home-made brown bread and butter, their famous fresh crab sandwiches, and more - all made on the premises. *Bar food Mon-Sat 12-9 (to 7pm in winter), Sun 12.30-8pm. Live music 3 days in summer. Closed Mon Nov-Mar; 25 Dec & Good Fri. CC.*

CROSSHAVEN

On the west side of Cork Harbour, 17km from Cork city, Crosshaven is a favourite seaside resort for Cork people and an important yachting centre. The seasonal nature of the town means that restaurants tend to come and go but there are several pubs of character including Cronin's (see entry).

  ## Cronin's Pub

Crosshaven Co Cork *021 483 1829 www.croninspub.com*

In the family since 1970, the Cronins' harbourfront pub has oodles of character; with its walls and high shelves crammed with maritime memorabilia, it's an unofficial exhibition of local history. They've always had a reputation for good food, especially seafood, and Ballymaloe-trained chef Denis Cronin sister Joeleen (front of house) and his partner Caroline Burgess are doing a great job with both the bar food and **The Mad Fish** restaurant. Genuine hospitality, the best local ingredients (suppliers credited) and consistently good, unfussy cooking make this a go-to destination. *Restaurant seats 35. L&D Tue-Sat. Bar food Mon-Fri L & Sat, 11.45-3.30pm. Restaurant closed Sun, Mon & Jan. CC.* **Directions:** *Straight into village, at car park.*

Bunnyconnellan

Crosshaven Area Myrtleville Crosshaven Co Cork ☎*021 483 1213 www.bunnyconnellan.ie*

Stunning sea views never fail to wow visitors to Paul and Julie O'Brien's friendly, beautifully located bar and restaurant near Crosshaven - and the food served here is pretty impressive too. Given the location, seafood is an obvious first choice and there's plenty to choose from, but there's much more to these extensive menus than fish, including some unusual meat and poultry evening dishes - and good vegetarian choices too. *Mon-Thu 12.30-11.30; Fri-Sat 12.30-12.30; Sun 12.30-11. CC.*

  Creagh House

Main Street Doneraile Co Cork ☎*022 24433 www.creaghhouse.ie*

Michael O'Sullivan and Laura O'Mahony's Regency townhouse was a renovation project and, since 2000, enormous amounts of TLC have paid off, as it has gradually been returned to its former glory. Accommodation is wonderful, in vast rooms with huge antique furniture, and crisp linen on comfortable beds. Anyone interested in architecture and/or history - or gardens - is in for a treat when staying here and Doneraile is well-placed for exploring a wide area. **Rooms 3.** *Supper on request (must book). Closed Oct-Mar. CC.* **Directions:** *Take N20 (Limerick road) from Mallow - 12.5km.*

 Doneraile Court Tea Rooms

Doneraile Co Cork ☎*087 251 5965*
www.heritageireland.ie/en/South-West/DoneraileWildlifePark/

Just off the main street of this quiet North Cork village, you'll find one of Ireland's hidden gems. Once home to the St. Leger family Doneraile Park's 400 acres of beautiful 18th century parkland are open to the public - and here in the old kitchen of the 'Big House', there is a lovely tea room. Tasty fare is offered all day from breakfast onwards, with quite a varied lunch menu. Well worth a visit. *Tea Rooms open 9.30-7 in summer, 10-4 in winter.*

  Glenilen Farm Dairy Products

Gurteeniher Drimoleague Co Cork ☎*028 31179 www.glenilen.com*

On their small West Cork dairy farm Alan and Valerie Kingston produce a growing range of excellent handmade products including farmhouse butter, clotted cream, double cream, low fat cream cheese (creme fraiche and quark), yoghurts and cheesecakes. All are made without preservatives, and delivered directly to shops and restaurants for faster distribution, and well worth looking out for.

  Cookies of Character

Dunmanway Co Cork ☎*023 885 5344 www.regale.ie*

In a little craft bakery just outside the West Cork market town of Dunmanway, patissier Richard Graham-Leigh uses the very best locally sourced ingredients to produce a wide range of handmade biscuits and cookies. A very successful recent addition to their range is their crackers for cheese, which were developed with Sheridans Cheesemongers (see entry). Available in good shops locally and in many of the best speciality food stores throughout Ireland.

DURRUS

Located in west Cork, 6 miles from Bantry, at the head of the Sheep's Head and Mizen Head peninsulas, the village retains its small pastoral atmosphere. Visitors will enjoy a trip to the Cool na Long Castle built by the McCarthy family, and the gardens of Cois Abhann and Kilvarock are nearby. Durrus is home to the award winning cheese of the same name made by Jeffa Gill (see entry), one of the many farmhouse cheeses that have made the west Cork region famous.

Blairscove House & Restaurant

Durrus Bantry Co Cork ☎ *027 61127 www.blairscove.ie*

In a stunning waterside location at the head of Dunmanus Bay, Philippe and Sabine De Mey's beautiful Georgian property is a very special place to eat – and to stay. Together with Sabine's brother Ronald Klotzer, who is head chef, the De Meys offer the wonderful food and service that this stylishly atmospheric restaurant is known for: their unique table d'hote dinner begins with the renowned buffet starter display, which is followed by a wide choice of meat and fish dishes simply cooked on the wood-fired grill. **Rooms 4**. *Restaurant seats 70; D Tue-Sat, 6-9.30pm. Closed Sun (except bank hol weekends), Mon & house closed early Nov-17 Mar. CC.* **Directions:** *3km outside Durrus on Crookhaven Road, blue gate on right hand side*

Carbery Cottage Guest Lodge

Durrus Bantry West Cork Co Cork ☎ *027 61368 www.carbery-cottage-guest-lodge.net*

With well-maintained gardens and beautiful views, Mike Hegarty and Julia Bird's purpose-built B&B and adjoining self-catering cottage creates a great first impression - and their hospitality extends to your four-legged friends too. Bedrooms are spacious, simply furnished and modern - not the height of luxury, but very comfortable - and everything about the house and the way it is run is guest focused. It's a real can-do place and would make a wonderfully relaxed holiday base, and with very good food too. **Rooms 3** *(1 with private bathroom). Residents D, Mon-Sat, 6-8. Must book meals in advance. Self catering also avail. No CC.* **Directions:** *Between Durrus and Ahakista.*

Gallán Mor

Kealties Durrus Bantry Co Cork ☎ *027 62732 www.gallanmor.com*

Noel and Lorna Bourke relocated here from London to start a new business and their boutique B&B, Gallán Mor (the mighty standing stone), is perched high on a hill with stunning views over Dunmanus Bay. No expense has been spared and rooms with smart en-suites and power showers also boast WiFi and satellite television - although many guests will be happy to leave television and laptops switched off. **Rooms 4**. *Self-catering also available.* **Directions:** *5.5km from Durrus on the Ahakista road.*

The Gateway Café & Brasserie

Main Street Durrus Bantry Co Cork ✆*027 61353*

In the centre of Durrus village, sharing the premises of Ryan's village shop, the ground floor of this welcoming restaurant is a family-friendly modern café serving good quality casual fare (smoked fish, meat or cheese platters, quiches, pizza, cakes) throughout the day. Upstairs, a smartly appointed evening restaurant serves local foods cooked with continental flair and gives real value. **Seats 60** *(outdoors, 14). Open B, L&D daily. CC.* **Directions:** *Centre of Durrus.*

 Good Things Café & Cookery School

Ahakista Road Durrus Co Cork ✆*027 61426* *www.thegoodthingscafe.com*

Carmel Somers, chef, teacher and author, does more than any other chef in the region to promote local produce and her menus at this little restaurant on the outskirts of Durrus village reflect this. Seasonality is a byword here: roasted summer vegetables, sea beet, lightly boiled, Kilcrohane new potatoes, the tartness of gooseberries with mackerel. A place where even the most demanding know they are in safe hands. **Seats 40** *(plus 10 outdoor in fine weather); Cafe open 2 wks Easter & from late Jun-Sep. Thu-Sun for L&D. Closed Tue, Wed and Sep-Easter. Reservations advised for dinner; a call to check times is wise, especially off-season. CC.* **Directions:** *From Durrus village, take Ahakista/Kilcrohane Rd.*

 **Thady Inn**

Farnanes Co Cork ✆*021 733 6379*

Formerly a barracks for British soldiers, this small whitewashed pub is set well back from the road. The owners, Den and Martha O'Flaherty, keep it simple and unspoilt, with a welcoming open fire. They offer a small menu and do a limited number of well-known dishes well - notably great steaks, served with perfectly cooked crispy chips. **Seats 40.** *Pub open 10.30am-11.30pm; food Mon-Sat, 12-9.45pm, Sun 4pm-9.45pm. No CC.* **Directions:** *Off N22 between Macroom and Cork.*

 Abbeyville House

Abercromby Place Fermoy Co Cork ✆*025 32767* *www.abbeyvillehouse.com*

Sean and Mary Lomasney's handsome and hospitable 19th century cut stone house offers the perfect place to stay in Fermoy, with very comfortable accommodation in spacious, elegantly furnished rooms - and delicious breakfasts to set you up for days exploring the many activities and attractions of the area (and indeed the whole Munster region). **Rooms 6** *(5 shower only). Closed 1 Dec - 31 Jan. CC.* **Directions:** *On the main road into town from the Dublin side, near the northern bank of the River Blackwater (across from town park).*

 Badger & Dodo

Fermoy Co Cork ✆*087 053 2660* *www.badgeranddodo.ie*

Badger & Dodo boutique coffee roasters was set up in 2008 by the highly experienced and coffee-educated Australian Brock Lewin who relocated here with his Irish-born wife. Their unusual range of quality fresh roasted coffees is gaining recognition through exposure gained in the high calibre cafés and restaurants they supply.

Charlie Mac's

20 McCurtain Street Fermoy Co Cork ✆*025 31740*

There's no shortage of either quality or quantity at Charlie Mac's pub, on the banks of the beautiful Blackwater River in Fermoy. Chef Fred Desormeaux has a following for his seafood cooking and it's as excellent (and sometimes surprising) as ever, but his culinary magic is fairly distributed - he even makes traditional liver & bacon look very inviting indeed. Understandably popular, so get there early. *Food Tue-Sun from 12 noon (Tue & Wed to 4, Thu-Sat to 9, Sun to 8). No food Mon.*

  Fermoy Natural Cheese Co

Strawhill Fermoy Co Cork ✆*025 31310 www.irishcheese.ie/members/fermoy*

Frank and Gudrun Shinnick have been making cheese on their farm near Fermoy since 1996. Their range of eight cows' milk cheeses varies from soft to mature hard, all made from the milk of Frank's herd of pedigree Holstein Friesians, fed on the fertile pastures of the Blackwater River valley. You'll see them on some of the area's best menus, also aold at speciality outlets, including The Pig's Back at the English Market.

  La Bigoudenne

28 MacCurtain Street Fermoy Co Cork ✆*025 32832*

At this little piece of France in the main street of a County Cork town, Noelle and Rodolphe Semeria's hospitality is matched only by their food, which specialises in Breton dishes, especially crêpes - both savoury (made with buckwheat flour) and sweet (with wheat flour). **Seats 36**. *D Tue-Sun, L Thu only. Closed Mon & 1-15 Oct. CC.* **Directions:** *On the main street, opposite ESB.*

      **Ballyvolane House**

Fermoy Area Castlelyons Fermoy Co Cork ✆*025 36349 www.ballyvolanehouse.ie*

Justin and Jenny Green are the current custodians of this gracious mansion. Surrounded by its own farmland and magnificent wooded grounds, it has formal terraced gardens, a trout lake and salmon beats on the River Blackwater. Justin's father Jeremy cares for the gardens and woodland - garden lovers will find a stay here especially rewarding. Justin and Jenny are an extremely hospitable couple, committed to continuing the standards of hospitality, comfort and food for which this lovely house is renowned - and working with other like minded local companies to create unique events. Families are made very welcome. **Rooms 6** *(1 shower only). D daily at 8pm, non residents also welcome (all by reservation). Closed 24 Dec - 1 Jan.CC.* **Directions:** *Turn right off main Dublin-Cork road N8 just south of Rathcormac (signed Midleton), following house signs on to R628.*

GLANDORE / UNION HALL

The attractive village of Glandore is beautifully situated in a sheltered location overlooking Glandore Harbour and its guardian rocks, Adam and Eve. The all year population is small and it will never be a place for mass tourism but there is comfortable accommodation to be found in the area. Looking west towards Union Hall, which is an important fishing port and within walking distance across a road bridge, this unspoilt village has a choice of pubs offering good food and traditional music and craic in the evenings - all quite different in character, each is equally charming.

Casey's of Glandore

Glandore Co Cork ✆*028 33716*

Run by Mary Casey, this gloriously old fashioned pub is at the 'top of the town'. A favourite destination for many regular visitors, it only opens in the evenings and is the place for impromptu sessions and late night craic. Open 6pm - late, nightly.

Glandore Inn

Glandore Co Cork ✆ *028 33468 www.theglandoreinn.com*

High up on the main street, with a clear view of Glandore Harbour, this atmospheric pub is run by chef David Wine and his wife Julie, so the focus is on good food. Both at lunchtime and in the evening, there's a continental tone to David's quite extensive menus, yet they also celebrate the local - especially seafood, of course, such as a big Seafood Platter or Glandore Fish Stew. Victorian beer bread is a speciality. ***Seats 40***. *L&D daily.* **Directions:** *High up on the main street.*

Hayes' Bar

The Square Glandore Co Cork ✆*028 33214 www.hayesbar.ie*

Beautifully located, with outdoor tables overlooking Glandore harbour, Hayes Bar has a cosy interior that is full of vintage charm - and Ada Hayes' famously 'different' bar food which. like the outstanding wines and unusual crockery collected on their frequent trips abroad, is inspired by their travels. Declan also paints and his work is exhibited here, from June to August. *Meals 12-6pm, Jun-Aug; Tapas Menu 6-9; weekends only off-season. Closed weekdays Sep-May except Christmas & Easter. No CC.* **Directions:** *The Square Glandore.*

The Marine

The Pier Front Glandore Co Cork ✆*028 33366 www.themarine.ie*

Right down beside the little harbour in Glandore village, the O'Brien family's 'new' Marine is a compact yet very complete complex, with lovely self-catering houses in addition to the original simple rooms. Above the bar and sunny terrace, an impressive first floor restaurant offers evening dining and proprietor Shane O'Brien heads up the kitchen team. The family also own The Rectory, a stylish private venue which may sometimes be open as a restaurant. ***Rooms 11*** *+ self catering. Restaurant* ***Seats 90***. *L Sun only. D daily, 6-8.30pm. Also bar meals. CC.* **Directions:** *On the pier front in Glandore.*

The Barn Restaurant

Glanmire Co Cork ☎*021 486 6211 www.barn-restaurant.com*

In an almost rural location at edge of the city, this long-established neighbourhood restaurant has a devoted local clientèle who love the old-fashioned atmosphere, good French/Irish cooking and warmly professional service under the guidance of proprietor/manager Abina Leahy. The traditional dessert trolley is a speciality. **Seats 100**; *D daily, L Sun only. Reservations advised (essential at weekends). Closed Mon. CC.*

  Vienna Woods Hotel & Mabel Crawford's Bistro

Glanmire Co Cork ☎*021 455 6800 www.viennawoodshotel.com*

Once the home of Lord and Lady Crawford, founders of the Beamish and Crawford Brewery, this attractively located hotel has retained an old world ambience and is known for friendly staff and traditional comfort - also for the hotel's atmospheric restaurant, **Mabel Crawford's Bistro**, which is a popular dining destination in its own right. Local suppliers are proudly highlighted - and there's even a Guaranteed Irish menu. **Rooms 48** *(some shower only). Restaurant* **Seats 80**. *L&D daily (Sun from 12.30). Bar menu also available.* **Directions:** *Eastern outskirts of Cork city, 1km from Glanmire roundabout.*

GLENGARRIFF

Famous for its mild Gulf Stream climate and lush growth - especially on nearby Garinish Island (Illnacullin Garden, 027 63040), with its beautiful gardens - Glengarriff has been a popular tourist destination since Victorian times and a little of that atmosphere still exists today. There are many things to see and do in the area and golfers will be more than satisfied with the challenge posed by nearby Bantry Bay Golf Club (Bantry, 027 50579).

  Casey's Hotel Glengarriff

The Village Glengarriff Co Cork ☎*027 63010 www.caseyshotelglengarriff.ie*

Glengarriff was a very popular destination with the first 'tourists' in Victorian times and Casey's Hotel dates back to that era, having been established in 1884, and it has been run by the same family ever since. A small, moderately priced and very hospitable hotel of the kind that gave Ireland a special reputation for hospitality, and that tradition has been at the core of their business down through the years. **Rooms 19.** *(10 shower only). Closed 15 Dec - 15 Feb. CC*

  Eccles Hotel

Glengariff Harbour Glengarriff Co Cork ☎*027 63003 www.eccleshotel.com*

The rather grand looking Eccles Hotel overlooks the harbour and is associated with Victorian times, although it actually dates as far back as 1745. Now run by the Hanratty hotelier family, who always keep a welcoming fire burning in the large reception, the accommodation is relatively modest but it's comfortable - and an appealing place to stop for a bite to eat in the bar, or to enjoy afternoon tea in the sun. **Rooms 66** *(14 shower only). Closed 23-28 Dec and midweek Nov-Feb. CC.*

 **The Rising Tide**

Glounthaune Co Cork ☎ *021 435 3233 www.therisingtide.ie*

Seen at its best at high water, the Murphy family's appealing pub/restaurant reflects the surroundings, with a maritime theme in the ground floor bar and eating area; upstairs, prints by renowned self-taught Irish artist, Ted Jones, compensate for any lack of view. Seafood is very much the star, with a lobster tank in situ, but other options are equally appealing and also feature local produce. *Seats 80 (outdoors, 30). Open daily for morning coffee (except Sun). Food 12.30-9.30pm (to 9pm Sun). Closed 25 Dec, Good Fri. CC.* **Directions:** *From Midleton/Waterford road take the Little Island/Glounthaune exit and follow signs to Glounthaune.*

 **The Heron's Cove**

The Harbour Goleen Co Cork ☎ *028 35225 www.heronscove.com*

When the tide is in and the sun is out there can be few prettier locations than Sue Hill's restaurant with rooms overlooking Goleen harbour, which has been a destination fish restaurant since 1985. Great ingredients, pleasing cooking, friendly attentive service from local staff make for a very enjoyable meal, and it's a lovely place to stay too. *Restaurant seats 30. Rooms 5 (4 shower only). Open all year except Christmas but bookings advisable, especially off season. Closed Christmas & New Year. CC.* **Directions:** *Turn left in middle of Goleen to the harbour, 100m from village.*

 Fortview House

Goleen Area Gurtyowen Toormore Goleen Co Cork ☎ *028 35324 www.fortviewhousegoleen.com*

Violet and Richard Connell's remarkable roadside farmhouse in the hills behind Goleen is immaculate and full of charm. Bedrooms beautifully furnished with antique beds have all sorts of thoughtful little details to surprise and delight, and Violet's idea of a 'standard Irish breakfast' - showcasing local produce - has to be seen to be believed. *Self-catering cottages also available. Rooms 3. Closed Oct-Apr. No CC.* **Directions:** *Between Schull and Goleen, 2km from Toormore on main Durrus-Bantry road (R591).*

 **Gougane Barra Hotel**

Gougane Barra Macroom Co Cork ☎ *026 47069 www.gouganebarrahotel.com*

In one of the most peaceful and beautiful locations in Ireland, Neil and Katy Lucey's delightfully old-fashioned family-run hotel overlooks Gougane Barra Lake, famous for its monastic settlements. Whether to stay or drop in for a meal in the bar or restaurant, it's a lovely place to visit - and Katy's great ingredients-led cooking is worth travelling for. *Rooms 26. Restaurant seats 70; L&D daily. Closed 20 Oct-7 Apr. CC.* **Directions:** *Situated in Gougane Barra National Forest; well signposted.*

 Innishannon House Hotel

Innishannon Co Cork ☎ *021 477 5121 www.innishannon-hotel.ie*

The Roche family's lovely house on the Bandon River was built in 1720 in the 'petit chateau' style, and both it and the riverside location and gardens have great charm. A good place to break a journey for a bite in the bar - or outside at a table overlooking the garden and river, if the weather is fine. *Rooms 13. Closed 25 Dec, late Jan/early Feb. CC.*

Ardrahan Dairy Products

Ardrahan Kanturk Co Cork ☎*029 78099 www.ardrahancheese.ie*

A clean environment and rich grasslands - the perfect requirements for the Burns family's wonderful Ardrahan, a pungent semi-soft cows' milk cheese, which they have made from the milk of their own herd of pedigree Friesians since 1983. They also produce a milder cheese, Duhallow, and the magical Lullaby Milk, which is milked before first light to retain the maximum amount of melatonin, a substance which helps the body to regulate sleep-wake patterns naturally.

 Jack McCarthy Butchers

Main Street Kanturk Co Cork ☎*029 50178 www.jackmccarthy.ie*

One of Ireland's most famous butchers; not only do Jack and Tim McCarthy stock an exceptional range of fantastic meats, but they're renowned for speciality products including spiced beef, air-dried beef and their amazingly successful black pudding, which has earned Gold Medal approval from like-minded butchers in Normandy, no less. An excellent online shop offers free delivery in Ireland, over a fixed limit. *Open Mon-Sat, 9-6. Closed Sun & bank hols. CC.*

 **The Glen House**

The Glen Kilbrittain Kinsale Co Cork ☎*023 884 9862 www.glencountryhouse.com*

Although classified (correctly) as a farmhouse, Guy and Diana Scott's home is an elegant period house and they have renovated it to a high standard for guests. Serving an excellent breakfast, it's a relaxed place where dogs are welcome to join the house spaniels (guests' horses are welcome too!) and teas and baby sitting are offered for children. *Rooms 5 (4 shower only). Closed Nov-Apr. CC. Directions: Signed off the R600, midway between Kinsale and Clonakilty.*

 **The Pink Elephant**

Harbour View Kilbrittain Co Cork ☎*023 884 9608 www.pinkelephant.ie*

Painted pink and set on a superb elevated site overlooking the sea and across the bay to Courtmacsherry, you can't miss Niall Hegarty's low bungalow-style bar and restaurant. It's open during the day as well as for dinner in summer, so it's a very useful place to know about - and what a lovely, friendly place it is too. Everything is cooked to order, and diets are accommodated at any time (advance notice is helpful, if possible). *Seats 80 (outdoors, 30); L&D daily. Open 7 days in summer, phone for opening times in winter. Closed Jan. CC. Directions: On R600 coast road near Kilbrittain.*

KINSALE

One of Ireland's prettiest towns, Kinsale sits at the mouth of the River Bandon and has the old-world charm of narrow winding streets and medieval ruins tucked in around Georgian terraces - all contrasting with the busy fishing harbour and marina of today. It has excellent leisure activities including yachting, sea angling, and golf - most notably the Old Head of Kinsale Golf Club (021 477 8444) - for culture lovers the town also has several art galleries. Kinsale, self-styled 'gourmet capital of Ireland' has a remarkable variety of good restaurants and and an exceptionally active programme of culinary activities- and, less widely recognised but of equal interest to the visitor, some of the best accommodation in the country.

 **Actons Hotel**

Pier Road Kinsale Co Cork ✆*021 477 9900* *www.actonshotelkinsale.com*

Overlooking the harbour and standing in its own grounds, this attractive quayside establishment is Kinsale's most famous hotel, dating back to 1946 when it was created from several substantial period houses. It is now in common ownership with The Trident Hotel; having re-opened in spring 2013 following refurbishment, this much-loved hotel operates as before. *Rooms 73 (1 shower only). Closed 24-26 Dec, all Jan. CC. Directions: On the waterfront, short walk from town centre.*

 The Black Pig Winebar & Café

66 Lower O'Connell Street Kinsale Co Cork ✆*021 477 4101*

Formerly of Ely Wine Bar (Ely Place, Dublin), Siobhan Waldron and Gavin Ryan's superb wine and artisan 'tapas' bar is hitting all the right notes in Kinsale. It's simple, but that is part of the charm; the buzz is good, there's a glowing stove in winter and outdoor seating for fine weather. The magnificent wine list includes a wide selection of organic, biodynamic and natural wines to partner the boards, slates and platters of artisan foods (also limited hot food). Very agreeable. *Thu-Sun 5.30-12. Booking recommended.*

 Blindgate House

Blindgate Kinsale Co Cork ✆*021 477 7858* *www.blindgatehouse.com*

Maeve Coakley's purpose-built guesthouse is set quietly in its own gardens high up over the town and with spacious rooms, uncluttered lines and a generally modern, bright and airy atmosphere. Bedrooms are thoughtfully furnished with elegant simplicity and Maeve is an hospitable host, known for her good breakfasts. *Rooms 11. Closed late Dec-mid Mar. CC. Directions: From The Pantry (formerly Fishy Fishy Café), take left up the hill, keeping left after St Multose Church. Blindgate House is after St Joseph's Primary School, on the left.*

 The Blue Haven Hotel

3/4 Pearse Street Kinsale Co Cork ✆*021 477 2209* *www.bluehavenkinsale.com*

This famous old hotel is attractively presented and hands-on proprietor Ciaran Fitzgerald has overseen a major refurbishment programme. Due to the nature of the building, public areas and rooms are quite compact, but space is well used and extra accommodation is offered at The Old Bank House (see entry), which is in common ownership. *The Blue Haven Food Company offers a range of quality products, available on site and online. *Rooms 17 (4 shower only). Restaurant seats 65. D daily, also casual menus. Open all year. CC. Directions: Centre of town.*

Carlton Kinsale Hotel & Spa

Rathmore Road Kinsale Co Cork ✆*021 470 6000* *www.carltonkinsalehotel.com*

Despite presenting an inscrutable, blocky exterior on arrival, this hotel is well-designed to ensure that guests get the best of the waterside location when looking out; the bright décor won't be to everyone's taste, but the view is the main focus in all of the public areas, including the Rockpool restaurant on the second floor, and many bedrooms. Good leisure facilities. *Rooms 70. Closed 21-27 Dec. CC. Directions: 5km from Kinsale town centre.*

Crackpots Restaurant

3 Cork Street Kinsale Co Cork ✆021 477 2847 www.crackpots.ie

All the pottery used at Carole Norman's attractive and unusual restaurant is made on the premises so, if you take a fancy to the tableware or any of the decorative pieces on the walls, you can buy that too. Menus are imaginative and considerate, with appealing options for vegetarians, and many of the specialities are seafood, notably shellfish. *Seats 65 (outdoors 25); L & D Mon-Sat; Sun L only. CC. **Directions:** Between Garda Station and Wine Museum.*

 Cucina

9 Market Street Kinsale Co Cork ✆021 470 0707 www.cucina.ie

A little gem in the heart of Kinsale, Ursula Roncken's appealing all-day café lies behind an attractive powder blue frontage with white lettering - crisply presented like the modern decor inside, it's friendly and welcoming and serves great tasting daytime food. Open some evenings too, serving delicious classics like charcuterie plates and excellent steaks. *Seats 38. Open Mon-Sat 8am-5pm (food served to 4pm); Sun 9-3; D Thu-Sat, to 9.30. Closed Bank Hols; 24 Dec-2 Jan. No CC. **Directions:** Centre of Kinsale Town.*

 Dalton's

3 Market Street Kinsale Co Cork ✆021 477 7957

Frances and Colm Dalton's cheerful little red-painted town-centre bar has a characterful, traditional-look interior and is well worth seeking out for good home cooking - more restaurant meals than usual bar food. Outside lunchtime, it operates normally, as a bar. *Seats 30. Closed 25 Dec, Good Fri. No CC. **Directions:** Town centre, opposite Market Place.*

 Finn's Table

6 Main Street Kinsale Co Cork ✆021 470 9636 www.finnstable.com

The closure of John and Julie Finn's much-loved restaurant Dillon's was a big loss to Timoleague, but it has proved to be Kinsale's gain since they opened their new venture, Finn's Table, in spring 2013 - and moved effortlessly into the top rank of a very competitive class. Lip-smackingly good food, together with a sense of personal care and value, ensures that every customer will want to revisit as soon as possible. *Thu-Mon, 5.30 till late. **Directions:** Centre of Kinsale.*

 **Fishy Fishy**

Crowley's Quay Kinsale Co Cork ✆021 470 0415 www.fishyfishy.ie

Martin and Marie Shanahan's almost-harbourside Fishy Fishy Café has become the benchmark for Irish seafood restaurants; their reputation for offering the widest possible range and freshest of fish is unrivalled, and their suppliers' list reads like a Who's Who of Co Cork fish and seafood specialists. The cooking is unfussy and known for clear, direct flavours that never fail to please; although big, by West Cork standards, it's invariably full to capacity at peak times and booking is always strongly recommended. *Seats 90 (outdoors, 60); open daily Mar-Oct, 12-9pm; Nov-Feb Sun-Wed 12-4pm, Thu-Sun 12-9pm. Closed Christmas 3 days. CC.*

   **Friar's Lodge**

Friar's Street Kinsale Co Cork ✆*021 477 7384 www.friars-lodge.com*

Maureen Tierney's friendly and exceptionally comfortable purpose-built guesthouse is very professionally operated, and offers an attractive alternative to hotel accommodation in the centre of Kinsale. Although large, it's a homely place to return to, with an open fire in the sitting room and drying room for wet gear. **Rooms 18** *(2 shower only). Closed 22-27 Dec. CC.* **Directions:** *Centre of Kinsale, next to parish church.*

                                    Jim Edwards

Short Quay Kinsale Co Cork ✆*021 477 2541 www.jimedwardskinsale.com*

The Edwards family are over 40 years in business at this characterful old place in the heart of Kinsale, which is known for its atmosphere and the good hearty food served in both bar and restaurant. Seafood is to the fore, but there are plenty of traditional dishes to please everyone - including great steaks and local Skeaghanne roast duck - and it offers good value. **Seats 75**; *food served daily 12-10pm (from 12.30 Sun). CC.* **Directions:** *Town centre.*

                                    Lemon Leaf Café

70 Main Street Kinsale Co Cork ✆*021 470 9792 www.lemonleafcafe.ie*

An appealing daytime spot in the centre of Kinsale, Tracy Keoghan's lovely Lemon Leaf Café is an oasis of calm in an already cool enough town. Quality local foods inspire lively menus that change throughout the day - and, while not licensed, the drinks list goes way beyond the usual. The great range of sweet treats make this just the place for an afternoon cuppa. *Mon-Fri 8.30-4.30, Sat & Sun 8.30-5pm.*

                                    Man Friday

Scilly Kinsale Co Cork ✆*021 477 2260 www.manfridaykinsale.ie*

Dating back to 1978, Philip Horgan's characterful restaurant high up over the harbour is one of Kinsale's longest-established and, with great atmosphere and a garden terrace, it is also one of the most popular. They major on seafood but offer plenty else besides - and, unlike many other restaurants area, they're open in the winter. **Seats 130** *(outdoors, 30). D Mon-Sat. Closed Dec 24-26. CC.* **Directions:** *Overlooking the inner harbour, at Scilly.*

                                    Max's Wine Bar

48 Main Street Kinsale Co Cork ✆*021 477 2443 www.maxs.ie*

Run by a young couple, Olivier and Anne Marie Queva - the chef and restaurant manager respectively - this smart contemporary restaurant has a loyal following in the locality, and it's a happy find for visitors too. Offering a pleasing balance of luxurious ingredients and the more homely, seafood from the pier is a key feature. **Seats 60**; *D daily, L special dates & high season.*

*Closed mid Dec - mid Mar. CC. **Directions:** Located parallel to tourist office, follow sign across from tourist office.*

 ## The Old Bank Town House

11 Pearse Street Kinsale Co Cork 📞*021 477 4075 www.oldbankhousekinsale.com*

A sister property to the Blue Haven Hotel, this fine townhouse is very golf friendly, with a lift and very comfortable, spacious bedrooms and lovely bathrooms. On the ground floor, there's a Gourmet Food Store and Café @ The Old Bank House offering casual daytime food, including treats from the in-house bakery. ***Rooms 17**. Cafe daily. Closed 25 Dec. CC. **Directions:** In the heart of Kinsale, next to the Post Office.*

 ## The Old Presbytery

43 Cork Street Kinsale Co Cork 📞*021 477 2027 www.oldpres.com*

This old house in the centre of Kinsale has provided excellent accommodation for many years and the current owners, Philip and Noreen McEvoy have made many improvements. All rooms have character and charm; a top suite has a lounge area with spiral staircase, and magnificent views. Breakfast showcases local produce; cosy sitting room and patio. ***Rooms 6** (2 shower only). Self-catering apartments avail (min 2 nights). Closed Nov-Mar. CC. **Directions:** Follow signs for Desmond Castle - in same street.*

 ## Perryville House

Long Quay Kinsale Co Cork 📞*021 477 2731 www.perryvillehouse.com*

Philip and Laura Corcoran's pretty house on the harbour front has been renovated to an exceptionally high standard and provides excellent, spacious accommodation. Breakfasts include home-baked breads, with Philip's own honey and local cheeses. Also on site is a Gift Shop, stocking unusual quality items, and the ***Garden Tea Room**, a delightful old world tea room with outdoor seating in fine weather. **Rooms 26**. Perryville Garden Tea Room, Mon-Sat 10-5. House closed 1 Nov-5 Apr. CC. **Directions:** Central location, on right as you enter Kinsale from Cork, overlooking marina.*

  ## Quay Food Company

Market Lane Kinsale Co Cork 📞*021 477 4000 www.quayfood.com*

David and Laura Peare's wholefood shop and deli near the Tourist Office has long been the place to pick up an artisan picnic (made to order), or for self-catering visitors to stock up with local goodies. Also carefully selected imported foods and speciality ingredients. Hamper service too. *Open Mon-Sat, 9.30-5.30.*

 ## The Spaniard Inn

Scilly Kinsale Co Cork 📞*021 477 2436 www.thespaniard.ie*

Characterful and friendly old pub located above Scilly. Best known for music (nightly), but offers bar food all year - traditional fare (Spaniard seafood chowder, smoked salmon platter, Oysterhaven mussels and oysters) and some more contemporary dishes. Restaurant in season, offering a more extensive menu. *Bar meals: L&D daily (all day Sat & Sun); Restaurant D daily. Closed 25 Dec & Good Fri, (restaurant also closes 2 weeks Nov & Jan). CC. **Directions:** At Scilly, about 0.5 kilometre south-east of Kinsale, overlooking the town.*

Stonewell Irish Craft Cider

Nohoval Belgooly Kinsale Co Cork ☎ *086 869 1148 www.stonewellcider.com*

Founded by Daniel Emerson and his wife Geraldine in 2010, Stonewell sources apples solely from premier Irish orchards, including Con Traas in Tipperary, to produce a medium-dry and a dry cider using traditional handmade methods and all-natural ingredients. Check the website for a list of stockists; features on menus in the region.

 **Trident Hotel**

Worlds End Kinsale Co Cork ☎ *021 477 9300 www.tridenthotel.com*

This blocky, zinc-and-wood fronted waterside hotel enjoys the best location in Kinsale town and hands-on GM Hal McElroy ensures that it is a well-run, hospitable and comfortable place to stay. The Wharf Tavern pub is a popular meeting place and Pier One restaurant, overlooking the harbour, serves above average food. **Rooms 75. Seats 80.** *D daily, L Sun only. Bistro menu avail 4-9; Bar Menu 12-9. CC.* **Directions:** *Take the R600 from Cork to Kinsale - the hotel is at the end of the Pier Road.*

 Ballinacurra House

Kinsale area Ballinacurra Kinsale Co Cork ☎ *021 477 9040 www.ballinacurra.com*

Des & Lisa McGahan's beautiful and immaculately presented country house estate is a luxurious venue, available for small weddings and civil partnerships, golfing groups and corporate events. Set within a walled garden with 10 foot-high stone walls, security gates and 40 acres of woodland and lawns, this elegant country mansion brings back old-world opulence and personal service. Private hire Georgian residence. **Rooms 22.** **Directions:** Two minutes from Kinsale on the Innishannon-Bandon Road.

 **Glebe Country House**

Kinsale Area Ballinadee nr Kinsale Bandon Co Cork ☎ *021 477 8294 www.glebecountryhouse.com*

Set in two acres of beautiful, well-tended gardens (including a productive kitchen garden), Gill Good's charming old rectory near Kinsale has a genuine country house feeling and hospitable ambience. Spacious reception rooms, stylishly decorated bedrooms and good food featuring home grown and local produce are all part of the appeal and it is well placed for exploring this wonderful area. **Rooms 4** *(2 shower only); D by arrangement. Closed Christmas. CC.* **Directions:** *N71 west from Cork to Innishannon Bridge, left at the bridge follow signs for Ballinadee 9km. At Ryans Shop, veer left, 2nd on the right.*

 **Toddies at The Bulman**

Kinsale Area Summercove Kinsale Co Cork ☎ *021 477 7769 www.toddies.ie*

Pearse and Mary O'Sullivan's very popular restaurant is located at the famous Bulman bar. Looking over to Kinsale, it has a uniquely sunny western aspect and offers interesting, good value bar food. Upstairs Toddies restaurant offers smart-casual dining; Pearse's seasonally-led menus showcase local and artisan produce in stylish contemporary dishes cooked with verve. *Restaurant: **seats 54**; L Tue-Sun; D Tue-Sat. Bar food Tue-Sun, 12.30-10.30pm. Restaurant closed D Sun, Mon. CC. **Directions:** Beside Charles Fort, near Kinsale.*

MACROOM

A well known market town, Macroom is a on the main Cork to Killarney route and is an ideal place to stop with a farmers' market every Tuesday (9-2) and good selection of shops and restaurants. The town centre is dominated by the walls of Macroom Castle; the gateway is the only remains of the castle left. There are enjoyable walks through the castle grounds. Bealick Mill Heritage Centre is also worth a visit (026 42811, open April to September).

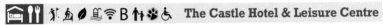 **The Castle Hotel & Leisure Centre**

Main Street Macroom Co Cork ☎ *026 41074 www.castlehotel.ie*

In the ownership of the Buckley family since 1952, this well-managed town centre hotel is ideally located for touring the scenic south-west and is equally attractive to business and leisure guests. It offers extensive leisure facilities and friendly staff take pride in making guests feel at home. Dan Buckley's Bar offers quality bar meals and is a popular place to break a journey. ***Rooms 60**. Closed 24-28 Dec. CC. **Directions:** On N22, midway between Cork & Killarney.*

 Coolea Farmhouse Cheese

Coolea Macroom Co Cork ☎ *026 45204 www.cooleacheese.com*

Dick & Helene Willems began making cheese here in the Cork Gaeltacht in 1979, and their famous gouda style cheese is now made by their son Dicky and his wife Sinead. Easily recognised by its shiny yellow rind and distinctive labelling, it is available plain and in several flavours (Herbs and Garlic; Cumin Seed); the deeply flavoured Coolea Mature is the best known. It is widely distributed and can be purchased from the farm.

 Granville's Bar & Restaurant

Castle Street Macroom Co Cork ☎ *026 20191 www.granvillesbarandrestaurant.com*

Known for its wholesome fare, notably great steaks and seafood, Paul and Leonie Granville's family-run bar and restaurant is full of character and equally popular with local diners and hungry travellers on the main Cork-Kerry road. The food style is hearty home cooking, based on fresh produce from local suppliers, with menus changing through the day and plenty of choices for children too. A great place to know about, this welcoming family-friendly restaurant gives good value. *Seats 76. Open Tue-Sun, from 12 noon-9.30 (9pm on Sun). Closed 25 Dec. CC.* **Directions:** *On the hill just off the town square on main Cork-Killarney road, N22.*

Macroom Oatmeal Mills

Massytown Macroom Co Cork ✆*026 41800*

The Macroom area is famous for milling - and these days it's famous for one simple yet outstanding product: traditional stone-ground oatmeal made by Donal Creedon at Macroom Oatmeal Mills. Although unfortunately not open to visitors, the product appears on some distinguished breakfast menus, notably Ballymaloe House at Shanagarry - whose steadfast support for this special product has probably done more than anything else to help achieve its present status. On sale in selective outlets, including the Ballymaloe Cookery School shop (and their online shop), along with wholemeal flour from the mills.

No 57 Gourmet Kitchen

57 Main Street Macroom Co Cork ✆*026 23457 www.no57gourmetkitchen.ie*

A lucky find for the food lover passing through this attractive market town. This nice little café serves wholesome all day food and its shelves are laden with Irish artisan products and appealing home-made ready meals - very handy for a self catering holiday cottage or if you're heading home to an empty house. Freshly baked breads and scones to go too, of course. *Mon 9-4, Tue-Fri 9-5, Sat 10-5. CC.*

Toons Bridge Dairy & The Real Olive Co

Old Creamery Toons Bridge Macroom Co Cork ✆*026 41471 toonsbridgedairy.blogspot.ie*

Here Toby Simmonds sells his familiar Real Olive Co imports, notably olives and cured meats, and also Ireland's only water buffalo products - which you can buy and taste in the little shop and a lovely conservatory café, operated by Toby's wife Jenny-Rose Clarke. Their deliciously simple food uses the ingredients they sell, including foods from other local artisan producers. Their own buffalo milk and cream stars in delicious mozzarella salad, ricotta cake, ice cream and the Toons Bridge cheese board. *Open: Fri-Sun, 11am-6pm.* **Directions:** *Heading west into Macroom on N22 take the Inchageelagh road, R584.*

MALLOW

A century ago Mallow was renowned as a spa, and is the oldest recorded warm spring in Ireland, discovered in 1724. Today this market centre is the largest town along the Blackwater Valley, and - along with the famous race course - the nearby Doneraile Wildlife Park (022 24244), which includes 166 hectares of 18th century landscaped park in the 'Capability Brown Style' is a popular place for visitors.

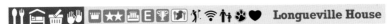 **Longueville House**

Mallow Co Cork ☎*022 47156 www.longuevillehouse.ie*

"The history of Ireland in miniature", the story of the O'Callaghan family's wonderfully productive estate and their beautiful yet relaxed 18th century house is very romantic. The river, farm and garden supply virtually all the fresh produce for William O'Callaghan's kitchen and for the artisan products he makes for sale, including delicious Longueville House Cider (see entry) and an apple brandy. It's a luxurious and relaxing place to stay, well located for exploring an exceptionally rewarding area including Cork city - and dining here is always a special treat. ***Rooms 20** (2 shower only). Seats 80. D Wed-Sun. House closed Mon, Tue & 2 weeks in Feb. CC.* ***Directions:*** *5km west of Mallow via N72 to Killarney. Turn right for Ballyclough, signed Longueville House.*

 Longueville House Cider

Longueville House Mallow Co Cork ☎*022 47156 www.longuevillehouse.ie*

Famous for many things, Longueville House produces its own cider and Ireland's only Vintage Apple Brandy. There are no colourings, additives or preservatives used at any stage during the production process – the naturally fermented amber-coloured cider is just filtered, lightly carbonated and pasteurised. Medium-dry, with a fresh appley flavour, it is naturally thirst quenching and is best served chilled, without ice – the perfect summer drink. Longueville House Cider and Vintage Apple Brandy can be purchased direct from Longueville House and it is retailed by off licences.

  Springfort Hall Hotel

Mallow Co Cork ☎*022 21278 www.springfort-hall.com*

Tracing its beginnings back to the 12th century, the Walsh family's friendly hotel has a welcome emphasis on comfort, with welcoming open fires warming the impressive public areas, and spacious individually decorated bedrooms. And this a place many guests want to return to for its relaxed atmosphere, friendly staff and good ingredients-led cooking. ***Rooms 49.** Baltydaniel Bar and Lime Tree Restaurant: Food served 12.30-9.30 daily. CC.* ***Directions:*** *A short distance outside Mallow on the Limerick Road.*

MIDLETON

Midleton is a busy East Cork market town and home of The Jameson Experience at the Old Midleton Distillery (021 461 3594; www.whiskeytours.ie), where you can find out all you every wanted to know about Irish whiskey, and get a bite to eat too. Food lovers will enjoy the Farmers Market on Saturday mornings (one of the best in the country). Midleton is well-placed for visiting Cork city, and also exploring the whole of east Cork, including Cobh (last port of call for the Titanic), Fota Wildlife Park & Arboretum and Youghal, famed for its connections with Sir Walter Raleigh. The pretty fishing village of Ballycotton merits a visit, and offers good coastal walking.

Ballycotton Seafood

46 Main Street Midleton Co Cork ☎*021 461 3122 www.ballycottonseafood.ie*

Second generation husband and wife team, Adrian and Diane Walsh, manage this famous company. Many products are made with fresh fish caught by their own boats landing into Ballycotton and processed in the company facility in Garryvoe near Ballycotton. Also at: The English Market, Cork.

  Dan Ahern Organic Chickens

Ballysimon Midleton Co Cork ☎*021 463 1058 www.daofp.com*

Dan and Anne Ahern are old hands at Midleton Market, where they sell their renowned organic chickens and other poultry, and also tender young grass-fed beef, which is hung for three weeks. You will see their products proudly proclaimed on the best menus in the area (and beyond).

 **Farmgate**

The Coolbawn Midleton Co Cork ☎*021 463 2771 www.farmgate.ie*

Older sister of Farmgate Cafe at the English Market in Cork (see entry), Marog O'Brien's unique shop and restaurant has been drawing people to Midleton in growing numbers since 1985 and - with a wonderful display of local produce, speciality foods and in-house baking leading through into the simple but evocatively decorated restaurant - it has lost none of its allure. **Seats 100** *(outdoors, 30). Open Mon-Sat, 9-5pm. Closed Sun, Bank Hols, 24 Dec-3 Jan. CC.* **Directions:** *Town centre near Jameson Heritage Centre.*

 Finíns

75 Main Street Midleton Co Cork ☎*021 463 1878*

Finín O'Sullivan's thriving bar and restaurant in the centre of Midleton town has long been a popular place for locals to meet for a drink and to eat some good wholesome food. An attractive, no-nonsense place, it offers a wide range of popular home-made dishes, mostly based on local produce notably steaks and fresh seafood - and perhaps a well-made Irish stew. *Bar food available Mon-Sat 10.30am-10pm, specials 12-6.30pm; Restaurant D Mon-Sat. Closed Sun, bank hols.* **Directions:** *Town centre.*

  Green Saffron Spices

Unit 16 Knockgriffin Midleton Co Cork ☎*021 463 7960 www.greensaffron.com*

Arun Kapil's sought-after spices are sourced by family connections in India. He and his Green Saffron team distribute them and do things which make them peculiarly Irish - eg creating unique mulled wine mixes and using them in Christmas puddings. They also work creatively with like-minded businesses (eg Dungarvan Brewing Company and Ballyvolane House, who hold special curry and beer nights). For stockists of spices and puddings, see greensaffron.com; also by mail order/online shop.

 **Jameson Experience Midleton**

Distillery Walk Midleton Co Cork ☎*021 461 3594 www.jamesonwhiskey.com*

Dating back to 1780, The Old Midleton Distillery is a fascinating place to visit and a tour of the old distillery is worthwhile - and consider buying a bottle of the unique Midleton Very Rare to take home. For sustenance, The Malt House Restaurant offers simple fare like Midleton beech-smoked Irish Atlantic salmon with brown soda bread and salad or perhaps some traditional Irish stew. *Seats 100. Food 10-4 daily (L 12-3pm). Distillery tours daily: 10-6 in summer, 11.30-4 in winter. Closed Christmas period, 1 Jan & Good Fri.*

 **Loughcarrig House**

Midleton Co Cork ☎*021 463 1952 www.loughcarrig.com*

Brian and Cheryl Byrne's relaxed and quietly luxurious country house is in a beautiful shore side location, ideally situated for bird-watching and sea angling. It also makes a wonderful base from which to explore the East Cork area, offering a pleasantly hospitable atmosphere - and an excellent breakfast. *Rooms 4 (all shower only). Closed 16 Dec-16 Jan. SC discretionary. No CC.* **Directions:** *From roundabout at Midleton on N25, take Whitegate Road for 3km; sign on left hand side.*

 **Midleton Park Hotel & Spa**

Old Cork Road Midleton Co Cork ☎*021 463 5100 www.midletonpark.com*

This pleasant hotel near the Old Midleton Distillery is very much the heart of events in the town. Popular with business visitors, it's also good for families - Fota Island wildlife park and Cobh harbour (last port of call for the Titanic) are among the nearby attractions; golf packages are arranged. *Rooms 80. Closed 25-26 Dec.*

  **O'Donovan's**

58 Main Street Midleton Co Cork ☎*021 4631255*

Pat O'Donovan's highly-regarded restaurant blends traditional and modern decor to good effect, but the most interesting feature is the hand-written menu which offers a varied and adventurous meal and excellent value. Nothing but the best ingredients are allowed in this kitchen, and they are locally sourced where possible. An early dinner menu offers particularly good value. *Seats 60. D Tue-Sat. Closed Sun, Mon. CC.* **Directions:** *At eastern end of Main Street, on right-hand side opposite entrance to Midleton Distillery.*

  The Pantry

Distillery Walk Midleton Co Cork ☎*021 463 3335*

Conveniently located for visitors to the Old Midleton Distillery, Gordon and Alison Callinan's café, foodstore and bakery has earned a following for its good traditional cooking and quality products - followers of good food will find plenty of familiar names here. Alison's an ace baker and even the lightest snack will be a pleasure. *Open Mon-Sat 9am-6pm. Closed Sun. CC.* **Directions:** *Distillery Walk is off the bottom of Main Street.*

Raymond's Restaurant

Distillery Walk Midleton Co Cork 📞*021 463 5235 www.raymonds.ie*

Attractively situated near the gates of the Old Midleton Distillery, opposite the river and a small park, Raymond Whyte's smart modern restaurant is an appealing place, known for excellent broadly Mediterranean-style cooking and good service, and while it has a loyal local following, it's especially convenient for visitors to the distillery. **Seats 55**; *L daily, D Tue-Sat; all day Sun. Closed Mon D & bank hol Mon L, 25 Dec - 1 Jan. CC.*

 Sage Restaurant

The Courtyard 8 Main Street Midleton Co Cork 📞*021 463 9682*

Local produce is a the heart of Chef Kevin Aherne's interesting restaurant, especially the famous 12 Mile Sunday lunch menus. But star of the show at Sage is Kevin himself who, while busy working in the open kitchen, also takes time to chat to customers as he transforms the wonderful ingredients of the area into beautiful, appetising - and unusual - dishes. **Seats 40** *(outdoors, 14). Open Tue-Sat from 9am, Sun from 11am. D Wed-Sat. Closed Mon. CC.* **Directions:** *Through a gated archway 100 metres on the left after you come off the main Midleton roundabout.*

 Ballymaloe Cookery School & Gardens

Midleton Area Shanagarry Co Cork 📞*021 464 6785 www.cookingisfun.ie*

Darina Allen's internationally renowned cookery school is situated in the picturesque East Cork countryside in the middle of a 100 acre organic farm and offers a wide range of courses for all levels. The Farm Shop sells organic treats including their own free range pork (fresh and frozen), homemade soups, sauce, stews etc and other selected produce, eg Gubbeen cheese and Smokehouse products; a selection of kitchen and gift items is also available online. *Farm Shop, Mon-Sat 11-5.30; online shop.]*

 Ballymaloe Country Relish

Midleton Area Hyde Ltd, Courtstown Park Little Island Co Cork 📞*021 435 4810 www.ballymaloecountryrelish.ie*

A consistently delicious, great tasting everyday accompaniment to just about everything, and we all like to have it handy in our kitchens. Based on a recipe developed by Myrtle Allen many decades ago, it is now made by to the same traditional methods by her daughter Yasmin Hyde. The range has grown and now includes a number of other tasty relishes and dressings, including a very nice mint jelly and a Bramley apple sauce.

 **Ballymaloe House**

Midleton Area Shanagarry Midleton Co Cork 📞*021 465 2531 www.ballymaloe.ie*

Ireland's most famous country house, Ballymaloe was one of the first to open its doors to guests when Myrtle and her husband, the late Ivan Allen, opened The Yeats Room restaurant in 1964. Managed today with discreet efficiency and warmth by Hazel Allen, assisted by other family members, the intensely restorative atmosphere of Ballymaloe is remarkable - and, although there are those who would say that the cooking is 'too homely', there are few greater pleasures than a fine Ballymaloe dinner followed by a good night's sleep in one of their thoughtfully furnished country bedrooms. Simply unique. **Rooms 30**. Restaurant **seats 110**; L&D daily. House closed 23-26 Dec, 2 weeks Jan. Self Catering Accommodation also available. CC. **Directions:** Take signs to Ballycotton from N 25. Situated 3km beyond Cloyne on the Ballycotton Road.

 Ballymaloe Shop Café

Midleton Area Ballymaloe House Shanagarry Co Cork ☎ *021 465 2032*

At the back of Wendy Whelan's magnificent crafts, kitchenware and gift shop at Ballymaloe House, there is a delightful family-run café offering wholesome soups and salads and delicious home-bakes - just the kind of light, nourishing fare that is needed to sustain you through a shopping expedition that may well be taking longer than you had planned. **Seats 25**; Open 10-5 daily, also Friday evening from 7pm. Closed 23-27 Dec. CC. **Directions:** 3.5km beyond Cloyne on Ballycotton road.

 Barnabrow Country House

Midleton Area Barnabrow Midleton Co Cork ☎ *021 465 2534 www.barnabrowhouse.ie*

Geraldine Kidd's sensitively restored seventeenth century house enjoys views across East Cork farmland to Ballycotton and - while mainly an events venue - it is open for Sunday lunch. Under Chef Stuart Bowes' influence, the food at Barnabrow focuses on local, organic and seasonal ingredients, including produce from the house's own garden and greenhouse. He also runs cookery courses and chef's table dinners for small groups. **Rooms 19** (17 shower only); L Sun Only 1-2.30; Chef's Table dinner by arrangement (groups of 8-10 adults). House closed 23-27 Dec. CC. **Directions:** From Cork N25 to Midleton roundabout, right for Ballinacurra, left for Cloyne, then on to Ballycotton road for 2km.

 Kilkenny Shop & Café

Midleton Area Shanagarry Design Centre Hegarty's Square Shanagarry Co Cork ☎ *021 464 5838*

If you can get through the barricade of temptations artfully arranged en route, a bright, relaxing area at the far end of the shop is home to the Kilkenny Café: you'll find all the ingredients-led salads, quiches, casseroles, home-baked breads and (especially) cakes that are the Kilkenny specialities, and everything has that home-cooked flavour. Mon-Fri 10-5, Sat & Sun, 10-6.

 Patrick & Mary Walsh's Vegetables

Midleton Area Shanagarry Co Cork ☎ *021 464 6836*

If you're visiting East Cork by car, swing round by Patrick and Mary Walsh's farm shop before heading home, and load up with their delicious seasonal vegetables and fruit. Depending on the month you're there, you'll find floury Golden Wonder and Kerrs Pink potatoes, all kinds of of vegetables, rhubarb and also soft fruit in season.

 Pepperstack Bistro at Rosies Bar

Midleton Area Lower Aghada Midleton Co Cork
☎ *021 466 1371 www.pepperstackbistro.com*

Opposite the pier in the pleasant village of Lower Aghada, Martin and Imelda Budden's attractive bar and bistro has a following for good food and hospitality. The warm welcome, peaceful surroundings, an appealing menu (with fresh local seafood a key speciality - give or take the occasional tiger prawn dish) - all this, plus attractive special offers, keeps drawing the regulars back. *Restaurant* **seats 70**. *Food served Tue 5-8.30pm, Wed & Thu 12.30-8.30pm; Fri & Sat 12.30-9.15pm; Sun 12.30-7pm. Mon – no food (bar opens 4pm).* **Directions:** *On the east side of Cork Harbour, R630 (Whitegate road).*

Shanagarry Smoked Salmon

Midleton Area Shanagarry Co Cork ✆*021 464 6955*

Shanagarry Smoked Salmon - more often referred to as Bill Casey's smoked salmon - has been gracing the tables at nearby Ballymaloe House and other discerning dining destinations since the 1980s. Bill uses only salmon organically farmed in deep Atlantic waters off Ireland's West coast for his traditional cold-smoked product, a beautiful deeply flavoured fish with excellent texture flavour that slices well. Available from: Bill Casey's smokehouse; Ballymaloe Shop; the Farm Shop at Ballymaloe Cookery School and other local outlets.

Stephen Pearce Pottery

Midleton Area Shanagarry Co Cork ✆*021 464 6807 www.stephenpearce.com*

Stephen Pearce's stunningly simple design style has a timeless appeal that works well with any style of décor - and the tableware pieces provide the perfect background for the lovely food served in the Tea Room. Good home baking is the tour de force of course, and the pared back style of the pottery sets off the simple goodness of the area's great artisan foods with panache. *Opening Times: Showroom Mon-Fri 10-5, Sat 10-6, Sun & bank hols 11.30-6. Tea Room Mon-Fri 11-3, Sat & Sun 11-4.*

Wildside Catering

Midleton Area Shanagarry Co Cork ✆*086 868 1863 www.wildsidecatering.ie*

Flagging his business as an 'alternative catering company' Ted Berner's aim is not just to provide delicious food for events, but to make it an event in itself. Like any good food, it all begins with the ingredients. His big speciality is spit roast pig, but it's not just any old spit roast, but Woodside Farm free range pork; cooked over a special frame, it looks and tastes amazing.

Woodside Farm

Midleton Area Old Court Ballincurrig Leamlara Co Cork ✆*087 276 7206 www.woodsidefarm.ie*

Slow Food farmers Martin and Noreen Conroy are renowned for the free range pork, bacon and sausages that they produce, with the help of their five children, on their small mixed farm near Midleton. Their wonderful pork is the meat of pure traditional Saddleback and Gloucestor Old Spot pigs, which they breed, rear, butcher and process themselves. Also Christmas turkeys. *Available from Midleton Farmers Market (Sat 9-2; Mahon Point Farmers Market (Thu 10-3) Douglas Court Farmers Marke (Sat 10-2) and the Ballymaloe Cookery School Shop.*

Ballinwillin House

Mitchelstown Co Cork ✆*025 84979 www.ballinwillinhouse.com*

Pat and Miriam Mulcahy's home, Ballinwillin House is extraordinary - right on the edge of Mitchelstown, a suburban cul-de-sac which ends in a security gate. Once inside the 80-acre estate, you see deer grazing and then a substantial 18th century country house and outbuildings – which house the farm shop, and also some unexpectedly modern and luxurious accommodation in a converted courtyard. A characterful old stone wine cellar reveals more surprises, as they also own a vineyard in Hungary. *Rooms 3 (all shower only). No CC. **Directions:** From Firgrove Hotel roundabout, take first exit left, to Mitchelstown; take next left into cul-de-sac before Maxol garage; large white gates at end.*

 ## Eight Degrees Brewing Company

Unit 3 Coolnanave Industrial Park Dublin Road Mitchelstown Co Cork
✆ *025 84933 www.eightdegrees.ie*

Located in the beautiful Ballyhoura region, the Eight Degrees mission is to make modern interpretations of traditional Irish ale and lager styles. The core beers include Howling Gale Ale, Sunburnt Irish Red, Knockmealdown Porter and Barefoot Bohemian Pilsner. The seasonal A Winter's Ale was developed using a custom-made spice blend from Green Saffron, also located in Cork. Available in bottles and on draught throughout Ireland. Check the website for stockists, also for tasting notes and beer and food pairing tips.

  ## O'Callaghan's Delicatessen, Bakery & Café

19/20 Lower Cork Street Mitchelstown Co Cork ✆ *025 24657 www.ocallaghans.ie*

The ideal place to break a journey, Patrick & Mary O'Callaghan provide a one stop shop for their many regulars, as they have an impressive deli and bakery as well as tasty fare for a snack or full meal in the café. Just the place to stock up with delicious home-baked breads and cakes, home-made jams and chutneys - and there's even a range of home-made frozen meals. *Seats 140 (outdoor 20). Food served Mon-Sat, 8.30 am- 5 pm. Closed Sun, bank hols, 24-27 Dec. CC. **Directions:** On main street, on right heading towards Dublin.*

 ## The Bosun

The Pier Monkstown Co Cork ✆ *021 484 2172 www.thebosun.ie*

Nicky and Patricia Moynihan's waterside establishment close to the both the car ferry across to Cobh and the Ringaskiddy ferries (France) has grown a lot over the years, with the bar as popular as ever and the restaurant and accommodation gaining new fans all the time. Seafood is the speciality, offered every which way, and there's always a good choice for vegetarians too. *Restaurant **Seats 80** (outdoors, 20); D daily, L Sun only. **Rooms 15** (9 shower only). Closed 25-26 Dec, Good Friday. CC. **Directions:** On sea front, beside the Cobh ferry and near Ringaskiddy port ferry.*

 ## Knocktullera Farm Produce

Newmarket Co Cork ✆ *029 60079*

John and Olive Forde's organic meats are produced on a traditional mixed farm, using working horses, and sold either directly from the farm or from Killavullen Farmers' Market at the Nano Nagle Centre, every 2nd Saturday 10.30am -1pm.

The Secret Garden Centre

Aghaneenagh Newmarket Co Cork 📞 *029 60084 www.thesecretgardener.com*

Brian and Sarah Paterson's unusual small plant-focused eco-friendly garden centre also offers local foods for sale (including their own honey, jams and preserves). There's also delicious local baking served in the charming little tea room, where 'they like to do things properly' so tea is served in a china pot and their freshly brewed coffee is from McCabes, roasted in Co Wicklow. Classics like chocolate cake and lemon drizzle cake feature all year round and there are seasonal treats too - including Murphy's Ice Cream (see entry) in summer.

Finders Inn

Nohoval Oysterhaven Co Cork 📞 *021 477 0737 www.findersinn.com*

Popular with local people, the McDonnell family's well-named old-world bar and restaurant is in a row of traditional cottages east of Oysterhaven, en route from Crosshaven to Kinsale. It can look uncared for from the road, but it's a very charming place, packed with antiques - and the cooking is good (seafood stars of course). *Seats 90. D Tue-Sun; L Sun only, 2-7pm. Closed Mon; Christmas week. CC. **Directions:** From Cork, take Kinsale direction; at Carrigaline, go straight through main street then turn right, following R611 to Ballyfeard; about 700 metres beyond Ballyfeard, go straight for Nohoval (rather than bearing right on R611 for Belgooly).*

Walton Court Café

Oysterhaven Co Cork 📞 *021 477 0878 www.waltoncourt.com*

In a scenic location overlooking Oysterhaven Bay, near Kinsale, Paul and Janis Rafferty's lovely old house is a listed building dating back to 1645, and in the courtyard you'll find this atmospheric café. Blackboards list all the temptations of the day - freshly baked breads are offered for sale, and in various hot and cold combinations (soup, hot sandwiches etc); dish of the day may be a beef & Guinness pie; delicious salads are laid out - and as for the desserts... great drinks too, including craft beer. A very useful place to know about if you are holidaying in the area. *Open Tue-Sun, 11am-5pm, closed Monday. No CC. **Directions:** 9km from Kinsale (Cork side); R600 to Belgooly, signs to Oysterhaven.*

Caherbeg Free Range Foods

Caherbeg Rosscarbery Co Cork 📞 *023 48474 www.caherbegfreerangepork.ie*

The Allshire family is well known for their free range pork products, including dry cure rashers, and they also offer Angus beef (frozen). Find Willie Allshire at Clonakilty Farmers' Market on Thursdays; also available from selected outlets, or order directly (can be delivered locally).

 **Celtic Ross Hotel**

Rosscarbery Co Cork ✆*023 884 8722 www.celticrosshotel.com*

This modern hotel is close to the sea, overlooking Rosscarbery Bay (although not on the sea side of the road), and well placed as a base for touring west Cork; the facilities in the leisure centre offer alternative activities for family holidays if the weather should disappoint. **Rooms 66** *(1 shower only); Closed mid Jan - mid Feb. CC.* **Directions:** *Take N71 from Cork City, 10 minutes drive west of Clonakilty.*

  Devoys Organic Farm

Garrane Rosscarbery Co Cork ✆*023 884 8763 www.devoysorganicfarm.com*

Look out for John and Sara Devoy's organic vegetables, fruit and eggs at farmers' markets (Clonakilty and Skibbereen, Fri & Sat respectively) and local shops including Scallys of Clonakilty, Fields of Skibbereen and URRU in Bandon. Local box delivery available; also weekly to Cork (value €25 or more).

   **O'Callaghan-Walshe**

The Square Rosscarbery Co Cork ✆*023 884 8125 www.ocallaghanwalshe.com*

Well off the busy main West Cork road, this unique restaurant on the square of the old village of Rosscarbery has a previous commercial history that's almost tangible. Its unique atmosphere is well-matched by proprietor-host Sean Kearney's larger-than-life personality and the simplicity of Martina O'Donovan's cooking is a joy - the superb West Cork Seafood Platter is a particular treat. **Seats 40**; *D Tue-Sun. Closed Mon, open weekends only in winter (a phone call to check is advised). CC.* **Directions:** *Main square in Rosscarbery village.*

  Pilgrim's Rest

The Square Rosscarbery Co Cork ✆*023 883 1796*

Just across the square from O'Callaghan-Walshe in Rosscarbery (and open at complementary times) Alec Suss and Joanne Durrant's charming, prettily appointed café gives out all the right vibes (Illy coffee and lovely home-bakes never fail to please) and is well worth checking out for a journey break. *Open daily in season 10am-5pm. More restricted times & offering off-season. CC.* **Directions:** *Off N71, on main square of Rosscarbery village.*

  De Barra Lodge

Rosscarbery Area Tineel Rosscarbery Co Cork ✆*023 885 1948 www.debarralodge.com*

Sinead and Dan Barry's purpose built B&B is worth a detour. Sinead's background is in hotels and what this hospitable couple offer is contemporary hotel standard accommodation at B&B prices - and, although (a very good) breakfast is the only meal served, Dan is happy to assist with lifts to and from restaurants in the village in the evening. **Rooms 5** *(3 shower only). Closed Christmas (and call in advance off season). No CC.* **Directions:** *From Clonakilty (N71) entering Rosscarbery turn right before bridge, travel to T junction and turn right, further 0.8km on right.*

SCHULL

Internationally known as a sailing centre, the seaside town of Schull attracts visitors from far and wide. The town includes some excellent craft shops, traditional pubs and local restaurants serving the freshest of locally caught seafood and visitors can sample the best of local produce at the Schull farmers' market every Sunday morning. Schull is home to Gubbeen Farmhouse (see entry), famous for cheese and smoked foods and the Schull Planetarium (028 28552, open June to September). Boat trips are available to the islands of Cape Clear and Sherkin, and other local activities include golf, sea angling, windsurfing, horse riding and cycling.

 **Corthna Lodge Country House**

Air Hill Schull Co Cork ✆ *028 28517 www.corthna-lodge.net*

Up the hill from Schull, Martin and Andrea Mueller's roomy modern house commands fine views. Bedrooms, although fairly compact, are comfortable and there's plenty of space elsewhere, including a terrace overlooking the garden towards the islands of Roaring Water Bay. Unusually, there's also a gym, a hot tub, a barbecue area - and a putting green. ***Rooms 6*** *(all shower only). Closed 15 Oct-15 April. CC.* **Directions:** *Through village, all signposted up hill, first left, first right - house is signposted.*

 **Grove House**

Colla Road Schull Co Cork ✆ *028 28067 www.grovehouseschull.com*

At their beautifully restored period house overlooking Schull Harbour, Katarina Runske and her son Nico offer relaxed surroundings and great food just a few minutes walk from the main street. A lovely dining room is set up stylishly with simple contemporary linen and cutlery - the restaurant has earned a following for its unique ingredients-led cooking with a distinctive Swedish flavour, and is regarded as the best place to dine in the area. *Restaurant* **Seats 40***; L Mon-Sat (phone call advised); D Mon-Sat. Closed D Sun except bank hol weekends. L Sun 1-5. Open weekend only off season, but can be opened on request. CC.* **Directions:** *On right beyond Church of Ireland Colla Road, 4 mins walk from village.*

  Gubbeen Farmhouse Products

Gubbeen House Schull Co Cork ✆ *028 28231 www.gubbeen.com*

Tom and Giana Ferguson are the fifth generation to care for this beautifully located dairy farm and production of the famed Gubbeen products is now a family affair. In addition to the original semi-soft Gubbeen cheese - made since 1979 and available both plain and smoked - their son Fingal's smoked foods range is much-admired (especially when using their own free range pork), and their daughter Clovisse produces organic vegetables and herbs for supply to local restaurants and shops. Their delicious foods are well distributed and Giana also does beautiful hampers.

 Gwens Chocolates

The Courtyard Main Street Schull Co Cork ✆ *028 27779 www.schullcourtyard.com*

French chocolatier Gwendall Lasserre's shop and patisserie has been a chocolate lovers' destination in the centre of Schull for many years. Since moving across the road to The Courtyard, they have space for a lovely café and a patisserie as well as the chocolate shop, and they can even offer the whole complex as a venue for private parties and events. No better people to undertake such a challenge, for wherever Gwen sells his exquisite chocolates, people will follow. Venue can take bookings for private parties of around 50 guests. *Open Wed-Mon, 9-5. Closed Tue; all Jan.*

   Stanley House

Schull Co Cork ✆*028 28425 www.stanley-house.net*

Nancy Brosnan's pristine modern house is a riot of flowers and provides a West Cork home from home for her many returning guests. Rooms are compact but very comfortable and a conservatory along the back of the house has wonderful sea views over a field where guests can watch Nancy's growing herd of deer, and sometimes see foxes come out to play at dusk. **Rooms 4** *(all shower only). Closed 31 Oct-1 Mar. CC.* **Directions:** *At top of main street, follow signs for Stanley House.*

   T J Newman's / Newmans West

Main Street Schull Co Cork ✆*028 27776 www.tjnewmans.com*

John and Bridie D'Alton's delightfully old-fashioned little pub has been a special home-from-home for regular visitors, especially sailors up from the harbour, as long as anyone can remember. Next door at the relaxing café-bar, Newman's West, a cleverly thought out menu offers all sorts of tempting bits and pieces, notably the Gourmet Choice and delicious desserts. **Seats 50**; *Food served all day 9-12 (Sun, 10am-11pm). Closed 25 Dec, Good Fri. No CC.* **Directions:** *Main West Cork route to Mizen Head.*

   West Cork Salamis

Derreenatra Schull Co Cork ✆*028 28579*

Constant experimentation resulted in the unique range of Frank Krawczyk products that food lovers are keen to seek out - and learn about - today. Frank sells his charcuterie at markets, and shares his hard-learned knowledge at 'Pig Out' demonstration classes, where he teaches basic home butchery, how to make products like brawn, country pate, bacon, kassler, speck, salamis, smoked ham - and how to make your own home smoker. For details of suppliers, and dates and locations of 'Pig Out' demonstration classes, contact Frank directly.

SKIBBEREEN

This bustling market town on the River Ilen has plenty of shops, crafts and restaurants to interest the visitor. Skibbereen Heritage Centre (028 40900) is interesting and so is the Skibbereen Trail to famine sites. The West Cork Arts Centre (028 22090) is also well worth a visit. The cattle mart on Wednesdays gives visitors a glimpse of traditional rural Ireland. On Fridays there is a Country Market in the town and a farmers' market is held on Saturdays - and Skibbereen is also the venue for the Taste of West Cork food festival which showcases the best of local farmhouse produce every September.

   Brown Envelope Seed Co

Ardagh Church Cross Skibbereen Co Cork ✆*028 38184 www.brownenvelopeseeds.com*

Madeline McKeever, who is also involved in Irish Seed Savers, grows her own organic vegetable, herb and edible flower seeds on her West Cork farm with her partner Mike Sweeney. Events are occasionally held on the farm, where they sometimes have their own Ardagh beef for sale. Good online shop for seeds, information, gift vouchers.

Fields SuperValu

Main Street Skibbereen Co Cork 📞*028 21400*

No ordinary supermarket - central to the community and supportive of local suppliers, Fields is a must-visit shop when in West Cork. It's an amazing shop, unlike most supermarkets it's right in the centre of the town and with its comfortably traditional coffee shop opening onto the main street. No matter what you are looking for, if it's good food and it's produced in the South-West you're pretty sure to find it here - and, if it's not here, just ask. *Open: Mon & Tue 8am-7pm, Wed &Thu 8am-9pm, Fri-Sun, 8am-7pm.*

  Kalbos Café

26 North Street Skibbereen Co Cork 📞*028 21515*

Siobhan O'Callaghan and Anthony Boyle's appealing café is long-established in the town. Based on well-sourced local ingredients, Siobhan's simple food is always wholesome and her dishes have real flavour. Whether just for a cup of delicious Illy coffee or a bowl of nourishing stew, Kalbo's is always a great choice - and good value too. **Seats 27**. Open Mon-Sat 9am-5pm; D Fri & Sat only. Closed Sun; Bank Hols; 25-27 Dec, 1 Jan. CC. **Directions:** In town centre a short walk from town square.

   **Liss Ard Estate**

Castletownshend Road Skibbereen Co Cork 📞*028 40000 www.lissardestate.com*

Outstanding features that will put this stunning property at the top of the shortlist for a West Cork break include the extensive grounds surrounding the elegant 19th century Liss Ard Country House (home to the artist James Turrell's fascinating Irish Sky Garden, 'The Crater'), activities to interest all ages, a holistic family-friendly philosophy and wholesome Slow Food focus on local foods - and GM Arthur Little's hospitable hands-on management. **Rooms 15**, Approval pending. (5 shower only). Self catering also available. Dining Room seats 40 (outdoors, 10) D daily. Non-residents welcome by reservation. Closed Nov. CC. **Directions:** N71 from Cork or Killarney. Liss Ard is 8km outside Skibbereen on the Tregumna Road.

 The Riverside Cafe

6 North Street Skibbereen Co Cork 📞*028 40090 www.riversideskibbereen.ie*

This well named café is a lovely, soothing retreat from this bustling market town. It's a real find for visitors to Skibbereen – and one with more than a hint of the Mediterranean about both the food and setting, especially on sunny summer days. A weekend evening tapas menu is appealing, also the speciality and artisan foods on sale, and freshly made snacks to go. *L Tue-Sat 12-3.30, D Fri & Sat 6-10.Closd Sun & Mon.* **Directions:** Off North Street, under a stone archway and through an iron gateway.

 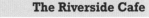 **West Cork Hotel**

Ilen Street Skibbereen Co Cork 📞*028 21277 www.westcorkhotel.com*

This welcoming hotel enjoys a pleasant riverside location beside the bridge, on the western side of Skibbereen town. With comfortable accommodation and friendly and helpful staff giving the hotel a homely feeling, it would make a good base for exploring the area. **Rooms 34** (10 shower only). CC. **Directions:** Follow signs N71 to Bantry through Skibbereen.

The Firehouse Bakery & Bread School

Skibbereen Area Heir Island Skibbereen Co Cork ☎ *085 156 1984 www.thefirehouse.ie*

Talented lawyer-turned-chef-and-baker Patrick Ryan, brought this imaginative venture to the quiet little island in Roaring Water Bay that is home to his partner Laura Moore's family. Unrushed handmade baking in a wood fired clay oven is the central focus, with crusty sourdough just one of a wide ranging repertoire. It's a magical setup and island visitors can call by to buy bread, or maybe enjoy a stone baked pizza, but courses must be booked ahead. *Also at: The Delgany, Co Wicklow (see entry).*

  ## Ummera Smokehouse

Inchybridge Timoleague Co Cork ☎ *023 884 6644 www.ummera.com*

Whatever Anthony Cresswell and his team turn their hands to at their iconic West Cork smokehouse they do it well. The range offered may vary depending on the availability of quality raw produce, but anything with the Ummera Smoked Products branding on it will be of an exceptionally high standard and with no artificial preservatives. Visitors welcome, also online sales.

 ## Drombeg Premium Irish Spirit

Union Hall Co Cork ☎ *028 34788 www.drombeg.org*

Like craft brewing, distilling is enjoying a revival in Ireland, and small craft distilleries such as this one established by childhood friends John O'Connell, Dennis McCarthy and Gerard McCarthy are opening for the first time in many years. Local spring water is an important ingredient and their first product, Drombeg, is an unusual brown spirit; lower in alcohol than whiskey, it can be drunk neat, over ice, in cocktails, or with a mixer as a long drink. Distrbuted by Barry & Fitzwillliam Ltd, Cork.

  ## The Fish Shop

Union Hall Co Cork ☎ *028 33818 www.irishprawns.com/Site_en/TheFishShop.html*

At this factory outlet overlooking the beautiful fishing harbour of Union Hall - one of Ireland's main fishing ports - Peter Deasy stocks a vast range of fish and shellfish straight from the boats. Live shellfish available from a tank in-store.

  ## Hegarty's Cheddar

Whitechurch Foods Church Road White Church Co Cork ☎ *021 488 4238*

Brothers Dan and John Hegarty have been making this traditional cloth-bound cheddar on their North Cork family farm since 2000. Hegarty's Cheddar is matured for at least 12 months before it goes on sale and is popular with consumers who want a real cheddar with character and appreciate its quality. Widely distributed, through supermarkets and independent food stores nationwide.

 **Aherne's**

163 North Main Street Youghal Co Cork ☎*024 92424 www.ahernes.com*

While John FitzGibbon supervises the front of house in this third generation business, his brother David reigns over a busy kitchen. Local seafood stars and it's worth planning a journey around a bar meal at Aherne's - or dine in the restaurant and have a restful night in their classy and extremely comfortable accommodation. *Bar food daily, 12-10. Restaurant **Seats 65**. D daily. **Rooms 12**. Closed 23-26 Dec. CC. **Directions:** on N25, main route from Cork-Waterford.*

 **Newtown House**

Kinsalebeg Youghal Co Cork ☎*024 94304 www.stayatnewtown.com*

In a quietly stunning waterside location, Georgina and Michael Penruddock's lovely and extremely comfortable nineteenth century house is actually on the Waterford side of the Blackwater estuary, with magnificent views across to Youghal - and its tranquil situation offers a degree of solitude that is becoming increasingly rare. A wonderful base for exploring unspoilt West Waterford and East Cork. This is a place you could fall in love with. *Rooms 2. Open 'most of the time'. No CC. **Directions:** From the N25 Dungarvan-Youghal road, take the R671 towards Ferrypoint. Newtown House is on the right just before you reach the estuary.*

 The Old Imperial Hotel

27 North Main Street Youghal Co Cork ☎*024 92435 www.theoldimperialhotel.com*

This old hotel the centre of Youghal has been given new life by proprietors, Mark Johnston and Mark Golden, who have undertaken extensive renovations. Bedrooms, which include a junior suite, have all the comforts demanded by today's travellers. Bistro fare has a welcome emphasis on local produce and this hotel's USPs include ample parking - and an old streetside bar, D. McCarthy: it's a gem. *Rooms 17. **Directions:** Centre of Youghal.*

 **Walter Raleigh Hotel**

Youghal Co Cork ☎*024 92011 www.walterraleighhotel.com*

Prominently located on the promenade of this heritage town, this smartly presented hotel overlooking Youghal Bay has its origins in three 18th century townhouses and has been run as an hotel since 1902. New owners Grace and Nick Ryan are now restoring it to its former glory and it has an upbeat vibe not felt for many a year. It is a pleasant place to eat, and Head Chef James Hallinan's appealing menus have an eye to seasonality and local produce; well cooked local seafood is a highlight, also 21-day aged steaks. *Rooms 38. Meals. A la carte bar-restaurant menu 12 noon- 9pm daily. 4-course Sun L (Green Park Restaurant) €19.95 (children €7.50) Also à la carte.*

  Yawl Bay Seafoods Ltd

Foxhole Industrial Estate Youghal Co Cork ☎*024 92290 www.yawlbayseafood.com*

Like his father before him, David Browne produces a range of home-smoked fish - salmon, from the West of Ireland and the Shetland Islands, and haddock - and sells a wide selection of other fish and shell fish from around the Irish coast. Some of the specialities with a longer shelf life are also available online, ie smoked salmon and vacuum packed crabmeat and crabtoes.

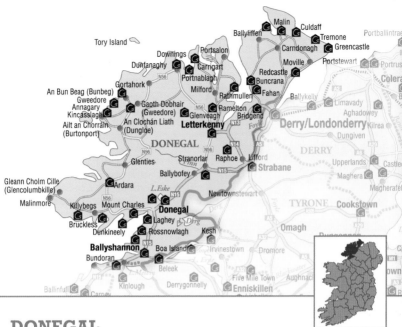

DONEGAL

Golden eagles are no mere flight of fancy in Donegal. Glenveagh National Park in the northern part of the county is the focal point of a programme for the re-introduction of this magnificent bird to Ireland.

Travel at sea level is also an increasingly significant element in visits to Donegal, one of Ireland's most spectacularly beautiful counties. It is much-indented by the sea, but the introduction of local car ferry services has shortening journeys and added interest.

For many folk, particularly those from Northern Ireland, Donegal is the holiday county par excellence. But in recent years, despite the international fluctuations of trading conditions, there has been growth of modern industries and the re-structuring of the fishing, particularly at the developing harbour of Killybegs, home port for the largest fishing vessels. This Donegal entrepreneurial spirit has led to a more balanced economy, with the pace being set by the county town of Letterkenny, where the population has increased by 50% since 1991. More recently. Letterkenny has become home to an impressive Arts Centre, a masterpiece of modern architecture.

But Donegal county is still a place of nature on the grand scale, where the landscape is challenged by the winds and weather of the Atlantic Ocean if given the slighest chance. Yet at communities like Bundoran and Rossnowlagh, where splendid beaches face straight into the Atlantic, enthusiastic surfers have demonstrated that even the most demanding weather can have its sporting uses.

For most folk, however, it is the contrast between raw nature and homely comfort which is central to Donegal's enduring attraction. For here, in some of Ireland's most rugged territory, you will find many sheltered and hospitable places whose amenities are emphasised by the challenging nature of their broader environment. And needless to say, that environment is simply startlingly utterly beautiful as well.

Danny Minnie's Restaurant

Annagry Co Donegal ✆*074 954 8201 www.dannyminnies.ie*

The O'Donnell family has run Danny Minnie's since 1962, and there's nothing about the exterior as seen from the road to prepare first-time visitors for the atmosphere of this remarkable restaurant. Brian O'Donnell's cooking (strong on local meats as well as seafood) matches the surroundings well: fine, with imaginative saucing, but not at all pompous. **Seats 80**; *D Mon-Sat.* **Rooms 5** *(unregistered). Closed Sun D (except prior to bank hols), 25/26 Dec & early week off season.* CC. **Directions:** *R259 off N56 - follow Airport signs.*

ARDARA

This colourful and scenically located small town is a popular holiday destination, and There are several successful festivals in the summer months, including the Ardara Walking Festival every March, and the 'Cup of Tae' traditional music festival held on the May bank holiday weekend. It is the home of hand woven tweed and knitwear, and the Ardara Heritage Centre (075 41704, with tea rooms) tells the story of Donegal tweed. Nearby scenic points include the Glengesh Pass, the Maghera Falls and the views out over the Atlantic from Loughros Point.

Nancy's Bar

Front Street Ardara Co Donegal ✆*074 954 1187*

Charlie and Ann McHugh's famous pub is a cosy, welcoming place in its seventh generation of family ownership. Everybody loves the higgledy-piggledy rooms and the wholesome home-made food, especially seafood, that - along with a good pint and live music - is now a big part of its charm. *Bar food daily 12-9, from Easter to September. Closed 25 Dec & Good Fri. No CC.* **Directions:** *In Ardara village.*

Woodhill House

Woodhill Ardara Co Donegal ✆*074 954 1112 www.woodhillhouse.com*

On the edge of this famous village and overlooking the Donegal Highlands, John Yates's large and hospitable house is full of character and would make a good base for exploring this fascinating area; garden rooms are slightly dearer but worth the premium. John's son James is the chef and the restaurant is popular locally, so booking is recommended. **Rooms 14** *(6 shower-only). Restaurant:* **Seats 50**. *D 6.30-10pm daily. Bar open normal hours (no food). House closed 20-27 Dec. CC.* **Directions:** *500m from Ardara village.*

Jackson's Hotel

Ballybofey Co Donegal ✆*074 913 1021 www.jacksons-hotel.ie*

Barry & Margaret Jackson's attractive hotel has been in the family since 1945 and an open fire in the comfortably furnished foyer sets a welcoming tone. Set in its own gardens, it enjoys a tranquil riverside position - a pleasant outlook from many of the spacious rooms, including the restaurant. There's an impressive conference and banqueting centre and the hotel is a very popular wedding Venue. *Rooms 138. Food available all day (9am-10.30pm); Restaurant: D 6-9.15 daily & Sun L. Open all year. CC. Directions: Beside the river, in centre of town.*

Kee's Hotel

Stranorlar Ballybofey Co Donegal ✆074 913 1018 www.keeshotel.ie

In the Kee family since 1892, this former coaching inn currently has the warmly hospitable Vicky Kee as General Manager. The very comfortable bedrooms are regularly refurbished and back rooms enjoy views of the Blue Stack Mountains; residents have direct access to a fine leisure centre. Food is wholesome and generous and an outstanding Sunday carvery is hugely popular. *Rooms 53. Bar food all day from 12.30. L&D daily; Children's manu. CC. On the main street in the village of Stranorlar.*

BALLYLIFFIN

This small village near the coast of North Donegal is set in the spectacular rocky surroundings of Malin Head and the impressive Inishowen coastline. It is a popular base for walkers, and home to the world famous Ballyliffin Golf Club (074 937 6119), which offers two eighteen hole links courses on the Glashedy links and the Old links. The Old links course was designed by Nick Faldo and is amongst the choice few courses that always attract discerning golfers from Europe and America.

Ballyliffin Lodge and Spa

Shore Road Ballyliffin Co Donegal ✆074 937 8200 www.ballyliffinlodge.com

With a beautiful view, space and comfort, this impressive hotel is a great asset to the area. General Manager and joint-proprietor, Cecil Doherty, has considered every detail including excellent on-site leisure facilities; spacious guest rooms are finished to a high standard with many extras. Jacks open-plan bar and restaurant offers modern evening dining, but a substantial carvery is served for Sunday lunch. Attracts big weddings. *Rooms 40. Seats 55. D daily. L Sun only. Bar meals from 12.30 daily. Closed 25 Dec. CC. Directions: In Ballyliffin village (signed).*

Glen House & Rose Tea Room

Ballyliffin Area Straid Clonmany Co Donegal ✆074 937 6745 www.glenhouse.ie

Beautifully located with an expansive view towards the sea, the McGonigle family's large guesthouse has a charming 18th century house at its heart and is stylishly comfortable and moderately priced. Sonia McGonigle is a thoughtful and hospitable host and there's a feeling of great personal care about the whole property. Rose Tea Room is open to all in summer. *Rooms 8 (all shower only). Rose Tea Room open weekends Mar-Jun and Sep-Oct, 10-6; daily in Jul & Aug, 10-6. D may be available at festival times, phone to check. Closed 24-27 Dec. CC.*

BALLYSHANNON

On the southern shores of Donegal Bay, Ballyshannon is the gateway to County Donegal and is one of the oldest towns in Ireland, having been made a Borough by Royal Charter in 1613. The poet William Allingham was born here - his father was a ship-owner and merchant - and it is also the birthplace of Rory Gallagher, the rock guitarist (there's a Rory Gallagher festival every summer). For golfers, the highly challenging County Sligo Golf Club (071 917 7134) is a short drive down the N15.

Donegal Brewing Company

Market Street Ballyshannon Co Donegal ✆ *071 985 1371 www.donegalbrewingcompany.com*

Launched in July 2012 on the banks of the River Erne, Donegal Brewing Company currently produces a single beer: Donegal Blonde Ale, with hints of biscuit, malt and a good balance of hop flavours.

Nirvana Restaurant, Wine Bar & Café

The Mall Ballyshannon Co Donegal ✆ *071 982 2369 www.nirvanarestaurant.ie*

Off the beaten track, on the Mall, Simon and Nicola Nightingale's stylish restaurant is a popular lunchtime spot and has a chic reception area, with soft seating and a smart designer bar where guests can relax both before and after dinner; a pleasant ambience in which to enjoy Simon's good contemporary cooking. **Seats 70**. L & D daily. **Directions:** *Turn left at the Mall, halfway up Main Street.*

Harry's Bar & Restaurant

Bridgend Inishowen Co Donegal ✆ *074 936 8444 www.harrys.ie*

Run by brothers Donal and Kevin Doherty and chef Raymond Moran, who have a real passion for the food of the area, there is a total dedication to showcasing local produce at Harrys - and the quality of both food and cooking has earned them a national reputation and inspired many others. Specialities like Greencastle fish, Donegal pasture-grazed beef and 'Best of Local Produce' dishes, change by season. Great value too: simply superb. **Seats 110**. L from 12.15; D from 4pm. Open all year. CC. **Directions:** *At junction of Buncrana-Derry and Letterkenny-Derry roads, 5km from Derry.*

Bruckless House

Bruckless Co Donegal ✆ *074 973 7071 www.bruckless.com*

Joan Evans's elegant 18th-century house and Connemara pony stud farm is set in 18 acres of woodland and gardens overlooking Bruckless Bay - an ideal place for people who enjoy quiet countryside and pursuits like walking, horse-riding and fishing. The two acre gardens are open to the public at certain times, as part of the Donegal Garden Trail. **Rooms 4**. Closed Oct-Mar. CC. **Directions:** *On N56, 18km west of Donegal.*

Ostan Gweedore

Bunbeg Co Donegal ✆ *074 953 1177 www.ostangweedore.com*

Although its blocky 1970s' architectural style may not be to today's taste, Ostan Gweedore was built to make the most of the location - and this it does exceptionally well. Most of the bedrooms have panoramic sea views and, while dated, they are comfortable. With a stunning beach and plenty of activities on site and nearby, it's appealing for families in high season. **Rooms 34**. L Sun only, 12-4pm; D daily from 7pm. Sundowner Tapas bar: 7pm-9.30pm daily. Snacks served 1-6pm, Mon-Sat. *Self-catering apartments also available. Open all year. CC.* **Directions:** *From Letterkenny, take coast road past hospital.*

BUNCRANA / INISHOWEN

Only a short distance from Derry City, Buncrana is a popular seaside resort on the eastern shore of Lough Swilly, and is the gateway to the Inishowen Peninsula which extends between Lough

Swilly and Lough Foyle and is a favourite destination for golfers and walkers. It is a beautiful, mainly mountainous area and Ireland's most northerly point, Malin Head, is at its tip; a 100-mile (161 km) circular scenic drive known as the 'Inis Eoghain 100' is signposted around the peninsula and makes a lovely outing on a good day and there are plenty of stopping places en-route: While in the area a visit to Glenveagh Castle & Gardens near Letterkenny (074 913 7090) is a must, and golfers have the fantastic championship courses at Ballyliffin Golf Club (Ballyliffin, 074 937 6119) within a short drive.

The Beach House Bar & Restaurant

The Pier Swilly Road Buncrana Co Donegal ✆074 936 1050 www.thebeachhouse.ie

Lovely views across Lough Swilly may be the trump card at Claire McGowan's smart-casual restaurant beside the Rathmullan ferry pier, but it has plenty else going for it too. Peter Cheesman's seriously tasty local food is cooked with panache, presented with flair and served by lovely staff in stylish surroundings - this is indeed a pleasant place to eat. **Seats 100.** *Open all year: Open 7 days high season, L 12-4pm, D from 5pm. Off Season - D Wed-Sun from 5pm; L Fri-Sun from 12pm. Closed Mon, Tue off season and Last 3 weeks in Jan. CC.* **Directions:** *Located on Buncrana Pier.*

BUNDORAN

Brennnans

Criterion Bar Main Street Bundoran Co Donegal ✆071 984 1810

The discerning drinker visiting this part of the country should make a point of calling in at this delightful pub in the centre of Bundoran town - it's as fine an unspoilt Irish pub as you'll find anywhere in the country: "no television, just conversation". Friendly, welcoming, just 'itself': magic.

The Coffee Dock

Unit 3 Building 2 Bundoran Retail Park Bundoran Co Donegal ✆071 983 3913

Julie Armstrong and her team have built up such a reputation for the quality and good cooking on offer at this modern shopping centre café that it attracts a steady stream of local business people and shoppers – and regulars travelling in the area will plan a detour off the main road for the pleasure of a meal here. **Seats 40** *(+10 outdoors). Open daily, all day from 9am. D Sat only from 7pm (tapas & live music), reservations essential. BYO. Closed 25 & 26 Dec. CC.* **Directions:** *At Bundoran Retail Park, off the main street, behind the cinema.*

BURTONPORT

Burtonport (Ailt an Chorrain) is a small fishing port and sea angling centre in The Rosses, renowned for its catches of salmon, lobster and crab in the summer months - fresh seafood which (along with many other varieties) finds its way onto menus in many of the local pubs and restaurants. Just off the town, the island of Arranmore is accessible by frequent car ferries.

The Lobster Pot

Burtonport Co Donegal ✆ *074 954 2012 www.lobsterpot.ie*

Easily recognised by the huge lobster on the side of the building, the Kelly family's atmospheric pub-restaurant is just the spot for a wholesome bite, whether it be a quick meal-in-a-soup bowl of chunky seafood chowder and home baked brown bread, or a full blown evening meal. The house speciality, "The Titanic", is a platter of lobster and other local fish and seafood - crab, smoked salmon, mussels, oysters - for two to share, while prime meats include Donegal beef. *Bar menu all day, D from 6pm.* **Directions:** *Down near the harbour.*

Quality Sea Veg

Cloughglass Burtonport Co Donegal ✆ *074 954 2159 www.qualityseaveg.ie*

Manus McGonagle has harvested seaweed on the Donegal coast since he was a child and his special hand harvested and air-dried products are now sought out by those in the know in Ireland and beyond. As well as dried sea vegetables, which you will see on some of the country's most interesting menus, Quality Sea Veg supply sea herbs and sea salt condiments for culinary use, and seaweed bath gels. Online and retail sales.

The Olde Glen Bar

Glen Carrigart Co Donegal ✆ *074 915 5130*

Just the sort of old pub advertising people dream about, this charming bar looks as it must have done a hundred, maybe two hundred years ago. Low ceilings, ancient weathered bar and furniture, fires in winter, a big old room and then another behind - and a great reputation for good food in the restaurant at the back, as well as craic in the bar. *Seats 50; D Tue-Sun, 6-9pm. Closed Mon (May-Sep) & occasional weekends May-Sep. MasterCard, Visa, Laser.* **Directions:** *5 minutes south of Carrigart village.*

Patisserie de Pascal

The Diamond Carndonagh Co Donegal ✆ *086 356 3134 www.patisseriedepascal.com*

French patissier Pascal brings continental style to the cooking at his popular café (aka Café Donagh) while using the best of local ingredients Specialities include an outstanding Croque Monsieur, along with delicious French desserts and pastries. Snacks such as vol-au-vents and panini are available too, and can also be bought to take away. A little bit of France in the centre of Carndonagh. *Mon - Fri 9am - 5pm. Sat 10 - 5pm.*

McGrory's of Culdaff

Culdaff Inishowen Co Donegal ✆ *074 93 79104 www.mcgrorys.ie*

An inn in the true sense of the word, offering rest and refreshment to travellers, the McGrory family's north-western institution was established in 1924; it remains a great place to stay, or to take a break when touring, as popular bar food is available throughout the day. But it is probably for music that McGrory's is most famous - as well as the regular sessions (Wed & Sat), it's a major venue for live shows featuring international names. *Rooms 17. D Tue-Sun, L Sun. Bar meals daily, 12.30-8.30. Restaurant closed Mon; house closed 24-26 Dec. CC.* **Directions:** *On R238 around Inishowen Peninsula.*

DONEGAL TOWN

Donegal Town was originally a plantation town and is now best known as the main centre for the tweed industry and crafts. A visit to the area would be unthinkable without calling into Magee's on The Diamond where there are hand loom weaving demonstrations.

Ard na Breátha

Drumrooske Middle Donegal Town Co Donegal ✆ *074 972 2288 www.ardnabreatha.com*

Theresa and Albert Morrow's welcoming guesthouse is tucked into a quiet corner of their busy working farm and has a pleasant view to the countryside beyond. It is, as they say on their brochure, 'a place worth finding', and was one of the first in Ireland to receive the EU flower award for Eco tourism. The restaurant is open to all by reservation in the evening; Albert offers a good, reasonably priced dinner, so many guests see no need to venture out in the evening during their stay. *Rooms 6. Restaurant Seats 25. D by reservation from 7pm; non-residents welcome. CC. Closed 1 Nov - 14 Feb.* **Directions:** *1.5km from Donegal town, on the Lough Eske road.*

Aroma

The Craft Village Donegal Co Donegal ✆ *074 972 3222*

Tom Dooley's smart little café at the Craft Village just outside Donegal Town has won a lot of friends for its warm and friendly atmosphere and excellent freshly cooked food that offers much more than would be expected of a coffee shop. Ingredients are impeccably sourced and everything both looks and tastes delicious. *Seats 30 (outdoors, 16); Open Mon-Sat, 9.30am-5.30pm. Closed Sun, 25-26 Dec, 1 Jan. CC.* **Directions:** *1.6km outside town on old Ballyshannon road.*

The Olde Castle Bar & Red Hugh's Restaurant

Donegal Co Donegal ✆ *074 972 1262 www.oldecastlebar.com*

It may seem a little touristy at first, but the O'Toole family offer real Irish hospitality in this restored stone building overlooking the ruins of O'Donnell Castle. Local seafood is the main speciality at this atmospheric traditional bar and restaurant especially in summer, and daily lunch specials include wholesome dishes such as a hearty bowl of Traditional Irish Stew. *Seats 70. Bar L Mon-Sat, 12-9pm. Restaurant open for D daily in summer, 6-9.15pm; D weekends in winter. CC.* **Directions:** *Centre of Donegal, opposite Donegal Castle.*

Donegal Cookery School

Clar Road Donegal Town Co Donegal ✆ *074 972 5222 www.donegalmanor.com*

At her purpose built cookery school just outside Donegal Town, Sian Breslin and an experienced team offer a range of cookery courses to suit varying skill levels, and can cater for up to 18 students per class. A daytime Afternoon Tea class may suit visitors who are interested in baking.

Le Fournil

Upper Main Street Donegal Town Co Donegal ☎*074 972 5684 www.lefournil.ie*

This a sister operation to the well-established business in Sligo Town, which French chef and baker Frank Pasquier supplies with fresh breads from his bakery. You'll find all the classics here, from crusty baguettes and rustic loaves to gleaming fresh fruit tartlets and precise macarons; also selected artisan foods, and unusual drinks, including French fruit cordials. Baking classes are offered. *Open Tue-Sat, 9.30-5.30.*

M McGettigan & Sons

Main Street Donegal Town Co Donegal ☎*074 972 1068*

This family-run butchers shop has awards a-plenty on its walls and is first port of call for many visitors to the town. Ireland's Supreme Champion Butchers Sausage winners on many occasions, Ernan and Diarmuid McGettigan celebrated the diamond anniversary of their business in 2012 with recognition from France (high praise indeed). And they offer a full range of top quality Irish meats too, of course.

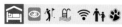

Rosapenna Hotel & Golf Resort

Downings Co Donegal ☎*074 915 5301 www.rosapenna.ie*

This renowned waterside golf hotel overlooking Sheephaven Bay is exceptionally spacious and comfortable, with guest rooms that have been thoughtfully designed down to the last detail. It is a very hospitable and relaxing place to stay. **Vardon Restaurant** is open to non-residents when there is room. **Rooms 60** *(3 shower only). Restaurant D daily, L Sun only. Hotel closed end Oct-mid Mar. CC.* **Directions:** *36km northwest of Letterkenny.*

DUNFANAGHY

Many people will have a soft spot for this traditional holiday area, often recalling family holidays spent at the famous old Arnold's Hotel (see entry), which has been in the same family for three generations. The local Killyhoey Beach features on many of the 18 holes at the scenic Dunfanaghy Golf Club, and Dunfanaghy makes an ideal base for touring Horn Head and the northern peninsulas. "McSwiney's Gun" is a natural blow hole which gives a loud report at certain conditions of the tide. The Dunfanaghy Workhouse Visitor Centre (074 913 6504) remembers this area in the Great Famine. One of the few places in Ireland where the corncrake can be heard in its natural habitat, Dunfanaghy is also a major centre for brown trout anglers and special interest holidays.

Arnold's Hotel

Dunfanaghy via Letterkenny Co Donegal ☎*074 913 6208 www.arnoldshotel.com*

Overlooking the spectacular scenery of Sheephaven Bay, Derek Arnold is the third generation to run this nice old-fashioned hotel in the picturesque village of Dunfanaghy. It's in a traditional holiday area that many have a soft spot for, and makes a comfortable, hospitable base for the (mainly) outdoor activities that bring visitors to this scenic place. **Rooms 30.** *Closed Nov-Easter. CC.* **Directions:** *In village of Dunfanaghy.*

The Green Man

Main Street Dunfanaghy Co Donegal ☎ *074 910 0800*

Eileen Gallagher and Neil Hougardy provide a great service for discerning residents and the many visitors to this popular holiday area, by offering a range of hard to find wines and carefully sourced foods, from Ireland and beyond. Many local goodies offered, from home baking to honey and artisan chocolate, from dry-cured bacon to seafood, salads and sea vegetables. *Open all year. Mon-Sat, 9.30-6, Sun 10-2. Also at local markets (Carrigart Wed am, Milford Wed pm, Ramelton Thu, Falcarragh Fri).*

    **The Mill Restaurant**

Figart Dunfanaghy Letterkenny Co Donegal ☎ *074 913 6985 www.themillrestaurant.com*

 Beautifully located on the shore of the New Lake, which is a special area of conservation, the mill was the home of Susan Alcorn's grandfather and, as they are a family of accomplished painters, the walls are hung with wonderful watercolours. Susan and her husband Derek, who is the chef, have earned a dedicated following here, as the location is superb, the welcome warm, the rooms lovely and the local ingredients-led cooking both imaginative and assured - and they also offer very good value. A magic place. **Rooms 6** *(2 shower only). Closed mid Dec-mid Mar. CC.* **Directions:** *N56 1km outside Dunfanaghy on Falcarragh road.*

  Starfish Cafe & Bistro

Main Street Dunfanaghy Co Donegal ☎ *074 910 0676 www.starfishcafeandbistro.com*

With its fresh blue frontage and relaxed seaside feel, Victoria Massey's small restaurant has simple charm and visitors will be delighted to find local foods featuring, along with homemade treats - especially baking, in the daytime café. The buzzy weekend bistro offers tasty cooking of local fish, poultry and beef, and good value. **Seats 28** *(+6 in courtyard). Café 9.30am-5.30pm daily, all year; Bistro Fri & Sat 6-9pm, (Easter and July & August bistro open 7 nights a week). BYO wine (corkage €4). CC.* **Directions:** *Centre of Dunfanaghy village.*

 The Cove

Dunfanaghy area Port na Blagh Dunfanaghy Co Donegal ☎ *074 913 6300*

An atmospheric dining room with a big open fire makes Peter Byrne and Siobhan Sweeney's restaurant warm and welcoming, and waiting for your table in the first floor bar with views over the harbour is no hardship. Siobhan's down-to-earth cooking is big on flavour and includes some less usual dishes - whitebait, perhaps, and a deeply delicious lamb tagine - along with favourites like a really good house chowder. **Seats 42**. *D Tue-Sun (& Bank Hol Mons), 6-9pm. Closed Jan - 16 Mar. CC.* **Directions:** *In Portnablagh, overlooking the harbour.*

Castle Murray House Hotel

St. John's Point *Dunkineely* Co Donegal ✆074 973 7022 www.castlemurray.com

The restaurant and most of the stylish bedrooms at Martin and Marguerite Howley's dramatically located hotel have wonderful sea and coastal views over the ruined castle after which it is named. It has a great reputation as a relaxing hideaway, and the restaurant (mainly local seafood in summer, more meat and game in winter) is a destination in itself. The wonderful location, friendly, helpful staff, comfort, and interesting food make this a place people return to time and again. **Rooms 10** (6 shower only). *Restaurant* **seats 80** *(outdoors, 20); D daily 6.30-9.30 (to 8.30 Sun), L Sun only, 1.30-3.30pm. Bar menu also available - Jun-Aug 12.30-3pm. Hotel closed mid Jan-mid Feb. CC.* **Directions:** *N56, 8km from Killybegs; first left outside Dunkineely village.*

The Red Door Restaurant

Carrowmullin *Fahan* Inishowen Co Donegal ✆074 936 0289 www.thereddoor.ie

Shay McCallion's beautifully located property on the eastern shore of Lough Swilly dates back to 1789, and it has retained its charm, especially in the little traditional bar with its open fire. While offering accommodation in individually styled rooms (including the funky 'Le Noir'...), the main emphasis remains on food, with a range of popular menus available throughout the day. **Rooms 4** (2 shower only). Room service (all day). Free parking. Closed 24-27 Dec. CC. **Directions:** In Fahan village, on sea side of R238 Derry/Buncrana road.

Filligans

Tullyard *Glenties* Co Donegal ✆074 955 1628 www.filligans.com

Sara and Philip Moss began making their small batches of jams and chutneys in 1997 for just one shop in Dublin, and - still made in the traditional way - their growing range is now available from a network of carefully selected specialist outlets. You'll spot them in quality shops, and also on menus in some of the nicest places to eat and stay in the area.

Highlands Hotel

Main Street *Glenties* Co Donegal ✆074 955 1111 www.highlandshotel.ie

The Boyle family's nice old fashioned hotel In the heart of the Bluestack Mountains is very much the centre of the local community - and more. Not only does it make a great base for the many outdoor activities that draw people to this beautiful area, but it also has literary, artistic and musical connections - and the annual Patrick MacGill Summer School is held here too. Quite a place. **Rooms 24. Directions:** Centre of Glenties.

GLENVEAGH NATIONAL PARK

Glenveagh National Park (Tel: 074 9137090; www.heritageireland.ie) is open to visitors all year, although visitor facilities are seasonal (mid March-early November). The Victorian castle, which is the focal point for visitors to the Park, was donated to the State by the last private owner, Henry Plummer McIlhenny, together with most of its contents - and the gardens are among the most interesting in Ireland, with many unusual and rare plants displayed in a series of garden rooms - the Pleasure Grounds, the Walled Garden, the Italian Garden and so on; garden tours are given regularly by experienced gardeners, but guests are also free to wander freely.

 ## Glenveagh Castle Tearooms

Glenveagh National Park Letterkenny Co Donegal
☎074 913 7090 www.glenveaghtearooms.com

There are catering facilities in the Visitor Centre, but this terrific tearoom in the castle courtyard is the place to head to for really tasty home cooking. Enjoy a bowl of hearty soup and some freshly baked brown bread perhaps, or a generous wedge of quiche with salads. Or have a lovely home baked scone or cake with your cuppa - outside when the weather is fine. **Seats 50** *(plus some outside). Open daily in summer, 11am-5.30pm. Open all year (limited opening in winter). NO CC.*

GREENCASTLE

The ruins of the castle that this "typical" Donegal holiday village and commercial fishing port was named after still stand on a rock overlooking the entrance to Lough Foyle. There is an 18-hole golf course and an excellent bathing beach locally, and a maritime museum in the village close to the place where the Greencastle - Magilligan ferry leaves from the harbour. The Inishowen Maritime Museum is an interesting place to visit - it runs exhibitions on maritime themes from Easter until October.

 ## Kealy's Seafood Bar

The Harbour Greencastle Co Donegal ☎*074 938 1010 www.kealysseafoodbar.ie*

It's a low-key little place where simplicity has always been valued and, even if it's just to pop in for a daytime bowl of Tricia Kealy's Greencastle chowder and some home-baked brown bread, don't miss the opportunity of a visit to Kealys. Those in the know plan their journeys around a meal at this excellent seafood restaurant. **Seats 65** *(outdoors, 20); Bar food served all day Wed-Sun; L & D Wed-Sun 12.30-2.45pm & 7-9.30pm. Closed Mon, Tue, 2 weeks Nov, 25 Dec, Good Friday. CC.* **Directions:** *On the harbour at Greencastle.*

 ## An Chuirt - Gweedore Court Hotel

Gweedore Gweedore PO Co Donegal ☎*074 95 32900*

The Doherty family's immaculate owner-run hotel is beautifully situated in the heart of the Donegal Gaeltacht and provides a very comfortable base for exploring the area. **Rooms 60.** *Closed 25-26 Dec. CC.* **Directions:** *N56 main road from Letterkenny to Gweedore.*

 ## Kitty Kellys

Largy Killybegs Co Donegal ☎*074 973 1925 www.kittykellys.com*

Heading out west on the scenic road towards Glencolumbkille, you can't miss Hugh O'Donnell's smartly presented former farmhouse, now an appealing bar and restaurant. A big oval logo set against wine-red walls is a clear invitation to investigate and the hungry traveller would do well to take it up, whether for a lunchtime bite or an evening meal in the (surprising) restaurant. *Open 1 May-last Sun Sep. Open daily in summer, 12-9. CC.* **Directions:** *On R263 Killybegs-Glencolumbkille road, west of Killybegs.*

Tara Hotel

Main Street Killybegs Co Donegal ✆*074 974 1700 www.tarahotel.ie*

Friendly and helpful staff ensure that guests immediately feel at home at this modern hotel, which is a recent addition to Killybegs and offers good facilities. A good choice for business travellers. ***Rooms 26. Directions:*** Centre of Killybegs, overlooking harbour.

 Iggy's Bar

Kincasslagh Co Donegal ✆*074 954 3112*

Just a short walk up from the harbour - it's also called the Atlantic Bar - Ann and Iggy Murray have run this delightfully unspoilt pub since 1986 and it's an all year home-from-home for many a visitor. Ann makes lovely simple food for the bar, mainly seafood - home-made soups, delicious crab sandwiches and Rombouts filter coffee. A classic Irish pub - you'll be glad you found it. *Bar open from 10am daily, light food available 12-6, Mon-Sat. Closed 25 Dec & Good Friday. No Credit Cards.* ***Directions:*** *On the corner of the Main Street, where the road turns off to the harbour.*

LETTERKENNY

The Letterkenny area - including Rathmullan and Ramelton - provides a good central location for exploring the county; a ferry between Rathmullan and Bundoran operates in summer (45 minutes). Originally a fishing village, which developed on the banks of Lough Swilly, Letterkenny town is now one of the largest and most densely-populated towns in Donegal - and until recently one of the fastest-growing towns in Ireland. The Donegal County Museum is in the town and worth a visit.

 **Castle Grove Country House Hotel**

Letterkenny Co Donegal ✆*074 915 1118 www.castlegrove.com*

Parkland designed by "Capability" Brown in the mid-18th century creates a wonderful setting for Raymond and Mary Sweeney's beautiful period house overlooking Lough Swilly. A lovely house with gracious reception rooms and spacious, comfortably appointed bedrooms, it has always had a name for promoting the good food of the area and produce from the gardens - and for Mary's warmly professional hospitality. ***Rooms 14***. *Restaurant seats 50; D 6.30-9pm daily; reservations required. Snacks available all day. Closed 23-29 Dec. CC.* ***Directions:*** *R245 off main road to Letterkenny.*

 La Fantasia

4 Roe House Justice Walsh Road Letterkenny Co. Donegal ✆*074 911 3421*

Established in 2008 but now in a new home, Davide Tullio's popular restaurant is a cross-cultural culinary gem: the best of Irish enhanced by an engaging Italian and attentive staff. Extensive menus offer plenty of favourites - pasta dishes and pizzas, chicken, fish and steak - as well as specials, including a wine of the month. Authentic cooking and a lovely ambience in the heart of Letterkenny. *Open 12:30 pm to 3:00 pm, 5:00 pm to 9:00 pm*

B   ### Lemon Tree Restaurant

39 Lower Main Street Letterkenny Co Donegal 📞*074 912 5788*

With its pretty lemon canopies, lemon painted and tiled frontage and colourful hanging flower baskets, this popular little restaurant in the centre of Letterkenny is easy to find. The house style is a mixture of traditional Irish and French classic, influenced by country house cooking and an open kitchen adds buzz as you can watch brothers, Gary and Christopher Molloy at work. **Seats 40**; *D daily from 5pm. Closed Good Fri, 24-26 Dec. CC.* **Directions:** *Centre of town.*

                        ### Radisson Blu Hotel Letterkenny

Paddy Harte Road Letterkenny Co Donegal
📞*074 919 4444 www.letterkenny.radissonblu.com*

This modern hotel on the edge of Letterkenny is well-placed for business travellers and also for short breaks in this beautiful area; although in a newly developed area (Marks & Spencer is a useful landmark just opposite the entrance), it is within easy walking distance of the town centre. Food is above average for hotel fare. **Rooms 114**. *TriBeCa:* **Seats 80**. *D Tue-Sat, 6-9.30; L daily 12.30-3.30. CC.* **Directions:** *Drive towards Letterkenny town, turn left at Tourist Office roundabout, turn left off roundabout (R250) - hotel is on right.*

                                 ### Sargasso

41 Port Road Letterkenny Co Donegal 📞*074 910 2277 www.sargasso.ie*

Colette Kelly and her talented team are upping the ante with a real commitment to local sourcing which could put Sargasso up there with the Donegal greats who have blazed the trail to make the county a destination for good food. Chef Martin Hernandez cooks creative modern bistro, including upbeat versions of the classics and local foods inspire almost every dish on seasonally driven menus. Nice little kids' menu too. *D Wed-Sun.*

                                    ### Yellow Pepper

36 Lower Main Street Letterkenny Co Donegal 📞*074 912 4133 www.yellowpepperrestaurant.com*

Since the early '90s Carol Meenan and Kieran Davis have done what they do best at the Yellow Pepper, providing consistently good fresh food and friendly service during the day and evening, seven days a week. Long before it became de rigeur, they promoted fresh, local food and credited their valued sources - including their own organic garden. There are no gimmicks at this caring and family friendly restaurant and it's a good place to know about. *Open Mon-Sun, 12-10.*

LOUGH ESKE

Lying beneath the Blue Stack Mountains with waterfalls at both the north and south ends, Lough Eske is a peaceful and picturesque area close to Donegal Town. The lough and the surrounding thickly-wooded mountains combine natural beauty with excellent fishing (for salmon, brown trout and sea trout) and a sense of history - Lough Eske has 12 islands, including the Isle of O'Donnell with the remains of an historic castle. Nearby Donegal Town offers the visitor much of interest including the 15th century Donegal Castle (074 972 2405, open March to October), the Old Franciscan Abbey and the Donegal Railway Heritage Centre (074 972 2655), with information on the history of the County Donegal railway. The beautiful beaches at Rossnowlagh and Murvagh are just a short drive away.

🍴🏠⬜⭐📖👁 🏃📶👫🐾♿❤ Harvey's Point Country Hotel

Lough Eske Donegal Co Donegal 📞*074 972 2208 www.harveyspoint.com*

Blessed with one of Ireland's most beautiful locations, the Gysling family's well-managed hotel on the shores of Lough Eske opened in 1989 and is now run by Marc Gysling and his wife Deirdre McGlone. The hotel is renowned for its special activity breaks, offered throughout the year, and recent changes have introduced luxurious accommodation - but the the friendliness and helpfulness of the staff remain its greatest asset. Good food is another focus and a choice of fine dining and less formal wine bar meals is offered, both with lake views. **Rooms 70**. Restaurant **seats 100**; L&D daily. Wine Bar menu also served daily, 12-9. Closed Jan, midweek Nov-Easter (except Christmas). CC. **Directions:** 6km from Donegal Town on N15 /N56.

🏠⬜€ 🏃👫   Rhu-Gorse

Lough Eske Co Donegal 📞*074 972 1685 www.lougheske.com*

Beautifully located, with stunning views over Lough Eske (and windows built to take full advantage of them), Grainne McGettigan's comfortable house has some very special attributes, notably the warmth and hospitality of Grainne herself - and a lovely room with picture windows and a big fireplace, where guests can relax. **Rooms 3** (2 shower only). Closed off season. CC. **Directions:** Take N15 /N56 to Lough Eske from Donegal Town.

🍴🏠⬜⬛ 🏃🚣🛁☕📶👫🐾♿❤ Solis Lough Eske Castle Hotel

Lough Eske Donegal Co Donegal 📞*074 972 5100 www.solislougheskecastle.ie*

At the heart of this impressive relatively new hotel there is indeed a castle and, although it does not have views of Lough Eske, it is surrounded by beautiful woodland and formal gardens and this is an exceptionally comfortable and relaxing hotel and a lovely place to stay. The aptly named Cedars Restaurant overlooks the garden; try the house speciality dessert: Frozen Tyrconnell Irish Coffee. **Rooms 96**. Cedars Restaurant **seats 100**. D daily from 6pm, L Sun 12-4pm. Closed at certain times off season, please call to check. CC. **Directions:** Donegal Town to Lough Eske, follow the signs from the N15.

MALIN

As the northernmost point of Ireland, unspoilt Malin offers rugged coastal scenery and beautiful beaches, excellent for walking, swimming or horse riding. The area is rich in wildlife and is a favourite spot for birdwatchers, whilst anglers will enjoy fishing from the beach or from rocky coastal points. This is a great base for the golfer as you are in easy reach of Inishowen's five magnificent golf courses. Malin town is small and charming, with a village green and a lovely old church.

 **Malin Hotel**

Malin Co Donegal 📞*074 937 0606 www.malinhotel.ie*

Although extensively upgraded in recent yeaars, Patrick and Fiona Loughrey's attractive hotel has lost none of its charm. While rooms are compact, they are inviting and comfortable - offering a friendly and moderately priced base for exploring this beautiful area. It's a popular short break destination - equestrian, kayaking and painting are among the themes - and a live music venue. **Rooms 18**. *Food available from 12 noon in high summer; phone to check off season. Closed 25 Dec. CC.* **Directions:** *Overlooking the village green in Malin town.*

 **Redcastle Hotel & Spa**

Moville Area Redcastle Moville Inishowen Co Donegal 📞*074 938 5555 www.redcastlehotel.com*

This modern hotel overlooking Lough Foyle is near the traditional holiday town of Moville yet, surrounded by extensive grounds and its own 9-hole parkland golf course, it's in a world of its own. Although some may be in need of refurbishment, rooms all have sea views. Popular wedding venue; can be very busy at weekends. **Rooms 93**. *Open all year except Christmas. CC.* **Directions:** *On east side of Inishowen peninsula (R238 from Letterkenny or Derry).*

RAMELTON

This beautiful old town, situated at the mouth of the River Lennon was built between 1609 and 1622. The O'Donnells had a castle here before the Gaelic chieftains were defeated in the 17th century and, in the Ulster plantation, the Stewarts built a town for the Scottish and English settlers; their history is evident in Ramelton's architectural heritage. There's an enjoyable walk from the tree-lined mall, following the river past the quay, then onto the guildhall and the ornate town hall, where country markets are held. Local attractions include the Ramelton Story exhibition (074 915 1266) housed in the recently renovated steamboat store; the Donegal Ancestry Centre is also housed here. Nearby, the magnificent Glenveagh National Park (074 913 7090), offers breathtaking scenery and includes wild deer, golden eagles, a castle and gardens. In nearby Gweedore, Ionad Cais Locha (074 953 1699, open March to November) is a two-storey farmhouse with a farm museum and a large collection of farm animals. Ramelton is an ideal base for exploring a wide area of this beautiful county, with walking, fishing, golf and horse riding all nearby, also shopping at Letterkenny.

 **Ardeen**

Ramelton Co Donegal 📞*074 915 1243 www.ardeenhouse.com*

Overlooking Lough Swilly, and set in its own grounds on the edge of this heritage town, Bert and Anne Campbell's lovely, immaculately maintained Victorian house is well-located for touring Donegal and Glenveagh National Park. Rooms are delightful, home baking is a speciality and it's very warm and comfortable, with open fires to return to after a day out. **Rooms 5**. *Self-catering also available in the 'Old Stables'. Closed Oct-Easter. CC.* **Directions:** *Follow river to Town Hall, turn right; 1st house on right.*

 Frewin

Rectory Road Ramelton Co Donegal 📞*074 915 1246 www.frewinhouse.com*

Thomas and Regina Coyle restored this large Victorian house with the greatest attention to period detail. Thomas specialises in restoring old buildings and is a collector by nature - much of his collection finds a place in this interesting house. Rooms have old-fashioned charm and a delicious breakfast, including freshly baked breads warm from the oven, is shared at a long table. *Rooms 4* (3 shower only); B&B €60-80 pps. Not suitable for children under 8. Closed 23 Dec-1 Jan. CC. **Directions:** 12km from Letterkenny (on R245).

  ## Donegal Rapeseed Oil

Oakfield Demesne Raphoe Co Donegal ✆ *074 914 5386 www.donegalrapeseedoilco.com*

Set up by Austin Duignan and Stephen Allen in 2009, this small, locally owned operation based at Raphoe has, in a short period of time, become established as a successful producer with a nationally recognised brand. Donegal Rapeseed Oil is promoted as a cooking oil - which is probably its best use - and its well balanced flavour has received plenty of independent recognition.

RATHMULLAN

This charming little port village on the shore of Lough Swilly in the north of Donegal offers stunning scenery from the 3km sandy beach to the Fanad Peninsula. In summer visitors can take advantage of the ferry which runs between Rathmullan and Buncrana, or perhaps take a horse ride on the beach. Other local attractions include the Flight of the Earls Heritage Centre (+353 (0) 74 919 4277) or for those who want to take home a few baking tips, then Kathleen Loughrey's School of Home Baking (+353 (0)74 915 8122) is a must do. Rathmullan is only an hour's drive from Glenveagh National Park (+353 (0)74 913 7090), which offers magnificent scenery, rich wildlife including deer, a castle and gardens.

 ## Belle's Kitchen / Salt n Batter

Pier Road Rathmullan Co Donegal ✆ *074 915 8800*

Just a short hop up Pier Road from the harbour, Ronnie Blake's neatly presented pair of businesses cater well to the informal dining needs of Rathmullan. The posher half is Belle's Kitchen, a nice buzzy little smart-casual spot to enjoy a quick bite of something wholesome and homemade, while Salt'n'Batter next door knows how to do the simple things really well: gleamingly fresh, succulent fish and perfect chips. And now, together with another local businessman Cormac Walsh, Ronnie has opened **The Ferry Gate Restaurant and Wine Bar** on the same street (074 9158779; D Thu-Mon).

  ## Kinnegar Brewing Company

Aughavannon Rathmullan Co Donegal ✆ *086 386 3455 www.kinnegarbrewing.com*

Kinnegar Brewing Company makes a small range of farmhouse beers on a nano rather than a micro scale, though that's set to change with a new 10-hectolitre brewery planned. They make three beers – Limeburner, a pale ale; Scraggy Bay, a red ale; and Devil's Backbone, an amber ale. Look out for them around Co. Donegal, eg Rathmullan House Hotel and The Ferry Gate restaurant Rathmullan; Mill Restaurant, Dunfanaghy; The Red Door, The Beach House and Kealy's on Inishowen; and at tasting events.

   ## Rathmullan House

Rathmullan Co Donegal ✆ *074 915 8188 www.rathmullanhouse.com*

Set in lovely gardens on the shores of Lough Swilly the Wheeler family's gracious nineteenth century house is fairly grand yet it has a laid-back holiday charm. Very comfortable accommodation includes ten appealing newer rooms. The food is a big attraction, in both restaurant and bars: head chef Kelan McMichael's modern Irish cooking is upbeat traditional, with meticulously-sourced menus based on the very best of local and artisan foods – including fresh produce from their own restored walled garden. Excellent breakfasts too. *Rooms 34*. *Restaurant seats 80*. D daily from 7pm. Informal meals in The Cellar Bar, 12.30-7pm Thu-Sun in summer and in Batts Bar 1-2.30pm daily. Closed 6 Jan-12 Feb. CC. **Directions:** From Letterkenny, far side of Rathmullan village.

ROSSNOWLAGH

Situated on the south side of Donegal Bay, this busy seaside holiday spot is famous for its beach. Extending to the north northwest for over 2km, from the cliffs at Coolmore in the south to the rock outcrop at Carrickfad, it is one of the most popular surfing beaches in Ireland. Other attractions include La Verna House (071 985 1342), a Franciscan Friary with attractive grounds and gardens, and the Donegal Historical Society's Museum (074 972 2874), open all year.

 **Sand House Hotel**

Rossnowlagh Co Donegal ✆*071 985 1777 www.sandhouse.ie*

This famous beachside hotel is now owned by longtime General Manager, Paul Diver, who has secured its long term future and kept the wonderful staff together as a team. Unrivalled sea views and easy access to the beach are the big attractions, but this immaculately maintained hotel also offers extremely comfortable accommodation, good food, a friendly bar and a spa. *Rooms 50*. Restaurant seats 80. D daily 7-8.30pm, L Sun only, 1-2pm. Closed Dec & Jan. CC. **Directions:** Coast road from Ballyshannon to Donegal Town.

 Smugglers Creek Inn

Cliff Road Rossnowlagh Co Donegal ✆*071 985 2367 www.smugglerscreekinn.com*

Offering panoramic view of Rossnowlagh Beach, Donegal Bay and the Blue Stack Mountains, Emily Browne's very popular inn is a breathtaking spot to unwind.To watch the sun go down over Donegal Bay while enjoying a straightforward and tasty meal such as traditional battered cod with mushy peas, homemade tartare sauce and chips is an unforgettable experience. *Seats 60* (outdoors, 26). Open daily from 12 (April-September) & Thu-Sun from 12 (October-March). Closed 24-26 Dec. CC. **Directions:** 10km north of Ballyshannon on coast road.

 **Trean House**

Tremone Lecamy Inishowen Co Donegal ✆*074 936 7121 www.treanhouse.com*

Way out on the Inishowen peninsula, Joyce and Mervyn Norris's farmhouse is tucked into a sheltered corner in stone-walled countryside beside the sea. Surrounded by a large garden with mature trees and welcoming flowers, it is a substantial house and offers a comfortable base for a relaxing away-from-it-all holiday in a homely atmosphere. *Rooms 4* (3 shower only). Closed 20 Dec-5 Jan. CC. **Directions:** From Moville follow R238 5km, turn right & follow house signs.

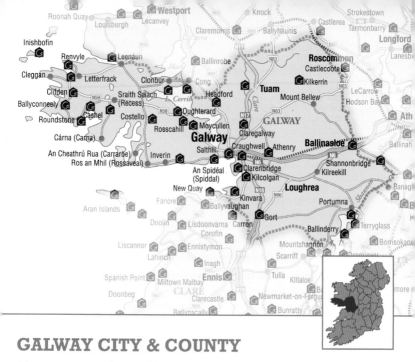

GALWAY CITY & COUNTY

Galway surpasses many other parts of Ireland in the spectacular variety and charm of its numerous scenic routes. But it also has more to offer in the way of offbeat expeditions and experiences, in addition to all the usual visual attractions of Ireland's Atlantic seaboard. Visiting the Aran Islands across the mouth of Galway Bay, for instance, can be done by air as well as by sea. However, as the much-visited Aran Islands have shown, the presence of an air service doesn't seem to lessen the popularity of the ferries, and people often seem to think that you haven't properly visited an island unless you go there by boat.

Then too, there are many coastal boat trips, including an informative seaborne tour from Killary Harbour on the county's northwest coast, Ireland's only genuine fjord, while Lough Corrib is also served by miniature cruise liners. As for sport ashore, the Galway Races at the end of July have developed into a six day meeting which is firmly established as Ireland's premier summer horse racing event, while the Ballinasloe International Horse Fair in the Autumn is simply unique. It dates back more than 280 years.

This has to be Ireland's most generous county, for in effect you get two counties for the price of one. They're neatly divided by the handsome sweep of island-studded Lough Corrib, with the big country of many mountains to the west, and rolling farmland to the east. As a bonus, where the Corrib tumbles into Galway Bay, we find one of Ireland's - indeed, one of Europe's - most vibrant cities. Galway is a bustling place which cheerfully sees itself as being linked to Spain and the great world beyond the Atlantic.

Lough Corrib is both a geographical and psychological divide. East of it, there's flatter country, home to hunting packs of mythic lore. West of the Corrib - which used itself to be a major throughfare, and is now a place of angling renown - you're very quickly into the high ground and moorland which sweep up to the Twelve Bens and other splendid peaks, wonderful mountains which enthusiasts would claim as the most beautiful in all Ireland.

Their heavily indented coastline means this region is Connemara, the Land of the Sea, where earth, rock and ocean intermix in one of Ireland's most extraordinary landscapes. Beyond, to the south, the Aran Islands are a place apart, yet they too are part of the Galway mix in this astonishing county which has its own magical light coming in over the sea. And yet, all its extraordinary variety happens within very manageable distances - Galway is a universe within one day's drive.

LOCAL ATTRACTIONS & INFORMATION

GALWAY CITY
- ▸ **Galway Races** (late July/early August, Sept & Oct)
  091 753870
- ▸ **Galway International Oyster Festival** (late September)
  091 527282

CO GALWAY
- ▸ **Heritage Centre** Aran Islands
  099 61355
- ▸ **Battle of Aughrim Centre** Aughrim *090 9673939*
- ▸ **International Horse Fair** (Sept/Oct) Ballinasloe
  090 9643453

- ▸ **Connemara Pony Show** (mid August) Clifden
  095 21863
- ▸ **Connemara Safari** - Walking & Islands Clifden
  095 21071

GALWAY

Galway is a vibrant, youthful city with an international reputation for exceptional foods - notably the native Irish oysters, which are a speciality of the Clarenbridge area and celebrated at the annual Oyster Festival there in September. The area is renowned for its seafood, especially shellfish, and speciality produce of all kinds - including local cheeses, fruit and vegetables, and specialities that do the rounds of other markets around the country - is on sale at the famous city centre Saturday Market (beside St Nicholas Church; Sat 8.30-4 also Sun, 2-6pm).

An Cupan Tae

8 Quay Lane Galway City ☎ *091 895 000 www.cupantae.eu/galway.html*

Alison McArdle's atmospheric tearoom is a younger sister of the popular café of the same name in Kenmare, Co. Kerry and is a delightful place of refreshment. Great range of loose leaf teas and baked treats served on mismatched china, but also more substantial meals including hot breakfasts and varied lunches (good soups and salads). **Seats 40**. *Food Mon-Sat 10am- 6pm; Sun 11am-6pm.* **Directions:** *Beside the Spanish Arch.*

Aniar Restaurant

53 Dominick Street Galway City ☎ *091 535 947 www.aniarrestaurant.ie*

Owned by well known restaurateurs JP McMahon and Drigin Gaffey, Aniar – meaning 'from the west' - has been the most talked about restaurant in Galway since opening in 2011. The name refers to the stated focus on seasonality, local suppliers, foraged foods from the wild and sustainably caught fish and, although there was a change of chef shortly before going to press, the established philosophy is shared by local man Ultan Cooke, who returned from a high profile position in London to take up the reins as head chef in March 2013. **Seats 30**; *Open Tue-Sat from 6pm. Closed Sun & Mon. CC.*

Antons

12 Father Griffin Road Galway City ☎ *091 582 067*

Anton & Grainne O'Malley's popular café is a simple place that's been feeding a loyal lunch time trade for many years, so it's just the kind of place visitors need to know about. Particularly recommended for home baking, consistently good salads and desserts in an unfussy atmosphere. Great coffees, teas, infusions and freshly squeezed juice too. **Seats 35**. *Open Mon-Sat, 8am-5pm. Closed Sun, 25 Dec. CC.* **Directions:** *5 mins walk from Spanish Arch, over the bridge from Jurys Inn, towards Salthill.*

 **Ard Bia & Nimmo's**

Spanish Arch Galway City ☎ *091 539 897 www.ardbia.com*

A wonderful stone-built medieval customs house overlooking the Claddagh Basin is home to Ard Bia (literally 'High Food') and sister restaurants, Ard Bia Café and Nimmo's, plus a constantly changing exhibition of modern art. Proprietor Aoibheann MacNamara's enthusiasm, energy and commitment to quality are evident throughout. Menus read lip-smackingly well, everything is cooked in house and 'striving to provide food that is 'Great for Galway', local suppliers are the stars of every deliciously meal served here. Great value for the quality too. *Seats 100 (outdoors, 10); Ard Bia Restaurant: Mon-Sat 6-10pm & Sun 10am-10pm. Ard Bia cafe Mon-Sat 9am-3.30pm & 6-10pm & Sun 10am-5pm & 6-10pm. Winebar Thu-Sat 6-11pm. Closed 25-26 Dec. CC. **Directions:** Harbour front, beside the Spanish Arch and Galway City Museums.*

 Ardawn House

College Road Galway City ☎ *091 568 833 www.ardawnhouse.com*

Mike and Breda Guilfoyle's hospitable guesthouse is convenient to the university and just a few minutes walk from Eyre Square. Accommodation is very comfortable, with good amenities and Mike and Breda take great pride in every aspect of the business, (including an extensive breakfast) and help guests to get the very best out of their visit to Galway. *Rooms 8 (all shower only). Closed 21-28 Dec. CC. **Directions:** Off N6, take city east exit; follow signs to city centre. First house on right after greyhound track.*

 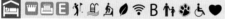 **The Ardilaun Hotel**

Taylors Hill Galway City ☎ *091 521 433 www.theardilaunhotel.ie*

A well-run establishment where friendly staff make a good impression from the outset, the Ryan family's famous old hotel dates back to about 1840 and, while considerably extended and constantly updated, it retains its gentle old-style atmosphere. Family- and pet-friendly, the style of both the hotel and its food is upbeat traditional; a popular wedding venue and equally suited to business and leisure breaks. *Rooms 125 (2 shower only). Closed 22-27 Dec. CC. **Directions:** 1.6km west of city centre (towards Salthill).*

 Asian Tea House Restaurant

15 Mary Street Galway City ☎ *091 563 749 www.asianteahouse.ie*

Terry Commons and Alan Wong's relaxed restaurant is loosely based on the ancient Chinese Tea House concept (a café centred around tea drinking); it offers something different in Galway city, and is good value. Menus representative of Malay, Vietnam, Thai, Japan and China, feature a large range of dishes, all MSG free and based mainly on locally sourced ingredients - and all dishes are cooked to order. Its success is well deserved. *Seats 46; L Thu-Sun from 12.30; D daily 5-10pm. CC. **Directions:** Galway City Centre, Mary Street is off the top of Eglinton Street.*

C R Tormey

Unit 17 Galway Shopping Centre Headford Road Galway City ✆*091 564 067*

Third generation family butchers involved in farming and retailing for over 65 years, with shops in Mullingar, Tullamore and Galway. All offer a combination of high quality traditional butchery and innovative products, earning them many accolades through the years.

Corrib House Tea Rooms & Accommodation

No. 3. Waterside Woodquay Galway City ✆*091 446 753 www.corribhouse.com*

Victoria and David Bohan's handsome waterside Georgian house was built in the early 1800's and sensitively restored before opening in 2011. Three of the four spacious, stylishly furnished guest rooms have river views, while the fourth overlooks an attractive courtyard, which is used for al fresco lunches in summer. One of Galway's most special daytime dining destinations, a visit is sure to be enjoyable. *Tea Rooms: Mon-Fri 8.30am- 5pm, Sat 10.30am-5pm, closed Sun. Unlicensed.* **Rooms 4**. **Directions:** *Centre of Galway, next to the Courthouse & Town Hall Theatre.*

Da Roberta

161 Upper Salthill Galway City ✆*091 585 808 www.darobertasalthill.com*

Roberta and Sandro Pieri's own 'piece of Italy' is still as popular as ever - and queues regularly form at the door. What you get here is charming hospitality, an authentic Italian atmosphere and good value - a great recipe for success. It is almost next to the sister restaurant, Osteria da Roberta, (157/159 Upper Salthill) which serves full meals - no pizza, so it is has less appeal for children and more for adults. *(Open Mon-Sat 5-11, Sun 12.30-11.* **Seats 90** *(outdoors, 18). Open daily 12-11.30. CC.* **Directions:** *Central Salthill, opposite the Church.*

Da Tang Noodle House

2 Middle Street Galway City ✆*091 561 443 www.datangnoodlehouse.com*

Widely recognised as Galway's most authentic Chinese restaurant, rated highly for quality and value. Du Han To, the personable owner-chef (his own art and calligraphy adorn the walls) has a loyal clientele who return again and again for outstanding noodle, dumpling, stir-fry and rice dishes. This little gem also offers a 'Lunchbox Take-Out'. *CHI Pan Asian take-away, is a sister enterprise (+353 (0)91 861687; Westside Enterprise Park, Le Chéile Road, Westside, Galway.) *Open from noon daily for L&D. Online ordering (see website).* **Directions:** *South of Eyre Square near Shop Street/Quay Street.*

The Dail Bar

41-42 Middle Street Galway City ☎*091 563 777 www.thedailbar.com*

This handsome traditional pub occupies a prominent corner position on Middle Street and Cross Street and proudly proclaims its establishment in 1759 beneath an elegant round clock. While not adventurous, cooking is above the standard normally expected in pubs, and includes plenty of vegetarian and gluten free options. Also known for TV sport and live music. *Seats 80. Open for food daily, 12-9.30pm. Children welcome. CC. **Directions:** Centre of Galway, corner of Middle and Cross streets.*

 Eat @ Massimo

10 William St. West Galway City ☎*091 582 239 www.eatgastropub.com*

Jp McMahon and team also run Galway's most talked about restaurant, Aniar, so the fact that they operate the food service here guarantees Massimo's status as one of the city's leading gastropubs. Also well known for good music, it's a pleasant and welcoming place to be (with an open fire) and it's popular with locals, especially for lunch and Sunday brunch. Ingredients-led menus offer imaginative meals, especially in the evening. Open daily, noon until late. CC. ***Directions:** City centre - Small Crane end of William Street.*

 EIGHT Bar and Restaurant

8 Dock Road Galway City ☎*091 565 111 www.eight.ie*

Tom Sheridan's EIGHT Bar & Restaurant overlooking busy Dock Road is known for its commitment to a quirky simplicity - and also to local suppliers, who are credited as members of the team. A meal here should be an enjoyable experience, and it's real value for money too - attentive service, good cooking and customer-friendly prices make for a great atmosphere, so the buzz is there. *Seats 50. Open Mon-Thu 4.30-11pm & Fri-Sun 12.30-11.30pm. **Directions:** Overlooking Dock Road.*

 The Fisherman

Galway Shopping Centre Headford Road Galway City ☎*091 561 966 www.fisherman.ie*

Proprietor Patrick O'Malley has been fishing since the age of 14 and now supplies much of the fish to The Fisherman from his own vessels. This chain of fresh fish shops based in the west of Ireland stocks a wide variety of fresh fish and shellfish from responsibly managed sources. *Open: Mon 8-6, Tue & Wed 9-6, Thu 8-8,, Fri 9-8, Sat 9-6, Sun 12-5.*

 The Front Door

Cross Street and High Street Galway City ☎*091 563 757 www.frontdoorpub.com*

Downstairs has all the intimacy of an inner city pub with cosy nooks and crannies for pint drinkers and casual dining. Upstairs is a young persons' hang-out with late night disco, big TV screens and tables for dining. The food is good, middle-of-the-road at reasonable prices, served by interested young staff. *Seats 90. L & D daily. Closed 25 Dec. CC. **Directions:** Middle of Galway's city-centre Latin Quarter.*

 **The G Hotel**

Wellpark Galway City ✆*091 865 200 www.theg.ie*

One of the finest hotels in the West of Ireland - and certainly the most original - the G is renowned for its interior by Galwegian milliner Phillip Treacy, who was given free rein to indulge his quirky creativity. Suites and guestrooms are much quieter in tone than the public areas, making for a restful stay, and there is a strong emphasis on food. A fun place that brings a smile to people's faces. *Rooms 101. Restaurant seats 72. Open daily for L & D. Closed 24-26 Dec. CC.* **Directions:** *East Galway city on the old Dublin Road, 5 mins drive from Eyre Square.*

 Galway Bay Brewery

Upper Salthill Road Galway City ✆*091 448 390 www.winefoodbeer.com/brewery*

Established in 2009, Galway Bay Brewery was Galway's first microbrewery and produces a range of five beers. Situated in the Oslo pub in Salthill village, an on-site building at the back of the pub allows for expansion to include brewery tours and talks on the craft of brewing with the brewer himself. Available at selected pubs in Galway and Dublin. See website for updates.

 **Galway Bay Hotel**

The Promenade Salthill Galway City ✆*091 520 520 www.galwaybayhotel.com*

This well-named hotel has views over Galway Bay to the hills of County Clare from public rooms on the upper ground floor as well as many of the well-equipped if, in some cases, slightly dated bedrooms. Its location and good leisure facilities make it a popular family holiday destination, but it is also a highly regarded conference centre. *Rooms 153. Open all year. CC.* **Directions:** *Located on Salthill Road beside Leisureland.*

  Gannet Fishmongers

Kiosk 17 Eyre Square Centre Eyre Square Galway City ✆*091 507 019 www.fishmongers.ie*

A familar sight at Galway Farmers' Market, Stephane Griesbach supplies "the best quality, best value in locally sourced, wild Irish fish" - and he is also responsible for creating a uniquely informative website about fish and the fish industry, fishmongers.ie Both interesting and useful, it's a "comprehensive source of information about fish and the fish industry both for the public and for participants in the various aspects of the industry".

 **Gourmet Tart Co.**

Monksfield Salthill Galway City ✆*091 861 667 www.gourmettartcompany.com*

Fintan and Michelle Hyland are best known in Galway for their high quality French style patisseries/delis and in 2010 they added this café/restaurant in Salthill. The shop offers the full range of beautiful handmade products - bakery, sandwiches, ready meals; behind it, in a minimalist room, talented head chef Damien O'Malley serves imaginative and deliciously seasonal meals. The cooking and service here out-perform many more expensive restaurants and it's probably the best value in town. *Seats 70. Open daily, from 7.30am-7pm (Fri & Sat to 'late'.) CC.* **Directions:** *Just off Upper Salthill road, opposite church. Bakery/delis also at: Galway Shopping Centre, Headford Road; Lower Abbeygate Street, Galway City; Raven Terrace, Claddagh, Galway City. Also Galway & Limerick farmers' markets.*

Gourmet Tart Company

65 Henry Street Galway City ☎*091 588 384 www.gourmettartcompany.com*

French bakers work through the night at Fintan and Michelle Hyland's bakery, to provide fresh croissants and other exquisite fare when the shop opens at 7.30a.m. This foodie haven of bakery, deli, and gourmet food shop celebrates good food at a fair price, all products are made from natural ingredients and are chemical-free. *Also at: 7 Abbeygate St Lr, Galway; Upper Salthill (opp. Seapoint); Galway SC. Open all day, times vary. Galway Farmers' Market & Limerick Milk Market (Sat). See also Gourmet Tart Co restaurant, Salthill.*

  Goya's

2/3 Kirwans Lane Galway City ☎*091 567010 www.goyas.ie*

If only for a cup of cappuccino or hot chocolate and a wedge of chocolate cake, or a slice of quiche, a restorative visit to Emer Murray's delightful contemporary bakery and café/deli is a must on any visit to Galway. Also specialises in wedding and special occasion cakes and seasonal baking. *Seats 56 (outdoor, 20). Open all day Mon-Sat. CC.* **Directions:** *Behind McDonaghs Fish Shop, off Quay Street.*

  Griffins Bakery

Shop Street Galway City ☎*091 563 683 www.griffinsbakery.com*

In business since 1876, fourth generation baker Jimmy Griffin is keeping up the family tradition in style and has won many an accolade, notably for the Griffin's Artisan range which includes allergy-specific, yeast-free and a collection of 'Galway' breads (try the whiskey brack). Buy from the shop, order online - or sample them in the charming traditional tea rooms. *Open 7 days (times vary).*

 **Harbour Hotel**

New Docks Road Galway City ☎*091 569466 www.harbour.ie*

Offering functional, comfortable accommodation with secure parking adjacent, and conveniently situated at the heart of the city, a fantastic harbourside location is this hotel's trump card. Galway city's main attractions are all within comfortable walking distance. *Rooms 96. Open all year except Christmas. CC.* **Directions:** *Beside the docks in Galway, 5 mins from Eyre Square.*

   The Heron's Rest B&B

Longwalk Spanish Arch Galway City ☎*091 539 574 www.theheronsrest.com*

The location of Sorcha Molloy's delightful B&B must be the best in Galway - right in the centre of the city just seaward of Spanish Arch and with everything within easy walking distance, yet quietly situated with views across the river and out to sea. And it is a charming house, with lots of TLC lavished on the sweet waterside rooms, and a lot of care in everything Sorcha does - including a typically generous and unusual breakfast menu. Magic. *Rooms 6 (3 shower only). Closed 30 Sep-1 May. CC.*

Hotel Meyrick

Eyre Square Galway City ℰ*091 564 041 www.hotelmeyrick.ie*

Formerly the Great Southern, this historic railway hotel was built in 1845 and has always had a special place in the hearts of Galway people. Although a contemporary style currently prevails, the older guestrooms still hint at the grandeur and elegance of its 19th century heyday. **Rooms 97**. *Closed 23-27 Dec. CC.* **Directions:** *In heart of the city overlooking Eyre Square.*

  **The House Hotel**

Spanish Parade Galway City ℰ*091 538 900 www.thehousehotel.ie*

This stylish hotel near Spanish Arch is homely at heart, with excellent facilities and many thoughtful touches which aim to make this your Galway 'home away from home'. Although styled 'boutique' - and all rooms are individually designed - it's bigger than it seems and accommodation includes a comfy, classy suite overlooking Galway harbour. **Rooms 40** *(some shower only). Closed 25-26 Dec. CC.* **Directions:** *Centre city, a block away from the Spanish Arch.*

 **The Huntsman Inn**

164 College Road Galway City ℰ*091 562 849 www.huntsmaninn.com*

Near the city centre and easily accessible by car, this busy spot near the G Hotel looks like a pretty row of houses and, with its colourful hanging baskets, the facade cleverly disguises a large interior. The smart, contemporary en-suite bedrooms offer great value, and it's a relaxed, comfortable place for flavoursome food at a reasonable price. Uncomplicated menus reflect a refreshingly down to earth philosophy, beginning with a good breakfast and later offer reliable favourites. Everything is cooked with care and well presented - and a separate children's menu doubles as a colouring competition. **Rooms 12** *(3 shower only).* **Seats 200** *(outdoors, 50); meals daily, 12.30-9.30 (Sun to 9). CC.* **Directions:** *Follow signs for Galway East, just before Eyre Square.*

 Il Folletto Ristorante Italiano

8 Quay Street Galway City ℰ*091 566 066 www.ilfolletto.ie*

On old Galway's busiest street, Chef Roberto Brasso's moderately priced restaurant Il Folletto ('pixie') is a lively, buzzy place. Atmospheric and friendly, it caters for all age groups and Roberto's menus represent several of Italy's many food regions and offer authentic renditions of many classics. Moderately-priced all-Italian wine list. **Seats 65**. *Open: Mon-Thu 5-10, Fri & Sat 5-10.30. Also L bank hol weekends and Mon-Sat in summer (Jun-Sep), 12-3.*

Il Vicolo

5 Buttermilk Lane Galway City ✆*091 535 922*

With downtempo jazz, large windows onto the street and keen staff there's a pleasant buzz at this tiny corner cafe/wine bar run by Gerry McMahon and his partner Aoife. Born out of Gerry's devotion to and experience of Italian food and wine, il Vicolo (alley in English), offers quality and value: with excellent coffee and rustic soups, you can snack well here for a tenner. **Seats 25**. *Open daily in summer 10am-10pm. More restricted winter opening. CC.* **Directions:** *Corner of Buttermilk Lane and Augustine Street, a couple of minutes walk from Shop Street.*

                               Joyces Supermarket

Shangort Road Knocknacarra Galway City ✆*091 589 300 www.joycesupermarket.com*

Support of local suppliers and locally produced goods distinguishes Joyces in the area; suppliers, many of them small producers, are credited on their website. Their efforts are rewarded with frequent accolades, including the the Glanbia Best in Fresh Awards in 2012. Also at: Athenry, Headford and Tuam.

                               Jurys Inn Galway

Quay Street Galway City ✆*091 566 444*

Magnificently sited to make the most of both the river - rushing past almost all the bedroom windows - and the buzz of the Spanish Arch area (just outside the door) this hotel, ike most Jurys room-only 'inns', it offers a good standard of basic accommodation without frills, although the high occupancy rate can sometimes show in wear and tear. **Rooms 128**. *Multi storey carpark adjacent.*

                                                K C Blakes

10 Quay Street Galway City ✆*091 561826*

Window tables downstairs are perfect for people-watching, while the outdoor tables (or upstairs dining room) offer a choice of ambience. Proprietor-chef John Casey sources ingredients for his wide-ranging menus with care and cooks with skill to offer something for every taste - and this remarkably consistent operation is fairly priced. *D daily, 5-10pm. Closed 25 Dec. CC.* **Directions:** *City centre, near Spanish Arch.*

                           Kai Café & Restaurant

Sea Road Galway City ✆*091 526 003 www.kaicaferestaurant.com*

Kai, meaning food in Maori, is run by chef Jess Murphy, a New Zealander, with her Irish husband David front-of-house. Menus at this rustic café and restaurant change daily and throughout the day, with home baking an early attraction; an excellent short à la carte dinner is dependent on the best ingredients available and carefully selected wines to accompany. Good value for the quality of the food and deservedly popular. **Seats 30**. Café open all day Mon-Fri. Restaurant D Wed-Sun 6.30-10.30pm. CC. **Directions:** Sea Road runs between Father Griffin Avenue and Upper Dominick Street.

Kellys Bar & Lounge

Bridge Street Galway City 📞*091 563804 www.kellysbar.ie*

This traditional pub in Galway's cosmopolitan city centre is a well run, customer-oriented pub with friendly staff, and there is a strong food component. Cooking is competent without being adventurous – "tasty, honest, homecooked food" is the promise, and it's available all day. An upstairs venue features live music, comedy nights and theatre. *Kitchen open 10.30am til 8pm.* CC. **Directions:** *Centre of Galway.*

 ### Kirwan's Lane Restaurant & The Seafood Bar

Kirwans Lane Galway City 📞*091 568 266*

Sister of the renowned seafood restaurant O'Grady's of Barna (see entry), Michael O'Grady's pleasing place in the city is a little oasis just off Galway's main shopping thoroughfare. It's known for smart cooking and, while there's a predictably strong showing of fish and shellfish, evening menus, especially, also take on board the tastes of vegetarians and meat-eaters. **Seats 90** (outdoors, 20). L& D daily. Closed 24-29 Dec. CC. **Directions:** Just off Cross Street and Quay Street.

  ### The Malt House Restaurant

Olde Malt Mall High Street Galway City 📞*091 567 866 www.themalthouse.ie*

 In a quiet, flower-filled courtyard off High Street, away from the often frenetic buzz of modern Galway, this smart-casual restaurant is a well run establishment, relaxed even at busy times; service never flags and there's a pleasant air of confidence about the operation. Many speciality Irish foods and organic ingredients feature on upbeat traditional seasonal menus and suppliers are listed; an outing here is always enjoyable and consistency has earned The Malt House local support. *The adjacent King's Head pub is in common ownership. **Seats 100** (outdoors, 30). Food served all day Mon-Sat from noon. Closed Sun, Bank Hols & Dec 25-Jan 2. CC. **Directions:** Located in a courtyard just off High Street.

  ### Martin Divilly

Westside Shopping Centre Seamus Quirke Road Galway City 📞*091 523 947 www.martindivillybutchers.com*

Third generation butcher Martin Divilly and his wife Audrey have won many an award over the years. While they concentrate on offering the very best meats and poultry - including dry-aged Angus and Hereford cross grass-fed beef from Galway farms; local spring lamb; low-salt home cured bacon; Carlow Free Range Chickens - they also have a very successful fresh fish counter.

Martines Restaurant

21 Quay Street Galway City ☎ *091 565 662 www.winebar.ie*

The smart facade of Martine McDonagh's long-established restaurant faces the family's famous fish restaurant, across the street. Local and artisan-produced seasonal ingredients are the foundation for cooking which is deliberately kept simple, with everything (including the ketchup) homemade. Menus give appealing choices for everyone, but their pride and joy is the 35 day dry-aged Irish Angus beef, cooked in a special charcoal oven that gives it that incomparable flavour. Service is friendly, there's a good buzz and it offers value too. *Seats 50 (outdoors, 20). Open daily, D only. Closed 25 Dec. CC. Directions: City centre, in the latin quarter near Jurys Inn Quay Street.*

                                         Maxwells Bistro

14 Williamsgate Street Galway City ☎ *091 568 974 www.maxwellsrestaurant.ie*

Galway's oldest restaurant, dating back to 1866, Paul O'Meara's lively bistro offers plenty of crowd pleasers, but the foundation is top quality local produce. It's easy to see why Maxwells is so popular – the staff are friendly and efficient, the portions are generous, the cooking is solid, and children are not only welcome, but very well looked after. A good place to know about. *Seats 85. Open 7 days, 10am-9.30pm. Directions: Williamsgate Street is just off west side of Eyre Square.*

                                                    McCambridges of Galway

38-39 Shop Street Galway City ☎ *091 562 259 www.mccambridges.com*

Established in 1925 and now run by siblings Eoin, Natalie and Norma, who take pride in continuing the family tradition, McCambridge's offers an ever-changing range of carefully selected food and wines from Ireland and abroad, including artisan jams, preserves, chutneys, Irish cheeses, speciality meats, ice creams - and irresistible Irish and continental chocolates including the gorgeous Skelligs from the Ring of Kerry. The first floor now operates as a restaurant, Upstairs @ McCambridges (see entry).

                                                  McDonaghs Seafood House

22 Quay Street Galway City ☎ *091 565 001 www.mcdonaghs.net*

In Galway's busiest restaurant street McDonaghs has been serving fish and chips 'for ever'. Nationally renowned, it is a thriving multi-faceted business: takeaway fish bar, indoor restaurant and boulevard seafood café in summer. The fish choice is wide and guaranteed fresh. What you get here is a definite local flavour of a bustling chipper, offering a pleasant experience at fairly reasonable prices. *Open 12-11 daily (Sun 4-10).*

Mortons of Galway

Lower Salthill Road Galway City ℂ*091 522 237 www.mortonsofgalway.ie*

A top-quality food store, Eric Morton's long experience in premium retail shows in the selectivity of this fine shop: freshly baked breads, pies, crumbles and quiches; fresh salads, cooked meats and deli foods, all prepared from scratch; fresh fruit and vegetables; traditional in-house butchery; fresh fish and seafood ("if we can't get it fresh we won't stock it"). Definitely a one-stop shop. *Open: Mon to Fri, 9-7; Sat, 9-6.30; Sun 10-5.30.*

Oscars Seafood Bistro

Dominick Street Galway City ℂ*091 582 180 www.oscarsbistro.ie*

Away from the bustle of the Spanish Arch area, husband and wife team Michael O'Meara and Sinead Hughes' theatrical restaurant has been wowing its many fans since 2000. Followers love Michael's originality and verve – and appreciate that this Euro-Toques chef's adventurous cooking is always based on the best of ingredients, notably ultra-fresh local seafood. Michael O'Meara's personality and wide-ranging interests add a lot to the pleasure of a visit to this friendly place, where good service goes hand-in-hand with exciting food. *Seats 45*. D Mon-Sat. Closed Sun (except Bank Hol weekends when they close Mon instead). CC. *Directions: 2 minutes across bridge from Jurys.*

Park House Hotel

Forster St. Eyre Square Galway City ℂ*091 564 924 www.parkhousehotel.ie*

If you want a thoroughly Irish welcome in the heart of Galway, you could not do better than stay at this cosy and central hotel. Park House Hotel has the individuality that comes with owner-management and provides an exceptionally friendly and comfortable haven from the bustle of Galway, which seems to be constantly in celebration. *Rooms 84*. Park Room Restaurant L&D daily. Closed 24-26 Dec. CC. *Directions: Located adjacent to Eyre Square.*

Radisson Blu Hotel & Spa

Lough Atalia Road Galway City ℂ*091 538300 www.radissonhotelgalway.com*

Attractively situated overlooking Lough Atalia, this fine contemporary hotel is more central than its scenic location might suggest. Excellent facilities for conferences and meetings are matched by outstanding leisure facilities, including a destination spa, Spirit One, while dining options include an authentic Japanese restaurant, RAW (see entry). *Rooms 261*, Restaurant *seats 220*; L Mon-Sat & D daily. Bar food also available daily. CC. *Directions: By lane from Lough Atalia, 3 minutes walk from bus & train station.*

RAW Restaurant Sushi in the Sky

Top Floor, Radisson Blu Hotel Lough Atalia Road Galway City
📞*091 538 212 www.sushiinthesky.ie*

Hisashi Kumagai is both the inspiration and the chef in RAW. The focus is on Japanese Sushi, showcasing the best of Galway's fresh raw seafood, fastidiously selected and prepared: sliced and artfully arranged as sashimi and as lightly vinegared rolls with rice and seaweed cut into bite-sized chunks. Guided by the very helpful, informed waiting staff, a meal in RAW is an adventure beyond the common ken and excellent value for such an unusual dining experience. *Open D only, Tue-Sat 6-10. CC.*

 Revive Café

35 Eyre Street Galway City 📞*091 533 779 www.revivecafe.ie*

Everything at Michael & Mary O'Reilly's popular day-time café is based on fresh produce daily, cooked simply; quality sandwiches, wraps, salads, panini are made to order, and dressings, pestos, salsa and relishes are also home-made. Although busy at lunchtime, it's a pleasant drop-in at any time, with a covered courtyard for summer, and staff are friendly and efficient. **Seats 60**. *Open daily 8am-5.30pm (Sun from 7.30). Closed 25-26 Dec, bank hols. CC.*

  The Seafood Centre

New Docks Galway City 📞*091 563 011 www.galwaybayseafoods.com*

This family-owned business was established in 1950 by John V. Holland and currently run by his two sons John Jnr and Noel. The shop at Galway Bay Seafoods offers a wide range of whitefish and shellfish, with live lobster, crab and oysters available from a tank in-store; they also have their own salmon smokery, and a purpose-built fish and seafood cookery school above the shop. *Open Mon-Wed 8.30-5, Thu-Fri 8.30-7.30, Sat 8.30-5. Closed Sun.*

  Sheridans Cheesemongers

14-16 Churchyard Street Galway City 📞*091 564 829 www.sheridanscheesemongers.com*

Synonymous with good cheese in Ireland, brothers Seamus and Kevin Sheridan started the business that is now a household name by selling cheese at Galway farmers' market many moons ago and their partner, Fiona Corbett, joined them in 1997. Here the current premises incorporates a wine shop and bar as well as the shop selling their incomparable cheeses and other speciality foods. Stocks reflect the seasons and are mainly Irish, but other equally carefully sourced European foods are also stocked. Also still selling from their original stall at the Saturday Galway Farmers' Market (held on the church square just outside the shop) and other markets in the Dublin area. *Shop: Mon-Fri 10-6, Sat 9-6 (also Sun 11.30-5 in summer). Wine shop and bar: Tue 5-10, Wed & Thu 1-10, Fri 1-12, Sat 12-12. Closed Sun & Mon.*

  Solaris Botanicals

Unit 3 Ballybane Enterprise Centre Castlepark Road Galway City
📞*091 750 020 www.solarisbotanicals.com*

Renowned medical herbalists Jorg Muller and Karin Wieland blend organic and herbal teas for discerning, health-conscious tea-lovers. Their products are outstanding: accolades include a Euro Toques award in 2009, for their organic whole leaf: "an innovative product, based on passion and expertise, with an environmental conscience..." Try the beautiful flowering teas, made in glass teapots. Available from specialist stores and online.

  ## Tigh Neachtain & Artisan Restaurant

17 Cross Street Galway City ✆*091 568 820 www.tighneachtain.com*

Tigh Neachtain (Naughton's) is one of Galway's oldest pubs. It has great charm, an open fire, a friendly atmosphere, impromptu music sessions - and their own seasonal craft beer. Above the pub, Artisan restaurant offers lovely simple lunches (freshly made soup and seafood chowder with speciality breads; an enticing array of sandwiches and salads featuring local produce). Dinner offers more substantial fare and pleasant, interested staff discuss the day's menu with enthusiasm. A useful place to know about and full of character. *Artisan seats 45 (outdoors, 20). L&D daily 12-3 & 6-10pm. Closed 25 Dec & Good Fri.*

 ## Tom Sheridans Bar & Restaurant

Clybaun Road Knocknacarra Galway City ✆*091 525 315 www.tomsheridans.ie*

In common ownership with two city sisters, The Front Door and The Dail Bar, this large traditional pub in Galway is at the heart of the western suburbs, catering mainly for a local trade. Friendly and customer-focused, it has wide screen TV for sporting events and offers an attractive restaurant as well as bar meals; barbecues are held in summer. *L & D daily. Closed 25 Dec. CC.* **Directions:** *West Galway, near Bearna, behind Clybaun Stores.*

 ## Travelodge Galway City

Joyce Roundabout Tuam Road Galway City Centre Co Galway ✆*091 781400*

Do not expect service at this spacious modern hotel but, for the budget conscious family, corporate guest or short break customer it will probably not be bettered on price. Other outstanding features include free off road car parking - and, very unusually for a city hotel, pets are allowed (book in online). Useful to know. **Directions:** *Coming south or east bound follow the R338 to Joyce roundabout, take the 3rd exit. Northbound take the N17 road into the city centre. The Travelodge is located on the R336, approximately 1 mile on the left hand side.*

  ## Upstairs @ McCambridges

38-39 Shop Street Galway City ✆*091 562 259 www.mccambridges.com*

Above the long-established wine shop and delicatessen, McCambridge's of Galway (see entry), this casual - but quality-conscious - restaurant uses only Irish meats and poultry and asserts its supports for local and artisan producers (albeit without crediting the suppliers by name). Constant supervision by the McCambridge family is noticeable, and the cooking should not disappoint. A great addition to the Galway dining scene, Upstairs@McCambridge's is warmly recommended. *Open all day Mon-Sat from 9am, Sun from 10.30. D Wed-Sat.*

The Westwood

Dangan Upper Newcastle Galway City ☎*091 521 442* *www.westwoodhousehotel.com*

A sister hotel to The Schoolhouse Hotel in Dublin and the Station House Hotel, Clifden (see entries) this 4* property is well located, on the edge of Galway and convenient to both the city and Connemara. Set well back from the road, it has a pleasant almost-in-the-country atmosphere and friendly, helpful staff. **Rooms 58**. *Closed 24-25 Dec. CC.*

   **Clayton Hotel**

Galway City Area Ballybrit Co Galway ☎*091 721 900* *www.claytonhotelgalway.ie*

Convenient to both Galway city centre and Galway Airport, this four star hotel is well located for business and leisure guests; with Galway Race Course and Rosshill Golf Course very close by (and a good choice of other golf courses within a short distance), it is an especially attractive destination for sports lovers. State of the art conference facilities. **Rooms 195**. *CC.* **Directions:** *Off the N6; at the Lynch roundabout take the R339, hotel entrance is on the right.*

🍴🏨🖥️📺👁️⛷️🏊🦺🌿📶 B 👫♿❤ **Connemara Coast Hotel**

Galway City Area Furbo Co Galway ☎*091 592 108* *www.sinnotthotels.com*

Sister property to the excellent Brooks Hotel in Dublin (see entry), Charles Sinnott's beautifully located hotel is on the sea side of the road, in its own grounds; it's hard to credit that Galway city is only 15 minutes' drive. Accommodation and food at this likeable hotel is of a generally high standard. The newer rooms are very spacious - and good facilities include an atmospheric bar, two restaurants, children's playroom (and playground) and leisure centre. Staff are invariably friendly and helpful. **Rooms 141**. *Gallery Restaurant* **seats 120**; *D 7-9.30pm daily. Open all year. CC.* **Directions:** *9km from Galway city on Spiddal road.*

🍴🍷   **Donnelly's of Barna**

Galway City Area Barna Co Galway ☎*091 592 487*

Donnelly's of Barna is a landmark at the crossroads in Barna. Established in 1892, this comfortable old world pub has little snugs, comfy corners and bric à brac as well as a more formal dining area. Strong on seafood, the same bar menu is served throughout and, although not inexpensive, the combination of good cooking, friendly attentive service and a relaxing ambience make this good value. **Seats 150**. *Mon-Sun 12-9.45pm (from 12.30 Sun). CC.* **Directions:** *On road that leads to harbour.*

  🛏️⛷️📶 B 👫♿❤   **Glenlo Abbey Hotel**

Galway City Area Bushypark Co Galway ☎*091 526 666* *www.glenlo.com*

Glenlo Abbey offers something different from other hotels in Galway and, while some may find it dated, others will embrace its old fashioned nature and friendly staff. **Rooms 46**. *Hotel closed 24-27 Dec. CC.* **Directions:** *4km from Galway on N59 in the Clifden direction.*

 **Maldron Hotel Galway**

Galway City Area Oranmore Co Galway ✆091 792 244 www.maldronhotels.com

Known for its excellent leisure facilities, this very family friendly hotel offers good value and is conveniently situated to visit Co Clare and Galway City, while good conference and business facilities also make it a popular venue for business guests. **Rooms 113**. *Closed 25-26 Dec. CC.* **Directions:** *at the Carrowmoneash roundabout on the main (N6) road.*

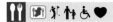 **Mulberrys Restaurant**

Galway City Area Unit 14 Barna Village Centre Barna Co Galway ✆091 592 123

www.mulberrys.ie

Inviting and welcoming, with bistro and tapas-style menus highlighting local ingredients (suppliers listed), James and Deirdre Cunningham's contemporary 'Italian and Seafood' restaurant features pasta and seafood, of course - and also meats from renowned Oughterard butcher, James McGeough, notably his superb sirloin steak. Quality, casual elegance and reasonable prices make Mulberrys a pleasant place to visit. **Seats 78** *(outdoors, 20). D only daily from 5pm. Closed Mon off season. CC.* **Directions:** *In the heart of Barna Village.*

 **O'Grady's on the Pier**

Galway City Area Sea Point Barna Co Galway ✆091 592 223 www.ogradysonthepier.com

In a stunning harbourside position, Michael O'Grady's charming restaurant is a favourite destination for seafood lovers. The best dishes are the simplest and, although the ubiquitous tiger prawn may make a surprising appearance, the wide range of fish and seafood is mainly fresh local produce, delivered daily: Cleggan crab, Rossaveal clams, Galway oysters (in season), Galway Bay lobster, local mussels, Aran salmon, locally caught mackerel, and sea fish landed at nearby Rossaveal. Well worth a visit. *Kirwan's Lane, a sister restaurant in Galway City, also has a strong focus on seafood. **Seats 85** *(outdoors 25); L & D daily. Closed 25/26 Dec. CC.* **Directions:** *7km west of Galway city on the Spiddal Road.*

The Twelve

Galway City Area Barna Village Co Galway ✆091 597 000 www.thetwelvehotel.ie

Fergus O'Halloran's unique hotel has achieved national recognition thanks to hands-on management and marketing by an inspired proprietor. The offering is highly unusual, from romantic rooms and West At The Twelve's exceptional fine wining and dining experience, to quality casual food, notably pizza, in the busy, child-friendly Pins Bar Bakery Bistro - and sales in the Pizza Dozzina artisanal shop next door - it sings of quality and innovation at every level. There is huge focus on the best local and artisan foods and craft beers, and this busy local and tourist venue is popular for sports on TV and weekend live music sessions too. A great destination. **Rooms 48**. *Restaurant **seats 90** (outdoors, 30); D Tue-Sun. Hotel closed 2-3 days Christmas. CC.* **Directions:** *At crossroads in Barna village.*

ARAN ISLANDS

Situated in Galway Bay, the Aran Islands of Inishmore, Inishmaan and Inisheer (Inis Mór, Inis Meáin and Inis Oirr), have a rugged splendour and a sense of time standing still, evident in the many thatch-roofed stone cottages that dot the landscape. Rich in history, the ruins of early Christian monasteries and fortifications dating back over 2000 years include the famous Dún Aonghusa ring fort. With sandy beaches, breathtaking cliffs, and twisting country lanes, the islands are well suited to walking or cycling. Visitors love the remoteness of the islands, the music and craic, and the glimpse of traditional island life that lies at the end of the short ferry trip. The largest of the islands, Inishmore, is also the most visited, so the true island experience may be more easily found on the smaller islands. The Aran Islands are easily accessible by ferry from Galway City, or the harbours at Rossaveal and Doolin, or by air from Galway (Aer Arann; www.aerarann.com; 091 541900).

 An Dún

Inis Meain Aran Islands Co Galway ☎*087 680 6251 www.inismeainaccommodation.ie*

At the foot of Dun Conchubhar (Connor's Fort) is Teresa and Padraic Faherty's restaurant and B&B, An Dún, with en-suite bedrooms (modern, comfortable, great views) and a mini-spa. In the restaurant, local foods star: fish straight from currachs; their own floury Inis Meain potatoes, fertilised in the traditional manner, with seaweed; organic vegetables grown in their polytunnel; scones, crumbles and tarts using local fruits. **Seats 40** *(outdoor seating 10). Closed 30 Nov-1 Mar. CC.* **Directions:** *Centre of island, near church, next door to JM Synge cottage.*

  **Inis Meáin Restaurant & Suites**

Inis Meain Aran Islands Co Galway ☎*086 826 6026 www.inismeain.com*

This wonderful place on the most tranquil and least visited of the Aran Islands group has earned an international reputation as one of Ireland's most desirable destinations. Chef Ruairi de Blacam, a native of Inis Meain, and his wife, Marie-Therese, offer a unique experience, serving beautifully simple food in a modern restaurant with a panoramic view of the island, sea and sky. Suites are designed to help guests discover the peace and quiet of the island, with fishing rods, bicycles and books instead of TV. *Restaurant* **Seats 30**. *D 7-9pm. Fri-Sat in May-June, Tues-Sat in July-Aug.* **Rooms 4** *& 1 suite apartment; Closed Oct-Apr. CC.* **Directions:** *After passing only pub on your right, take next right, then take first left.*

 Kilmurvey House

Kilronan Inis Mor Aran Islands Co Galway ☎*099 61218 www.kilmurveyhouse.com*

Treasa Joyce's 150-year old stone house stands out as a beacon at the foot of the Aran islands' most famous attraction, Dun Aonghasa. It's a fine house and well kept; spacious bedrooms are stylish and beautifully finished, with great views. Dinner for groups only, by arrangement; free transport for B&B guests to Kilronan, for dinner there. **Rooms 14** *(4 shower only). Closed 31 Oct-1 Apr. CC.* **Directions:** *7km from Kilronan.*

 Mainistir House

Inis Mor Aran Islands Co Galway ☎*099 61169 www.mainistirhousearan.com*

Joel d'Anjou's hostel and restaurant is open twenty years and still the most talked about place on the islands. It generally provides more comfort than the hostel rate implies - but the food is the main attraction, and you don't need to stay here to experience it. Lovingly cooked by a well-travelled foodie, Joel's famous 'Vaguely Vegetarian Buffet' (changes daily) is served nightly and this fun and funky restaurant continues to give amazing value. *Restaurant Seats 45. D daily, 8pm. Accommodation: (8 private rooms plus hostel accommodation for up to 70). CC. Directions: 1.5km along the main road from the harbour.*

 ## Man Of Aran Cottages

Kilmurvey Inis Mor Aran Islands Co Galway ✆*099 61301 www.manofarancottage.com*

Despite its fame - this is where the film Man of Aran was made - Joe and Maura Wolfe make visiting their home a genuine and personal experience. Basic little bedrooms are full of quaint, cottagey charm and meals will be enhanced by home-grown produce such as beautifully sweet cherry tomatoes from Joe's garden - somehow productive, even in this exposed location. Magic. *Rooms 3 (1 en-suite). Residents' D 7-8pm, by arrangement. Closed Nov-Feb. No CC. Directions: Minibus or cycle from Kilronan, 6.5km.*

 ## Ostan Inis Meain

Inis Meáin Aran Islands Co Galway ✆*099 73020 www.ostaninismeain.com*

Páraic & Gobnait O'Fátharta's hotel is the only one on the central island and their traditional Irish hospitality is very relaxing for visitors. The bedrooms all have magnificent views and the hotel is a focus for activities on the island, offering not just food and drink, but also music and the craic that goes with it. *Rooms 10. Directions: Centre of Inis Meain island.*

 ## Pier House Guest House

Kilronan Inis Mor Aran Islands Co Galway ✆*099 61417 www.pierhousearan.com*

In a new building, right on the pier where the boats arrive, Maura and Padraig Joyce run this large well-kept guesthouse; rooms are comfortable, with more facilities than most island accommodation. As they are beside the ferry, the Joyces concentrate on mainstream food in the restaurant, based mainly on good local ingredients. *Rooms 10. Restaurant seats 45 (also outdoor seating on pier) Open all day from 11am. Reservations advised. CC.*

  ## Radharc An Chlair

Castle Village Inis Oirr Aran Islands Co Galway ✆*099 75019*

Brid Poil's welcoming dormer house has views of the Cliffs of Moher and Galway Bay, and she has a great reputation so you need to book well ahead. Rooms are comfy (no tv) and, although no dinner is offered, there are treats a-plenty for breakfast - Brid's philosophy is 'simple and in season'. Her son Owen operates a walking tour business on the island. *Rooms 4 (3 shower only). Closed 1 Nov - 17 Mar inc. No CC. Directions: At Castle Village.*

  ## South Aran House & Restaurant

Inishere Aran Islands Co Galway ✆*099 75073 www.southaran.com*

Inis Oirr, the smallest and most easterly of the Aran Islands is a tranquil place, perfect for quiet contemplation, relaxed walks and swimming in crystal clear waters. Maria and Enda Conneely are Slow Food members and their Fisherman's Cottage (restaurant/cookery school) and South Aran House (accommodation) reflect the personality of the island for adult guests. *Seats 54 (outdoors, 25). L&D daily. Rooms 4. Closed Nov-Mar. CC. Directions: Turn right at the pier and 400 metres on.*

Teach an Tae Tea Rooms & Café

Inis Oirr Aran Islands Co Galway ✆*099 75092 www.teachantae.com*

Michael and Alissa O'Donoghue understand the value of doing homely things well, and the menu at their charming tea room is very simple. Their hens provide beautiful, fresh eggs for the baking, and the organic garden - replenished each year with sand and seaweed from the shore - is the source of vegetables and salads. Everything is made from scratch and they sell homemade preserves and locally made crafts. **Seats 40**. *Open 10am-5pm daily, Easter to Oct. No CC.* **Directions:** *In the centre of the island; about 100m from the beach.*

 Teach Nan Phaidai

Kilmurvey Inis Mor Aran Islands Co Galway ✆*099 20975*

Catherine Concannon's pretty cottage is just the kind of place that visitors to Ireland dream of finding - a delightful daytime restaurant, where an open turf fire is lit on cold days. Delicious homemade food is listed on a large blackboard, while an array of wonderful cakes and buns and Fair Trade coffees take over the counter... **Seats 65** *(outdoors, 12). Open 11am-5pm, daily. Closed 20-26 Dec. CC.* **Directions:** *Just around the corner from Man of Aran Cottage.*

 **Tig Congaile**

Moore Village Inis Meain Aran Islands Co Galway ✆*099 73085 www.inismeainbb.com*

Sitting outside on a fine day, the peace and the view make Vilma and Padric Conneely's restaurant the best spot on the island. Vilma loves to use organic and sea vegetables, and her wonderful Sea Vegetable Soup is a speciality known well beyond the islands. Dinner here is really good and, even though less publicised than some of the restaurants on the islands, Vilma's cooking is on a par with the best. **Seats 45**; *L&D daily; reservations required. Closed Nov-Feb. CC.* **Directions:** *Thirty minutes walk from the pier.*

 Tigh Fitz

Killeaney Inis Mor Aran Islands Co Galway ✆*099 61213 www.tighfitz.com*

Over 100 years ago Penny Fitzpatrick's grandfather opened his bar in the village of Killeaney on the Aran Islands, little knowing then that the island's airport would be a few fields away. Although the bar has since closed, accommodation is very comfortable and the food - notably Penny's Aran-style bouillabaisse - is top quality and probably the best value on the island. **Rooms 11** *(all shower only). Restaurant open Mon-Sat, 12-6 (will also cook dinner for groups, on reservation). Guesthouse closed Nov-late Dec. CC.* **Directions:** *1.5km from Kilronan village.*

  The Foods of Athenry

Oldcastle Kilconieron Athenry Co Galway ✆*091 848 152 www.foodsofathenry.ie*

Former dairy farmers Paul and Siobhan Lawless started their 'free-from' farmhouse bakery in a converted bicycle shed in 2000.They have since continued making the same healthily delicious home bakes with no additives (including salt and yeast), have planted an organic orchard of native apples, developed biodegradable packaging and earned a national reputation, notably for their gluten-free range. Widely available.

The Friendly Farmer

Knockbrack Athenry Co Galway ✆*087 620 3765 www.thefriendlyfarmer.blogspot.com*

Ronan Byrne, aka The Friendly Farmer, is a familiar figure at Galway and Moycullen farmers' markets, where he sells the free range meat and - especially - award-winning poultry - produced on the 35 acre farm outside Athenry in East Galway where he grew up. An on-farm abattoir ensures total control and minimal food miles. Sells directly to restaurants, and at local markets, farmgate by arrangement. *Sold at Galway and Moycullen Farmers' markets; from the farm and selected retailers.*

 The Old Barracks Pantry Bakery & Restaurant

Cross Street Athenry Co Galway ✆*091 877 406 www.oldbarracks.ie*

Cathal O'Malley and Fiona King's atmospheric restaurant and bakery offers good home cooking of well-sourced foods including home-reared meats (Angus steaks, Saddleback pork) and local produce. Keenly priced for the quality, booking advised. BYO. **Seats 50** *(outdoors, 10). Open Mon-Sat 9am-6pm, Sun 12-7pm. Supper at The Barracks, Thu-Sat 6.30-9.30pm. Closed 25 Dec. CC.* **Directions:** *In the centre of Athenry, with parking at the rear.*

 **Raheen Woods Hotel**

Athenry Co Galway ✆*091 875 888 www.raheenwoodshotel.ie*

Useful for business travellers and families, this modern hotel has good facilities and friendly staff; within walking distance of this Heritage Town, yet attractively situated in a woodland setting with landscaped gardens. **Rooms 50**. *Closed 25-26 Dec. CC.* **Directions:** *M6 exit 17.*

BALLINASLOE

Ballinasloe is County Galway's second largest town, after Galway City. Situated off the M6 linking Dublin and Galway it is one of the principal gateways to the West. Its position on the River Suck, a tributary of the Shannon, has historical importance and, in modern terms, allows access to the inland waterways – there is a marina in the town. The event the town is most famous for is the Ballinasloe Horse Fair; held every October it is one of Europe's oldest and largest, dating back to the 1700's, and attracts up to 100,000 visitors from all over the world. Other equestrian activities also take place throughout the year. It is an interesting area but, because of its location, many visitors will stay only briefly. Ballinasloe Farmers Market is held every Friday 9am-2pm (Croffey Centre, Main Street).

 Beechlawn Organic Farm

Beechlawn Ballinasloe Co Galway ✆*086 179 9007 www.beechlawnfarm.org*

Husband-and-wife team Padraig Fahy and Una Ní Bhroin run their renowned National Organic Demonstration Farm in a very open, visitor-friendly way and hold courses and farm walks several times a year; mainly geared towards other growers, but group visits can be arranged at any time. They pack home delivery boxes on Tuesdays, when visitors are welcome at the farm to buy vegetables. Beechlawn produce is sold at markets (Loughrea Thu am, Moycullen Fri pm); box delivery scheme (home or business addresses).

 **Carlton Shearwater**

Marina Point Ballinasloe Co. Galway 📞*090 9630400 www.shearwaterhotel.com/*

There's a wide region to be enjoyed from Ballinasloe and this modern four star hotel would make a good base for exploring it. While not exactly waterside, it's an agreeable place to stay whether on business or leisure, with short breaks and special offers frequently available. Meals, including a good breakfast, are served in several pleasing areas, and cooking is above the standard usually expected of an hotel. *Rooms 104. Opening Times L&D available daily. CC.*

 **Ballinderry Park**

Ballinasloe Area Kilconnell Ballinasloe Co Galway 📞*090 968 6796 www.ballinderrypark.com*

George and Susie Gossip have worked wonders, creating a comfortable home out of a ruin. Their smallish but perfectly proportioned early Georgian house is now a place of of timeless elegance, and George is not only a thoughtful host but well known in Ireland as a terrific cook (notably game, in season) whose imaginative, flavoursome, ingredients-led meals never strive for effect. *Rooms 4 (2 shower only). Residents' D at 8pm (not always available Sun, Mon). Closed 1 Nov - 31 Mar except for groups. CC. Directions: R348 from Ballinasloe, through Kilconnell, take left for Cappataggle, immediately left & continue until road turns into one avenue.*

BALLYCONNEELY

Home to the world famous Connemara Pony, the tranquil, unspoilt village of Ballyconneely is situated on a peninsula jutting into the Atlantic between Clifden, to the north, and the pretty fishing village of Roundstone, to the east. The peninsula is ringed by beautiful beaches, which are ideal for both bathing and shore angling. Other local attractions include the Roundstone bog, rich in undisturbed wildlife and habitat, whilst golfers will enjoy the 27 hole course at Connemara Golf Club (095 23 502/23 602).

 Connemara Smokehouse

Bunnowen Pier Ballyconneely Co Galway 📞*095 23739 www.smokehouse.ie*

Graham and his wife Saoirse Roberts' beautifully located smokehouse near Clifden offers an appealing range of products with a reputation for excellence based on "following a simple recipe: fresh fish, natural ingredients, and traditional smoking methods that have stood the test of time." The whole process is demonstrated, with tastings, at weekly smokehouse tours. Visitors welcome on weekdays (except lunch hour, 1-2pm); smokehouse tours Wed in season (at 3pm - booking advised); group tours all year. Shop; online shop. Closed seasonal hols & bank hols.

 Emlaghmore Lodge

Ballyconneely Co Galway 📞*095 23529 www.emlaghmore.com*

Built in 1862 as a small fishing lodge, Nicholas Tinne's magically located house is situated halfway between Roundstone and the 18-hole links golf course at Ballyconneely, in a Special Area of Conservation. Comfortably furnished in keeping with its age, it feels gloriously remote yet there are sandy beaches, good pubs and restaurants nearby. *Rooms 4 (1 shower only). Closed Nov-Easter. CC. Directions: 10 km from Roundstone, 4km from Ballyconneely.*

BARNA

Just west of Galway city, Barna is known for its fine beach, the Silver Strand; the village is clustered around an attractive little harbour and it's a popular place of escape for Galwegians at weekends and on summer evenings. Recent developments have brought a major change of scale, but it remains a pleasant destination, and a rewarding one for food lovers.

 Ali's Fish Shop

Unit 20 Barna Village Centre Barna Co Galway ☎091 596 623

Popular fishmonger Ali Galivandy supplies a good range of ultra fresh local fish daily, and is known for giving good customer service.

  Connemara Abalone

Aille Barna Co Galway ☎091 591 307 www.abalone.ie

Known as much for their beautiful iridescent shells as for the delicately flavoured meat, this exotic shellfish is unexpected in the rugged West of Ireland - but Cindy O'Brien has been farming them here since 2002. Although most of the production is exported, there's demand in Ireland at the Chinese New Year - and Connemara Abalone is sometimes showcased in local restaurants too.

CASHEL

Lying at the head of the beautiful Cashel Bay, the townland owes its name to the ring fort which borders the graveyard. Cashel Hill stands at the top of the bay; it is a pleasant walk to the top of this hill, where you will be rewarded by breathtaking views of the surrounding area. The area offers a number of historical sites, including a megalithic tomb, and the varied landscape offers walkers and pony trekkers some beautiful trails amid the many lakes and bogs, over the Twelve Bens and Maamturks Mountains, or along the secluded coves of Bertaghboy Bay. Activities in the area include golfing at Connemara Golf Club in Ballyconneely (095 23 502/23 602), horse riding, deep sea and also freshwater fishing - the area is known for its excellent salmon fishing.

 **Cashel House Hotel**

Cashel Connemara Co Galway ☎095 31001 www.cashel-house-hotel.com

Relaxed hospitality combined with professionalism have earned an international reputation for the McEvilly family's outstanding hotel. Cosy and restoring, its many high points include the very comfortable accommodation; many open fires and comfy places to unwind; wonderful gardens (open to the public; gardening courses); equestrian connections (the 'Justice' Connemara and Irish Sport Horse stud and show jumping yard, which has an Equestrian Shop on site, is run by a family member); mainly classic cooking of local foods (including a great breakfast) and, especially, Kay McEvilly's warm hospitality. **Rooms 29**. *Restaurant seats 85. L & D daily. Bar food available. Closed 30th Nov - mid Feb except Christmas & New Year. CC.* **Directions:** *South off N59 (Galway-Clifden road), 1.5km west of Recess turn left.*

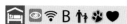 **Zetland Country House**

Cashel Bay Cashel Co Galway ☎*095 31111 www.zetland.com*

Colm Redmond's friendly and attractive small hotel was originally a sporting lodge and has a light and airy atmosphere and spacious public areas. Most bedrooms have sea views or overlook the lovely gardens. A public bar, opened in the current ownership, contributes a livelier atmosphere than usually expected at country houses. *Rooms 20 (1 shower only) Light lunches available daily, bar food 12-9pm. Traditional music / dancing some evenings. CC. Directions: N59 from Galway. Turn left after Recess.*

CLAREGALWAY

Just north-east of Galway on the junction of the N17 and N18 roads, Claregalway is a fast-growing satellite town for Galway city; only 10km from the city, it is very convenient to Galway airport. Visitors interested in history should see the ruins of a Franciscan abbey built by John de Cogan in 1290, among the most beautiful of its kind in the country. The area is also notable as the origin of the Irish ancestors of Che Guevara (Patrick Lynch). Garden enthusiasts will enjoy Ardcarraig (Bushypark, 091 524 336) and Brigit's Garden & Café (see entry for café, Roscahill, 091 550 905), which are only a short drive away, while golfers will be challenged by the recently re-developed Galway Bay Golf Club (091 790 711) in Oranmore.

 **The Claregalway Hotel**

Claregalway Claregalway Village Co Galway ☎*091 738 300 www.claregalwayhotel.ie*

Convenient to Galway city yet without the hassle, Paul and Nora Gill's modern hotel is a popular venue for conferences and business meetings. Good leisure facilities also make it attractive for families visiting Galway but preferring not to stay in the city. *Rooms 48 (3 shower only); Closed 24-25 Dec. CC.*

CLIFDEN

The main town of Connemara, Clifden nestles on the edge of the Atlantic with a dramatic backdrop of mountains. Although it has been somewhat over-developed recently, it remains an excellent base - not only for golfing, but for exploring this exceptionally scenic area; the quality of food and accommodation available in and around the town is very high, and non-golfers will find plenty to do: walking, horse riding, and bathing are all on the doorstep, the Connemara Garden Trail is relaxing and educational, and the island of Inishbofin can be visited by ferry from Cleggan.

 **Abbeyglen Castle Hotel**

Sky Road Clifden Co Galway ☎*095 21201 www.abbeyglen.ie*

Set romantically in its own parkland valley overlooking Clifden and the sea, the crenellated Abbeyglen Hotel is run in a uniquely hands-on style by legendary hoteliers Paul and Brian Hughes. From the minute of meeting Gilbert the parrot at reception, it's clear that this place is different; it's big and comfortable and laid-back - not perfect, but endearing, with a charming generosity of spirit. *Rooms 45. Restaurant seats 70; set D daily 7-9pm. Closed 6 Jan-1 Feb. CC. Directions: About 300 metres out of Clifden on the Sky Road, on the left.*

 **Ardagh Hotel & Restaurant**

Ballyconneely Road Clifden Co Galway ☎ *095 21384 www.ardaghhotel.com*

Beautifully located, overlooking Ardbear Bay, Stéphane and Monique Bauvet's family-run hotel is a modest-looking modern bulding and could easily be passed by - but that would be a mistake as it is well known for quiet hospitality, low-key comfort and Monique's excellent food. *Rooms 17. Restaurant seats 55. D 7.15-9.30pm daily. Closed Nov-Mar. CC.* **Directions:** *3km outside Clifden on Ballyconneely Road.*

 Clifden Station House Hotel

Clifden Co Galway ☎ *095 21699 www.clifdenstationhouse.com*

Built on the site of the old railway station and convenient to the town, this large modern hotel is known for its friendly and helpful staff and short breaks; it suits those who require a leisure centre and conference/banqueting facilities. The complex includes a railway museum and a range of upmarket shops and boutiques. *Rooms 78. CC Closed 25 Dec.*

  The Connemara Hamper

Market Street Clifden Co Galway ☎ *095 21054 www.connemarahamper.com*

Eileen and Leo Halliday's well-stocked little shop sells handmade Connemara baskets, and provides a showcase for many excellent artisan products, both local and from further afield, but mainly Irish. Also local organic produce in season, and Illy coffee to go. Well worth a visit. *Closed Sun. No online sales, but mail order service for delivery within Ireland/EU.*

 Derryclare Restaurant

Market Square Clifden Co Galway ☎ *095 21440*

Tommy and Lee Flaherty's restaurant overlooking the square is one of the few in Clifden with outdoor seating to the front, making it a good choice in fine weather. Friendly and reasonably priced, it's popular with families, who have pasta and pizza options (also available to take away), while blackboard menus offer day-long specials, including fish. *Seats 90. 12-10pm daily.* **Directions:** *Centre of Clifden.*

 Foyles Hotel

Main Street Clifden Co Galway ☎ *095 21801 www.foyleshotel.com*

Eddie Foyle's handsome 19th century hotel in Clifden town centre has played a central role in the hospitality of the area for many a year. Comfortably old-fashioned, with good beds and modern bathrooms, it is in a wonderful time warp. The hotel's Marconi Restaurant combines quality and atmosphere with good value and is one of the most popular in the town. *Rooms 25. Restaurant open 6-9pm daily. Hotel closed Christmas & Jan. CC.* **Directions:** *Centre of Clifden.*

 Mallmore Country House

Ballyconneely Road Clifden Co Galway ☎ *095 21460 www.mallmore.com*

Alan and Kathleen Hardman's restored Georgian home near Clifden is set in 35 acres of woodland grounds; Connemara ponies are bred here, and old woodland has been retained so the grounds are teeming with wildlife. Warm and welcoming, with a turf fire in the lovely drawing room and individually decorated rooms, it is a lovely, peaceful place to stay. *Rooms 6 (all shower only). Closed 1 Nov-1 Mar. No CC. Directions: 1.5 km from Clifden; signed off Ballyconneely road.*

 Mitchell's Restaurant

Market Street Clifden Connemara Co Galway ✆095 21867 www.mitchellsrestaurantclifden.com

JJ & Kay Mitchell's attractive and well-managed restaurant offers efficient, welcoming service and consistently pleasing, stylishly simple "good home cooking" all day, every day throughout the season. The emphasis is on local fish from sustainable sources, but there's a fair choice for non-fish eaters, especially on the all-day menu which offers a wide range of lightish fare. *Seats 70; Open daily, 12-10. Closed Nov-Feb. CC. Across the road from SuperValu supermarket.*

 **The Quay House**

Beach Road Clifden Co Galway ✆095 21369 www.thequayhouse.com

 The Quay House is the oldest building in Clifden and was built around 1820 and, since 1993, has been relishing its most enjoyable phase, in the incomparable hands of long-time hoteliers, Paddy and Julia Foyle. It's a fine house, with spacious rooms, including a stylishly homely drawing room with an open fire and exceptionally comfortable accommodation in wittily decorated and sumptuously furnished rooms. Breakfast is a treat to relish and Paddy and Julia are consummate hosts, making a stay here a luxuriously enriching experience. Irish hospitality at its best. *Rooms 14. Closed Nov-mid Mar. CC. Directions: 2 minutes from town centre, overlooking Clifden harbour - follow signs to the Beach Road.*

 Sea Mist House

Clifden Connemara Co Galway ✆095 21441 www.seamisthouse.com

Offering stylish and comfortable accommodation, Sheila Griffin's attractive house just off the square in Clifden was built in 1825, and retained its character while recent renovations added modern comforts. Guests can relax in a large conservatory overlooking the lovely cottage garden, which produces some of the delicious things appearing at breakfast. *Rooms 4 (all shower only). Closed Nov-Mar. CC. Directions: Left at square, a little down on right.*

 Steam Café

Station House Courtyard Clifden Co Galway ✆095 30600

There's plenty of interest at the Station House Courtyard, including seriously tasty food at this bright and welcoming daytime restaurant, where familiar-sounding dishes often have a twist - and that special fresh, home cooked flavour. Aromatic freshly-ground coffee, warming soups, punchy salads and delicious cakes and desserts are just a few of the good reasons to drop in. *Open Mon-Sat 10-5.30. Directions: In courtyard in front of Station House Hotel.*

CLONBUR

The picturesque village of Clonbur is quietly located in a Gaeltacht area at the centre of scenic west Galway, just east of Mount Gable and beautifully situated between Lough Corrib and Lough Mask - a perfect base for hill and forest walking holidays to suit all levels of experience (or none), and fishing on two of Ireland's most famous loughs. It's a place with a great sense of community, and many will prefer it to the more obvious tourist destinations and beauty spots.

 ### Ballykine House

Clonbur An Fhairce Co Galway ☎*094 954 6150 www.ballykinehouse-clonbur-cong.com*

Very comfortable accommodation and Ann Lambe's warm hospitality make this an appealing base for a peaceful holiday. With a library room, a pool table, a drying room for anglers and a comfy sitting room and conservatory for lounging and chatting it's a sociable house. A patio/barbecue area enjoys a lovely view on fine evenings - when guests also like to walk to a local pub or restaurant and get a lift back later. A lovely place to stay. **Rooms 5** *(4 shower only)*. *Closed 1 Nov-17 Mar. No CC.* **Directions:** *3 km from Cong, on Cong/Clonbur Rd - R345.*

 ### Fairhill House Hotel

Main Street Clonbur Co Galway ☎*094 954 6176 www.fairhillhouse.com*

In the centre of this pretty village, the Lynch family's friendly Victorian hotel dates back to 1830; sympathetic refurbishment has added modern comforts without loss of character and accommodation is very comfortable for a country hotel. You'll get pleasing meals too in Eddie's Bar, where there's an open fire, lots of memorabilia, music and craic. A very pleasant place to stay. **Rooms 20**. *Closed 24-25 Dec. CC.* **Directions:** *Centre of Clonbur (4km from Cong).*

 ### John J. Burke & Sons

Mount Gable House Clonbur Co Galway ☎*094 9546175 www.burkes-clonbur.com*

Everybody loves Burkes pub in Clonbur - this characterful old family-run pub is one of this attractive village's greatest assets, well known for atmosphere, music and homely food. It's a friendly, welcoming place no matter when you might drop in, and very much the heart of the community and sporting activities. **Seats 140** (outdoors 20); Food from 10am daily. Closed 24-26 Dec, Good Fri; weekends only Oct-Mar. CC. **Directions:** 5km from Cong (R345).

Connemara Hill Lamb

Connemara Hill Lamb Corr na Móna Connemara Co Galway
☎*094 9548798 www.connemarahilllamb.ie*

Born and bred on the beautiful hills of West Galway, Connemara Hill Lamb is a prestige seasonal product (late summer/autumn) and one of very few Irish foods to have European Protected Geographical Indication (PGI) status. It has a unique flavour, resulting from its diet and terrain; look out for it on menus, and local butchers (notably McGeoughs of Oughterard). Connemara Hill Lamb can be purchased online and their website lists stockists.

Raftery's The Blazers Bar

Craughwell Co Galway 📞*091 846 708 www.rafterysbar.ie*

Now in its third generation of family ownership, Donald and Therese Raftery's famous pub is the meeting place for the legendary Galway Blazers Hunt, who are kennelled nearby. Immaculately maintained and full of character, this friendly pub has open turf fires and a cosy stove for chilly days, a sunny patio for fine weather - and good popular bar food whatever the weather. *Bar Food from 9.30 daily (11 on Sun). Closed 25 Dec & Good Fri. CC.* **Directions:** *On old Galway-Dublin road (R446) between Loughrea and Galway.*

The Gallery Café Restaurant

Queen Street Gort Co Galway 📞*091 630 630 www.gallerycafe.ie*

It is well worth leaving the M18 for a bite at Sarah Harty's famously funky all day café, an entertaining place where the food is all about the locality. Sustainability and seasonality inform chef Pawel Karnafel's cooking. They're famed for great pizzas (a dozen to choose from), which go down a treat with families, while adventurous evening menus feature foods foraged from land and sea. *Open Tue 10-3, Wed & Thu 10-9, Fri & Sat 10-9.30, Sun 11-9. Closed Mon.*

Lisdonagh House

Headford Caherlistrane nr Headford Co Galway 📞*093 31163 www.lisdonagh.com*

About 20 minutes drive north of Galway city in the heart of hunting and fishing country, John and Finola Cooke's early Georgian house enjoys beautiful views overlooking Lake Hackett. A lovely property, with large well-proportioned reception rooms, very comfortable bedrooms decorated in period style and impressive marbled bathrooms to match, it is surrounded by a wooded estate where guests are free to wander. **Rooms 9** *(2 shower only); Closed 1 Nov-1 May. CC.* **Directions:** *N17 to within 7km of Tuam, R333 to Caherlistrane.*

INISHBOFIN

Inishbofin, 'the island of the white cow', is located 11km (7 miles) off the coast of Galway and it is estimated that it has been inhabited for as long as 6,000 years. The island is home to five small villages, where the main industries are farming, fishing and tourism. Ideal for an away-from-it-all holiday, the island is known for its sandy beaches and clear waters, which are ideal for shore angling, swimming, snorkelling and diving, and the interior of the island provides mountain walks and gentle hill climbing. Sailing is a popular activity too, and, as you sail into the harbour, you will see Oliver Cromwell's 16th century barracks, which were used a prison for Catholic priests. The Inishbofin Heritage Centre (095 45 861) houses an interesting exhibition, illustrating island life in bygone days.

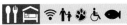 **The Dolphin Hotel & Restaurant**

Inishbofin Co Galway 📞*095 45991 www.dolphinhotel.ie*

Set in landscaped grounds, Patrick & Catherine Coyne's Dolphin Hotel grew from their popular restaurant and has proved a wonderful addition to this beautiful unspoilt island. As well as very comfortable accommodation, there's also a lovely residents' lounge, with access to decking and great views - and, of course, the restaurant, where menus change throughout the day and (subject to availability) there's a focus on locally caught seafood. Inishbofin lobster is often available - order by noon. **Rooms 11**. *Restaurant* **seats 100** *(outdoor seating, 20). Open daily in summer: L 12.30-5; D 7-9.30. Establishment closed Nov-Mar. CC.* **Directions:** *10 minute walk from the pier.*

 **Doonmore Hotel**

Inishbofin Island Co Galway 📞*095 45804 / 14 www.doonmorehotel.com*

Locally known as 'Murray's' and in the family for three generations, the hotel overlooks the sea and sand dunes of Inishbofin. With geraniums along the front lounge, this family-friendly place looks more like a traditional guesthouse than an hotel, and offers good home cooking and old fashioned comfort. Simply special. **Rooms 20** *(15 shower only); Restaurant* **seats 45**, *D daily from 7pm. Bar food 12-9pm. Establishment closed Oct-Mar. CC.* **Directions:** *10 minute walk from harbour.*

  **Inishbofin House Hotel & Marine Spa**

Inishbofin Island Co Galway 📞*095 45809 www.inishbofinhouse.com*

Everything about the Day family's hotel delights visitors, who love the good food that it has always been known for - and, especially, Bridie Day and the lovely staff who look after everyone so well. Although now a large luxury hotel (a first for the island), with a spa and beauty salon, it has lost none of its easy going island appeal. **Rooms 34**. *Closed Nov-Feb. CC.* **Directions:** *Beside harbour.*

 Coyne's Bar and Bistro (Tigh Chadhain)

Kilkerrin Connemara Co Galway 095 33409 *www.coynesbar.com*

Friendly donkeys amble over to the wall as you park at Michael and Annemarie Coyne's neatly presented pub overlooking Kilkerrin Bay - a typical welcome to the Connemara Gaeltacht and this real old-fashioned Irish pub. A proper informal dining experience is offered, with accessibly priced bi-lingual menus catering for all tastes and everything cooked to order. The house speciality is a delicious seafood chowder: thick and plentiful with good chunks of fresh local fish and served with a homemade brown scone, it's a meal in itself. **Seats 40**. *Opening Times Food times: summer (Jun-Aug) 10-8.30, off season 10-5. Bar open Mon-Thu 10.30am-11.30pm, Fri & Sat 10.30am-12.30am, Sun 12.30pm-11.00pm. CC.*

  Kelly Galway Oysters

Tyrone Kilcolgan Co Galway 📞*091 796 120 www.kellyoysters.com*

Kilcolgan is synonymous with native oysters, the famed 'Galway Bay oysters'. Michael Kelly's company is not only a highly respected supplier to hotels and restaurants in Ireland and abroad (including Rick Stein), but you can also buy from them online (Oct-Apr) in smaller quantities - anything from 25 oysters, and very good value too.

 **Moran's Oyster Cottage**

The Weir Kilcolgan Co Galway ☎*091 796 113 www.moransoystercottage.com*

As pretty as a picture, with a well-kept thatched roof and a lovely waterside location, fans beat a path to Morans at every available opportunity for their wonderful local seafood, especially the native oysters (from their own oyster beds) which are in season from September to April (farmed Gigas oysters are on the menu all year). *Seats 120 (outdoor seating, 60). Meals 12 noon - 10pm daily. Closed 3 days Christmas & Good Fri. CC. **Directions:** Just off the Galway-Limerick road (N18), signed between Clarenbridge and Kilcolgan.*

KINVARA

Situated in south County Galway, just on the edge of the Burren, this picturesque seaside village has become a lively community, with a strong pride of heritage and culture. The village offers lots of local arts and crafts such as bog wood sculptures and ceramics, along with village festivals such as the Galway Hooker Festival and numerous music festivals. Local attractions include Dunguaire Castle (which hosts medieval banquets April to October, Tel: 1800 269 811), which was built in the 1500s and is still in excellent condition today, whilst visitors have easy access to the Burren, the Cliffs of Moher and the Aran Islands. Coole Park (091 631 804, open all year), near Gort, the famous meeting place of Irish literary figures from the 20th century, is only a short drive away too. Other activities available locally include golf (scenic championship cours at Gort), walking, cycling and scuba diving, and the famous Oyster Festivals held in the Clarinbridge area each autumn are also within easy reach.

 Keogh's Bar & Restaurant

Main Street Kinvara Co Galway ☎*091 637 145 www.keoghs.eu/index.php*

Padraig Brennan's popular pub in Kinvara village has a cosy bar with an open fire - and an informal restaurant with plenty of traditional character too. It's a welcoming scene - and a perfect setting for down to earth meals. Also music - the schedule is given on their website. *Seats 50 (outdoor seating, 18). Food available daily 9.30am-10pm (Sun from 12). Closed 25 Dec, Good Fri. CC. **Directions:** Kinvara village.*

 Kinvara Smoked Salmon

Kinvara Co Galway ☎*091 637 489 www.kinvarasmokedsalmon.com*

In this picturesque village on the south side of Galway Bay, Declan Droney's smoked salmon is made using traditional smoking methods and the best organic Irish salmon (see Clare Island Organic Salmon), and known for its firm flesh and subtle smoking. Available in good stores, eg Superquinn, and from their online shop.

 The Pier Head Bar & Restaurant

The Quay Kinvara Co Galway ☎*091 638 188 www.pierhead.ie*

Mike Burke's harbourside bar and restaurant has lots of maritime character. Whether eating casually downstairs or in the first floor restaurant this is an enjoyable place to visit, both for its good cooking (including plenty of seafood) and friendly service - and the lovely harbour view. Also music at weekends, all year. *Seats 100 (outdoors, 24). L&D daily. Closed 25 Dec & Good Fri. CC. **Directions:** Kinvara harbour front.*

LEENANE

There can be few more spectacular locations for a village than Leenane, which is tucked into the shoreline at the head of Ireland's only deepwater fjord, backed by dramatic mountains. Leenane was the setting for the film of John B Keane's story, The Field, (starring Richard Harris), a fact celebrated by several pubs in the village, which is also home to The Sheep & Wool Centre (095 42323) with sheep and wool museum, café and gift shop.

 ## Blackberry Café & Coffee Shop

Leenane Co Galway ✆ *095 42240*

Everything is freshly made each day at Sean and Mary Hamilton's lovely little restaurant, where reliable daytime food includes substantial snacks and good baking - freshly-baked bread to go with home-made soups and chowders, for example, and tasty fruit tarts. Extra dishes such as hot smoked trout and a chicken main course may be offered in the evening. **Seats 40**. *Open 12-4 and 6-9 daily in high season. Closed Tue in shoulder seasons & end Sep-Easter. CC.* **Directions:** *On main street, opposite car park.*

 ## Delphi Lodge

Leenane Co Galway ✆ *095 42222 www.delphilodge.ie*

Owned since 2011 by Michael Wade, this beautifully located 19th century sporting lodge is large and impressive in a relaxed, understated way. Although most famous for salmon and trout fishing, Delphi Lodge is also an ideal holiday hideaway for those who simply seek a quiet rural retreat. **Rooms 12**. *Generally closed, 15 Oct – 15 Jan. Open all year to private groups of 18+. CC.* **Directions:** *13km northwest of Leenane on the Louisburgh road.*

 ## Delphi Mountain Resort & Spa

Leenane Co Galway ✆ *095 42208 www.delphimountainresort.com*

Stunningly located in a beautiful and unspoilt area, this sensitively designed hotel, restaurant, spa and adventure centre is owned and managed by husband and wife team Rory and Aileen Concannon, who emphasise its remoteness ('no TV and limited phone coverage') and aim to make it a complete away from it all experience for guests. **Rooms 38**. *Restaurant seats 50 (outdoors, 12), open to non-residents L&D daily. Bar food 12.30-9pm daily. Closed Jan. CC.* **Directions:** *From Galway take the N59 to Leenane - then 12km to Delphi.*

 ## Portfinn Lodge

Clifden Road Leenane Co Galway ✆ *095 42265 www.portfinn.com*

Run by the Daly family since 1977, Portfinn Lodge overlooks picturesque Killary harbour. It has particular appeal for visiting fishing and scubadiving enthusiasts, and seafood lovers, but with its wonderful location, pleasant staff, simple but comfortable rooms and good food cooked by owner-chef Oran Daly, a visit here should be enjoyable for everyone. **Seats 40** *(outdoors, 12). D Tue-Sun. Rooms 11. House closed 20 Dec-1 Mar. CC.* **Directions:** *Midway between Westport and Clifden (N59).*

LETTERFRACK

Founded by Quakers in the mid 19th century, the village of Letterfrack is close to Connemara National Park (095 41 054), which offers 2,957 hectares of beautiful countryside and a rich habitat for wildlife. The park also includes an exhibition centre and visitors can take a guided walk along one of the many nature trails. Letterfrack is host to Connemara Bog Week, which is a varied festival held in June, including guided walks, fun runs and traditional music. Anglers will find some of the best salmon fishing in the country.

 Avoca Letterfrack

Letterfrack Co Galway ✆ *095 41058 www.avoca.ie*

A useful place to know about when you are exploring this beautiful area, the 'Possibly shop' ('possibly the most interesting craft shop in the west') is not huge, but it offers lovely clothing and crafts to buy - and some wholesome treats in the well known Avoca style on sale, albeit on a smaller scale (no café). On main Clifden-Westport road overlooking Ballinakill Bay at Letterfrack.

  **Kylemore Abbey Restaurant & Tea House**

Kylemore Letterfrack Co Galway ✆ *095 41155 www.kylemoreabbey.ie*

Providing you are tolerant of tour buses and high season crowds, this dramatically located Abbey offers a surprising range of things to see, do, buy - and eat. Produce from their farm and Victorian Walled Garden is used in the many jams and preserves made by the Bendictine community, and features in three food outlets (Mitchell's Cafe, Henry's Express Coffee Shop and the Garden Tea House), all specialising in traditional home cooked food and baking. *Seats 200* (outdoors, 60). *Mitchell's Café meals daily 9.30-5pm. Open all year except Christmas week. (The Garden Tea House, in the restored walled garden, is open Easter-Hallowe'en, 10.30-5; entry fee applies.) CC.* **Directions:** *3km from Letterfrack, on the N59 from Galway.*

 **Rosleague Manor Hotel**

Letterfrack Co Galway ✆ *095 41101 www.rosleague.com*

Energetic young owner-manager, Mark Foyle, is gradually working his way through a major renovation programme at this lovely, graciously proportioned, pink-washed Regency house, which looks out over a tidal inlet through gardens planted with rare shrubs and plants. Although the area also offers plenty of energetic pursuits, there is a deep sense of peace at Rosleague and it's hard to imagine any better place to recharge the soul. *Rooms 20. Restaurant Seats 60 (Private Room seats 12). D 7.30-9 daily. Closed mid Nov-mid Mar. CC.* **Directions:** *On N59 main road, 11km (7 miles) north-west of Clifden.*

LOUGHREA

Loughrea is a substantial town in east Galway and takes its name from the adjacent lake, the second largest limestone lake in County Galway, after Lough Corrib. Loughrea has a number of hotels including the old family-run town centre O'Deas Hotel (091 841611; www.odeashotel.com); popular as a base for fishing holidays, there is much of interest in the area. Loughrea Lake is an important bird sanctuary and popular for fishing, (trout, pike and perch), water-sports and swimming. The town centre Cathedral of St. Brendan is of interest, and The Turoe Stone, an important Celtic monument, is in nearby Bullaun, where you will also find Turoe Pet Farm and Leisure Park (091 841-580; www.turoepetfarm.com). Dartfield - Ireland's Horse Museum & Park (091 843-968) is a short distance east of the town, and horseriding and trekking are also available in the area.

Taste Matters

Millennium House Westbridge Loughrea Co. Galway ☎*091 880010*

Taste Matters has a following of locals and also visitors to this charming lakeside town. It's a no-frills operation, yet with a certain style, and Jirka Hanka from the Czech Republic and Slovakian chef Michal combine to make this a cheerful and hospitable restaurant with friendly, welcoming staff, good broadly European food and a small but excellent wine list. **Seats 24**. *Open Wed-Sun. L 12-3, D 6-9.30. CC.* **Directions:** *Situated at the traffic lights on the corner of the Galway road out of Loughrea.*

 Slieve Aughty Centre

Kylebrack West Loughrea Co Galway ☎*090 974 5246 www.riding-centre.com*

Slieve Aughty Centre is a tranquil, remote eco-friendly guesthouse and certified organic restaurant, equestrian centre, and venue in East County Galway. Most rooms have balconies and they're surprisingly luxurious for an eco-destination. Or you can just visit the organic restaurant and wine bar, The Organic Kitchen. Interesting, friendly and 'alternative': don't expect the same kind of service as in conventional destinations.

 'Enjoy' at White Gables

Moycullen Co Galway ☎*091 868 200 www.enjoy.whitegables.com*

Next door to their charming White Gables restaurant (see entry), Kevin and Ann Dunne have this lovely deli/bakery offering a welcome range of artisan products, home-cooked seasonal foods, breads and cakes for sale - and, more recently, a café 'Enjoy More'. It's all so charmingly presented that it would be hard to pass through Moycullen without stopping to have a peep at what's on offer. *Open Tue-Sun, from 9am; closed Mon. Online shop.* **Directions:** *On N59 in Moycullen village, 11km (8 m) from Galway city.*

 The Forge

Moycullen Co Galway ☎*www.theforgepubmoycullen.com*

On the Galway side of Moycullen village, a landmark corner building is home to The Forge, a large pub, restaurant and entertainment centre. While menus tend towards the predictable bar/restaurant style, what makes The Forge stand out is the amount of care taken with sourcing (suppliers are listed in detail), and the standard of cooking is reliably good. Open daily from 9.30am (Sun, from 12). CC. **Directions:** Centre of Moycullen village (Galway side).

 White Gables Restaurant

Moycullen Village Moycullen Co Galway ☎*091 555 744 www.whitegables.com*

Kevin and Ann Dunne have run this atmospheric cottagey restaurant since 1991, and it remains one of the area's most consistently popular places to eat. Kevin's cooking is refreshingly traditional and features local meats including Connemara lamb and excellent beef, both from the famous butchers McGeoughs of Oughterard, alongside seafood - and the trademark roast half duckling à l'orange. The Dunnes also run "'Enjoy' at White Gables", next door (see entry). **Seats 45**. *D Tue-Sat; L Sun only. Closed Mon, Tue & 23 Dec-10 Feb. CC.* **Directions:** *Centre of Moycullen village.*

ORANMORE

Between Galway city and Athenry, first impressions of Oranmore are that it is dominated by busy roads. But Oranmore itself is a pleasant place and offers good food and hospitality, notably the seafood, especially shellfish, the area is renowned for.

 Basilico Restaurant

Main Street Oranmore Co Galway ✆*091 788 367 www.basilicorestaurant.ie*

Owners Paolo Sabatini and Fabiano Mulas - head chef and restaurant manager respectively - work hard to create points of difference in their restaurant, including original art works by Fabiano, which add atmosphere and make a great talking point. Renowned especially for their pizzas, this is a popular, comfortable restaurant and their support of local food producers is commendable. ***Seats about 60***. *Open Mon- Sat 5-10, Sun 12.30-9.30.*

 The Boathouse Seafood & Grill

Main Street Oranmore Co Galway ✆*091 788 525 www.theboathouse.ie*

With a big blue sailboat motif set into its handsome stone frontage you can't miss Rudi and Frances Rabasse's smartly renovated restaurant. Rudi's years of experience show in a welcoming sense of professionalism, and he and Scottish chef Anthony Printer make a good team, offering modern Irish food - notably seafood - but with a strong French bias. Even that old faithful chowder has a touch of French chic about it, and very good it is too. ***Seats 70***. *D Tue-Sat, L Sun & Tue-Fri. Closed Mon except for groups.*

 Péarla na Mara

Unit 10 Howley Square Oranmore Co Galway ✆*091 483 900 www.pearlanamara.ie*

There's an air of care about Justina Kocjan and Kamel Ourdache's town centre restaurant. The couple have built a local reputation for good value and it is well earned. Offering varying menus throughout the day, and with Kamel's cooking bringing a little Mediterranean sunshine to Irish ingredients, the long opening hours make this a very useful place to know about when visiting the Oranmore area. *Open Mon-Sat 8-11, Sun 10-11. CC.* **Directions:** *Oranmore town centre, next to Bank of Ireland.*

OUGHTERARD

Oughterard is a charming riverside village, known as the Gateway to Connemara, an area of natural beauty renowned for outdoor activities notably fishing, but also horseriding, walking and watersports - and Oughterard is a sociable place, known for live music in the pubs at night. There are many interesting gardens to visit in the area; Connemara Garden Trail leaflets are widely available in tourist information offices and hotels; otherwise, for up to date details, contact the Connemara Garden Trail directly (095 21148).

 **Corrib Wave Guesthouse**

Portcarron Oughterard Co Galway ✆*091 552 147 www.corribwave.com*

A fisherman's dream, Michael and Maria Healy's unpretentious, neatly maintained waterside guesthouse is in a stunningly beautiful location and offers warm, family hospitality, comfortable accommodation, an open turf fire to relax by and real home cooking. Everything to do with fishing is organised for guests, there's golf and horse riding nearby, and music in the village pubs at night. ***Rooms 10*** *(4 shower only); Residents D 7pm. Closed 1 Dec-1 Feb. CC.* **Directions:** *From Galway, signed from N59, 1 km before Oughterard.*

 **Currarevagh House**

Glann Road Oughterard Co Galway 📞 *091 552 312 www.currarevagh.com*

Tranquillity, trout and tea in the drawing room - these are the things that draw guests back to Henry and Lucy Hodgson's gracious, but not luxurious, early Victorian manor overlooking Lough Corrib. Offering old-fashioned service and hospitality, it's more like a private house party than an hotel and country pursuits, especially fishing, are the ruling passion. Lucy, a Prue Leith trained cook, showcases fresh local produce in season, maintaining the Currarevagh motto 'keep it simple, unfussy and ultimately delicious'. **Rooms 12** *(2 shower only). 4 course D €45, at 8pm. Closed Nov-mid-Mar (house available for private hire in winter). CC.* **Directions:** *Take N59 to Oughterard. Turn right in village square and follow Glann Road for 6.5km.*

  **McGeoughs Connemara Fine Foods**

Camp Street Oughterard Co Galway 📞 *091 552 351 www.connemarafinefoods.ie*

Established by Eamonn McGeough in 1971 and now run by his son, James - a German-trained master butcher - this butchers shop and fine food retailers has achieved national renown. Specialities to look out for include the famed Connemara Hill Lamb (see entry), dry-aged beef, gourmet sausages and the McGeough's unique air-dried and smoked meats and salamis that take up to six months to cure, and are showcased at leading restaurants. Butchery classes offered. *Open Mon-Sat. Closed Sun. Online shop.*

 Railway Lodge

Canrower Oughterard Co Galway 📞 *091 552 945 www.railwaylodge.net*

Carmel Geoghegan's haven of warmth and relaxed charm is named after the railway which once ran from Galway to Clifden. Combining the best of old and new, the comfortable bedrooms have orthopaedic beds made up with Irish linen and downstairs there are open fires, a cosy sitting room and a nice old fashioned kitchen where Carmel will happily make dinner (by reservation) as well as rustling up home-baked bread for breakfast. A delightful place to stay and well located for exploring Connemara. Self catering also available. **Rooms 4.** *Open all year. CC.* **Directions:** *N59 from Galway; in Oughterard, turn left after Corrib Hotel, and then immediately right, following signs to Railway Lodge.*

Ross Lake House Hotel

Rosscahill Oughterard Co Galway ✆*091 550 109 www.rosslakehotel.com*

Quietly located in six acres of beautiful gardens, Henry and Elaine Reid's charming country house was built in 1850 and, sensitively refurbished, now offers elegant accommodation in spacious rooms and suites. While graciously proportioned and impressively furnished, the warm interest of the proprietors and their staff ensure a welcoming and homely atmosphere. **Rooms 13** *(1 shower only); D 7-8.30 daily. Closed 1 Nov-15 Mar. CC.* **Directions:** *Signed off Galway-Oughterard road; 10km from Moycullen village.*

 **Brigit's Garden Café**

Oughterard Area Pollagh Roscahill Co Galway ✆*091 550 905 www.brigitsgarden.ie*

Jenny Beale's beautiful themed garden near Oughterard reflects the Celtic festivals and, in addition to woodland trails, a ring fort and a stone chamber, there's a lovely café overlooking the gardens. Everything is kept pleasingly simple, serving wholesome fare - big soups, platters, quiches and salads for lunch, great home bakes for afternoon tea. Well worth a visit. **Seats 50** *(outdoors, 35). Open 1 May-30 Sep, 10.30-5 daily; April, open Sun only;. Closed Oct-mid Apr but tea & coffee available and caters for groups by arrangement. CC.* **Directions:** *Just off the N59 between Moycullen and Oughterard.*

PORTUMNA

Portumna is a substantial town on the River Shannon in south-east Galway, with a large bridge (opened periodically for river traffic to pass through) linking it to County Tipperary. It is a popular base for river cruising (there is an Emerald Star cruiser base near the bridge) and coarse fishing. The town is most famous for the 17th century Portumna Castle, which is scenically located near Portumna (or 'New') Harbour on Lough Derg, with Portumna Forest Park to the west of it. The castle was gutted by fire in 1826 and has recently been extensively restored and parts of it opened to the public; restoration included the 17th century walled kitchen garden, which has now been organically planted with fruit trees, flowers, herbs and vegetables, following the original plan.

 Dyson's Restaurant

Patrick Street Portumna Co Galway ✆*0909 742 333*

Good food, pleasing surroundings and friendly service make for an enjoyable outing to John and Heather Dyson's bright contemporary restaurant. Sophisticated cooking may include some dishes with traditional influences and John takes pride in sourcing the best of ingredients locally, with an emphasis on organic foods and their own produce. Fish daily from Galway too. **Seats 40**. *Outdoor seating (deck). L&D Wed-Sat; Sun 1-8pm. Closed Mon, Tue, Bank Hols. CC.* **Directions:** *Town centre, a couple of doors from the Post Office, opposite Credit Union.*

  Killeen Farmhouse Cheese

Killeen Millhouse Loughanroe East Ballyshrule Portumna Co Galway ✆*090 974 1319*

East Galway cheesemaker Marion Roeleveld is known for the excellent gouda-style cheese which she makes in two varieties using both goat's milk and cow's milk. You'll see plain and flavoured version of these versatile cheeses at varying stages of maturity at Sheridans, other speciality shops in Galway and at On the Pig's Back in Cork, also at farmers' markets - and on menus, especially in the West.

RECESS

Source of the famous Connemara green marble, which has been quarried here for some 400 years, Recess is in an area of bog land, forest and lakes dominated by the mountain peaks of the impressive 12 Bens. Recess boasts the magnificent 18th century Ballynahinch Castle Hotel & Gardens (see entry), which is set in 450 acres of woodlands and salmon fishing rivers in the heart of Connemara. Local activities include golf at the Connemara Golf Club (095 23 502/23 602), fishing, horse riding and heritage centres.

 **Ballynahinch Castle Hotel**

Recess Co Galway ✆*095 31006 www.ballynahinch-castle.com*

 Renowned as a fishing hotel, this wonderful place was the Guide's 2012 Hotel of the Year. A crenellated Victorian mansion, it enjoys a most romantic position in 450 acres of ancient woodland and gardens on the banks of the Ballynahinch River. Despite the impressive scale, hands-on General Manager Patrick O'Flaherty and his outstanding staff make sure the atmosphere is relaxed, and a high level of comfort and friendliness combined with huge open fires, excellent local food from head chef Head Chef Xin Sun and his team, and a little quirkiness (plus an invigorating mixture of residents and locals in the bar at night), keeps bringing people back. Magic. **Rooms 40**. *Owenmore Restaurant open daily for D. Bar meals daily. Closed Christmas & Feb. CC.* **Directions:** *N59 from Galway - Clifden; left after Recess (Roundstone road), 6 km.*

 Breaking Eggs

Recess Co Galway www.breakingeggs.com

Championing family cooking, well known chef Cliodhna Prendergast's innovative online cookery programme is for parents and children. Her 10-minute videos feature her three young children sourcing ingredients – maybe mushroom foraging, gathering eggs or fishing for mackerel – before helping cook up a simple and tasty family meal. The step-by-step recipes are fun for children to follow.

 **Lough Inagh Lodge**

Recess Connemara Co Galway ✆*095 34706 www.loughinaghlodgehotel.ie*

Maire O'Connor's former sporting lodge on the shores of Lough Inagh makes a delightful and exceptionally comfortable small hotel, with a country house atmosphere. While it has special appeal to sportsmen, Lough Inagh makes a good base for touring Connemara - or for a bite to eat in the appealing bar, where there's a welcoming open fire. **Rooms 13**. **Seats 36**; *L & D daily. Bar meals 12.30-4 & 6.30-9pm daily. Closed mid Dec-mid Mar. CC.* **Directions:** *N59 from Galway city, take right N344 after Recess; 5km on right.*

 **Renvyle House Hotel**

Renvyle Co Galway ☎*095 46100 www.renvyle.com*

In one of the country's most appealingly remote and beautiful areas, this famous Lutyens-esque house has a romantic and fascinating history, having been home to people as diverse as a Gaelic chieftain and Oliver St John Gogarty. Its setting and quirky charm is unrivalled in Ireland and, with outstanding hospitality and food from legendary General Manager Ronnie Counihan and head chef Tim O'Sullivan respectively, it's no wonder it has developed a cult following. A wonderfully away-from-it-all pace to stay - and a great place to plan a break when touring the area. *Rooms 68. Roisin Dubh Restaurant D daily. Bar meals 12-8 daily. Closed 1-23 Dec & 1 Jan-14 Feb. CC. Directions: 18km north of Clifden.*

ROUNDSTONE

This charming village is clustered around its traditional stone-built harbour, so seafood is very much the speciality in every bar and restaurant. Nearby, Connemara Golf Club (Ballyconneely, 095 23502) will prove to be a stern test for any golfer, while garden lovers would enjoy spending some time in nearby Cashel House Hotel & Gardens (Cashel, 095 31001), and Ballynahinch Castle Hotel & Gardens (Recess, 095 31006). Connemara Garden Trail leaflets are available in tourist information offices and hotels; or contact the Connemara Garden Trail directly (095 21148). The hill climber will also feel at home here, for Roundstone lies beneath Errisbeg Mountain, an easy climb for most, with fantastic views of sea, lakes and mountains waiting as a reward.

 **O'Dowd's Bar & Restaurant**

Roundstone Co Galway ☎*095 35809 www.odowdseafoodbar.com*

The O'Dowd family's much-loved pub overlooking the harbour remains one of those simple places, with the comfort of an open fire and a good pint, where people congregate in total relaxation - spilling out to sit on the low stone wall in the busy summer months. A reasonably priced bar menu majors in seafood or, for more formal meals, the restaurant next door does the honours: the seafood chowder is ace. *Restaurant seats 36. Meals 12-10 daily (to 9.30 in pub). Closed 25 Dec. CC. Directions: On harbour front in Roundstone village.*

Roundstone House Hotel & Vaughan's Restaurant

Roundstone Connemara Co Galway ☎*095 35864 www.roundstonehousehotel.com*

The Vaughan family's classic village hotel is in the heart of Roundstone and enjoys a great view over the harbour and distant Connemara hills, from public areas and many of the comfortable en-suite rooms. In summer the busy bar offers a separate menu, as well as formal dining in the hotel restaurant, both with an emphasis on local seafood and traditional cooking. *Restaurant seats 40. CC. Directions: Centre of Roundstone.*

 **The Anglers Return**

Roundstone Area Toombeola Roundstone Connemara Co Galway
📞 *095 31091 www.anglersreturn.com*

Built as a sporting lodge in the eighteenth century, Lynn Hill's charming and unusual house on the Ballynahinch River near Roundstone offers comfort, peace, tranquillity, delicious food and a caring atmosphere. Fishing remains a major attraction, and it would be perfect for a painting holiday in this stunningly beautiful area, or for garden lovers; a Connemara Garden Trail member, the three acres of natural gardens are open daily in spring and summer (best in late spring). Best of all, there is Lynn herself: an original. ***Rooms 5*** *(4 with shared bathrooms). Closed mid Dec-Feb. No CC.* **Directions:** *N59 from Galway; left onto R341 Roundstone road for 6.5km; house is on the left, after Ballynahinch Castle.*

 **Builín Blasta Café & Bakery**

Ceardlann Craft & Design Centre Spiddal Co Galway 📞 *091 558 559 www.spiddalcrafts.ie*

 New Zealander owner-chef Jamie Peaker (he spells it J-me) runs this attractive café-cum-bakery with infectious enthusiasm. Although the menu at Builin Blasta (The Tasty Loaf, in Irish) appears to be made up of familiar dishes, there are some nice original touches and the high standard of cooking - and pleasantly gentle and caring service by local girls - make for an experience that ensures plenty of returning customers. Baking is a genuine forte here, and there is also a selection of House chutneys, jams and dressings for sale. Just the kind of place that every visitor to Connemara hopes to happen on. ***Seats 40*** *(outdoors, 16). Open Tue-Sat 10am-5pm; Sun 11am-5pm. Closed Mon, Jan. CC.* **Directions:** *Galway side of Spiddal village on the main road west (R336).*

  The Winehouse

Bishop Street Tuam Co Galway 📞 *093 42512*

Cathal Reynolds, a Euro-Toques chef, was the original owner of Cré na Cille restaurant (established by him and his wife Sally in 1979), which earned fame throughout Ireland for good cooking and an outstanding and moderately priced wine cellar. Now his focus is on wine, especially the wines of France; a real wine enthusiast, he imports many wines directly and still offers good value too.

 Finns Bar & Restaurant

Tuam Area Milltown Tuam Co Galway 📞 *093 51327*

John and Lucy Finn's attractive bar and restaurant is on the river, in a charming little award-winning tidy town a few miles north of Tuam - a welcome sight for hungry travellers between Galway and Sligo. Known for great steaks, John cooks an eclectic mix of international and traditional dishes - reasonably priced and served in a relaxed atmosphere. ***Seats 70****. D Tue-Sun, 5-9pm. No bookings. Closed 3 days Christmas & Easter. CC.* **Directions:** *16km from Tuam, on main N17 to Sligo.*

KERRY

It's something special, being Kerry. This magnificent county in the far southwest has Ireland's highest and most varied mountains, and certain favoured areas also have our longest-lived citizens. Then, too, it's a region which has long been a global pioneer in the hospitality business - in 2004, the scenically-blessed town of Killarney celebrated 250 years in the forefront of Irish tourism.

So visitors inevitably arrive with high expectations. But Kerry can confidently face the challenge. This magnificent county really is the Kingdom of Kerry. Everything is king size. Not only has Kerry mountains galore - more than anywhere else in Ireland - but there's a rare quality to Carrantuohill, the highest of all.

By international standards, this loftiest peak of MacGillicuddy's Reeks (try pronouncing it "mackil-cuddy") may not seem particularly notable at just 1038 m. But when you sense its mysterious heights in the clouds above a countryside of astonishing beauty, its relative elevation is definitely world league. And all Kerry's mountains sweep oceanwards towards a handsome coastline which rings the changes between sheltered inlets and storm tossed offshore islands. Visually, Kerry has everything.

But these days, spectacular scenery isn't enough on its own. Like other leading visitor destinations, Kerry is well aware of the need to provide accessible entertainment and an increasing choice of places with cultural and historical interest. Here too, the Kingdom can oblige. And it can also oblige those with sporting interests - the place is sports mad. As for history, the oldest fossil footprints in the Northern Hemisphere are in Kerry, and they're about 350 million years old. You'll find them way down west, on Valentia Island, and they're reckoned one of the seven wonders of Ireland.

The town of Killarney, among the lakes and mountains where they're re-establishing the enormous white-tailed sea eagle, has long been a magnet for visitors, but Killarney is determined to reinvent itself from time to time, while retaining all that is best from the past. And across the purple mountains from Killarney, the lovely little town of Kenmare in South Kerry is both a gourmet focus, and another excellent touring centre. As one of the prettiest places in Ireland, Kenmare puts the emphasis on civic pride.

ANNASCAUL

Annascaul, on the Dingle peninsula, is one of the most-photographed villages in Ireland mainly because of the colourful and humorous frontage painted onto his pub by the late Dan Foley (which is still a fine pub). It was also the birthplace of the Antarctic explorer Tom Crean, who was part of Robert Scott's ill-fated attempts to reach the South Pole. The South Pole Inn (see entry) was once owned by Crean, and statue just across the road was erected in his honour. The area is particularly good for walking and hill walking. Nearby Dingle hosts a farmers market every Friday (10am-4pm) and the links at Tralee Golf Club (066 713 6379), about 25km, is the nearest recommended championship golf course.

Ashes Butchers

Annascaul Co Kerry ✆*066 915 7127 www.annascaulblackpudding.com*

Renowned for its smooth, dense texture, Annascaul Black Pudding has been made here by hand since Ashe's shop was established in 1916; still made to the original recipe, it is now joined by white pudding and homemade sausages, all made by Thomas Ashe using fresh natural ingredients. Annascaul Puddings are proudly showcased by many restaurants, so look out for them on menus in the area. Buy from the shop, other selected retailers, and online.

South Pole Inn

Annascaul Co Kerry ✆*066 915 7388 www.thesouthpoleinn.com*

Not only a delightful well-run pub, but also well worth a visit to view its fascinating collection of memorabilia connected with the great Irish explorer Sir Ernest Shackleton and his second officer, Tom Crean of Annascaul, who ran this pub on his return from the Antarctic. *Seats 52 (outdoors, 50). Bar food 12-8 daily. Closed 25 Dec & Good Fri. CC.* **Directions:** *On the main road between Tralee & Dingle.*

Kate Browne's Pub

Ardfert Co Kerry ✆*066 713 4055*

A sister property to the lovely Cahernane House Hotel in Killarney, the Browne family's friendly and attractive pub has an old world ambience with welcoming open fires creating a cosy atmosphere and adding to the charm. Wholesome fairly-priced food is served, especially local seafood, and it's very family-friendly. *Seats 100 (outdoors, 20); food daily, 12-10pm. Closed 25 Dec, Good Fri. CC.* **Directions:** *5 km north of Tralee, on the left as you enter Ardfert.*

Cill Rialaig Café

Cill Rialaig Arts Centre Dun Geagan Ballinskelligs Co Kerry
✆*066 947 9277 www.cillrialaigartscentre.org*

One of Ireland's most interesting visitor destinations, offering exhibitions, workshops and events all year; also an excellent place to shop for unusual items - and you'll find quality food at the Cill Rialaig Café. Open: Off-season (Oct to mid-May) Thu-Sun, 11 to 5; summer season (mid May-Sep), open daily 11-6. **Directions:** *On the R566 Ballinskelligs road, via the N70 Ring of Kerry Road 14.5km from Caherciveen or 11km from Waterville.*

 **Skelligs Chocolate Co**

The Glen Ballinskelligs Iveragh Peninsula Co Kerry ✆ *066 947 9119* *www.skelligschocolate.com*

Colm O h-Ealai's high quality chocolate operation is in a remote location at St Finian's Bay on the Ring of Kerry, overlooking the mystical Skellig islands. Re-built following a fire and re-opened in 2012, complete with a smart new café, its unique appeal has made the Skelligs and Cocoa Bean Chocolates factory an equally appealing destination for families on holiday and food lovers. *Open Mon-Fri all year except Jan, weekends in Jul-Aug only. Online shop. Café.*

BALLYBUNION

Situated in north County Kerry, at the mouth of the river Shannon estuary, Ballybunion faces west to the north Atlantic and across the Shannon estuary to the shores of County Clare. The first transatlantic telephone transmission was made from the Marconi wireless station here in 1919 to Louisbourg, Cape Breton Nova Scotia, by W. T. Ditcham, a Marconi Engineer. Ballybunion is in an unspoilt area of great natural beauty, with a wide range of flora and fauna, resident and migratory birds and marine animals, including sea otters, seals, porpoises and dolphins, which can be observed along the coast. The clean waters of the area also make it ideal for harvesting sea vegetables, such as dulse (dillisk/ sea grass/ Palmaria palmata) and Irish moss (carrageen moss/ Chondrus crispus). To many visitors Ballybunion is synonymous with golf - the links courses here are ranked among the top golf courses in the world, and attract many famous visitors including President Bill Clinton of the United States of America (August 1999).

 Harty-Costello Townhouse Bar & Restaurant

Main Street Ballybunion Co Kerry ✆ *068 27129* *www.hartycostellos.com*

Although styled a townhouse, Davnet and Jackie Hourigan's welcoming Ballybunion town centre property is really an inn. Encompassing all the elements of hospitality within its neatly painted and flower bedecked yellow walls, it makes a relaxing and hospitable base for a golfing holiday, or for touring the south-west. **Rooms 8**. *B&B. Meals Tue-Sat, 12-4 (bar); 6.30-9 (restaurant). No food on Sun & Mon; establishment closed 30 Oct-30 Mar. CC.* **Directions:** *Centre of Ballybunion.*

 Kilcooly's Country House

Main Street Ballybunion Co Kerry ✆ *068 27112* *www.golfballybunion.com*

Formerly known as Iragh Tí Connor ("the inheritance of O'Connor"), John and Joan O'Connor's fine establishment dates back to the 19th century and now has a quality country house feeling, with exceptionally large, comfortable bedrooms - while the old bar and lounge areas have been transformed to make a welcoming space with a modern bistro vibe. **Rooms 17**. *Food daily, 12.30-9.30pm. Closed Christmas week. CC.* **Directions:** *Top of main street, opposite statue of Bill Clinton.*

Teach de Broc

Links Road Ballybunion Co Kerry ☎*068 27581 www.ballybuniongolf.com*

You don't have to play golf to appreciate this outstanding guesthouse, but it certainly must help as it is almost within the boundaries of the famous Ballybunion links. Aoife and Seamus Brock offer great hospitality, an extremely high standard of comfort - and excellent food, in both the bistro and little wine bar, too. **Rooms 14** *(2 shower only)*. Bistro **seats 40**. *D daily, 5-10pm; Sun 3-8pm. Closed 1 Nov - 15 Mar. CC.* **Directions:** *Directly opposite entrance to Ballybunion Golf Club.*

CAHIRCIVEEN

Midway way round the Ring of Kerry, this small market town in the shadow of the Benetee Mountain overlooks Valentia harbour on the Iveragh Peninsula. Cahirciveen offers a wealth of stunning scenery, historical sites, and sporting activities; in the town itself there are intimate traditional pubs, and good food shopping, including a farmers' market in the summer months. The many places of historical interest to visit include the 19th century Daniel O'Connell memorial church, the Cahirciveen Heritage Centre in the old Irish Constabulary Barracks (066 947 2777), and the 15th century Ballycarbery Castle (066 947 2777). There is a marina and local activities include sailing and other watersports, mountaineering, walking, cycling and horse riding. Deep sea anglers are well catered for, with boats available for charter.

O'Neills - The Point Bar

The Point Bar Renard Point Cahirciveen Co Kerry ☎*066 947 2165*

In the same family for 150 years, Michael and Bridie O'Neill's pub is beside the Valentia Island car ferry and renowned for its seafood. It's immaculately clean, full of character and has a great friendly atmosphere - and the secret of its success is simple food based on top quality ingredients. *Food daily April to October & weekends only in winter: L Mon-Sat, D daily. Closed L Sun; Nov-mid Dec; midweek in Spring. NO CC.* **Directions:** *Beside the Valentia Island ferry slip.*

QC's Seafood Bar & Townhouse

3 Main Street Cahirciveen Co Kerry ☎*066 947 2244 www.qcbar.com*

With original features including a rugged stone wall and an enormous fireplace, Kate and Andrew Cooke's sensitively renovated bar and restaurant in the centre of Cahirciveen has oodles of character. Ultrafresh local fish and seafood - supplied by the family company, Quinlan's Kerry Fish at Renard's Point - stars on both bar and restaurant menus, and the adjoining townhouse offers splendidly spacious and stylish accommodation. **Seats 50** *(outdoors, 20). L&D daily in summer; Thu-Sun in winter.* **Rooms 5**. *Closed 25 Dec, Good Fri; 8 Jan - mid Feb. CC.* **Directions:** *In the centre of Caherciveen.*

The Quarry Restaurant

Kells Post Office Cahirciveen Co Kerry ☎*066 947 7601 www.patscraftshop.com*

Pat Golden's family run "one stop shop" on the Ring of Kerry is extremely useful to know about - not only will you get good home cooking here, but there's a post office and foodstore, filling station, tourist information point and bureau de change. The 'Golden Mile Nature Walk' up behind the quarry, is just the place to walk off your lunch. *Seats 86. Open daily 9am-6pm, Easter-Oct. Closed Oct-Easter.* **Directions:** *Midway between Glenbeigh & Cahirciveen.*

 ## Quinlans Kerry Fish

Renard Point Cahirciveen Co Kerry ✆ *066 947 2177 www.kerryfish.com*

The Quinlan family's processing plant at Renard Point, outside Cahirciveen supplies their four shops with fresh fish daily, some from their own boats. *Also at: Cahirciveen, Killorglin, Tralee and Killarney.*

  ## Ring of Kerry Quality Lamb

c/o South Kerry Development Partnership Ltd Bridge Street Cahirciveen Co Kerry
✆ *1890 252 978 www.ringofkerryqualitylamb.ie*

Lamb is one of Kerry's most iconic products. It is always reassuring to know exactly where your food is coming from and this direct sales scheme is great for both farmers and their customers - everyone gets a fair deal. Anyone can buy this quality lamb online; and it is traceable from farm to fork.

CAHERDANIEL

Beyond Westcove, near the shore of Derrynane Bay, the small village of Caherdaniel makes an excellent base to explore the Ring of Kerry, with its breathtaking scenery - mountains, beaches and fantastic views over Kenmare Bay. There are excellent walking routes in the nearby Derrynane National Park (066 947 5113), where a visit to the former home of Daniel O'Connell 'The Liberator', Derrynane House (with good tearooms at Easter and in summer, 066 947 5252), is a must and pony trekking is available in the mountains, woodlands or on the beach. Golfers are well catered for by both the Waterville (066 947 4102) and Skellig Bay golf clubs (066 947 4133). During the summer there's a farmers' market on Fridays.

 ## Derrynane Hotel

Caherdaniel Co Kerry ✆ *066 947 5136 www.derrynane.com*

Activity holidays are a big draw at his unassuming 1960s-style hotel, which would be well worth a visit for its superb location alone. Under the excellent management of Mary O'Connor, this hospitable, family-friendly place is a home from home for its many returning guests. While quite modest, the accommodation is very comfortable. The stunninng view from bar and restaurant (overlooking an outdoor pool and gardens running down to a sandy beach) makes the wholesome food served all the more enjoyable. *Rooms 70. Restaurant seats 100. D 7-9pm daily. Bar snacks available during day. Hotel closed Oct-Easter. CC.* **Directions:** *In village of Caherdaniel, midway on Ring of Kerry.*

Iskeroon

Caherdaniel Co Kerry ✆*066 947 5119 www.iskeroon.com*

Approaching Geraldine Burkitt and David Hare's beautiful property overlooking Derrynane Harbour is an adventure and the effort taken to get there makes it all the more restful once settled in. Amazing sub-tropical gardens in this wonderfully wild place - and beautiful suites (with kitchen, for self-catering option). **Rooms 2** *(both suites and no smoking). *Self-catering studio apartment for two also available. Closed Oct-Apr. CC.* **Directions:** *Between Caherdaniel and Waterville (N70), turn off at the Scariff Inn, signed to Bunavalla Pier. Go to the pier and left through "private" gate; cross beach and enter through white gate posts.*

James Ashe

Camp Co Kerry ✆*066 713 0133*

This fine old pub just off the Tralee-Dingle road has been in the family for 200 years. It's a delightful place, full of genuine character and hospitality - ideal for a drink and a chat. *Closed 25 Dec & Good Fri. Phone ahead to check opening times, especially off season.* **Directions:** *On the main Tralee-Dingle road, 16km from Tralee.*

CARAGH LAKE

Beautiful Lough Caragh – or Caragh Lake as it is usually called - is near Killorglin, on the Ring of Kerry. Its clear waters originate in the MacGillycuddy Reeks, providing the perfect environment for healthy fish for game anglers, notably salmon and trout. Walkers love the the impressive scenery, while golfers will enjoy the tranquil 18 hole links course at Dooks (066 976 8205), which is close to nearby Glenbeigh, where the blue flag Rossbeigh beach is ideal for families, and popular with sea anglers too. Both the lake and the nearby strand provide the opportunity for water sports such as canoeing, windsurfing and swimming. Special events held in the area in the summer include the Puck Fair in Killorglin in August, and the summer races on Glenbeigh beach.

Ard na Sidhe Country House

Caragh Lake Killorglin Co Kerry ✆*066 976 9105 www.ardnasidhe.com*

One of the most impressive Arts and Crafts houses in Ireland, this charming revivalist Elizabethan style country house hotel is in a beautiful mountain location overlooking Caragh Lake. Set in woodland and delightful gardens, this romantic sister hotel to The Europe Hotel & Resort and The Dunloe (see entries), makes a peaceful retreat. **Rooms 18**. *Fairyhill Restaurant seats 45, open Tue-Sun for D. Hotel closed mid Oct-May. CC.* **Directions:** *Off N70 Ring of Kerry road, signed 5 km west of Killorglin.*

Carrig Country House & Restaurant

Caragh Lake Killorglin Co Kerry ✆*066 976 9100 www.carrighouse.com*

At the heart of Frank and Mary Slattery's sensitively extended Victorian country house lies a hunting lodge once owned by Lord Brocket - and he chose well, as it is very attractive and handsomely set in fine gardens with the lake and mountains providing a dramatic backdrop. There are not so many 'proper country houses' like this any more, and it is a quietly luxurious and serene place to stay – a perfect escape from the modern world, and with excellent food served in a lovely dining room overlooking the lake. **Rooms 17**. **Seats 50** *(outdoors, 20); D daily, 7-9. Establishment closed Dec-Feb. CC.* **Directions:** *Left after 4km on Killorglin/Glenbeigh Road N70 (Ring of Kerry), then turn sharp right at Caragh Lake School (2.5km), 1km on the left.*

  ## Westcove Farmhouse Shop

Westcove Road Castlecove Iveragh Peninsula Co Kerry ✆*066 947 5479 www.westcove.net*

At this gem just off the Ring of Kerry, Danish confectioner Jane Urquhart has a craft shop (with speciality foods on sale in summer), a small bakery and even a self-catering apartment to let.

  ## Dingle Peninsula Cheese

Kilcummin Beg Castlegregory Co Kerry ✆*066 713 9028*

Using summer milk from cows grazing the natural grasses and herbs on the south-west tip of the Dingle Peninsula, Maja Binder makes cheeses of real character and they have won many accolades. Maja also runs The Little Cheese Shop in Dingle (see entry); this gorgeous little speciality store stocks a wide range of cheeses and everything to do with them, along with wines - and, of course, all of her partner Olivier's wonderful meat and seafood products.

Harbour House & Islands Restaurant

Scraggane Pier Road Castlegregory Co Kerry ✆*066 713 9292 www.maharees.ie*

Waterworld dive centre is located at Pat & Ronnie Fitzgibbon's guesthouse at Scraggane Pier; they run diving courses here (and their facilities include a swimming pool). Aside from offering comfortable accommodation, this is a useful place to know about when touring, as the restaurant is open to non-residents and they are usually open for lunch as well as dinner (a phone call is advised). **Rooms 8**. *CC.* **Directions:** *Dingle Peninsula, north of Castlegregory.*

  ## Milesian Restaurant

Main Street Castlegregory Co. Kerry ✆*087 979 4337 www.milesianrestaurant.com*

Full of character and old world charm, chef Greg O'Mahoney's atmospheric restaurant in a 200 year old Irish cottage is the stuff that holiday dreams are made of - and luckily the experience lives up to the surroundings. Local foods, notably seafood and Kerry mountain lamb, take pride of place and Greg's background in fine dining shows in carefully sourced ingredients and delicious cooking. Great value too - and there's even traditional music. *Opening times (seasonal): Café 8am-2pm, Brunch (Sat & Sun) 10-2, L 12-2, D 5-10.*

  On The Wild Side

Kilcummin Beg Castlegregory Co Kerry ☎087 792 2468

Olivier Beaujouan's unique range of products comes from (and is inspired by) the local environment, especially the sea and foreshore. Home-smoked fish (smoked salmon with dill is a favourite) and seaweeds – especially the seaweed terrines - are his pièces de resistance, and he is also famed for his range of pickled sea vegetables. Sold at markets and at The Little Cheese Shop in Dingle (see entry).

 **Spillanes**

Fahamore Maharees Castlegregory Co Kerry ☎066 713 9125 www.spillanesbar.com

It's a long way down from the main road to reach the Maharees, but many would make the journey just for a visit to Marilyn and Michael Spillane's great traditional pub – it's been in the family since 1875 and they work hard at both the food and hospitality, earning a loyal following as a result. Wide ranging menu - ideal for families. **Seats 90**; *Meals daily in high season from 1pm; low season from 6pm. Closed Nov-Mar. CC.* **Directions:** *Dingle Peninsula,5km north of Castlegregory, between Bandon and Tralee bays.*

Crag Cave - Garden Restaurant

Castleisland Co Kerry ☎066 714 1244 www.cragcave.com

Just east of Tralee, this limestone show cave is one of Kerry's biggest attractions - a wonderful outing for families, and weatherproof too. It also has a very pleasant restaurant, offering good home cooking - freshly prepared light lunches and snacks - in attractive surroundings, with seats by an open fire for chilly days. **Seats 50** *(outdoors, 50). Food daily 11am-5pm (from 10am Sun). Closed Mon & Tue in Jan & Feb. CC.* **Directions:** *2km outside Castleisland town just off the N21.*

Jam Castleisland

Castle Lighting Killarney Road Castleisland Co Kerry ☎066 714 2816 www.jam.ie

Just a short drive from their former premises in Ballyseedy, James Mulchrone's Castleisland café opened in 2013 and is well worth seeking out. Offering the full menu in the comfortable cafe, or outdoors, it has the trademark warm friendliness and casual chic of Jam with lovely simple, fresh food and more-ish home baking, also the full range of delicious take home items. **Seats 40**. Open Mon-Sat 8.30-5.30, Sun 12-5.30. Also at Kenmare, Killarney and Cork.

Cloudberry Bakery

Shanahill East Castlemine Co Kerry ☎Tel: 066 976 6910 www.cloudberrybakery.com

Anyone who has seen and tasted even the smallest example of Samantha ('Sam') Harrison's Cloudberry Bakery products will know that this is something out of the ordinary. Specialities include wedding cakes, and an impressive array of cupcakes, beautifully precise continental macarons, Guinness Brownies), cake pops, tarts and a popular Red Velvet cake. *Available from: Markets and events; online ordering planned.*

DINGLE

Dividing the bays of Tralee and Dingle, Kerry's most northerly peninsula is an appealing destination, with stunning scenic drives, fine beaches and the town of Dingle itself which is full of character. A lively all-year destination, it is renowned for its music, crafts, fishing and, for over twenty years, for its most famous inhabitant, Funghi the friendly dolphin - you can take a boat to watch him playing in the bay. This Gaeltacht (Irish speaking area) is of great historical interest, and there are many ancient remains, especially in the Ventry / Slea Head / Ballyferriter area west of the town. Dingle town (which is twinned with Santa Barbara) has much to offer, including interesting shopping - specialities as diverse as leather goods, tweeds, pottery, gold and musical instruments are all made locally - and an equally appealing range of great places to stay, eat and enjoy traditional music and craic.

 **Ashes Bar & Restaurant**

Main Street Dingle Co Kerry ✆*066 915 0989 www.ashesbar.ie*

This nice old pub in the centre of Dingle goes back to 1849 and has a smart traditional frontage. Now owned by Sinead Roche and Thomas Ashe, the emphasis is on local fish and seafood, with a good seafood chowder and homebaked brown bread and excellent fish and chips among the specialities. **Seats 52**. *L&D daily in summer. Closed last 2 weeks Jan, 25 Dec. CC.*

 Bambury's Guesthouse

Mail Road Dingle Co Kerry ✆*066 915 1244 www.bamburysguesthouse.com*

Just a couple of minutes walk from the centre of Dingle, Jimmy and Bernie Bambury's well-run, purpose-built guesthouse has spacious modern rooms. A natural host, Bernie enjoys making sure her guests get the very best out of a stay in Dingle - and her breakfasts will set you up for the day. **Rooms 12** *(all shower only). Open all year. CC.* **Directions:** *On N86, on the left after the Shell garage, on entering Dingle.*

 Béile le Chéile

Dick Mack's Yard Green Street Dingle Co Kerry
✆*087 915 1350 www.foodiefancies.blogspot.com*

Well known for the cupcakes and other comforting Farmers' Market treats she baked in recent years, journalist, teacher and food lover Sharon Ni Chonchuir now runs her own café in this quaint spot behind Dick Mack's pub. It has a pretty tea room look that's perfect for the tasty ingredients-led daytime food she serves and there's space outside for sunny days - visitors are delighted to find it and locals love it too. *Open daytime.* **Directions:** *Behind Dick Mack's pub.*

 Caifé na Caolóige @ Louis Mulcahy Pottery

Clogher Ballyferriter Dingle Co Kerry ✆*066 915 6229 www.louismulcahy.com*

You might plan a stop for the children to have a go at the pottery and then feel like a coffee – but what you'll find here is certain to exceed all expectations, and well worth a special visit. Everything is homemade and delicious and the Mulcahys' support for their area, and for artisan producers and suppliers throughout Ireland, is clear to see on the menu, where you are invited to 'savour a Taste of West Kerry', and the provenance of all food is listed. **Seats 30**. *Open 10-5pm daily. CC.* **Directions:** *16km west of Dingle on the gorgeous Slea Head Drive.*

Castlewood House

The Wood *Dingle Co Kerry* ✆ 066 915 2788 www.castlewooddingle.com

Just five minutes' walk west of Dingle Town, this luxurious purpose-built guesthouse is run by Brian and Helen Heaton - for whom nothing is too much trouble to ensure that their guests enjoy the very best of Irish hospitality. Attention to detail is seen in everything they do, from the outstanding in-room facilities provided to the delicious breakfasts freshly cooked to order from a wide-ranging menu. *Rooms 12*. *Closed Dec-mid Feb (open few days over New Years day). CC.* **Directions:** *Take* Milltown road from Dingle, 500m from town centre on the right.

The Chart House

The Mall *Dingle Co Kerry* ✆ 066 915 2255 www.thecharthousedingle.com

Jim McCarthy's attractive stone-built restaurant has been one of Dingle's favourite dining destinations since opening in 1997. Jim, ever the perfect host, ensures that everyone is well looked after and generally having a good time, while head chef Noel Enright's menus are steadfastly based on the best of local foods - always kept simple to allow the special qualities of ingredients to take centre stage. *Seats 45*; *D 6-10, daily in summer (Jun-Sep), restricted opening in winter. Closed 6 Jan-13 Feb. CC.* **Directions:** *Left at the roundabout as you enter the town.*

Dingle Benners Hotel

Main Street *Dingle Co Kerry* ✆ 066 915 1638 www.dinglebenners.com

This 300-year old centrally-located hotel makes a very comfortable base within easy walking distance of the whole of Dingle town - and it is full of character. *Rooms 52*. *Closed 20-27 Dec. CC.* **Directions:** *Town centre, half way up Main Street on left beside Bank of Ireland.*

Dingle Brewing Company

Spa Road *Dingle Co Kerry* ✆ 066 915 0743 www.dinglebrewingcompany.com

This fascinating craft brewery is located in the old Dingle Creamery building and it makes an atmospheric Visitor Centre. Self-guided Tour and sample pint of Tom Crean's, €6. **Directions:** Edge of Dingle Town, on Conor Pass road.

Dingle Skellig Hotel

Dingle Co Kerry ✆ 066 915 0200 www.dingleskellig.com

It may be modest-looking from the road, but this 1960s hotel enjoys a superb shoreside location on the edge of Dingle town and has won many friends over the years. While not luxurious, it's a well-run, family-friendly hotel with organised entertainment for children in school holidays, and a good leisure centre and spa - and also makes an excellent off season business destination. *Rooms 111*. *D daily in summer, 6.30-9. Bar meals, 12.30-9pm. Self-*

catering in the adjacent Dingle Marina Cottages. Hotel closed mid-week Nov & Dec, all Jan. CC. **Directions:** *On the sea side of the road as you approach Dingle from Tralee & Killarney.*

 The Dingle Whiskey Distillery

Milltown Dingle Co Kerry ✆*www.dinglefoundingfathers.com*

With only three distilleries in operation, all of which are owned by international drinks giants, distilling has been neglected in Ireland recently... but not any more, as a new craft distillery is now operating in Dingle.

 Doyle's Seafood Restaurant

5 John Street Dingle Co Kerry ✆*066 915 2674 www.doylesofdingle.ie*

Established over a quarter of a century ago Doyle's was originally a small pub built in 1790; full of cottagey charm, it was the restaurant that first made Dingle's name as a dining destination. This iconic establishment is now run by by Sean Roche and Anna Scanlon, who have retained its reputation as a premier seafood destination. *Seats 40. D only, Mon-Sat. Closed Sun (except bank hol weekends), bank hol Mon & 3 weeks Nov/Jan.* **Directions:** *On way in to town, take last exit on 2nd roundabout; take next right after 200m; restaurant is 25m on left.*

 Fenton's of Dingle

Green Street Dingle Co Kerry ✆*066 915 2172 www.fentonsrestaurantdingle.com*

Patricia Fenton's charming restaurant has everything that visitors look for in this fascinating town - including a nice folksy atmosphere, a pretty patio garden where you can eat in fine weather and and a cosy fire for chilly days. Although mainly a seafood destination, other choices may include local beef and lamb from the family farm. *Seats 50 (outdoors, 12). Closed Mon & Nov-Mar. CC. At lower end of Green Street, near the harbour.*

 The Garden Café

Green Street Dingle Co Kerry ✆*087 781 5126 www.thegardencafedingle.eu*

With its homely surroundings of 'rescued' furniture and an open fire, Sheila Egan's friendly café is the heart of Dingle, where people meet to catch up with all the news - and have some comforting and very tasty food. Don't miss the daily 'Dingle Dog', made with Jerry Kennedy's much-celebrated sausages; you can even read local baker-bard Gene Courtney's poem, Ode to the Dingle Dog, while you eat. *Open Wed-Sat 10-4.30, Sun 12-4 (may open longer hours in summer).* **Directions:** *Opposite the church on Green Street.*

 **The Global Village**

Upper Main Street Dingle Co Kerry ✆*066 915 2325 www.globalvillagedingle.com*

There's an air of quiet confidence about Martin Bealin and Nuala Cassidy's long-established restaurant and Martin's cooking is sure-handed, exceptionally creative and consistently well-judged. Nothing is over the top here but everything – the local provenance and seasonality, the cooking, the balance of flavours, the pride in service - works together to make a memorable experience. One not to be missed. *D 5.30-10pm Mar-mid Nov.* **Directions:** *Dingle town centre - top of Main Street on the right, opposite turning to Green Street.*

The Goat Street Café

Goat Street Dingle Co Kerry ✆*066 915 2770 www.thegoatstreetcafe.com*

"Slow food and fast service" is the admirable aim at this popular little ingredients-led café on the aptly-named steep street up the hill from Main Street in Dingle town. It's a laid-back spot offering extremely good value for the quality of both casual daytime fare and evening meals. **Seats 45**; *Open daily, 10am-4pm; D Thu-Sat only, 6-9pm. Closed Sun. CC.* **Directions:** *Top of the Main Street on the left.*

   **Greenmount House**

Upper John Street Dingle Co Kerry ✆*066 915 1414 www.greenmounthouse.ie*

Just five minutes walk from the centre of Dingle, John and Mary Curran have run one of Ireland's finest guesthouses since the mid-70s. An exceptionally comfortable place to stay, it's quietly located on the hillside, with private parking and uninterrupted views across the town and harbour to the mountains across the bay - and ousanding breakfasts too. **Rooms 14** *(3 shower only). Closed 20-27 Dec. CC.* **Directions:** *Turn right and right again on entering Dingle.*

 The Half Door

John Street Dingle Co Kerry ✆*066 915 1600 www.halfdoor.ie*

Denis and Teresa O'Connor's cottagey restaurant in Dingle is one of the prettiest and consistently popular in town, and well-known for great seafood. **Seats 50.** *D Mon-Sat. Closed Sun; Christmas. CC.* **Directions:** *On entering Dingle, turn right onto The Mall at roundabout, then right onto John Street.*

   **Heatons House**

The Wood Dingle Co Kerry ✆*066 915 2288 www.heatonsdingle.com*

Cameron and Nuala Heaton's fine purpose-built guesthouse is set in well-maintained gardens just across the road from the water and, although convenient to Dingle town, it's beyond the hustle and bustle of the busy streets. An impressive foyer-lounge area offers space for relaxation, as do the regularly refurbished bedrooms, which include junior suites and superior rooms. Great breakfasts too. **Rooms 16.** *Closed 29 Nov-27 Dec. CC.* **Directions:** *600 metres beyond marina, at front of town.*

  Jerry Kennedy Butchers

Orchard Lane Dingle Co Kerry ✆*066 915 2511 www.dinglebutcher.com*

No ordinary butchers, this traditional shop run by Associated Craft Butchers of Ireland member Jerry Kennedy has been in the same family for generations - and it's where, among many other fine Irish meats and speciality in-house products, you will find that special Blasket Islands lamb in late summer and autumn. *Open Mon-Sat, 8-6.* **Directions:** *Just off the main street in Dingle Town.*

The Little Cheese Shop

Grey's Lane Dingle Co Kerry 📞 *087 625 5788 www.thelittlecheeseshop.net*

Maja Binder, the acclaimed Swiss-trained producer of the Dingle Peninsula Cheese range, runs this gorgeous little cheese and speciality food shop and it's a 'must-visit' destination for food lovers when in Dingle. Stocks the best Irish and European cheeses, her husband Olivier Beaujouan's 'On the Wild Side' products and other excellent speciality foods. *Open Tue-Fri 11-6, Sat 11-5. Closed Sun.* **Directions:** *Off Green Street in the centre of Dingle town – opposite the library.*

 **Lord Baker's Restaurant & Bar**

Dingle Co Kerry 📞 *066 915 1277 www.lordbakers.ie*

Dating back to 1890, John Moriarty's excellent bar and restaurant is believed to be the oldest pub in Dingle and is full of character. Local seafood stars and tables are set up in front of an open fire in the front bar, where speciality dishes include a very good chowder with home-baked soda bread. John is an excellent host, caring and watchful - no detail escapes his notice, ensuring that every guest in Dingle's largest restaurant will leave contented. *Seats 120*; L & D Fri-Wed Rest. closed Thur, house closed 24-26 Dec. CC. **Directions:** Town centre.

 **Murphys Ice Cream & Café**

Strand Street Dingle Co Kerry 📞 *066 915 2644 www.murphysicecream.ie*

Many would make the trek to Dingle solely for the pleasure of tucking into one of the treats on offer at Kieran and Séan Murphy's cheerful blue and white fronted café down near the harbour. They've made ice cream here with fresh Kerry milk and cream since 2000 and, although the café offers only coffees and ice cream, the range is growing all the time. *Seats 25 (outdoors, 8). Open daily high season, 11-10pm; low season, 11-6.30pm. No CC.* **Directions:** *In town centre.*

  Number Fifty Five

55 John Street Dingle Co Kerry 📞 *066 915 2378 www.stelladoyle.com*

Stella Doyle's charming B&B is a hidden gem in the centre of Dingle offering accommodation with character - and a high level of comfort - at a very affordable price. *Rooms 2*; *Closed 30 Sep-mid Apr. No CC.* **Directions:** *At main road roundabout, turn right up the mall; turn right up John Street - the house is at the top on the left side.*

  O'Cathain Iasc Teo Fish Shop

The Quay Dingle Co Kerry 📞 *066 915 1322 www.iascteo.com*

There's plenty of locally caught fish and shellfish to choose from at this quayside shop, including live Blasket lobster. Reasonable prices are another bonus of the quayside purchase, with daily special offers frequently giving a real bargain. And good service too - knowledgeable staff are happy to advise on storage, preparation and cooking your purchase. *Closed Sun, also Mon in winter.*

Out of the Blue

Waterside Dingle Co Kerry ✆066 915 0811 www.outoftheblue.ie

You can't miss Tim Mason's bright blue seafood restaurant on the Dingle harbour front - and it's an absolute delight. Everything depends on the fresh fish supply from the boats that day and if there's no fresh fish, they don't open (their motto is "No chips. Nothing frozen. Everything fresh or alive."). Just the kind of place that visitors dream of finding - it is not unusual to hear a different language spoken at every table. **Seats 35** *(outdoors, 30). D daily in summer, L Sun & bank hol w/e only. May close when no fresh fish is available; Closed Nov-mid Mar. CC.* **Directions:** *Opposite the pier on Dingle harbour.*

Pax House

Upper John Street Dingle Co Kerry ✆066 915 1518 www.pax-house.com

Just outside Dingle, John O'Farrell's modern house enjoys what may well be the finest view in the area, and it is also one of the most comfortable and relaxing places to stay. Thoughtfully furnished bedrooms have every amenity; two suites have their own terraces - and so does the stylish lounge. Eggs for breakfast are supplied by free-range chickens that strut around the garden. **Rooms 13** *(5 shower only); Closed 1 Nov-1 Apr. CC.* **Directions:** *Turn off at sign on N86.*

Ted Browne (De Brun Iasc Teo)

Ballinaboula Dingle Co Kerry ✆066 915 1933

A certified member of the Organic Trust, Ted Browne of Dingle is a name that you will see proudly displayed on menus, especially in the South-West of Ireland. He is an especially interesting producer, renowned for quality organic smoked salmon, prawns and crab - especially the crab.

Gorman's Clifftop House

Dingle Area Glaise Bheag Ballydavid Dingle Peninsula Co Kerry
✆066 915 5162 www.gormans-clifftophouse.com

Beautifully situated near Smerwick Harbour on the Slea Head scenic drive and Dingle Way walking route, Sile and Vincent Gorman's guesthouse is, as they say themselves "just a great place to relax and unwind". Laid-back and welcoming with open fires, very comfortable rooms, great views - and a lovely restaurant where Vincent's good cooking introduces guests to the life of the area through the local foods. **Rooms 8**. **Seats 35**. *Set D daily, 7-9pm. House open Nov-Feb by reservation only; Closed 1 Jan-10 Feb. CC.* **Directions:** *12.5km from roundabout west of Dingle Town - sign posted An Fheothanach. Keep left at V.*

Dovinia Chocolates

Dingle Area Baile Ghainín Beag Ballydavid Co Kerry ✆*086 193 6574 www.dovinia.com*

Saorla Ó Corráin uses the very best of ethically sourced and fresh local ingredients in her handmade creations, which are named after a local pre-Christian goddess. Hot chocolate spoons are the speciality and there are also bars, seasonal treats and novelties - and classic chocolates with gorgeous fillings in unusual flavour combinations. Saorla's chocolate has the perfect gloss which is a sign of quality and professionalism, and her products are beautifully branded and packed as gifts. Also offered individually. *Dingle Farmers' Market (Fri 10-2); local shops including The Little Cheese Shop.*

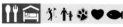 **The Old Pier**

Dingle Area An Fheothanach Ballydavid Dingle Co Kerry ✆*066 915 5242 www.oldpier.com*

Overlooking the Atlantic and the Blasket Islands, Padraig and Jacqui O'Connor's friendly restaurant is so popular with locals that (unusually for these parts) punctuality is important - as you may find the restaurant already choc-a-bloc with people if you arrive late. Local seafood is the star of this big-hearted restaurant, and the comfortable rooms offer good value. *Seats 40 (outdoors, 20); D Wed-Mon. Restaurant closed Tue, Nov-Feb. Rooms 5 (all shower only), year round; CC.* **Directions:** *11.5km west of Dingle.*

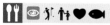 **The Skipper**

Dingle Area Ventry Dingle Peninsula Co Kerry ✆*066 915 9853 www.ventryskipper.com*

French cooking and charming service at realistic prices may not be what you'd expect to find in this remote area, but hungry visitors doing the scenic Slea Head drive west of Dingle town should be pleasantly surprised to happen on Paddy Chauvet's rustic roadside seafood restaurant. *Seats 90 (outdoors, 25). Open daily 12-10pm. Closed 1 Oct - 15 Mar. CC.* **Directions:** *7km west of Dingle, on the Slea Head drive.*

 Tig Bhric

An Riasc Ballyferriter Slea Head Dingle Peninsula Co Kerry ✆*066 915 6325 www.tihbhric.com*

Way west of Dingle town on the Slea Head scenic drive, Adrienne Heslin & Paul Lynch's atmospheric pub has everything any visitor could hope to find - and more. There's a little traditional shop at the front, a cosy bar with an open fire, simple wholesome food, music and craic. And this is also home to the West Kerry Brewery (see entry). *Open: Wed-Mon, closed Tue.* **Directions:** *Northwest of Dingle town.*

 West Kerry Brewery (Beoir Chorca Dhuibhne)

An Riasc Ballyferriter Slea Head Dingle Peninsula Co Kerry
✆*087 682 2834 www.westkerrybrewery.ie*

The West Kerry Brewery (also known as Beoir Chorca Dhuibhne) is the smallest brewery in Ireland and the most westerly brewery in Europe and they have been brewing cask-conditioned ale since 2008 using their own spring water. It is located at Tig Bhric (see entry) and this partnership between two pubs produces three beers. One (Carrig Dubh) is bottled for pubs and restaurants in the area.

 **The Tankard**

Kilfenora Fenit Tralee Co Kerry ☎*066 713 6164*

Easily spotted on the seaward side of the road from Tralee, the O'Sullivan family's pub and restaurant has a great reputation, especially for seafood. There are wonderful sea and mountain views from the restaurant, which has a patio area and a path down to the sea. Seafood cooking in the restaurant can be exceptional. *Seats 130. L&D daily. Bar meals daily, 2-10pm. Closed Good Fri. CC.* **Directions:** *8km from Tralee on Spa/Fenit road.*

 **West End Bar & Restaurant**

Fenit Tralee Co Kerry ☎*066 713 6246 www.westendfenit.ie*

Good food is offered both in the cosy bar and the restaurant of the O'Keeffe family's pub, which was built by chef Bryan O'Keeffe's great grandmother, in 1925. It has a sound reputation for traditional cooking - "classic French with Irish popular cuisine" - notably local seafood. Also offers moderately priced B&B. *Bar/restaurant Meals 5.30-10pm daily in season (bar food 2-10pm weekends). Rooms 10. Closed Jan-Mar. CC.* **Directions:** *11km from Tralee, well signposted.*

KENMARE

Renowned for its fine restaurants and outstanding accommodation (the range and quality is exceptional for a town of its size), The Heritage Town of Kenmare (Neidín/ 'little nest') is pleasingly designed and ideally sized for comfortable browsing of its quality shops and galleries. It also has a full complement of characterful pubs, and makes an excellent base for exploring both south Kerry and the near parts of west Cork. Kenmare Farmers Market is held on The Square, on Wednesday mornings. For golfers, Kenmare Golf Club and Ring of Kerry are the closest, with championship golf courses a little over 20km away - Killarney Golf & Fishing Club (Killarney, 064 663 1034) and Bantry Bay Golf Club (Bantry, 027 50579). The exceptional climate means there are wonderfully exotic sub-tropical gardens to visit – Derreen Garden (064 668 3588) at Lauragh, off the Kenmare Castletownbere road, for example. For families, the Star Sailing & Adventure Centre (064 664 1222; www.staroutdoors.ie) is outside the town at Dauros; it offers courses or just a good family day out all year round – and their first floor restaurant is open to everyone. Excellent walking is available, with Glen Inchaquin Park nearby and the both Kerry Way and the Beara Way in the wider area. There is also a very pretty harbour from where you can swim, fish or take boat trips on the Seafari (064 664 2059) to view the sea life in the area. There's a good Tourist Information Office on the square in Kenmare, with details of everything that's going on.

 The Boathouse Winebar & Bistro

Dromquinna Manor Kenmare Co Kerry ☎*064 664 2889 www.dromquinnamanor.com*

John "At Your Service" Brennan's stylish waterfront restaurant and wine bar is beautifully situated in a 19th century boathouse overlooking a little harbour. Offering quality casual food all day and an atmospheric wine bar and restaurant at night, it's a great amenity for the families holidaying in the "glamping" tents in the grounds and is also open to the general public. *Seats 70* (outdoors, 40). *Open Jue-Aug Mon-Sun 12.30-9; May-Jun & Sep Tue-Sun 12.30-9 (closed Mon); Oct Thu-Sun 12.30-9 (closed Mon-Wed). CC.* **Directions:** *Dromquinna Manor is 5km west of Kenmare, on the N70.*

The Breadcrumb

New Road O'Shea's House Kenmare Co Kerry ☎*064 664 0645 www.thebreadcrumb.com*

Manuela Goeb specialises in robust traditional German sourdough breads at her little bakery and cafe off the main street but, although that is a speciality well worth seeking out for itself, there is much more on offer including tempting cakes and pastries; vegetarian and coeliac options; good soups and coffees. *Open Mon-Sat, 8.30-6.30 (7 days in high season) Also at markets: Dingle (Fri); Milltown (Sat).*

 **Brook Lane Hotel**

Kenmare Co Kerry ☎*064 664 2077 www.brooklanehotel.com*

A short walk from the town centre, Una and Dermot Brennan's smart boutique hotel is sleek and modern, offering all the flair and comfort of a custom-built hotel but with the service and intimacy of the very best kind of B&B. A popular smart-casual food destination (all day bar and evening bistro), it has also become known for traditional Irish music. *Rooms 21*. *Closed 24-26 Dec. CC.* **Directions:** *Just outside Kenmare on the Ring of Kerry Road (take the turn off for Sneem).*

 Cupan Tae

26 Henry Street Kenmare Co Kerry ☎*064 664 2001 www.cupantae.eu/menus.html*

Right in the centre of this lovely planned town, Mary O'Leary's traditional Tea Shop is dainty and chintzy. Freshly cut sandwiches, home baking and a huge range of beverages are the specialities, with several versions of Afternoon Tea offered. Light meals, eg smoked salmon salads and a variety of quiches, also available all day. *Seats 45 (outdoors, 20). Open daily 10am-5.30pm (to 5pm Sun). Closed 24 Dec - Easter.* **Directions:** *Near junction of Henry Street and Shelbourne Street.*

 The Horseshoe

3 Main Street Kenmare Co Kerry ☎*064 664 1553*

This pleasingly old-fashioned bar and restaurant is a cosy and atmospheric place, known for the unpretentious and wholesome good food served in the informal oil-cloth-tabled restaurant at the back, with an open fire and original cattle stall divisions. *Seats 35. Open for L & D daily. Open all year. CC.* **Directions:** *Centre of Kenmare.*

  Kenmare Select Smoked Salmon

Kilmurry Kenmare Co Kerry ☎*064 664 1422*

If you see Kenmare Salmon on a menu in Kerry - especially the Smoked Salmon with Seaweed - try it, as you will be in for a treat. The Benoit family's certified organic smoked salmon is known for its high quality, light smoke and 'sashimi' fresh texture; the thick fillets offered are unusual, and intended for chunky vertical slicing. They also produce smoked oysters. *Online shop.*

Jam

6 Henry St Kenmare Co Kerry 064 664 1591 www.jam.ie

Eat in or take away, James Mulchrone's delightful bakery and café is the original of a small group of 'Jams' in Kerry and Cork. Everything is homemade using the best of local produce and, with affordable prices and friendly service, it's a winning combination. A great spot to stock up on goodies for a picnic. **Seats 55**; Open daily 8am-6pm. Closed Sun in Oct-Mar, 4 days Christmas. CC. **Directions:** Lower Henry Street on the left.

 **Lime Tree Restaurant**

Shelburne Street Kenmare Co Kerry 064 664 1225 www.limetreerestaurant.com

A former head chef, Michael Casey, has returned and taken over as chef patron at the Lime Tree, Kenmare's landmark restaurant, where he is making the best of the stunning local produce from the nearby ocean and from the rivers and lands of Kerry and West Cork. A comprehensive wine list and excellent service add to the experience, where a sense of place really comes through. *Open Thu-Mon, 6-9pm, closed Tue and Wed.* **Directions:** *Top of town, next to Park Hotel.*

  The Lodge

Killowen Road Kenmare Co Kerry 064 664 1512 www.thelodgekenmare.com

Rosemarie Quill's large, purpose-built guesthouse is just 3 minutes walk from the centre of Kenmare town. At pocket-friendly prices, it offers hotel-style accommodation with king size beds, good bathrooms, plenty of space and a lovely breakfast. **Rooms 10**. Closed Nov-Mar. CC. **Directions:** *Cork road, 150m from town opposite golf course.*

  Lorge Chocolates

Bonane Kenmare Co Kerry 064 667 9994 www.lorge.ie

In a former post office between Kenmare and Glengarriff, French master chocolatier Benoit Lorge makes exquisite chocolates for some special restaurants and hotels, bespoke orders for special occasions and also a range for retail sale. Courses also offered. On sale at the factory shop, online from the website and from selected retail outlets.

 **Mulcahy's**

36 Henry Street Kenmare Co Kerry 064 664 2383

Bruce and Laura Mulcahy's stylish contemporary restaurant has long been one of Kenmare's most consistently pleasing dining venues. Informative staff are genuinely welcoming and Bruce's compact menus are fresh and imaginative; his trademark spicy dishes are inspired by travel but with a firm foundation of seasonal local foods, notably seafood - and some dishes are offered in two sizes. **Seats 35**. D daily, 5.30-10pm. Closed 24-26 Dec and one week in autumn/winter. CC. **Directions:** Top of Henry Street.

Muxnaw Lodge

Castletownbere Road Kenmare Co Kerry 📞*064 664 1252 www.muxnawlodge.com*

Set in lovely gardens, Hannah Boland's wonderfully cosy and homely house was built in 1801 and enjoys beautiful views across Kenmare Bay. Recent renovations and refurbishments have brought about great improvements, without changing the warm and tranquil character of this pleasant house in any way - and it remains very much a home where you can relax. *Rooms 5. Residents D by arrangement. Closed 24-25 Dec. No CC.* **Directions:** *2 minutes drive from Kenmare Town (first right past the double-arched bridge towards Bantry).*

                                           Number 35

35 Main Street Kenmare Co Kerry 📞*064 664 1559 www.no35kenmare.com*

In common ownership with Brook Lane Hotel this atmospheric restaurant has plenty going for it, even in a town with so much competition. Kenmare salmon, Kerry lamb and local organic produce feature among the the good food served and, with lots of wood and open stone, it has a warm and welcoming feeling. *Seats 40. D only Wed-Mon, 6-10. Closed Mon & Tue. CC.* **Directions:** *Town centre.*

                                           P F McCarthys

14 Main Street Kenmare Co Kerry 📞*064 664 1516*

Paul & Breda Walsh's fine pub, previously known as the Fáilte Bar, goes back to 1913 and is now known for its tasty food, traditional music and craic. Although brighter and more spacious since renovations, an open fire creates a cosy atmosphere and the wholesome, fresh-tasting food is based on carefully sourced ingredients. *Seats 60; Food served Mon-Sat 12-9pm. Closed 25 Dec, Good Fri. CC.* **Directions:** *First pub/restaurant on the right hand side as you travel up Main Street.*

   **Packie's**

Henry Street Kenmare Co Kerry 📞*064 664 1508*

In a town blessed with an exceptional choice of wonderful eating places, the Foley family's buzzy little restaurant in Kenmare has long been a favourite for returning visitors. Oozing with atmosphere, it's an informal and relaxed place to eat - "honest, clean cooking with genuinely friendly service" is the stated promise and and an underlying discipline of professionalism from proprietor-chef Martin Hallissey and his team ensures that it is delivered every time. *Seats 35; D Tue-Sun. Closed Mon; Feb. CC.* **Directions:** *Town centre.*

 **Park Hotel Kenmare**

Kenmare Co Kerry ✆ *064 664 1200 www.parkkenmare.com*

For even the most jaded traveller, a stay at Francis and John "At Your Service" Brennan's renowned hotel is always a treat. A magnificent waterside location, with mountain views over gardens, belies its convenience at the heart of this Heritage Town. Luxury and hospitality are the bywords here - also outstanding food, overseen by a talented new Head Chef, James Coffey since spring 2013. **Rooms 46**. *Restaurant seats 80 (outdoors, 20). D, 7-9 daily. CC.* **Directions:** *Top of town. Hotel closed late Oct-mid Apr, except for Christmas/New Year.*

 The Purple Heather

Henry Street Kenmare Co Kerry ✆ *064 664 1016*

Open since 1964, Grainne O'Connell's informal restaurant/bar was among the first to establish a reputation for good food in Kenmare, and is a daytime sister restaurant to Packie's (see entry). This is a great place, serving wonderfully wholesome food in a relaxed atmosphere - and it's open almost all year. **Seats 45**. *Meals Mon-Sat, 11-5.30pm. Closed Sun, Christmas, bank hols. CC.* **Directions:** *Town centre - mid Henry Street (on right following traffic flow).*

 The Rose Garden

Gortamullen Kenmare Co Kerry ✆ *064 664 2288 www.rosegardenkenmare.com*

A neat bungalow set in landscaped gardens, Vladimira and Jerome's café and bakery is well worth the few minutes walk from Kenmare town. Jerome is a pastry chef and their USP is the seriously delicious food served in their café and also the patisserie that's very impressive for a small bakery and sold at very reasonable prices. *Open all day. No CC.* **Directions:** *On the N70 Sneem road, on the edge of Kenmare town.*

 **Sallyport House**

Kenmare Co Kerry ✆ *064 664 2066 www.sallyporthouse.com*

John and Helen Arthur's pleasing Edwardian house on the edge of Kenmare is in a beautiful setting overlooking the harbour, with fine garden and mountain views at the rear. Quietly located yet within walking distance of shops and restaurants, it's spacious, comfortable, well maintained - and does a good breakfast too. **Rooms 5**. *Closed 1 Nov-1 Apr. No CC.* **Directions:** *500m south of town on N71 (Glengarriff road), between town and bridge.*

Sea Shore Farm Guest House

Tubrid Kenmare Co Kerry ✆ *064 664 1270 www.seashorekenmare.com*

Owen and Mary Patricia O'Sullivan's well-named farm guesthouse is beautifully situated overlooking the Beara peninsula - and Mary Patricia (a veritable mine of local information) provides old-fashioned Irish hospitality at its best, with welcoming and efficient reception and spotlessly clean accommodation. **Rooms 6** *(4 shower only). Closed 15 Nov-1 Mar. CC.* **Directions:** *Off Ring of Kerry N70 Kenmare/Sneem road; signposted at junction with N71.*

Sheen Falls Lodge

Kenmare Co Kerry ☎ *064 664 1600 www.sheenfallslodge.ie*

Set in a 300-acre estate across the river from Kenmare town, this gently contemporary hotel is beautiful inside and out with its waterside location, welcoming fires burning in the handsome foyer and in elegant reception rooms, including a lounge bar which - like the highly-regarded La Cascade restaurant - overlooks the tumbling waterfall. **Rooms 66**. Restaurant **seats 120** *(outdoors, 12). D daily 7-9. Hotel closed Jan 2 - Feb 4 & midweek Nov, Dec, Feb & Mar. CC.* **Directions:** *Take N71 Kenmare (Glengarriff road); turn left at Riversdale Hotel.*

Shelburne Lodge

Cork Road Kenmare Co Kerry ☎ *064 664 1013 www.shelburnelodge.com*

The oldest house in Kenmare, Tom and Maura Foley's house is a fine stone building with lovely gardens, and it has great style and attention to detail. Elegant and extremely comfortable, with an inviting log fire and interesting books to read, the feeling is of being a guest in a private country house. Their superb breakfasts are legendary and at night guests are directed to the family's restaurant, Packie's. **Rooms 10** *(3 shower-only). Closed Dec 1-mid Mar. CC.* **Directions:** *500 metres from town centre, on the Cork road R569.*

Tom Crean Fish & Wine

Main Street Kenmare Co Kerry ☎ *064 664 1589 www.tomcrean.ie*

In a former bank - dating back to the early 19th century and full of character - Aileen d'Arcy recently renamed this popular restaurant after her grandfather, the Antarctic explorer Tom Crean. Local foods - especially seafood, and her own organic produce - are central to the cooking, and there's a great buzz in the big and airy room. **Seats 100** *(outdoors, 36). D daily 5-10pm. Closed Tue (May-Sep), 7 Jan-end Mar. CC.* **Directions:** *Main Street, corner of R569.*

Truffle Pig Fine Foods

Henry Street Kenmare Co Kerry ☎ *064 668 9624 www.trufflepigkenmare.com*

This excellent deli and café has become a destination for discerning shoppers. You can stock up with goodies from a wide range of artisan delicatessen products, farmhouse cheeses and gourmet salads, together with the breads, pies, cakes and other treats that are cooked on site. Perfect for a picnic. *Open Mon-Sat, 9.30-6*

Virginia's Guesthouse

36 Henry Street Kenmare Co Kerry ☎ *086 372 0625 www.virginias-kenmare.com*

Neil and Noreen Harrington are superb hosts and guest comfort comes first with them. Guestrooms have lovely big beds, and everything you could need, and each winter sees regular refurbishment – new mattresses, whatever is necessary. And their breakfasts are a point of honour too, offering many delights. A lovely place to stay. **Rooms 8** *(all shower only). Closed 22-25 Dec. CC.* **Directions:** *Town centre; shares an entrance with Mulcahy's Restaurant.*

Avoca Handweavers Kenmare

Kenmare Area Moll's Gap Kenmare Co Kerry ✆*064 663 4720* *www.avoca.ie*

Located at a famous viewing point on the Ring of Kerry, this outpost of the Pratt family's County Wicklow weaving company sells its fine range of clothing and crafts. Upstairs, in a first floor self-service restaurant with stunning views, it offers consistently wholesome and appealing home-made fare to sustain the weary sightseer. *Restaurant* **seats 80**. *Food service all day 10-5. Closed 25/6 Dec, Jan-Mar. CC.* **Directions:** *On Ring of Kerry at famous panoramic crossroads.*

 The Strawberry Field

Kenmare Area Moll's Gap Blackwater Killarney Co Kerry
✆*064 668 2977* *www.strawberryfield-ireland.com*

High up in hills on the road between Moll's Gap and Sneem, Peter and Margaret Kerssens specialise in making tempting pancakes - to the delight of the travellers seeking sustenance on this lonely but lovely road. *Open daily, year round, 11am-6pm.*

KILLARNEY

Famous throughout the world for its romantic beauty (Lakes of Killarney, Killarney National Park, the Ring of Kerry), the Killarney area has long been a source of inspiration for poets, painters and writers. Despite the commercial tone of the town itself - which has been a centre of tourism since before the days of the Victorian Grand Tour - the surroundings are stunning and, with a number of the country's finest hotels in the town and immediate area, it remains an excellent base for exploring the area, or for leisure activities, notably golf (Killarney Golf & Fishing Club, 064 663 1034), walking and fishing. Visiting Muckross House and the National Park (native red deer; traditional farm) is always a highlight.

 **Aghadoe Heights Hotel**

Lakes of Killarney Killarney Co Kerry ✆*064 663 1766* *www.aghadoeheights.com*

This stylish contemporary property enjoys stunning views of Killarney's famous lakes and the mountains beyond, and also overlooks the town's two 18-hole championship golf courses. It is one of the country's most luxurious hotels and, under the caring management of Pat and Marie Chawke and their welcoming staff, it is a very special place. Good food has always been a feature of the hotel and the view from the restaurant is wonderful. *Rooms* **74**. *Restaurant* **seats 110** *(outdoors, 40); D daily; L Sun only. Informal menus also offered 10am-9.30pm daily in summer. Closed mid-week Nov-Mar. CC.* **Directions:** *3.2km north of Killarney; signposted off N22.*

Arbutus Hotel

College Street Killarney Co Kerry ☎ *064 31037 www.arbutuskillarney.com*

In the Buckley family since 1926, this lovely old hotel has the charm and personality that so many newer ones lack. There's an emphasis on genuine hospitality and good home cooking – fresh home baking and a great breakfast - and traditional music and craic next door, at Buckleys Bar. **Rooms 35**. **CC**. **Directions:** *Town centre; within walking distance of railway station.*

 The Brehon

Muckross Road Killarney Co Kerry ☎ *064 663 0700 www.thebrehon.com*

Everything at this five-storey hotel, conference centre and spa next to the Irish National Events Centre (INEC) is on a grand scale. The design, decor and furnishings of the public spaces are striking, featuring some interesting modern art and sculpture, and it is a popular conference and wedding venue. Accommodation is luxurious and the restaurant is airy and bright, with a wide ranging breakfast menu offered. **Rooms 123**. *Open all year. CC.* **Directions:** *Located opposite the National Park (N71) 1.5km from town centre.*

 Bricín

26 High Street Killarney Co Kerry ☎ *064 663 4902 www.bricin.com*

Upstairs, over a craft shop (interesting to browse if you like Irish pottery), Paddy & Johnny McGuire's country-style first-floor restaurant has been delighting visitors with its warm atmosphere and down-to-earth food since 1990. Features traditional dishes like boxty (potato pancakes), too rarely seen in Irish restaurants. **Seats 29**; D Mon-Sat, 6-9. Closed Sun, Mon and Feb. CC. **Directions:** *On the High Street, Killarney.*

 Cahernane House Hotel

Muckross Road Killarney Co Kerry ☎ *064 663 1895 www.cahernane.com*

A great dining destination, the Browne family's attractive hotel is in a lovely quiet location, convenient to Killarney town, yet - thanks to a long tree-lined avenue and parkland which stretches down to the water - with a charmingly other-worldly atmosphere. With comfortable accommodation and David Norris's good cooking of local foods, it makes an appealing base. **Rooms 38**. *Restaurant: D daily. Also bar food, 12.30-9.30pm. Closed mid Dec-mid Jan. CC.* **Directions:** *Ouskirts of Killarney, off the N71 near Muckross Park.*

 Coolclogher House

Mill Road Killarney Co Kerry ☎ *064 663 5996 www.coolclogherhouse.com*

Mary and Maurice Harnett's beautiful early Victorian house is just on the edge of Killarney town and yet, tucked away on its 68-acre walled estate, it is an oasis of peace and tranquillity. Impressive and relaxed. They quite reasonably call it 'perhaps the most exclusive accommodation available in Killarney'. ***Rooms 6***. *CC*. ***Directions:*** *Leaving Killarney town, take Muckross Road; turn left N72, onto Mill Road (signed); gates on right after 1km.*

Cucina Italiana

St. Anthony's Place Killarney Co Kerry ☎*064 662 6575*

Tucked away down a laneway, Marcello Cesariello's smartly presented Italian restaurant is one of the town's most popular. Quality ingredients are the foundation for an appealing menu offering an extensive range of dishes – and not only in the familiar categories; unusually for an Italian restaurant, a separate vegetarian menu is also offered. ***Seats 60***. *D daily. Closed Jan. CC.* ***Directions:*** *Opposite East Avenue.*

Earls Court House

Woodlawn Junction Muckross Road Killarney Co Kerry
☎*064 663 4009 www.killarney-earlscourt.ie*

Although Roy and Emer Moynihan's purpose-built guesthouse quite near the town centre is now classified as an hotel, its essential qualities of hospitality, professionalism, comfort and character remain unchanged. Emer gives personal attention to the details that make for real comfort, and breakfasts are superb. ***Rooms 30***. *Closed 15 Nov - 1 Mar. CC.* ***Directions:*** *Take the first left at the traffic lights on Muckross road (signed), then 3rd premises.*

Gaby's Seafood Restaurant

27 High Street Killarney Co Kerry ☎*064 663 2519*

One of Ireland's longest established seafood restaurants, this is also one of the great classic Irish kitchens. Proprietor-chef Gert Maes' menus are offered in classic French style and in three languages; although expensive, absolute freshness is clearly the priority, and it has a pleasantly informal atmosphere. ***Seats 75***. *D only. Closed Sun (& Mon, Tue - Jan-Mar). CC.* ***Directions:*** *On the main street.*

The German Butcher Shop

Aghadoe Killarney Co Kerry ☎*064 33069 www.germanbutchershop.com*

A food lovers' destination at Fossa since the 1980s, Armin Weise's highly respected butchers supplies local venison from the Killarney National Park as well as excellent charcuterie, German meat cuts and other specialities including tempting continental patisserie. Gluten free products are included in the range. Open Mon-Sat. Closed Sun. Mail order service available.

Jam

Old Market Lane Killarney Co Kerry ☎*064 663 7716 www.jam.ie*

This branch of James Mulchrone's highly regarded Kenmare bakery, delicatessen and café lies behind a smart frontage in an attractive pedestrianised laneway. And, of course, the same basic principles apply here: affordable prices, friendly service and real home-made food using the best of local produce. ***Seats 70***. *Open Mon-Sat, 8am-5pm. Closed Sun from Oct-Apr, 4 days Christmas. CC.* ***Directions:*** *Town centre, between Main Street and the Glebe public car park.*

Just Cooking

Killahane Firies **Killarney** *Co Kerry* ☎ *066 979 3660 www.justcooking.ie*

Well known chef Mark Doe and his wife Bernie run this cookery school near Farranfore (Kerry airport). They offer consultancy services and, in their purpose built kitchen for classes of up to 12 students, a wide range of courses on themes as diverse as Basic Cookery, Men Only and Kids Summer Camps. *Directions: Near Farranfore (Kerry airport).*

  Kathleens Country House

Madams Height Tralee Road **Killarney** *Co Kerry* ☎ *064 663 2810 www.kathleens.net*

If you like staying in a quietly situated owner-run establishment of character rather than an hotel, Kathleen O'Regan Sheppard's long-established guesthouse outside Killarney could be the place for you. It's just at the beginning of the Ring of Kerry route, convenient for a wide range of outdoor pursuits - and serves an excellent breakfast. *Rooms 17.* Closed 1 Oct - Easter. CC. *Directions: 1.6km north of Killarney Town off N22 (Tralee road).*

  Killarney Lodge

Countess Road **Killarney** *Co Kerry* ☎ *064 663 6499 www.killarneylodge.net*

Run by a member of one of Killarney's most respected hotelier families, Catherine Treacy's fine purpose-built guesthouse is set in private walled gardens just a couple of minutes walk from the town centre and is a very comfortable place to stay. Large rooms have all the amenities expected of an hotel, plus the care that only hands-on owner management can give - and a good Irish breakfast, including home-baked breads and scones. *Rooms 16* (1 shower only). Closed 1 Nov-1 Mar. CC. *Directions: 2 minutes walk from town centre off Muckross Road.*

Killarney Park

Town Centre **Killarney** *Co Kerry* ☎ *064 663 5555 www.killarneyparkhotel.ie*

Set in extensive gardens shared with the adjacent Malton, the Treacy family's luxurious, well-run hotel is deceptively modern - despite its classical good looks, it only dates from the 1990s. Since then constant improvement has been the theme, with a destination spa among the amenities - and excellent food (some of it from their own gardens) served in all areas. *Rooms 72.* Restaurant *seats 90*; D daily. Food also served in The Garden Bar, 12-9pm daily. Hotel closed 24-27 Dec. CC. *Directions: Town centre, near railway station.*

 Killarney Plaza Hotel

Kenmare Place **Killarney** *Co Kerry* ☎ *064 662 1100 www.killarneyplaza.com*

In seeking to regain the glamour of the grand hotels, the Plaza offers an alternative to the modernism that has taken over in Irish hotels in recent years. Very centrally located and with good amenities including underground parking and spa, at relatively reasonable rates. *Rooms 198.* Open all year. CC. *Directions: Town centre.*

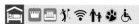

Killarney Royal Hotel

College Street Killarney *Co Kerry* ☎*064 663 1853* *www.killarneyroyal.ie*

Proprietors Joe and Margaret Scally have lavished care and investment on the Royal. This sister property to Hayfield Manor, Cork, is a beautiful hotel furnished in an elegant period style that enhances the age and design of the building. While luxurious, a warm and friendly atmosphere prevails throughout. **Rooms 29**. *Closed 25-26 Dec. CC.* **Directions:** *In Killarney town centre on College Street, off the N22.*

Killeen House Hotel

Aghadoe Killarney *Co Kerry* ☎*064 663 1711* *www.killeenhousehotel.com*

10 minutes from Killarney (5 from Killeen and Mahony's Point golf courses), this 19th century rectory is now Michael and Geraldine Rosney's "charming little hotel". Unique features include a pubby little bar, where guests' golf balls are accepted as tender, and 'Rozzers' restaurant, which is very popular locally as well as with residents. **Rooms 23**. **Seats 50**. *D daily. Closed mid Oct-mid April. CC.* **Directions:** *6.5km from Killarney town centre - just off Dingle Road.*

Lake Hotel Killarney

Muckross Road Killarney *Co Kerry* ☎*064 663 1035* *www.lakehotel.com*

Adjacent to the National Park and Muckross House, on a prime lakeshore site with mountain views, Niall Huggard's historic hotel lays fair claim to 'the most beautiful location in Ireland' - and Niall does everything possible to ensure that the visitor's experience matches up to the scenery. **Rooms 131** *(2 shower only). Closed Dec & Jan. CC.* **Directions:** *2 km from Killarney town centre, on the Muckross Road.*

Lord Kenmare's Restaurant

College Street Killarney *Co Kerry* ☎*064 663 1294* *www.lordkenmares.com*

The Murphy family's cosy first floor restaurant's polished floors and bare tables add up to a good bit of noise, but nobody seems to mind. Good food, together with great service and value ensure that this cheerful place is always packed - even on weekdays, when other restaurants are quiet, there's lots of buzz. Booking advised. **Directions:** *Town centre, above Murphy's Bar and Squire's Pub.*

The Malton

Town Centre East Avenue Road Killarney *Co Kerry* ☎*064 663 8000* *www.themalton.com*

Although much of the interior has received a modern makeover, this classic Victorian railway hotel remains a pleasant place to stay. The pillared entrance, ivy-clad facade and welcoming open fire still convey a sense of occasion, and its convenience to town and station is unchanged. There has been renewed focus on the gardens recently; they now supply produce to the kitchens and also some of the ingredients for the hotel's in-house product range The Malton Pantry. *Rooms 172. Open all year. CC.* **Directions:** *In the heart of Killarney town beside Railway Station.*

  ## Miss Courtney's Tea Rooms

8 College Street Killarney Co Kerry ✆*087 610 9500 www.misscourtneys.com*

Sandra Dunlea is the fourth generation of her family to run a business here, and Miss Courtney's Tea Rooms has all the elegance and charm of a bygone age, offering harrassed visitors the perfect antidote to the pushy modern world outside. *Seats 50 (outdoors, 16). Open 7 days in summer, 10am-8.30pm (Sun to 6).* **Directions:** *Town centre, directly opposite Glebe car park.*

  ## Murphys Ice Cream & Café

37 Main Street Killarney Co Kerry ✆*087 052 3145 www.murphysicecream.ie*

This cheerful blue and white fronted café in the centre of Killarney was the first branch of the popular Dingle Murphys Ice Cream to be opened by the eponymous American brothers Kieran and Séan. While offering only coffees and ice cream, the range of flavours is very wide - and some are limited edition seasonal specialities. *Seats 25 (outdoors, 8). Open 7 days a week. No CC.* **Directions:** *In town centre.*

 ## Pay As You Please

New Market Lane High Street Killarney Co Kerry ✆*086 306 8253*

Located in an old warehouse in the town centre, Rob O'Reilly and Barry McBride's funky restaurant opened with no name but it's become known as 'Pay As You Please' thanks to the novel system of inviting diners 'to pay what you think the food is worth'. The menu is limited, but what comes out of Barry's kitchen is good - and everybody loves it. *Seats 40 (outdoors, 10). Open 10am-4pm daily in summer (check off season), D Thu-Sat. No CC.* **Directions:** *Off High Street, on the laneway behind Quill's Woollen Market.*

  ## Quinlans Seafood Bar

77 High Street Killarney Co Kerry ✆*064 662 0666 www.kerryfish.com/index.php/seafoodbar*

A cousin business of the famous Quinlan's Fish Shops, Liam Quinlan's basically-appointed but bright and airy town centre restaurant doubles as a takeaway - and it merits recommendation for its outstanding selection of very fresh fish, good simple cooking, reasonable prices - and a menu in four languages. *Open from 12 noon, 7 days a week.* **Directions:** *Town centre, opposite Quill's Woollen Market.*

 ## Randles Hotel

Muckross Road Killarney Co Kerry ✆*064 663 5333 www.randlescourt.com*

The Randles' well located, family-managed hotel has developed around an attractive Edwardian house and its combination of period features and modern appointments make it a very pleasant and comfortable place to stay. A good breakfast is served and there's a choice of restaurants for evening meals. *Rooms 78. Bar meals & D daily. Closed 22-27 Dec. CC.* **Directions:** *5 mins walk from town centre on Muckross Road.*

 **The Ross**

Town Centre Killarney Co Kerry 📞*064 663 1855 www.theross.ie*

Lovers of contemporary style will adore the Treacy family's impressive boutique hotel. Eerie electric-green lighting at reception prepares the first-time guest for a funky stay, although the exceptionally comfortable accommodation is quieter in tone. The Lane Café Bar serves good casual fare while the theatrical **Cellar One** restaurant provides a stunning setting for great cooking. **Rooms 29**. **Seats 60**; *D daily. Bar food daily, 12.30-8.30pm. Hotel closed 24-27 Dec. CC.* **Directions:** *Town centre.*

 The Smoke House

8 High Street Killarney Co Kerry 📞*064 663 7877 www.thesmokehouse.ie*

Right in the centre of Killarney, Sandra Dunlea's smart-casual restaurant is a sister operation to Miss Courtney's Tea Rooms. Specialising in steaks and seafood, its good honest food, long hours of opening and stylish laid-back atmosphere make it very popular with tourists and locals alike. **Seats 44**. *Open 7 days 9-"late". CC.* **Directions:** *Town centre.*

 Treyvaud's Restaurant

62 High Street Killarney Co Kerry 📞*064 663 3062 www.treyvaudsrestaurant.com*

Brothers Paul and Mark Treyvaud's attractive and friendly town-centre restaurant has a well-deserved following, both locally and beyond the area. Consistently good cooking of fresh and local foods, moderate pricing, long opening hours and well-trained staff with a clear desire to send customers away happy with their meal have proved a winning formula. **Seats 80**; *L Tue-Sun; D daily. Closed Mon & Tue off season (Nov-Feb). CC.* **Directions:** *500 yards up main street, on the left.*

 West End House

Lower New Street Killarney Co Kerry 📞*064 663 2271 www.westendhouse.com*

This listed building has a fascinating history and a huge feature fireplace in the end wall (remaining from the Fassbenders' time here) sets an atmospheric tone for the series of romantically cottagey rooms that provide an unusual setting for some admirably seasonal cooking. **Seats 70**. *D Tue-Sat, Sun by reservation only. CC. Closed Mon & Tue.* **Directions:** *Opposite St Mary's Church.*

 **The Beaufort Bar & Restaurant**

Killarney Area Beaufort Killarney Co Kerry 📞*064 664 4032 www.beaufortbar.com*

In the fourth generation of family ownership, Padraig O'Sullivan's attractive pub near the Gap of Dunloe is always a pleasure to visit with its open stonework and welcoming fire, in both the bar and atmospheric first floor restaurant. There's bias towards fish but also plenty of other choices, usually including Kerry lamb. *Restaurant* **Seats 60**; *D Tue-Sat; L Sun only (closed D Sun, all Mon). Bar D Tue-Thu. Establishment closed Bank Hols, Nov, Christmas week. CC.* **Directions:** *Follow the N72 to Killorglin. Left at Beaufort bridge, first stone building on left in village.*

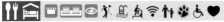

The Dunloe

Killarney Area Beaufort Killarney Co Kerry ☎ *064 664 4111 www.thedunloe.com*

Sister hotel to the Europe Hotel & Resort, Fossa and Ard na Sidhe Country House at Caragh Lake (see entries), this beautifully located hotel is mainly modern (although the original castle is part of the development) and has much in common with the larger Europe: the style is similar, the scale is generous, and standards of maintenance and housekeeping are exemplary. Perhaps surprisingly, it is a good choice for families - and also the family pet. *Rooms 102. Restauratn D daily. Closed 1 Nov- 6 April. CC. Directions: Off main Ring of Kerry road.*

The Europe

Killarney Area Fossa Killarney Co Kerry ☎ *064 667 1300 www.theeurope.com*

Open since 1965, this impressive hotel may now be around fifty years old, but its spacious style, quality furnishings, beautiful views and balconies all along the lake side of the hotel are timeless qualities and it has continued to outshine many a new top level hotel - notably since the seriously impressive ESPA was added, along with a new conference and events centre. Both restaurants are popular dining destinations and, like all public areas, share the stunning views. *Rooms 187. Panorama Restaurant (D Mon-Sat exc Nov-Dec); Brasserie Bar, with terrace (all day daily). Closed mid Dec - early Feb. CC. Directions: On main Ring of Kerry road, N72.*

Muckross Park Hotel & Cloisters Spa

Killarney Area Muckross Killarney Co Kerry ☎ *064 662 3400 www.muckrosspark.com*

Located within the Killarney National Park, handy to all the championship golf courses in the area, and ideally situated for exploring south Kerry, this luxurious hotel makes an ideal base on the edge of Killarney town. The interior mood ranges from romantic to smart contemporary, with warmly Irish service and fine food to match. *Rooms 68. CC. Directions: 4km from Killarney, on main Kenmare/Ring of Kerry road, almost opposite entrance to Muckross House.*

Killorglin Cheese

Ardmoniel Killorglin Co Kerry ☎ *066 976 1402*

Wilma O'Connor has made the traditional gouda-style cheeses of her native Holland here since the 1980s; look out for her plain and flavoured cheeses on restaurant menus and at markets in the area, and speciality shops around the country.

 **Nick's Seafood Restaurant & Piano Bar**

Lr Bridge Street Killorglin Co Kerry ✆ *066 976 1219*

Anne and Nick Foley's pair of attractive stone-faced townhouses are home one of the famous old restaurants of Ireland and it is is clearly thriving. Local seafood is the big draw (grilled Cromane mussels, lobster thermidor), although other choices, include prime Kerry beef and lamb - and Nick's classic French cooking with an Irish accent has earned a lot of friends. *Seats 60. D Wed-Sun. Closed Mon & Tue, all Nov, Christmas. CC.* **Directions:** *On the Ring of Kerry road, 20 km from Killarney.*

 **Sol y Sombra Wine & Tapas Bar**

Old Church of Ireland Lower Bridge Street Killorglin Co Kerry ✆ *066 976 2347 www.solysombra.ie*

Atmospheric is one of the things they do best in the Foley family and this younger sister restaurant to Nick's, run by Clíodhna Foley, proves the point. Located in a former Church of Ireland premises, it's a fantastic setting for music and 'raciones', a larger size of tapas based jointly on local produce and Spanish specialities that suits Irish tastes perfectly. *Seats 80 (outdoors, 20). Open Tue-Sun 5-11pm. Food served 6-10pm (to 10.30pm Fri & Sat; 9.30pm Sun). Closed Mon (& Tue in winter), Feb. CC.* **Directions:** *On left as you drive through town. Set back from road next to Nick's Restaurant.*

    **Jack's Coastguard Restaurant**

Killorglin Area Waters Edge Cromane Killorglin Co Kerry ✆ *066 976 9102 www.jackscromane.com*

Just a stone's throw from the sea at Cromane, where the famous mussels are landed, this handsome stone building sends out all the right signals - as does the restaurant, which is fresh and original. Head chef is Jonathan Keary, brother of the owner of Jacks, Brian Keary, and he's doing an excellent job with fresh produce that includes the meats of the area - Kerry lamb and beef, speciality foods such as Annascaul puddings - and, most notably, fish and seafood. Bookings advised. *Seats 130. Hours vary; closed Tue. CC.* **Directions:** *Waterside in Cromane.*

LISTOWEL

A lively traditional market town on the banks of the River Feale in north Kerry, Listowel is probably most famous for its writers, notably John B. Keane and Brian MacMahon, and the Writers Week literary festival held in the town in June; the famous John B Keane pub in William Street is now run by his son Billy, also an author, who keeps on the family traditions. Interesting features of this Heritage Town include a beautiful five arch bridge over the River Feale, which dates back to 1829, Listowel Castle (086 385 7201, open May to September) and The Garden of Europe, located in the town park, where more than 2,500 trees and shrubs from all over Europe are grown. Local activities include golfing at the Listowel Golf Course (068 21592), excellent salmon and trout fishing on the River Feale, and horse riding at the Listowel Equestrian Centre (068 23 734, open six days a week, closed Mondays). The famous Listowel Races horse-racing festival takes place in in September. The town offers interesting shopping including local crafts of pottery, candles, jewellery and knitwear.

There's a farmers' market every Friday in the square (9-2), and the annual Listowel Food Fair is held in the town in November.

 **Allo's Restaurant Bar & Bistro**

41/43 Church Street Listowel Co Kerry ☎068 22880

Helen Mullane and Armel Whyte's traditional feeling café-bar is the type of contemporary, self-confident Irish eating house that visitors hope for but do not always find in every provincial town. Armel's team source great raw materials and cook them with flair, while Helen is an impressive hostess. Even a quick bar lunch can be memorable. *Seats 50 (outdoors, 20). Open Tue-Sat, 12-9. Closed Sun & Mon, 25 Dec & Good Fri. CC.* **Directions:** *Coming into Listowel on the N69, located half way down Church Street on the right hand side (almost opposite Garda Station).*

  John Rs Home Bakery & Delicatessen

70 Church Street Listowel Co Kerry ☎068 21249 www.johnrs.com

Pierce Walsh's impressive shop is the kind that every town should have but few do. The home baking range includes all the old favourites; then there are the tasty homemade meals to go, the hampers - and Café Hannah, next door, which offers a wholesome menu including many of the products from the shop. *Open Mon-Sat, 9-6.*

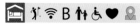 **Listowel Arms Hotel**

Listowel Co Kerry ☎068 21500 www.listowelarms.com

Kevin O'Callaghan's much-loved old hotel is rich in history and especially famous as the main venue for the annual Listowel Writers Week. Some of the very comfortable bedrooms overlook the River Feale - and the race course too, so these are at a premium in Listowel Race Week. *Rooms 42. Closed 25-26 Dec. CC.* **Directions:** *In the corner of the historic old square in Listowel town centre.*

 Beal Organic Cheese

*Listowel Area Beal Lodge Organic Farm, Asdee Listowel Co Kerry
☎068 41137 www.bealorganiccheese.com*

Kate Carmody's distinctive North Kerry organic cheddar cheeses are all made with vegetarian rennet and the two cheese made on the farm use only the milk of Beal Lodge's pedigree Holstein-Friesian herd. Mature Béal Organic Cheddar is handmade on the farm using pasteurised milk matured for nine months and Raw Milk Béal Organic Cheese is an outstanding variation. Béal Handmade Cheddar is a milder block cheese produced in an off-farm artisan cheesemaking facility. *Available from: Selected butchers and speciality food stores throughout Ireland including Avoca, Donnybrook Fair, Fresh Supermarkets and Mortons in Dublin (see website for current list).*

   **The Moorings**

Portmagee Co Kerry ☎066 947 7108 www.moorings.ie

With open fires, and music at night, Gerard and Patricia Kennedy's quayside bar and restaurant is full of character - and it's known for excellent local seafood. Just arrived catch of the day is posted on blackboards, while provenance and named suppliers lead menus featuring the likes of pan-fried Valentia scallops and Cahirciveen smoked salmon. Comfortable accommodation includes some seafront rooms. *Restaurant: D Tue-Sun. Bar food 12-8.30pm.* **Rooms 16.** *House closed 25/26 Dec. CC.* **Directions:** *Turn right for Portmagee 5km outside Caherciveen on the Waterville Road (N70) onto R565, bear left after 10km before bridge.*

SNEEM

Situated on the Ring of Kerry between Kenmare and Waterville, Sneem is "a knot" in Irish, and this colourful, immaculately kept village is divided in two by the River Sneem, creating an unusual "hour-glass" shape ("The Knot in the Ring"). The first week of August sees Sneem at its busiest with the "Welcome Home Festival", in honour of those who emigrated from Ireland.

 Burns Butchers

North Square Sneem Co Kerry 064 664 5139 *www.sneemblackpudding.com*

The popular Sneem black pudding originated in this little butchers and is still made here by fourth generation butcher Kieran Burns, baked like a big cake and sliced as required.

 O'Sullivan's Butchers

North Square Sneem Co Kerry 064 664 5213 *www.sneemblackpudding.ie*

Peter O'Sullivan carries on the proud tradition of the family meat business, which dates back to 1958, and continues to make their family recipe for Sneem Black Pudding by hand.

 **The Parknasilla Resort & Spa**

Parknasilla Sneem Co Kerry 064 667 5600 *www.parknasillahotel.ie*

Set in 500 acres of sub-tropical parkland, overlooking Kenmare Bay, this classic Victorian hotel is blessed with one of the most beautiful locations in Ireland; it opened under new ownership in 2013, with many key staff retained. Open fires and comfy lounging furniture sum up the indoor mood, while hotel and estate offer a very wide range of activities. Rooms vary greatly offering both traditional and contemporary styles, some - like the formal dining room - with sea and mountain views.

Rooms 83. *Restaurant* **seats 180** *(outdoors, 40). L&D daily. Self catering villas also available. Hotel open weekends only 15th November-20th December; Closed 5 Jan - 7 Mar. CC.* **Directions:** *25 km west of Kenmare, on Ring of Kerry.*

 **Tahilla Cove Country House**

Tahilla Cove Sneem Co Kerry 064 664 5204 *www.tahillacove.com*

Although much added to over the years (with a blocky annexe in the garden), this comfortable family-run guesthouse has an old house in there somewhere. And it's a refreshingly low-key place with two very special features: the location, which is genuinely waterside (own harbour); and the owners, James and Deirdre Waterhouse. **Rooms 9** *(1 shower only). Closed mid Oct-Easter. CC.* **Directions:** *16km west of Kenmare and 8km east of Sneem (N70).*

TRALEE

Co Kerry's largest town, Tralee is a busy and lively spot. Home to the world famous Rose of Tralee International Festival (066 712 3227), Tralee town boasts many visitor attractions including Kerry County Museum (066 712 7777, open all year), Europe's only working windmill the Blennerville Windmill (066 712 1064, open April to October) and Siamsa Tire (066 712 3055), the national folk theatre of Ireland. The town park covers 80 acres and includes an award winning rose garden. Walkers are well accommodated as both the Dingle way and the North Kerry way start in Tralee and include breathtaking scenery of the one of the most scenic counties. Golfers will enjoy the 18 hole links at Tralee Golf Club (066 713 6379), while sailing enthusiasts can use the 100 berth marina.

 **Ballygarry House Hotel & Spa**

Killarney Road Tralee Co Kerry ✆ *066 712 3322 www.ballygarryhouse.com*

Now in the third generation of ownership by the McGillicuddy family, this is an appealing hotel, with exceptionally friendly and helpful staff, and it is moderately priced for the high standard of accommodation, food and service offered. ***Rooms 64***. ***Seats 80***. *L & D daily. Bar meals 12.30-9.30pm daily. Closed 21-28 Dec. CC.* **Directions:** *1.5km from Tralee, on the N21 Killarney road.*

 **Ballyseede Castle**

Ballyseede Tralee Co Kerry ✆ *066 712 5799 www.ballyseedecastle.com*

Set in 35 acres of parkland and garden on the edge of Tralee town, this very likeable hotel has 15th century origins. It is spacious, and comfortable, with quirky features that give a sense of fun - as at its sister hotel, Cabra Castle in Co Cavan (see entry), you may well be greeted by the resident Irish wolfhound (or a less prestigious but equally friendly canine companion). ***Rooms 23***. *Closed 4 Jan - 4 Mar. CC.* **Directions:** *Just off the Tralee-Killarney Road (N21).*

 **The Brandon Hotel**

Princes Street Tralee Co Kerry ✆ *066 712 3333 www.brandonhotel.ie*

Overlooking a park and the famous Siamsa Tire folk theatre, and close to the Aquadome, Tralee's largest hotel is at the heart of activities throughout a wide area and a popular business destination. ***Rooms 185***. *Closed 15-28 Dec. CC.* **Directions:** *Town Centre.*

 **Brook Manor Lodge**

Fenit Road Tralee Co Kerry ✆ *066 712 0406 www.brookmanorlodge.com*

Set back from the road in its own grounds, Sandra and Jerome Lordan's large purpose-built guesthouse offers immaculate and particularly spacious accommodation. There's plenty of lounging space and breakfast - cooked to order from an extensive menu - is served in a big conservatory with sun blinds fitted. Sandra and Jerome are genuinely hospitable, making this a sociable place to stay, with a friendly can-do atmosphere. ***Rooms 8*** *(2 shower only). Closed 1 Nov - 1 Feb. CC.*

Directions: *2 km from town centre on Fenit road (R558).*

Grand Hotel

Denny Street Tralee Co Kerry ✆*066 712 1499 www.grandhoteltralee.com*

Established in 1928, the Grand is one of the town's most comfortable and popular hotels; it's at the heart of the local community and there's always a buzz. It's a pleasant place to stay and the Pikeman Bar is especially useful to know about - this fine traditional bar has an open fire and serves wholesome food all day. *Rooms 43 (some shower only). Bar food 8.30am-9.30pm daily. Samuel's Restaurant breakfast, L&D daily. CC. **Directions:** Town centre.*

 Kingdom Food & Wine

Oakpark Tralee Co Kerry ✆*066 711 8562 www.kingdomstore.ie*

Easy to spot in a former church, you will be glad you found Maeve Duff's treasure trove of good things. The well-chosen range of Irish and international foods (and wines) on sale includes local specialities not widely stocked and 'free-from' baked goods. ***Directions:*** Near Meadowlands Hotel.

 Mary Annes Tea Rooms

17 Denny Street Tralee Co Kerry ✆*066 712 7610*

Everybody loves the tea room that Eileen Nolan has dedicated to her grandmother Mary Anne Hickey - with its charming period furnishings, oilcloth or linen-covered tables and delightful mismatched chairs and china, it's an oasis of old world gentility in the heart of Tralee, and everything is freshly baked by Eileen herself. *Open Mon-Sat, 9-6. Closed Sun. **Directions:** Centre of Tralee, above Finnegan's Restaurant & Wine Cellar.*

 **Meadowlands Hotel**

Oakpark Rd Tralee Co Kerry ✆*066 718 0444 www.meadowlandshotel.com*

This friendly and comfortable hotel is set in 3 acres of grounds and landscaped gardens, yet handy to the town centre. Unusual features include interesting furniture, commissioned from Irish craft manufacturers, and a rustically-themed restaurant that is supplied by owner Paddy O'Mathuna's own fishing boat. *Rooms 58. Restaurant **seats 100**; D Mon-Sat, L Sun only. Restaurant closed Sun D. Closed 24-25 Dec. CC. **Directions:** 1km from Tralee town centre on the N69, but usually accessed by N21/N22.*

  **Spa Seafoods Deli & Café**

The Spa Tralee Co Kerry ✆*066 713 6901 www.spaseafoods.com*

The Walsh family have not only a fishmongers shop, but also a delicatessen - and, above it, a seafood café with views across the bay. Very simple in décor and ambience, the cafe has earned a following for its good food, value and friendly staff. Except for offering a single vegetarian starter and main course, the menu is all fish. *Seats 47 (outdoors, 12). L & D Tue-Sun. Closed Mon, also other days off season (call ahead to check). CC. **Directions:** 6km west of Tralee on the Fenit road, opposite the Oyster Tavern.*

The Oyster Tavern

Tralee area The Spa Tralee Co Kerry ☎*066 713 6102*

James McGrath's well-maintained bar and restaurant halfway between Tralee and the village of Fenit (a busy fishing port and excellent base for sailing), is easily spotted by its large roof sign. A convivial atmosphere in the bar and large selection of skilfully prepared seafood in the restaurant ensure a strong local following. *Seats 140*. *D daily, L Sun only. Closed 25 Dec, Good Fri. CC.* **Directions:** *6km outside Tralee, on the Fenit road.*

 **The Phoenix**

Tralee Area Shanahill East Castlemaine Co Kerry ☎*066 976 6284 www.thephoenixorganic.com*

Lorna Tyther's unusual restaurant exudes charm with its rambling gardens - you can choose whether to eat beneath trailing honeysuckle and fairy lights, or inside in the relaxed and cheerful dining area. The imaginative vegetarian menu, which includes local fish from Dingle harbour, offers organic wines and the best of local and organic produce. *Seats 45; Open 11am-11pm in high season; low season Wed-Sun 11am-6pm and also D Sat. Closed Feb (except 14th). No CC.* **Directions:** *7km west of Castlemaine on the R561 coastal road to Dingle. (N70 from Killarney or Tralee).*

VALENTIA ISLAND

Situated off the coast of the Ring of Kerry, Valentia Island is the most westerly point of Western Europe and is accessible by road via the Portmagee Bridge or by frequent car ferry leaving from Cahirciveen daily between April and October. Valentia combines natural beauty with a rich history that includes many Celtic church remains, standing stones, tombs and forts. The Valentia Heritage Centre (066 947 6411) near the main village of Kingstown tells the story of how the first ever transatlantic link was laid in Valentia in 1857, putting Cahirciveen in direct contact with New York. Local attractions include the Skellig Experience (066 947 6306, open April to November), an exhibition about the monks who used to live on the island. The island is a popular spot for scuba diving, with three diving centres, and other activities available include hill walking, cycling, canoeing, deep sea angling and shore fishing.

 Knightstown Coffee

Knightstown Valentia Island Co Kerry ☎*066 947 6373*

This bright and funky coffee shop in Knightstown village is a great place to break a journey when touring the area. Aside from terrific coffees, good home cooking is the great strength, especially baking - and a great little 'gently used' bookshop also stocks unusual and inexpensive toys, books and games for children. *Open Easter - October. No CC.*

  Valentia Island Farmhouse Ice Cream

Kilbeg Valentia Island Co Kerry ☎*066 947 6864 www.valentiadairy.com*

Made with pasteurised (but not homogenised) full fat milk and cream from their Friesian herd, the Dalys' ice cream conrains no artificial flavourings, colours or preservatives. The wide variety of flavours can be bought or sampled along with soft drinks, teas and coffees in their rustic little half-doored Ice Cream Parlour. Also look out for it on on menus locally. *Open in summer only.*

WATERVILLE

This traditional seaside village lies at the very south west of Kerry between Lough Currane and Ballinskelligs Bay. Although it is world famous for reasons as diverse as communications (Waterville is the site of one of the Kerry cable stations recognised as World Heritage Communications Sites); famous visitors (notably Charlie Chaplin); sporting heroes (home of Gaelic footballer Mick O'Dwyer) and of course golf (Waterville golf links is recognised as one of the top courses in Britain and Ireland), Waterville remains largely untouched from development with breathtaking scenery. It also offers a rich list of historical sites such as Staigue Fort (066 947 5127), Cill Rialaig and nearby Derrynane House (066 947 5113). With such close proximity to the sea, water sports such as canoeing, sailing and diving are easily accessible, while other activities on offer include horse riding and golf. Walkers will enjoy the scenic walk up to Coomakista Pass, or a quiet meander along the sandy beach of Skelligs Bay.

 Brookhaven House

New Line Road Waterville Co Kerry ✆066 947 4431 www.brookhavenhouse.com

Overlooking the Atlantic Ocean and Waterville Championship Golf Course and peacefully set in its own attractive garden, Mary Clifford's family-run custom-built guesthouse lays the emphasis on comfort and personal service. The spacious en-suite bedrooms are very comfortable and most have lovely views over the bay. **Rooms 6** *(1 shower only). Closed 15 Nov - 1 Mar. CC.* **Directions:** *Less than 1km from Waterville on the north side.*

 **Butler Arms Hotel**

Waterville Co Kerry ✆066 947 4144 www.butlerarms.com

Peter and Mary Huggard's fine hotel dominates the seafront at Waterville; it is one of several to have strong links with Charlie Chaplin and like many hotels that have been owner-run for several generations, it has established a special reputation for its homely atmosphere and good service - and good food too, in both bar and restaurant. **Rooms 40**. *Restaurant* **Seats 70**; *D daily. Bar food daily, 12-3 & 6-9pm. Hotel closed late Oct-end Mar, except for special bookings. CC.* **Directions:** *on Ring of Kerry road.*

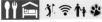 **The Old Cable House**

Milestone Heritage Site Old Cable Station Waterville Co Kerry
✆066 947 4233 www.oldcablehouse.com

Alan and Margaret Brown's Old Cable House has Victorian character and the added interest of its transatlantic cable history. Set high above the town to give clear Atlantic views, some of the simply furnished rooms are small by modern standards with an emphasis on authenticity. Alan cooks 'unpretentious good food with character'. **Rooms 13**. *Restaurant* **seats 32**. *D daily in summer. Closed 24-25 Dec. CC.* **Directions:** *In Waterville town.*

 **The Smugglers Inn**

Cliff Road Waterville Co Kerry ✆066 947 4330 www.thesmugglersinn.ie

Lucille and Henry Hunt's famous clifftop inn enjoys a remarkable location right beside the world famous championship Waterville Golf Links and the homely rooms are comfortable, some with spectacular views. Local ingredients, especially seafood, star in Henry's cooking for both bar and restaurant. *Restaurant/Bar* **Seats 90**. *Restaurant L&D daily. Bar food 12-8.30, (snack menu only 3-6 pm).* **Rooms 13** *(9 shower only); Closed 7 Jan-2 Apr & 22-28 Dec. CC.* **Directions:** *Before village of Waterville, on coast road next to Waterville Golf Links.*

KILDARE

As would be expected of an area which includes the famed racecourses of The Curragh, Punchestown and Naas among its many amenities, Kildare is the horse county par excellence. The horse is so central and natural a part of Irish life that you'll find significant stud farms in a surprisingly large number of counties. But it is in Kildare that they reach their greatest concentration in the ultimate equine county. Thus it's ironic that, a mere 400 million years ago, Kildare was just a salty ocean where the only creatures remotely equine were the extremely primitive ancestors of sea horses.

But things have been looking up for the horse in County Kildare ever since, and today the lush pastures of the gently sloping Liffey and Barrow valleys provide ideal country for nurturing and training champions. Apart from many famous private farms, the Irish National Stud in Kildare town just beyond the splendid gallops of The Curragh is open for visitors, and it also includes a remarkable Japanese garden, reckoned the best Japanese rock garden in Europe, as well as the Museum of the Horse.

The development of Ireland's motorway network has been particularly beneficial to Kildare, as it has lightened the traffic load through the county's towns. In fact, with its proximity to Dublin, getting off the main roads is what enjoyment of life in Kildare is all about. It's surprisingly easy to get away from the traffic, and you'll quickly find areas of rural enchantment and unexpected swathes of relatively untamed nature.

LOCAL ATTRACTIONS & INFORMATION

▸ **Quaker Museum & Library**
Ballitore
059 8623344
▸ **Castletown House**
Celbridge *01 6288252*

▸ **Larchill Arcadian Gardens**
(follies) Kilcock
01 6287354
▸ **Irish National Stud**
Kildare (Tully) *045 521617*

▸ **Japanese Gardens** Kildare
(Tully) *045 521251*
▸ **Steam Museum** Straffan
01 6273155
▸ **Irish Pewtermill** Timolin-
Moone *059 8624164*

Trouble Brewing

Allenwood Co Kildare ✆*087 908 6658 www.troublebrewing.ie*

Trouble Brewing was founded in 2009 by three enthusiasts, Paul O'Connor, Stephen Clinch and Thomas Prior (Head Brewer), who wanted to create the kind of quality beers they'd like to see in their local pubs: ones packed with flavour and presented in a spirit of fun and good humour. There are three beers in the core range. Check their website for a list of where to find their beer, both on draught in pubs and in bottles.

ATHY

Athy is pleasantly situated alongside the River Barrow and the Grand Canal, which has three locks in the town, descending to the river. Athy Farmers Market and Craft Fair is held on Emily Square on Sunday (10am - 3pm).

 Castlefarm

Narraghmore Athy Co Kildare ✆*059 863 6948 www.castlefarmshop.ie*

A vibrant farm shop, an open farm policy (tours arranged) and the energetic communication skills of Peter and Jenny Young make this a perfect stop for those wanting to know about and buy freshly farmed and produced food with a real "taste sensation". Farm tours offered. *Farm Shop usually last weekend of month in summer; occasional off season - phone to check.* **Directions:** *Half way between Athy and Kilcullen, just off the L8016.*

 **Coursetown Country House**

Stradbally Road Athy Co Kildare ✆*059 863 1101 www.coursetown.com*

This welcoming 200-year-old house attached to a large farm is immaculately maintained inside and out, with a beautiful garden and an extensive natural history library special features. Jim and Iris Fox's dedication to the comfort of their guests is exemplary. Delicious healthy eating and local produce for breakfast stand out. **Rooms 4**. *Closed 14 Nov - 14 Mar. CC.* **Directions:** *Just outside Athy, on R428. Turn off N78 at Athy, or N80 at Stradbally; well signposted.*

 The Ballymore Inn

Ballymore Eustace Co Kildare ✆*045 864 585 www.ballymoreinn.com*

It's the fantastic food that keeps people coming to the O'Sullivan family's stylish pub-restaurant. Nobody understands the importance of careful sourcing better than Georgina O'Sullivan, and their policy of using only the very best ingredients, careful cooking and providing a relaxed ambience has proved a winning formula. Well-balanced choices include smashing speciality pizzas and fresh fish, but this is beef country and they're renowned for their steaks - chargrilled aged sirloin or fillet at night, a juicy steak sandwich at lunchtime, perhaps. Also small artisan foods shop. **Seats 100** *(+16 outside); Food served daily, L 12.30-3, D 6-9. Closed 25 Dec & Good Fri. CC.* **Directions:** *Centre of Ballymore Eustace.*

Nurney House

Nurney House Carbury Co Kildare ☎*046 955 3337*

Deirdre O'Sullivan & Norman Kenny's long-established and unusually self-sufficient mixed organic farm supplies a wide range of products including fruit, vegetables and cereals, honey and eggs. Sold at markets (Dublin Food Co-Op and Trim) and the farm shop; also stocks other artisan products, eg Mossfield cheeses. Open Friday afternoons.

CELBRIDGE

Celbridge is attractively situated on the River Liffey, 22 kilometres (13 miles) from Dublin, and is the third largest town in Kildare. The town is of historical interest for many reasons, ranging from Celbridge Abbey (and its association with Jonathan Swift) to Castletown House.

The Village at Lyons

The Village at Lyons Celbridge Co Kildare ☎*01 630 3500 www.villageatlyons.com*

Beautifully situated and landscaped alongside the Grand Canal, this complex features a welcoming conservatory restaurant for fine dining, luxurious accommodation, facilities for corporate events and exclusive weddings (including a small chapel that has to be seen to be believed), a retail area with a café and a cookery school where guest chefs offer courses. Restaurant **Seats 73** *(outdoors, 20); open Wed-Sat for L&D, Sun L only 12-7pm. Closed Mon & Tue, 25-26 Dec, Good Fri. CC.* **Directions:** *Left turn for Ardclough just before bridge in Celbridge village. Follow road about 2 miles, to section with warning signs for tight bends; left turn shortly after (look for a small pale green sign opposite turn); over hump back bridge - on the right with 2 big lions on pillars flanking gate.*

CLANE

Clane is a fast-growing small town halfway between Maynooth and Naas; via the motorway it is about an hour from Dublin city centre at off-peak times. The River Liffey, the Grand Canal and Mondello Racing Circuit (045 860 200), home to Irish Motor Racing, are all close by. Abbeyfield Equestrian Centre (045 868 188) in Clane caters for people of all ages and for all levels; the nearby Donadea Forest Park, on the road to Kilcock, offers a variety of forest walks and facilities.

 Westgrove Hotel & Conference Centre

Clane Co Kildare ☎*045 989 900 www.westgrovehotel.com*

This friendly and well-run 4* hotel contributes welcomes facilities to the town and makes a good base for business or sporting activities in the area. It includes a leisure club with an Elemis spa. Notable for helpful staff who make guests feel at home. **Rooms 99**. *Closed 24-26 Dec. CC.*

 **Zest Café & Restaurant**

Unit 6/7 Clane Shopping Centre Clane Co Kildare
☎*045 893 222 www.zestcafeandrestaurant.ie*

Owner Mark Condron, head chef Alan O'Regan and a talented young team have built up a loyal local following for Zest. A hidden gem, it's well worth seeking out by the visitor. The secret of its success is great cooking, consistent quality and good value over a wide range of options.

That quality is maintained over its long opening hours, starting with interesting breakfasts. **Seats 54**; café Mon-Sat, 8.30am-4pm; restaurant D 5.45-10pm & L Sun, 1-9pm. CC. **Directions:** Off Main Street - turn at AIB, left hand side.

 ## Ballysax Organic Chicken

Ballysax Farm Martinstown Road Curragh Co Kildare ✆087 210 8895

Margaret McDonnell's birds are reared on The Curragh and renowned for quality and flavour. They are the chicken of choice for many discerning chefs, including Georgina O'Sullivan of the Ballymore Inn and Coolanowle Country House (see also also online shop www.organicmeat.ie). Ballysax chickens are available from Kilternan Country Market, and selected Dublin, Wicklow and Galway butcher shops. Farmgate sales are available, and private orders can be supplied.

 ## Martinstown House

Curragh Co Kildare ✆045 441 269 www.martinstownhouse.com

Edward Booth and his wife Roisin's delightful 200-year-old 'Strawberry Hill' gothic house is set in 170 acres of beautifully wooded land. The lovely walled kitchen garden provides seasonal ingredients for the table: fine food, comfort and the warmth of welcome will ensure an enjoyable stay. **Rooms 4** (1 with private bathroom). Closed Christmas. CC. **Directions:** Kilcullen exit off M9 then N78 towards Athy. Sign at 1st crossroads.

 ## Rathsallagh House

Dunlavin Co Kildare ✆045 403 112 www.rathsallagh.com

The O'Flynn family's large, rambling country house is just an hour from Dublin, but it could be in a different world. While modern amenities have been added, including the 18-hole golf course, and it is very professionally run, it retains a classic country house atmosphere. Twice the national winner of our Irish Breakfast Awards, good food is central to Rathsallagh, starting with seasonal produce from the farm and walled garden. **Rooms 29. Seats 120**. D daily. L Sun only 1-3pm. Food served at Rathsallagh Golf Club, 9-9 daily (to 7pm in winter). CC. **Directions:** 24km south of Naas off Carlow Road, take Kilcullen Bypass (M9), turn left 3km south of Priory Inn, follow signposts.

 ## O'Keeffe's Bar & Restaurant

13 The Harbour Kilcock Co Kildare ✆01 628 7225 www.okeeffesbar.com

Visitors are sure to be cheered by the open fires and friendly staff in Thomas & Bernie O'Keeffe's harbourside pub, featuring a handsome traditional bar and a larger comfortable lounge. Unlike many establishments offering meals under the carvery banner, the food not only offers good value but is fresh, well-cooked and appealingly displayed. The good food, service and value all ensure that customers will return. **Seats 145**. L (carvery) & D (à la carte) served daily. **Directions:** Centre of Kilcock, by the canal harbour.

 **Fallons of Kilcullen**

Main Street Kilcullen Co Kildare 📞*045 481 063 www.fallonb.ie*

A smartly understated exterior leads into the beguiling interior of this atmospheric restaurant and buzzy bar which offers food with a sense of place and personality. Owned by Brian Fallon (of Fallon & Byrne, Dublin), Fallons have set a benchmark when crediting their suppliers, presenting information in a very engaging way. The quality of the produce is matched by commitment and talent in the kitchen, and friendly service. **Seats 65**; *food served daily 12.30-10pm (to 9pm Sun). Closed 25 & 26 Dec, Good Fri. CC.* **Directions:** *Centre of village.*

  Jane Russell's Original Irish Handmade Sausages

Link Business Park Kilcullen Co Kildare 📞*045 480 100 www.straightsausages.com*

"No off cuts. No short cuts. Just prime cuts." is her motto and this philosophy is the simple reason for the success of Jane Russell's Original Irish Handmade Sausages. The fifth generation of a prize-winning pork and bacon curing family, she credits her grandfather with the recipe. Others have followed, always consistent with her philosophy for quality and flavour. Sold at: Farmers' Markets (Naas, Dun Laoghaire, Red Stables, Marlay Park, Farmleigh & BrookLodge) and at selected speciality stores.

  Nolans Butchers

Main Street Kilcullen Co Kildare 📞*045 481 229 www.nolansofkilcullen.tripod.com/main.html*

Renowned for their meats, their friendly knowledgeable staff, and simply for being the social hub of the village, Nolan's has been getting it right since 1886. With fourth generation butcher James Nolan you get total traceability and trust. Also well-stocked with other topnotch foods – fish, vegetables, breads, artisan cheeses and wine. *Open Mon-Sat, 8am-6pm.*

 Hartes Bar & Grill

Market Square Kildare Co Kildare 📞*045 533 557 www.hartesbar.ie*

Behind Paul Lenehan and Ronan Kinsella's traditional flower-decked pub frontage lies a very modern hybrid, combining the qualities of the classic Irish bar with something altogether different - and it's all to do with good food. The main event is cooking your own 'steak on a stone' but, while this may be fun, it would be a pity to miss Barry Liscombe's excellent cooking. This is a great dining destination - and the commitment to support Irish producers is commendable... *Mon-Thu 12-9.30, Fri & Sat 12-10, Sun 12-9. CC.* **Directions:** *Town centre.*

 **L'Officina by Dunne & Crescenzi**

Kildare Retail Village Kildare Co Kildare 📞*045 535 850 www.dunneandcrescenzi.com*

Located in Kildare Village designer shopping centre, this outpost of the Dunne and Crescenzi restaurants bears the hallmark of the group – simple, authentic Italian cooking based on the best ingredients (many of them proudly local and seasonal) allied to consistently high quality. Whether it's a wholesome snack (try their famous antipasti) or a relaxed dinner, it's done with style. **Seats 150** (*also outdoor seating); food daily from 9.30am-5.30/6pm (Fri-Sat to 7.30). CC.* **Directions:** *Within walking distance of Kildare town, exit 13 M7.*

Mary Kathryns Deli

6 Academy Street Kildare Co Kildare ☎045 530 588 www.marykathryns.com

High-quality ingredients and good cooking make for tasty eating at Mary Kathryn Murphy's pristine deli and food shop. Notable for wholesome salads and tempting home baking, Mary-Kathryn's offers a range of freshly-prepared ready meals - and she stocks some local artisan products. Closed Sun.

 Becketts Hotel

Cooldrinagh House Leixlip Co Kildare ☎01 624 7040 www.beckettshotel.ie

This handsome property, once the home of Samuel Beckett's mother, is now an unusual hotel offering contemporary style and a high level of service for business guests. Away from the business suites, the restaurant and bar area score strongly for atmosphere and style. The early evening menu offers particular value for the quality. **Rooms 10**. **Seats 130**. L Mon-Fri & Sun; D daily. Closed Christmas; restaurant closed bank hol Mondays. CC. **Directions:** Take N4, turn off at Spa Hotel, next left after Springfield Hotel.

 The Courtyard Hotel

Main Street Leixlip Co Kildare ☎01 629 5100 www.courtyard.ie

Excellent views of the River Liffey from the restaurant, bar and many of the suites are an attractive feature of this privately owned 4* hotel. Dating from the 18th century, it now offers contemporary comfort. The black stuff was originally brewed here before Arthur Guinness moved the business to Dublin – you can savour it in Arthur's Bar. **Rooms 40**. Open all year. CC. **Directions:** Centre of Leixlip.

   **Leixlip House Hotel**

Captains Hill Leixlip Co Kildare ☎01 624 2268 www.leixliphouse.com

 This fine Georgian house overlooking Leixlip village is furnished and decorated to a high standard in period style. The strong, simple decor particularly pleases business guests and, with a welcome emphasis on service, the atmosphere at this well managed hotel is one of discreet opulence. In the Bradaun Restaurant, carefully sourced ingredients are cooked with imagination, creativity and flair. **Rooms 19** (14 shower only). **Seats 50**. Food served daily 12-10. Restaurant closed Mon-Wed (except for group bookings). Hotel closed 25-26 Dec. CC. **Directions:** Leixlip exit off M4 motorway. Take right in Leixlip village at traffic lights.

MAYNOOTH

Attractively situated beside the Royal Canal, Maynooth is a busy university town and the centre for the training of Catholic diocesan clergy in Ireland. The grounds of St. Patricks College run parallel to the canal and there are pleasant waterside walks.

Avenue Café

Main Street Maynooth Co Kildare ☎*01 628 5003 www.avenuecafe.ie*

Just across from the gates into Carton House and its beautiful tree-lined avenue, Robert and Bronagh Kennedy, along with head chef John Cole, have earned a loyal following at this appealing family-friendly restaurant. Although stylishly updated, the old building has retained its character, and the cooking style is modern smart-casual, with a healthy respect for Irish producers. *Open Mon-Sat from 12 (last orders 9.45pm); Sun 1-8pm.* **Directions:** *Dublin end of Main Street.*

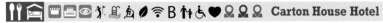 **Carton House Hotel**

Maynooth Co Kildare ☎*01 505 2000 www.cartonhouse.com*

Once the residence of the Dukes of Leinster, Carton House is an imposing mansion set in one of Ireland's finest country estates – and home to two championship golf courses. The public areas lend themselves to entertainment on a grand scale while the accommodation is luxurious and contemporary. Prices are not unreasonable for a hotel of this calibre. The Linden Tree restaurant offers fine dining presented in a classical style. **Rooms 165**. *Restaurant seats 160. D daily. CC.* **Directions:** *Close to Maynooth and signed from the town.*

                                                    Greenes Restaurant

Main Street Maynooth Co Kildare ☎*01 654 8000 www.greenes.ie*

This appealing restaurant beside Maynooth Castle has a cosy atmosphere, with a French ambience - and friendly staff. Evening menus lean towards fish but, as befits a restaurant in a university town, all tastes and budgets are well catered for. Overall, good food at fair prices. *Open daily; Mon-Fri 12-10, Sat & Sun 11am-10pm. CC.*

                                                    Fureys Bar

Moyvalley Co Kildare ☎*046 955 1185*

Just off the M4 but insulated from traffic noise by hedges, this charming and immaculately maintained bar has something of the Victorian country railway station about it. The welcoming bar has cosy sections, one with a stove and canal views. Good home cooking is the basis of its reputation - try one of their famous steaks, with 'all the trimmings'. NB: groups must book ahead. *Meals Mon-Sat, 12-7.50pm; no food Sun. CC.* **Directions:** *Leave M4 just west of toll booths, junction 8 (signed Kilcock). Travel through Enfield, on old Dubiln-Galway road, look out for sign. Located where the road, railway & canal meet between Enfield & Moyvalley.*

  Moyvalley Estate

Balyna Estate Moyvalley Co Kildare ☎*046 954 8000 www.moyvalley.com*

A modern hotel on the 530-acre Balyna Estate (includes luxurious Balyna House - exclusive use). A spacious reception area and friendly staff set a welcoming tone and dining choices include the first floor Sundial Bar (golf course views), which is pleasant for casual food. Accommodation offers well-appointed modern rooms and appealing courtyard 'townhouses'. **Rooms 64**. *Restaurant* **seats 100** *(outdoors, 50); Food served daily 12-10pm. CC.* **Directions:** *Just off the M4 (exit 8, signed Enfield).*

NAAS

Although the casual visitor may not be especially aware of it, as this bustling town turns its back on its most attractive amenity - Naas is pleasingly situated on a branch of the Grand Canal and has a proper little harbour. It's a fast-growing place and Naas is well located for many of the county's sporting activities including horse racing (three courses nearby - Punchestown 045 897704, The Curragh 045 441 205 and Naas 045 897 391). There's also golf a-plenty, car racing (Mondello Park, 045 860 200) and attractions such as the Wicklow Mountains are not far away. The Japanese Gardens (045 521 617) and The National Irish Stud (045 521 251) are at nearby Kildare Town.

 Brady Family Ham

Timahoe Donadea Naas Co Kildare 📞*045 863 650 www.traditionalham.com*

Specialists in the production of premium quality, hand-crafted traditional, Irish hams and breakfast meat products. Some products are available from their online shop.

 The Brown Bear Restaurant

Two Mile House Naas Co Kildare 📞*045 883 561 www.thebrownbear.ie*

Owner Eugene Brennan welcomes guests personally to this pleasing bar and restaurant, where the personal touch extends to all of the friendly and knowledgeable staff. Head chef Josef Zammit has cooked with acclaimed Masterchef judge and restaurateur, Dylan McGrath, and the cooking is of a very high standard. *Seats 72 (outdoors, 15). D Wed-Sat, L Sat & Sun. Bar open from 12.30 daily. Restaurant closed last 2 weeks Feb. CC.* **Directions:** *From Naas - Kilcullen road, turn right for Two Mile House, through the Village, past the church and on the right hand side.*

 East Coast Seafood

Unit 8 Friary Business Park Naas Co Kildare 📞*087 125 5833*

Specialising in fresh Dublin Bay Prawns and Irish smoked salmon, this quality-conscious fishmongers sells wide variety of fish and shellfish (plaice, cod, haddock, whiting, mackerel, mussels & clams) sourced mainly from the boats in Clogherhead. You may also find sea vegetables (edible seaweeds) on offer in season. *Open: Tue-Fri 9-6, Sat 9-4.*

Harvest Kitchen

1 Sallins Road Naas Co Kildare 📞*045 881 793 www.harvestkitchen.ie*

Food and wine shop with a difference offers a catering service and food gifts, including hampers for all occasions. The colourful canopies and pavement tables will draw you in to explore the wide selection of artisan products offered from Ireland and further afield - also soups, coffees, freshly prepared snacks and home baking to eat on site or take away. *Open: Mon-Fri 8-5, Sat 8-6, Sun 9-5.*

 Indie Spice Naas

3 New Row Naas Co Kildare 📞*045 883 660 www.indiespice.ie*

The original home of a chain of highly-regarded Indian restaurants, the stylish interior in Naas promises something special. Service is prompt and courteous, with poppadoms and dips brought right away. The main menu offers a wide variety of dishes in familiar styles (Tandoor, Biriyani etc) while the lunch specials are very good value. *Seats 85; Open all day 12-11.15pm (Sun 1-11pm). Closed 25 Dec. CC.* **Directions:** *New Row is just off the bottom of Main Street.*

 ### Killashee House Hotel & Spa

Old Killcullen Road Naas Co Kildare ✆*045 879 277 www.killasheehouse.com*

Set in impressive gardens and woodland just outside Naas, highlights of this attractive hotel include the spa; lovely traditional rooms (four-posters in some); and a large first floor lounge overlooking the grounds, which is pleasant for afternoon tea and informal socialising. Popular for business events and weddings. *Rooms 141. Closed 24-25 Dec. CC.* **Directions:** *N7 Dublin - Naas, then 2km on R448, Kilcullen road.*

Maudlins House Hotel

Dublin Road Naas Co Kildare ✆*045 896 999 www.maudlinshousehotel.ie*

Situated on the outskirts of Naas, this mainly modern hotel has a restored country house at its heart and retains some of the charm and atmosphere of the large family home it once was. It offers good food, including fine dining in The Virginia Restaurant, and conference/banqueting facilities. *Rooms 25. Restaurant seats 85. D daily, L Sun only. Bar menus daily. Closed 24-26 Dec. CC.* **Directions:** *M7 South to Naas, left at second roundabout for Naas, on right hand side.*

Tenors Grill Room

Fairgreen Street Naas Co Kildare ✆*045 881 595 www.tenorsgrillroom.ie*

Although it is best known for giving great value, your budget shouldn't be the only motive for coming to this pleasant smart-casual restaurant (the name has more to do with the price of all main courses, viz, a tenner, than with famous singers). The happy and well-trained waiting staff and tasty, unpretentious cooking make it a solid choice for any occasion. *Open for L&D daily.*

Thomas Fletcher

Commercial House Main Street Naas Co Kildare ✆*045 897 328*

This great old pub has been in the Fletcher family since Tom Fletcher's father ran it in the 1930s. It puts Irish theme pubs to shame, with its simple wooden floor and long, plain mahogany bar broken up with mahogany dividers and stained glass panels. *Open daily 4pm-closing; from 12 Sat. Closed 25 Dec, Good Fri & Bank Hols.* **Directions:** *At the Dublin end of town, beside Penneys.*

 ### Trax Brasserie

Friary Lane Naas Co Kildare ✆*045 889 333 www.traxbrasserie.ie*

Set atmospherically in a 130-year-old cut stone railway building, this welcoming venue has oodles of charm. Menus suggest a good range of modern classics including, of course, the great steaks that are de rigeur in these parts; also appealing vegetarian and seafood choices. Good food cooked simply with flair, smart service and good value. *D Mon-Sun, L Sun only; early D 5-6.45 daily. CC.* **Directions:** *Off the main street - behind Lawlors Hotel.*

Vie de Chateaux

The Harbour Naas Co Kildare ☎045 888 478 www.viedechateaux.ie

This sociable harbourside French restaurant has struck a chord with local diners. Platters of charcuterie, soups and tartines, terrific lunchtime 'big plates' (starter & main course on one plate), cheerful bistro classics like moules frites and an à la carte menu make for a lively range of choices. Good choice of mainly French wines by the glass. *Seats 50; L Mon-Fri; D Mon-Sun. CC. **Directions:** Beside the canal harbour. Also at: VDC@Home 2 Castle Building, Friary Road, Naas [(045) 889200; vdchome.ie; Food to go, outside catering and an office delivery menu.*

  Hadji Bey

L.C. Confectionery Cutlery Road Newbridge Co Kildare ☎045 431 318 www.hadjibey.ie

The iconic Hadji Bey's Turkish Delight was a Cork speciality for many years until production ceased in the 1970s, and was recently revived by L.C. Confectionery. Available in Original Rose and Rahat Lokoum (rose, orange and lemon flavours) the nostalgically designed re-usable gift packs include an article on Hadji Bey's Turkish Delight first published in The Guardian in 1964. A great product and a perfect gift. Buy at English Market, Cork, and speciality stores.

 Hanged Mans

Milltown Newbridge Co Kildare ☎045 431 515 www.hangedmans.ie

Right beside a lovely old stone canal bridge, Pat Keane's cosy bar and restaurant is full of charm and draws regular customers from a wide area. Fairly traditional food with an emphasis on good meat dishes is served in attractively rustic rooms at the back. Service and presentation are first class, with imaginative side dishes noteworthy. Charm and wholesome food make a winning combination. *D daily, L Sun only. Closed 24-30 Dec. CC. **Directions:** Beside the stone hump-backed canal bridge in Milltown.*

Keadeen Hotel

Newbridge Co Kildare ☎045 431 666 www.keadeenhotel.ie

The O'Loughlin family's long-established hotel is set in landscaped gardens on the edge of Newbridge town. The centre of local activities, it is a favoured venue for both business and leisure, offering quality accommodation and extensive conference and event facilities, along with a comfortably furnished lounge bar, popular restaurant and a romanesque Fitness Club with 18-metre swimming pool. *Rooms 75. Closed 23 Dec - 4 Jan. CC. **Directions:** From Dublin take N7 off M50, take sliproad sign posted Curragh race course & follow signs for Newbridge.*

  Nick's Fish Newbridge

Moorefield Road Newbridge Co Kildare ☎045 440 055 www.nicksfish.ie

Younger sister to Nicholas Lynch's well known fish shop in Ashbourne Co Meath, Nick's Fish Newbridge offers the same high standards of seafood and service. Nick, a former fisherman himself and an environmentally aware supplier, sources much of the fresh fish directly from fishermen and the range offered is impressive. Also offers ready meals, sauces and seasonings, plus a selection of organic and artisan products from Ireland and abroad. *Open: Tue-Fri 9-6, Sat 10-5. **Directions:** Opposite Credit Union.*

The Silver Restaurant

Athgarvan Road Newbridge Co Kildare ✆*045 488 439*

Ballymaloe-trained Natalie Collins brings excellence to the Silver Restaurant at the must-visit Newbridge Silverware Visitor Centre. Local ingredients are used wherever possible in the lunch menu of homemade staples such as soups, lasagne and quiches. Baking is also a strength. Afternoon tea served on pretty Newbridge bone china is a delight. *Seats 100*. *Open Mon-Sat 9am-4.45pm & Sun 11.30am-5pm. Closed 3 days Christmas, 1 Jan. CC. Directions: Athgarvan Road is South of the town centre and runs parallel to Main Street.*

Barberstown Castle

Straffan Co Kildare ✆*01 628 8157 www.barberstowncastle.ie*

Barberstown Castle has been occupied continuously for over 400 years and current owner Kenneth Healy has added a new wing in keeping with its style. Several suites are in the ancient Castle Keep, but most rooms are modern, some with four-posters. An elegant bar, two drawing rooms and big log fires are among the comforts of this historic venue, which also offers traditional afternoon tea and fine dining of character. *Rooms 57*. *Seats 100; D Fri & Sat only. Tea Rooms, 10am-4pm daily. Closed 24-26 Dec, Jan and Easter week. CC. Directions: West M4 - turn for Straffan exit at Maynooth - follow signs for Naas/Clane.*

K Club

Straffan Co Kildare ✆*01 601 7200 www.kclub.ie*

Its origins date back to the 6th century but it was the Barton wine family who established the tone of the elegant Straffan House in the 19th century. Set in lush countryside, and overlooking formal gardens and two championship golf courses, today's hotel boasts unrivalled opulence; the interior is magnificent, with superb furnishings and a wonderful collection of original paintings by famous artists, including Jack B.Yeats. The hotel and two clubhouses offer a range of dining experiences; The River Room offers a dining experience based on the best of local and estate-grown seasonal produce, and a signature list of 250 wines. *Rooms 92*. *Light bar lunches available daily. CC. Directions: 29km south west of Dublin airport and city (M50 - N4).*

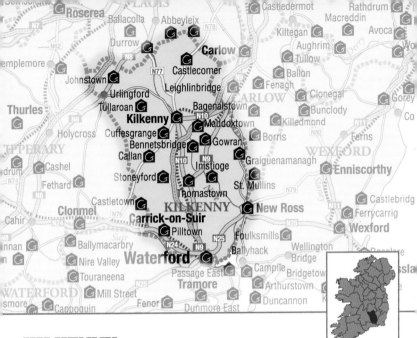

KILKENNY

Kilkenny is a land of achingly beautiful valleys where elegant rivers weave their way through a rich countryside spiced by handsome hills. So naturally it's a place whose people care passionately about their county, and the miniature city at its heart. For Kilkenny - the Marble City - is one of Ireland's oldest cities, and proud of it. Its array of ancient buildings is unrivalled. But, by today's standards of population, this gem of a place is scarcely a city at all. Yet it's a city in every other way, with great and justified pride in its corporate status.

Civic pride is at the heart of it, and the city is benefitting from the refurbishment of its ancient quay walls along the River Nore, and the increase in pedestrian zones. Enjoying its reputation as a major centre for civilisation and culture for well over 1500 years, Kilkenny city thrives on a diverse mixture of public debates about conservation, arts festivals, and a comedy festival of international standing.

Rivers define the county. Almost the entire eastern border is marked by the Barrow, which becomes ever more spectacularly lovely as it rolls gently through the beautiful Graiguenamanagh, then thrusts towards the sea at the tiny river port of St Mullins. The southern border is marked by the broad tidal sweep of the Suir, and this fine county is divided diagonally by the meandering of the most beautiful river of all, the Nore.

LOCAL ATTRACTIONS & INFORMATION

▸ **Gowran Park Racecourse**
Gowran *056 7726225*

▸ **Woodstock Gardens** Inistioge
056 52699

▸ **Cushendale Woollen Mills**
Graiguenamanagh
059 9724118

▸ **Kilkenny Castle** Kilkenny
056 7721450

▸ **Rothe House** (16c house, exhibitions) Kilkenny
056 7722893

▸ **Jerpoint Abbey** Thomastown
056 7724623

▸ **Kilfane Glen & Waterfall**
Thomastown
056 7724558

Kells Wholemeal

Danesfort Road Bennettsbridge Co Kilkenny 📞*056 772 7399? www.kellswholemeal.ie*

Milling is a proud tradition along the great river valleys of this beautiful region, and seven generations of the Mosse family have stoneground local wheat to make the famous Kells Wholemeal Flour. Look out for it on menus, particularly in the South-East - discerning chefs value their unique texture and flavour and credit the supplier - you'll notice the difference.

Nicholas Mosse Irish Country Shop

The Mill Bennettsbridge Co Kilkenny 📞*056 772 7505 www.nicholasmosse.com*

Two floors of pottery, including a large seconds area where good bargains are to be found, constitute one excellent reason to visit this venue in a lovely rural setting on the banks of the River Nore. Another is the food offering in the café, featuring appealing savoury dishes and good home baking. **Seats 35**; Cafe: Mon - Sat 11am - 5pm; Sunday 1.30 - 4pm. Closed 25-27 Dec & 1 Jan. CC. **Directions:** 7km south of Kilkenny, just before bridge turn off.

Ballaghtobin

Ballaghtobin Callan Co Kilkenny 📞*056 772 5227 www.ballaghtobin.com*

Set in parkland on a large working farm, this immaculately maintained house has been in the Gabbett family for 350 years. Catherine Gabbett has maintained it in style, whilst adding every modern comfort in the bedrooms. No dinners, but Catherine will direct you to good restaurants close by. **Rooms 3**. Closed Nov-Feb. CC. **Directions:** Past Callan Golf Club on left, 4km, bear left; bear left at junction, entrance on left opposite Gate Lodge.

Keoghs Model Bakery

Lower Bridge Street Callan Co Kilkenny 📞*056 772 5254 www.keoghsmodelbakery.com*

In the family for over a century, William Keogh, his father and wife, Ann, use the best ingredients in tried and tested recipes to produce everything from sliced pan bread to wedding cakes, novelty cakes, and handmade chocolates. *Open Mon-Sat, 7-5.*

CASTLECOMER

An attractive town with wide tree-lined streets, Castlecomer takes its name from the local castle which was built by the Normans in 1171. Today it is a thriving town with and many fine old buildings including the recently renovated Estate Farmyard at Castlecomer Discovery Park (www.discoverypark.ie). The Park attracts many visitors for a day out and has woodland walks, two fishing lakes (rainbow trout), a collection of wooden sculptures, picnic areas, a children's adventure playground among its attractions. Many people come especially to visit the design craft yard; refreshments are available here at Jarrow Café (see entry).

Jarrow Café

Discovery Park Castlecomer Demesne Castlecomer Co Kilkenny
☎ *056 444 0019 www.discoverypark.ie/visitor-centre*

Castlecomer's fantastic Discovery Park counts exciting tree top walks among its attractions, and also a recently built but sympathetically designed Visitor Centre, where you will find a spacious exhibition area - and Evan and Anna Stewart's excellent café. Renowned for the wholesome meals and great home baking that they provide from breakfast onwards every day, it has become a destination in itself. Well worth a detour. *Open: 10-5 daily (also open for groups in the evening, by arrangement). CC.*

  Wandesforde House

Dublin Road Castlecomer Co Kilkenny ☎ *056 444 2441 www.wandesfordehouse.com*

Anyone looking for somewhere hospitable and relaxing to stay in the South-East should consider Wandesforde House - hosts Michael and Anna McDonald extend a warm welcome to their charming early 18th century home and are always happy to share their local knowledge. The delightful bedrooms are individually furnished with old family furniture and very comfortable beds. **Rooms 5.** *Closed 14 Dec - 14 Jan.* **Directions:** *5km from Castlecomer on the right heading towards Athy.*

  Highbank Organic Orchards

Farmley Cuffesgrange Co Kilkenny ☎ *056 772 9918 www.highbankorchards.com*

The limestone-rich soil of Co Kilkenny, where Rod and Julie Calder-Potts have farmed since 1969 (organically since 1994), is particularly suitable for apple growing. Their shop now offers a staggering range of apple-based Highbank products - including a wonderful syrup, non-alcoholic Drivers' Cider - and Proper Cider. *Organic Farm Shop (Mon-Fri, 8-5, Sat by appointment, closed bank hols). Also sell at selected farmers' markets, and from Iago's at the English Market, Cork.*

 Ryeland House Cookery School

Cuffesgrange Co Kilkenny ☎ *056 772 9073 www.ryelandhousecookery.com*

Anne Neary has offered cookery classes at her lovely 19th century farmhouse near Kilkenny since 1991 and they have never been more popular. Well known from her weekly radio slot (KCLR 96FM), the great ingredients produced on the farm and surrounding area provide a delicious foundation for her demonstrations and practical classes.

  Kilbawn House

Dungarvan Co Kilkenny ☎ *056 779 3883 www.kilbawnhouse.com*

Elizabeth and Jim Byrne's immaculate B&B is surrounded by beautifully maintained grounds on a rise just outside the village of Dungarvan (not to be confused with the Co Waterford town of the same name). A welcoming cuppa, great baking and attractive views of Mount Leinster from all four bedrooms make this a great touring base. **Rooms 4.** *Closed 20 Dec - 10 Jan. CC.* **Directions:** *On the (N9) R448, between Gowran and Thomastown, 1km south of Dungarvan Village.*

Glasrai & Goodies

Main Street Gowran Co Kilkenny ✆*056 773 3799 www.glasraiandgoodies.com*

With its colourful display of fresh local produce around the doorway like gleaming fruits spilling out from a classic cornucopia, Siobhán Lawlor's tiny shop in the pretty village of Gowran is a treasure trove for food lovers. This place brims with the vitality of its passionate owner. *Open Mon-Fri 8.45-6.30, Sat 9.30-6, Closed Sun.*

GRAIGUENAMANAGH

Situated in the Barrow Valley, an area of outstanding natural beauty, Graiguenamanagh offers the visitor beautiful walks along the tow paths, boating too and there's even a swimming place along the quay. In fact the perfect little river port of Graiguenamanagh has everything, notably several hostelries of character. Points of interest include Duiske Abbey (059 972 4238), which dates back to the Cistercian monks who built the town and weirs on the river which were active again in recent years until the current blanket ban on eel fishing came into force. It's not really a shopping place but Cushendale Woollen Mills (059 972 4118; www.cushendale.ie) is of particular interest - one of Ireland's oldest woollen mills, this family-run business goes back to the 17th century; the Mill Shop is open all year.

 **Waterside**

The Quay Graiguenamanagh Co Kilkenny ✆*059 972 4246 www.watersideguesthouse.com*

An attractive old stone warehouse on the quayside of the River Barrow makes a characterful setting for Brian and Brigid Roberts' well-run guesthouse and restaurant. A comfortable reception area leads into the stylish restaurant, where Brigid offers varied menus and good home cooking – in very pleasant waterside surroundings. On fine summer days there are tables outside on the quayside. Bikes for hire (collection/delivery service). **Rooms 10. Seats 45**. *D daily; L Sun only 12.30-3. *In summer there's also a light Daytime Menu available, 11-4. Restaurant open weekends only in winter. Establishment closed Jan, 25 Dec. CC.* **Directions:** *Centre of Graiguenamanagh.*

 The Motte Restaurant

Plas Newydd Lodge Inistioge Co Kilkenny ✆*056 775 8655 www.inistioge.ie*

Rodney and Deirdre's Doyle's restaurant is situated in a classically proportioned lodge. Although small in size, this unique country restaurant has great charm and the slightly retro feel to Rodney's cooking makes a welcome change from the now almost universal multi-national menus. An imaginative vegetarian dish is always included. **Seats 40**. *Open for group bookings only. CC.* **Directions:** *Opposite village "name sign" on Kilkenny side of village.*

 Murphy Fisheries

Ballinabarna Inistioge Co Kilkenny ✆*051 423 917*

If you are ever see Murphy Fisheries salmon listed on a menu, thank your lucky stars and order immediately. When salmon fishing on the River Nore reopened following a conservation closure, fisherman Mick Murphy and his wife Trisha established Murphy Fisheries to market the wonderful wild salmon caught by local snap-net fishermen for just two months each year. A very special seasonal product.

The Inn @ Ballilogue Clochan

Ballilogue The Rower Inistioge Co Kilkenny ✆*051 423 857 www.ballilogueclochan.com*

Pat McCarthy's sensitively converted cluster of traditional buildings in deepest south Kilkenny makes for a boutique B&B that's the height of rural chic – and heaven for design lovers. The large semi-conservatory living area with an open fire that opens onto a sensory garden is just one special feature of this charming location. A unique cottage museum and shop, Mrs M's, is exclusively open for residents. **Rooms 6** *(some shower only); D summer weekends only, by arrangement.* **Directions:** *Located 12km south of Inistioge in New Ross direction (R700).*

Gathabawn Farmhouse Ice Cream

Johnstown Area Brennan's Dairy Products Gathabawn Co Kilkenny ✆*086 351 6880*

The Brennan family's Gathabawn Farmhouse Ice Cream is one of the most outstanding of Ireland's excellent artisan ice creams - and it really is freshly made. Dairy farmers Liam and Anthony Brennan convert their dairy herd morning's milking into luscious dairy ice cream in no time, ready for delivery to some of Ireland's best-known restaurants. If you see any of their wide range of ice creams (and sorbets) on a menu don't miss the chance to try it.

KILKENNY

Kilkenny straddles the River Nore, and is named after the sixth-century church founded by St Canice; it is a city of great historical interest and its narrow winding streets and old buildings add an old-world dimension to the busy life of a modern city. Kilkenny Castle, the magnificent thirteenth century seat of the the Butlers (the Earls and Dukes of Ormonde), is owned by the state and open to the public, and the Kilkenny Design Centre workshops are across the road, in the old castle stables. Kilkenny city and county is renowned for its outstanding craft workers (pottery, woodwork, linens, knitwear, hand-blown glass, jewellery); a shopping trip to nearby Bennettsbridge is also recommended and local tourist offices will have details of the Kilkenny Food and Craft Trails. Dunmore Cave, just a few miles north of the city, is worth an outing.

A Slice of Heaven

62 High Street Kilkenny Co Kilkenny ✆*087 953 3870 www.asliceofheaven.ie*

Renowned baker Mary McEvoy has a national following for her gorgeous creations, which are astonishingly detailed and exquisitely presented in decorative boxes. She pays great attention to the ingredients, which are all natural and local if at all possible and, together with her husband the well known chef Neil McEvoy, she also offers baking and general cookery classes including courses for kids.

Butler House

16 Patrick Street Kilkenny Co Kilkenny ✆*056 776 5707 www.butler.ie*

This elegant Georgian townhouse was restored with interesting results in the 1970s in a style combining contemporary design and period architecture. Unusually spacious bedrooms are a happy outcome of this redesign. Breakfast is served in the Kilkenny Design Centre across the gardens. **Rooms 13** *(1 shower only). Closed 24-29 Dec. CC.*

Café Sol Restaurant

William Street **Kilkenny** *Co Kilkenny* ✆*056 776 4987 www.cafesolkilkenny.com*

The house style of Noel McCarron's popular daytime café and evening restaurant is colourful and punchy, showing international influences but based on the best local produce. Vegetarians always do well here, too – and the lovely homely desserts are delicious. **Seats 50**. *Open Mon-Sat, 12-10, Sun 12-9. Closed 25/26 Dec, 1 Jan. CC.*

 **Campagne**

The Arches 5 Gashouse Lane **Kilkenny** *Co Kilkenny* ✆*056 777 2858 www.campagne.ie*

This well-named French-inspired restaurant, run by chef Garrett Byrne and his wife, restaurant manager Brid Hannon, has chosen a pastoral style in tune with the owners' passionately held food philosophy of involving local food producers in the cooking. This is not show-off food but well-chosen ingredients cooked to perfection and beautifully presented. **Seats 75** *(outdoors, 16). Open L&D Tue-Sat. L only Sun. Closed Sun D, Mon; 2 weeks Jan. MasterCard, Visa, Laser.*

 Chez Pierre

17 Parliament Street **Kilkenny** *Co Kilkenny* ✆*056 776 4655*

Pierre Schneider's cosy little daytime Kilkenny restaurant has long been popular with people for serving honest and appetising bistro fare. But Pierre's kitchen talents really show through in his evening menus with some seriously flavoursome choices. Willing service by staff smartly dressed in black. **Seats 25**; *D Tue-Sat. Closed Sun, Mon; 24 Dec - 2 Jan. CC.*

 Cillín Hill

Kilkenny *Co Kilkenny* ✆*056 772 1407 www.cillinhill.com*

For a very different kind of outing, why not visit Ireland's flagship livestock sales centre, Kilkenny Mart. See cattle and sheep being bought and sold in the fine new sales rings - it's great fun watching the auctioneers at work, and then you can queue up with the farmers for a bite at Langtons @ Cillín Hill. *Café open Mon-Sat 7.30-4, Sun 9.30-4.*

 The Courtyard Bar and Grill

No 3 Workhouse Square MacDonagh Junction SC **Kilkenny** *Co Kilkenny*
✆*056 777 2559 www.thecourtyardbarandgrill.com*

Located within the stylish MacDonagh Junction shopping complex, David Rouse's inviting modern restaurant has introduced a new level of daytime dining to the Kilkenny area. Suppliers are referenced, the cooking from this well known chef is excellent and overall the Courtyard scores highly in quality and value for money, notably the early dinner menu. **Seats 90**. *Mon-Sun 10am-7pm (Sun from 11am), D Thu-Sat 6-9pm.*

 Cramers Grove Ice Cream

Cramers Grove Farm **Kilkenny** *Co Kilkenny* ✆*056 772 2160 www.cramersgrove.com?*

Nigel and Carol Harper produce one of the best of this region's premium handmade ice cream ranges. Made from the milk of their own dairy herd, the secret of this brand's success is that traditional methods and ingredients are used in small batches, and no shortcuts are taken. They're sold at their own Kilkenny café and selected speciality food stores, and also feature on leading restaurant menus; once tasted, you will want to seek them out. Treats by Cramers Grove, McDonagh Junction. *Open: Mon-Wed & Sat 9am-6pm, Thu & Fri 9am-7pm. Sun & Bank Holidays 12-6pm.*

 ## Foodworks Café

7 Parliament Street **Kilkenny** *Co Kilkenny* ✆*056 777 7696 www.foodworks.ie*

The focus at Peter Greany and Maeve Moore's popular café has always been on local ingredients. This really means local, as much of the food served comes from the family farm on the outskirts of Kilkenny City. An attractive venue, in a former bank, Foodworks offers a satisfying eating experience presented in a friendly casual style. **Seats 50**. *Tue-Wed 12-3pm, Thu-Sat 12-10pm. Closed Sun, Mon. CC.*

 ## The Gourmet Store

56 High Street **Kilkenny** *Co Kilkenny* ✆*056 777 1727 www.thegourmetstorekilkenny.com*

One of Kilkenny's most popular casual fresh food destinations, Padraig and Irene Lawlor offer a well-chosen range of Irish and continental deli fare, plus a wide range of freshly prepared food to go and good coffee.

 ## Hotel Kilkenny

College Road **Kilkenny** *Co Kilkenny* ✆*056 776 2000 www.griffingroup.ie*

Dubbed 'the four star with flair', Hotel Kilkenny is set in award-winning gardens and its excellent leisure facilities are a big draw. Comfortable accommodation includes newer deluxe rooms as well as refurbished original rooms, and an exceptional speciality drinks menu is a feature of the attractive bar. **Rooms 138**. *Open all year. CC.*

 ## Kilkenny Design Centre

Castle Yard **Kilkenny** *Co Kilkenny* ✆*056 772 2118 www.kilkennydesign.com*

Situated in what was once the stables and dairy of Kilkenny Castle, this deservedly popular restaurant is situated above temptations of a different sort, on display in the famous craft shop. Wholesome and consistently delicious fare is the hallmark of Kilkenny Design, but at the self-service daytime café and the evening restaurant. Look out for the local Lavistown cheese in salads. Very reasonably priced too. **Seats 70** *(outdoors, 12); Self service meals daily 11-7; restaurant D Thu-Sat. Closed Sun & banks hols off-season (Jan-Mar). CC.*

 ## Kilkenny Hibernian Hotel

1 Ormonde Street **Kilkenny** *Co Kilkenny* ✆*056 777 1888 www.kilkennyhibernianhotel.com*

Formerly the Hibernian Bank, this Georgian building has been restored to its former glory to become the Kilkenny Hibernian Hotel. The nine older rooms are particularly spacious and furnished to a very high standard while the old banking hall makes an impressive traditional bar. With a street entrance, the popular City Bar & Grill is designed to avoid the feel of a hotel dining room. **Rooms 46**. *Closed 24-25 Dec. CC.*

 **Kilkenny Ormonde Hotel**

Ormonde Street Kilkenny Co Kilkenny ✆ *056 772 3900 www.kilkennyormonde.com*

Kilkenny city's leading hotel enjoys an outstandingly convenient central location for both business and leisure guests, beside (but not adjacent to) a multi-storey carpark. A popular city meeting place, it has all the facilities of a good hotel – rooms ranging from standard to a presidential suite – excellent business and conference facilities, a health club and spa and a choice of eating areas. *Rooms 118*. *Restaurant seats 75*. *D daily, L Sun only. CC.*

Kilkenny River Court Hotel

The Bridge John Street Kilkenny Co Kilkenny ✆ *056 772 3388 www.rivercourthotel.com*

Beautifully situated just off the narrow, bustling streets of the city centre, this fine hotel is equally attractive for business or leisure. The Riverside Restaurant has lovely views of Kilkenny Castle and the River Nore. With chef Gerard Dunne in charge, good cooking is guaranteed; the main courses are especially interesting and he also offers seasonal syllabubs for dessert. *Rooms 90*. *Seats 80* (outdoors, 50). *D daily, L Sun only. Food is also served in the Riverview Bar, 12.30-8pm daily. Closed 24-25 Dec. CC.*

 B **Langton House Hotel**

69 John Street Kilkenny Co Kilkenny ✆ *056 776 5133 www.langtons.ie*

Although mainly famous for its maze of bars, with seating areas and restaurants that stretch right through this substantial building to a garden and private car park, Langtons is also an hotel of some character. Good-sized rooms are furnished to a high standard with well-appointed bathrooms, making it a good city centre choice. Also offers a lively middle of the road dining experience. *Rooms 30*. *Closed 25 Dec. CC.*

 Laragh House

Waterford Road Kilkenny Co Kilkenny ✆ *056 776 4674 www.laraghhouse.com*

John and Helen Cooney's guesthouse (only built in 2005) is now well established as it offers a very reasonably priced alternative to an hotel while being within walking distance of the city centre. The eight bedrooms are individually styled with all modern conveniences. *Rooms 8* (5 shower only). *Closed 24-26 Dec. No CC.*

Lautrecs Tapas & Winebar

9 St. Kieran Street Kilkenny Co Kilkenny ✆ *056 776 2720 www.lautrecs.com*

Jim & Anthony Smith's attractive two-storey restaurant and bar has a smart and appealing frontage on this lovely pedestrianised street, with a bright awning over outside tables and a blackboard menu listing some of the treats to be had. Once inside you'll find a warmly informal wine bar with an atmospheric vibe. Everything on the sociable and seasonally changing 'tapas' menus is cooked to order and based on locally produced ingredients. Good value and enjoyable. *Wed-Thu 5-10, Fri 5-12, Sat 2-12, Sun 12-8. CC.*

Lavistown House

Centre for Creative Living Kilkenny Co Kilkenny 📞*056 776 5145 www.lavistownhouse.ie*

The original producers of Lavistown Cheese, Roger and Olivia Goodwillie still make superb food - a true free-from product, Lavistown Gourmet Sausages are made from pure Irish pork, without any preservatives, nitrates or nitrites - and no fillers (rusks, bread) so they are also gluten free and suitable for coeliacs - and they freeze well, so stock up when you find them. And there's freshness and fun about all of their courses, which are unlike anyone else's.

 ### Lyrath Estate Hotel & Convention Centre

Dublin Road Kilkenny Co Kilkenny 📞*056 776 0088 www.lyrath.com*

Set in 170 acres of mature parkland, this modern hotel has a 17th century house at its heart, now extended to become a large hotel with a conference centre and spa. The resulting blend has considerable character and accommodation is spacious and well appointed in a modern classic style. The range of bars and eating areas includes an attractive bar with terrace, and an oriental restaurant. *Rooms 137. Closed 20-26 Dec. CC. Directions: 2km from Kilkenny city on the Dublin/Carlow road.*

 ### Marble City Bar

66 High Street Kilkenny Co Kilkenny 📞*056 776 1143 www.langtons.ie*

The Langton family's historic bar was re-designed a few years ago by the internationally acclaimed designer, David Collins and, although initially controversial (especially the ultra-modern stained glass window which now graces an otherwise traditional frontage), it is a wonderful space to be in and attracts a varied clientèle. Enjoy the vibrant atmosphere and the ingredients-led contemporary European bar food. Downstairs, the Marble City Tea Rooms offers lighter fare. *Food service from 10am; main menus from 12 noon-10 pm. Closed 25 Dec. CC.*

 ### Newpark Hotel

Castlecomer Road Kilkenny Co Kilkenny 📞*056 776 0500 www.newparkhotel.com*

At the heart of local activities, this popular 1960s hotel on the N7 is just a ten-minute walk to the city centre. It enjoyed a major extension and renovation programme in recent years, with an upgrading of all facilities; bedrooms are modern and there's a choice of bars and restaurants. An established business and conference destination, good leisure facilities have appeal for family breaks. *Rooms 111 (16 shower only). Open all year. CC.*

  ### Pembroke Hotel & Stathams Bar & Grill

Patrick Street Kilkenny Co Kilkenny 📞*056 778 3500 www.kilkennypembrokehotel.com*

Sister to the Ormonde Hotel, this 4* boutique hotel just a stone's throw from all the Kilkenny landmarks is a good base for business or pleasure. Contemporary rooms provide ample workspace, withl ittle extras (robes, slippers) in superior rooms. Stathams Bar & Grill offers a notable eating experience, with South-East produce, particularly Kilkenny beef and Kilmore Quay seafood, prominent. *Rooms 74. CC.*

Ristorante Rinuccini

1 The Parade Kilkenny Co Kilkenny ☎ *056 776 1575 www.rinuccini.com*

The closely packed tables at Antonio and Marion Cavaliere's Italian restaurant opposite Kilkenny Castle are an indication of its popularity, with the room quickly filling up. The secret of its success is consistently good classic Italian cooking of fresh mainly local ingredients, together with great service and outstanding value for money. **Seats 100** (outdoors, 10). L & D daily. Closed 25-26 Dec. CC.

Rosquil House

Castlecomer Road Kilkenny Co Kilkenny ☎ *056 772 1419 www.rosquilhouse.com*

Just across the road from the Newpark Hotel, Phil and Rhoda Nolan's handsome guesthouse is easy to find and a short walk from the city centre. Their dream was to combine the best attributes of a small hotel with the personal care and good value associated with Ireland's best guesthouses. The result is an exceptionally comfortable and hospitable place to stay - with superb breakfasts showcasing local artisan foods. **Rooms 7.** CC.

Swans Chinese

101 High Street The Parade Kilkenny Co Kilkenny ☎ *056 772 3088*

A bright room with red alcoves and charming Chinese waitresses contribute to the relaxing ambience at Swans. With an entrance off High Street, it is a very agreeable venue for enjoying well prepared and presented oriental cuisine. **Seats 56**; L & D Mon-Fri; Sat/Sun & Bank Hols all day. Closed 25 Dec, Good Fri. CC.

Zuni Restaurant & Boutique Hotel

26 Patrick Street Kilkenny Co Kilkenny ☎ *056 772 3999 www.zuni.ie*

Although Zuni is an hotel ('boutique', and with a youthful style of accommodation), the atmosphere is more restaurant with rooms: an oasis of contemporary chic in this bustling city, it is favoured by discerning Kilkenny diners. Talented chef Maria Raftery offers international dishes, but her creative use of local ingredients lends a distinctive Irish tone. *Restaurant* **seats 70** (outdoors, 24). L Tue-Sun; D daily. **Rooms 13** (8 shower only). Hotel closed 23-27 Dec. CC.

Blanchville House

Dunbell Maddoxtown Co Kilkenny ☎ *056 772 7197 www.blanchville.ie*

Monica Phelan's elegant Georgian house is easy to spot - there's a folly in its grounds. A friendly, welcoming place, it has classic dining and drawing rooms and the comfortably furnished bedrooms in period style all overlook attractive countryside. An excellent breakfast is served – dinner if pre-arranged. The renovated Coach Yard offers four self-catering coach houses. **Rooms 5** (1 with private bathroom, 2 shower only). Closed 1 Nov-1 Mar. CC.

Directions: From Kilkenny take N10 (Carlow-Dublin road), 1st right 1km after 'The Pike Pub'; 3km to crossroads (Connolly's pub). Take left, large stone entrance 1.5km on left.

 Little Irish Apple Co

Clonmore House Piltown Co Kilkenny 📞*051 567 872*

Although most of their production is sold directly to Bulmers and to packers for sale in supermarkets, the Little family also sell apples and their delicious pasteurised pressed juice at markets. They are members of the Taste of Kilkenny Food Trail and visitors are welcome by appointment.

 **Knockdrinna Farm House Cheese**

Stoneyford Co Kilkenny 📞*056 772 8446 www.knockdrinna.com*

If you want to buy some seriously good artisan produce and to see an outstanding example of rural diversification, a visit to Robert and Helen Finnegan's farm in Stoneyford village is highly recommended. A kitchen experiment has blossomed into a fascinating business with a wide range of cheeses and their own whey fed free range pork on sale, along with other deli and local products. Tours and courses offered. Café. *Open: Tue-Sat 11-6 (also Sun in summer).*

THOMASTOWN

Thomastown is an early medieval town with charming streets and picturesque views of the River Nore, and also happens to be the birthplace of the 18th century philosopher George Berkeley. Local attractions include Jerpoint Abbey (056 772 4623, open March to November), a Cistercian abbey established in the second half of the 12th century. The abbey has Romanesque details; an impressive sculpted cloister arcade features unique carvings. There is also an informative visitor centre and exhibition. Visitors will enjoy a trip to Kilfane Glen and Waterfall (0772 4558; www.kilfane.com), a recently discovered romantic era garden featuring a superb waterfall and a cottage orné. Garden lovers should also make a point of seeing Mount Juliet Gardens (056 777 3000), and the restored Woodstock Gardens (056 779 403) at Inistioge are not far away. Golfers, of course, are well catered for with the championships golf course at Mount Juliet (056 777 300.

 **Ballyduff House**

Thomastown Co Kilkenny 📞*056 775 8488 www.ballyduffhouse.com*

Set in fine rolling countryside, Breda Thomas's 18th century house overlooking the River Nore is blessed with an utterly restful location. Breda is a relaxed host who enjoys sharing her home with guests who have the use of large well-proportioned day rooms as well as spacious bedrooms furnished with antiques. There are beautiful walks on the estate. *Rooms 5.* *Self-catering accommodation adjacent. Open all year. No CC. **Directions:** 5km south of Thomastown.*

 The Blackberry Café

Market Street Thomastown Co Kilkenny 📞*086 775 5303 www.theblackberrycafe.ie*

Formerly a cobbler's workshop, Jackie Hoyne's café with its immaculately maintained paintwork and lovely Georgian windows presents an attractive face to the passer-by. Inside blackboard menus offer familiar café fare but tip-top ingredients, careful preparation (and the welcome aroma of home baking coming from the semi open kitchen) make this café stand out from the crowd. *Mon-Sat 9.30-5.30pm (Sat from 10.30). Closed Sun & Bank Hols. No CC.* **Directions:** *On the corner of Main Street.*

 Goatsbridge Premium Irish Trout

Thomastown Co Kilkenny ✆*086 818 8340 www.goatsbridgetrout.ie*

Previous generations of Margaret and Gerard Kirwan's family business took over where the Cistercian monks left off in this area, ensuring there's trout aplenty in the Arrigle River in the Nore valley. They welcome visitors to see their eco-friendly working environment and to try their Premium Fresh and Smoked Trout - and also their delicious Irish Trout Caviar, which is perhaps a first for Ireland. Open all year; farm tours, direct sales, just call ahead. **Directions:** *Signed at Thomastown.*

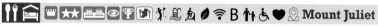 **Mount Juliet**

Thomastown Co Kilkenny ✆*056 777 3000 www.mountjuliet.ie*

Lying amidst 1,500 acres of unspoilt woodland, pasture and formal gardens beside the River Nore, beautiful Mount Juliet House is one of Ireland's finest Georgian properties. Yet it has a uniquely restful atmosphere, and General Manager William Kirby and his enthusiastic staff are keen to make guests feel at home. Outstanding food is sure to be a highlight of a visit; excellent choices are offered and the Lady Helen Dining Room is a serious dining destination. Also exceptional facilities for sporting activities and the Spa & Health Club for pampering. **Rooms 58**. *Lady Helen dining room* **seats 50**. *D Mon & Wed-Sat. Al Fresco Menu and Afternoon Tea (1-6 daily). Kendals, in Hunters Yard, D daily 6-0pm. Informal dining in The Club, Presidents Bar (12 noon-9pm). Hotel open all year. CC.* **Directions:** *Signed from Thomastown.*

 Sol Bistro

Low Street Thomastown Co Kilkenny ✆*056 775 4945 www.restaurantskilkenny.com*

This cheerful daytime café and evening bistro is a younger sister of the well-established Kilkenny city favourite and you will find the same winning format here: attractive, relaxed surroundings and well executed modern cooking based on well-sourced ingredients. Evening reservations are recommended. **Seats 50**. *Open Mon-Tue 11-5, Wed-Thu 11-9, Fri-Sat 11-10, Sun 12-8.* **Directions:** *Centre of Thomastown.*

 The Truffle Fairy

Chapel Lane Thomastown Co Kilkenny ✆*087 286 2634 www.trufflefairy.com*

There is indeed a touch of magic about chef Mary Teehan's chocolate creations, and visitors are welcome to the production kitchen, shop and café (where you may even get a complimentary truffle with your coffee). Whether in luscious truffles and chocolate fudge, or the chocolate bars and barks (with dried fruits and/or nuts), cakes and cookies, the freshness and quality of ethically sourced ingredients stands out.

Oldtown Hill Bakehouse

Oldtown Tullaroan Co Kilkenny ☎ *056 776 9263*

Joy Moore's craft bakery is on the family's dairy farm. Using high quality ingredients they make all the good things that are traditionally baked in farmhouse kitchens, including a famously delicious wholemeal soda bread that is not only made using their own milk but, very unusually, the wheat has been grown locally too - and this bread is sugar free, yeast free and egg free with no artificial additives or preservatives. *Open by appointment, and available in selected outlets in the South-East and East.*

Happy Heart Rapeseed Oil

Drumeen Farm The Islands Urlingford Co Kilkenny ☎ *087 926 5423 www.secondnatureoils.com*

Produced on the longest-established organic farm in Ireland, which was established by her parents Ben and Charlotte in 1976, Kitty Colchester's 'Second Nature' Happy Heart extra virgin rapeseed oil was an early success story in the new wave of Irish-produced oils and is admired as much for its purity as for its fine flavour and culinary versatility.

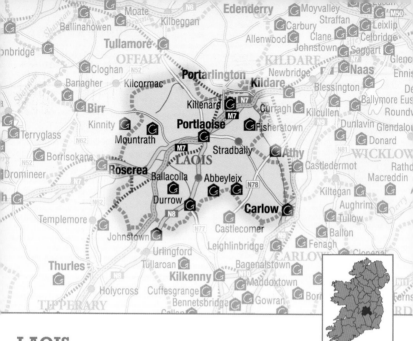

LAOIS

With its territory traversed by the rail and road links from Dublin to Cork and Limerick, Laois is often glimpsed only fleetingly by inter-city travellers. But as with any Irish county, it is a wonderfully rewarding place to visit as soon as you move off the main roads. For Laois is the setting for Emo Court and Heywood, two of the great gardens of Ireland at their most impressive. And it's a salutary place to visit, too. In the eastern part, between Stradbally and Portlaois, there's the Rock of Dunamase, that fabulous natural fortress which many occupiers inevitably assumed to be impregnable. Dunamase's remarkably long history of fortifications and defences and sieges and eventual captures has a relevance and a resonance for all times and all peoples and all places.

But there's much more to Laois than mournful musings on the ultimate vanity of human ambitions. With its border shared with Carlow along the River Barrow, eastern Laois comfortably reflects Carlow's quiet beauty. To the northwest, we find that Offaly bids strongly to have the Slieve Bloom Mountains thought of as an Offaly hill range, but in fact there's more of the Slieve Blooms in Laois than Offaly, and lovely hills they are too. And though the River Nore may be thought of as quintessential Kilkenny, long before it gets anywhere near Kilkenny it is quietly building as it meanders across much of Laois, gathering strength from the weirdly-named Delour, Tonet, Gully, Erskina and Goul rivers on the way.

ABBEYLEIX 📍

Founded in the 18th century by Viscount de Vesci, as an estate town, Abbeyleix takes its name from a 12th century Cistercian abbey and today it is an attractive Heritage Town own with tree-lined streets and plenty to interest the visitor, including Abbeyleix Heritage House (057 873 1653) and the Sensory Gardens (057 873 1325). The town has a golf course (057 873 1450), a tennis club, a Polo Club - that offers great entertainment in the summer - and many delightful walks including one starting from the grounds of St. Michael & All Angels Church of Ireland, known as The Lords Walk. There are also beautiful gardens to visit nearby including Heywood Gardens (Ballinakill, 057 873 3563) and Gash Gardens (Portlaoise, 057 873 2247), and wonderful fishing on the internationally renowned River Nore.

G's Gourmet Jams

Abbeyleix Co Laois ✆*057 873 1058 www.gsgourmetjams.ie*

Making a good old-fashioned product with natural flavour is the main selling point for Helen Gee's traditional handmade jams, chutneys and relishes. Local fruits, including home grown rhubarb and raspberries, are used, with no additives, and all the family are involved with the business, growing it carefully to protect the real homemade flavours that are its USP.

The Gallic Kitchen

Main Street Abbeyleix Co Laois ✆*086 605 8208 www.laois.gallickitchen.com*

Acclaimed baker, food producer and caterer Sarah Webb is the power behind this delightful little shop in Abbeyleix. Alongside her own delicious baked goods and salads, she also offers other premium delicatessen foods. There are a few tables where you can enjoy temptations such as a freshly brewed coffee and meringue roulade, for example. *Seats 10*. *Open Mon-Sat 10-6, Sun 11-6*. **Directions:** *Centre of Abbeyleix.*

McEvoys

Main Street Abbeyleix Co Laois ✆*057 875 7500 www.macsabbeyleix.ie*

Formerly a pub, this smart 'steak & wine bar' lies behind a classic black shopfront. Run by the Stokes family, proprietors of nearby Castle Durrow, it offers a satisfying, fun and affordable dining experience based on locally sourced ingredients. Great steaks are a point of pride and the standard of cooking and presentation is high throughout. *Seats 60*. *Food Wed-Sat 5-10pm, Sun 3-9pm. Closed Mon & Tue, 25 Dec. CC.* **Directions:** *Main street Abbeyleix.*

Morrissey's

Main Street Abbeyleix Co Laois ✆*057 873 1281*

One of Ireland's finest and best-loved pubs, Morrissey's is a handsome building on the wide main street of this attractive little town. It first opened as a grocery in 1775 and, with its high shelf-lined walls and a pot belly stove to gather round on cold days, it's a great place to lift the spirits. True to the old tradition, food is not its strength - and television, cards and singing are not allowed. *Closed 25 Dec & Good Fri.* **Directions:** *In village on right heading south.*

Sandymount House

Oldtown Abbeyleix Co Laois ✆*057 873 1063 www.abbeyleix.info*

A charming mid 19th century house set in mature woodlands, Avril Bibby and Robin Scott's country house B&B has all the advantages of old and new – bedrooms have smart en-suites and broadband as well as television and clothes-pressing facilities. And they'll see you off with a good breakfast... *Rooms 4 (all shower only); Closed 20 Dec-2 Jan. CC.* **Directions:** *2km down Ballacolla/Rathdowney (R433) road from Abbeyleix, on right hand side.*

D.P.Connolly & Sons

Abbeyleix Area Shanahoe House Shanahoe Abbeyleix Co Laois
✆*057 873 9991 www.dpconnollyandsons.ie*

The lovely retro branding on the Connolly family's products will catch your eye in the shops and restaurants where they are on sale - different from anything else on the market, they're well worth a try. Natural juices, pure and blended, are the core products - notably with elderflower - and you'll also find jars of old fashioned sweets, a few preserves and hand cooked crisps in the range. *Widely distributed.*

 ## Abbey Cheese Company

Cuffsborough Ballacolla Portlaoise Co Laois 📞*057 873 8599*

Pat 'Paddy Jack' Hyland makes the Abbey Organic Cheese range on the family farm, using pateurised milk from a single herd. Best known is Abbey Blue, a mild Cambozola style cheese that gains flavour with age; plain and smoked versions are available, also a feta-style cheese, St Canice, and Paddy Jack, a hard gouda style cheese coated in black ash. Sold at farmers' markets, notably the Saturday market at Temple Bar in Dublin, and featured on menus locally. *Cheeses Produced: Abbey Blue Brie, Abbey Smoked Brie, Paddy Jack Cheese.*

 ## The Fishermans Thatched Inn

Fisherstown Ballybrittas Co Laois 📞*057 862 6488* *www.the-fishermans.com*

All are welcome at Sean Ward's picturesque pub. With a welcoming fire in the grate and the front bar packed with bric-a-brac, it's delightful. Not a daytime place, except at weekends and it makes no pretence of being a food destination either: a range of gourmet pies is the only food served – but it is a magic spot. Music sessions on Tuesdays and Sundays in summer. *Usually open from 6pm midweek, Sat from 2pm, Sun 12.30-11.*

  ## Ballyfin House

Ballyfin Co Laois 📞*057 875 5866* *www.ballyfin.com*

Chicago businessman Fred Krehbiel, his Irish wife Kay and managing director Jim Reynolds put in eight years of restoration before opening this Regency mansion in the foothills of the Slieve Bloom mountains as a luxurious hotel. It offers complete privacy thanks to its reservations-only, full-board policy and, although the daily rate seems high, it also offers value. While certainly impressive, hospitable General Manager Aileesh Carew keeps the tone relaxed and it is emphatically not stuffy. With so much on site, many guests never feel the need to leave the estate: prepare yourself to fall in love. **Rooms 15**. *Open all year. CC.* **Directions:** *M7 junction 18, signposted Mountrath/Portlaoise, on entering Mountrath turn right at the traffic lights, 7km on left.*

 ## Castle Durrow

Durrow Co Laois 📞*057 873 6555* *www.castledurrow.com*

Set in lovely gardens, Peter and Shelley Stokes's substantial 18th century country house has magnificent period features, and offers comfort and relaxation with style. Spacious accommodation is in high-ceilinged, individually decorated suites in the main house with views over the parkland, while two wings offer pleasing rooms in two styles. In the Castle Restaurant policy is for careful local sourcing – and the cooking of fish is especially impressive. **Rooms 40**. *Restaurant* **seats 60**. *D Wed-Sun. Bar meals, 12-7 daily. Closed 31 Dec-15 Jan. Closed*

24-26 Dec. CC. **Directions:** *Durrow is off the main Dublin-Cork road, M8, entrance to hotel from village green.*

 ## Dunmore Country School

Swan Road Durrow Co Laois ✆*087 125 8002 www.dunmorecountryschool.ie*

French couple Tanguy and Isabelle de Toulgoët specialise in gardening courses - notably 'helping you to grow tasty vegetables in an organic, sustainable, intensive and cost effective way'. They also offer 'Seed to Table' cookery classes based on whatever is in season at the time - a delicious way to learn as you prepare a 'typically French' three-course lunch, and then have the pleasure of eating it. Customised courses available, also courses conducted in French...

 ## The Heritage Golf & Spa Resort

Killenard Co Laois ✆*057 864 5500 www.theheritage.com*

Great staff and exceptional leisure facilities are the trump cards at this luxury hotel and golf resort set in rural Laois. Not only the destination golf course and spa, but indoor and outdoor bowls, tennis and a 4-mile floodlit jogging and walking track. Spacious accommodation is very comfortably furnished. Fine dining is offered in the Arlington Room with informal options elsewhere in this attractive venue. **Rooms 98**. *12 Self catering houses available. Restaurant seats* **Seats 100**. *D Mon, Tue, Thu-Sat. Food also available in other areas including the bar 12-9pm daily. Hotel closed 22-26 Dec. CC.* **Directions:** *M7 exit no. 15 to Killenard.*

 ## Roundwood House

Mountrath Co Laois ✆*057 873 2120 www.roundwoodhouse.com*

It is hard to see how anyone could fail to love this unspoilt early Georgian house, which lies secluded in mature woods, at the foot of the Slieve Bloom mountains - a sense of history and an appreciation of genuine hospitality are all that is needed to make the most of a stay here. Restored by Frank and Rosemarie Kennan over many years, it is now run by their daughter Hannah and her husband Paddy. **Rooms 10**. *D at 8pm (7pm Sun). Establishment closed 24 & 25 Dec. CC.* **Directions:** *On the left, 5km from Mountrath, on R440.*

PORTLAOISE

Not a lot of people know this, but the county town of Laois was previously called Marybrough (it was first established by Queen Mary in 1556 as "the Fort of Maryborough") and was only re-named 'Portlaoise' in 1922. Today it is a major commercial, retail, and arts centre for the Midlands and there is much of interest to visitors, including the old jail which is now an Arts Centre (057 866 3355), the ruins of an 800-year old hill-top castle at Dunamaise, a large Georgian estate home and surrounding gardens at Emo (057 862 6587), a Georgian square at Mountmellick, and especially - the unspoilt Slieve Bloom Mountains & Forest Park. The championship golf course nearby at The Heritage (Killenard, 0502 45500) provides a particularly tough challenge, and garden lovers will be interested to visit the nearby Gash Gardens (Castletown, 057 873 2247) or Heywood Gardens (Ballinakill, 057 873 3563).

 **Ivyleigh House**

Bank Place Church Street Portlaoise Co Laois ✆*057 862 2081 www.ivyleigh.com*

This lovely early Georgian house is a listed building and the present owners, Dinah and Jerry Campion, have restored it immaculately and furnished it beautifully. Bedrooms are the essence of comfort and elegance - but it is at breakfast time that this superb guesthouse is at its best: it has more than once been recognised in our Breakfast Awards. *Rooms 6 (all shower only). Closed Christmas period. CC. Directions: Centre of town follow signs for multi storey car park, 30 metres from carpark.*

Portlaoise Heritage Hotel

Jessop Street Portlaoise Co Laois ✆*057 867 8588 www.theheritagehotel.com*

This popular hotel, right in the town centre, has particularly good facilities for conferences and business travellers. Accommodation, in several grades of room, is very comfortable, with all the amenities expected of a good hotel. Offers a fun experience at Kellys Foundry Grillhouse (hot rock steaks), also fine dining at The Fitzmaurice and an informal Italian bistro. *Rooms 110. Closed 24-27 Dec. CC. Directions: Centre of Portlaoise.*

Stradbally Fayre Café and Foodhall

Main Street Stradbally Co Laois ✆*057 864 1697 www.stradballyfayre.ie*

Just across the road from Stradbally Estate (home of the Electric Picnic and Annual Steam Rally), Chris Maguire's delightful daytime café and food hall offers delicious homemade and organic fare, served with charm by knowledgeable staff, in appealing and unusual contemporary surroundings. Top-notch fresh and dried goods can be bought in the Foodhall. *Seats 52 (outdoors, 12). Open Mon-Sat 9am-5.30pm Sun & Bank Hols 10am-5pm. Closed 25/26 Dec, 1 Jan, Easter Sun. CC. Directions: Centre of Stradbally.*

LEITRIM

In times past, Leitrim was known as the Cinderella county. Official statistics admitted that Leitrim did indeed have the poorest soil in all Ireland, in places barely a covering of low fertility. Back in the sad old days of the 1950s, the county's population had fallen to 30,000. It was doubted that it was still a viable administrative entity.

Today, Leitrim quietly prospers. The county town, Carrick-on-Shannon, is one of Ireland's brightest and best, a bustling river port. Admittedly, there are drawbacks. The town's very first traffic lights came into action in the summer of 2004. Formerly, there were no traffic lights in all Leitrim county. Or at least, not on the roads. The modern automated locks on the restored Shannon-Erne Waterway - whose vitality has contributed significantly to Leitrim's new prosperity - may have had their own boat traffic lights since the waterway was reopened in 1994. But it took another ten years before the roads followed suit.

Leitrim is rightly seen as a pleasantly away-from-it-all sort of place which has many attractions for the determined connoisseur, not least enthusiasts for traditional music, But is it really so remote? Popular perceptions may be at variance with reality. For instance, Leitrim shares the shores of Lough Gill with Sligo, so much so that Yeat's legendary Lake Isle of Innisfree is within an ace of being in Leitrim rather than Sligo of Yeatsian fame. To the northward, we find that more than half of lovely Glencar, popularly perceived as being one of Sligo's finest jewels, is in fact in Leitrim. As for the notion of Leitrim being the ultimate inland and rural county - not so. Leitrim has an Atlantic coastline, albeit of only four kilometres, around Tullaghan.

LOCAL ATTRACTIONS & INFORMATION

▸ **Waterways Ireland**
Carrick-on-Shannon
071 9650898
▸ **Sliabh an Iarainn Visitor Centre** Drumshanbo
071 9641522

▸ **Glens Arts Centre**
Manorhamilton
071 9855833
▸ **Lough Rynn House and Gardens** Mohill
071 9631427

▸ **The Organic Centre**
(Ecotourism) Rossinver
071 9854338

Cannaboe Confectionery

Willowfield Road Ballinamore Co Leitrim ✆ *071 964 4778 www.cacamilis.com*

Fans of the RTE TV Nationwide programme may already be familiar with Sharon Sweeney's impressive special occasion cakes and cupcakes. She makes both classic and novelty cakes for every conceivable occasion - and gives cake decorating and sugarcraft classes at Athlone IT. Details of current courses are given on her website, where you will also find Cake Decorating for Beginners dvds for sale online.

 Glenview House

Aghoo Ballinamore Co Leitrim ✆ *071 964 4157 www.glenview-house.com*

Both locals and holidaymakers enjoy visiting Brian and Teresa Kennedy's farm guesthouse which, unusually, not only offers good food and accommodation, but also Leitrim's only museum - an extraordinary private collection of over 7,000 rural artefacts, ranging from pre-famine Ireland to the recent past. Teresa's 5-course dinners are legendary and a stay here is a taste of real traditional Irish hospitality. *Rooms 6 (5 shower only). Restaurant: Seats 40; D daily., subject to demand. L Sun only; reservations essential. Museum open 7 days (small charge). CC. Open all year. Directions: 3.5km south of Ballinamore.*

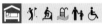 **Riversdale Farm Guesthouse**

Ballinamore Co Leitrim ✆ *071 964 4122 www.riversdale.biz*

The Thomas family's farm guesthouse is a truly rural escape, yet its USP is that it offers exceptional amenities (an indoor heated swimming pool and squash court, for example) for a country B&B. It's ideal for teenagers and there are family suites in the courtyard and spacious bedrooms with lovely views over the waterway and the colourful barges moored below the house - which Riversdale offer for holidays afloat. *Rooms 9 (2 shower only); Closed 1 Dec-31 Jan. CC. Directions: Just outside Ballinamore (signposted from R204), beside Aghoo Lock, on Shannon-Erne Waterway.*

CARRICK ON SHANNON ♨

An ideal location on the River Shannon has resulted in Carrick-on-Shannon becoming one of the most popular destinations for cruise holidays and fishing in Ireland. There is also a golf course (071 966 7015) on the outskirts of the town and just a short drive away the wonderful Strokestown Park House & Gardens (Strokestown, 071 963 3013) is a historic house and estate, with restored walled gardens and famine museum. This thriving town is cosmopolitan in its outlook, with a growing range of restaurants and some fascinating shops. The characterful old Market Yard Centre is always a good browsing spot; it's right at the heart of this vibrant town, and the hub of local activities including Farmers Markets (Thursdays), Crafts Markets (Saturdays), and many special events. The Dock (071 9650828; www.thedock.ie) is Carrick's cultural centre - housed in the beautiful 19th century former Courthouse building, overlooking the River Shannon, it has been wonderfully restored as Leitrim's first integrated centre for the arts, with a 100+ seat performance space, three art galleries, artists' studios, an arts education room; it is also home to The Leitrim Design House.

 **Bush Hotel**

Town Centre Carrick-on-Shannon Co Leitrim ✆*071 967 1000 www.bushhotel.com*

Joseph Dolan's much-loved hotel is best known for old-fashioned hospitality and exceptionally pleasant and helpful staff but, as the first Irish hotel to achieve an EU 'Flower' award for sustainable tourism, there's nothing backward-looking about the management. Whilst recently refurbished and extended, there's a pleasing sense of history, especially in the public areas - and in the food, although bistro-style dishes are offered alongside the comfortingly familiar. *Rooms 60. Seats 100; L&D daily. Closed Christmas. CC. **Directions:** Town centre.*

 Courtyard Kitchen

Main Street Carrick on Shannon Co Leitrim ✆*071 967 1894 www.courtyardkitchen.com*

Although Joe O'Gorman & Ciaran Reidy's smart-casual restaurant is one of the newer businesses in the town, pleasant and helpful staff create a relaxed atmosphere and a policy of offering quality with value soon earned this modern café-restaurant a local following. Look out for the traditional potato dish Leitrim Boxty, perhaps partnered with Donegal smoked salmon; steaks always feature but vegetarians are well looked after too. *Open: L&D daily. **Directions:** Off the upper end of the main street; (not obvious from the road).*

 Cryan's Hotel

The Quay Carrick-on-Shannon Co. Leitrim ✆*071 967 2066/7/8 www.cryanshotel.ie*

Set in an enviable location on the banks of the Shannon and just a couple of minutes' walk from the town centre, this welcoming and friendly hotel is popular with locals and tourists alike. Bedrooms are modern and stylish and rooms at the front overlook the river, while a reputation for great steaks and fine fish makes for a busy dining room with a good buzz. *Rooms 24. L&D daily. CC.*

 **Hollywell Country House**

Liberty Hill Cortober Carrick-on-Shannon Co Leitrim ✆*071 962 1124*

Just across the bridge from the town, Ronan and Grainne Maher's charming period house has its own river frontage and beautiful views over the Shannon. With a long reputation for the comfort and warm hospitality offered by the Maher family, this is one of the region's most delightful places to stay and its re-opening following restoration is very welcome. A pathway through lovely gardens leads down to the river and there is coarse fishing on site. *Rooms 4 (2 shower only). Closed Dec & Jan (open for New Years). CC. **Directions:** From Dublin, cross bridge on N4, keep left at Gings pub. Hollywell entrance is on left up the hill.*

 **The Landmark Hotel**

Dublin Road Carrick-on-Shannon Co Leitrim ✆*071 962 2222 www.thelandmarkhotel.com*

This aptly named hotel just across the road from the river has a dramatic lobby with fountain feature, creating a certain expectation. It offers extensive conference and banqueting facilities and bedrooms are spacious and comfortable, many with views over the Shannon. Well presented smart-casual food served in the Boardwalk Café is good value. *Rooms 60 (2 shower only). Boardwalk Cafe **seats 140** (outdoors, 20), L&D daily. Aromas Café, 9-6pm; Bar food served daily. Hotel closed 25 Dec. CC. **Directions:** Centre of town.*

The Oarsman Bar & Café

Bridge Street Carrick-on-Shannon Co Leitrim ✆ *071 962 1733 www.theoarsman.com*

This characterful pub, run by brothers Conor and Ronan Maher, is very welcoming and efficiently run, even at the busiest times. The bar is solidly traditional. with two welcoming fires and a pleasant outside seating area at the back. A strong kitchen produces consistently excellent food with evening menus offered upstairs. One of Ireland's pleasantest pubs and it just goes on getting better - definitely worth a detour. Bar food Tue-Sat 12-9pm. *Restaurant* **seats** **40**; D Thu-Sat. Closed Sun, Mon, 25 Dec, Good Fri. CC. **Directions:** Town centre. *The Mahers also operate a café at Ardcarne Garden Centre.*

Shamrat Restaurant

Bridge Street Carrick-on-Shannon Co Leitrim ✆ *071 965 0934*

Uncluttered contemporary decor and well-spaced tables with comfortable high-back chairs make a pleasing setting for a varied and well cooked selection of authentic Indian and Bangladeshi dishes - and attentive service from friendly and helpful staff adds to the enjoyment. L&D daily. (BYO permitted, no corkage). *Closed 25 Dec. CC.* **Directions:** *Near the bridge, on right-hand side walking into town.*

Victoria Hall

Quay Road Carrick-on-Shannon Co Leitrim ✆ *071 962 0320 www.victoriahall.ie*

This stylish contemporary restaurant is in an imaginatively restored and converted, almost-waterside Victorian building beside the Rowing Club, and it offers well-executed and good value meals served by smart, attentive staff. Menus offer a wide range of broadly Asian and European dishes but local food features too; traditional boxty is innovatively presented in a range of boxty wraps. **Seats 70** (outdoors, 25). Open daily, 12.30-10. Closed 25 Dec, Good Fri. CC. **Directions:** On Boathouse Quay, beside the Rowing Club and town park.

Vittos Restaurant & Wine Bar

Market Yard Centre Carrick-on-Shannon Co Leitrim
✆ *071 962 7000 www.vittosrestaurant.com*

Husband and wife team Jason and Jo O'Brien's attractive stone-built restaurant on the corner of Market Yard offers good cooking and extensive mainly Italian menus. It's a friendly place with a full bar, offering pizza, pasta, salads, plus grills including steaks and fish in the evening. Very family friendly and many items available to take away. **Seats 70** (outdoors, 25). Open D Tue-Fri & all day Sat & Sun 12.30-10.30pm. Closed Mon. CC. **Directions:** Centre of town.

Harkins Bistro

Dromod Harbour Dromod Co Leitrim ✆ *071 965 8718 www.harkinsbistro.com*

Right beside Dromod harbour, Adrian and Emma Harkins' attractive restaurant is popular for locals and visitors alike, especially those boating on the Shannon. Emma is the chef and modern Irish cooking the stye, with appealing menus offering something for everyone and sometimes including unusual dishes. Also caters for parties, including weddings. *Seats 50 (outdoors, 20). Open Wed-Sun (& Bank Hols) 4-last orders at 9pm. CC. Directions: N7 Sligo road to Dromod, on harbour.*

Riverbank Restaurant & Club House Bar

Dromohair Co Leitrim ✆*071 916 4934 www.riverbankrestaurant.ie*

The Kelly family's hospitable two-storey bar and restaurant is a well-established dining destination within the greater Sligo area. Chef John Kelly spent several years with Neven Maguire at MacNean Restaurant, Co Cavan (see entry) so you can count on careful sourcing of quality local ingredients; he offers an imaginative range of generous dishes, including great steaks with upbeat trimmings - and good value. *Seats 70. D Fri-Sun. Bar food daily, 12.30-9pm. Restaurant closed Mon-Thu, 24-26 Dec, Good Fri. CC. Directions: Sligo side of Dromohair village.*

Lough Allen Hotel & Suites

Drumshanbo Co Leitrim ✆*071 964 0100 www.loughallenhotel.com*

Although the approach is not appealing, this contemporary waterside hotel outside the characterful village of Drumshanbo will quickly win you over. Accommodation is spacious and comfortable and - like the attractive bar and deck - many rooms have lake views. The staff are brilliant and, with a relaxed ambience and good amenities, it's a good base for activity holidays. Self-catering also available. *Rooms 72 (4 shower only); Open all year. CC. Directions: 15 km from Carrick-on-Shannon, on Drumshanbo-Sligo road.*

The Cottage Restaurant

Jamestown Carrick on Shannon Co Leitrim ✆*071 962 5933 www.cottagerestaurant.ie*

Well known local chef, Shamzuri Mohid Hanifa, offers excellent modern European and Asian food at this cheerful white-washed restaurant on the edge of the pretty village of Jamestown and it has become a firm favourite with local diners and visitors, many of whom arrive by boat. Although not essential, reservations are strongly advised, especially at weekends. *Seats 40 (outdoors 16). L & D Thu-Sun. Closed Mon-Wed. CC. Directions: On right just before entering Jamestown village.*

Canal View Restaurant

Keshcarrigan Carrick on Shannon Co Leitrim ✆*071 964 2111*

Overlooking the canal and with a small marina just across the road, enthusiastic owner/manager Steve Taylor provides a personal dining experience that puts as much emphasis on customer enjoyment as on the good home cooked food – which is based on fresh, seasonal local produce (suppliers credited). Guests from all over the world just love it. *Open Fri-Sat 6-10, Sun 4-8 in summer; also other nights if there are bookings. Live music on Friday nights.*

The Courthouse Restaurant

Main Street Kinlough Co Leitrim 071 984 2391 www.thecourthouserest.com

Owner-chef Piero Melis offers excellent contemporary Mediterranean cooking at this popular and very highly-regarded restaurant. Atmospheric, with a welcome open fire on chilly days, it's a hospitable place and full of charm. Piero's philosophy is to keep it simple and allow his carefully sourced local foods to take centre stage, but this simplicity is skilfully achieved. Booking is strongly advised, especially at weekends. **Seats 40.** *D Wed-Mon. L Sun only. Closed - Tue, 2 weeks after Feb 14, Christmas. CC.* **Directions:** *Off main Donegal-Sligo road (N15), 5 km towards Sligo from Bundoran. Take turning directly opposite Tullaghan House.*

 # An Caife Bia Sláinte

Upper Main Street Manorhamilton Co Leitrim 071 985 6500 www.ancaifebiaslainte.com

Karen Feehily's attractive daytime café in the centre of Manorhamilton has a sense of down to earth quality. Despite the reasonable prices, everything on their wide ranging menu is made with the very best of ingredients - and it shows in the taste. But they have some less predictable USPs too - award-winning Italian coffee, for a start, and amazingly pretty special occasion cakes from their Roses & Bows Cakery. *Open: Mon-Fri 9.30-5, Sat 10-4. Closed Sun.*

 # Lough Rynn Castle Hotel & Estate

Lough Rynn Mohill Co Leitrim 071 963 2700 www.loughrynn.ie

Set amongst 300 acres of rolling countryside, historic Lough Rynn Castle has seen major restoration with a view to making it a perfect country haven, and no expense or effort has been spared. Opulently appointed lounges, drawing rooms and a library are remarkably intimate for public rooms in an hotel. Bedrooms include luxurious castle rooms with wonderful views of the estate and surrounding countryside. A beautiful and peaceful place. **Rooms 43**; *Open all year. CC.* **Directions:** *Signed from Mohill village.*

  # The Organic Centre

Rossinver Co Leitrim 071 985 4338 www.theorganiccentre.ie

This extraordinary place is well worth a visit whether to attend one of its courses - covering a wide range of life skills, including cookery courses, and offered on a regular basis - or just to have a look. Their Eco-Shop offers seasonal produce from their own gardens as well as a range of gardening and home items, books and organic herb tinctures, and there's a coffee shop too. *Open Tue-Sun, closed Mon. Online shop. CC.*

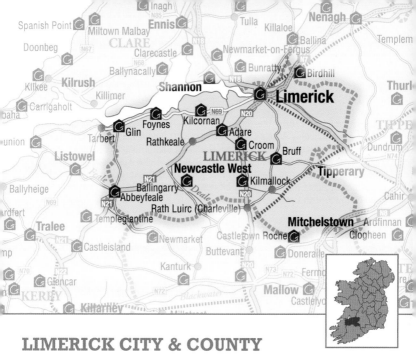

LIMERICK CITY & COUNTY

The story of Limerick city and county is in many ways the story of the Shannon Estuary, for in times past it was the convenient inland access provided by Ireland's largest estuary - it is 80 kilometres in length - which encouraged the development of life along the estuary's sea shores, and into the fresh water of the River Shannon itself.

Today, the area's national and global transport is served by air, sea and land through Shannon International Airport, the increased use of the Estuary through the development of Foynes Port and other deepwater facilities, improvement and restoration of rail links, and a modern road network augmented by a tunnel under the Shannon Estuary immediately seaward of Limerick city. Within the city, the opening of improved waterway links through the heart of town has seen the welcome regeneration of older urban areas continuing in tandem with the attractive new developments.

Inland from the river, the very richness of the countryside soon begins to develop its own dynamic. Eastern Limerick verges into Tipperary's Golden Vale, and the eastern county's Slieve Felim hills, rising to Cullaun at 462 m, reflect the nearby style of Tipperary's Silvermine Mountains. Southwest of Limerick city, the splendid hunting country and utterly rural atmosphere of the area around the beautiful village of Adare makes it a real effort of imagination to visualise the muddy salt waters of the Shannon Estuary just a few miles away down the meandering River Maigue, yet the Estuary is there nevertheless.

LOCAL ATTRACTIONS & INFORMATION

▸ **Flying Boat Museum**
Foynes
069 65416
▸ **Hunt Museum**
Limerick
061 312833

▸ **King John's Castle**
Limerick
061 360788
▸ **Interpretive Centre**
Lough Gur
061 360788

LIMERICK

Of great historical and strategic importance, Ireland's fourth city is also renowned for its rich cultural tradition, with many excellent museums, galleries and theatres to visit - and Ireland's first purpose-built Concert Hall (contact Tourist Information Office, 061 317 522, for details of events): other attractions in the city centre include King John's Castle (1212), St. Mary's Cathedral (1168), The Hunt Museum (Rutland Street; 061 312 833), several (seasonal) tours including Angela's Ashes walking tour (from Arthurs Quay, 061 317 522), hop on-hop off sightseeing tour, the historical walking tour of Limerick (from Arthurs Quay, 061 317 522) and boat tours along the River Shannon. There is a Farmers' Market in the Milk Market every Saturday (8am-2pm) and golfers might like to try the championship course at nearby Adare Manor Hotel & Golf Resort (061 395 044) which has several times been home to the Irish Open.

  **Absolute Hotel**

Sir Harry's Mall Limerick City ✆ *061 463 600 www.absolutehotel.com*

Located on the far side of the River Shannon where the Abbey River flows into it, this stylish modern hotel enjoys a great site with a waterside bar and restaurant, decked outdoor seating area and views of the hills - and a peaceful situation in what is still a city centre area. Three grades of rooms are offered with no shortage of style at any level and only a modest premium for more spacious 'Cosy' rooms. With fine amenities and complimentary parking, Absolute represents real value for money for anyone visiting Limerick city. **Rooms 99** *(all rooms shower only). Open all year. CC.*

  Azur

8 Georges Quay Limerick City ✆ *061 314 994 www.azurcafebrasserie.ie*

Good cooking and simple presentation by owner-chef Ken Stembridge make a confident partnership in this prime riverside location. While well-balanced menus offer choice to all, seafood is the speciality and Seafood Platter the house special. Exciting dishes, menus offering very good value, efficient service and a relaxed setting make this a good choice. **Seats 75.** *L Mon-Fri, D Tue-Sat, open all day Sun from 2pm. CC.*

  Blas by Cafe Noir

Irish World Academy of Music and Dance University of Limerick Limerick City
✆ *061 234 904 www.cafenoir.ie*

This Limerick-based group of French-inspired coffee houses has made superb baked goods and patisserie its hallmark from the beginning. This outlet in the Irish World Academy of Music and Dance at the University of Limerick maintains this tradition with delightful breakfast and lunch offerings. *Open Mon-Fri, 8.30am-5.30pm.*

Bobby Byrne's Bar

3 O'Connell Avenue Limerick City ✆ *061 316 949 www.bobbybyrnesbar.com*

One of Limerick's best-known sporting pubs, Bobby Byrne's is celebrating 50 years in business. Opened in 1963 by the original Bobby and his wife Helen, it quickly became a great supporter of local teams, particularly rugby. Operated since 2003 by son Robert and family, its original character remains despite major refurbishment. Tasty home cooked food is served throughout the day. *Food served daily. Mon-Fri 8.30-8.30, Sat 9.30-8.30, Sun 12-7.30. Carvery L daily; evening menu from 3pm (Sun 'teatime menu' 4-7.30). No food bank hol Mondays. Bar closed Good Fri & 25 Dec. Christmas Day. Beer garden. CC.*

Café Noir

Robert Street Limerick City ✆ *061 411 222 www.cafenoir.ie*

Featuring the outstanding baked goods and patisserie that distinguish the Café Noir brand, this branch opens late on Thursday, Friday and Saturday nights when a full Tapas-style menu is rolled out. Cheerful efficient service is the result of careful in-house training by the group. *Open Mon-Wed 9am–5.30pm; Thu-Sat 9am–12 midnight.*

Cafe Noir

Park Point Centre Castletroy Limerick City ✆ *061 423 901 www.cafenoir.ie*

The two-level Castletroy Café Noir outlet adjoining the Travelodge Hotel has expanded the quality daytime format to full evening service. From 6pm, when a full brasserie style menu is rolled out, it is transformed with subtle lighting and table service. French onion soup en croûte is a signature dish on menus that highlight local produce; Chef's special and fish dishes change daily. *Open Mon-Sun, 7.30am-10.30pm. Directions: Just off Dublin road on outskirts of city.*

Castletroy Park Hotel

Dublin Road Limerick City ✆ *061 335 566 www.castletroy-park.ie*

Well maintained gardens, a large and warmly furnished foyer and welcoming staff create a good first impression at this pleasant four star hotel near the University of Limerick and its cultural and sporting amenities. Spacious and comfortable, it has a lot to offer including good food - diners expecting a typical hotel meal in McLaughlins Restaurant should be pleasantly surprised. **Rooms 107** *(2 shower only). Restaurant* **seats 70**. *L & D daily. Hotel open all year. CC.* **Directions:** *Dublin road, directly opposite the University of Limerick.*

Clarion Hotel Limerick

Steamboat Quay Limerick City ✆ *061 444 100 www.clarionlimerick.com*

This dramatic cigar-shaped 17-storey riverside hotel enjoys panoramic views over the city and the Shannon region, with Sinergie Restaurant right on the waterfront. A clean-lined contemporary style prevails, with comfortable bedrooms varying due to the unusual shape of the building. Good business facilities appeal to midweek guests, but weekends attract a far livelier crowd. Parking can be problematic, especially for late arrivals. **Rooms 158.** *Closed 24-26 Dec. CC.*

Copper & Spice

2 Cornmarket Row Limerick City ✆ *061 313 620 www.copperandspice.com*

Well situated near the restored Milk Market buildings, this attractively named restaurant would be hard to miss; you have to ring a bell to get in, so you are assured of immediate attention from agreeable staff. This stylish restaurant offers a different experience from other ethnic restaurants in the city, and gives value for money. **Seats 75**; *D Mon-Sat, L Sun only. Closed Sun D, 25 Dec, Good Fri. CC.*

Cornstore at Home

42 Thomas Street Limerick City ✆ *061 609 905 www.cornstoreathome.com*

'Restaurant Quality at Home' is the promise at Padraic Frawley's Aladdin's cave of a shop and ready meal takeaway - and every freshly prepared dish is made in a dedicated kitchen at their popular restaurant The Cornstore, across the road. Known with good reason as 'Limerick's Fallon & Byrne', it offers a fantastic choice of homemade ready meals (as well as dressings, breads, preserves etc) plus fresh produce and and an extensive and carefully selected range of delicious foods from other artisan producers. Cookery demos too. A must-visit when in Limerick. *Open Mon-Fri 10-7, Sat 10-6. Closed Sun. CC.*

The Cornstore Winebar & Restaurant

19 Thomas Street Limerick City ✆ *061 609 000 www.cornstorelimerick.com*

A sister restaurant to Padraic Frawley's great dining venue The Cornstore in Cork (see entry), the same stylish mix of quality, accessibility and buzz works equally well in his home city. Steaks and seafood are the specialities - and their unique in-house steak ageing unit ensures exceptionally tender meat - but there is much more to The Cornstore than surf'n'turf. Locally produced organic and artisan ingredients feature on wide ranging menus and the cooking has flair. With its emphasis on atmosphere, quality and value, together with carefully selected wines and good service, Limerick is lucky to have the Cornstore. **Seats 200**. *L & D daily. Closed 25 Dec. CC.*

The Curragower Seafood Bar

Clancys Strand Limerick City ✆ *061 321 788 www.curragower.com*

Cian Bourke's atmospheric bar on the County Clare side of the River Shannon is said to be one of the oldest pubs in the city; it has character by the bucketful and a splendid view across the Curragower Falls to King John's Castle from the attractive terrace. The food style is homely, which suits the surroundings; the emphasis is on freshly cooked food using local ingredients and speciality dishes are all seafood, but the offering overall is evenly balanced. *Open daily 12-11; Food served Wed-Sun 12-9. CC*

Freddy's Bistro

Theatre Lane Glentworth Street Limerick City ℰ *061 418 749 www.freddysbistro.com*

Run by sisters Liz Phelan and Caroline Kerely, the long established Freddy's Bistro is part of the fabric of Limerick dining and this friendly and atmospheric hideaway consistently delivers great food. Ecelectic menus - which, unusually, include a full coeliac menu - span several continents, but local produce is highlighted and good value given. This Limerick gem has lots of character and is well worth seeking out. *Seats 60. D 5.30-late. CC.*

The French Table

1 Steamboat Quay Limerick City ℰ *061 609 274 www.frenchtable.ie*

French chef Thomas Fialon and and his Limerick-born wife Deirdre run this excellent, pleasingly understated restaurant near the Clarion Hotel. Well-trained, welcoming staff convey a sense of order, in preparation for the serious business of enjoying a good meal, and francophiles will be in their element, as Thomas interprets classic French dishes with finesse - and offers outstanding value. A lunchtime warm steak sandwich with plum tomato salad and sautéed potatoes (€9)is the best buy in town. *Seats 52; L Tue-Fri; D Tue-Sun. Closed Sat L, Sun L, & Mon, 24-26 Dec, 1 Jan, Good Fri. CC.*

George Hotel

O'Connell Sreet Limerick City ℰ *061 460 400 www.thegeorgeboutiquehotel.com*

This boutique hotel right in the heart of the city is a welcoming place in a relaxed modern style. Contemporary bedrooms have some nice touches including Egyptian cotton sheets, and guests have concessional use of a nearby pool and leisure centre. Its location in the heart of the commercial and shopping centre makes it a handy meeting place. *Rooms 125. CC.*

Gingergirl

Limerick City ℰ *087 611 6360 www.gingergirl.ie*

'Local, seasonal, and simple' is the mantra for redhead Helen Keown's aptly named 'Gingergirl' products. She sells her excellent handmade jams, chutneys and home baking at markets and in speciality food stores, where she also offers tastings. An online hamper service delivers within Ireland, and this former marketing executive offers related services to businesses too.

The Glasshouse Restaurant

Riverpoint Building Lower Mallow Street Limerick City
ℰ *061 469 000 www.glasshouserestaurant.ie*

In the dramatic Riverpoint development overlooking the river at Shannon Bridge, owner-chef David Corbett's chic contemporary restaurant and bar is an exciting place to dine. Known for its extensive cocktail and (non-Irish) craft beer list, the ground floor lounge offers informal dining, while the upstairs restaurant conveys a sense of occasion and (although provenance of clearly well-sourced ingredients is not mentioned) the excellent cooking matches the atmosphere. *Seats 100* (outdoors, 30). *Open D only Tue-Sat (& bank hol Sun). Closed Sun & Mon. CC.*

Greenhills Hotel

Caherdavin Ennis Road Limerick City ✆ *061 453 033 www.greenhillsgroup.com*

Welcoming is the byword at the comfortable Greenhills Hotel, where Daphne Greene is the third generation of the family to head up front of house. Brother Hugh is in charge of the food, with homely touches like freshly baked cookies, and the restaurant's selling point is quality local produce. Banqueting rooms overlook landscaped grounds and a flower-hung courtyard with splashing fountain. It would be all too easy to miss this pleasant hotel when speeding by on the Limerick - Shannon road, but it's well worth a stop.

 Hamptons Grill

Henry Street Limerick City ✆ *061 609 325 www.hamptonsgrill.ie*

This large, stylish restaurant grill with plenty of buzz offers a good range of meat, fish and vegetarian options on the lunch and dinner menus. Desserts, though the portions seem small, are densely and deliciously rich (prices also small). There is a real desire to please here. *Seats 150; Open 12-10.30pm daily. CC.*

 Jim Flavin Butchers

Dublin Road Castletroy Limerick City ✆ *061 331 977*

No stranger to awards, ACBI (craftbutchers.ie) member Jim Flavin is 'Limerick's sausage king'. He's been a fixture in Castletroy since 1996 and has earned a loyal following for his excellent meat and butchery products, notably beef raised on the family farm at Grange - the Flavins take great pride in 'farm to fork' traceability. They also sell fish and fresh fruit and vegetables and have a second shop at Greenpark. *Open Mon-Sat 7am-7pm, Sun 9am-6pm.*

 La Cucina

5 University Court Castletroy Limerick City ✆ *061 333 980 www.lacucina.ie*

Bruno and Lorraine Faneran's delightful little café/deli offers casual dining with a difference. They specialise in authentic Italian food, while also taking pride in using fresh Irish ingredients - and there's a very high standard of cooking coming out of the semi-open kitchen. Great tasting food offers outstanding value for money and it's a place where you'll find smiles all round (from both staff and customers!). *Open Mon-Fri 11am–9.30pm; Sat 12-9.30pm.*

 **Limerick Strand Hotel**

Ennis Road Limerick City ✆ *061 421 800 www.strandlimerick.ie*

Just across the Sarsfield Bridge from the main commercial heart of Limerick, this well-appointed modern hotel is especially well equipped for business travellers, but all guests also enjoy the pleasant ambience (and great views from the upper floors), excellent leisure facilities and - unusually for a large hotel - the opportunity to explore the foods of the region. Head chef Tom Flavin makes provenance and seasonality a point of difference in The River

Restaurant, and the kitchen team also produces a homemade pantry range, The Secret Ingredient, allowing diners to bring home a taste of Limerick. *Rooms 184*. *Restaurant: L Mon-Fri & Sun. D daily. Bar snacks from 7am Mon-Fri; 9am Sat & Sun. Parking (fee applies). CC.*

Micheal O'Loughlin Butchers

6 Upper William Street Limerick City ✆*061 414 102 www.michaeloloughlinbutchers.ie*

Proudly styled 'Old World Master Butchers', Michael O'Loughlin's shop is a reminder of the way butchers used to be, with lots of character, proper local supplies and an emphasis on service. You'll find 21-day dry-aged beef here, lamb from The Burren across in Co Clare, ham and bacon from Tipperary and a whole lot of unusual things too, ranging from almost-forgotten tripe, skirt and pig's tails, to rabbit or game in season - and, if you're planning a big party, this is the place to get a pig on a spit. *Open Mon-Sat, 8-6. Online shop.*

Mortell's Delicatessen & Seafood Restaurant

49 Roches Street Limerick City ✆*061 415 457 www.mortellcatering.com*

A sandwich board welcomes in hungry passers-by with an offer of three fresh fish of the day – all Irish caught, and cooked to order by your chosen method in view of the public. A full breakfast menu also includes a seafood breakfast. Freshness, friendly service and an interested and eagle-eyed proprietor Michael Mortell make this appealing deli and casual daytime restaurant/coffee shop a place to return to. *Seats 30*. *Open Mon-Sat 8.30-4.30. Closed Sun. CC.*

No. 1 Pery Square Hotel & Spa

Pery Square Limerick City ✆*061 402 402 www.oneperysquare.com*

A stunning property on the city's most gracious Georgian square, this is Limerick's premier boutique hotel. Immaculately restored by owner Patricia Roberts in celebration of its original architectural features, the warmth of welcome and pampering of guests at this luxurious hotel now match the care devoted to the building. Fine public rooms and sumptuous bedrooms are a delight and the holistic Spa @ No.1 offers the ultimate in pampering. Scottish head chef Alan Burns has earned national acclaim for the smart Brasserie One, offering ingredients-led cooking style that achieves simplicity in both classic and rustic dishes. Wine is also a special focus, with tastings held and retail sales offered. *Rooms 20*. *Brasserie seats 70 (outdoors, 20). L & D Tue-Sat. Sun brunch 11am-7pm. Closed Sun D, Mon & house closed 25-27 Dec. CC.*

The Pavilion

North Campus University of Limerick Limerick City ✆*061 213 369 www.pavilion.ie*

Located within the University's Conference & Sports Campus, this striking modern bar/restaurant caters for students as well as the dining public but they do it with style. There are all day offers for €5, for example, while the short but appealing evening menu is more sophisticated - although, surprisingly, there may be no vegetarian option. The Pavilion Tapas

Plate makes a sociable starter, and the good cooking includes a great rendition of traditional fish & chips - go for it. *Open daily from 10am (Mon-Thur to 11.30pm, Fri & Sat to12.30am, Sun to 11pm); L 12-3 (Sun to 4), D 5-9.*

 ## Radisson Blu Hotel & Spa Limerick

Ennis Road Limerick City 📞 *061 456 200 www.radissonblu.ie/hotel.limerick*

Although just a short drive from the city centre, this hotel enjoys an almost rural setting and views of the Clare hills. Offering fine conference and business facilities, it also has a well-appointed spa with an outdoor Canadian hot tub. It is exceptionally spacious, both in public areas and accommodation, with all rooms styled deluxe. **Rooms 154.** *CC.*

  ## René Cusack Fish

St. Alphonsus Street Limerick City 📞 *061 440 054*

This family business was founded by René Cusack and is now run by his son Paul. They offer a wide range of whitefish and shellfish with live lobster and oysters available from a tank in-store - the shop is supplied daily from the company's plant in Raheen Industrial Estate, Limerick. *Open Tue-Sat 9-5.30. Closed Sun & Mon. Also at: The Milk Market (Unit C; Wed-Fri 9-5.30, Sat 9-4).*

 ## The River Bistro

4 George's Quay Limerick City 📞 *061 400 990 www.theriverbistro.ie*

Well known local chef Diarmuid O'Callaghan and his wife Carmel run this smartly presented riverside restaurant, where food takes centre stage. Diarmuid is a well-travelled man known for his commitment to using the best seasonal ingredients, and for unpretentious cooking that offers a mix of old favourites and more adventurous dishes - focusing on flavour above all else. Not cheap but you'll get good value, especially midweek. **Seats 50** *(outdoors, 10). D only Tue-Sat. Closed Sun & Mon. CC.*

  ## The Sage Cafe

67/68 Catherine Street Limerick City 📞 *061 409 458 www.thesagecafe.com*

 Mike & Siobhan Hogan's centrally located café near the Milk Market is easy to spot by the smart green and white striped awning (with tables underneath on fine days) - and the queues of people waiting to lunch on their healthy food. They do lovely fresh-flavoured lunch dishes - Caesar salad in two sizes, great soups with homemade brown bread or spelt bread, oriental dishes - and gorgeous home bakes, including gluten-free choices, maybe served with a dollop of whipped cream and a giant strawberry. A quality-driven place, everything's made from scratch. **Seats 50.** *Mon-Sat, 9-5.30 (breakfast 9-11.30, L 12-4). Closed Sun, Bank Hols, Christmas week. CC.*

Savoy Hotel

City Central Henry Street Limerick City ✆ *061 448 700 www.savoylimerick.com*

While not Limerick's largest hotel, it is one of the most luxurious and scores highly on service. With excellent in-room and leisure facilities it's mainly aimed at the business guest; terrace gardens enjoy views of the city and river, and the pleasant Savoy Bar echoes the site's previous life as a cinema. The Savoy Restaurant is open for all meals, and highly regarded chef Bryan McCarthy now heads the kitchen team. *Rooms 94. CC.*

1826 Adare

Main Street Adare Co Limerick ✆ *061 396 004 www.1826adare.ie*

Top chef Wade Murphy and his wife Elaine's rustic chic restaurant is in one of this postcard-pretty village's most charming cottages. Moving away from his fine dining background, Wade offers keenly-priced gastropub style casual dining "but without being a pub!". Monthly-changing menus are built on seasonal local produce, with daily blackboard specials offering extras such as whole sole and braised meats. Top notch cooking in a relaxed style - and at a very accessible price. Another must-visit destination for Adare. *Open: D Tue-Sat, all day Sun, 12-6. May open L Thu-Sat in summer. A la carte.*

Adare Farm

Adare Co Limerick ✆ *087 296 2626 www.adarefarm.ie*

Far from being the commodities they once were, Adare Farm foods are now valued as niche products. Adare Farm Fresh Country Milk - pasteurised but non-homogenised and available in traditional glass bottles - is taking the country by storm. Adare Farm Ice Cream features on some of the best menus in the Mid- and South-West. And there's the pig-on-a-spit, a crowd pleaser at Limerick's historic Milk Market and the centrepiece of countless big get togethers around the country. An amazing success story - and that's just the half of it.

Adare Manor

Adare Co Limerick ✆ *061 396 566 www.adaremanor.com*

This magnificent neo-Gothic mansion is set in 900 acres beside the River Maigue, its splendid chandeliered drawing room and cloistered dining room look over formal box-hedged gardens towards the famous golf course. Accommodation varies; some rooms are luxurious, with impressive marble bathrooms; a 'golf village' suits groups and families. The Oak Room offers modern classical cuisine with local ingredients featuring. *Rooms 62. Oak Room Restaurant seats 70; D daily. Carriage House Restaurant, daily, 7am - 9.30pm. Open all year. CC. Directions: Centre of Adare village.*

Berkeley Lodge

Station Road Adare Co Limerick ✆ *061 396 857 www.adare.org*

Situated on a quiet road just off the centre of Adare village, and within easy walking distance of the Heritage Centre, shops and restaurants, Bridie Herlihy's B&B offers a quiet and comfortable base for visiting this pretty place. Bridie is a caring host; this quality shows very much in the breakfast which goes well beyond the usual favourites. *Rooms 6. Open all year. CC. Directions: Coming from Limerick take a right at the roundabout in the centre of the village.*

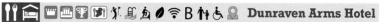 **Dunraven Arms Hotel**

Adare Co Limerick ✆ *061 605 900 www.dunravenhotel.com*

Established in 1792, the Murphy family's large hotel retains the comfortable ambience of a country inn – albeit a very luxurious one. An unrivalled reputation for the quality and value of short breaks offered, and a dedication to giving personal service, make Dunraven Arms an outstanding example of contemporary Irish hospitality at its best. The delightfully old fashioned Maigue Restaurant showcases the best of local produce, with rib of beef carved from a trolley at your table - and is set up as smartly for the excellent breakfast as it is for dinner. *Rooms 86*. *Seats 50*; *D daily, L Sun only. Bar food daily. Open all year. CC.*

 Fitzgeralds Woodlands House Hotel & Spa

Knockanes Adare Co Limerick ✆ *061 605 100 www.woodlands-hotel.ie*

Just outside Adare, the Fitzgerald family's welcoming 3* hotel is set in well-kept gardens and is now in an energetic second generation ownership, who have systematically upgraded and developed the whole hotel. With good conference/banqueting and leisure amenities it's always been a popular venue for weddings and suited to large gatherings. *Rooms 93 (11 shower only).*

 Miss Crumpets Tea Rooms

Adare's Old Creamery Blackabbey Adare Co Limerick ✆ *061 395 734 www.oldcreameryco.com*

Adare's Old Creamery and its owner, Helen Mackessy, go back a long way. Her grandfather, Michael Hanley, was one of the founders of this co-operative creamery in the early 1900's - and her father was a milk supplier in later years. Having been resued from dereliction by Helen, it now houses an 8,000 square foot shop and this charming tea room, serving simple but very good quality baking. *Open Mon - Sat 10-6, Sun 2-6.*

 **The Wild Geese Restaurant**

Rose Cottage Main Street Adare Co Limerick ✆ *061 396 451 www.thewild-geese.com*

In one of the prettiest cottages in Adare, David Foley and Julie Randle's atmospheric restaurant offers consistently excellent modern Irish cooking and caring service, making an irresistible package. David, a Euro-Toques chef, sources the best local ingredients with meticulous care and presents them with pride - everything is made from scratch and the niceties of a special meal, such as presenting an amuse-bouche, are observed. *Seats 60 (outdoors, 10). D Tue-Sat, L Sun only. Closed Mon & Sun D; 24-26 Dec; 8-26 Jan. CC. Directions: Top of Adare village, opposite Dunraven Arms Hotel.*

 Tuscany Bistro

9 Newtown Centre Annacotty Castletroy Co Limerick ✆ *061 333 444 www.tuscany.ie*

Bright and enticing, this super little neighbourhood restaurant near Limerick University is warm and buzzy with a nice Italian feel to it, and friendly hands-on owner Sabarina Amodeo very much in evidence. Fairly priced menus offer freshly prepared, tasty versions of all the Italian favourites and professional and attentive service is a highlight. **Seats 34** *(outside, 12). Open Tue-Sun 12.30-9pm (to 10pm Thu-Sun). Closed Mon. CC.* **Directions:** *In a small shopping centre in Annacotty.*

  ## The Green Apron

Derryclough Ballingarry *Co Limerick* ✆ *087 980 8853 www.thegreenapron.ie*

Started by her parents in the 1970s, Theresa Storey and her family now run this small artisan preserves company, which has a special reputation for wonderful traditional jellies made from fruits foraged in nearby hedgerows - and many of the ingredients for other seasonal products still come from the walled garden of her parents' 18th century castle nearby. They also offer courses in kitchen gardening and hold home preserving workshops. *Available from: Limerick Milk Market (Saturday) and shops in the area.*

 ## The Mustard Seed

Echo Lodge Ballingarry *Co Limerick* ✆ *069 68508 www.mustardseed.ie*

What can be said about Dan Mullane's wonderful restaurant The Mustard Seed at Echo Lodge that has not been said before? Having started life in Adare in 1985, it moved just twenty minutes drive away to this very special and hospitable Victorian country residence set on seven acres of lovely gardens - including the organic kitchen garden and orchard that supply their seasonal bounty to an outstanding kitchen. When staying, choose between traditionally sumptuous rooms (old house) and contemporary style (new suites), all equally luxurious. A one-off - and with exceptional warmth and personal service. **Rooms 16**. *The Mustard Seed* **seats 50** *(outdoors, 6). D 7-9.30 (6-9pm Sun). Closed 24-26 Dec and 1st 2 weeks Feb. CC.* **Directions:** *From top of Adare village take first turn to left, follow signs to Ballingarry - 11km; in village.*

  ## Pandora Bell

Killonan Ballysimon *Co Limerick* ✆ *061 339 300 www.pandorabell.ie*

Nicole Dunphy's artisan confectionery range is a relatively recent addition to the market for high quality treats in Ireland, but the simple philosophy ('the best ingredients') and visual appeal – the big handmade lollipops in particular – have made a big impact. This original and beautifully presented range is hugely successful - and deservedly so. Available from selected outlets nationwide; also to buy from the online shop.

 ## Old Bank House

Bruff Co Limerick ✆ *061 389 969 www.theoldbank.ie*

Very close to Lough Gur and the Ballyhoura Mountains (popular for cycling and walking breaks) Bruff is a lovely village within easy distances of a lot of interesting places, and Miriam Sadlier Barry's unusual and very hospitable B&B would make a great base for exploring the area. Formerly a bank, it's been well converted to offer a high standard of accommodation at reasonable price. *Rooms 9 (2 shower only); Closed 23-27 Dec. CC. **Directions:** Bruff is located southeast of Limerick City (on the R512 road).*

O'Shaughnessy's

Glin Co Limerick 068 34115

Not to be missed while in the Glin area, is O'Shaughnessy's pub, just outside the walls of Glin Castle. One of the finest pubs in Ireland, it is now in its sixth generation of family ownership and it is easy to imagine that precious little has changed in the last hundred years. *Open limited hours (usually Fri night & weekends only).* **Directions:** *Up into village, take right turn; pub is on your left before the gates to Glin Castle.*

Rigneys Farm

Curraghchase Kilcornan Co Limerick 087 283 4754 *www.rigneysfarm.com*

Caroline and Joe Rigney rear rare breed pigs such as Tamworth and Saddlebacks on their west Limerick farm. Look out for their their Curraghchase Meats products - notably dry cured bacon and ham, and homemade sausages, puddings and burgers - they are truly outstanding, and have rightly won numerous awards. You won't find a better rasher anywhere. *Available from: Farm shop, Sun, 10-6. Farmers' Markets: The Crescent Limerick (Wed 9.30-2.30), Listowel (Fri 9-2). Also some local and specialist retailers.*

Flemingstown House

Kilmallock Co Limerick 063 98093 *www.flemingstown.com*

Just two miles from the medieval village of Kilmallock, up a long drive flanked by fields of grazing cattle, Imelda Sheedy King's comfortable farmhouse is a lovely place to stay. The standards of service and the magnficent breakfast spread at Flemingstown are remarkable; it is representative of the very best rural Irish welcome. **Rooms 5** *(all shower only); D by arrangement. Likely to be closed Nov-Mar. CC.* **Directions:** *R512 to Kilmallock from Limerick; then towards Fermoy for 3.5km. House set back from road, on left.*

Market Place Brasserie

Carnegie Centre Market Place Newcastle West Co Limerick 069 66900 *www.marketplacebrasserie.ie*

Liam and Cathy Corbett's smart neighbourhood restaurant has a few outside tables overlooking the old market square - a nice spot to enjoy coffee and a cake in the sun. Staff are very nice and welcoming, and everything on the customer-friendly menu is made from scratch, so most dishes can be adapted, eg for coeliacs. Plenty of local - or at least Irish - ingredients feature and the simple things are done well. A good place to know about. **Seats 48**. *Open D Wed-Sat, L Thu, Fri and all day Sun 12.30-7pm.* **Directions:** *Town centre. Also at: Adare.*

LONGFORD

Longford is mostly either gently undulating farming country, or bogland. The higher ground in the north of the county up towards the intricate Lough Gowna rises to no more than 276m in an eminence which romantics might call Carn Clonhugh, but usually it's known as Corn Hill. The more entertainingly named Molly Hill to the east provides the best views of the lake in an area which arouses passionate patriotism - a few miles to the north is Ballinamuck, scene of the last battle in the Rising of 1798 in a part of Longford renowned for its rebellions against foreign rule.

By contrast, the southern part has peaceful associations - along towards that fine village of Ballymahon and through its territory on the Westmeath border, Longford takes in part of the Goldsmith country. Goldsmith himself would be charmed to know that, six kilometres south of the road between Longford and Edgeworthstown, the tiny village of Ardagh - a place of just 75 citizens - is so immaculately maintained that it has been the winner of the Tidiest Village in the Tidy Towns awards.

Another award-winner is Newtowncashel in the southwest of the county, atop a hill immediately eastward of Elfeet Bay on northern Lough Ree, where the scenery becomes more varied as County Longford has a lengthy shoreline along the Shannon's middle lake. West of Longford town at Clondra, the attractive Richmond Harbour is where the Royal Canal - gradually restored along its scenic route from Dublin - finally reconnnected with the Shannon in 2010, having been closed since 1954.

LOCAL ATTRACTIONS & INFORMATION

▸ **Heritage Centre** Ardagh
043 75277
▸ **1798 Memorial & Visitor Centre** Ballinamuck
043 24848

▸ **Bog Lane Theatre**
Ballymahon *0902 32252*
▸ **Carrigglas Manor** (Gandon stableyard, lace museum)
Longford *043 41026*

▸ **Heritage Centre**
Newtowncashel *043 25021*

PBELL'S IRELAND

ChocOneill

~~~~ 2 8067 www.choconeill.ie

Jam... chocolate company from their home workshop.
Speci... ... n, seasonal ingredients, the range is variable. But
a consta... 086 21... - is their Boite en Chocolat (Chocolate Box), made
like an Eas... nell encasing fresh chocolates, truffles and pralines...
Irresistible. ...ys by appointment. Online shop.

Aubergine Gallery Café

1st Floor The White House 17 Ballymahon Street Longford Co Longford ☎ *043 334 8633*

Brother and sister Stephen and Linda Devlins' popular and long-established first floor restaurant has a vibrant, youthful atmosphere. Stephen is an accomplished chef and his menus are Irish/Mediterranean, offering delicious, fresh-flavoured dishes that cater for everyone but place an unusual emphasis on tasty vegetarian food - although a good steak is de rigeur in these parts too. The cooking is invariably creative and seafood lovers will be well pleased too. *Seats 45 (+20 in lounge area). L Mon-Sat; D Fri/Sat & Sun L 2-7.30pm. Closed D Mon-Thu, Bank Hols, Dec 23-Jan 2. CC.* **Directions:** *First floor premises, town centre.*

Longford Arms Hotel

Main Street, Longford Co Longford ☎ *043 334 6296* www.longfordarms.ie

Old-fashioned hospitality is done well in the Longford Arms, which is the hub of community activities and popular with locals and visitors alike. The good-sized bedrooms are modern and stylish, with everything needed for business travellers, and the leisure centre has a 22-metre saltwater pool, which is unique in the south of Ireland. Food available all day. *Rooms 58. Opening times: Bistro/carvery is open Mon-Fri 7.30am-3pm, Sat-Sun 8am-6pm. Bar menu from 5pm-8pm daily. CC.*

Torc Café & Foodhall

1 New Street Longford Co Longford ☎ *043 334 8277* www.torccafe.com

Chocoholics will love Ruth McGarry-Quinn's relaxed modern café as (exceptionally good) chocolate is the speciality. Seating, servery and foodhall blend seamlessly, so it's tempting to pick up some treats while waiting for your order of healthy home-made food. Other highlights include real food for kids - and an imaginative choice of cold drinks, including traditional lemonade. *Open Mon-Thu 9am-6pm, Fri & Sat 9-am-8pm. Closed Sun, bank hols, 25-26 Dec. CC.* **Directions:** *From Dublin direction, on the left after St Mel's cathedral.*

Viewmount House

Dublin Road Longford Co Longford ☎ *043 334 1919* www.viewmounthouse.com

Since opening VM Restaurant at the lovely Georgian Viewmount House in 2008, James and Beryl Kearney and Head Chef Gary O'Hanlon have taken the midlands by storm, making Longford a must-visit destination for food lovers. Gary is from Donegal (proud source of most of his fresh fish) and, while this is a special destination, his cooking is grounded in the familiar products of the region, and is not overly cheffy. VM is a lovely restaurant, and certainly worth a journey Accommodation offered (unregistered). *Seats 55; D Wed-Sat, Sun L only 1-4.30pm. Restaurant closed Mon, Tue. CC.* **Directions:** *From Longford R393 to Ardagh. 1km, up sliproad to right following signs. Entrance 200m on right.*

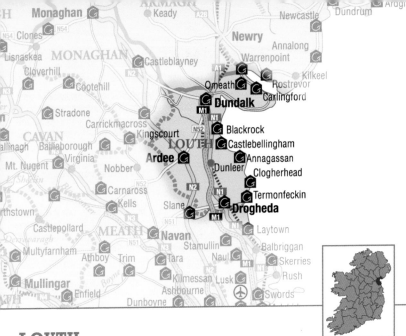

LOUTH

Strategically located in the middle of the main East Coast corridor between Dublin and Belfast, Louth has been enthusiastic about the opportunities provided by the opening of the M1 motorway which now runs smoothly west of Drogheda and Dundalk. Much of the county is fine farmland, at its most productive in the area west of the extensive wildfowl paradise of Dundalk Bay, on whose shores we find the attractive village of Blackrock, one of Ireland's better kept secrets. But as well there are the distinctive uplands in the southwest, whose name of Oriel recalls an ancient princedom which is also remembered in Port Oriel, the busy fishing port at Clogherhead.

In the north of the county, the Cooley Mountains sweep upwards in a style which well matches their better-known neighbours, the Mountains of Mourne, on the other side of Carlingford Lough. Its name might suggest that this is a genuine fjord, but it isn't. However, its beauty is such that there's more than enough to be going along with, and on its Louth shore the ancient little port of Carlingford town used to be a best-kept secret, a quiet little place imbued with history, but today it is happily prospering both as a recreational harbour for the Dundalk and Newry area, and as a bustling visitor attraction in its own right.

The county's three main townships of Ardee, Dundalk and Drogheda each have their own distinctive style, and all three have been finding fresh vitality in recent years. Dundalk is the county town, while the historic borough of Drogheda is the main commercial port, its river valley crossed by the Boyne Railway Viaduct of 1855 vintage, a remarkable construction that it is reckoned one of the seven engineering wonders of Ireland.

LOCAL ATTRACTIONS & INFORMATION

▸ **Carlingford Adventure Centre**
Carlingford
042 9373100

▸ **Beaulieu House and Garden**
Drogheda
041 9838557

▸ **Millmount Museum**
Drogheda
041 9833097

337

The Glyde Inn

Annagassan Dunleer Co Louth 📞 *042 937 2350 www.theglydeinn.ie*

Overlooking Dundalk Bay, with the Mourne and the Cooley Mountains in the background and a long sandy beach just outside the windows, the O'Neill family's inn is simply stunning on a fine day. A nice traditional bar offers character and cosiness on one side, while the restaurant has the view; lobster is a speciality and they do a very good chowder - craft beers too. *L&D daily. CC.* **Directions:** *On seafront in Annagassan.*

  Callaghans Butchers

58 Market Street Ardee Co Louth 📞 *041 685 3253 www.callaghansbutchersardee.ie*

Fourth-generation butcher Peter Callaghan still does things much the same way his great-grandfather did: buying cattle and sheep from local farmers and dry ageing it for up to 28 days for the best flavour. And award winning products to seek out here include the popular garlic and herb sausage - and the real stars, the black and white puddings, which have gained recognition both at home and in Europe. Tasty lasagnes and pies too. *Open all day Mon-Sat.*

 **Fuchsia House**

Dundalk Road Ardee Co Louth 📞 *041 685 8432 www.fuchsiahouse.ie*

Owner-chef Sarajit Chanda from Bangladesh and his Irish wife Sarah Nic Lochlainn have created a restaurant combining Asian authenticity and excellent service. Curries are a star attraction but throughout the varied menu top-class Irish ingredients are turned into mouth-watering dishes. The excellent Aruna sauces are made here too, and cookery classes offered. **Seats 42** *(outdoors, 12). L Fri only. D Tue-Sat; all day Sun & bank hol Mon, 12-9. CC.*

  Hickeys Farm Shop

Kells Road Ardee Co Louth 📞 *041 685 6471*

This good-sized family farm shop just outside Ardee sells potatoes, carrots, turnips, broccoli and cauliflower directly from the Hickeys' own farm as well as a wide range of other fresh fruit and veg, freshly baked goods, some pantry staples and a small selection of local and artisan products. A busy shop doing a brisk trade and useful to know about. *Mon to Sat, 9-6.*

The Brake

Main Street Blackrock Co Louth 📞 *042 932 1393*

A smart frontage with colourful well-maintained window boxes entices customers into The Brake - and, once inside, it's all warmth and country charm, with old pine and rural bric-à-brac, open fires and friendly staff. It has a well-deserved reputation for good bar meals at moderate prices - but be aware this is not a lunchtime spot. **Seats 120.** *Bar open 5-11.30. D daily. Closed 25 Dec, Good Fri. CC.* **Directions:** *Turn off the main Dublin-Belfast road 5km south of Dundalk.*

CARLINGFORD

This delightful medieval village is set amongst spectacular scenery with views across Carlingford Lough to the Mountains of Mourne in County Down. It is a small place and, although off the beaten track, has been 'discovered' so it is best to avoid busy times like festivals, if you want to see it at its best.

The Bay Tree Restaurant

Newry Street Carlingford Co Louth ✆ *042 938 3848 www.belvederehouse.ie/baytree.htm*

Proprietor and accomplished chef Conor Woods takes pride in using the best fresh local produce (some grown in a polytunnel at the back of the premises) at this attractive restaurant. The foundation is classical – but you will find a sprinkling of lighter, more contemporary dishes. The overall result is consistently delicious meals served in a welcoming atmosphere. **Seats 50**. *Open daily in summer, from 6pm-late, and Sun L. Closed Mon & Tue in winter. Group bookings welcome at other times.* **Directions:** *Centre of village.*

 Beaufort House

Ghan Road Carlingford Co Louth ✆ *042 937 3879 www.beauforthouse.net*

This immaculate property takes full advantage of its quiet waterside location with wonderful sea and mountain views, while being just a few minutes walk from Carlingford village. Michael and Glynnis Caine were previously restaurateurs, and dinner is available by arrangement for parties of eight or more. **Rooms 5** *(2 shower only). Closed 25 Dec. CC.* **Directions:** *Approaching from Dundalk, turn right just before the village and harbour; house on shore.*

 Belvedere House

Newry Street Carlingford Co Louth ✆ *042 938 3848 www.belvederehouse.ie*

Belvedere House offers attractive moderately priced accommodation above the Bay Tree Restaurant – where breakfast is served. While homely and comfortable rather than luxurious, the themed rooms have been refurbished in a pleasant country style and have all the modern facilities. **Rooms 7** *(6 shower only). CC.* **Directions:** *Centre of village.*

 **Carlingford House**

Dundalk Street Carlingford Co Louth ✆ *042 937 3118 www.carlingfordhouse.com*

Discerning visitors to Carlingford will love Peter and Irene Finegan's fine 19th century house in the heart of this charming medieval village. It offers great hospitality and a stylish mix of old and new – reception rooms are smartly traditional while bedrooms have a more contemporary airy feel. No dinners, but Irene sends guests off with an excellent breakfast. **Rooms 5** *(all shower only). Closed part of September. CC.* **Directions:** *M1 Dublin-Belfast, take Exit 18 to R173 Carlingford.*

 Food for Thought

Trinity Mews Dundalk Street Carlingford Co. Louth ✆ *042 938 3838*

Tom Hayes's gourmet store, deli and café is one of the most popular daytime eating places in the village. Everything is cooked using fresh, local ingredients where possible and great versions of crowd pleasers like lasagne, pizza, fish cakes and quiche are accompanied by a delicious range of salads. The small shop stocks artisan jams, chutneys, relishes, chocolate and delicacies of all kinds. *Open Mon-Thu & Sat 9-6, Fri 9-7, Sun 10-6. CC.*

Ghan House

Carlingford Co Louth ✆ *042 937 3682 www.ghanhouse.com*

One of the village's oldest and most interesting houses, the Carroll family's 18th century property is attractively situated in its own walled grounds on the edge of the medieval village and with views across Carlingford Lough to the Mountains of Mourne. Atmospheric rooms in the main house have sea or mountain views and an adjacent building offers newer accommodation. Guests - whether resident or in for dinner - can mingle in the welcoming bar, or relax beside the drawing room fire. As well as an evening restaurant, the Carrolls also run a cookery school here. **Rooms 12** *(1 shower only).* **Seats 60**; *non-residents welcome by reservation. D only, "most days". House closed 24-26 Dec and 31 Dec & 1-3 Jan. CC.* **Directions:** *On entering Carlingford from Dundalk direction, after 50 kph sign on left hand side.*

Kingfisher Bistro

Darcy McGee Courtyard Dundalk Road Carlingford Co Louth
✆ *042 937 3716 www.kingfisherbistro.com*

Mark and Claire Woods' appealing restaurant at the heritage centre in Carlingford has a well-earned loyal local following. An attractive space with an open kitchen and some very pleasant outside seating area, it packs a mighty punch, offering great cooking and modern menus including, of course, some tempting seafood specials. Pricing is very reasonable, including the interesting wine list. **Seats 45**. *D daily, L Sun only.* **Directions:** *Dundalk road, Carlingford.*

Magees Bistro

Tholsel Street Carlingford Co Louth ✆ *042 937 3751 www.mageesbistro.com*

This lively venue has a varied bistro menu with some unusual choices – deep fried frogs legs with herb butter, perhaps – alongside popular dishes like cajun chicken Caesar and a wide range of seafood including lobster (fairly priced), and grilled seafood platter. Extensive cocktail menu too. The ancient walls with castle windows add to the atmosphere - it's easy to see why this restaurant is so popular. *Tue-Fri, 10-3.30pm (from 1pm on Sun), D Tue-Sun 7-9. Closed Sat L and Mon.* **Directions:** *On the paved street of Tholsel, near the gate tower.*

The Oystercatcher Bistro

Market Square Carlingford Co Louth ✆ *042 937 3989 www.theoystercatcher.ie*

Lots of satisfyingly deep gutsy flavours are the hallmark of Harry and Marian Jordan's bright and stylishly simple restaurant on the square. Chef Harry describes their food as "a cornucopia of influences, spices from North Africa and the Middle East, blended with Mediterranean flavours using Irish ingredients". A refreshing alternative. **Seats 28**; *D daily (from 4pm Sun). Closed Mon & Tue in winter, 21-27 Dec, Jan. CC.* **Directions:** *In the centre of Carlingford village.*

The Oystercatcher Lodge

Market Square Carlingford Co Louth ✆ *042 937 3922 www.oystercatcherlodge.com*

Very well located, Brian and Denise McKevitt have been doing great business on the square in Carlingford village since 1996. Guest rooms are quite minimallst but bright, spacious and very clean, with all the necessary facilities. **Rooms 8** *(all shower only). CC.*

PJ O'Hares

Tholsel Street Carlingford Co Louth ✆ *042 937 3106 www.pjoharescarlingford.com*

A fine old pub whose heart seems resistant to change – a grocery at the front and an unspoilt hard-floored pub with an open fire at the back. New areas respect the spirit of the old and, while the food is not as simple as it used to be, the speciality is still Carlingford oysters – with a pint of stout of course. **Directions:** *Centre of village.*

Lily Finnegans

Carlingford area Whitestown Co Louth ✆ *042 937 3730*

What a delight this pretty, traditional pub is – although now predictably popular with a young set who bring life and plenty of noise at busy times, it is a friendly and welcoming place without a sense of cliquishness. Any visitor will feel at home here, sipping a pint or a glass of whiskey in the bar or a little room at the back that feels as if it hasn't changed in fifty years. Open evenings. *Closed 25 Dec, Good Fri.*

Derrycamma Farm Rapeseed Oil

Derrycamma Farm Castlebellingham Co Louth ✆ *087 822 3875 www.rapeseed-oil.ie*

In 2010 Carol and Patrick Rooney moved on from existing product lines (free range chickens and eggs, and traditional crops of wheat, barley and oats) to growing oilseed rape for culinary use. They have since added the first flavoured Irish rapeseed oils, infused with garlic, chilli and lemon. A fine local alternative to olive oil. From some butchers, food shops and supermarkets.

Glyde Farm Produce

Mansfield Castlebellingham Co Louth ✆ *042 937 2343 www.bellingham.ie*

Peter and Anita Thomas make their excellent semi-hard, raw milk, natural rind cheese Bellingham Blue Farmhouse Cheese here, using milk from a single herd and vegetarian rennet. This robust cheese has won many awards, including 2010 Supreme Champion Irish Cheese in the British Cheese Awards, and you will see it on some of the country's top menus. Find it, and Bellingham Bawn soft goat cheese, at speciality food stores, and local markets and festivals, or buy it from the farm.

CLOGHERHEAD

The fishing village of Clogherhead is about 12km south of Drogheda, and easily accessed from the M1 Dublin-Belfast motorway. From the Clogherhead peninsula just north of the village (designated a Natural Heritage Area under the 1997 Louth County Development Plan), there are clear views of the Cooley and Mourne Mountains to the north and to Lambay Island to the south; it is popular for many activities including, fishing, walking, sightseeing and water based activities. The village is close to the historic town of Drogheda, the Boyne Valley and Newgrange

Heritage site, and the standing stones around Newgrange are made of Clogherhead rock. Clogherhead is mainly known for fishing - the harbour, known as Port Oriel, was built in 1885 and recently extended.

 **Fishermans Catch**

Unit 4 Port Oriel The Harbour Clogherhead Co Louth ✆ *041 988 9706 www.fishermanscatch.ie*

Owned by fourth generation fisherman John Kirwan jnr, this popular fish shop is right on the harbour at Port Oriel, with the spanking fresh fish supplied by his son Jonathan, skipper of their boat Argonaut IV. The Kirwans also make their own homemade sauces and fish cakes, and a great seafood chowder - which you can buy to enjoy at the picnic table outside or to take away. *Open daily, 9-6 (including Bank Holidays).* **Directions:** *At Clogherhead Harbour.*

 Little Strand Restaurant

Strand Street Clogherhead Co Louth ✆ *041 988 1061*

Local seafood is the thing at Catherine Whelahan's popular restaurant in a neat modern building in Clogherhead village. House specialities include beautiful Clogherhead scampi, cooked and served the traditional way with sauce tartare, although a range of meat and vegetarian options is also available. Closed during the winter months. *Seats 60. Open Thu-Sun (high season) & Bank Hols, Thu & Fri 6pm-"late"; Sat & Sun all day 12-8/8.30pm (depends on demand). Closed Mon, Tue (& Wed/Thurs off-season). CC.* **Directions:** *5km from Termonfeckin village.*

DROGHEDA

A bustling town straddling the River Boyne, Drogheda is one of the most historically interesting towns in Ireland, as many groups of settlers (pre-historic, Celtic, Vikings, and Norman) were instrumental in its formation, and it is associated with many of Ireland's most significant events, the most famous being The Battle of the Boyne. Although now a Dublin commuter town, the street plan has not changed significantly since the 13th century. Local attractions that may be of interest to visitors to Drogheda include the Martello Tower and St Peter's Church, which contains the preserved head of St Oliver Plunkett, kept as a shrine to the Saint who was martyred for his faith at Tyburn, England, in 1681.

 Brown Hound Bakery

2 Bryanstown Centre Dublin Road Drogheda Co Louth ✆ *041 983 3792 www.brownhound.ie*

Jeni Glasgow and Reuven Diaz, who also own the Eastern Seaboard Bar & Grill just a few shops down, have brought their unique flair to the Brown Hound, a craft bakery with an American vibe. It has become a foodie destination for everything from cupcakes to pumpkin doughnuts, from rustic galettes to classy sandwiches. *Opens late on Thurs, Fri and Sat as The Swine Bar, serving charcuterie plates at candlelit tables. Tue–Sat, 8am-7pm; Sun 10-3; also open Thu-Sat night, as The Swine Bar. CC.* **Directions:** *Leave Drogheda (heading south) on Dublin Road, take right at traffic lights after railway station.*

 **Bru Bar Bistro**

Northbank 1 Haymarket Complex Drogheda Co Louth ✆ *041 987 2784 www.bru.ie*

This stylish and relaxed venue, located in an unusual building erected on stilts over the river, has a large bar and informal restaurant on the ground floor and an exclusive cocktail and martini bar upstairs. Trusted suppliers and local produce inform the cooking and the style is colourful, modern and family-friendly. Deservedly popular. *Seats 120 (outdoors, 40). Food served daily, 12-10.30pm (to 10pm Sun). Closed 25-26 Dec, Good Fri. CC.*

D Hotel

Scotch Hall Drogheda Co Louth ✆*041 987 7700 www.thedhotel.com*

This cool hotel is part of an impressive waterfront development in Drogheda, about 30 minutes from Dublin Airport; its contemporary lines contrast pleasingly with the old town, and the interior is bright, clean-lined and spacious. Helpful staff create a friendly atmosphere and many bedrooms have views over the river. Good facilities for business meetings and events. *Rooms 104. Open all year except Christmas. CC. Directions: The entrance to the hotel is c. 300 metres on the left adjacent to the Scotch Hall Shopping Complex.*

D'Vine Winebar & Restaurant

Distillery House Dyer Street Drogheda Co Louth ✆*041 980 0440*

There's an instant feel-good factor about Sonia Micalef and Damien Leddy's relaxed basement restaurant and wine bar. And the food is good too, in a simple Italian style that is full of flavour. Delicious desserts, good coffee - and, especially, the good-humoured staff - make for an enjoyable outing. *Seats 40. Open Wed-Sun: noon-close. Closed Mon & Tue; 25/26 Dec, 1 Jan. CC. Directions: Centre of town, northside of river.*

Eastern Seaboard Bar & Grill

1 Bryanstown Centre Dublin Road Drogheda Co Louth ✆*041 980 2570 www.easternseaboard.ie*

Husband and wife team Reuven Diaz and Jeni Glasgow offer hugely stylish modernity, professionalism and excellent food in this American-inspired venture on the edge of Drogheda. Quality food sourcing is immediately obvious in Reuven's flexible and interesting menus, and the value is great for food cooked and served with such style. Excellent children's menu also. *Seats 100. Open Mon-Sat 12-10pm, Sun 12-8.30. Closed 25 Dec, Good Fri. CC. Directions: Leave Drogheda (heading south) on Dublin Road, take right at traffic lights after railway station.*

Kirwans Fish Cart

55 Laurence Street Drogheda Co Louth ✆*041 983 0622*

The Kirwan family used to sell fish from a stall just across from the present shop, hence the name 'Kirwan's Fish Cart'; now operated by Patrick Kirwan, this popular shop offers a wide range of fresh whitefish and shellfish, mainly sourced directly from the local trawlers in Clogherhead. *Closed Sun & Mon.*

The Kitchen Restaurant

2 South Quay Drogheda Co Louth ✆*041 983 4630 www.kitchenrestaurant.ie*

Unassumingly located across the road from a shopping centre, The Kitchen on the quays in Drogheda might look like a regular bistro, but open the menu and you're in for a surprise, as its culinary style reflects the influences of Spain, Morocco, Turkey and Egypt. It offers a intriguing range of tapas, starters and mains. Strangely the Eastern Med and Middle East theme does not extend to the desserts, but the quality remains. Staff are friendly and attentive. A real find. *Open Wed-Sat 11-10; Sun 12-9.*

 **Scholars Townhouse Hotel**

King Street Drogheda Co Louth ✆ *041 983 5410 www.scholarshotel.com*

Located in a listed 19th century building in Drogheda, Martin and Patricia McGowan's small hotel creates a good impression from the outset. Although compact, the bedrooms have been sensitively modernised. A large formally appointed restaurant and a bar with a nice old-fashioned atmosphere on the ground floor offer a range of eating and drinking options, with a consistently high standard of cooking and service. **Rooms 16** *(14 shower only).* **Seats 70** *(outdoors, 24). Restaurant L & D daily. Food service 12-9.30 daily. Restaurant closed 25/26 Dec. CC.* **Directions:** *Just outside town centre.*

  Stockwell Artisan Foods

No 1 Stockwell Lane Drogheda Co Louth ✆ *041 981 0892 www.stockwellartisanfoods.ie*

Gwen Fearon and Orlaigh Callaghan, the dynamic duo behind this aptly named business, have received many accolades for their enterprise and respect for artisan producers and local suppliers informs everything they do, both at the original Stockwell Lane premises - with its outstanding grocery-deli and café next door - and the newer café-restaurant in the north quay area. Two must-visit destinations when visiting Drogheda. *Open Mon-Sat 8am-5pm. Also at: Stockwell Cafe-Restaurant, 1 Mayoralty Street, Drogheda (041 9841574).*

 The Tower Winebar & Grill

Millmount Drogheda Co Louth ✆ *041 987 3777 www.millmount.net*

Located next to the historic Millmount fort (Drogheda Museum, Millmount), you'll find the best views in town here - the conservatory offers panoramic views of the Boyne River and Drogheda area - and good food too. The small menu mainly focuses on crowd pleasers, but assured cooking elevates dishes beyond the everyday - coq au vin,for example, lifted from its rustic origins by a wild mushroom and red wine reduction. While adequate, the wine list is less extensive than expected of a wine bar. *Open for lunch and dinner.*

 Traders Coffee House

1 St Laurence Street Drogheda Co Louth ✆ *087 224 2765*

Small but mighty - everything from the coffee to the crisps in Niamh Fagan and Eoin Holmes' little café has been carefully sourced. The sandwiches aren't your usual ham and cheese – here it's Jack McCarthy's free-range dry-cured ham with an Irish artisan cheese. The music is mellow and indie, the staff relaxed and friendly. *Open Mon-Sat, 8-6.* **Directions:** *Centre of Drogheda. (Also at: 1 Railway Street, Navan, Co Meath. Tel: 087 242 4138. Open Mon-Fri 9.30-4, Sat 10-4.)*

 Dunany Organic Flour

Drogheda Area Dunany Togher Drogheda Co Louth ✆ *041 685 2242*

Fourth generation farmers Andrew and Caroline Workman have grown certified organic cereals - including low gluten rye and spelt - on their coastal farm since 2006. They later started milling it on the farm, where it's packaged in simple brown paper bags, complete with a do-able recipe that's sure to encourage new bakers. A great quality product, well worth seeking out; now distributed by the speciality artisan foods distributors, Taste The View (www.tastetheview.ie), it may be nearer than you think.

DUNDALK

The county town of Louth, Dundalk is in an area rich with historical folklore, and is convenient to the Cooley Peninsula and the charming medieval town of Carlingford on the southern shore of Carlingford Lough. Architecturally, Dundalk town is dominated by a massive seven-storey windmill, which begs restoration.

Ballymascanlon House Hotel

Carlingford Road Dundalk Co Louth ✆ *042 935 8200 www.ballymascanlon.com*

Set in 130 acres of parkland, this destination hotel has developed organically around a large Victorian house. The public areas have been renovated with considerable panache in a warm contemporary style, and the spacious bedrooms are equally attractive. Popular for business, it also offers impressive leisure facilities, including an an 18-holf golf course and a 20-metre pool. **Rooms 90**. *Open all year. CC. **Directions:** M1 from Dublin (exit 18); on the Carlingford road, 5km north of Dundalk.*

Crowne Plaza Dundalk

Green Park Dundalk Co Louth ✆ *042 939 4900 www.crowneplazadundalk.ie*

This striking modern 4* hotel, conveniently located close to the M1 halfway between Dublin and Belfast, has particular appeal for business guests. However, the area has plenty to offer leisure visitors, and the remarkable top floor Fahrenheit Rooftop Restaurant – with views over the Cooley Mountains and Irish Sea – is a local destination and booking is advisable. **Rooms 129** *(7 shower only). Fahrenheit Grill: Seats 140; D daily, L Sun only. CC. **Directions:** M1 Dundalk South exit (jct 16), continue towards Dundalk and hotel is on the left.*

Eno Bar Grill & Wood-Fired Pizza

5 Roden Place Dundalk Co Louth ✆ *042 935 5467 www.eno.ie*

This quality-focused family-friendly restaurant scores highly for tasty food at a very reasonable price. Really good basics convey the philosophy – the house minestrone, for example, is jam-packed with good things - and the wood-fired oven put to good use, and not just for pizza: it gives a special flavour to the gorgeous breads such as piadina. **Seats 85**. *Open 7 days, 12-10pm. CC. **Directions:** Directly opposite St. Patrick's Cathedral which has a large car park.*

Johnny Morgans Fish Shop

7 Eimer Court Market Square Dundalk Co Louth ✆ *042 932 7977*

This long-established family-run business was founded by Johnny Morgan and is now operated by his son Colm. Morgan's offers a wide range of fresh whitefish and shellfish sourced from the nearby port of Kilkeel. *Closed Sun & Mon.*

McKeown's Bar & Lounge

16 Clanbrassil Street Dundalk Co Louth ✆ *042 933 7931*

This well-run pub of character has a great atmosphere and friendly staff – just the place for a pint and welcome reassurance that the great Irish pub is alive and well in Dundalk. *Open daily. Food (soup & freshly made sandwiches) served daily, 10.30-6.30. Closed 25 Dec, Good Fri. No CC. **Directions:** Town centre - middle of the main street.*

Restaurant Number Thirty Two

32 Chapel Street Dundalk Co Louth ✆ *042 933 1113 www.no32.ie*

Attractively situated in a leafy corner of town, Susan Heraghty's great little place is the neighbourhood restaurant par excellence. There has always been a terrific generosity of spirit here, in quality of food and service. Also exceptionally good value, especially the early evening menu. **Seats 60**; D Mon-Sat. Closed Sun, bank hols. CC. **Directions:** *First left turn after courthouse at "home bakery".*

The Spirit Store

George's Quay The Harbour Dundalk Co Louth ✆ *042 935 2097 www.spiritstore.ie*

This pub of great character and friendliness is right on the quay where coasters dock, so you never know what country visiting sailors may come from. But everyone mixes well in the wackily-furnished bars downstairs and it's always worth popping in, even if only for a cup of tea to break a journey. Regular music sessions (often famous names) are held in the upstairs bar. Closed 25 Dec, Good Fri. CC. **Directions:** *On the quayside, beside the bridge.*

Strandfield House

Ballymascanlon Dundalk Co Louth ✆ *087 777 8750 / 042 937 1856*

Old farm sheds have found a new lease of life at Hannah Byrne's unusual farmyard venture, which includes a café showcasing local foods in tasty fare and a retail operation offering an eclection combination of products, including some of the ingredients featuring on the menu. Some tables and a patio have lovely views of the sweeping Cooley mountains and surrounding fields and there's also a flower shop. A quirky, interesting place to visit. Open Mon-Sun, 9am-6pm. CC. **Directions:** *Just outside Dundalk off R173, Carlingford road.*

Fitzpatrick's Bar & Restaurant

Dundalk Area Rockmarshall Jenkinstown Dundalk Co Louth
✆ *042 937 6193 www.fitzpatricks-restaurant.com*

Masses of well-maintained flowers draw attention to Danny and Dympna Fitzpatrick's well-run old-world bar and restaurant on the Carlingford Road. What's on offer is traditional home-cooked food (sometimes with a modern twist, notably on evening menus); the wide range offered includes a good selection of local seafood. It can seem expensive, especially at lunch time, but it is real food and portions are generous. **Seats 90** (outdoors 150). Open daily in summer, otherwise Tue-Sun 12.30 -10pm (Tue-Wed to 9pm), Sun 12.30-3.30 & 5.30-9pm. Closed Mon Oct-Apr (except bank hols), 25 Dec, Good Fri. CC. **Directions:** *Just north of Dundalk town, take Carlingford road off main Dublin-Belfast road. About 8km on left.*

Glebe Brethan

Glebe House Dunleer Co Louth ✆ *041 685 1157*

Using unpasteurised milk from Montbeliarde cows originating from the Jura region of eastern France, this extraordinary thermophilic gruyère-style cheese was produced on the family farm until recently by the late David Tiernan. Made in great 45-kilo wheels and matured for up to 18 months, this wonderful multi-award winning cheese is still available. It is distributed through Sheridans Cheesemongers (see entry) and may also be seen on restaurant menus around Ireland.

Morgans Fine Fish

Omeath Co Louth ✆ *042 937 5128 www.morgansfinefish.com*

In the fish retail business for five generations, the Morgan family has been fishing for salmon and herring since the 1890s. The present day shop, attached to the processing plant overlooking Carlingford Lough, offers a wide range of fresh whitefish and shellfish. *Closed Sun & Mon.*

TERMONFECKIN

Termonfeckin is a picturesque little village 8km (5 miles) north-east of Drogheda, and the nearby Baltray and Seapoint golf courses attract many visitors.

  ## An Grianan

Termonfeckin Co Louth ✆ *041 982 2119 www.an-grianan.ie*

Situated in parkland beside the sea, An Grianán House at Termonfeckin is an Edwardian manor held in trust by the Irish Countrywomen's Association, who use it as a residential Adult Education Centre and the programme includes cookery courses. Open to non members (men as well as women), it is available all year round for weekend, mid-week breaks and conferences (sleeps up to 125).

 ## McEvoys Farm Shop

Nunneryland Termonfeckin Co Louth ✆ *041 988 1242*

David McEvoy sells carefully reared and aged meats and is especially know for his free range poultry - both chickens and the organic free range bronze turkeys reared for Christmas. Also stocks other products, including Sowans organic bread mixes. *Closed Sun.*

 ## The Tasty Tart

Sandpit Termonfeckin Co Louth ✆ *087 98 93871 www.thetastytart.ie*

Tara Walker trained at Le Cordon Bleu in Paris and now offers cookery classes from her purpose-built kitchen in this attractive seaside village. Tara runs hands-on and demonstration classes in a fun, informal home atmosphere, where participants can relax with a glass of wine and see how dishes come together. Bespoke classes for private groups are also available. *CC.*

 ## Triple House Restaurant

Termonfeckin Co Louth ✆ *041 982 2616*

In the pretty village of Termonfeckin, Pat Fox's long-established restaurant is in a 200-year-old converted farmhouse set in gardens with mature trees. The rather neglected exterior is off-putting, the décor is overdue a makeover, and the menu may not change much, but the very reasonably priced food here is produced in a kitchen that knows what it is doing – and you can settle in front of a log fire in the reception area on cold evenings with the menu and a glass of wine. **Seats 40**. *D Tue-Sun, L Sun only. Closed Mon, Christmas. CC.* **Directions:** *8km north east of Drogheda.*

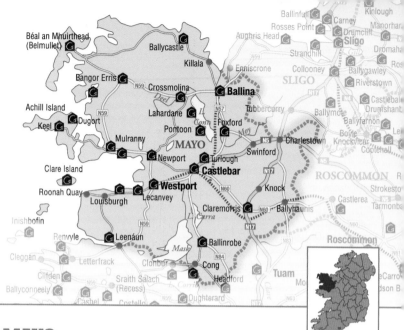

MAYO

Mayo is magnificent. All Ireland's counties have their devotees, but enthusiasts for Mayo have a devotion which is pure passion. In their heart of hearts, they feel that this austerely majestic Atlantic-battered territory is somehow more truly Irish than anywhere else. And who could argue with them after experiencing the glories of scenery, sea and sky which this western rampart of Ireland puts on ever-changing display, particularly over Achill Island.

Yet among Mayo's many splendid mountain ranges we find substantial pockets of fertile land, through which there tumble fish-filled streams and rivers. And in the west of the county, the rolling hills of the drumlin country, which run in a virtually continuous band right across Ireland from Strangford Lough, meet the sea again in the island studded wonder of Clew Bay, where the neat town of Westport is a byword for hospitality, and a key staging post on the popular Great Western Greenway Cycle Track

Along Mayo's rugged north coast, turf cutting at the Ceide Fields near Ballycastle has revealed the oldest intact field and farm system in existence, preserved through being covered in blanket bog 5,000 years ago. An award-winning interpretive centre has been created at the site, and even the most jaded visitor will find fascination and inspiration in the clear view which it provides into Ireland's distant past. A few miles eastward, the charming village of Ballycastle is home to the internationally-respected Ballinglen Arts Foundation, creative home-from-home for artists worldwide, and nearby, the lively town of Ballina is where the legendary salmon-rich River Moy meets the sea in the broad sweep of Killala Bay.

LOCAL ATTRACTIONS & INFORMATION

- ▶ **Turlough House** Castlebar
  094 9031589
- ▶ **Interpretive Centre** Ceide
  Fields *0996 43325*
- ▶ **Woollen Mills Visitor Centre**
  Foxford *094 9256756*

- ▶ **Traditional Farm Heritage
  Centre** Killasser(Swinford)
  094 9252505
- ▶ **Museum of Country Life**
  Turlough *094 9031589*

- ▶ **Great Western Greenway**
  Westport *098 25711*
- ▶ **Westport House & Children's
  Zoo** Westport
  098 25430/27766

ACHILL ISLAND

Achill island is the largest island in Ireland so don't forget to top up with fuel as you're driving on to it; there's a large service station, Lavelle's Esso Garage, on the right - and it is open on Sundays. It is a place of great beauty, with mountains, lakes, valleys, magnificent sea-cliffs, wild moors and spectacular scenery. It has a number of small attractive villages, several unpolluted sandy beaches ideal for bathing, excellent deep sea, shore and lake angling and opportunities for all kinds of outdoor activities. An interesting place that is also useful to know about is Seasamh O'Dalaigh's workshop and gallery, Dánlann Yawl (098 36137), at Owenduff (on the right coming from the mainland); it has a teashop during gallery hours, making a pleasant place for a break - and also a 2-bedroom apartment with magnificent views.

Gray's Guest House

Achill Dugort Dugort Achill Island Co Mayo ✆*098 43244 www.grays-guesthouse.ie*

A legendary guesthouse in the attractive village of Dugort, the qualities of peace and gentle hospitality have had appeal - especially to artists and writers - for a century. Bedrooms and bathrooms vary due to the age of the premises - the emphasis is on old-fashioned comfort and there are facilities for families. Residents' dinner is served in a large, quite formally appointed dining room with lovely old-fashioned cooking. **Rooms 14** *(1 with private bathroom, 13 shower only). Closed 24-26 Dec. No CC.*

The Cottage Coffee Shop

Dugort Achill Island Co Mayo ✆*098 43966*

Karan and Paul McNamara's purpose-built cottage-style restaurant is dedicated to providing quality daytime food for visitors. It is charming in its simplicity, serving wholesome, genuinely home-made food and fresh flavours. Everything is supplied locally, especially fish, and they take particular pride in their home baking. Right beside Dugort's lovely beach, this is just the kind of place that holidaymakers like best. **Seats 50** *(outdoors, 20); Open June-September. CC.*

The Beehive

Achill Keel Keel Achill Island Co Mayo ✆*098 43134*

At their informal restaurant and attractive craft shop in Keel, husband and wife team Michael and Patricia Joyce take pride in the careful preparation and presentation of the best of Achill produce, especially local seafood. Offering great all-day self-service food – which you can have indoors, or take out to a patio overlooking Keel beach – everything is home-made and baking is a speciality. The shop is interesting also, with some quality gift items and clothing lines not found elsewhere. **Seats 100** *(outdoors, 60). Meals 9.30-6pm daily, Easter-early Nov. Closed Nov-Easter. CC.* **Directions:** *Situated in the centre of Keel village overlooking beach and Minuan cliffs.*

Bervie

Achill Keel Keel Achill Island Co Mayo ✆*098 43114 www.bervieachill.com*

John and Elizabeth Barretts' magical beachside house is a low, tucked-in kind of a place with a little wicket gate giving direct access to the beach, and an other-worldliness which is very rare these days. Since 1932 it's been the ultimate escape for the many guests who have stayed here. While meals are primarily for residents, extra guests are very welcome for dinner when there is room - and it's a delightful place to call into for afternoon tea, with Elizabeth's delicious hot-buttered scones and home-made jam. **Rooms 14** *(Registration pending).* **Seats 32**.*D daily 7-8.30 (Mon closed to non-residents), Afternoon Tea daily 2-4.30. Closed early Nov-Easter.*

  Ferndale

Achill Keel Crumpaun Keel Achill Island Co Mayo ✆*098 43908 www.ferndale-achill.com*

Located on a hillside overlooking Keel Village and Bay, Jon Fratschoel's B&B must have some of the most stunning and ever-changing views in the West of Ireland. Contrasting with the rugged island setting, the flamboyant, historically themed bedrooms are lavishly furnished. A wacky place, it's very different from anything you're likely to encounter elsewhere. **Rooms 6**. **Seats 40**. *D daily in summer, 6-10.30; after Hallowe'en open weekends only (Thu-Sun) except fully open over Christmas. CC.* **Directions:** *Signed up the hill from Keel village. Take a right at the Annexe Inn, signposted on the left after 400m.*

BALLINA

The largest town in Co. Mayo dates back to the 15th Century and is home to the River Moy, internationally renowned as an exceptional salmon river. It has become a busy commercial and tourist centre, but is rich in heritage with numerous stone age tombs dotted throughout the area. Local places of interest to visit include the ruins of Moyne Abbey, the Father Peyton Memorial Centre, which shows a multimedia presentation telling the story of the Rosary Priest (0964 5374) and the 15th century Belleek Castle (0962 2400), which includes 1,000 acres of beautiful woodland on the banks of the River Moy. A street festival in July (096 70905), includes a heritage day when the town's traders transform their shop fronts to replicate the way they would have looked in Victorian times. The festival also showcases traditional foods, crafts and open air entertainment is provided. A weekly farmers' market is held at the Market Square on Saturdays (9-2 in summer. 10-2 in winter).

  **Belleek Castle**

Ballina Co Mayo ✆*096 22400 www.belleekcastle.com*

Situated just outside Ballina amidst 1,000 acres of woodland and forestry, on the banks of the River Moy, Paul Doran's castle was the ancestral home of the Earl of Arran and, with a 16th century armoury, big open fires, quirky Armada Bar and massive chandeliers, it now makes an unusual small hotel. It manages to combine old world charm with modern comforts - and, while atmospheric, the candlelit restaurant offers much more than character, as

Head Chef Stephen Lenahan's faultless cooking has made this an impressive dining destination. *Rooms 11 (5 shower only). Restaurant Seats 60, D only daily. Afternoon Tea (bar, from 2pm daily). Closed Dec-Feb. CC.* **Directions:** *Follow signs on way into Ballina for Belleek.*

 Brennans Lane

Garden Street Ballina Co Mayo ✆*096 74971 www.brennanslane.ie*

Located on the first floor of a busy bar and night-club venue in the heart of Ballina, Siobhán and Keith Brennan's restaurant is quite a hit for both its modern decor and high quality food. French Chef David Gouman's creative menus and good cooking attract a loyal clientèle, as he offers something appealing to suit everyone. Meats are Irish, and the house policy is to source fresh, local and in season. With such pleasant surroundings, seamless service and seriously good cooking, it is hardly surprising that so many customers feel that one visit is not enough. *Restaurant Tue-Sat 5-late, Sun-late. Bar food 12-5pm daily. CC.* **Directions:** *Facing the Market Square, with plenty of parking.*

  Clarkes Salmon Smokery & Seafood Delicatessen

O'Rahilly & Connolly Streets Ballina Co Mayo ✆*096 21022 www.clarkes.ie*

Renowned throughout the North-West and beyond, 'Clarke's Master Fishmongers & Salmon Smokers since 1945' is now Clarke's Seafood Delicatessen, a bright modern shop offering wines, Irish farmhouse cheeses and other speciality foods as well as ultra fresh seafood, shellfish and an innovative range of prepared seafood. Services include smoking salmon and trout for anglers, who can have their catch smoked, sliced and packaged to order. *Open Mon-Sat. 9-6. Closed Sun. Online shop.*

 Crockets on the Quay

Ballina Co Mayo ✆*096 75930 www.crocketsonthequay.ie*

The Murphy family's well-known hostelry is attractively situated on the quay in Ballina, overlooking the River Moy, with seating outside for fine weather and a pleasant old-style front bar as well as a modern one at the rear. Interesting bar meals are served all day by friendly staff and it's a hospitable place that leaps into life at night. More formal evening meals and Sunday lunch are available in the restaurant, which overlooks the river. *Seats 60 (outdoors, 40). Food Mon-Fri 4-9.30, Sat & Sun 12.30-9.30. Closed 24-26 Dec, Good Fri. CC.* **Directions:** *On the edge of Ballina; from town, take main Sligo road, turn left after the Bunree Bridge towards the Quay Village.*

🏠 🕴 ♨ ⚓ 🛜 B ♥♥ ♿ ♥ **Downhill House Hotel**

Downhill Road Ballina Co Mayo ✆*096 21033 www.downhillhotel.ie*

In the Moylett family for three generations, Downhill House Hotel is known for its hands-on hospitality and relaxed, friendly atmosphere. Quietly situated on the banks of the River Brosna, it enjoys an almost-rural location just a short walk from the town centre. A good base for fishing holidays with golf also nearby; families have on-site leisure facilities, a children's club and interesting places for outings. **Rooms 60** (5 shower only). Closed 22-27 Dec. CC. **Directions:** 1.5km from Ballina on the main Sligo road (N59).

Gaughans

O'Rahilly Street Ballina Co Mayo ☎096 70096

One of the great old bars of Ireland and in the family since 1936. It's now run as a wine bar by Edward Gaughan and his wife Mary, who is a great cook and offers homely specialities like quiche Lorraine with salad, lovely old-fashioned roasts and local seafood including open smoked salmon or crab sandwich (in season) and ploughman's lunch - all unpretentious, wholesome fare. **Seats 40**. Food served Mon-Sat, 10am-6pm (to 5pm off season). Closed Sun, bank hols, 23 Dec - 2 Jan. CC. **Directions:** Up to the post office, on the left.

Heffernans Fine Foods

4 Market Square Ballina Co Mayo ☎096 21218 www.heffernansfinefoods.com

Anthony and Geraldine Heffernan's long-established family butchers, café, deli, and bakery, Heffernans Fine Foods, has developed considerably of late. Butchery remains the core business - they have their own abattoir, and the range of fresh meats displayed in the shop is impressive. However, in addition to delicatessen fare and home bakes there is now a smart café, the Heifer & Hen, offering wide ranging menus with an emphasis on provenance. Butchers open Mon-Sat 9-6. Café D Thu-Sat 5.30-9.30, Sun 12.30-6.

The Ice House Hotel

The Quay Ballina Co Mayo ☎096 23500 www.theicehouse.ie

Bring your binoculars when heading for this quirky hotel, as the wildlife in the River Moy and wooded banks beyond your room is perhaps its most fascinating feature. The lovely 150 year old building is now a funky mix of traditional and bold contemporary design, sporting a spa and riverside hot tub. Hands-on manager Ken Bergin extends real Irish hospitality and both day time fare and destination dining are offered in the atmospheric, light-filled Pier Restaurant, where highly regarded chef, Matt Fuller, heads up the kitchen team. **Rooms 32** (4 shower only). **Seats 70** (outdoors, 40). L&D daily. Food available all day, 12.30-9.45pm. Closed 25-26 Dec. CC. **Directions:** N59 to Ballina, through town, turn down by the river.

Market Kitchen at Murphy Brothers

Clare Street Ballina Co Mayo ☎096 78538 www.marketkitchen.ie

Above Murphy Brothers buzzy bar, overlooking the River Moy, is one of Ballina's best restaurants. Run by husband and wife team Susan Walsh and chef Kieran Sweeney, fresh, seasonal and local is the motto - and the quality and value offered explain its popularity. Great cooking is key but friendly, efficient service, a proper children's menu and a good wine list also add to the appeal of this attractive restaurant. Open: Tue- Sat 3-9; Sun 1-9 (L1-3). CC.

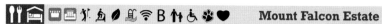 **Mount Falcon Estate**

Foxford Road Ballina Co Mayo ✆096 74472 www.mountfalcon.com

Once a romantic family home, Mount Falcon is now a 32-bedroom luxury hotel with some beautiful period features. Accommodation is mainly modern but includes six deluxe rooms in the original house with original features. The 100-acre estate offers double bank salmon fishing on the River Moy and lovely lakeside and woodland walks. The classically appointed restaurant is in the original kitchen, storeroom and pantry; with Philippe "Irish Produce, French Heart" Farineau cooking you should have a treat in store. **Rooms 32**. Self catering also available. **Seats 72** *(outdoors, 20). L&D daily. Bar menu daily, 12.30-7pm. Hotel closed 24/25 Dec, Jan. CC.* **Directions:** *Look out for discreet black and white signage on the right, about 6.5km outside Ballina on the N26 to Foxford.*

 **Enniscoe House**

Ballina Area Castlehill Ballina Co Mayo ✆096 31112 www.enniscoe.com

In parkland and mature woods on the shores of Lough Conn, Susan Kellett's charming and historic Georgian mansion offers crackling log fires, warm hospitality and good home cooking. A very special place for anglers and all with an empathy for the untamed wildness of the area, its large public rooms have period style, and Susan's delightfully simple dinners are served in the intimate dining room. Converted outbuildings offer a genealogy centre, small agricultural museum with working blacksmith, and conference facilities, and the restored wall gardens (with tea rooms) are open to the public. **Rooms 6.** Restaurant: **Seats 20**. *D daily, non-residents welcome by reservation. Closed Oct-Mar. CC.* **Directions:** *3km south of Crossmolina on R315.*

 Devour Bakery

3 Church Lane Ballinrobe Co Mayo ✆094 952 1626 www.devourbakery.net

Yvonne and James Murphy's slightly scarily named Devour Bakery turns out to be a little honey once you get there, with cheery greetings for the steady stream of customers coming in to buy from their daily baking of delicious breads, scones and pastries, to enjoy a coffee and a bun at one of the two tables squeezed into this little shop, or to collect or order the special occasion cakes that attract business from a wide area. A great place to know about.

BALLYCASTLE

Ballycastle, 'the town of the stone fortress', is on the scenic rugged coast of north Mayo, where sandy beaches and towering cliffs are exposed to the force of the Atlantic Ocean. An unspoilt small town, with a rich history going back 5000 years and many historical sites including megalithic tombs, early Christian and medieval ruins, its special attraction is the nearby Ceide Fields Interpretive Centre (096 43325) which was built at the world's most extensive stone age monument; here, preserved beneath the wild blanket bog, is a 5000 year old landscape of farms, stone dwellings and megalithic tombs. The surrounding area of Ballycastle lies largely untouched, with a variety of natural habitats including bog, mountains, meadows, rocky shores, cliffs and beaches. Simplicity, natural beauty and remoteness are the unique attractions of this area, which has attracted a vibrant artistic community (Ballinglen Arts Foundation; 096 43184/43366) but there are plenty of active pursuits too, including swimming, scuba diving, excellent shore angling, bog rambling and hill walking, and horse riding at the Heathfield Stables (096 43350). Golfers can play world class championship links golf to the east at Enniscrone Golf Club (096 36297) or to the west in Belmullet (Carne Golf Links, 097 82292).

Mary's Bakery & Tea Rooms

Main Street Ballycastle Co Mayo ✆ *096 43361*

Mary Munnelly's homely little restaurant is the perfect place to stop for some tasty home cooking. Baking is the speciality but she does "real meals" as well - a full Irish breakfast, which is just the thing for walkers, home-made soups and free-range chicken dishes. If you strike a chilly day, it's very pleasant to get tucked in beside a real fire - and there's also a garden with sea views for fine weather. *Seats 30 (outdoors 12). Open 10am-6pm daily in summer (may open later - to 8-ish - in high season; shorter hours off season). Closed Sun off-season (Oct-Easter), & first 3 weeks Jan. No CC. Directions: Centre of Ballycastle.*

Stella Maris Country House Hotel

Ballycastle Co Mayo ✆ *096 43322 www.stellamarisireland.com*

Formerly a coastguard regional headquarters and then a convent - and named Stella Maris by the Sisters of Mercy - the hospitable owners Terence McSweeney and Frances Kelly have made this fine property into a very special small hotel, with a warm and stylish interior. Comfortable bedrooms and a vast conservatory take full advantage of the majestic sea views. Frances's good cooking is based on local ingredients, organic produce from nearby Enniscoe and also from the hotel's gardens, making breakfast and dinner very enjoyable experiences. *Rooms 12 (6 shower only). Restaurant seats 26. D 7-9, non-residents welcome (reservations recommended). Restaurant closed Mon (to non-residents); hotel closed Oct-Mar. Closed Oct-Apr. CC. Directions: West of Ballina on R314; 2km west of Ballycastle.*

BELMULLET

Positioned on the strip of land between Blacksod and Broadhaven bays, Belmullet is the entrance to the Mullet peninsula, a district of untouched beauty with many secluded beaches and coves and a number of islands off its coast. (Inishkea Island Tours; 097 85741) The town is a centre for shopping, serving the Erris region, and is one of the leading sea angling centres in Europe with both excellent shore and deep sea fishing available, and also excellent fresh water angling in the many local lakes and rivers, all with healthy stocks of salmon and trout. Nearby heritage sites of interest to the visitor include megalithic tombs, Iron Age cliff forts and castles from the 16th, 17th, and 18th century. Golfers relish the challenge of the 18 hole championship links course at Carne (097 82292), whilst other local activities on offer include walking, abseiling, pony trekking, scuba diving, windsurfing, sailing and canoeing.

Broadhaven Bay Hotel

Ballina Road Belmullet Co Mayo ✆ *097 20600 www.broadhavenbay.com*

This large three-star hotel enjoys commanding views over Broadhaven Bay and offers not only accommodation but extensive bar, restaurant and banqueting facilities - all much needed services in the area. Well appointed bedrooms, friendly, helpful staff and a leisure centre and spa make this is a comfortable place to be based when visiting this beautiful and remote area. *Rooms 90. CC. Directions: On the road into Belmullet.*

Talbot Hotel

Barrack Street Belmullet Co Mayo ✆ *097 20484 www.thetalbothotel.ie*

Situated in the heart of one of Ireland's furthest flung towns this friendly place has long been popular for its famous bar, An Chéibh ("the anchor"). It now also offers luxurious accommodation with glamorous decor that's far from traditional. The Barony restaurant, where breakfast is served, is the in-place in the area for special meals - which naturally favours local seafood. *Restaurant seats 40, open Wed-Sat 6.30-9.30pm. Bar food daily, 7.30am (from 8am Sat/Sun) to 9pm in summer, to 8pm in winter. Rooms 21. Bar/rest closed Good Fri, hotel closed 25 Dec. CC. Directions: Hotel on the left on main entrance into Belmullet.*

CASTLEBAR

This bustling market was originally a garrison town, deriving its name from a settlement around the De Barra Castle in the 11th century. Its central location is ideal for touring the county and visiting local attractions such as Ballintubber Abbey (094 903 0934), the Céide Fields (096 43325), Croagh Patrick mountain and the Foxford Woollen Mills (094 925 6756, open all year). Visitors can take a guided historical walk around the town or can pay a visit to the 18th century Turlough Park House (094 903 1755), which is home to the National Museum of Country Life and the grounds include formal gardens and an artificial lake. Reflecting the area's strong artistic tradition, the Castlebar Linenhall Arts Centre (094 9023733) is an interesting place to visit, and the energetic will find plenty of outdoor pursuits available locally, including cycling, horse riding, walking, golf and fishing. After a tiring day of exploring the area, visitors could consider a trip to the Kachina Natural Spa in Mayo Leisure Point (094 902 7110).

                                                                    Bar One Gastro Pub

Rush Street Castlebar Co Mayo ✆094 903 4800

In the same family ownership as Dublin's stylish Saba (see entry), Mark Cadden's gastropub is the busiest bar food venue in the Castlebar area. Modern and well designed, the welcome is warm and friendly with high standards maintained throughout. Daytime specials change daily, with gluten free and vegetarian versions of several dishes offered, and children are well catered for. At weekend this is Castlebar's nighttime hotspot. *Seats 80; food served all day Mon-Sat 12-9pm. No food on Sun, Bank Hol Mon. CC. Directions: Around the corner from the Linenhall Arts Centre (turn left).*

                                                                              Café Rua

New Antrim Street Castlebar Co Mayo ✆094 902 3376 www.caferua.com

Ann McMahon's vision was very clear when she set up here over a decade ago and, while she is still very involved, it must be rewarding to see her son and daughter, Aran and Colleen McMahon, carrying on and developing the philosophy - they are very serious about the food they serve, but the tone is light-hearted. Wholesome, home-made fresh food is the order of the day - and careful sourcing of ingredients is a point of pride. There's an interesting drinks menu and 'because we know that they love food too', there's also a special children's menu, one of many thoughtful touches. *Seats 35. Open Mon-Sat, 9am-6pm. Closed Sun; Bank Hols, 1 week at Christmas. CC. Directions:Near the Linenhall Arts & Exhibition Centre and Welcome Inn, opposite Supervalu carpark.*

                                                                      Helena Chocolates

8 Cavendish Lane Castlebar Co Mayo ✆094 902 2755 www.helenachocolates.ie

Having lived here for over a quarter of a century, Dirk Schonkeren is by now an honorary Mayo man. Together with his wife Elaine, this Belgian chef and chocolatier was one of the pioneers in Irish chocolate making when they first set up business in 1980s Castlebar. Alongside beautiful handmade chocolates, cakes, desserts and one-off pieces, they also run their shop and café as 'a chocolate experience'. Online sales & telephone mail order service offered.

Rua Café & Deli

Spencer Street Castlebar Co Mayo ℰ*094 928 6072 www.caferua.com/ourshop-deli.shtml*

The younger retail sister of the McMahon family's excellent Café Rua on New Antrim Street, this brilliant deli & café stocks a wide range of the delicious foods and ingredients that have been served in the café for over a decade. International speciality foods feature too, of course, but most local of all, there are the foods they make themselves - including a range of chutneys, relishes and dressings. *Closed Sun & bank hols. CC.* **Directions:** *Near courthouse & the mall.*

Cuinneog Dairy Products

Castlebar Area Shraheen's Balla Castlebar Co Mayo ℰ*094 903 1425 www.cuinneog.com*

Thanks to the Butler family, who farm near Castlebar, Mayo is home to some once familiar dairy products, which had all but disappeared but are now beginning to be made again – Irish farmhouse country butter and natural buttermilk. The butter, especially, has caught the public imagination, because country butter was once made routinely on most small-scale Irish dairy farms and both of these fuller-flavoured products have attracted well-earned acclaim. Available from good supermarkets and speciality food stores; also on some restaurant menus.

Clare Island Organic Salmon

Clare Island Co Mayo ℰ*074 919 2820*
www.marineharvest.com/en/products1/Atlantic-salmon/Organic-Salmon/

With the ever-growing threat to fish stocks in the wild this operation in Clew Bay, six miles off the Mayo coast, is an encouraging success story. Produced at the world's most exposed salmon farm, in pure waters where the Atlantic tidal exchange provides strenuous exercise, it is renowned for its superb flavour, lean flesh and firm muscle texture. Certified organic since 1997 the consistently excellent quality makes Clare Island salmon an ingredient of choice for leading restaurants and fish smokers.

The Food Store

Ballyhaunis Road Claremorris Co Mayo ℰ*094 936 2091*

Easily spotted by its smart facade, quality is key at Niall Heffernan's thriving store. It began as Heffernan Meats and is still known especially for quality meat, but this surprising place is actually a latter day version of the traditional country shop that stocked everything. There's an in-house bakery, a deli section specialising in home cooked meats, fresh local organic produce and a carefully selected range of niche products including organic ranges - and a second store at the town's Silverbridge Shopping Centre. *Open Mon-Thus 7.45-6.30,Fri-Sat 7.45-7, Sun 9-5.*

Old Arch Bar & Bistro

James Street Claremorris Co Mayo ℰ*094 936 2777 www.theoldarchbistro.com*

Fergus and Anne Maxwell's inviting bar and informal restaurant has a welcoming atmosphere in the comfortable, low-ceilinged reception area and bar. The restaurant is relaxed and friendly, portions are generous, the cooking is good and prices are moderate: ideal for a family-friendly restaurant in a growing town. There's a large garden area too, with gas heaters, barbecue and plenty of seating. **Seats 80** *(outdoors, 30). L &D daily. Pub food served 12-9pm daily. Closed 25-26 Dec, Good Fri. CC.* **Directions:** *Beside railway bridge, on the main street.*

The Bay Leaf

Castlebar Area Horkan's Garden Ctre Turlough Co Mayo ✆094 928 9743 *www.thebayleaf.ie*

A few hundred metres along the road from the wonderful Museum of Country Life, Horkan's is a garden centre with a difference, offering happy hours of browsing for garden and homewares - and the delightful bright and airy Bay Tree restaurant, serving good food. Some local and artisan foods feature in carefully prepared dishes that taste as good as they look. A useful place to know about. *Open 7 days. Mon-Sat, 9.30-6. Sun, 12-6. CC.*

Derrymore Farmhouse

Claremorris Area Derrymore Partry Claremorris Co Mayo ✆094 954 3173

About a kilometre from Partry on the road to Westport, you'll see The Blue Teapot signposted on the left turnoff for Tourmakeady. This will lead you to Derrymore Farm farm (known locally as The Blue Teapot) where Vincent and Manita van Dulmen serve wonderful homemade breads, scones, tarts and so on in their little daytime café and sell their own products such as cheese and honey. It's a gem for walkers, and fun for visitors to find. *Open 10.30-6 daily in summer.*

CONG

This picturesque village on the edge of Connemara is beautifully situated on Lough Corrib, and world-famous as the setting for the John Wayne film 'The Quiet Man'. Guided tours and memorabilia associated with the film are an inevitable feature today, but there is more to Cong than The Quiet Man: historical sites include Cong Abbey, the remnants of the Augustinian abbey founded in the 12th century by Turlough O'Connor, King of Connaught and High King of Ireland. Ashford Castle & Gardens south of Cong is worth a visit just to see the beautiful estate. Cong is an excellent base for golfers who want to play some of the best golf courses in the west of Ireland, not only the course at Ashford Castle, but Westport Golf Club (098 28262), and also championship links at Connemara (095 23502/23602), Enniscrone Golf Club (096 36297) and Galway Bay Golf Club (098 36262). A wealth of other activities on offer includes boat cruises, horse riding, canoeing and walking in the rich diverse landscape of the west taking in rivers, lakes, mountains and forests. Cong River also provides the keen angler with excellent salmon and brown trout fishing.

Ashford Castle

Cong Co Mayo ✆094 954 6003 *www.ashford.ie*

Set in 350 acres Ireland's grandest castle hotel dates back to the early 13th century. Grandeur, formality and tranquillity are the essential characteristics, from the immaculately maintained grounds to the impressive public rooms and luxurious accommodation. The hotel is noted for its extensive outdoor pursuits, attentive service and good food - Executive Head Chef, Stefan Matz, has won many accolades for the hotel and he's a keen supporter of artisan producers and independent suppliers. The castle has three restaurants: The Connaught Room (private hire only); the George V Dining Room, which offers pricey fine dining and Cullen's Cottage, in the grounds, which offers accessible all-day informal dining. **Rooms 83**. *George V Dining Room:* **Seats 160**. *D daily. Cullen's at the Cottage: Seats 65 (outdoors 48). Open daily high season, a phone call to check is advised, especially off-season. Hotel open year round. Cullens at the Cottage, closed Oct-May. CC.* **Directions:** *Signed from Cong.*

 **Ballywarren Country House**

Cross Cong Co Mayo ☎094 954 6989 www.ballywarrenhouse.com

Diane and David Skelton's hospitable country house is in a pleasant rural area of gentle farming countryside, near Cong and Ashford Castle. Large and well proportioned, with just three charming bedrooms, it has a welcoming feeling from the minute you arrive. Diane and David have received many accolades for their food and a wholesome five-course dinner based on seasonal local ingredients is served, by arrangement, in the lovely Garden Room. *Rooms 3. Residents' D is by arrangement only at time of booking. Closed 2 weeks Apr, 2 weeks Oct. CC.* **Directions:** *East of Cong, on the Headford road.*

 Hungry Monk Café

Abbey Street Cong Co Mayo ☎094 954 5842

Fiona McMahon's attractive all-day café is just the place to drop in for a wholesome meal or snack in this delightful village, at any time of day. Cottagey and friendly, it has rough walls and brightly coloured mismatched chairs giving it a relaxed and homely feeling, and there's a great aroma of really good coffee as you arrive–perfect to go with the gorgeous home bakes for which this pleasant café is renowned. *Seats 30; summer hours Easter- end August, Mon-Sat, 10-6pm & Sun 11-5pm. Closed Jan/Feb. CC.* **Directions:** *Centre of Cong village.*

 **Lisloughrey Lodge**

The Quay Cong Co Mayo ☎094 954 5400 www.lisloughreylodge.com

The heart of this boutique hotel is a fine period house, which offers the best accommodation and views down Lough Corrib, however rooms - and especially the junior suites - in the new development are comfortable and stylish, and there's a great hot tub too. At Wildes Restaurant head chef Jonathan Keane serves wonderfully imaginative cuisine based on the best seasonal local produce. Backed up by an interesting wine list and knowledgeable service in a lovely space, you may expect a special dining experience. *Seats 56. D daily; L Sun only. Bar food daily, 12.30-10pm. Closed 24-28 Dec. CC.* **Directions:** *Just outside Cong, on Ashford Castle estate.*

FOXFORD

Nestling between the Ox and Nephin mountains, Foxford is situated on the River Moy, famous for its fishing. Foxford is synonymous with woollens, especially 'the Foxford blanket'; established in 1892, vistors today will find a newly revitalised business at Foxford Woollen Mills Visitor Centre (094 925 6104; www.museumsofmayo.com/foxford) which is very much the centre of the local community and hosts a café, two art galleries, a jewellery workshop, Christmas Craft Fair and Saturday Farmers' Market as well as showcasing their own updated ranges of homewares and clothing.

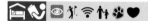 **Pontoon Bridge Hotel**

Pontoon Foxford Co Mayo ☎094 925 6120 www.pontoonbridge.com

The Geary family have run this friendly and beautifully located hotel since 1964. Extensive public areas make the most of the setting – notably in the Waterfront Bar, (music on some nights), and two restaurants. Rooms vary a great deal, however, so it is necessary to discuss your requirements when booking – many of the better ones have private terraces or balconies. Activity breaks include cookery courses. *Rooms 58 (2 shower only). Closed 23-27 Dec. CC.*

Tiernan Brothers

Upper Main Street Foxford Co Mayo ✆*094 925 6731 www.themoy.com*

For many, angling is the lifeblood of Co Mayo and the River Moy is its heart. A one stop shop of a very different kind is Michael and PJ Tiernan's 'Mayo Angling Advice Centre', an extraordinary place with a century and a half's experience of providing everything that could possibly be needed by anglers hoping to bag one of the noble river's wild Atlantic salmon or sea trout. *Online shop.*

Leonard's

Lahardane Ballina Co Mayo ✆*096 51003*

This unspoilt roadside traditional pub and grocery shop was established in 1897 and continues as the centre of local activities. There's a large dining area behind the pub, where all the area's get-togethers take place – if only those walls could talk. And, if you get hungry when travelling, there's always the makings of a picnic on the shelves. *Closed 25 Dec & Good Fri.*

T.Staunton

Lecanvey Westport Co Mayo ✆*098 64850/64891*

Thérèse Staunton runs this great little pub near the beginning of the ascent to Croagh Patrick – genuinely traditional, with an open fire, it has the feeling of a real 'local'. Not really a food place, but homemade soup and sandwiches or plated salads are available every day until 9pm. Occasional traditional music sessions - and frequent impromptu sing-songs. *Closed 25 Dec & Good Fri. No CC.* **Directions:** *12.5km from Westport on Louisburgh Road.*

Hudson's Pantry

Long Street Louisburgh Co Mayo ✆*098 23747 www.hudsonspantry.ie*

Richard and Tricia Hudson ran the highly regarded Hudson's Bistro, in Navan Co Meath, for many years before 'retiring' to Co Mayo. But here they are, back at their old tricks with Hudson's Pantry, a lovely unpretentious place near the Diamond serving honest food with international influences. Wonderful home-made desserts, a proper children's menu and interesting wine list complete the attraction. *Seats 24*. D Mon-Sat from 4.30pm; check for off season times. Closed Sun; 2 weeks Oct & Jan. CC. **Directions:** On the square.

MULRANNY

This tranquil seaside village is located on the strip of land between Clew Bay and Blacksod bay, home to colourful giant fuchsias and exotic plants - a rich natural heritage which is celebrated each summer during the Mulranny Mediterranean Heather festival. Mulranny is on Ireland's longest off road cycling and walking route, the Great Western Greenway (www.greenway.ie), and has a blue flag sandy beach, which is ideal for swimming and shore fishing. The Corraun Peninsula offers three mountain peaks with incredible views, and golfers will enjoy the links at Mulranny Golf Course (098 36262).

Mulranny Park Hotel

Mulranny Westport Co Mayo ✆ *098 36000 www.mulrannyparkhotel.ie*

Set in wooded grounds, this former railway hotel dates back to 1897 (the line is now the Great Western Greenway walking and cycling route) and, while mainly modern, has retained some of its original character. Rooms are well appointed and amenities include a 20-metre pool, but the central focus is food: Head Chef, Ollie O'Regan, has been closely involved with the development of the Gourmet Greenway (showcasing the wonderful artisan food in the vicinity) and his commitment to local produce is reflected in lovely menus served, notably in the elegant Nephin Restaurant with stunning views. *Rooms 61 (7 shower only). Restaurant seats 50; D daily. Waterfront Bistro: Seats 80; food 12.30-9pm. Bar food, 12-9pm. Closed 18-26 Dec. CC.* **Directions:** *In Mulranny village on the N59.*

Nevins Newfield Inn

Tiernaur Mulranny Co Mayo ✆ *098 36959 www.nevinsinn.com*

While John and Anne Nevin's pleasant traditional pub is known for the wholesome, generous fare served throughout the day, the real USP is genuine hospitality – nothing is ever too much trouble here, and every visitor is truly welcome. Cosy, with a real turf fire, there's also outside seating for fine weather dining and varied menus offer something for everyone. *Seats 70, Open Mon-Sun 9am-9pm. CC.* **Directions:** *On the main road N59, between Newport and Mulranny.*

A Taste of Days Gone By

Furnace Newport Co Mayo ✆ *098 41717 www.pattishomemadejam.com*

Patti Moss's background is in marketing and - with recipes inspired by her Irish grandmother's cookery book and products all named after friends and relatives - her experience is put to good use in this relatively young company. Her flavoursome handmade jams, marmalade, relishes, sauces, and salad dressings are much in demand. *Available from: Sligo, Johnston Court (Wed), Castkebar farmers' market (Fri), Ballina farmers' market (Sat). Online shop.*

NEWPORT

This pleasant town on the Brown Oak River is well known as an angling centre, and close to the attractive and unspoilt coastline of Clew Bay famous for its 365 islands. Anglers have a wide choice of lake and river fishing, (on loughs Feegh and Furnace, the Newport River and Lough Beltra) and boats for deep sea fishing can be chartered from Clew Bay. Walkers will enjoy varied trails over mountains and hills, including cultural/historical tours such as the Old Bangor Trail Walk (48km), which is regarded as one of the finest walks in the country.

The Blue Bicycle Tea Rooms

Main Street Newport Co Mayo ✆ *096 984 1145*

The Great Western Greenway brings a lot of people to Newport, and many visitors who are looking for a bite to eat while they're passing through the town head straight here, to Phil Chambers' delightful old-world tea room. In an impressive stone building with steps leading up to it, this atmospheric spot is a real blast from the past, with its dainty china and home baking, but the focus on local and home grown ingredients is timeless. *Open 10.30-6 daily to end Sep.* **Directions:** *Top of the main street, opposite Kellys butchers.*

Kelly's of Newport

Main Street Newport Co Mayo ✆*098 41149 www.kellysbutchers.com*

An excellent traditional butchers with a licensed abattoir where they slaughter all their own locally sourced lamb and beef, Kelly's of Newport has been in the family since the 1930's and the larger-than-life Sean Kelly is one of Ireland's most famous butchers. Although many of their products are now widely distributed, people love the shop and travel great distances for a bit of banter and to buy Kelly's multi-award-winning black and white puddings and sausages – and, especially, their traditional 'putog' black pudding, a unique product similar to haggis. Kelly's innovative Greenway Pudding celebrates the Gourmet Greenway Food Trail (which goes through Newport), its magic ingredient is seaweed from the nearby Atlantic shoreline and it sports a map of the Greenway trail on the label. How could you resist? *Open: Mon-Thu 9-7, Fri-Sat 8-8. CC.*

Newport House

Newport Co Mayo ✆*098 41222 www.newporthouse.ie*

Kieran Thompson's distinctive creeper-clad Georgian house was once the home of the O'Donnells, Earls of Tir Connell. Today this riverside gem symbolises all that is best about the Irish country house, and has been close to the hearts of fishing people for many years. John Gavin, head chef since 1983, is one of Ireland's unsung food heroes; the lovely dining room makes the perfect backdrop for "cooking which reflects the hospitable nature of the house" in fine meals made with home-produced and local foods - and Kieran's renowned wine list adds an extra magic. **Rooms 16** *(2 with private (non connecting) bathrooms).* **Seats 38**. *L & D daily. Non-residents welcome by reservation. House closed 1 Nov-18 Mar. CC.* **Directions:** *In village of Newport.*

WESTPORT

A great example of good town planning - Westport was designed by the Georgian architect James Wyatt - this charming town is a delightful place to spend some time: The Mall, with its lime trees flanking the Carrowbeg River, is especially pleasing to the eye, and nearby Westport House is open to the public in summer and well worth a visit. High standards of accommodation and restaurants in and around Westport make it a very agreeable base, and there is plenty to do in the surrounding area - Achill Island is just a short drive, for example, and the Great Western Greenway (www.greenway.ie) offers Ireland's longest off-road walking and cycle route.

An Port Mór

1 Brewery Place Bridge Street Westport Co Mayo ✆ *098 26730 www.anportmor.com*

Named after the proprietor-chef's home town, Portmor House in Blackwatertown, Co Armagh, Frankie Mallon delights customers with his no nonsense cooking. Acknowledged as cooking some of the best food in the area, noted for good saucing and great flavour, he is clearly achieving his stated aim: 'to give the customer the very best in local fresh produce and value for money'. Front of house staff are locals with a knowledge of the food producers featured on the menu; there's a strong emphasis on fish and, true to Euro-Toques principles, suppliers are enthusiastically credited. **Seats** *34. D Tue-Sun. Closed Mon.* **CC. Directions**: *Half way up Bridge Street in Brewery Lane opposite McCormack's butchers.*

Ardmore Country House Hotel

The Quay Westport Co Mayo ✆ *098 25994 www.ardmorecountryhouse.com*

Pat and Noreen Hoban's small family-run hotel is quietly located in immaculately maintained gardens near Westport harbour, with views over Clew Bay, and it offers warm hospitality, very comfortable accommodation and good food. Spacious, individually decorated guest rooms are furnished to hotel standard and Pat offers accomplished evening meals with charming service in the long-established fine dining restaurant - where an outstandingly good breakfast is also served. **Rooms** *13.* **Seats 50**. *D 7-9 (daily in summer). Closed Nov-Mar. CC.* **Directions:** *1.5 kms from Westport town centre, on the coast road.*

Carlton Atlantic Coast Hotel

The Quay Westport Co Mayo ✆ *098 29000 www.atlanticcoasthotel.com*

Behind the traditional stone facade of an old mill on Westport harbour, this bright modern hotel has good-sized bedrooms, and an excellent leisure centre and spa. Staff are exceptionally friendly and efficient and the hotel's Fishworks Café-bar offers mainly seafood menus with reliable cooking. **Rooms 85**. *Restaurant* **seats 90**. *Food served 12.30-9 daily. Closed 22-27 Dec. CC.* **Directions:** *Located at Westport harbour, 1.5km from town centre on main Louisburgh road.*

Clarkes Seafood Delicatessen

Lower Peter Street The Octoagon Westport Co Mayo ✆ *098 24379 www.clarkes.ie*

In the centre of town beside the Octagon, you'll find the Westport branch of the Clarke brothers' renowned Ballina business (see entry). Ultra fresh fish and seafood, of course, along with a great range of wines and deli fare headed up by their smoked salmon. Look out for the local Gouda-style cheese, Carrowholly, made just outside the town by Andrew Pelham-Byrne. *Open Tue-Sat, 10-6. Closed Sun & Mon.*

Hotel Westport

Newport Rd *Westport Co Mayo* ✆ *098 25122 www.hotelwestport.ie*

Just a short stroll from Westport town centre, this well run modern hotel offers excellent facilities for both tourists and business guests. Extensive leisure facilities are a major attraction for families, who also appreciate the kids club (summer and mid term). Spacious rooms are regularly refurbished and the hotel's Islands Restaurant serves upbeat traditional menus, which are imaginative for a hotel and strong on local ingredients. Service is charming and efficient. **Rooms 129**. Restaurant **seats 140**; D daily; L Sun only. Bar food also served daily, 12-9.30pm. Open all year. CC. **Directions:** From Castlebar Street, turn right onto north mall (do not go over the hump back bridge), then turn onto Newport Road, 1st left and at the end of the road.

Kate McCormack & Sons

Bridge Street *Westport Co Mayo* ✆ *098 25619*

John McCormack is currently the main man at Kate McCormack's sixth generation butchers shop in Westport and not only is this Associated Craft Butchers of Ireland member continuing the tradition of supplying the people of Westport with excellent meats, but his locally reared meats go into specialities in the family restaurant upstairs - like bacon and cabbage, and a casserole of spring lamb - and many of the deli dishes from the shop are also on the menu.

Knockranny House Hotel

Knockranny *Westport Co Mayo* ✆ *098 28600 www.khh.ie*

Set in landscaped grounds overlooking Westport town, Adrian and Geraldine Noonan's Victorian-style hotel offers spacious bedrooms, many with fine views of Croagh Patrick, and excellent leisure facilities including treatment rooms, a swimming pool, gym, and hair salon. A popular short break destination and wedding venue, the hotel has an enviable reputation for good food at La Fougère, where critically acclaimed Euro-Toques chef Seamus Commons favours local ingredients and classic French techniques. His showpiece special occasion meals are renowned and the eight-course tasting menu is a culinary highlight; with a professional front-of-house team, and extensive wine list, this has become a destination restaurant. **Rooms 97**. Restaurant **seats 120**. L&D daily. Hotel closed 22-27 Dec. CC. **Directions:** Take N5/N60 from Castlebar. Hotel is on the left just before entering Westport.

Mangos Restaurant

Bridge Street Westport Co Mayo ✆*098 24999 www.mangoswestport.com*

Owned by chefs Pat Kelly and Peter Carroll, you can't miss the bright blue frontage of this cosy and welcoming restaurant at the top of Westport's main street. Fish is very much to the forefront on extensive menus that offer something for everyone. The food is good and the friendly, efficient staff are local or in Westport for a good number of years, which adds to the atmosphere. There is a great buzz and this is a place where everybody seems to have a good experience. **Seats around 40**; D Mon-Sat. Closed Sunday. CC. **Directions:** Top of Bridge Street on the left going up the hill.

  Marlenes Chocolate Haven

James Street Car Park James Street Westport Co Mayo ✆*098 24564 www.chocolatehaven.net*

Handmade with the best Belgian chocolate, Marlene's Chocolates offer a range of sweet indulgences, with no additives or preservatives added. Wedding favours, children's party novelties and corporate gifts are a speciality and there's a wide range to choose from in the shop, along with a café offering diabetic chocolates, a range of coffees and the speciality of the house - Marlene's Hot Chocolate. *Open Mon-Sat 9.30-6. Closed Sun.*

 Matt Molloy's Bar

Bridge Street Westport Co Mayo ✆*098 26655*

If you had to pick one pub in this pretty town, this soothingly dark atmospheric one would do very nicely - not least because it is owned by Matt Molloy of The Chieftains, a man who clearly has respect for the real pub: no TV (and no children after 9 pm). Note that it's an afternoon into evening place, not somewhere for morning coffee. *Closed 25 Dec & Good Fri.*

  McCormack's at The Andrew Stone Gallery

Bridge Street Westport Co Mayo ✆*098 25619*

Above Kate McCormack's sixth generation butchers shop (see entry) this small, unpretentious restaurant showcases works by local artists and serves soups, quiches, patés and home-baked cakes, the product of generations of family recipes and particularly of Annette McCormack's table. Here, her two daughters, Katrina and Mary Claire, carry on the tradition. Simple everyday dishes that might be quite ordinary elsewhere are memorable here, thanks to the quality of the ingredients used and the care taken in their preparation. Don't leave without one of the gloriously home-made desserts. **Seats 34**. *Open all day 10.15am-4.45pm, Thu-Sat and Mon. Closed Sun & Wed. CC.* **Directions:** *Westport town centre - on the main street.*

The Pantry & Corkscrew

Peter Street The Octagon Westport Co Mayo ☎*098 26977 www.thepantryandcorkscrew.com*

Dermott Flynn and Janice O'Rourke's little café-restaurant offers 'a small food menu and some good wine selections', with everything made on the premises and plenty of local produce. Dermott's cooking is good, and so is the value and quality, while Janice's very pleasant and helpful service helps the restaurant to give off a cosy, comfortable feeling - in tune with their aim 'to bring a casual and fresh slow food dining experience to the town'. **Seats 24**. *L & D Tue-Sun. Closed Mon. CC.* **Directions:** *On Peter Street just off the Octagon.*

 Quay Cottage Restaurant

The Harbour Westport Co Mayo ☎*098 50692 www.quaycottage.com*

Run by the original owner, Kirstin McDonagh, together with a previous manager, Pascal Sonal, and chef Michel Nagy, a native of Paris, this atmospheric restaurant on Westport harbour's charming quayside is a key destination for diners in the Westport area. The cooking is impressive, showcasing the best of local ingredients, notably fish, with French flair - and this, together with warm hospitality and the charm of Quay Cottage itself, make for a magic combination. **Seats 80**. *D 6-10pm. Closed Sun (& Mon off season); Christmas & January. CC.* **Directions:** *On the harbour front, at gates to Westport House.*

 Sage

10 High Street Westport Co Mayo ☎*098 56700 www.sagewestport.ie*

A new team has instilled fresh life into this attractive restaurant, since chef Shteryo Yurukov and front of house partner Eva Ivanova took on the ownership in 2013. Formerly noted for authentic Italian cooking (and a few of the popular pasta dishes remain) the focus is now on seafood and contemporary Irish cooking. It's encouraging to see local foods highlighted and Shteryo's cooking is very good; main courses, especially, are quietly impressive. A very pleasing restaurant and good value too. **Seats 45**. *Mon-Sun 5.30-10. CC.* **Directions:** *Just beyond the clock at the top of the main street, up the hill on the right.*

 The Sheebeen

Rosbeg Westport Co Mayo ☎*098 26528 www.croninssheebeen.com*

Just outside Westport, the Cronin family's popular old world thatched pub overlooking Clew Bay enjoys an almost-waterside location, and there's a warm welcome extended to all by the friendly local staff. Relaxed and characterful, there's a welcoming fire, several rooms and hideaway corners in the bar and an atmospheric first floor restaurant; menus can be predictable but it provides an enjoyable experience. *Food served daily 12-9.30 high season (4-9.30 Nov-Mar). CC.* **Directions:** *Far side of Westport harbour.*

 Sol Rio Restaurant & Cafe

Bridge Street Westport Co Mayo ☎*098 28944 www.solrio.ie*

Euro-Toques chef José Barroso from Portugal and his Westport-born wife Sinead Lambert run this lively first floor restaurant, where José takes pride in sourcing local and organic food and highlighting suppliers. Well priced lunch and dinner menus offer a wide range of popular dishes and local staff are helpful and welcoming. Try to get a window table so that you can watch the comings and goings of Bridge Street. **Seats 75**. *L&D Wed-Mon. Closed Tue. CC.* **Directions:** *In the heart of Westport opposite Matt Molloys pub.*

Westport Plaza Hotel

Castlebar Street Westport Co Mayo 📞*098 51166 www.westportplazahotel.ie*

Adjoining its larger sister property the Castlecourt Hotel, in the centre of Westport, this smart, contemporary hotel has spacious stylishly furnished public areas, including a comfortable bar, and impressive accommodation. Guests have use of the 'Spa Sula' and the C Club leisure facilities next door. A destination for local diners, Restaurant Merlot offers consistently good modern international cooking and food is well presented and enjoyable - although, with two sittings most nights, it may not be a place to linger. *Rooms 87 (5 shower only). Restaurant seats 120. D daily. Open all year. CC.*

Westport Woods Hotel

Quay Road Westport Co Mayo 📞*098 25811 www.westportwoodshotel.com*

Michael Lennon is the affable, hands-on owner manager who seems to be everywhere at this eco-friendly 1960s hotel near Westport House. The décor may not be especially impressive but don't let this put you off. Rooms are generous, with comfortable beds and the staff are notably attentive and friendly. Favoured by families, Westport Woods has excellent leisure facilities and provides a complimentary "go!kids!" Club to entertain all ages. *Directions: Louisburgh road.*

Carrowholly Cheese

Westport Area Carrowholly Westport Co Mayo 📞*087 237 3536*

While this is not be a major dairy farming area, it is home to some outstanding dairy products. Andrew Pelham-Burn's beautiful hard gouda style cheese is hand-made by traditional methods near Westport, using raw cows' milk and vegetarian rennet. Available plain and aged (the nutty 'Old Russet), also flavoured with Nettle; Garlic and Chive; Cumin; and the intriguing Pepper (green, black and 'a hint of cayenne'). Try it on local menus, and buy some to take home.

The Tavern Bar & Restaurant

Westport area Murrisk Westport Co Mayo 📞*098 64060 www.tavernmurrisk.com*

Myles and Ruth O'Brien have been running this fine bar and restaurant just outside Westport, at the foot of Croagh Patrick, since 1999 and have built up an enviable reputation for their hospitality - and Myles's good cooking, which showcases the best of local foods. Bar menus are extensive and the fine dining restaurant, Upstairs At The Tavern, offers several very attractive menus with local seafood from Clew Bay the speciality. Well-informed staff, who are nearly all local, are welcoming and know the menu and the nightly specials. *Seats 75. D Wed-Sun in summer, also L Sun. (Weekends only off-season, although bar food is served daily all year, 12.30-9). Establishment closed Good Fri, 25 Dec. CC. Directions: At the foot of Croagh Patrick, 5 mins from Westport.*

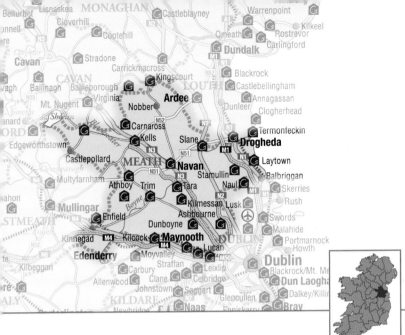

MEATH

Royal Meath. Meath of the pastures. Meath of the people. Meath of many people.......its key location near Dublin means Meath is one of the fastest-growing counties. The numbers aren't huge in today's overcrowded and city-oriented world, perhaps, but nevertheless Meath is a county which finds itself living in interesting times. The proximity of Dublin can be challenging. But it also brings benefits. With an increasingly affluent and discerning population, Meath is able to support a wide variety of hospitable establishments ranging from glossy restaurants of international quality, to characterful pubs deep in the heart of the country.

And the inevitable changes - for instance, the need to find ways through the county for new major roads - are projects which you feel Meath can absorb. There were some very vocal objections raised when the M3 was created through the valley beside the Hill of Tara, Royal Tara, ancient seat of the High Kings. But now that the road is running smoothly and safely, and largely hidden by trees, it's appropriate to remember that Tara's power was based on being the meeting point of the six great roads of ancient Ireland. How better to honour Tara in the 21st Century than with a modern motorway which takes today's traffic harmlessly to the east, well clear of the main sacred site with its wonderful views westward ?

Anyone with an interest in the remote past will find paradise in Meath, for along the Boyne Valley the neolithic tumuli at Knowth, Newgrange and Dowth are awe-inspiring, Newgrange in particular having its remarkable central chamber which is reached by the rays of sun at dawn at the winter solstice.

LOCAL ATTRACTIONS & INFORMATION

▸ **Bru na Boinne Visitor Centre** Donore *041 9880300*

▸ **Grove Gardens & Tropical Bird Sanctuary** Kells *046 9234276*

▸ **Sonairte (National Ecology Centre)** Laytown *041 9827572*

▸ **Newgrange (inc Dowth & Knowth)** *041 9880300*

▸ **Loughcrew Historic Gardens** Oldcastle *049 8541922*

▸ **Loughcrew Passage Tombs** Oldcastle *049 8542009*

▸ **Interpretive Centre** Tara *046 25903*

▸ **Trim Castle** Trim *046 9438619*

ASHBOURNE

Convenient to Dublin airport and on the edge of countryside offering rural activities including horse riding and racing (Fairyhouse Racecourse, 01 825 6167), golf at Ashbourne Golf Club (01 835 2005) or the championship course at nearby Roganstown Golf & Country Club (Swords, 01 843 3118) as well as the historical sites of County Meath.

Broadmeadow Country House

Bullstown Ashbourne Co Meath ✆*01 835 2823* *www.irishcountryhouse.com*

The Duff family's country guesthouse near Dublin airport is situated on 100 acres and surrounded by beautiful landscaped gardens. A fine equestrian centre is run as a separate business. Whatever the reason for your visit, it's a friendly and very comfortable place to stay, with elegant public rooms and spacious en-suite bedrooms furnished to hotel standards. **Rooms 8** *(2 shower only). Closed 24 Dec-2 Jan. CC.* **Directions:** *Off N2 at R125 towards Swords village.*

Chocolate Boutique

Main Street Ashbourne Co Meath ✆*01 835 1021* *www.chezemily.ie*

This chic shop and café sells the superb Chez Emily chocolates handmade by Ferdinand Vandaele and Helena Hemeryck at The Ward, Co Dublin since 1996. They use only top quality Belgian chocolate (for flavour, gloss and 'snap'), and the freshest local ingredients. Some are unlike anything else available in Ireland - the divine cherry liqueurs, containing whole cherries complete with stones, for example. *Open Mon-Sat 10-6. Also at: The Ward. Online shop.*

Cinnamon Garden

Above Hunters Moon Pub Main Street Ashbourne Co Meath
✆*01 835 2777* *www.cinnamongarden.ie*

With its pleasing setting, authentic cooking and courteous service from well-trained staff, this contemporary restaurant brings a little piece of India to Ashbourne's main street. The extensive menu represents a number of India's regions and is modern in style, while daily spice blends and locally grown seasonal produce bring real freshness to the flavours. An asset to the area – and offers good value too. **Seats 70.** *D Mon-Sat. Sun 12.30-10.30pm. Closed 25 Dec. CC.* **Directions:** *Centre of Ashbourne, opposite church above Hunters Moon Pub.*

Eatzen Chinese Restaurant

Unit 4 Building 3b Ashbourne Town Centre Ashbourne Co Meath ✆*01 835 2110* *www.eatzen.ie*

Cantonese cuisine with a twist is the specialty at this bright design-led restaurant – which is highly regarded by the Chinese community and known for imaginative presentation and good service. Owner chef Simon Tsang has wide experience in Asian cooking and you may find some less usual ingredients and dishes on the menu. **Seat 100**; *Open Mon-Sat 5.30-11.30; Sun 1-10. CC.* **Directions:** *Above Ashbourne Tesco.*

Hugh Maguire Craft Butchers

Unit 3-4 Town Centre Main Street Ashbourne Co Meath
✆ *01 849 9919 www.hughmaguirebutchers.com*

A prominent member of the Associated Craft Butchers of Ireland, Hugh Maguire's modern shop has much to recommend it with accolades including a Euro-Toques Award. The fresh blood black pudding is a speciality and his sausages have won acclaim in Europe. *Open: Mon-Wed 8am-7pm, Thu 8am-8pm, Fri 8am-9pm, Sat 8am-6pm.*

  ## Nick's Fish Ashbourne

Unit 9 Ashbourne Town Centre Ashbourne Co Meath ✆ *01 835 3555 www.nicksfish.ie*

Nicholas Lynch's popular fish shop is well known for its high standards of seafood and service. Nick, a former fisherman himself and an environmentally aware supplier, sources much of the fresh fish directly from fishermen and the range offered is impressive. Also offers ready meals, sauces and seasonings, plus a selection of organic and artisan products from Ireland and abroad. *Open: Mon-Sat 10-5. Closed Sun.*

 ## Pillo Hotel Ashbourne

The Rath Ashbourne Co Meath ✆ *01 835 0800 www.pillohotelashbourne.com*

Conveniently located for business travellers who need to be near Dublin city and the airport, this 4* hotel (formerly the Marriott Hotel Ashbourne) offers a high level of amenities and comfort. Also very family-friendly, with leisure centre, Kids Club in Jul-Aug and attractions including Tayto Park and Funtasia nearby. **Rooms 148**. *Closed 24-26 Dec. CC.* **Directions:** *North side of Ashbourne.*

  ## Man of Aran Fudge

Station House Ballivor Co Meath ✆ *086 256 6542 www.manofaranfudge.ie*

The man behind this evocatively named product is Aran Islands native Tomás Póil. You'll see him at markets and events selling award-winners like Granny's Nutty Fudge, Irish Coffee Fudge, Strawberries & Cream Fudge and many others - even a Christmas Pudding Fudge. Quality is the secret of its success - all are made with real Irish butter and fresh cream. *Widely available; online shop.*

  ## The Forge

Pottlereagh Carnaross Kells Co Meath ✆ *046 924 5003 www.theforgerestaurant.ie*

This delightful old forge is home to Irene and Pauric White's restaurant, where they use local produce in both traditional and innovative dishes and Sunday lunch is one of the most popular meals. Everything is very appetising and the enjoyment of a meal here is enhanced by excellent service from warm and friendly staff. An early dinner menu offers especially good value. **Seats 50** *(outdoors, 10). D Wed-Sat. Open: L Sun only. Closed Sun D, Mon & Tue; 2nd week Aug; 24-26 Dec. CC.* **Directions:** *7km north of Kells.*

Sheridans Cheesemongers

Virginia Road Station Carnaross Co Meath ✆ *046 924 5110 www.sheridanscheesemongers.com*

An old railway building provides an atmospheric warehouse, shop and headquarters for cheesemonger brothers Kevin and Seamus Sheridan, who have changed the way we buy and care for cheese in Ireland. The shop sells all manner of good artisan things as well as cheese, and is the venue for their annual Irish Food Festival. One of the true greats in Irish food. *Visitors welcome Thu-Sat when the shop is open a weekly farmers' markets held Sat 10-3. Also at: Galway, Dublin and Waterford (Ardkeen).*

CLONEE/DUNBOYNE

The population of the Clonee/Dunboyne area has grown a lot in recent years, and garden lovers will find plenty of interest within a short drive, including Larchill Arcadian Gardens (01 628 7354, Kilcock), and Primrose Hill (Lucan) which are both nearby.

Dunboyne Castle Hotel & Spa

Dunboyne Co Meath ✆ *01 801 3500 www.dunboynecastlehotel.com*

The original 18th-century country house remains the dominant feature of this stylishly developed 4* hotel. It's a popular wedding venue, with an impressive spa, excellent banqueting/conference and meeting facilities, dedicated exhibition complex and golf nearby. Spacious, luxuriously furnished rooms are mainly in the new section, and a choice of restaurants and bars includes The Ivy for fine dining. **Rooms 145** *(6 shower only). Open all year. CC.* **Directions:** *N3 into Dunboyne village, left at Slevins pub, a few hundred metres down the road on the left.*

The Mint Leaf

Summerhill Road Dunboyne Co Meath ✆ *01 801 3866 www.themintleaf.ie*

At this light, bright, family-friendly café, the food is simple and good, and the menu and the staff are full of information on its preparation and origin. Offering tasty daytime fare and lunch specials, dinner is a slightly more formal affair on late week evenings, when a more elaborate menu is offered - suiting the classics on the wine list. **Seats 60** *(outdoors, 20). Cafe open Mon-Sun until 5.30pm. Restaurant D Thu-Sat. Closed Bank Hols. CC.* **Directions:** *Dunboyne village, through lights, 2nd building on left.*

ENFIELD

This small town to the west of Dublin is situated on the Royal Canal and was believed to have been on the main road to Tara, seat of the High Kings of Ireland. Since then its history has been continuously interwined with roads, rail and the canal as transport requirements have changed over the years. Today the canal is an attractive feature and, despite its close proximity to the motorway (which has relieved traffic in the town itself), the harbour area has been pleasantly developed as a public park. Garden lovers will find several properties of interest within 20km, including Ballindoolin House & Garden (Carbury, 046 973 2377), Williamstown Garden (Carbury, 046 955 2971) and Lodge Park Walled Gardens (Straffan, 01 628 8412). Golfers are spoilt for choice with several top championship courses nearby including The K Club (Straffan, 01 601 7200), Carton House (Maynooth, 01 505 2000) and Palmerstown House PGA National (Johnstown, 045 906 901).

🏠 🍴 ♨ 🌡 🛋 📶 B 👫 ♿ ♨ ♨ ♨ The Johnstown House Hotel & Spa

Enfield Co Meath 📞*046 954 0000 www.johnstownhouse.com*

This mainly modern hotel has a mid-18th-century house at its heart and something of its country house atmosphere lives on, notably in a drawing room with a plasterwork ceiling by the renowned Francini brothers. It's well suited to corporate events and business meetings, but the spa and leisure club and shopping outlets also appeal to private guests. **Rooms 126**. CC. **Directions:** *Take M4 from Dublin - exit at Enfield.*

KELLS

Famously associated with the Book of Kells, this busy market town has much of historical interest to offer, including a Round Tower and High Crosses. The Kells Heritage Centre (046 924 7840, open all year) is located in the old Courthouse on the Navan Road and provides an interesting summary of Kells' ancient monastic history to visitors, who may also enjoy The Kells Heritage Trail, a walk of the town that takes in all the monastic sites. For those interested in rural and social history, Causey Farm (046 94434135) gives presentations on activities such as ceili dancing, turf cutting and traditional bread baking, along with traditional meals and live music. Grove Gardens & Open Farm with tropical bird sanctuary (046 943 4276), an informal garden on 6 acres with exotic animals and fowl, walks, roses and clematis is well worth a visit and makes a great family outing. Golfers can enjoy a round at Headfort Golf Club (046 9240146), which is one of Ireland's most scenic courses. The town includes some interesting craft shops and art studios, and visitors can buy the best of local farmhouse produce at the Farmers' Market held every Saturday (10-4).

🍴 👫 The Bective

Bective Square Kells Co Meath 📞*046 924 7780 www.thebective.ie*

A popular spot with locals, this atmospheric place is eclectically done up, and the wide-ranging menu offers plenty of familiar choices - with the proud claim that 90% of the tasty, attractively presented food is sourced in County Meath. Friendly, attentive staff and outdoor seating are further reasons for visiting this family-friendly place. **Seats 90**. *Wed-Sat, 5-10; Sun 3-9.*

🍴 🏠 📺 🍴 B 👫 Headfort Arms Hotel

Headfort Place Kells Co Meath 📞*046 924 0063 www.headfortarms.ie*

Set in the Boyne Valley, an area rich with tradition, the historic Headfort Arms has been trading for over 200 years. Now owned by the Duff family, this three star hotel offers comfortable accommodation and true hospitality. An ideal base to explore the 'Royal County', golf and family breaks are offered, also an appealing Meath Food Trail Package, including dinner in The Vanilla Pod (see entry) and visits to local food producers. An interesting one to try. **Rooms 45**.

🍴 📺 🍴 ✐ 📶 B 👫 ♨ Vanilla Pod Restaurant

Headfort Arms Hotel Kells Co Meath 📞*046 924 0063 www.headfortarms.ie*

This long-established and popular bistro-style restaurant is run independently of the hotel and offers good food based on carefully sourced ingredients, many of them local. Quite a few contemporary dishes are offered, including some vegetarian; the cooking is excellent, including homemade desserts, and the presentation delightful. Wine evenings are sometimes held. **Seats 80**. *D daily, Sun all day, 12.30-9.30. Closed 24-26 Dec.* CC. **Directions:** *On main Dublin-Cavan road, left section of black & white building on right.*

Kilbeg Dairies

Kells Area Horath Carlanstown Kells Co Meath ✆046 924 4687 www.kilbegdairies.ie

Using rich buttery-coloured milk supplied buy local farmers, Kieran and Jane Cassidy make a sophisticated range of products on their farm near Kells, - including soft cream cheese, crème fraiche, fromage frais, quark, sour cream, Greek style yogurt, fruit flavoured yogurts and mascarpone cheese - most of which are available in fat-free versions, as well as the original gorgeously creamy and full flavoured products. Versatile in cooking and popular with chefs, the Cassidys also run a recipe service on their website.

Ryan's Farm

Kells Area Ballinlough Kells Co Meath ✆087 985 7480 www.ryansfarm.com

Ryan's Farm may be 'suppliers of farm fresh food since 1928', but there is nothing old-fashioned about Jim Ryan's business. They supply top quality beef, lamb, pork (including sausages and black and white pudding) and free range chicken directly to hotels and restaurants - and sell from their own farm shop, and when attending markets and food fairs with their cheerful mobile food unit. Well worth a visit. **Directions:** *R163 west of Kells.*

The Station House Hotel

Kilmessan Co Meath ✆046 902 5239 www.stationhousehotel.ie

The Slattery family's unique establishment is an old railway junction, and all the various buildings were converted to a make a hotel full of charm and character. An interesting and unusual place to visit, with lovely gardens, it makes a pretty wedding venue and the traditional Signal Restaurant is especially popular for Sunday lunch. **Rooms 20** *(1 shower only).* **Seats 90**. *(outdoors, 50). L&D daily. Bar Menu Mon-Sat, 11-6. Open all year. CC.* **Directions:** *From Dublin M3 to junction 6 Dunshaughlin and follow signposts.*

Sonairte National Ecology Centre

The Ninch Laytown Co Meath ✆041 982 7572 www.sonairte.ie

An interesting place for an outing with an organic farm shop, Mustard, offering vegetables, herbs and fruit in season as well as jams, cordials and pickles based on the garden produce. There's also a café, plants for sale, a farmers' market on the last Sunday of the month, and courses and classes running throughout the year.

NAVAN

Situated on the banks of the River Boyne, Navan, is the main town and administrative capital of County Meath. The Blackwater river meets the river Boyne on the eastern side of the town at the ancient Poolbeg bridge and there are many attractive riverside walks. Famous for its fine furniture and carpets, it's a good shopping town and also hosts an open air market every Friday. Nearby gardens to visit include Grove Gardens (near Kells, 046 943 4276) which is an informal garden on 6 acres with exotic animals and fowl, walks, roses and clematis (especially good for a family day out) and Rockfield House (Drumconrath, 046 905 2135), a charming old walled garden with a stream and a collection of herbaceous plants. For sporting folk, there's Navan Racecourse (046 902 1350), and Headfort Golf Club (Kells, 046 928 2001) has championship golf over two 18 hole courses.

Athlumney Manor

Athlumney Road Navan Co Meath ☎ *046 907 1388 www.athlumneymanor.com*

At this modern B&B surrounded by lovely gardens, Pat Boylan is front-of-house and has all the local information at his fingertips, while Pauline Boylan presides over the kitchen. Back rooms have views over Athlumney Castle and are more spacious than those at the front. Genuine hospitality and good value – a handy place to stay when visiting Navan. *Rooms 7 (all shower only). CC.* **Directions:** *East side of Navan town off R153.*

Earls Kitchen

Old Corn Market Navan Co Meath ☎ *046 905 9678 www.earlskitchen.com*

Good homemade food is the hallmark of Sandra Earl's café in the Old Cornmarket. Menus include daily specials and a display counter offers appealing savoury dishes and salads to one side and Sandra's glorious desserts on the other. Presentation is excellent and everything looks as delicious as it tastes. A cut above the rest, Earl's Kitchen is a little gem. *Seats 21, open Mon-Sat 9-5.30pm. Closed Sun, Bank Hols, Christmas, New Year. No CC.* **Directions:** *Off N51 Ludlow Street.*

The Loft Restaurant

26 Trimgate Street Navan Co Meath ☎ *046 907 1755*

Exceptionally pleasant, helpful staff and a lively global menu at reasonable prices that emphasises accessibility – this is a place for all ages and every (or no particular) occasion. The main menu offers cosmopolitan dishes and daily blackboard specials. Downstairs, the Tapas Bar serves a range of cold and hot tapas, with wine available by the glass and bottle. *Seats 90. D daily. Closed Good Fri, 25/26 Dec. CC.* **Directions:** *Centre of Navan, corner of Trimgate Street and Railway Street.*

The Russell Restaurant

15-16 Ludlow Street Navan Co Meath ☎ *046 903 1607*

An ultra glamorous restaurant that wouldn't look out of place in a chic boutique hotel. Everything is made on the premises, including good breads, excellent pasta and impressive sorbets and ice cream. Stylish presentation suits the smart décor, and most of the dishes can be ordered as tapas portions and enjoyed in the main dining room or bar. *Seats 50; D Tue-Sun. CC.* **Directions:** *Centre of town, off Market Square, parallel to N3.*

Ryan's Bar

22 Trimgate Street Navan Co Meath ☎ *046 902 1154*

This pleasant, well-run and popular pub is a good meeting place for a drink or a light lunch: soups, hot panini, wraps (including a vegetarian option) and toasties (honey baked ham, perhaps, with a salad garnish), plus there's always a dessert among the daily specials. It's good value and the airy bar makes for a comfortable atmosphere. *Open from 11.30 am. Closed 25 Dec & Good Fri. CC.* **Directions:** *Main Street Navan.*

Bellinter House

Navan area Navan Co Meath 📞 *046 903 0900 www.bellinterhouse.com*

Transformed into a chic Meath bolthole, this Palladian gem offers some luxurious accommodation with beautiful surrounds and leisure centre. In addition to all-day dining in the Drawing Room, Eden Restaurant in the vaulted basement offers quality fresh produce imaginatively cooked in contemporary combinations. *Rooms 34 (19 shower only). Seats 90 (outdoors, 20). Restaurant L Sun only, D daily. Food served all day, 11am-11pm in the drawing room. Restaurant closed 24-26 Dec. CC.* **Directions:** *Off N3 near the Hill of Tara.*

Burkes Farm Ice Cream

Navan Area Corbalton Tara Navan Co Meath 📞 *046 902 5232 www.burkesfarmicecream.com*

Bernie and John Burke make a gorgeous range of luscious ice creams with the cream-laden milk from their herd of beautiful Jersey cows. Bernie Burke makes a lot of flavours, including classics like vanilla and chocolate but also unusual ones such as clotted cream & strawberry, and the very popular apple crumble. Some are seasonal, such as plum pudding ice cream for Christmas, and there's a range of sorbets, including that refreshing essence of early summer, elderflower.

Teltown House

Navan Area Teltown Navan Co Meath 📞 *046 902 3239 www.teltownhouse.com*

Overlooking the River Blackwater in the heart of the Boyne Valley and convenient to Navan, Kells and Slane, Bertie and Renée Clarke's lovely creeper-clad 17th-century country house offers elegant reception rooms with open fires. The big en suite bedrooms enjoy views of their rich pastureland and Renée makes hearty breakfasts on her trusty Aga. *Sleeps 8-10. Open all year.* **Directions:** *Off N3 northwest of Navan.*

Fairyhouse Food & Wine School

Fairyhouse Road Ratoath Co Meath 📞 *01 689 6476 www.fairyhousecookeryschool.com*

Self-confessed food lover Billie O'Shea owns and runs this beautifully located purpose built cookery school, offering a wide range of cookery classes and courses for everyone from beginners to experienced cooks wishing to upgrade their skills. Demonstration and hands-on classes are offered. with tastings and wine matching an integral part of courses, where relevant.

SLANE

This appealing village is well placed for visitors to the historic sites of the area, notably the Brú na Bóinne complex of Neolithic chamber tombs, which lies on the River Boyne 5km down river from the village. This includes Newgrange, a passage tomb built c. 3200 BC that is of special interest on the morning of the winter solstice. Garden lovers should consider a visit to Listoke Gardens (Drogheda, 041 983 2265), a 6 acre Edwardian garden with walled garden, herbaceous borders and woodland walks, or Beaulieu House, Gardens and Car Museum (Drogheda, 041 983 8557) a beautifully located three hundred year old walled garden with herbaceous borders, fruit and vegetables. Championship golf beckons at nearby Headfort Golf Club (Kells, 046 928 2001), County Louth Golf Club (Drogheda, 041 988 1530) and Seapoint Golf Club (Termonfeckin, 0982 2333).

 **Conyngham Arms Hotel**

Slane Co Meath ✆ *041 988 4444 www.conynghamarms.ie*

This former 17th-century coaching inn, now owned by Tricia and Brian Conroy of nearby Tankardstown House (see entry), was tastefully refurbished in 2012 and the pretty bedrooms are just what you would hope for in a rural hotel. Dining is informal, but features local, seasonal produce and specialist suppliers. A great choice if you're touring the Boyne Valley, whether for a stay or for a memorable meal break. *Rooms 15*. Restaurant: Mon-Thu 10- 8; Fri 10-9; Sat & Sun 9-9.

 **Georges Patisserie**

Chapel Street Slane Co Meath ✆ *041 982 4493 www.georgespatisserie.com*

You're in for a real treat at this continental-style bakery, where much-admired patissier George Heise bakes a wide range of fresh breads and scones (the brown bread and blueberry scones are especially good) superb cakes and desserts. With five small tables to enjoy a coffee and a delicious bite, it's a great spot for locals and a wonderful place for visitors to know about - and travellers on the N2, to break a journey or buy goodies to take home. *Open Wed to Sat, 9:00 to 6:00*. **Directions:** *Centre of Slane.*

 Newgrange Gold Premium Irish Seed Oils

Crewbane Slane Co Meath ✆ *041 982 4273 www.newgrangegold.ie*

Most of the crop that goes into John Rogers's cold-pressed rapeseed oil comes from fields that lie in the shadow of Newgrange, and all of it is sourced from the Boyne Valley. The product range includes rapeseed oil as well as two flavoured versions (garden herbs and chilli garlic). John is also Ireland's only producer of camelina oil, extra rich in omega-3. Widely distributed to specialist outlets, see website for list.

 **Rossnaree**

Slane Co Meath ✆ *041 982 0975 www.rossnaree.ie*

Perched above the River Boyne, overlooking the famous megalithic passage tombs of Knowth and Newgrange, Aisling Law's handsome Victorian and Italianate house is the perfect place for history-lovers, with four individually themed bedrooms. Breakfast is a grand affair, served in the elegant dining room in front of a crackling log fire. An enchanting bolthole too, ideal for a quick escape from Dublin. *Rooms 4 (some with private bathrooms). Open all year*. **Directions:** *M1 north, exit for Bru na Boinne, through Donore, past Newgrange visitors centre, entrance on sharp bend on left.*

 **Tankardstown House**

Rathkenny Slane Co Meath ✆ *041 982 4621 www.tankardstown.ie*

Tricia and Brian Conroy's magnificent Georgian country house is available for individual bookings or to hire for exclusive use including weddings. There are six elegant bedrooms in the house, plus cottages in the charming 18th-century stable yard. Also a dining destination of note: choose between The Bistro (smart casual, with outdoor seating) and the sophisticated rustic fine dining Brabazon Restaurant; both are charming and serve excellent food. *Rooms 18*. The Bistro: Wed-Sun 12-6pm. Brabazon Restaurant: Thu-Fri, D; Sat & Sun open all day from noon. Open all year. CC. **Directions:** *7km from Slane.*

Boyne Valley Blue Farmhouse Goats Cheese

Slane Area Mullagha Farm Slane Co Meath ☎*086 384 4162*

Made from the milk of their 300 goats since 2010, Michael Finegan's magnificent unpasteurised semi-hard blue veined goats cheese is the only one of its kind in Ireland. Matured for 3 to 6 months before sale, allowing the goats milk flavour to balance with the blue, it packs a real punch at six months; while superb on the cheeseboard, Michael commends it especially as a cooking cheese, with pasta, perhaps, or for the classic steak and blue cheese combo.

 Clarke's Fresh Fruit

Clinstown Stamullen Co Meath 01 841 3262 www.clarkesfreshfruit.ie

The Clarke family's 56 acre soft fruit farm is one of the largest in Ireland. Renowned grower Pat Clarke produces strawberries, raspberries, blackberries and blueberries for distribution to multiples and independent stores and a same-day pick, pack and dispatch system allows their fruit to reach the shops in peak condition. Also for sale at the farm shop, where jams made with their fruit by Folláin in Co Cork (see entry) are available too. *Available from: Seasonal Farm Shop, May-Nov. Mon-Fri 9-5, Sat & Sun.* **Directions:** *West of the village of Stamullen (M1 Exit 7).*

 O'Connell's

Tara Area Skryne Hill of Tara Co Meath ☎*046 902 5122*

Four generations of O'Connells have been caretakers of this wonderfully unspoilt country pub. It's all beautifully simple: two little bars with no fancy bits, lots of items of local interest and a welcoming fire in the grate. What more could anyone want? *Closed 25 Dec & Good Fri. No CC.*

 Franzini O'Briens

French's Lane Trim Co Meath ☎*046 943 1002*

Modern and spacious, this smart, popular restaurant beside Trim Castle has light-hearted menus that offer an excellent range of choices in the international style and an interesting wine list (supplied by Jim Nicholson). Together with an informal, buzzy atmosphere, it's a place for a good night out. *See also O'Briens Good Food & Drink House, near Navan. **Seats 110**. D daily, L Sun only. Closed Tue, Mon off-season (Sept-May), 24-26 Dec. CC.* **Directions:** *Beside Trim Castle.*

 Knightsbrook Hotel & Golf Resort

Trim Co Meath ☎*046 948 2100 www.knightsbrook.com*

Convenient to Dublin and also well placed for visiting the county's historical and cultural attractions, this relatively new golf hotel and spa just outside Trim is a popular destination for short breaks, conferences and weddings. Bedrooms are large and luxuriously furnished, and there are excellent leisure facilities. Several dining options are offered. ***Rooms 131**. Closed 25 Dec. CC.* **Directions:** *About a mile from Trim town, on the Dublin Road.*

MONAGHAN

Of all Ireland's counties, it is Monaghan which is most centrally placed in the drumlin belt, that strip of rounded glacial hills which runs right across the country from Strangford Lough in County Down to Clew Bay in Mayo. Monaghan, in fact, is all hills. But as very few of them are over 300 metres above sea level, the county takes its name from Muineachain - "Little Hills". Inevitably, the actively farmed undulating country of the little hills encloses many lakes, and Monaghan in its quiet way is a coarse angler's contemplative paradise.

Contemplation of a different sort is the theme at Annaghmakerrig House near the Quaker-named village of Newbliss in west Monaghan. The former home of theatrical producer Tyrone Guthrie, it is a busy centre for writers and artists who can stay there to complete 'work in progress', or defer deadlines in congenial company.

In the east of the county at Castleblayney, there's a particularly attractive lake district with forest park and adventure centre around Lough Mucko. Southwards of Castleblayney, we come to the bustling town of Carrickmacross, still famous for its lace, and a Tidy Towns awardee.

Monaghan's pretty village of Glaslough towards the north of the county is worth a visit, and at Clontibret in northeast Monaghan, there's gold in them thar little hills. Whether or not it's in sufficient quantities to merit mining is a continuing matter of commercial debate, but the fact that it's there at all is another of Monaghan's more intriguing secrets.

LOCAL ATTRACTIONS & INFORMATION

▸ **Carrickmacross Lace Gallery**
Carrickmacross
042 9662506

▸ **Dun a Ri Forest Park**
Carrickmacross
042 9667320

▸ **Lough Muckno Leisure Park**
Castleblayney *042 9746356*

▸ **Clones Lace Exhibits** Clones
047 51051

▸ **Castle Leslie Gardens**
Glaslough *047 88109*

▸ **Patrick Kavanagh Centre**
Inniskeen *042 9378560*

▸ **Rossmore Forest Park**
Monaghan Town *047 81968*

▸ **Annaghmakerrig** (Tyrone
Guthrie Centre) Newbliss
047 54003

Courthouse Restaurant

Monaghan St Carrickmacross Co Monaghan 📞*042 969 2848 www.courthouserestaurant.ie*

Beside the handsome cut limestone courthouse, well known chef Conor Mee and Charlotte Carr's atmospheric and friendly restaurant caters well for the daily changing needs of their local clientele. Conor's menus combine quality and value, offering imaginative choices. Specialities include a delicious lamb hotpot and many lighter dishes; basics like breads and soups are excellent – also classics such as fish and chips: sea-fresh and perfectly made. Vegetarian and vegan menu offered too. Well worth a detour. **Seats 50**. *L Wed-Sun; D Wed-Sun. Closed Mon (except bank hols), Tue, 1st week Jan. CC.*

 **Nuremore Hotel**

Carrickmacross Co Monaghan 📞*042 966 1438 www.nuremore.com*

The Gilhooly family's fine owner-managed country hotel is set in a parkland estate, with its own 18-hole golf course. Bedrooms may seem a little dated but are generous and comfortable; some have views over the gardens and lakes, as do spacious and public areas areas including the fine dining Restaurant. There's a full leisure centre and a wide range of related facilities. **Rooms 72**. **Seats 100**. *L Sun-Fri; D daily. Closed L Sat. Open all year. CC.*

 Christmas Made Easy

Lough Egish Food Park Lough Egish Castleblayney Co Monaghan
📞*041 981 3837 www.christmasmadeeasy.ie*

Euro-Toques chef Neil McFadden and his wife, Hazel, who is a tutor at the Kitchen in the Castle cookery school at Howth Castle, Co. Dublin, run this innovative company, which supplies pre-prepared Christmas dinners, all based on the very best ingredients. There are six menus to choose from, each with detailed cooking instructions and timetables.

 Kirks Seafood

Main Street Castleblayney Co Monaghan 📞*087 855 6059*

Mary and Jim Kirk, from the major fishing port of Clogherhead in Co. Louth, now run this retail outlet in Co. Monaghan, where they offer a fine range of seafood sourced from their own home port. *Open Wed-Sat.*

 **Hilton Park**

Clones Co Monaghan 📞*047 56007 www.hiltonpark.ie*

Once described as a "capsule of social history" because of their collection of family portraits and memorabilia going back 250 years or more, the Madden family's wonderful 18th century mansion is set in beautiful gardens (open to the public by arrangement), amidst 200 acres of woodland and farmland. Four-poster beds make for a special country house stay, and Lucy, an enthusiastic organic gardener, supplies freshly harvested produce for meals in the house. A visit here is a rare treat. *Rooms 6. Residents D Tue-Sat; 24 hours notice required. Open all year by arrangement. CC. Directions: 5km south of Clones on Scotshouse Road.*

 ## Silver Hills Foods

Emyvale Co Monaghan 📞*047 87124 www.silverhillfoods.com*

Having taken over from his parents, Ronnie and Lyla, Stuart Steele now runs this environmentally responsible farm and produces a unique breed of Pekin duck – good enough, in fact, to attract special praise from super-chef Heston Blumenthal. The farm shop sells the full duck range as well as luxurious feather and down items and other local artisan products. *Shop open 9-6, daily; phone 047 87124 to order and collect.*

 ## Lodge at Castle Leslie

Glaslough Co Monaghan 📞*047 88100 www.castleleslie.com*

Guests can choose between rooms in the extraordinary castle or in the Lodge at Castle Leslie Estate, a modern 4-star hotel built around a stable courtyard, complete with a spa and equestrian centre. Dining options for both residents and non-residents are the hotel's informal Conors Bar or Snaffles Brasserie, where Andrew Bradley cooks up a storm in a wood-burning stone oven. *Castle Leslie: Bedrooms 20. Dining Room at Castle Leslie: D only for groups. The Lodge: Rooms 29. Snaffles Brasserie in The Lodge: Seats 80 (outdoors, 20). D daily. Bar food served daily in Conor's Bar, 12.30-8.30pm. Restricted opening winter (closed midweek). CC. Directions: 10 mins from Monaghan Town: Monaghan-Armagh road-Glaslough.*

 ## Andy's Bar and Restaurant

12 Market Street Monaghan Co Monaghan 📞*047 82277 www.andysmonaghan.com*

At the Redmond family's handsome Victorian-style bar, substantial bar meals include a range of specials on a blackboard as well as a concise written menu. The restaurant upstairs, which has a pleasingly old-fashioned ambience, offers a much more extensive range of tasty popular and classic dishes. This is good, generous cooking based on quality ingredients, offering value - and great service. *Restaurant: Seats 50. D only, Tue-Sun (Sun 1.30-9.30). Bar meals Tue-Sun. Closed Mon, Bank Hols, 25 Dec, Good Fri. CC. Directions: Town centre, opposite the Market House.*

 ## Hillgrove Hotel

Old Armagh Rd Monaghan Co Monaghan 📞*047 81288 www.hillgrovehotel.com*

Overlooking the town from a fine hillside location, this privately owned hotel offers good business and leisure facilities and spacious public areas. The contemporary bedrooms have pleasant views - as does the stylishly informal restaurant, Vettriano, serving lunch and dinner every day. *Rooms 87. Closed 25 Dec. CC. Directions: Take N2 from Dublin to Monaghan town.*

  ## Meadowsweet Apiaries

Doon Ballinahown Co Offaly 📞*086 884 4938*

The unspoilt Slieve Bloom Mountains and bogland in this unique and interesting area are perfect for honey - as shown by third generation apiarist Andrew McGuinness, at Meadowsweet Apiaries. Produced here since 1956, their beautiful honey is natural (no heat filtration), with distinct regional flavour; both the honey and their beeswax products have achieved well-deserved national recognition. If you see them on sale, snap them up!

OFFALY

At the heart of the old Ely O'Carroll territory, Offaly is Ireland's most sky-minded county. In the grounds of Birr Castle, there's the Parsons family's famous restored 1845-vintage 1.83m astronomical telescope - rated one of the Seven Wonders of Ireland - through which the 3rd Earl of Rosse observed his discovery of the spiral nebulae. And in Tullamore, there's a thriving amateur Astronomical Society whose members point out that the wide clear skies of Offaly have encouraged the regular observation of heavenly bodies since at least 1057 AD, when astronomy was the province of moon-minded monks.

On a more modern note, the Tullamore Dew Heritage Centre is housed in the restored 1897 canal-side bonded warehouse, which formerly stored the famous local whiskey. The Centre explores Tullamore's distilling, canal and urban history with entertaining style. Style is also the theme of the new County Hall in Tullamore, which has been awarded the An Taisce Sustainable Building accolade.

The Grand Canal finally reaches the great river at Shannon Harbour in Offaly, after crossing Ireland from Dublin through Tullamore, and on the river itself, waterborne travellers find that Offaly affords the opportunity of visiting Clonmacnoise, where the remains of an ancient monastic university city give pause for thought.

In the south of the county, the Slieve Bloom Mountains rise attractively above Offaly's farmland and bogs. These are modest heights, as they attain just 526 m on the peak of Arderin. However, it is their understated charm which particularly appeals, and nestling in a valley of the Slieve Blooms is the unspoilt village of Kinnitty, where Offaly's gentle quality of life is most in evidence.

LOCAL ATTRACTIONS & INFORMATION

▸ **Birr Castle Demesne &**
Historic Science Centre Birr
0509 20336/22154

▸ **Visitor & Interpretive Centre**
Clonmacnoise
090 9674195

▸ **Tullamore Dew Heritage**
Centre Tullamore
0506 25015

BANAGHER

This small town on the western edge of County Offaly was originally built to protect a crossing point on the river Shannon - impressive fortifications guarding the river crossing are still to be seen. Today, angling and all watersports are attractions; there is a marina, it is a popular stopping place for cruisers and boats can be hired here. Along the river banks, the Shannon Callows are home to a wealth of wild flowers and bird life, and river buses take visitors along the river to Clonmacnoise (Visitor & Interpretive Centre 090 967 4195), and other places of interest. For those who seek the 'real Ireland' this is an interesting small town to be based, and always was - it provided a wealth of inspiration for author Anthony Trollope who wrote his first novels here.

  ## Bo Bristle Brewing Company

Unit 5 Enterprise Centre Banagher Co Offaly ✆*086 125 0283 www.bobristle.com*

Located on the banks of the River Shannon, the name of this brewery comes from Celtic legend, where great importance is attached to the bristles of the boar. The IPA is their flagship beer and the amber ale is their latest brew. The beers aren't widely available, but check their website for stockists.

  ## Coolfin Gardens Organic Bakery

Unit 3 Banagher Enterprise Centre Banagher Co Offaly ✆*087 204 5593*

Swiss baker Jonas Hein and his Irish wife Layla O'Brien run this certified organic bakery and, thanks to the excellence of their rustic continental breads and their hard work selling directly to the public through farmers' markets and the Lough Boora Farm (see entry) vegetable boxes, this small bakery's reputation is impressive.

 ## Flynns Bar & Restaurant

Main Street Banagher Co Offaly ✆*057 915 1312*

Established in 1914, this welcoming family-run pub and restaurant has come a long way since it started off as a traditional grocery-bar, but it has lost none of its friendly appeal. An open fire immediately makes visitors feel at home in the cosy bar, and their steaks are renowned. There's music at weekends too. *L&D daily. CC.* **Directions:** *Centre of Banagher.*

  ## The Harbour Master's House

Shannon Harbour Banagher Co Offaly ✆*057 915 1532 www.theharbourmastershouse.ie*

If a B&B in a quiet and picturesque waterside setting with a pub serving good food only yards away takes your fancy, you won't do better than Grainne Kirwan's charming and hospitable Harbour Master's House at Shannon Harbour. The bedrooms vary in character, as rooms in old houses do, and are all en suite. A delightful place, full of history. **Rooms 5** *(all shower only). Closed 10 Dec-1 Apr. CC.*

 ## J.J.Hough

Main Street Banagher Co Offaly ✆*057 915 1893*

Hidden behind a thriving vine, Michael and Sheila Hough's charming 250-year-old family-run pub is soothingly dark inside. A world-famous music pub, it's authentic and unique, with a wealth of Irish art on the walls. It's a great local and also popular with people from the river cruisers, who come up from the harbour for pints, music and craic. *Open 10.30 am - 1 am. No food. Closed 25 Dec & Good Fri.* **Directions:** *Lower Main Street.*

BIRR

Birr is a lovely old town steeped in history and it makes a good holiday centre, with plenty to do and see locally - Birr Castle, with its observatory and magnificently restored gardens to visit (and a cefé-bistro on site), also golfing, fishing and riding. River excursions are available and Birr Outdoor Education Centre (057 912 0029) has a range of watersports education courses including canoeing, sailing and board sailing.

  ### Brambles Café & Deli

Mill Street Birr Co Offaly ✆ *087 745 3359 www.bramblesbirr.ie*

There's no better place to enjoy a good coffee and excellent home-baked produce than Gillian Delahunt's inviting café. Gillian makes and sells her own soda bread, carrot cake, chocolate biscuit cake, scones and other treats along with homemade soup and deep-filled pies. She also sells her own organic duck eggs and lettuce from her family farm and a range of quality local produce. Absolutely delicious. ***Seats 18*** *(outdoors, 4); Mon-Sat, 9am-6pm; Sun 12-6. Closed Sun in winter, bank hols. No CC.*

  ### The Chestnut

Green Street Birr Co Offaly ✆ *www.thechestnut.ie*

Clodagh Fay operates this old pub, which poured its first pint in 1823. It's a good place to while away a Sunday afternoon reading the papers by the fire with a great cappuccino or pint of Guinness. They host mouth-watering BBQs in summer and the eclectic 'full moon market' is held in the courtyard (beside a beautiful secret garden) on the third Saturday of each month. *Open from 8pm Mon-Thu, from 5pm Fri, from 3pm Sat-Sun - closing. Closed 25 Dec, Good Fri.* **Directions:** *Just off the Main Square, Emmet Square.*

  ### Emmas Café & Deli

31 Main Street Birr Co Offaly ✆ *057 912 5678*

This delightful Heritage Town is blessed with excellent choices when it comes to buying local foods and enjoying casual daytime fare, and Adrian Shine and Debbie Kenny's well-known cafe-deli is one of the longest established. Combining an attractive café and a deli counter, it offers a tempting range of artisan products, including cheeseboards and hampers that are made to order all year round.

 ### The Loft Café & Craft Shop

O'Connell Street Birr Co Offaly ✆ *057 912 0063*

This bright, airy café above Mulholland Pharmacy serves breakfast, lunch and a tempting range of homemade desserts. The menu offers straightforward café fare: freshly made sandwiches, wraps, bagels and paninis as well as a good selection of salads, homemade soups and breads and a savoury tart of the day. Fresh ingredients, friendly service and a menu with plenty of choice means there's something for everyone.*Seats 34 (+16 outdoors). Open: Mon-Sat, 9-6. Closed Sun. Licensed. NO CC.* **Directions:** *Off Emmet Square at the top of O'Connell Street.*

The Organic Store

Main Street Birr Co Offaly ☎*057 912 5881*

Jonathan Haslam's shop sells a carefully selected range of organic and eco-friendly products, many of them local. And this is the retail arm of Mossfield Organic Farm, well known for their organic dairy products, notably Ralph Haslam's magnificent Gouda-style cheeses. Of the five cheeses currently made (two plain and three flavoured), the mature plain is especially outstanding for its rich nutty flavour. *Open: Mon-Sat 10-6.30.*

The Stables Emporium & Tea Rooms

6 Oxmantown Mall Birr Co Offaly ☎*057 912 0263 www.thestablesbirr.com*

The Boyd family's characterful gift emporium is in a lovely old Georgian house overlooking the tree-lined mall. Now run by Caroline Boyd, she serves delicious light lunches, snacks, drinks (including wine) and homemade desserts in the elegant drawing room, complete with open fire and comfortable armchairs. There's also a nice little front garden for sitting out in fine weather. *Open Tue-Sat, 10.30-5.30 and Sun 1-5.30 (Nov, Dec, Jun, Jul & Aug). Closed Dec 25-29. CC.* **Directions:** *Town centre, between St Brendan's church & private gates of Birr castle.*

The Thatch Bar & Restaurant

Crinkle Birr Co Offaly ☎*057 912 0682*

This little thatched pub and restaurant outside Birr shows just how pleasing a genuine, well-run country pub can be. Des Connole, proprietor since 1991, has a well-earned reputation for the immaculate maintenance and atmosphere of the pub, and both bar food and restaurant meals offer generous portions at a reasonable price. *Seats 50. D daily, L Sun. Bar meals Mon-Sat, 12.30-3 & 5-7.30. Restaurant closed D Sun, establishment closed 25 Dec, Good Fri. CC.* **Directions:** *1.5km from Birr (Roscrea side).*

Townsend House Guesthouse

Townsend Street Birr Co Offaly ☎*057 912 1276 www.townsendhouse-guesthouse.com*

Martin and Lorraine Kearns's impressive guesthouse has kept original period features (and open fires), yet offers all the comforts and conveniences demanded by today's travellers. Bedrooms vary in size due to the age of the building, which is part of the charm, and all are en suite. There's even a bar at this atmospheric place and it's a great base for exploring the town and its environs. *Rooms 12.* **Directions:** *Centre of Birr.*

Coolnagrower Organic Produce Ltd

Birr Area Fortal near Birr Co Offaly ☎*057 912 1562 www.coolnagrower.ie*

One of Ireland's biggest and most successful organic growers, Philip Dreaper has been producing a range of vegetables since 1992 and is renowned for his expertise. He is famed for his top quality carrots, potatoes and turnips and the other main crops grown are leeks, onions and beetroot. Look for the Coolnagrower products in supermarkets as well as organic stores and farmers' markets. Open days are sometimes held on the farm (www.teagasc.ie).

Mossfield Organic Farm

Birr Area Clareen Birr Co Offaly 📞*057 913 1002 www.mossfield.ie*

Ralph Haslam's herd of 80 Friesian cows graze herby limestone pastures and their milk to makes magnificent cheeses. Five gouda style cheeses are made - Mossfield (young and mature), flavoured young Mossfield (tomato & herbs; garlic & basil; cumin) - and the newer Mossfield Slieve Bloom (mild creamy cheddar style). Mossfield Mature (8 months+) is the standout cheese, with wonderful depth of flavour. They now also produce non-homogenised bottled milk, buttermilk and yoghurt, all using their own milk. Available from their shop in Birr town (see entry) and selected stockists.

  Clanwood Farm

Cush Cloghan Co Offaly 📞*087 649 4477 www.clanwoodfarm.com*

Orla and Sean Clancy produce organic beef, pork and eggs on their family farm, selling them directly to customers and at markets, along with speciality products including soups, sauces, salads and pickles. Orla's excellent Clanwood Farm Organic Soups are a great success, also their catering trailer The Organic Kitchen, where they team up their organic burgers with other local producers' foods - effectively it's a Taste of Offaly burger. Good thinking - and absolutely delicious.

 **Eden Deli Café**

84 JKL Street Edenderry Co Offaly 📞*046 973 3994*

Breads, cakes, stocks, soups and sauces are all made from scratch at Niall & Niamh Walsh's two-storey deli and café near the harbour, and the best of ingredients (local where possible) are used in their deliciously, wholesome fare. They dry cure bacon, dry age beef sirloins - and even churn butter and culture buttermilk in-house - and the difference is in the taste. Eden Deli promises 'breakfast, lunch, cakes & treats', and this it does exceptionally well. *Seats 40 (outdoors, 10). Open Mon-Sat from 8.30 (Mon, Tue, Sat to 5.30, Wed-Fri to 6). Closed Sun, Bank Hols, Christmas week. No CC. **Directions:** Opposite the canal harbour in the centre of Edenderry.*

  Quarrymount Free Range Meats

Quarrymount Killeigh Co Offaly 📞*086 833 1006 www.freerangemeats.ie*

Third-generation farmer Ray Dunne's refrigerated cabinet is a familiar sight at farmers' markets, where he sells his grass-fed 21-day dry-aged beef, free-range chickens and specialty beef sausages from his 100-acre farm near Killeigh on the Laois/Offaly border. Available from markets (can order & collect); order form on website (pay by cheque, free delivery in some areas).

 Ardmore Country House

The Walk Kinnitty Co Offaly 📞*057 913 7009 www.kinnitty.com*

Walking holidays are a speciality at Christina Byrne's stone-built Victorian house and it offers very welcome old-fashioned comforts: brass beds, turf fires and homemade bread and preserves for breakfast. The lovely bedrooms are deliberately left without amenities to make a visit here a real country house experience and to encourage guests to mix with each other – tea is available downstairs at any time in this hospitable house. *Rooms 5 (3 shower only). Closed 23-27 Dec. No CC. **Directions:** In village of Kinnitty.*

 **Kinnitty Castle Hotel**

Kinnitty Co Offaly 📞*057 913 7318 www.kinnittycastlehotel.com*

In this famously wacky Gothic Revival castle, eclectically furnished public areas include a library bar, Georgian-style dining room, Louis XV drawing room and an atmospheric Dungeon Bar. Bedrooms vary - the best are big and romantic, which befits this successful wedding venue. The castle is haunted (of course) and at its best a stay here can be great fun, but make sure you don't leave your sense of humour at home. **Rooms 37**. *Closed 24-26 Dec. CC.* **Directions:** *On the R422- Emo to Birr Road,off main N7 Limerick Road.*

  Derryvilla Blueberries

Portarlington Co Offaly 📞*057 864 2882 www.derryvillablueberries.com*

The high bush American blueberries produced on John Seager's Derryvilla Blueberry Farm near Portarlington are a seasonal treat, and all the more precious for that. No pesticides are used at Derryvilla farm, which is managed by Nuala O'Donoghue. Fresh blueberries and products made with them (a tangy tonic and preserves) are for sale at the farm shop, and you can pick your own in August and September.

 The Village Tavern

Main Street Shannonbridge Co Offaly 📞*090 967 4112*

Weary travellers can be restored at J.J. Killeen's wonderful pub and shop, particularly by the house special of hot rum and chocolate – perfect after a damp day on the river. Meanwhile, you can also top up on groceries, fishing bait and gas. Music nightly from May to September; weekends only during the off season. **Directions:** *On the main street of Shannonbridge, between Ballinasloe and Cloghan.*

TULLAMORE

This thriving canalside town is perhaps best known for its most famous product, Tullamore Dew and, while it may no longer be made here, the Tullamore Dew Heritage Centre (057 9325015) on the banks of the Grand Canal focuses on the distilling, canal and urban history of the town (tours available daily). Nearby, the splendid Gothic Charleville Forest Castle stands in beautiful parkland - the Charleville oak is one of the biggest and oldest in the country and, botanically, an important survivor of primeval stock. Tullamore is also an ideal base for discovering the Slieve Bloom Mountains, with many beautiful walking and cycling trails, and picnic areas with panoramic views of the surrounding lowlands. Also nearby are the unique 'Lough Boora' parklands; the boglands habitat supports a wide range of flora and fauna and now also hosts some of the most innovative land and environmental sculptures in Ireland - the artists, inspired by the rich natural and industrial legacy of the boglands, have created a series of large-scale sculptures that are now part of the Parklands permanent collection. Garden lovers should make a point of visiting Birr Castle (057 912 0336), with its observatory and magnificently restored gardens. Tullamore is an excellent short break destination with everything in the compact town within walking distance. There is a country market at the Millenium Square on Saturday (9-4).

 The Blue Apron

Harbour Street Tullamore Co Offaly 📞*057 936 0106 www.theblueapronrestaurant.ie*

This little restaurant near the canal is well worth seeking out for owner-chef Kenan Pehlivan's interesting cooking. Menus cover all the bases, yet also offer something different – some unusual combinations work well, and all dishes are attractively presented. Combining quality of food and service with good value, the cooking is among the best to be found in a wide area. *Open Wed-Sat 5.30- 9.30pm (to 10 Fri & Sat), Sun 12.30-9pm. Closed Mon & Tue.* **Directions:** *Centre of Tullamore.*

Bridge House Hotel

Bridge Street Tullamore *Co Offaly* ☎*057 932 5600 www.bridgehouse.com*

This recently redeveloped centrally located 4-star hotel is popular with locals and a comfortable place to stay, with spacious public areas, and a leisure centre with pool and gym among the facilities. Suites are offered as well as compact and well equipped standard rooms. A very good breakfast is a highlight - as are the mostly Irish staff, who are particularly friendly and helpful. **Rooms 70.** *Closed 25 Dec. CC.* **Directions:** *Centre of Tullamore on Bridge Street.*

C.R. Tormeys Butchers

Bridge Street Tullamore *Co Offaly* ☎*057 932 1426*

Associated Craft Butchers of Ireland members, these third-generation farmers and family butchers are well known in the west and midlands, with shops in Mullingar, Tullamore and Galway. Recognised for their high standards and combining tradition with innovation, they have achieved numerous awards for excellence, notably for their beef. *Open: Tue-Sat, 9-6.*

Farm Factory Direct

Kulcruttin Business Park Spollenstown Road Tullamore *Co Offaly*
☎*057 932 9405 www.farmfactorydirect.ie*

Margaret and Ivor Deverell's business is a direct sales outlet for top-quality locally produced meat. Grass-fed Irish Hereford beef is supplied by Hereford Prime, a breeders' group that promotes the raising and management of the breed, which is known for the well-marbled meat that gives it its tenderness and flavour, and also lamb from the Offaly Lamb Producers Group.

Jamie's Restaurant

Main Street Tullamore *Co Offaly* ☎*057 935 1529*

This lively restaurant is a home from home for many local diners and serving good food at reasonable prices. Jamie Owens runs the show from the kitchen and it's a family affair front of house. The early bird menu is great value and the à la carte menu offers an appealing variety of dishes, with 'a great steak' consistently popular. **Seats 40.** *D Wed-Sun; L Sun only. Closed Mon & Tue. CC.* **Directions:** *Main Street.*

Lough Boora Farm

Leabeg Tullamore *Co Offaly* ☎*057 934 5005*

Tony Garahy runs a long-established organic box scheme in West Offaly and North Tipperary, supplying vegetables in season (a wide range of varieties is grown) and home-produced beef and lamb (mainly frozen) as well as organic bread from Coolfin Gardens Bakery in Banagher. The farm produce is also sold at markets and selected stores.

SiRocco's Restaurant

Patrick Street Tullamore Co Offaly ☎*057 935 2839 www.siroccos.net*

This popular Italian restaurant, owned and managed by Paula Moran-Tahraoui, is warm and welcoming. The extensive menu features a wide range of dishes and a real bonus is that many dishes can be ordered as a main course or as a (generous) starter. Service is spot on, it's very family friendly and good value for money. Visitors to Tullamore would be happy to find this place. **Seats 70** *(outdoors, 10); D Mon-Sat, L Thu & Fri only; Sun all day, 1-10pm. Closed 25-26 Dec, 1 Jan, Good Fri. CC.* **Directions:** *Adjacent to Tullamore Garda Station (town centre).*

 ### Tullamore Court Hotel

O'Moore Street Tullamore Co Offaly ☎*057 934 6666 www.tullamorecourthotel.ie*

An attractive building, set back from the road a little and softened by trees, this large modern hotel is welcoming, with bright and cheerful public areas. With an excellent leisure centre and fine banqueting facilities it serves the local community well. Its business and conference facilities are a great strength and it's also a comfortable and hospitable base for short breaks, within easy walking distance of the whole town. **Rooms 104**. *Closed 24-26 Dec. CC.* **Directions:** *South end of town.*

 ### Annaharvey Farm

Tullamore Area Tullamore Co Offaly ☎*057 934 3544 www.annaharveyfarm.ie*

Equestrian activities are the main attraction at Henry and Lynda Deverell's restored grain barn near Tullamore, where very comfortable accommodation is offered and good home cooking has always been a central feature. This appealing equestrian centre and farm B&B is a delightful place to stay, and cookery classes are available too, adding an extra dimension to a rural break. **Rooms 7** *(6 shower only). Meals available for residents only Mon-Sat. Closed Dec & Jan. CC.* **Directions:** *R420 Tullamore - Portarlington.*

  ### Glenisk Organic Dairy

Tullamore Area Newtown Killeigh Co Offaly ☎*057 934 4000 www.glenisk.com*

Situated beside the Cleary family's farm at Killeigh, Glenisk is Ireland's largest organic dairy producer. Working with about 50 organic farmers, they produce cows' milk and yogurt, a children's range – yogurt and fromage frais – and also goats' milk and yogurt. The scale of their operation means their award winning range can compete effectively with mainstream products, bringing organic production to a widely accessible level.

  ### O'Donohue's Bakery

Tullamore Area Kilcruttin Centre Tullamore Co Offaly ☎*057 932 1411*

Although quite a large scale operation, this award-winning fifth generation craft bakery is known for its outstanding quality and is currently run by Cathal O'Donohue and family. Buttermilk soda, batch bread, spelt & honey bread, low GI multiseed bread and wholewheat soda are among the most popular products. Their success is down to a combination of traditional methods and innovative products – all of which have a genuine home-baked flavour.

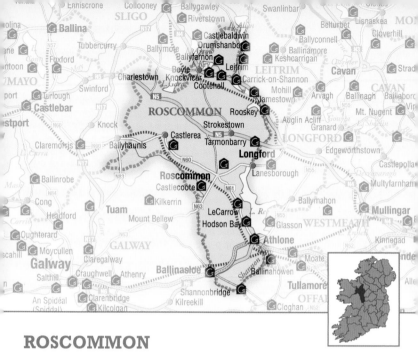

ROSCOMMON

It could be said that Roscommon is a county much put upon by the counties about it. Sometimes it seems that just as Roscommon is on the verge of becoming significant, it becomes somewhere else. In one notable example - the hotel complex at Hodson's Bay on the western shores of Lough Ree - the location is actually in Roscommon, yet the exigencies of the postal service have given it to Athlone and thereby Westmeath.

But Roscommon is a giving sort of county, for it gave Ireland her first President, Gaelic scholar Douglas Hyde (1860-1949), it was also the birthplace of Oscar Wilde's father, and the inimitable songwriter Percy French was a Roscommon man.

Roscommon town itself has a population of 1,500, but it's growing, though the presence of extensive castle ruins and a former gaol tell of a more important past. The gaol was once noted for having a female hangman, today it has shops and a restaurant. Northwestward at Castlerea - headquarters for the County Council - we find Clonalis House, ancestral home of the O'Conor Don, and final resting place of O'Carolan's Harp.

In the north of the county, the town of Boyle near lovely Lough Key with its outstanding Forest Park is a substantial centre, with a population nearing the 2,000 mark. Boyle is thriving, and symbolic of this is the restored King House, a masterpiece from 1730. Reckoned to have been the most important provincial town house in Ireland, it is today filled with exhibits which eloquently evoke the past. And nearby, the impressive riverbank remains of Boyle Abbey, the largest Cistercian foundation in Ireland, date from 1148.

LOCAL ATTRACTIONS & INFORMATION

▸ **Boyle Abbey** Boyle
071 9662604
▸ **King House**
Boyle *071 9663242*

▸ **Strokestown Park** House,
Garden & Famine Museum
071 9633013

▸ **Clonalis House** Castlerea
094 9620014

 **Kilronan Castle**

Ballyfarnon Co Roscommon ✆*071 961 8000 www.kilronancastle.ie*

A 5-star hotel at the heart of a 40-acre estate overlooking Lough Meelagh; the original castle has been restored with style in the public areas and, while most rooms are new, accommodation is luxurious. The beautifully appointed and intimate Douglas Hyde Restaurant makes a fine special occasion dining destination. With a leisure club and spa, it's a popular wedding and short break venue. **Rooms 84**. *Open all year. CC.* **Directions:** *Follow R280/284 north from Carrick on Shannon.*

BOYLE

The attractive town of Boyle lies beneath the Curlew Mountains on the main pass connecting the plains of Connaught with the North and straddles the Boyle River. A good fishing area, it has its own harbour, where Shannon cruisers can overnight. Known for its fine music pubs, Boyle also offers much of historical interest, notably King House (500 years of Irish life, 071 966 3242).

 Lough Key House

Boyle Co Roscommon ✆*071 966 2161 www.loughkeyhouse.com*

Frances McDonagh's lovely small Georgian residence is ideally placed to explore the wonderfully wild North-West. The three best rooms in the house are kept for guests and all are quite different. A happy house, with lots of animals around; Frances is a great hostess and breakfast is a high point, including freshly-laid eggs from their own hens. **Rooms 6** *(3 shower only). Closed 9 Dec-9 Jan. CC.* **Directions:** *Located on the N4, 5km from Boyle.*

 Castlecoote House

Castlecoote Co Roscommon ✆*090 666 3794 www.castlecootehouse.com*

Even if you aren't staying at Kevin Finnerty's fine Georgian house, this Hidden Ireland property is a beautiful place to visit – guided tours of the house and grounds are offered from April to October and afterwards you can have afternoon tea in the Old Ballroom. Bright and airy guest rooms have marble fireplaces and four-poster beds. A wonderful place to stay for both individuals and groups. **Rooms 5** *(1 with private bathroom, 1 shower only); Closed 31 Oct - 17 Mar. CC.* **Directions:** *into village, cross bridge, bear right, gates are directly ahead.*

🏨 📺 🛏 🎿 ♥ **Clonalis House**

Castlerea Co Roscommon ✆*094 962 0014 www.clonalis.com*

Despite the grandeur, there's a warm and homely atmosphere at Pyers and Marguerite O'Conor-Nash's stunning 45-room Victorian Italianate mansion. Everything is on a huge scale: open fires burn in the vast yet comfortable reception rooms, and luxurious bedrooms have massive four-poster and half-tester beds. The beautiful dining room makes an impressive setting for Marguerite's good home cooking, but an informal alternative is also offered in a 'country kitchen' setting.

History is everywhere - even in a small museum (open to the public). A magnificently rewarding place to stay. **Rooms 4** (1 with private bathroom). Residents D Tue-Sat (24 hrs notice required). Closed Oct-Apr. CC. **Directions:** N60, west of Castlerea.

M. J. Henry

Cootehall Boyle Co Roscommon ✆071 966 7030

M.J. Henry hasn't changed in at least 30 years (except for the new smokers' area at the back), and in true country Irish fashion, this pub is also a food store. Get in beside the fire with a hot whiskey and the world will do you no harm. A visit to Cootehall would be unthinkable without checking on this little gem. Not really a food place, but there may well be music. Open evenings only midweek, from midday at weekends. Closed 25 Dec & Good Fri. **Directions:** 3km off N4 Sligo - Dublin road, between Boyle & Carrick-on-Shannon.

Bruno's Restaurant

Tara Marina Knockvicar Boyle Co Roscommon ✆071 966 7788

Bruno Boe's stylish contemporary restaurant enjoys views over the river and is equally popular with local diners and boating visitors to the marina alongside. Expect a warm welcome, authentic Italian cooking and fair prices at this relaxing and family-friendly restaurant, which makes a great destination for a Sunday out. **Seats 70.** D Tue-Sun, Sun open from 1pm-'late'. Closed Mon & a few weeks Oct-Nov & Feb. CC. **Directions:** Near Carrick-on-Shannon, on the Knockvicar-Cootehall road.

St Johns House

Rinnagan Lecarrow Co Roscommon ✆090 666 1748 www.stjohnshouse.biz

In a beautiful rural waterside location overlooking Lough Ree, Richard and Liz Collins's lovely understated late Georgian country house may well be Roscommon's best kept secret. The rooms are very different but all have charm and breakfast is served in a fine formal dining room with an open fire. With warm hospitality, a wonderful setting, and so many things to do and explore right on the doorstep, it's a magical place and you'll soon be wishing you could stay longer. What a find.

Rooms 3. Self catering also available. Closed Oct-Mar unless by arrangement. **Directions:** From Lecarrow (N61) follow signs for St John's House / Rinn Duin Castle.

The Yew Tree

Lecarrow Co Roscommon ✆090 666 1255

Just off the main road and near Lecarrow's attractive little harbour, Nicola Slattery and Aidan Murray's smartly presented and welcoming restaurant is deservedly popular. Open from lunchtime onwards in the second half of the week, this pleasant neighbourhood restaurant offers generous portions of good food on a short lunch menu and more elaborate dishes in the evening. Good value and a great asset to the area. **Seats 65**. Open Wed-Sun,12.30-9. CC. **Directions:** From Athlone, N61 Roscommon road, about midway between the two towns.

 **Abbey Hotel & Leisure Centre**

Abbeytown Galway Road Roscommon *Co Roscommon* ✆*090 662 6240 www.abbeyhotel.ie*

The heart of this pleasing 4-star hotel is an old manor house and some of this ambience remains. While mainly modern, the spacious bedrooms are all of a high standard, some with a view of the 13th century abbey. Although known for its conference and business facilities, the high level of comfort, leisure facilities and good value offered also make it appealing for short breaks. **Rooms 50** *(2 shower only). Hotel closed 25-26 Dec. CC.* **Directions:** *N4 to Roscommon, Galway Road; next to the library, on the left.*

  Castlemine Farm

Castlemine Fourmilehouse Roscommon *Co Roscommon* ✆*090 662 9886 www.castleminefarm.ie*

Sean Allen and his two sons, Derek and Brendan, are the latest generations to run this family farm with animal welfare at its heart - which has made a mark nationally for quality and marketing innovation. The Allens' pasture-fed beef, lamb, rare breed pork, poultry and vegetables are sold directly in their farm shop, at Galway and Moycullen Farmers' Markets and online. Visitors are welcome; occasional farm walks and activities (check website). *Farm Shop (Athlone Road, Roscommon Town, Mon-Thu & Sat 9-6, Fri 9-7); online shop.*

  Galway Hooker

Roscommon Business Park Racecourse Road Roscommon *Co Roscommon*
✆*087 236 6186 www.galwayhooker.ie*

First cousins Aidan Murphy and Ronan Brennan have received numerous awards for their Irish pale ale since they established their brewery in 2006, including being twice crowned Ireland's Best Beer. The beer is named after a traditional type of sailing boat used by local fishermen. Check their website for a listing of where to find the beer.

  **Gleeson's Townhouse**

Market Square Roscommon *Co Roscommon* ✆*090 662 6954 www.gleesonstownhouse.com*

Overlooking the square, Mary and Eamonn Gleeson's townhouse and restaurant provides just what every visitor requires: a warm welcome, comfortable rooms and first-class food. The Gleesons place great emphasis on food, offering wholesome fare in their popular coffee shop and extensive à la carte menus in the Manse Restaurant; they buy local where possible, including produce from the the weekly farmers' market. Allow time to visit their specialist food and wine shop next door, as it is well worth a look. **Rooms 19**. *Restaurant* **seats 55** *(outdoors, 30). L&D daily. Also café open 8am-6pm daily. Closed 25-26 Dec. CC.* **Directions:** *Town centre, next door to Tourist Office / County Museum.*

  The Tattie Hoaker

14 Goff Street Roscommon *Co Roscommon* ✆*086 157 5623*

This well-known health food store sells organic wholefoods as well as a wide range of health supplements and health and beauty products. They operate a weekly home delivery organic fruit and vegetable box scheme and trade at farmers' markets, including the Market Yard at Carrick-on-Shannon (Thursdays).

The Old Fort

Shannonbridge Co Roscommon ✆*090 967 4973 www.theoldfortrestaurant.com*

In a pleasant and historically interesting site right beside the Shannon, Fergal Moran's restaurant in a restored fort has oodles of character. Head chef Marie Haverty offers a number of menus and, as ever, the simplest dishes are often best – a juicy local steak, cooked as ordered, is a very good meal, and together with attentive service and lovely surroundings can make for a memorable outing. ***Seats 80**. D Fri-Sat; L Sun. (A phone call to check is advised). Closed Nov-Feb inc. CC.* **Directions:** *Beside the bridge in Shannonbridge.*

Keenans Hotel & Restaurant

Tarmonbarry (via Clondra) Co Roscommon ✆*043 332 6052 www.keenans.ie*

Just beside the bridge over the Shannon in Tarmonbarry, Barry and Annette Keenan's friendly, well-run bar and restaurant is full of character; it's a favourite watering hole for river folk and makes a great place to break a journey between Dublin and the north-west. Informal meals are mostly quite traditional, but with more international influences in the evening dishes, while à la carte bar menus offer hearty fare that pleases all age groups – the steak sandwich is not to be missed. Smart en-suite accommodation is offered, with some of the 12 rooms overlooking the Shannon. ***Rooms 12**. Restaurant **seats 100**. Food daily 12.30-8.30. Restaurant closed D Sun. Establishment closed 25/26 Dec. CC.* **Directions:** *On N5, west of Longford town.*

The Purple Onion Bar & Restaurant

Tarmonbarry (via Clondra) Co Roscommon ✆*043 335 9919 www.purpleonion.ie*

Paul Dempsey and Pauline Roe's busy roadside pub has an old-world feeling and it doubles as an art gallery, so good original paintings add interest and charm. The choice offered is impressive for a small restaurant, with a core of popular dishes but a few to tempt more adventurous diners too. The food is interesting and offers something different from other choices in the area – the wild boar sausage alone is reason enough to return. ***Seats 55**; L Sun only; D Tue-Sun. Closed Mon. CC.* **Directions:** *13km west of Longford on Dublin-Westport road.*

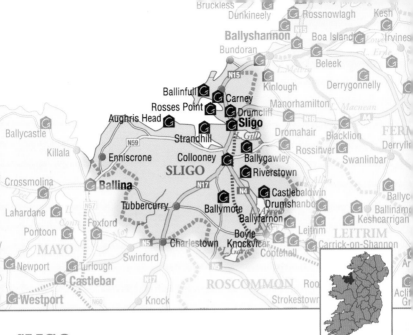

SLIGO

There's a stylish confidence to Sligo which belies its compact area as one of Ireland's smallest counties. Perhaps it's because they know that their place and their way of life have been immortalised through association with two of the outstanding creative talents of modern Ireland, W.B.Yeats and his painter brother Jack. The former's fame seems beyond question, while the latter's star was never higher than it is today.

The town and the county have many associations with Yeats, but few are more remarkable than Lissadell House, the former home of the Gore-Booths, best known as the family of Constance Gore-Booth. As Countess Markievicz, she was much involved with the Easter Rising of 1916. But whatever the reason for Sligo's special quality, there's certainly something about it that encourages repeat visits. The town itself is big enough to be reassuring, yet small enough to be comfortable. And the countryside about Sligo town also has lasting appeal, with its impressive scale set by the heights of Ben Bulben.

Mankind has been living here with enthusiasm for a very long time indeed, for in recent years it has been demonstrated that some of County Sligo's ancient monuments are amongst the oldest in northwest Europe. Lakes abound, the mountains are magnificent, and there are tumbling rivers a-plenty.

Yet if you wish to get away from the bustle of the regular tourist haunts, Sligo can look after your needs in this as well, for the western part of the county down through the Ox Mountains towards Mayo is an uncrowded region of wide vistas and clear roads.

LOCAL ATTRACTIONS & INFORMATION

▸ **Largest Megalithic Cemetry in Ireland** Carrowmore
071 9161534

▸ **Drumcliffe Church & Visitor Centre** Drumcliff
071 9144956

▸ **Seaweed Bath House**
Inniscrone *096 36238*

▸ **Model Arts & Niland Gallery**
Sligo *071 9141405*

 **Beach Bar/Aughris House**

Aughris Head Templeboy Co Sligo ☎071 917 6465 www.thebeachbarsligo.com

The McDermott family's picturesque thatched pub seems too good to be true when you first find it in this quiet and unspoilt place. It's a lovely stopping place with wholesome, home-cooked food like seafood chowder, great steaks, bangers and mash and homemade desserts too. The McDermotts also offer comfortable, inexpensive, family-friendly B&B accommodation in a neat bungalow just beside the pub and overlooking the ocean. Bar opens at noon daily. Bar food daily 1-8 in summer (food served weekends only off season). Rooms 6 (1 with private bathroom (not connected)). *Open all year. CC.* **Directions:** *Off N59 Sligo/Ballina Road, Coast road to Aughris Head/Pier.*

 Castle Dargan Hotel & Golf

Castle Dargan Estate Ballygawley Co Sligo ☎071 911 8080 www.castledargan.com

Named after the ruins of the ancient castle which remain within its Darren Clarke-designed championship golf course, the bar of this contemporary hotel is a pleasant spot to enjoy a bite, with golf and countryside views and extensive decking. Bedrooms are finished to a high standard, with suites in the old house enjoying a special atmosphere. It would make a magnificent wedding venue. ***Rooms 54.*** *Open all year. CC.* **Directions:** *10 minutes from Sligo town - take the R284 to Ballygawley.*

    **Temple House**

Ballinacarrow Ballymote Co Sligo ☎071 918 3329 www.templehouse.ie

 A Georgian mansion situated in 1,000 acres of farm and woodland, overlooking the original lakeside castle which was built by the Knights Templar in 1200 A.D. The Perceval family has lived here since 1665, and Roderick and his wife Helena now welcome guests to their home, which is a fascinating place where everything has a history, log fires warm the huge rooms and bedrooms are furnished with family antiques. Evening meals, served in a beautiful dining room, are a real treat. Activity breaks, cookery demonstrations, music and traditional dancing nearby. ***Rooms 6*** *(2 shower only). Residents D (book by 1pm, not available Sun). Closed Dec-Mar. CC.* **Directions:** *Signposted off N17, 0.5 km south of Ballinacarrow.*

  **Clevery Mill**

Castlebaldwin Co Sligo ☎071 912 7424 www.cleverymill.com

From the moment you push open the door of Brian and Pamela Conboy's converted mill, you get a sense of warmth and relaxation and, whether staying in one of the charming country bedrooms or just in for a meal, you'll enjoy the old-world country ambience in the bar area. The restaurant overlooks the old waterwheel and tempting menus offer a wide selection of dishes, with suppliers - mostly local and many organic - credited. ***Seats 54*** *(outdoors, 8); D Thu-Sat, L Sun only. Rooms 6. Closed D Sun, Mon-Wed; house closed Christmas & New Year. CC.* **Directions:** *20km from Sligo, N4 towards Dublin.*

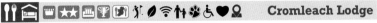 **Cromleach Lodge**

Lough Arrow Castlebaldwin via Boyle Co Sligo ☎*071 916 5155 www.cromleach.com*

Christy and Moira Tighe's hotel enjoys stunning views over Lough Arrow - and a stay in one of the ten original rooms offers a luxurious retreat for discerning guests, with genuine hospitality from the Tighe family and their staff. Diners travel great distances to Moira's Restaurant, where meticulously sourced ingredients are transformed into beautiful dishes, with memorable attention to detail. Also a popular wedding venue. *Rooms 57. Restaurant seats 100. L & D daily. Light food served throughout the day. House closed Mon & Tue, Nov and 5 days at Christmas. CC. Directions: Signposted from Castlebaldwin on the N4.*

 **Markree Castle**

Collooney Co Sligo ☎*071 9167800 www.markreecastle.ie*

 Sligo's oldest inhabited house has been home to the Cooper family for 350 years. Set in magnificent park and farmland, this quirky place is a proper castle - a huge portico leads to a covered stone stairway that sweeps up to an impressive hall, where an enormous log fire burns. It is a popular wedding venue and accommodation varies but, thanks to the determined restoration work of current owners Charles and Mary Cooper, this is a place with real heart - and they are generous with the heating. Knockmuldowney Restaurant is very beautiful and the food has always been good here. *Rooms 30. Restaurant seats 90. D daily & L Sun; bar menu also available. Hotel closed 24-27 Dec. CC. Directions: Just off the N4, take the Dromohair/R290 exit at Collooney roundabout.*

Davis's Restaurant & Yeats Tavern

Drumcliff Co Sligo ☎*071 916 3117 www.yeatstavernrestaurant.com*

Owned by the Davis family since 1970, this stylish and cheerful modern restaurant's warm welcome and wide-ranging menu of tasty, fresh, locally sourced food has earned it a well-deserved reputation as a popular and affordable eating place for both locals and visitors. Bar food is also available every day in the Yeats Tavern. *Seats 200 (outdoors, 30). Food served Mon-Sat 10.30am-9.30pm, Sun & Bank Hols 12-9pm. Closed Good Friday, 25/26 Dec. CC. Directions: 7km north of Sligo Town on the main Donegal road (N15).*

 Carraig Fhada Seaweed

Cabra Rathlee Easky Co Sligo ☎*096 49042 www.carraigfhada.com*

In addition to its traditional use to enrich farmland, seaweed is harvested commercially in Ireland for culinary and therapeutic use, particularly in Co Sligo. Frank and Betty Melvin of Carraig Fhada Seaweed are long-established experts and their range includes the seaweeds most widely used in cooking, carrageen moss (carraigín) and dillisk (duileasc), also kombu (the Japanese term for kelp). Carraig Fhada Seaweed also prepare products for therapeutic use, including their popular Atlantic Seaweed Bath.

Eithna's by the Sea

Mullaghmore Co Sligo 086 851 5607 www.bythesea.ie

A favourite destination for seafood lovers for many a year, fans will be delighted to find Eithna O'Sullivan's atmospheric harbourside restaurant is back. Mainly a daytime place, she offers classic seafood and quality light meals using the best from sea and land, including seaweeds. Seafood salad on brown bread with dressed salad, perhaps, or grilled mackerel with seaweed pesto. Also vegetarian options - and delicious desserts. Simply masgic. *Open daily in summer, 10-5, D Sat and other evenings if booked. NO CC.*

Coopershill House

Riverstown Co Sligo 071 916 5108 www.coopershill.com

Undoubtedly one of the most delightful and superbly comfortable Georgian houses in Ireland, this sturdy granite mansion is a warm and friendly place under the management of Simon O'Hara, who runs it with the seamless hospitality born of long family experience. Rooms are sumptuous and, as well as seasonal home grown fruit and vegetables, you may well find their own venison on the dinner menu, along with other delicious dishes cooked up by Simon's partner, Christina McCauley. And, at breakfast, you can watch red squirrels scampering around outside. A particularly perfect country house. **Rooms 8** *(1 shower only, 1 private bathroom). Dining Room* **Seats 30**. *D 8.15pm daily (non-residents welcome by reservation). Closed end Oct-1 Apr. (off-season house parties of 12-16 people welcome.) CC.* **Directions:** *Signposted from N4 at Drumfin crossroads.*

Coopershill House Irish Venison

Riverstown Co Sligo 071 916 5108 www.coopershill.com

Established by Lindy and Brian O'Hara in 1995, Coopershill Venison is the tender meat of the O'Hara family's young grass-fed fallow deer; often served to guests at this beautiful place, it is also seen on some of the best restaurant menus in Ireland. Animal welfare is a high priority and farm visits are welcome by arrangement. Offered in a wide range of cuts, including delicious sausages and smoked haunch, the meat is available to purchase direct from the farm, from selected retailers and from the Sligo farmers' market (Sat 9-1). Recognition for Coopershill Venison includes an Irish Food Writers' Guild Good Food Award in 2011. The price list is on the website and there's a recipe booklet to help home cooks get the best from this delicious and versatile meat.

ROSSES POINT

This seaside village is set against the impressive backdrops of spectacular mountains and Sligo Bay. Rosses Point offers visitors two magnificent sandy beaches, great for windsurfing and sea angling, whilst golfers can take advantage of an 18 hole championship golf club. Although small, the village has good eating places and friendly atmospheric pubs.

 The Waterfront

Rosses Point Co Sligo ✆*071 917 7122 www.waterfrontrestaurant.ie*

This popular restaurant boasts fine views of Oyster Island and Coney Island, and owner-chef Brian Fox's cooking combines traditional and more adventurous flavours, with a focus on seafood. Light meals are available during the day, with products from the in-house bakery a highlight. On the pricey side, but ingredients are fresh, mainly local and good quality - and the setting is priceless. *Seats 120 (outdoors, 20). Open 12 noon-10pm. Open 7 days in summer, closed Mon & Tue off season. Music Fri night. Closed 25 Dec, Good Fri. CC. **Directions:** In Rosses Point village, looking out on the bay.*

SLIGO

A fascinating town, with a rich heritage, Sligo has a rich cultural heritage and, in the town, the Model Arts & Niland Gallery is especially worth visiting; there are many associations with the poet W.B. Yeats and his brother, the painter Jack Yeats - the most notable connection was with Lissadell House & Gardens (Ballinfull; 071 916 3150; not open to the public at time of going to press), the former home of the Gore-Booths, of whom the best known was Constance Gore-Booth who, as Countess Markievicz, was much involved with the Easter Rising of 1916. The County Sligo (Rosses Point, 071 917 7134) championship golf course provides a tough test for golfers of all abilities. There is a Farmers Market in Sligo IT on Saturdays (9am -1pm).

 **Clarion Hotel Sligo**

Clarion Road Sligo Co Sligo ✆*071 911 9000 www.clarionhotelsireland.com*

This large hotel dates back to 1848 but has emerged as a modern classic following recent redevelopment. Accommodation is of the usual Clarion standard, with a high proportion of suites, and dining options include the well-appointed Sinergie restaurant or casual dining Asian style in the Kudos Bar. Good business and conference facilities are an attraction, and leisure and pampering facilities include a pool, gym and spa treatments. *Rooms 312. CC. **Directions:** Follow N16 signs for Enniskillen.*

Coach Lane Restaurant @ Donaghy's Bar

1-2 Lord Edward Street Sligo Co Sligo ✆*071 916 2417 www.coachlane.com*

Orla and Andy Donaghy's attractive restaurant has earned a well-deserved place as one of the best in the area and its atmosphere and consistently good food never fail to please. Andy's menus are lively and attractive and his cooking is confident. An active supporter of local produce, he offers a wide choice and does a great line in well-aged Angus steaks and sustainably sourced seafood. *Seats 120 (40 outdoors). D daily. Also bar food daily 3-10pm. Traditional music Sun night.Closed 25 Dec, Good Fri. CC. **Directions:** N4 to Sligo, left at Adelaide Street, right into Lord Edward Street.*

Cosgroves

32 Market Street Sligo Co Sligo ✆*071 914 2809*

Third-generation grocer Michael Cosgrove's delightful traditional shop has been trading since 1898. It not only sells all manner of good things but also offers a level of personal service that's becoming increasingly rare. They take pride in the fact that it's a place where regular customers are known by name, and 'you'll find more real choice than in any of the big multiples'. How true. *Open Mon-Sat, 9.30am-7pm. Closed Sun.*

                                                          Eala Bhan

Rockwood Parade Sligo Co Sligo ✆*071 914 5823 www.ealabhan.ie*

Following on the success of their Strandhill seafood restaurant, Trá Bán (see entry), Anthony Gray and Cedric Roussilhe opened this town centre restaurant Eala Bhàn ('White Swan') in an attractive riverside premises in 2011. Steak and seafood are the stated specialities (try the lunchtime chargrilled sirloin steak sambo), but menus offer plenty of choice, with upbeat versions of many crowd pleasing dishes including delicious vegetarian and children's choices. Offering delicious food, pleasing surroundings, great staff and real value for money, it's easy to see why this restaurant is so successful. *Seats 65. D daily, L Tue-Sun. Closed L Mon, 25-26 Dec & Good Fri. CC.*

                                            The Embassy Wine Bar & Grill

JFK Parade Sligo Co Sligo ✆*071 916 1250 www.embassygrill.eu*

Although not enticing from the street, this town centre restaurant on the banks of the Garavogue River is stylishly appointed and an extensive à la carte menu offers plenty of favourites and homemade desserts. Generous servings of good-quality food, served efficiently in a relaxed environment and giving good value for money explain the Embassy's popularity. *Seats 60. D daily, L Sun only. Closed Good Fri, 24-26 Dec. CC.*

                                                  The Glasshouse Hotel

Swan Point Sligo Co Sligo ✆*071 914 9170 www.theglasshouse.ie*

A contemporary hotel with glass featuring heavily to take advantage of the 140 metres of frontage on the Garavogue River, it's a short walk from the shops, bars and restaurants – the style will not be to everybody's taste but locations don't come much more convenient than this. Some of the 116 bedrooms have balconies overlooking the river and city centre. *Rooms 116. Closed 24-26 Dec. CC.*

The Gourmet Parlour

Bridge Street Sligo Co Sligo ✆*071 914 4617 www.gourmetparlour.com*

Catherine Farrell and Annette Burke, both Ballymaloe-trained chefs, turn out some very tasty fare using carefully sourced, mainly local ingredients at their shop and deli. As well as offering an extensive menu, including wholesome ready meals, soups, salads and sandwiches (and some seriously tempting cakes and desserts), they also do catering and wedding cakes. *Open Mon-Sat, 9-6.*

Hargadons

4 O'Connell Street Sligo Co Sligo ✆*071 915 3709 www.hargadons.com*

 This famous and much-loved traditional grocery-bar is a listed building dating back to 1864 and today it has a great reputation for food too. Managed by Joe Grogan and Miriam Harte, there's a commitment to quality produce and showcasing the very best from the immediate locality. The emphasis is on hearty, home-cooked, traditional food, especially at lunchtime, but with a cosmopolitan twist. The old-world ambience, quality ingredients cooked well, pleasing presentation and lovely service from smartly dressed staff with black aprons all make for a really enjoyable meal here. A must-visit when in Sligo. *Restaurant seats 60. L&D Mon-Sat. No food on Sun.*

Kates Kitchen

3 Castle Street Sligo Co Sligo ✆*071 914 3022 www.kateskitchen.ie*

Sisters Kate, Beth and Jane O'Hara source and sell a wide range of the finest foods available, including baked goods and treats from local bakers and specialty meats from around Ireland. Along with fine wines and European specialities, Irish artisan producers are very well represented, including many from the immediate area - and they also offer a small selection of snacks and meals to go. *Open Mon-Sat, 8.45-6.15.*

Le Fournil

Tobergal Lane Sligo Co Sligo ✆*087 137 2724*

French chef Franck Pasquier established this popular continental bakery in 2008; he now runs the newer Donegal Town branch (which bakes breads for both outlets), but he has left it in the good hands of Clotilde Rambaud, who worked with him for several years. As well as their superb sourdough loaves made with specially sourced hard flour, they produce delectable patisserie and continental chocolate - and you will also find many other treats not easily sourced in Ireland. *Open:Tue-Thu 9.30-6, Fri 8.30-6, Sat 8.30-5.30.*

Lyons Café

Quay Street Sligo Co Sligo ☎ *071 914 2969 www.garystafford.com*

A visit to to the magnificently traditional Lyons Department Store (est. 1835) is de rigeur when visiting Sligo; it's a joy - and, on the first floor, is Gary Stafford's terrific café-restaurant. While their great home baking and enticing homemade desserts are legendary, Gary and his team also take seasonal, local produce and transform it into both gorgeous comfort food and a wide range of colourful, fresh-flavoured dishes, often influenced by his travels. Great salads and sandwiches too - and a lovely cookery book on sale. A place to savour. *Seats 125. Open Mon-Sat 9am-6pm (L 12.30-3pm). Closed Sun, Bank Hols, 25/26 Dec. CC. Also at: Slice@The Model.*

Montmartre

1 Market Yard Sligo Co Sligo ☎ *071 916 9901 www.montmartrerestaurant.ie*

Although out of the way, this pleasant, unpretentious French run restaurant has a strong local following and is well worth seeking out. Proprietor-chef Stéphane Magaud's varied menus offer French cuisine in a light, colourful style, with local produce featuring, especially seafood. Vegetables feature more than is usual in French restaurants, including imaginative vegetarian dishes; also game in season. Sound cooking, attractive presentation and reasonable prices ensure repeat customers. *Seats 50. D Tue-Sat, also bank hol Sundays. Closed Mon, 24-26 Dec. CC.*

Osta Café & Wine Bar

Garavogue Weir View (near Hyde Bridge) Stephen Street Sligo Co Sligo
☎ *071 914 4639 www.osta.ie*

Brid Torrades is well-known for her ardent support of local organic food and small producers, and the food at her attractive riverside café has immediacy and real depth of flavour. Breads and pastries from Brid's bakery are a specialty, as are Irish cheeses and charcuterie; daily specials include panini and wraps, also a spectacular array of homemade cakes. Good choice of wine by the glass (tapas offered in the evening). *Seats 35 (outdoors, 10). Open daily from 8am- 8pm (Thu-Sat, to 9.30pm), Sun 12- 5pm. Closed Winter Bank Hols. No CC.*

Slice @ The Model

The Model Arts & Niland Gallery The Mall Sligo Co Sligo ☎ *071 914 1405 www.themodel.ie*

Chef Gary Stafford operates this contemporary café in the atrium of the Model Arts Gallery and, although the kitchen is tiny, it works in tandem with his other business, Lyon's Café (see entry). Expect the same principle of using locally sourced ingredients in simple, great-tasting food, including a daily soup, vegetarian hot special, sandwiches, desserts, baked treats and a popular Sunday brunch. *Seats 125. Food served Tue-Sat 11.30-4.30pm, Sun 12-4pm. Closed Mon, 25/26 Dec. No CC.*

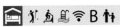 **Sligo Park Hotel**

Pearse Road Sligo Co Sligo ✆*071 919 0400 www.leehotels.com*

Set in parkland on the edge of Sligo town, this fairly modern hotel is known for its conference and leisure facilities, and appeals to those who prefer a quiet location and easy parking. Recent refurbishment has paid off, making this a much more attractive hotel; now that it has regained its cared-for feeling, it's a budget-conscious destination to consider for business and leisure.

 Source Sligo

1/2 John Street Sligo Co Sligo ✆*071 914 7605 www.sourcesligo.ie*

Ray and Eileen Monahan's glass-fronted landmark building houses several stylishly presented complementary businesses (a retail area, an informal restaurant, a wine and tapas bar and a stunning top floor cookery school), each reflecting a different aspect of the ideology behind Source – which, as the name implies, is a celebration of local foods and suppliers. A must-visit place for foodies when travelling in the North-West. *Open daily. Breakfast 9.30-12; Full menu 12-9.30pm. CC.*

  Tir na nOg

Grattan Street Sligo Co Sligo ✆*071 916 2752*

Sligo is a great town for good old-fashioned shopkeeping, and Mary and Norah O'Donnell's excellent wholefood store is one of its best-loved institutions, having supported local producers and supplied the town with a great range of health foods, organic vegetables and homeopathic remedies for many years. There's advice a-plenty and plenty of goodies to tempt you too – there's even vegan ice cream in the freezer. *Open Mon-Sat 9-6.*

   **Radisson Blu Hotel & Spa Sligo**

Sligo Area Ballincar Rosses Point Sligo Co Sligo ✆*071 914 0008 www.radissonblu.ie/hotel-sligo*

Views over Sligo Bay are the USP at this spacious and very comfortable hotel a short distance outside the town - views can be enjoyed to the full from the Classsiebawn Restaurant. Popular for weddings and short breaks, leisure facilities are good and the various room combinations include family rooms. The Radisson reputation for reliability and environmental awareness is a plus. **Rooms 132**. *Restaurant: D daily, L Sat & Sun. Bar meals also available, 12-7 daily. Open all year. CC.* **Directions:** *From Sligo town, follow signs for Rosses Point; the hotel is on the right after 3km.*

  Fabios

2a Wine Street Sligo Town Co Sligo

Perhaps Ireland's only authentic Italian gelateria, Fabio Boni's terrific little place has taken Sligo by storm. The fare is simple but of the best and everything is homemade. Using mainly local ingredients in season, plus some imported specially from Italy, Fabio makes all his own ice creams (gelato) and sorbets, which match the best you would find anywhere in Italy. *Open: Mon-Sat, 11am-6pm. No CC.*

Shells Bakery Café

Seafront Strandhill Co Sligo ℰ071 912 2938 www.shellscafe.com

Jane and Myles Lamberth's pretty little seafront café is the first port of call for many regular visitors to Strandhill. There's an obvious pride in using and producing the best and the menus offered for breakfast, lunch and snack times are surprisingly extensive. All breads and baked treats are made in-house and afternoon tea is a big treat. A great little spot, and with its own cookbook - and a shop next door too. *Open 7 days 9.30am-6pm. CC.* **Directions:** *On the sea front.*

Strand House Bar

Strandhill Co Sligo ℰ071 916 8140

Just 10 minutes' drive from Sligo and close to one of Europe's most magnificent surfing beaches, this well-known bar has a big welcoming turf fire, cosy snugs and friendly staff. Bar meals are served from noon to 4pm. (The first floor restaurant, Trá Bán, is operated separately.) *Bar meals served 12-4pm. Closed 25 Dec & Good Fri. CC.* **Directions:** *Follow signs to Sligo airport (Strandhill). Strand House is situated at the end near the beach.*

Strandhill Lodge & Suites

Top Road Strandhill Co Sligo ℰ071 912 2122 www.strandhilllodgeandsuites.com

Aimed at the discerning yet budget-conscious traveller, the Lodge has all of the advantages of quality hotel standard accommodation without the price tag associated with service. Rooms all have ocean views over the village and everything travellers could wish for: it's equally suited to couples seeking a romantic getaway, families who need the space and freedom not normally associated with hotels, and business guests. An exceptional place to stay, at exceptional value - and good food, music and craic available next door too. A great asset to Strandhill. **Rooms 22**, *1 self-catering apartment. CC.* **Directions:** *Located on the R292 road 7km from Sligo Town, well signed.*

Trá Bán Restaurant

Strandhill Co Sligo ℰ071 912 8402 www.trabansligo.ie

Located above the Strand House Bar but operated independently, proprietor Anthony Gray's hidden gem of a restaurant specialises in steak and seafood. Chef Cedric Roussilhe is committed to using only the finest local ingredients and takes pride in crediting his suppliers on wide ranging menus that are carefully crafted to combine quality with popular appeal. This relaxed and well-run restaurant combines good food with good value and is deservedly popular. *Eala Bhán in in Sligo Town is a sister restaurant (see entry). **Seats 60** (outdoors, 24). D Tue-Sun. Closed Mon; 25 Dec, Good Fri. CC. **Directions:** On seafront in Strandhill above Strand House Bar.

 ## The Venue Bar & Restaurant

Top Road Strandhill Co Sligo ✆071 916 8167 www.venuestrandhill.ie

 Shoreside properties tend to claim the attention in seaside towns, but the inquisitive visitor will find this lovely pub up the hill, overlooking Strandhill Bay. Beyond the cosy, old-world front bar, the restaurant is a big, bright room with panoramic views – a pleasant setting to enjoy good down-to-earth food, notably steaks and local seafood. Everything is wholesome and homemade which, together with the lovely location, friendly atmosphere and pocket-friendly prices, explains its well-deserved popularity. It's a great music pub too, with regular sessions (free entry). Bar open, 12.30pm – "Late". Restaurant **Seats 120**, Open daily 12.30-9.30. Closed 25-26 Dec & Good Fri. CC. **Directions:** Located on the R292 road 7km from Sligo Town, next door to Strandhill Lodge & Suites.

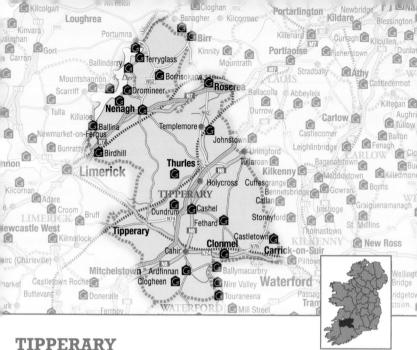

TIPPERARY

The cup of life is overflowing in Tipperary. In this extensive and wondrously fertile region, there's an air of fulfillment, a comfortable awareness of the world in harmony. And the placenames reinforce this sense of natural bounty.

Across the middle of the county, there's the Golden Vale, with prosperous lands along the wide valley of the River Suir and its many tributaries, and westwards towards County Limerick across a watershed around Donohill. The Vale be so named because the village of Golden is at its heart, but then it could be the other way round - that's the kind of place it is

The county's largest town, down in the far south under the Comeragh Mountains, is the handsome borough of Clonmel - its name translates as "Honey Meadow". Yet although there are many meadows of all kinds in Tipperary, there's much more to this largest inland county in Ireland than farmland, for it is graced with some of the most elegant mountains in the country.

North of the Golden Vale, the Silvermine Mountains rise to 694 m on Keeper Hill, and beyond them the farming countryside rolls on in glorious profusion to Nenagh and Tipperary's own riviera, the beautiful eastern shore of Lough Derg. Inevitably, history and historic monuments abound in such country, with the fabulous Rock of Cashel and its dramatic remains of ancient ecclesiastical buildings setting a very high standard for evoking the past.

But Tipperary lends itself every bit as well to enjoyment of the here and now. Tipperary is all about living life to the full, and they do it with style in a place of abundance.

LOCAL ATTRACTIONS & INFORMATION

‣ **Tipperary Crystal Visitor Centre** Birdhill *061 379066*

‣ **Bru Boru Culture Centre** Cashel *062 61122*

‣ **Holy Cross Abbey** Thurles *0504 43241*

Brocka-on-the-Water Restaurant

Kilgarvan Quay Ballinderry Nenagh Co Tipperary ☎*067 22038*

Anthony and Anne Gernon's almost-waterside restaurant in their home has attracted a following disproportionate to its size over the years. The atmosphere is very much a 'proper restaurant', but with a warm family welcome. Hens cluck around a garden stocked with the fruit and vegetables that will inspire the night's dinner - which also offers popular specialties showcasing local products. **Seats 30**; *D Fri-Sat, other nights according to demand (call to check opening times off-season). Closed Sun, Mon, Wed. No CC.* **Directions:** *Lough Derg drive, half way between Nenagh and Portumna.*

  Seymour Organic Farm

Sheepwalk Organic Farm Finnoe Road Borrisokane Co Tipperary
☎*086 400 0680 www.sheepwalkfarm.com*

Organic since 1999, the animals on Michael Seymour's farm are allowed to mature naturally on old limestone pastures, producing wonderfully flavoursome meat (Texel cross lamb and Aberdeen Angus beef) all year round. Both fresh and frozen meat is available whether small or large quantities; freezer boxes of lamb or beef, or a combination, are offered, also bespoke orders. *Available from: Sheepwalk Farm (call Michael on 086 400 0680 to arrange a time). Farmers' Markets: Ennis (Fri 8-2), Nenagh (Sat 10-3). Phone or email order for collection or delivery.*

  The Apple Farm

Moorstown Cahir Co Tipperary ☎*052 744 1459 www.theapplefarm.com*

Con Traas is one of Ireland's best known apple growers, and not only does he grow about 60 varieties of apples on this beautiful farm, but also pears, plums, cherries, strawberries and raspberries. A large farm shop offers fresh fruit in season, fruit juices (including a unique sparkling apple juice), preserves and other artisan products. Visitors are welcome to visit the orchards and there's even a caravan/camping site on the farm. The bottled products are also available online. *Shop open daily: Apr-Oct, 8am-6pm; Nov-Mar 8am-5pm, Sun 10-5. Also online sales for some products. CC.*

  Ballybrado Ltd

Ballybrado House Cahir Co Tipperary ☎*052 746 6206 www.ballybrado.com*

Established in1983 by one of Ireland's most famous organic activists, Josef Finke, and his wife Marianne, Ballybrado has always been known for its stoneground organic flour - and, more recently, also for baked products and mixes. The Ballybrado brand has passed down to their daughter, Julia, who is adding new lines of organic products, notably mueslis, baking mixes and quality snack foods.

  Good Herdsman Organic Meats

Clogheen Road Cahir Co Tipperary ☎*052 744 5500 www.goodherdsmen.com*

Established in 1989 by organic veteran Josef Finke, in order to coordinate the supply, processing and marketing of organic livestock in Ireland, Good Herdsmsan is the largest organic meat processor in Ireland and the UK. It coordinates the supply, processing and marketing of around 200 certified organic farmers, allowing organic Irish meats to take their place competitively in the chill cabinets of mainstream retailers.

  O'Briens Farm Shop

Outrath New Inn Cahir Co Tipperary

Pat O'Brien and family grow a range of floury potatoes and apples for their O'Briens Apple Juice. These are sold in this popular farm shop, along with home-produced pork, bacon and other local food products, including vegetables, free-range eggs, Baylough cheese and William's honey.

 River House Restaurant & Café Bar

1 Castle Street Cahir Co Tipperary ☎*052 744 1951 www.riverhouse.ie*

Jennifer Bailey's stylish café is in a lovely location, overlooking the River Suir and weir with a view of one of Ireland's most famous visitor attractions, Cahir Castle. A pleasing place for both tourists and locals to have a bite when visiting Cahir, the blackboard menus offer a range of popular dishes - smoothies, sandwiches, homemade quiches, hot dishes and desserts/cakes; food has homemade flavour and is fairly priced. *Open from 9am daily; L 12-3 daily; D Thu-Sun (to 9.30, except Sun to 7pm).*

CARRICK ON SUIR

This beautifully located medieval town is set in the ancient Golden Vale (Gleann an Oir), with the Comeragh Mountains to the south and the Walsh Mountains to the southeast, making this unspoilt area a wonderful base for outdoor activities. The river has always been central to the life and development of the town, formerly for trade and now mainly for pleasure. Although tidal, Carrick-on-Suir is navigable from any part of Ireland's inland waterways and a landing pontoon allows access to the town by boat. The Blarney Woollen Mills/Meadows & Byrne development, Dove Hill Design Centre (5km outside town on the N24/Clonmel road), attracts shoppers to the area and there is a farmers' market on Fridays in the Heritage Centre (Main St., 10am-2pm). Garden Lovers are spoilt for choice in this area, with several gardens of note nearby and there is golf at Carrick Golf Club (051 640 047) while challenging championship golf is available in nearby Mount Juliet Golf Club (Thomastown, 056 777 3064).

 **Kilkieran Cottage Restaurant**

Kilkiernan Castletown Carrick-on-Suir Co Tipperary ☎*051 645110 www.kilkierancottage.ie*

This pretty white cottage with its cheerful red half door enjoys views of the Comeragh mountains. Loyal customers enjoy the location and the ambience as well as the good seasonally inspired food prepared by highly regarded Kilkenny chef Neil McEvoy.Perfectly cooked food with a local bias, friendly service and the lovely rural setting make this an ideal place to bring visiting guests. *D Wed-Sun; L Sun only. CC.* **Directions:** *Castletown is a few km north of Carrick on Suir on the R697 beside Kilkieran High Crosses.*

CASHEL

Visitors flock here to see the famous the Rock of Cashel, a site hosting a ruined church and fortifications, formerly the seat of the Irish kings of Munster; King Cormac built his superb Royal Chapel in the 12th century and it can be seen on the Rock - nearby were Cistercian, Dominican and Franciscan abbeys, two of which may still be viewed. And the town itself also has much to offer, including archaeology and architecture of great historical significance (information available at the Heritage Centre on Main Street), and also some of the best food and hospitality to be found in Ireland (see entries). Golfers will find a Philip Walton designed 18 hole championship course nearby, at Dundrum House Hotel & Country Club (www.dundrumhousehotel.com).

 Baileys Hotel Cashel

Main Street Cashel Co Tipperary ✆*062 61937 www.baileyshotelcashel.com*

Set back from the road, with an attractive planted plaza in front, this fine early-18th century building in the heart of Cashel is a very pleasant place to stay and to experience Irish hospitality and good cooking. Although larger than it looks, with 19 bedrooms, a spacious restaurant, a cosy cellar bar and a leisure centre, the hotel's Delaney family give it a homely, welcoming feeling. *Rooms 20. Restaurant seats 60 (outdoors, 15); D daily, L Sun only. Bar food served daily 12.30-9.30. Establishment closed 24-28 Dec. CC. Directions: Centre of town, opposite post office.*

 **Café Hans**

Moor Lane Cashel Co Tipperary ✆*062 63660*

Brothers Hans and Stefan Matthia run this smashing little contemporary café in Cashel, and it's the ideal complement to the evening restaurant, Chez Hans, next door. A short menu offers perfect daytime food: colourful, sassy dishes including lots of salads, open sandwiches that come with homemade French fries, and half a dozen hot dishes. Everyone travelling the Dublin–Cork route should make a note of this place - and get there early. *Seats 43. Open Tue-Sat, 12-5.30pm (advisable to check off-season). Closed Sun & Mon, 2 weeks end Jan. No CC. Directions: Off N8 in Cashel, 50m in Rock of Cashel direction.*

 **Cashel Palace Hotel**

Main Street Cashel Co Tipperary ✆*062 62707 www.cashel-palace.ie*

Patrick and Susan Murphy, owners of this former bishop's residence since 1998, have given it TLC and it it exudes that old-fashioned atmosphere and hospitality that modern hotels cannot emulate.The lovely reception rooms, and main bedrooms overlook the gardens and the Rock of Cashel at the rear. The atmospheric vaulted Bishops Buttery restaurant and Guinness Bar serve meals daily. *Rooms 23. Restaurant: Outdoor seating, 20; L & D daily. Food is also available in the Guinness Bar, 10am-8pm. Hotel closed 24-26 Dec. CC. Directions: just off Main Street.*

Chez Hans

Moore Lane Cashel Co Tipperary ✆*062 61177 www.chezhans.net*

Opening a restaurant in a church was highly original when Hans-Peter Matthia did it in 1968, providing an atmospheric setting for his seriously fine food (it was our Atmospheric Restaurant of the Year in 2009). Still the leading restaurant in a wide area, it's now run by son Jason and his wife Louise who make an equally formidable team. The cooking is outstanding and the early dinner menu represents some of the best value to be found in Ireland; there's an extensive à la carte, either is worth a special journey. Booking ahead is essential. *Seats 70. D Tue-Sat. Closed Sun, Mon, last 2 weeks Sept & last 2 weeks in Jan. CC. Directions: First right from N8, 50m on left; at foot of Rock of Cashel.*

Hill House

Palmer Hill Cashel Co Tipperary ✆*062 61277 www.hillhousecashel.com*

Enjoying magnificent view of the Rock of Cashel, Carmel Purcell's welcoming Georgian house was built in 1710 and has great character. The large rooms (some with four posters) are very comfortable, with television, radio and tea/coffee facilities and good bathrooms; while Carmel shows guests to their room, she gives the lowdown on local attractions and settles them in very hospitably. Breakfast is a high point, with freshly baked breads and home preserves. **Rooms 5** *(all shower only); CC.* **Directions:** *2 minutes walk from Cashel town centre.*

  The Spearman

97 Main Street Cashel Co Tipperary ✆*062 61143 www.spearmanstearoom.com*

Brother and sister JD and Elaine Spearman's bakery and tea room is a charming old-style place to take a break for a bite to eat and 'freshly ground coffee or a grand cup of tea'. They do light lunches as well as all day snacks and all their confectionery and traditional breads and scones are freshly made on the premises every day. Some items, including soup, are available gluten-free. **Seats 25**. *Open Mon-Sat, 8.45-5. Closed Sun & bank hols.* **Directions:** *Opposite turn for Clonmel on the main street.*

 Dualla House

Cashel Area Dualla Cashel Co Tipperary ✆*062 61487 www.duallahouse.com*

Set in 300 acres of rolling Tipperary farmland in the Golden Vale, Martin and Mairead Power's Georgian manor house near Cashel faces south towards the Slievenamon, Comeragh, Knockmealdown and Galtee Mountains. its special appeal is peace and tranquillity which, together with comfortable accommodation in large, airy bedrooms, great hospitality and Mairead's home cooking keep guests coming back time and again. **Rooms 4** *(3 shower only). Closed Nov-Mar. CC.* **Directions:** *5km from Cashel on R691.*

 **Old Convent Gourmet Hideaway**

Mount Anglesby Clogheen Co Tipperary ✆*052 746 5565 www.theoldconvent.ie*

The perfect destination for couples seeking a short 'get away from it all' experience, Dermot and Christine Gannon's stylish restaurant with accommodation is in one of the most beautiful and unspoilt parts of the country. Dermot's nightly-changing tasting menus offer stunning cooking of their own and local produce, while sumptuously appointed rooms and relaxation areas have wonderful views of the gardens and countryside. A true gourmet hideaway. *Restaurant:* **Seats 50**; *D Thu-Sat (& Bank Hol Sun).* **Rooms 6** *(1 shower only). Closed Sun-Wed, 23 Dec-end of Jan. CC. Directions:From Clogheen take the Vee/Lismore road, 0.5km on right.*

 Bay Lough Cheese

Mount Anglesby Clogheen Co Tipperary ✆*052 746 5275*

In the foothills of the Knockmealdown mountains, Dick and Anne Keating use the milk of a neighbouring farmer's herd and vegetarian rennet to make their excellent raw cows' milk cheddar style cheese. It's available as Bay Lough Cheddar (3+ months), Bay Lough Mature (8+ months) and Bay Lough Cheddar Smoked (3+ months); the young cheeses have flavoured variations, with garlic & herbs. Typical well made traditional cheddar, Mature Bay Lough develops a good 'bite'. Available from markets and selected shops, also seen on menus.

CLONMEL

Clonmel derives its name form Cluain Meala, meaning the meadow of honey, and today it is a prosperous town on the river Suir, known especially for its apple orchards and cider production. Clonmel is rich in heritage: the town walls were built in the 14th century and the quays date back to medieval times; also of interest is the heritage site of St Patrick's Well which includes the remains of a 17th century church; and the White Memorial theatre which was formerly a Methodist church, built in 1843. Surrounded by the Comeragh and Knockmealdown Mountains, it is an excellent base for climbing and walking. Local attractions include the town's poppy field, which is best in July and August. Golfing enthusiasts can play the 18 holes at Slievenamon Golf Course (052 32213). Every Saturday the best of local produce is on display at the Clonmel Farmers' Market (9.30-12.30).

Befani's Mediterranean & Tapas Restaurant

6 Sarsfield Street Clonmel Co Tipperary ✆052 617 7893 www.befani.com

In a restored listed building near the quays, this stylish Mediterranean restaurant has become a favourite spot for local diners. Co-owner and chef Adrian Ryan and business partner and restaurant manager Fulvio Bonfiglio offer flavoursome, seasonally-led food and also lunchtime tapas; quality ingredients, good cooking and service plus a relaxed atmosphere and real value for money have won them many friends. *Seats 55 (outdoors 15); Food served Mon-Sun, 9am-9.30pm; Tapas Mon-Sat 12.30-2.30. Closed 25 Dec, 1 Jan. CC.* **Directions:** *Town Centre.*

Hickeys Bakery & Café

West Gate Clonmel Co Tipperary ✆052 612 1587 www.hickeysbakery.com

Visitors to this medieval town are delighted to find this charming fourth generation craft bakery and café, which has been pleasing customers (including the author, William Trevor) since 1901. Nuala Hickey continues the family tradition, baking her unique traditional crusty bread, artisan bread and cakes, including the famous Hickey's barm brack, which is also available online. Beside the bakery counter, the little café is set up with closely packed tables, where locals and visitors mingle cheerfully, enjoying the wholesome food and atmosphere. *Open Mon-Sat 9-6.* **Directions:** *Town centre.*

Hotel Minella

Coleville Road Clonmel Co Tipperary ✆052 612 2388 www.hotelminella.ie

Dating back to 1863, the Nallen family's pleasant hotel is attractively located in its own grounds, overlooking the River Suir. This is the main hotel in the area, with good conference facilities and a fine leisure centre, and is popular for weddings. Many of the suites and (recently refurbished) rooms overlook the river and there's a welcoming tone, with complimentary local apples offered at reception. *Rooms 90. Closed 23-29 Dec. CC.* **Directions:** *Edge of Clonmel town.*

James Whelan Butchers

Oakville Shopping Centre Clonmel Co Tipperary ✆052 618 2477 www.jameswhelanbutchers.com

Fifth generation butcher Pat Whelan is one of Ireland's best known butchers, and one of the most innovative. Specialising in dry-aged, grass-fed Hereford and Aberdeen Angus beef from their own family farm, they also offer wagyu beef and lamb (home produced), pork and bacon, and some smoked fish; certified organic meat retailers, Whelans also sell organic chicken. An extensive range of prepared meals and artisan products is offered, made in-house and by other small producers. They have their own licensed abattoir and were among the first to sell online. *Open Mon-Wed 8-6.30, Thu-Fri 8-7, Sat 8-6, Sun 10-5. Online shop. Also at: Avoca Food Market, Monkstown, Co Dublin.*

  ## O'Donnell's Crisps

Seskin Farm Kilsheelan Clonmel Co Tipperary ✆*052 613 9016* *www.odonnellscrisps.com*

Since 2010, seventh generation farmer Ed O'Donnell has used the potatoes grown on the family's Golden Vale farm to produce O'Donnell's Crisps. Handmade to his specification, they are very different from mass market crisps, and the flavourings used are artisan - including Con Traas's Irish cider vinegar, made nearby at The Apple Farm near Cahir, and Mount Callan Cheddar, from Co Clare.

  ## Omega Direct Irish Organic Beef

Clashavaugha Ballymacarbry Clonmel Co Tipperary ✆*087 273 5447* *www.omegabeefdirect.ie*

Joe and Eileen Condon's organic hill farm on the edge of the Knockmealdown Mountains is a model farm for Farming with Altitude, a state initiative to encourage sustainable use of commonage in Ireland. Their Galloway cattle thrive under these conditions and their company, Omega Beef, employs a modern traceback system and an open farm gate policy, meaning customers are welcome to visit by arrangement and see this unique, low-impact organic beef farm first-hand. Available from: online shop. Also from Ardkeen Quality Food Store, Waterford.

 ## Sean Tierney

13 O'Connell Street Clonmel Co Tipperary ✆*052 612 4467*

This tall, narrow pub is a mini-museum of artefacts of bygone days – but there's also a giant TV screen discreetly hidden around a corner, for watching matches. Upstairs (and there are a lot of them; this is a four storey building) there's a relaxed, traditional family-style restaurant serving popular, good value food. *Food served daily, 12.30-9. Closed 25 Dec, Good Fri.CC.* **Directions:** *Situated half way down O'Connell St. on the left opposite Dunnes Stores.*

 ## Stonehouse Restaurant

29 Thomas Street Clonmel Co Tipperary ✆*052 612 8877* *www.stonehouserestaurant.ie*

In the very building where the late Michael Clifford set the region's culinary bar a decade ago, Jim and Anthony Smith of Lautrecs in Kilkenny city (see entry), have made this fine old 3-storey building into a bright and stylish setting for very fine food from talented young Head Chef Mark Ahessy. Excellent wine list too; all the elements work well together for a memorable dining experience. **Seats 70.** *D Tue- Sat (& bank hol Sun), L Thu, Fri & Sun. CC.*

  ## Kilmaneen Farmhouse

Clonmel Area Ardfinnan Newcastle Clonmel Co Tipperary ✆*052 613 6231* *www.kilmaneen.com*

As neat as a new pin, Kevin & Ber O'Donnell's delightfully situated farmhouse is on a former dairy farm, surrounded by three mountain ranges - the Comeraghs, the Knockmealdowns and the Galtees - and close to the rivers Suir and Tar, making it an ideal base for walking and fishing holidays. Genuinely hospitable hosts and homely comforts all add up to a real country break. **Rooms 3** *(2 shower only). Residents' D 7pm except on Sun (must book in advance). Closed 1 Nov-1 Mar. CC.* **Directions:** *In Ardfinnan, follow signs at Hill Bar.*

Cloughjordan Wood-fired Bakery

Cloughjordan Co Tipperary ✆*085 182 2777 www.cloughjordanwoodfiredbakery.com*

In his beloved and highly efficient Alan Scott designed oven, Joe Fitzmaurice bakes a range of beautiful handmade organic breads, flavoured only with natural sea salt - and without any of the artificial flour improvers, enhancers, colourings, bleachings or other artificial or chemical additives that are commonplace in bread today. Not just a healthy product, artisan breads have real flavour, texture and keeping qualities that ordinary commercial baking can't deliver. Supplies selected retailers. Bread Club for local customers.

 ## Sarah Baker Cookery School

Cloughjordan House Cloughjordan Co Tipperary
✆*0505 42492 / 087 969 0824 www.sarahbaker.ie*

Based in the converted Coach House at her 17th century family home, Sarah Baker's cookery school offers classes which are designed to interest a wide range of students. Many of them seasonal, are showcasing their own home produce and and that of other local producers. Both demonstration and hands-on cookery classes are given and there is a walled kitchen garden - you can even learn how to grow your own vegetables combined with a cookery demonstration and lunch in a day. Classes packaged with overnight accommodation are also offered. CC

DROMINEER

Dromineer is an appealing little place on Lough Derg, with a pretty harbour and lovely woodland walks. It's a popular destination for Shannon cruisers, sailing folk and families out for the day at weekends. Fishing is a popular activity on both the lake and the nearby Nenagh river. One of Dromineer's claims to fame is the Lough Derg Yacht Club, which dates back to 1835, yet acts as a contemporary community centre for the village. There is a Farmers' Market nearby in Nenagh on Saturdays (10am-3pm).

 ## Crowes Farm

Gurtussa Dundrum Co Tipperary ✆*062 71137 www.crowefarm.ie*

Renowned for its excellent cooking quality and flavour, free-range pork produced at Crowe's Farm is processed at their on-farm butchery for sale as fresh meat and to make natural, homemade bacon and ham products, puddings and sausages. This environmentally aware family also produce organic bronze turkeys for Christmas and offer a range of services including spit roasts, butchery classes and courses, and an abattoir service for home-reared pigs. Available from good shops nationwide (eg Nolans, Dublin, Ardkeen Good Food Store, Waterford; selective SuperValu stores), see website for details. *Online shop. CC.*

  ## Cashel Blue & Crozier Blue Cheese

J&L Grubb Ltd Beechmount Fethard Co Tipperary ✆*052 31151 www.cashelblue.com*

Ireland's most famous blue cows' milk cheese, Cashel Blue, has been made by Jane and Louis Grubb and family on their farm near Fethard since 1984. Their nephews, Henry and Louis Clifton Brown, have been making the excellent Crozier Blue (one of the very few blue Irish sheep milk cheeses) from the milk of their sheep grazed on pasturelands near Cashel since 1999. Both cheeses are consistent award winners in Irish and international competition and Cashel Blue, in particular, is well distributed internationally. Widely available from cheese shops, delis and food stores.

Mobarnane House

Fethard Co Tipperary 📞 *052 613 1962 www.mobarnanehouse.com*

Richard and Sandra Craik-White's gracious 18th century country house makes a wonderfully spacious retreat for guests: the aim is to provide peace and quiet in great comfort, with very personal attention to detail. Richard's excellent food is served in a lovely dining room and all the rooms have everything you could need for a relaxing stay. Woodland walks and other activities on site. **Rooms 4**. *Residents' D; advance reservation essential. Closed Nov-Mar. CC.* **Directions:** *From Fethard, take Cashel road for 6km; turn right, signed Ballinure and Thurles; 2.5km on left.*

Larkins Bar & Restaurant

Garrykennedy Portroe Nenagh Co Tipperary 📞 *067 23232 www.larkinspub.com*

You can't miss Maura and Cormac Boyle's pretty white cottage pub with its cheerful red paintwork at Garrykennedy's charming little harbour. Lunch offers old favourites - homemade soup, seafood chowder, chicken wings, steak sandwich and a roast of the day - and local beef is the backbone of the evening menu, which takes things up a gear. Full of character, it's an attractive spot, with music at weekends and on Wednesday in summer (with Irish dancing). *Food in summer: Mon-Sat 10.30am-9.30pm & Sun 12.30-9.30pm (in winter food daily from 5pm, all day at weekends). Closed Good Fri, 25 Dec. CC.* **Directions:** *12km from Nenagh.*

NENAGH

This thriving town in the heart of Ireland's best farmland can provide a convenient base within easy reach of many attractions in the mid-west, including Lough Derg. Chief amongst the town's attractions is Nenagh Castle, constructed by the Fitzwalter (also known as Butler) family in the 13th Century, and one of the finest of its kind in Ireland. Nenagh makes a handy place to break a journey, and there is a farmers' market in the town each Saturday (10am-3pm).

Country Choice

25 Kenyon Street Nenagh Co Tipperary 📞 *067 32596 www.countrychoice.ie*

Peter and Mary Ward are among Ireland's most famous artisan shopkeepers - Country Choice is a treasure trove of the very best foods from Ireland and abroad, so food lovers plan their itineraries with care to take in a a light meal of simple, seasonal, home-cooked food and a little serious shopping. Local, seasonal fresh foods reflect the agricultural economy of Tipperary, and Peter's cheeses are legendary. Mary, an exceptional cook, quietly produces magnificent terrines from the family's saddleback pigs, thousands of jars of jam in season and vast numbers of handmade Christmas puddings - and Peter is one of the most energetic and dedicated movers and shakers in the wonderful world of artisan foods. Definitely worth a detour. **Seats 35**; *Open all day (9-5.30). Closed Sun. CC.* **Directions:** *Centre of town, on left half way down Kenyon Street.*

Lough Derg Chocolates

Newtown Nenagh Co Tipperary 📞*087 968 3534 www.loughdergchocolates.ie*

Although only operating since 2011, Malachy and Elaine Dorris's Lough Derg Chocolates hit the ground running and quickly reached a chocolate-hungry market. Their developing range of smartly packaged handmade confectionery includes luscious traditional truffles with fresh cream fillings, cute chocolate lollies and milk chocolate bars - and these Tipperary Food Producers members use as many local ingredients as possible.

  Oldfarm

Redwood Lorrha Nenagh Co Tipperary 📞*086 810 0125 www.oldfarm.ie*

At Oldfarm, Margaret O'Farrell and Alfie McCaffrey's stated mission is to bring you the taste of real pork, and that they do – they rear free range Saddleback pigs on a natural gm-free diet to produce tasty, succulent, free-range pork, bacon and preservative-free sausages that can be delivered directly to your door. They also offer pig rearing courses - and piglets for sale (when available). They're the first free range producer to get the Bord Bia Quality Assured Mark for their pork and bacon. Read all about it in Margaret's prize-winning blog, A Year in Redwood. Visitors welcome. *Online and telephone orders.*

 The Pantry

12 Quintin's Way Nenagh Co Tipperary 📞*067 31237 www.thepantrycafe.ie*

Selling home-baked bread, quiches, cakes and gateaux alongside hot lunches, breakfasts, brunches and afternoon teas, Grainne Moylan's bright and attractive bakery-café is always buzzing. While home baking and their own range of preserves are specialities, many of the delicious dishes offered showcase local foods - Crowe's Farm sausages and rashers in the breakfast, for example. An enjoyable place to take a break. *Seats 70 (outdoors, 20); Open Mon-Sat, 8.30am-6pm. Closed Sun. CC. Directions: Town centre, in shopping precinct.*

The Pepper Mill

27 Kenyon Street Nenagh Co Tipperary 📞*067 34598 www.thepeppermill.ie*

With interesting, well-sourced food, good cooking and combining value with a sense of occasion, it's no wonder Mairead and Robert Gill's restaurant, The Peppermill is so popular. A tapas menu is served downstairs in the smart, comfortable wine bar and there's a fine contemporary restaurant on the first floor. Refreshingly straightforward menus show world influences, but there's a welcome leaning towards Irish themes and an emphasis on fish, delivered daily from West Cork. Pleasing choices and good cooking keep satisfied customers coming back. *Seats 75 (outdoors, 10); D Tue-Sun. Closed Mon, 24-26 Dec & Good Fri. CC. Directions: Nenagh town centre.*

Quigleys

9 Kenyon Street Nenagh Co Tipperary ✆067 31454 www.quigleys.ie

Established by Michael Quigley in 1890, this family-owned bakery is run by his great-great grandson John and his wife Margaret. Now with shops and cafés in 15 locations, including Athlone, Tullamore, Roscrea and Carlow, and over 150 employees, they have grown dramatically - but the family business ethos hasn't changed and the craft bakery and food kitchen in Nenagh supplies all of the outlets with their freshly baked breads, cakes and savouries every day.

The Scullery

Kilkeary Norwood Nenagh Co Tipperary ✆086 174 4402 www.thescullery.ie

Florrie Purcell started making simple, old-fashioned 'free-from' foods with a contemporary twist at The Scullery in 2004, and now has over twenty products in her range, from high quality handmade Christmas puddings, to a wide range of condiments, sauces, relishes, pickles and glazes. Her individual Christmas puddings, especially, have gone down a treat.

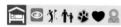

Ashley Park House

Nenagh Area Ardcronney Nenagh Co Tipperary ✆067 38223 www.ashleypark.com

Margaret and P.J. Mounsey's home is one of those beautiful 18th-century houses where all is elegance, comfort and charm. Each of the handsome rooms enjoys a fine view and a hearty breakfast is served in the splendour of the double dining room. Surrounded by woodland, and with views of Lough Ourna and the distant Slieve Bloom Mountains, it's just the place for anyone seeking peace and comfort in really splendid surroundings - and it makes a highly romantic wedding venue. **Rooms 5** *(all with private bathrooms, 2 shower only). Residents L&D available by prior arrangement only. Open all year. No CC.* **Directions:** *On the N52, 7km north of Nenagh.*

Coolbawn Quay

Nenagh Area Coolbawn Nenagh Area Co Tipperary ✆067 28158 www.coolbawnquay.com

This unique resort on Lough Derg is modelled on a 19th-century Irish village, with understated and, in some cases, surprisingly luxurious accommodation scattered throughout the pretty cottages in the village. The mini spa, small conference facilities, berthing for cruisers and the charming little bar and restaurant all contribute to making this a destination of choice. It's also a romantic location for weddings. **Rooms 48** *(2 shower only).* **Restaurant Seats 40**. *D Tue-Sat. Non-residents welcome by reservation. Bar food daily in high season, 12.30-2.30. Closed Christmas. CC.* **Directions:** *located exactly 3.2km past Coolbawn village.*

The Fairways Bar & Orchard Restaurant

Nenagh Area Kilruane Nenagh Co Tipperary ✆*067 41444 www.thefairwaysbar.ie*

While offering choices to please all tastes, the speciality at Geoff Jones's characterful country pub is seafood. Whether as a destination for a tasty meal or a journey break for travellers, it's a pleasant and laid-back venue - the friendly and efficient staff have been working as a team since opening in 2006 and there's a clear commitment to quality, fresh food, excellent service, consistency and price. **Seats 55** *(outdoors, 16); L & D daily. Closed Good Fri, 25 Dec. CC.*

Directions: *Three minutes drive from Nenagh town on the Cloughjordan Road.*

ROSCREA

Roscrea (Ros Cré - "wood of Cré") is a small town in the south midlands where, in ancient times, the five main routes in Ireland, or the Slighe Dhála, converged, and is quite near the Slieve Bloom Mountains. Designated a Heritage Town, it has many architectural features of note, including the Round Tower, Roscrea Castle and Damer House Complex (050 521 850). The town grew around its monastery and The Round Tower, on Church Street, has a doorway 15 feet from the ground and is the oldest surviving part of the ancient monastery. A Heritage Trail, with accompanying booklet in three languages, is freely available to help you explore this historic town (Roscrea Heritage - Castle & Damer House, 050 521 850). There are some exceptional gardens nearby: Birr Castle Demesne (Birr, 057 912 0336) is a large demesne with important collections of trees, lake, walks, and formal garden while Gash Gardens (Portlaoise, 057 873 2247) is a garden for plant enthusiasts that will inspire those making new gardens.

Boulabane Ice Cream

Boulaban Farm Boulabane Roscrea Co Tipperary ✆*086 262 6348 www.boulabanefarm.ie*

Michael and Kate Cantwell use milk and cream from their pedigree Holstein/Friesian herd to make their delicious Boulabane Ice Cream. An adventurous range, it offers lots of flavours including fruit sorbets, diabetic ices and soya ices - and is picking up awards a-plenty. Although not widely retailed, they feature on restaurant menus in the region and you will find the 500ml tubs in some local shops such as SuperValu in Nenagh.

Monaincha House & Health Spa

Roscrea Co Tipperary ✆*050 523 757 www.monainchahouse.com*

Tom and Carmel Moore's 18th-century house is well situated for exploring this beautiful part of the country, but with a health spa, tennis court, 5 acres of gardens and farmland walks on site, you might not want to venture out very much at all. The rooms are all south facing and have views over the gardens to the countryside beyond. A good choice for a short break. **Rooms 3**. **Directions:** *3 km from Roscrea on the N7 (Dublin road).*

GEORGINA CAMPBELL'S IRELAND

  Fiacrí House Restaurant & Cookery School

Roscrea Area Boulerea Knock Roscrea Co Tipperary ✆*0505 43017 www.fiacrihouse.com*

Enda and Ailish Hennessy's lovely country house style restaurant and cookery school is well worth seeking out as it offers excellent cooking and the caring service that makes a special experience. Ailish showcases the food of the area and, while menus are balanced, local meats are especially good. Cookery classes are offered throughout the year and Ailish aims to teach cooking skills in an atmosphere in which students will also make new friends. A very popular restaurant – advance booking is essential. **Seats 70**. D Wed-Sat. *Closed Sun, Mon, Tue and 25 Dec, Good Fri. *Cookery classes run throughout the year, suitable for individuals, groups and team building packages etc. 1 day courses are also held at other times eg Christmas and Easter.* **Directions:** *10km from Roscrea.*

  White Gypsy

Shelta Beer Ltd 14 Priory Place Templemore Co Tipperary ✆*086 172 4520 www.whitegypsy.ie*

Experienced brewer Cuilán Loughnane established The White Gypsy Brewery in 2009. The philosophy is about getting back in touch with the things that made Ireland famous for its beer but have been forgotten, and they source as many ingredients as possible locally. Stocked by pubs and restaurants; buy online at Drinkstore.ie and Bradleys Off Licence.

 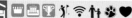 **Saratoga Lodge**

Templemore Area Barnane Templemore Co Tipperary ✆*0504 31886 www.saratoga-lodge.com*

In a particularly unspoilt and peaceful part of the country, just below the famous Devil's Bit in the Silvermine mountain range, Valerie Beamish's lovely house on a working stud farm is well-situated on an open, sunny site looking out over the hills. Bedrooms are very comfortable and peaceful and Valerie takes great pride in giving guests a good breakfast and can provide picnics too. An extremely hospitable house all round. **Rooms 3**. *Residents' D daily (on request). Closed 23 Dec-3 Jan. No CC.* **Directions:** *From Templemore, take the Nenagh road for 3km; take 2nd turn right at the B&B sign. Take left at next junction (2.5km); house is on the left.*

  The Derg Inn

Terryglass Co Tipperary ✆*067 22037 www.derginn.ie*

Michael and Joyce Soden's popular country pub is one of the area's best for food - everything is sourced with care, including organic ingredients when possible. Whether in fine weather, when the sturdy outdoor tables beckon, or beside the fire on chilly days, the thought of a good meal here quickly gets hungry guests into a relaxed mood. Wide-ranging menus include some surprises but local Hereford steaks are always a winner; there's a very pleasant bar and an interesting little wine list to enjoy with or without food. Sunday lunch is also quite a speciality. *Seats 150*. *Open daily: food available 11-10. Music Fri-Sun in summer (Sun traditional). Closed Good Fri, 25 Dec. CC.* **Directions:** *In the heart of Terrryglass Village.*

Kylenoe House

Terryglass Area Ballinderry Terryglass Nenagh Co Tipperary ✆*067 22015*

Virginia Moeran's old stone house offers homely comfort and real country pleasures close to Lough Derg. The farm is home to an international stud and the woodlands are a haven for wildlife; with beautiful walks, riding (with or without tuition), golf and water sports available on the premises or close by, this is a real rural retreat. Spacious, airy bedrooms overlook beautiful rolling countryside and Virginia's breakfasts are a treat. *Rooms 3 (1 with private bathroom). Residents D (book by noon). Closed 15 Dec-15 Jan. No CC.* **Directions:** *N7 to Moneygall, Cloughjordan, Borrisokane, take road for Ballinderry/Terryglass and straight 10km on right.*

THURLES

In the heart of the Suir Valley – a beautiful area renowned for its world class farmland - Thurles is the largest town in North Tipperary. There are many castles and monastic settlements in the surrounding and area and, with the Silvermines mountains to the north-west and the Slieveardagh Hills to the south-east, it has much to offer walkers and trekkers.

Cooleeney Cheese

Cooleeney Moyne Thurles Co Tipperary ✆*0504 45112 www.cooleeney.com*

The Maher family make an astonishing range of cow and goat milk cheeses, including the trademark raw cows' milk Cooleeney (Camembert style), which has become a benchmark for the very best of Irish farmhouse cheeses. Others include Dunbarra (semi soft range), Gortnamona (goat) and Maighean (powerful, raw cows' milk). They export their own and other farmhouse cheeses and offer hampers which include homemade preserves. The better-known cheeses are widely available from specialty stores. Order form available on website for direct sales.

Crossogue Preserves

Crossogue House Ballycahill Thurles Co Tipperary
✆*0504 54416 www.crossoguepreserves.com*

Veronica Molloy's outstanding jams, jellies, chutneys, curds and marmalade are all based on family recipes handed down through the generations and are still made by hand in small batches. Jams include such tempting varieties as strawberry and champagne, blackcurrant and Irish stout and gooseberry and elderflower, while more unusual preserves include an Irish coffee curd and a parsley jelly. Well worth seeking out. Widely available from speciality food stores. Direct orders taken by email or phone.

Inch House Black Pudding

Bouladuff Thurles Co Tipperary ✆ *0504 51348 www.inchhouse.ie*

Nora Egan makes this much-admired fresh blood pudding by traditional methods, using a family recipe handed down from mother to daughter. Recognition includes a bronze medal at the Concours International du Meilleur Boudin 2011 in Mortagne-au-Perche, France. Nora has also developed a gluten-free pudding as well as a wide range of chutneys and dressings, all of which are highly recommended. Widely available from butchers and specialist food stores including Ardkeen, Waterford; Avoca branches; Donnybrook Fair, Dublin; Country Choice, Nenagh; selected SuperValu stores and many more; check Inch House website for full list of retailers.

  **Inch Country House & Restaurant**

Thurles Area Bouladuff Thurles Co Tipperary ✆ *0504 51348 www.inchhouse.ie*

This magnificent Georgian house outside Thurles was built in 1720 and managed to survive some of the most turbulent periods in Irish history - but it is current owners, John and Nora Egan, who have made it the handsome, comfortably furnished period house which guests enjoy today. Big log fires burn in period fireplaces and reception rooms include an impressive William Morris-style drawing room with a tall stained glass window, plasterwork ceiling and adjoining library bar. A lovely traditional dining room, which is also used for breakfast, is transformed into a restaurant at night - a fine setting for delicious dinners that showcase Inch House and other local and artisan produce. A lovely place to stay, and to dine. *Rooms 5 (1 shower only). Restaurant seats 50. D Tue-Sat. Restaurant closed Sun & Mon; house closed 2 weeks Christmas. CC. Directions: 6km from Thurles on Nenagh Road.*

 Mitchel House

Mitchell Street Thurles Co Tipperary ✆ *050 490 776 www.mitchelhouse.ie*

Proprietor Michael O'Dwyer is the third generation to operate a business from this property and his bright modern restaurant is an attractive venue. Several menus (tapas, early bird, à la carte) are offered and, while the range includes plenty of traditional favourites, the cooking style is modern and fresh. Offering variety and value, it's a popular restaurant and has a good buzz of happy punters enjoying good cooking in pleasant surroundings. *Seats 86. Open D Wed-Sun & L Sun. Directions: Off Cathedral Street (N75).*

  Irish Piemontese Beef

Thurles Area Two Mile Borris Thurles Co Tipperary ✆ *087 913 5349 www.irishpiemontesebeef.ie*

Originating from Northern Italy, Piemontese cattle have been reared in Ireland since the 1980s and their meat is available from good butchers. Being naturally low in cholesterol, lean and tender, Piemontese beef is rapidly growing in popularity. John Commins and Michael Fennelly's company 'Irish Piemontese Beef' is a leading supplier.

WATERFORD

On the quays of Waterford city, we are witness to a trading and seafaring tradition which goes back at least 1,150 years. But this sense of history also looks to the future, as Waterford is popular as a Tall Ships assembly port. Today's larger commercial ships may be berthed downstream on the other side of the river at Belview, but the old cityside quays on the south bank retain a nautical flavour which is accentuated by very useful marina berthing facilities in the heart of town.

This fine port was founded in 853 AD when the Vikings - Danes for the most part - established the trading settlement of Vadrefjord. Its strategic location in a sheltered spot at the head of the estuary near the confluence of the Suir and Barrow rivers guaranteed its continuing success under different administrators, particularly the Normans, so much so that it tended to overshadow the county of Waterford, almost all of which is actually to the west of the city.

But for many years now, the county town has been Dungarvan, which is two-thirds of the way westward along Waterford's extensive south coast. This spreading of the administrative centres of gravity has to some extent balanced the life of the Waterford region. But even so, the extreme west of the county is still one of Ireland's best kept secrets, a place of remarkable beauty between the Knockmealdown, Comeragh and Monavullagh mountains, where fish-filled rivers such as the Bride, the Blackwater, and the Nire make their way seawards at different speeds through valleys of remarkable variety and beauty, past pretty towns and villages such as romantic, castle-bedecked Lismore.

LOCAL ATTRACTIONS & INFORMATION

▶ **Nire Valley & Comeraghs on Horseback** Ballymacarbry
052 36147

▶ **Mount Melleray Activity Centre** Cappoquin
058 54322

▶ **Lismore Castle & Gardens** Lismore *058 54424*
▶ **Waterford Crystal Glass Centre** Waterford *051 332500*

ARDMORE

This picturesque village and popular seaside resort overlooking Ardmore Bay was originally a 5th century monastic settlement; founded by St. Declan in 416 AD, it is reputed to be the first such settlement in Ireland pre-dating St. Patrick. Today, the Ardmore Round Tower and Cathedral still attract visitors, as they always did, and St. Declan's Way, a 94km long-distance pilgrim's way walk to Cashel, follows the old routes as faithfully as possible. Ardmore is on the Gaeltacht & Galltacht Scenic Drive and there's a lovely 5km circular cliff walk, which takes about an hour. A highlight of the village is Ardmore Pottery and Craft Shop (024 94152) which is just below the Cliff House Hotel (see entry), looking down to the pier and boat cove; Ardmore's charming trademark blue and white pottery is made here, and they also stock a range of quality Irish crafts.

 **Cliff House Hotel**

Ardmore Co Waterford ☎*024 87800 www.thecliffhousehotel.com*

A bold and modern boutique hotel with spectacular sea views, this chic bolthole draws guests as much for the culinary offerings as the setting overlooking Ardmore Bay. Dutch head chef, Martijn Kajuiter, strives for perfection using meticulously sourced local and seasonal produce to deliver stunning cooking. General Manager Adriaan Bartels is well known for his warmth and discreet customer care, and this luxury hotel has earned a reputation for service too. The Well spa offers a stunningly positioned outdoor infinity pool and a Jacuzzi, sauna, steam room and gym, all overlooking the bay. *Rooms 39. Restaurant seats 64 (outdoors, 20). L & D daily. Bar food daily, 12-9pm. Restaurant closed Sun, Mon, Tue off season. Hotel closed 24-26 Dec. CC. Directions: Hotel is located at the end of Ardmore village (N25-R673) via the Middle Road*

 White Horses Restaurant

Ardmore Co Waterford ☎*024 94040*

Christine Power and Geraldine Flavin's delightfully bright and breezy café-restaurant is open for all the little lifts that visitors need – morning coffee, afternoon tea – as well as imaginative lunches (plus Sunday lunch, which runs all afternoon) and a more ambitious à la carte evening menu. Offering a good balance between traditional dishes and more adventurous fare, it's equally good for a reviving cuppa and a sweet treat from the luscious homemade selection on display, or a full meal. Attractive and pleasant, service at this well-run establishment is well-organised and efficient, even at its busiest. *Seats 50. May-Sep: Tue-Sun 11-'late'; Winter weekends only: Fri from 6 pm, Sat 11-11 & Sun 12-6. Closed Mon all year, except bank hols (bank hol opening as Sun), 1 Jan-13 Feb. CC. Directions: Centre of village.*

BALLYMACARBRY

Popuar with walkers, this small village is beautifully situated between the Knockmealdown and Comeragh Mountains, an unspoilt area with terrain to suit every level of walker; the Comeragh Mountain Walking Festival is held here every October, with graded walks led by very experienced guides. Anglers will enjoy Clonanav Farmhouse (053 913 6141), which provides tuition for game angling, whilst horseriding can be arranged by Nire Valley Equestrian Trail-Riding & Trekking (052 36147), with treks through some of the most beautiful scenery in Waterford. Golfers will find that many pleasing Co Waterford courses are convenient to Ballymacarbry, including the Eddie Hackett designed Williamstown Golf Club (051 853131), Waterford Golf Club (051 876 748), Dunmore East Golf Club (051 383 151), and Tramore Golf Club (051 386 170).

  **Glasha**

Glasha Ballymacarbry via Clonmel Co Waterford ✆052 613 6108 www.glashafarmhouse.com

Olive and the late Paddy O'Gorman made their hospitable farmhouse into the kind of relaxed country retreat visitors to Ireland dream of finding. Bedrooms are luxurious for a farm stay, there's comfortable lounging room for guests, and the nearest pub is just 3 minutes' walk. Olive makes a delicious home-cooked dinner for guests, by arrangement, and the food is gorgeous in its simplicity. A lovely place to stay, and a perfect antidote to the stresses of urban life. **Rooms 6** *(2 shower only). Residents' D by arrangement. Closed D Sun, 20-27 Dec. CC.* **Directions:** *Off 671 road between Clonmel and Dungarvan, 3.5km from Ballymacarbry.*

   **Hanora's Cottage**

Nire Valley Ballymacarbry Co Waterford ✆052 613 6134 www.hanorascottage.com

This charming country guesthouse is a very special place – equally wonderful for foot-weary walkers, or desk-weary city folk in need of clear country air. The hospitality of the Wall family is matched by luxurious accommodation and people travel from far and wide to dine here too. Euro-Toques chefs, Eoin and Judith Wall, are enthusiastic supporters of small suppliers; they use local foods whenever possible and credit them on the menu. Overnight guests begin the day with Hanora's legendary breakfast buffet (National Winner of our Irish Breakfast Awards in 2002); it takes some time to get the measure of this feast, so make sure you get up in time to make the most of it. **Rooms 10.** *Restaurant seats 40. D Mon-Sat. Closed Christmas week. CC.* **Directions:** *Take Clonmel/Dungarvan (R671) road, turn off at Ballymacarbry.*

Melody's Nire View Bar

Nire View Bar Ballymacarbry Co Waterford ✆052 36169

A great place to take a break if you're walking or simply touring the area, this well-run pub traditional in the upper reaches of the Nire Valley has a stable yard nicely set up with outside tables for sunny days and welcoming open fires for winter. *Barfood 10.30-9. Closed 25 Dec & Good Fri. CC.* **Directions:** *On Nire Valley scenic drive, R671, Dungarvan/Clonmel road.*

Barrons Bakery & Coffee Shop

Cook Street Cappoquin Co Waterford ✆*058 54045 www.barronsbakery.ie*

Esther and Joe Barron's business dates back to 1887, and this wonderfully traditional bakery still uses the original Scottish brick ovens to make breads with real flavour and an old-fashioned crust; the range is wide but the Waterford 'blaas' are unique. Barron's is one of four bakeries awarded by Euro-Toques for their production of this traditional square white yeasted roll. The coffee shop serves lunch and wholesome daytime snacks. *Mon-Sat 9-5.30.*

  Crinnaghtaun Apple Juice

Cappoquin Estate Tivoli Cappoquin Co Waterford ✆*058 54258 www.irishapplejuice.ie*

"Apple juice is only as good as the apple", say David and Julia Keane, whose 90 acre orchards have been the source of their natural cold-pressed apple juice since 1992. The apples - including Bramley, Cox's and Egremont Russet - are hand picked, milled and pressed; the only addition is vitamin C (to prevent oxidation). The cloudy, golden juice is then pasteurised to prevent spoilage - and that's it, pure and simple.

 Knockalara Farmhouse Cheese

Knockalara Farmhouse Cappoquin ✆*Co Waterford024 96326*

In custom built cheese-making premises at their farm in beautiful West Waterford, Agnes and Wolfgang Schliebtz make a range of sheeps' cheeses and a cows' milk feta style cheese, Waterford Greek Cheese. The milk for their well known Knockalara range of cheeses is supplied by Henry Clifton Browne of Crozier Blue (see entry) and all of the cheeses are hand made using traditional methods and vegetarian approved rennet substitute. Locally available.

  La Touche Organics

Dromore Aglish Cappoquin Co Waterford ✆*024 96729 (work);086 394 0564*

Siobhán La Touche produces organic fruit and vegetables, apples, juice and flowers. Vegetables include heritage and indigenous Irish varieties and they offer quality bagged mixed leaves; a far cry from the standard supermarket offering, they include about ten different varieties of lettuce and are available all year round. Also sells organic produce from other Irish growers, and imports. *Available from Farmers' Markets: Dungarvan (Thu 9.30-2), Clonmel (Sat 10-2).*

   **Richmond House**

Cappoquin Co Waterford ✆*058 54278 www.richmondhouse.net*

Genuine hospitality, high standards of comfort, caring service and excellent food are all to be found in the Deevy family's fine 18th century country house and restaurant just outside Cappoquin. Claire or Jean Deevy will usually be there to welcome guests, and show you to one of the nine individually decorated bedrooms. The restaurant is the heart of Richmond House, with Paul an ardent supporter of local produce. Menus balance traditional country house cooking and more adventurous dishes inspired by international trends. Service is attentive and discreet and the Deevys make sure you will have a memorable breakfast to see you on your way too. Cappoquin is a wonderful area to explore, and Richmond House makes an excellent base. **Rooms 9.** *Restaurant **seats 45.** D daily (early menu Tue-Fri). Closed 22 Dec-10 Jan. CC.* **Directions:** *1km outside Cappoquin on N72.*

The Suir Inn

Cheekpoint Co Waterford 📞*051 382 220 www.mcalpins.com*

An immaculately maintained 300-year old inn run by the McAlpin family since 1972, this characterful place is more like a traditional bar than a restaurant. Seasonal menus offer a good choice - half a dozen starters (mostly seafood) and about ten main courses - and there's a moderately priced wine list. Specialities include a generous and reasonably priced seafood platter and seafood pie. All meals come with brown soda bread and a side salad. **Seats 62**; *D Mon-Sat. Closed Sun. CC.* **Directions:** *11km east of Waterford, on harbour front.*

DUNGARVAN

Dungarvan is the county's main town except for Waterford city and is beautifully located on Dungarvan Harbour (renowned for its wildlife), with much of interest nearby: the Gaeltacht of Ring is just a few miles away, for example, and the lovely Nire Valley (walking, pony trekking) runs deep into the Comeragh Mountains north of the town. West of Dungarvan, the Heritage Town of Lismore, with its fairytale castle and gardens, is just a short drive.

Cairbre House

Strandside North Abbeyside Dungarvan Co Waterford 📞*058 42338 www.cairbrehouse.com*

Brian Wickham's fine old guesthouse is attractively situated just across the bridge from Dungarvan town centre. Of great historical interest, it is set in wonderful gardens, right on the water. Recently redecorated bedrooms are bright and cheerful and guests have a dedicated sitting room with an open fire. Breakfast is a high point, especially when served in the back garden in fine weather. The gardens are Brian's greatest love and a source of great pleasure to guests. A lovely spot. **Rooms 4** *(all shower only). Closed mid Dec-mid Jan. CC.* **Directions:** *From Waterford take right exit off N25 at Strandside roundabout, house 200m up on the left.*

The Country Store

3 Shopping Arcade Mitchell Street Dungarvan Co Waterford 📞*058 43061 www.thecountrystore.ie*

With local suppliers including The Tannery, Eunice Power of Powersfield House and Baldwin's Ice Cream from Knockanore, you'll find an exceptional choice of local speciality foods alongside everyday items at Conor Lannen's terrific store. Central to the life of the town, this well-named shop reflects the seasonal production of farmers, growers and artisan producers in the area, offering everything from potatoes, carrots, apples and honey, to free range eggs, cheeses and home baking. A great shop. *Open Mon-Sat, 8-6.*

Dungarvan Brewing Company

Unit 5 No. 2 Westgate Business Park Dungarvan Co Waterford
📞*058 24000 www.dungarvanbrewingcompany.com*

Dungarvan Brewing Company was founded by brothers-in-law Cormac O'Dwyer and Tom Dalton along with their wives, Jen and Claire, with a view to offering the Irish beer drinker a greater choice in craft beers, with an emphasis on quality, craft and tradition. Three beers make up the core range; brewed in small batches, unfiltered, unpasteurised and naturally carbonated, they bears little resemblance to mass-produced beers. Available nationwide, check website for stockists. Tours by arrangement.

  ## John David Power Butchers

57 Main Street Dungarvan Co Waterford ✆*058 42339*

Renowned for his dry-cured bacon and sausages, the fine products sold by this traditional butchers have a strong local following - and have graced the menu of the town's leading restaurant, The Tannery, since it opened. *Open Mon-Sat, 9-5.30.*

 ## The Moorings

Davitts Quay Dungarvan Co Waterford ✆*058 41461 www.mooringsdungarvan.com*

Whether you arrive when it's busy and the atmosphere is lively, or at a quiet time when there are just a few people relaxing in the bar, this friendly family-run establishment is a welcoming and interesting place to have a drink or enjoy something to eat. Outdoor tables on the quay enjoy a wonderful view of Dungarvan harbour, and seafood features heavily on the bar and restaurant menus. Bar food available all day. *Restaurant D Fri & Sat.* **Directions:** *On the quays in Dungarvan.*

 ## Nude Food

86 O'Connell Street Dungarvan Co Waterford ✆*058 24594 www.nudefood.ie*

London-born Louise Clark's smashing café restaurant and deli off the square in Dungarvan may be small, but it packs a mighty punch. Drop in to pick up some of the freshly made and artisan products on sale, or to eat and you'll find integrity – simply written menus, suppliers names that guarantee impeccable provenance and a children's menu with 'real food'. The atmosphere is transformed by candlelight in the evening when the menu expands. *Seats 30 (outdoors, 21). Open Mon-Sat, all day (D Thu-Sat). Closed Sun, Bank Hols, 25-26 Dec, 1 Jan. CC.* **Directions:** *Right at traffic lights in square at exit to Cork.*

 ## Powersfield House

Ballinamuck West Dungarvan Co Waterford ✆*058 45594 www.powersfield.com*

Although recently built, the traditional country house style of Edmund and Eunice Power's fine guesthouse outside Dungarvan gives a sense of maturity and bedrooms have been individually decorated to a high standard. Eunice is an enthusiastic professional cook (she gives cooking classes in-house and at The Tannery Cookery School, nearby) and runs a successful outside catering company; it's worth staying for the seasonally-led breakfast alone. **Rooms 4** *(all shower only). Residents' D by arrangement. Cookery Courses available, details on application. CC.* **Directions:** *Take the Killarney road R672 from Dungarvan at Kilrush roundabout; second turn left, first house on right.*

 ## Quealy's Café Bar

82 O'Connell Street Dungarvan Co Waterford ✆*058 24555*

Just off the main square in Dungarvan town, Andrew Quealy's café-bar is a friendly, buzzy place with simple, good quality table settings in the smart bar. Food is well above the usual expectation of "bar food" in terms of sourcing, cooking and presentation and they offer a modern menu of good dishes at very reasonable prices. Well turned out staff ensure a relaxed ambience even at busy times. *Bar meals: All day Mon-Sun. CC.* **Directions:** *Town centre, west of the main square.*

 **The Tannery**

10 Quay Street Dungarvan Co Waterford ✆*058 45420 www.tannery.ie*

For over a decade, discerning diners from all over Ireland (and beyond) have been making a beeline for Paul and Maire Flynn's stylish contemporary restaurant in Dungarvan. Menus are wonderfully simple yet, paradoxically, the food tastes very exciting; Paul's exceptional cooking uses the best local ingredients to produce delicious eclectic fare with a strong Irish slant. Attentive and efficient service and an interesting and kindly priced wine list enhance this standout experience. Comfortable, stylish and very convenient accommodation is offered nearby, in The Tannery Townhouse in Church Street (registration pending). *Restaurant* **seats 60**. *L Fri & Sun only, D Tue-Sat.* **Rooms 14** *(12 shower only). CC.* **Directions:** *End of lower main street beside old market house.*

 The Tannery Cookery School

10 Quay Street Dungarvan Co Waterford ✆*058 45420 www.tannery.ie*

Just around the corner from Paul and Maire Flynn's renowned restaurant The Tannery, The Tannery Cookery School is beside the Glanbia Organic Garden, which supplies both the restaurant and the school. Deservedly acclaimed chef Paul Flynn offers an exciting range of courses reflecting his down to earth philosophy, suited to all tastes and abilities from evening demos to a five-day hands-on course. Market garden courses also offered.

 Gortnadiha Lodge

Dungarvan Area Ring Dungarvan Co Waterford ✆*058 46142 www.gortnadihalodge.com*

Eileen and Thomas Harty's house is west of Dungarvan in the Ring Gaeltacht (Irish speaking) area and is in a lovely, quiet setting, with woodland gardens and wonderful land and sea views. Accommodation in the family home is spacious, furnished with quality, and very comfortable. Eileen is a warm and interested host, and breakfasts offer a very wide selection of local and home produce. **Rooms 3** *(2 shower only). Closed 21 Dec - 21 Jan. CC.* **Directions:** *N25 Rosslare to Cork, 3 km from Dungarvan: follow the sea.*

DUNMORE EAST

This small fishing village located in Co. Waterford on an unspoiled coastline, with coves and beaches is an ideal base for touring the south east. The harbour in Dunmore is one of the five designated National Fishery harbours and holds the world record for the largest tuna caught on a rod. The housing in the village is built in the Breton style, with several thatched cottages giving the village an unique and attractive character. Local historic sites include the 12th century Anglo Norman castle and the Church of St Andrew built in 1815. Above the town is a lovely wooded park with pleasant walks and there is a protected beach called Counsellor's strand, which is an ideal spot for sea angling and swimming, whilst the harbour is a popular spot for the yachting community. Dunmore East Adventure Centre (051 383 783) offers both land and water based activities, such as sea kayaking which is a unique fun way to explore the coast.

Azzurro at The Ship

Dock Road Dunmore East Co Waterford ☎*051 383 141 www.azzurro.ie*

The Cavaliere family's appealing family-friendly bar and restaurant is well worth trying for its inexpensive Italian and broadly Mediterranean cooking, welcoming atmosphere and high standards. Menus based on quality local ingredients offer great choice and everything, including ice creams, is homemade. While Azzurro is pitched as a cost-conscious dining destination, the quality and flavour of everything served is likely to exceed expectations. **Seats 70** *(private dining room 50); heated deck. Open all year D Mon-Fri, Sat & Sun all day noon-11. Also L daily May-Sep. CC.* **Directions:** *On the right as you head into Dunmore East from the Waterford side.*

Beach Guesthouse

1 Lower Village Dunmore East Co Waterford ☎*051 383316 www.dunmorebeachguesthouse.com*

Breda Battles' smart modern guesthouse in Dunmore East has easy accessibility to the beach, and offers a moderately priced base for exploring the area. Front rooms, including the breakfast room, lounge, and some bedrooms have a sea view. Everything is very clean and well maintained though hard flooring throughout can be noisy. Tasty breakfasts include lovely scones and preserves. **Rooms 7** *(2 shower only). Closed 1 Nov - 1 Mar. CC.* **Directions:** *First left in village; house facing sea wall.*

Lemon Tree Café

Seacliff Coxtown Dunmore East Co Waterford ☎*051 383 164 www.lemontreecatering.ie/cafe.asp*

Joan Power's gem of a café is just outside Dunmore East village, but well worth the effort of seeking out for lovely fresh fish and home baking. Low-key décor is enhanced by original art works (for sale) and there's a welcoming decking area. They do breakfast and afternoon tea, and at lunchtime spanking fresh fish, salads and soups feature, together with a tempting snack menu. Staff are very friendly and efficient and it's good to see all the restaurant suppliers chalked up on a blackboard on the wall. **Seats 43** *(outdoors, 20), open all day daily (D Fri & Sat only). Closed Mon & Nov. CC.* **Directions:** *Past the harbour, 200m up the hill, on the left.*

The Spinnaker Bar

Lower Village Dunmore East Co Waterford ☎*051 383 133 www.thespinnakerbar.com*

With its rustic nautical theme and sturdy, practical tables the Edmondsons' attractive neighbourhood pub/restaurant is enjoyable for all. Menus have a sense of place and local seafood stars, of course - their speciality is seafood chowder, with beer-battered fish & chips and a great seafood pie also very popular - but there's plenty of choice for all tastes. Special offers (including 'kids eat free') are well worth checking out. *Open all day, daily from 11am. CC.* **Directions:** *Centre of village.*

Strand Inn

Dunmore East Co Waterford ✆ *051 383 174 www.dunmoreeast.com*

Dating back to 1750 this beachside inn is now run by Clifden and Louise Foyle together with Clifden's mother, Edwina. Food is served in the bar which was always the heart of the inn, and also in The Strand Seafood Restaurant, where concessions for non-seafood eaters include steaks and vegetarian options. Nearby, the Foyles also own The Cliff, a casual family-friendly pizza/pasta restaurant in summer a venue for special events, notably weddings, in winter. **Seats 120** *(outdoor, 40). L daily in summer, D daily all year. Bar food daily 12.30-9pm. Rest closed Jan & Mon-Tue in Nov-Mar. CC.* **Directions:** *Left after petrol station in village; beachside building.*

Gaultier Lodge

Dunmore East Area Woodstown Co Waterford ✆ *051 382 549 www.gaultier-lodge.com*

Snugged down in sand dunes for shelter beside Woodstown Strand, Sheila Molloy's early 19th century lodge offers wonderful views from the upper windows, right across the Suir estuary, to Duncannon and the Hook. Set in large gardens it has great style and, like Sheila herself, this lovely house will lift the spirits. When dinner is unavailable the restaurants of Dunmore East are just three miles away. **Rooms 3** *(1 shower only). D by arrangement (book 24 hours in advance; not always available Sun or Thu). Closed Oct - end Apr. No CC.* **Directions:** *From Waterford take R684, Dunmore East road. Take left for Woodstown after 4km. Right at beach, last house on left behind high wall.*

The Copper Hen

Fenor Co Waterford ✆ *051 330 300 www.thecopperhen.ie*

A lovely restaurant in the small village of Fenor, where talented chef Eugene Long is proud to name the quality Irish ingredients used in his excellent and stylishly presented cooking. Service in this appealing and wallet-friendly casual restaurant is friendly and informed. They serve lunch and dinner through a long weekend, which is a big plus for people travelling, or holidaying in the area. *L & D Thur-Sat, Sun L only.* **Directions:** *About 6km from Tramore, above Mother McHugh's pub.*

Vogelaars Apple Farm

Mullinabro Ferrybank via Waterford Co Waterford ✆ *051 872 544*

Apples and fresh juices available at the farm shop, when in season, and you are welcome to call and enquire about 'pick-it-yourself' in the autumn. It makes a lovely day out.

Flahavans Oats

Kilnagrange Mills Kilmacthomas Co Waterford ✆ *051 294 107 www.flahavans.com*

One of Ireland's oldest family businesses, this sixth generation family firm has been milling oats here for over 200 years and their iconic and mainly locally grown products go into almost every Irish shopping trolley. Lauded both for their combination of tradition and innovation and their products' consistent excellence, recognition includes business awards and many food awards including Irish Food Writers' Guild and Great Taste Awards. To demonstrate the versatility of oats, Flahavan's commission recipes from celebrity chefs, including Kevin Dundon; also an excellent Simple Oat Recipes booklet by Mary Flahavan.

Comeragh Mountain Lamb

Kilmacthomas Area Comeragh Lemybrien Co Waterford
☎051 291 533 www.comeraghmountainlamb.ie

Irish mountain lamb is one of Ireland's most sought after most sought after speciality foods - and is increasingly seen under regional branding. A unique product of a rugged terrain with heathers and wild herbs, Comeragh Mountain Lamb is prepared locally by an artisan butcher and dry aged for ten days before being sold in late summer through winter as a fresh, not frozen, product. These factors combine to give this lamb its unique, delicately herbal flavour.

  ## Baldwins Farmhouse Ice Cream

Killeenagh Knockanore Co Waterford ☎086 322 0932 www.baldwinsicecream.com

Innovative young dairy farmer Thomas Baldwin established this alternative enterprise on the family farm near Knockanore village in beautiful West Waterford, where he and his parents, John and Maria have a 70 cow herd of Holstein/British Friesian cross. Their milk and cream is transformed into superb ice cream made on a traditional crème anglaise base in small batches. It's showcased in good restaurants and cafés in the region, including Richmond House, Cappoquin, and The Old Convent, Clogheen, Co Tipperary. Available from quality shops in the Waterford/Cork area (see website for list of stockists).

 ## Knockanore Farmhouse Cheese

Ballyneety Knockanore Co Waterford ☎024 97275 www.knockanorecheese.com

Knockanore Farmhouse Cheese is made near Villierstown and it's very much a family operation, headed up since 1987 by passionate cheesemaker Eamonn Lonergan and his wife Patricia, who produce the Knockanore Cheese range using the raw cows' milk of the Lonergan family's pedigree Friesian herd and vegetarian rennet. The cheddar style cheese comes plain, or flavoured with spices and herbs such as black pepper and chives - or in a powerful oakwood smoked version. *Available from Sheridans Cheesmongers and selected stores; also on local menus.*

LISMORE

Beautifully positioned on the banks of the River Blackwater and at the base of the Knockmealdown Mountains, most of this attractive Heritage Town town was planned and built in the 19th century, whilst its historic roots go back over a 1000 years earlier to the establishment of a monastery by St Carthage in 636 AD. Local attractions include the fairytale Lismore Castle (058 54424), dating back to 1127 and with gardens open to the public; other gardens nearby include Cappoquin House Garden (Cappoquin, 058 54290) and Ballyvolane House (appointment only, Fermoy, 025 36349). Lismore Heritage Centre (058 54975) houses an award winning display of Lismore's history and features of St Carthage's Church of Ireland include an impressive spire and Celtic tombstones.

 ## Ballyrafter Country House Hotel

Lismore Co Waterford ☎058 54002 www.ballyrafterhouse.com

Ballyrafter was built by the Duke of Devonshire as his estate manager's residence and overlooks the Duke's fairy tale Lismore Castle. Today Joe and Noreen Willoughby run it as a welcoming country house hotel where fishing is a big draw but a relaxing laid-back atmosphere, log fires and good home cooking also add up to an appealing package for all guests - as many new fans have discovered recently. The great charm of Ballyrafter (aside from its owners) is that it has escaped over-energetic refurbishment and remains itself. *Rooms 14 (5 shower only). Restaurant seats 30. D daily in summer (Mon residents only), Sat only in winter (bar & restaurant). L Sun only. Bar Meals: 12-6.30 daily. CC. Directions: On the edge of Lismore town.*

  ## Michael McGrath Butcher

Main Street Lismore Co Waterford ☎ *058 54350*

This highly-prized fourth generation butcher is of the old school, where traditional methods decree that meats will hang in the shop awaiting the customer's order. They slaughter their own cattle, and offer the facility to other local farmers. You'll find McGrath's meat on many a fine table, including The Tannery, in Dungarvan and Ballyvolane House near Fermoy.

  ## The Summerhouse

Main Street Lismore Co Waterford ☎ *058 54148 www.thesummerhouse.ie*

An appealing lifestyle store offering homewares and gifts, The Summerhouse is known equally for the edible delights on offer in the informal all-day café at the back - goodies aplenty, including freshly baked breads, lunches and other treats from their own bakery. Using only the best ingredients is a point of pride here, and it shows. Proprietor Gael Byrne is also a highly regarded florist. *Open Tue-Sun 10-5.30. Closed Mon. CC. Directions: At the east end of Main Street, across from the Post Office and supermarket.*

 ## The Castle Country House

Millstreet Dungarvan Co Waterford ☎ *058 68049 www.castlecountryhouse.com*

Set in landscaped gardens overlooking the River Finisk, the Nugent family's unusual and wonderfully hospitable 18th century farmhouse was built around the remains of a 16th century castle. The spacious bedrooms are thoughtfully furnished and Joan Nugent is renowned for her meticulous housekeeping. There's a guest sitting room with an open fire and excellent breakfasts are served in a lovely room that's more like a small restaurant than a farmhouse dining room. A wonderful place to stay. *Rooms 5 (all shower only). Dining Room: Seats 20 (+5 outside); Residents D 7pm, by arrangement. Closed 1 Nov-31 Mar. CC. Directions: Off N25 on R671.*

 ## Triskel Cheese

Killowen Orchard Portlaw Co Waterford 086 0744534

Triskel Cheeses are hand-ladled French-style soft goats cheeses (Pyramid, Crottin and Bouche), and a semi-hard cow's cheese, Gwenned, made by Breton woman Anna Leveque. Anna's partner is the apple farmer Philip Little, and she makes her cheeses at a small production unit at their home in Portlaw, West Waterford, using locally sourced milk. Available at Farmer's Markets (Midleton, Mahon Point, Kinsale, Mallow and Douglas), from Sheridans Cheesemongers and other selected outlets.

  ## The Grand Hotel

Tramore Co Waterford ☎ *051 381 414 www.grand-hotel.ie*

This big old hotel is not perhaps quite as grand as it once was, but it has enviable views of Tramore Bay and will be enjoyed by guests who like quirky older properties. Friendliness and old-fashioned comfort are the order of the day here and, just a few minutes' walk from all the amenities of this holiday town, it's popular with families and is especially child-friendly. *Rooms 80. CC. Directions: Above the town of Tramore.*

 ## The Market Street Restaurant

2 Market Street Tramore Co Waterford ✆ *051 338 495 www.themarketst.com*

Popular chef Michael Mee relocated with his team from Carrick-on-Suir to the holiday town of Tramore, bringing his terrific cooking with him. Committed to sourcing local, preferably organic, produce where possible, there's an emphasis on fish, most of it landed in nearby Dunmore East, and portions are generous. Set on quiet Market Street, the welcome is warm at this smart dining room, which offers great value. *D Wed-Sun, Sun L. Directions: Centre of Tramore.*

WATERFORD

Known around the world as the home of the Waterford Crystal (Waterford Visitor Centre, The Mall; www.waterfordvisitorcentre.com; 051 317000) (051 33 2500), Waterford City has many other attractions too, including the Waterford Christ Church Cathedral (051 858 958), the Waterford Heritage Museum (051 876 123), the 13th century Reginald's Tower (051 304 220) and Waterford Treasures at the Granary (051 304500, open all year), which houses gold, silver and bronze treasures, along with historical documents and a treasure trail that takes you through 1000 years of Waterford's history. Only recently designated a city, its centre is now developing attractively around the river - which, with a marina and walkways along the quays, is a pleasant place to explore.

  ## Ardkeen Quality Food Store

Dunmore Road Waterford Co Waterford ✆ *051 874 620 www.ardkeen.com*

The fact that Ireland's premier cheesemongers, Sheridans, have partnered with Ardkeen says a lot about the special nature of this extraordinary store. Locally owned and managed by the Jephson family, there's a serious and impressive commitment to quality and community. A one-stop-shop for all your gourmet needs, this independent supermarket's shelves are stocked with the finest local artisan produce alongside a butcher's counter, fish counter, fresh fruit and vegetables, delicatessen, barista coffee bar, juice bar, florist, off-licence offering over 300 wine and cookshop offering fresh meals to take home. Their website also merits a special visit- their Food Heroes menu alone will blow you away. Open Mon-Sat, 8am-9pm, Sun & public hols 9am-6pm. Also Producers' Market, second Sunday of every month.

  ## Athenaeum House Hotel

Christendom Waterford Co Waterford ✆ *051 833 999 www.athenaeumhousehotel.com*

Guests feel very much at home in this 4-star boutique hotel, set in 10 acres of parkland overlooking the River Suir, just outside Waterford city. Owner-managed by Stan Power, a former General Manager of Mount Juliet House in County Kilkenny, and his wife Mailo, the chic contemporary decor, luxurious rooms, the smart Zaks restaurant and good service will appeal to discerning travellers. *Rooms 28*. Closed 25-27 Dec. CC. **Directions:** *Leaving railway station on N25 in the direction of Wexford, take the first right after the traffic lights on to Abbey Road, half a mile later take the first right.*

Becketts Bar & Restaurant

Dunmore Road Waterford *Co Waterford* 051 873 082

A well maintained garden with plenty of seating make a good impression on arrival at this large family-friendly pub on the outskirts of Waterford city. The main menu is perhaps too long but prices are very reasonable and, with very good staff and pleasing surroundings, this is a useful place to know about. *Food served daily 12.30-9.30pm (to 8.30pm Sun). Closed 25 Dec, Good Fri. CC.* **Directions:** *Follow Dunmore East signs out of city.*

Bellissimo

Cedar House Ardkeen Dunmore Road Waterford *Co Waterford*
051 879 178 www.bellissimo-waterford.com

A pleasant family-friendly restaurant specialising in Italian favourites, notably pasta and pizza, and with daily specials usually including seafood. Well-trained staff, colourful decor and a bill that's modest for the quality delivered sends customers away happy. *Seats 50 (outdoors, 20). Open noon daily, to 9pm Sun-Tue & 10pm Wed-Sat. CC.* **Directions:** *Off R683 Dunmore Road, 500m from Waterford Castle.*

Berfranks

86 The Quay Waterford *Co Waterford* 051 306 032 www.berfranks.ie

Overlooking the quays, Frank and Bernadette Treyvaud's lovely delicatessen, wine shop and café is full of character and jam-packed with good things. Speciality sandwiches may on the famous Waterford Blaa (roll) and they have earned a following for their cakes and sweet things. Frank and Bernadette have a keen eye for quality and a commitment to stocking Irish artisan products along with other carefully selected speciality products and wines. *Seats 36 (outdoors, 8). Open Mon-Sat 8.30am-5pm. Closed Sun, Bank Hol Mon & 25 Dec. CC.* **Directions:** *Near the clock tower on the quay in Waterford City.*

Bodéga!

54 John St. Waterford *Co Waterford* 051 844 177 www.bodegawaterford.com

With its warm Mediterranean colours, this place would bring the sun out on the darkest of days. Proprietor Cormac Cronin has a high regard for the raw materials in the region; 85-90% of their ingredients are produced locally, suppliers are proudly name checked on menus and the drinks list includes Irish craft beers. Firmly established as a Waterford favourite that delivers quality and value, it's always busy. At lunchtime it attracts young people, some with children – who are made especially welcome – and, while prices rise later, the early dinner menu is a snip. Regular live music too, including big names like Mary Coughlan, Freddie White and Eleanor McEvoy. *Seats 70; L&D Mon-Sat. Closed Sun (open Sun bank hol weekends); Good Fri, 25/26 Dec, 1 Jan, Bank Hol Mons. CC.* **Directions:** *A few doors down from the Applemarket, in city centre.*

 ## Diamond Hill Country House

Slieverue Waterford Co Waterford 📞*051 832 855 www.stayatdiamondhill.com*

Set in one and a half acres of landscaped gardens, the Smith-Lehane family's long established and moderately priced guesthouse is just outside Waterford city. The house has been completely refurbished and most of the well-equipped bedrooms have king-size beds. A good base for exploring the area and, with ten courses within half an hour's drive, it's ideal for golfing breaks. *Rooms 17 (14 shower only). Closed Dec. CC.* **Directions:** *Off the N25 - 1km outside Waterford.*

 ## Foxmount Country House

Passage East Road Waterford Co Waterford 📞*051 874 308 www.foxmountcountryhouse.com*

David and Margaret Kent have been hosting guests in their lovely 17th century home on the edge of Waterford city for 45 years. It's a haven of peace and relaxation, so don't expect phones or TVs in bedrooms, or a very early breakfast. Margaret's home bakes are a treat - afternoon tea in the drawing room, freshly baked breads for breakfast - and you're welcome to bring your own wine and enjoy a glass at the log fire before going out for dinner. Luxury dog accommodation is offered too. *Rooms 4. Closed mid Nov-mid Mar. CC.* **Directions:** *From Waterford city, take Dunmore Road - after 4 km, take Passage East road for 1.5km.*

 ## The Gingerman

6/7 Arundel Lane Waterford Co Waterford 📞*051 879 522*

This hospitable pub in a pedestrianised lane in the main shopping area is a useful place to drop into for a drink, a cuppa, or a casual bite to eat. It can be very busy but, at quieter times is a pleasant spot, with welcoming open fires in several bars. This lovely ambience, together with pleasant staff, a good-humoured hands-on owner and commitment to serving wholesome food has earned it a loyal local following. *Open 10am-11.30pm. Food served Mon-Sat, 10-6 (to 7 Fri & Sat); Sun L 12.30-6pm. Closed 25 Dec, Good Fri. CC.* **Directions:** *Off John Roberts Square.*

 ## The Granary Cafe

The Granary Hanover Street Waterford Co Waterford 📞*051 854 428 www.granarycafe.ie*

Chef Peter Fowler's food at this bright and pleasing café has real homemade flavour. A self-service operation, the food is simple – breakfast, sandwiches, quiches, pies, soups, and good desserts and cakes - but it's a pleasant spot with a spacious seating area with couches, reading material and tables, and also an outdoor eating area for fine weather. *Mon-Sat 8am-5pm.*

 ## Granville Hotel

The Quay Waterford Co Waterford 📞*051 305 555 www.granville-hotel.ie*

The Guide's Hotel of the Year 2013 and one of the country's oldest hotels, this much-loved quayside establishment is owner-run since 1979 by the Cusack family, who have restored the old building to its former glory. The overall food style is proudly traditional, with some local specialities featuring. The hotel's Bianconi Restaurant delivers good value and excellent cooking by Executive Head Chef Stephen Hooper, so reservations are essential. As elsewhere in the hotel, it is the warm Irish hospitality and service that really make a visit here memorable. *Rooms 98. Restaurant seats 140. L Sun only 12.30-5.30, D daily 5.30-9.30 (Sat to 10). Bar meals 10.30am-9pm daily. Closed 25-27 Dec. CC.*

 ## Harlequin Cafe & Winebar

37 Stephen Street Waterford Co Waterford *051 877 552 www.harlequin-cafe.com*

This tiny café serves authentic Italian food at very reasonable prices and has become a favourite with locals. The menu, like the proprietors, is Italian and can transport you to a back street in Rome or Venice. A delightful choice when eating out in Waterford, it serves all sorts of meals and snacks from morning to night. Its Italian croissant and cappuccino for breakfast are a real treat. *Seats 20; Open daily 12-9.30pm. Closed Sun in winter, Bank Hols, 2 weeks at Christmas. CC.*

  ## Henry Downes

8-10 Thomas St. Waterford Co Waterford ℓ*051 874 118*

Established in 1759, and in the same (eccentric) family for six generations, John de Bromhead's unusual pub is one of the few remaining houses to bottle its own whiskey. Not the easiest of places to find, once visited it certainly will not be forgotten. Friendly, humorous bar staff enjoy filling in customers on the pub's proud history and will gladly sell you a bottle of Henry Downes No.9 to take away. No food is served and the pub is not suitable for children. *Open from 5pm to normal closing time. Closed 25 Dec & Good Fri. No CC.*

  ## Hickeys Bakery

59 Barrack Street Waterford Co Waterford ℓ*051 375 388*

The Hickey family has been running this bakery in Waterford city centre for over half a century, and it was one of four bakeries honoured by Euro-Toques for maintaining the tradition of making the 'Waterford blaa' the floury yeast roll that is peculiar to the area.

L'Atmosphère

19 Henrietta Street Waterford Co Waterford ℓ*051 858 426 www.restaurant-latmosphere.com*

With delicious, keenly priced food and friendly service from mainly French waiting staff, the whole impression in Arnaud Mary and Patrice Garreau's restaurant is of eating in a really good French bistro. Menus include an early dinner offering extremely good value, and may even include a glass of house wine. Expect typical French bistro and 'gran'mère' cooking at its best (including excellent breads – Arnaud has a French bakery in the town). While menus may offer luxurious items like foie gras, or lobster, there is a high level of skill here and a good old-fashioned sense that cheaper cuts of meat will also be used, and properly. *Seats 48; L&D Mon-Fri; D only Sat, Sun. Closed L Sat & Sun and bank hol Mons. CC.*

La Bohème

2 George St. Waterford Co Waterford 📞*051 875 645 www.labohemerestaurant.ie*

Christine and Eric Thèze's elegant restaurant in the basement of Waterford's Chamber of Commerce building is smart and stylish with a lovely French vibe. Warm and friendly French waiters give one a feeling of being in expert hands and gleaming glass, silver, and crisp white linen are perfect in this room where seasonally changed menus are offered. The cooking style is modern classic French, with menus offering Irish meats, seafood, rabbit and veal in dishes that typify French restaurants. A strongly French wine list offers value in regional wines – and service is excellent. This is a restaurant that is serious about its food and is a great asset to Waterford city. *D Tue-Sat. Closed Sun, Mon, 25-27 Dec. CC.*

La Palma on the Mall

20 The Mall Waterford Co Waterford 📞*051 879 823 www.lapalma.ie*

Offering 'formal dining in a relaxed setting' the Cavaliere family's popular Italian restaurant is in a graceful Georgian building on Waterford's Mall. Specialities include Irish rose veal parmigiana style, with tomato, basil and fresh oregano salsa, and house variations on Italian classics are based on carefully sourced Irish ingredients, including local seafood. Service is very pleasant and attentive and the bill should be agreeably reasonable. [The old Palma, now the Espresso, serves pizza and pasta.] *Seats 75 (outdoors, 10); D only Mon-Sat; Sun 1-7pm. Closed 25-26 Dec, 1 Jan, Good Fri. CC.* **Directions:** *Opposite Bishop's Palace & Theatre Royal.*

M&D Bakery

34 Mount Sion Avenue Waterford Co Waterford 📞*051 378 080*

Named after two brothers and third generation bakers, Michael and Dermot Walsh, this highly regarded bakery is one of the four bakeries recognised by Euro-Toques for continuing to include the traditional Waterford blaa in their range. They supply many catering and retail businesses.

Metalman Brewing Company

Unit 14 Tycor Business Centre Tycor Waterford Co Waterford
📞*087 250 9638 www.metalmanbrewing.com*

Born of a desire to see more beer produced by independent brewers in Ireland, Metalman Brewing is the brainchild of beer enthusiasts Gráinne Walsh and Tim Barber, who were frustrated by the lack of availability and choice of tasty, authentically Irish beer. The flagship Metalman Pale Ale is available all year, with seasonals released. Check website for stockists.

Sion Hill House & Gardens

Sion Hill Ferrybank Waterford Co Waterford 📞*051 851 558 www.sionhillhouse.net*

George and Antoinette Kavanagh have been welcoming guests to their lovely hillside house above Waterford city since 1996. Immaculately maintained and with classically proportioned

rooms furnished with fine antiques, anyone who enjoys beautiful old things will find this a wonderful place to stay- especially garden lovers, as it is more a garden with a house in it, rather than a house with a garden attached. But what a house, all the same. *Rooms 4 (2 shower only). Closed 22-27 Dec. CC.*

Tom Kearneys Butchers

37a John Street Waterford Co Waterford ✆*051 874 434*

Waterford has more than its fair share of good butchers. Tom Kearney's stands out especially for their beef; they raise their own animals for supply to some of the city's most discerning customers and you will see the name proudly credited on many of the area's top menus.

Tower Hotel Waterford

The Mall Waterford Co Waterford ✆*051 875801 www.towerhotelwaterford.com*

Enjoying a central location within easy walking distance of everything in Waterford city, there are excellent business and leisure facilities are at this big hotel, the flagship of the FBD Hotels Group and a sister property to the beautifully located Faithlegg House Hotel (see entry). Recent years have seen an improvement in standards throughout, including many refurbished bedrooms. *Rooms 136. Closed 24-26 Dec. CC.*

Waterford Castle Hotel

The Island Ballinakill Waterford Co Waterford ✆*051 878 203 www.waterfordcastle.com*

Serenely situated on its own wooded island (complete with 18-hole golf course) this characterful and romantic hotel dates back to the 16th century, and is reached by a private ferry. Combining the elegance of earlier times with modern comfort, service and convenience, it also offers beautiful, natural food. As elsewhere in the hotel, discreet, well-trained staff look after guests magnificently. A very special place. *Rooms 19. Restaurant seats 60. D daily, L Sun only. Open all year. CC. Directions: Outskirts of Waterford City just off Dunmore East road.*

Faithlegg House Hotel

Waterford Area Faithlegg Co Waterford ✆*051 382 000 www.faithlegg.com*

Set in wooded landscape with magnificent views over its own golf course and the Suir estuary, this lovely 18th century house boasts graciously proportioned rooms alongside more practical modern hotel rooms in a new wing (self-catering accommodation is also offered in the grounds). Activities on site include golf, a swimming pool, and numerous health and beauty treatments. There is a choice of restaurants nearby and the hotel's fine dining restaurant, The Roseville Rooms, offers classical cuisine. *Rooms 82. Hotel closed 25 Dec. CC. Directions: Off Dunmore East Road 10km outside Waterford city.*

The Fitzwilton Hotel & ChezKs Restaurant

Bridge Street Waterford City Co Waterford ✆*51 846 900 www.fitzwiltonhotel.ie*

Centrally located close to the quay, this pleasing modern four star hotel is within comfortable walking distance of all the main visitor attractions in Waterford City; good facilities and generously sized single rooms make it popular with business travellers. The restaurant, Chez-K's, offers good cooking based on top quality local ingredients (including breakfast). *Rooms 88. CC.*

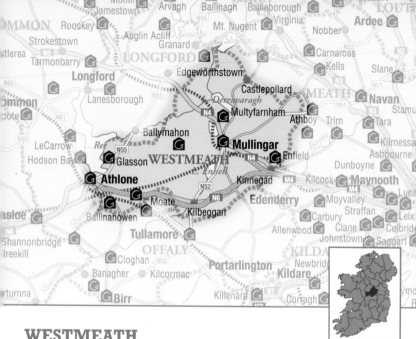

WESTMEATH

As its name suggests, in the distant past Westmeath tended to be ruled by whoever held Meath, or perhaps it was the other way around. But today, Westmeath is a county so cheerfully and successfully developing its own identity that they should find a completely new name for the place. For this is somewhere that makes the very best of what it has to hand.

Its highest "peak" is only the modest Mullaghmeen of 258 m, 10 kilometres north of Castlepollard. But this is in an area where hills of ordinary height have impressive shapes which make them appear like miniature mountains around the spectacularly beautiful Lough Derravaragh, famed for its association with the legend of the Children of Lir. Turned into swans by their wicked step-mother, they were swans for 900 years until saved by the coming of Christianity.

Westmeath abounds in lakes to complement Derravaragh, such as the handsome expanses of Lough Owel and Lough Ennell on either side of the fine county town of Mullingar, where life has been made even more watery in recent years with the restoration of the Royal Canal, which loops round town on its way from Dublin to the north Shannon.

Meanwhile, Athlone on the Shannon to the southwest has a real buzz, and north of it there's the wide lake of Lough Ree in all its glory, wonderful for boating in an area where the Goldsmith country verges towards County Longford, and they've a monument to mark what some enthusiasts reckon to be the true geographical centre of all Ireland. You really can't get more utterly rural than that.

LOCAL ATTRACTIONS & INFORMATION

▸ **All Ireland Amateur Drama Festival** (May) Athlone
090 6473358

▸ **Athlone Castle Visitor Centre**
Athlone *090 6492912*

▸ **Tullynally Castle & Gardens**
Castlepollard *0*
44 49060

▸ **Ballinlough Castle Gardens**
Clonmellon *046 9433135*

▸ **Locke's Distillery Museum**
Kilbeggan
0506 32134

436

ATHLONE

Athlone makes a perfect break for anyone crossing the country, but it's much more than a handy stopover and has become a destination town for weekend breaks. There's a growing supply of quality accommodation in the area and this bustling, youthful centre town of Ireland has much to offer. Although other towns along the mighty Shannon might challenge this, Athlone could be seen as the culinary capital of the inland waterways, with a cluster of good eating places in the town itself and surrounding area. A Farmers' Markets is held on Saturdays (Market Square 10am-3pm). There's plenty of historical interest in the area, including Athlone Castle, and other popular visitor attractions include the award winning Glendeer Open Farm (090 6437 147) and the Viking Cruise (090 647 3383/ 086 262 1136) of the Shannon. Lakeside championship golf is found nearby, at the beautifully located Glasson Golf Hotel (Glasson, 090 648 5120).

Al Mezza

6 Bastion Street Athlone Co Westmeath ✆ *090 649 8765*

This atmospheric little Lebanese/Mediterranean restaurant on Athlone's 'left bank' has earned a following for its friendliness and for offering something different from other restaurants. Proprietor-chef Milad Serhan's menus are quite extensive, so mixed dishes are probably the best bet on a first visit. Service is friendly and the charming old building adds to the fun of a visit here. Great value too. *Seats 40 (outdoors, 12). D Wed-Mon. Closed Tue; Good Fri, 25 Dec. CC.* **Directions:** *Between High Street and O'Connell Street.*

Hodson Bay Hotel

Hodson Bay Athlone Co Westmeath ✆ *090 644 2000 www.hodsonbayhotel.com*

With lovely lake and island views and a wide range of leisure activities on site - including a destination spa and leisure centre, as well as golf and water-based activities - this family-friendly hotel is in great demand as a venue for both business and social occasions. Newer bedrooms are bright and comfortable and many also have views of Lough Ree. *Rooms 133. Open all year. CC.* **Directions:** *Roscommon road (N61) - off N6 Athlone bypass.*

Kin Khao Thai Restaurant

1 Abbey Lane Athlone Co Westmeath ✆ *090 649 8805 www.kinkhaothai.ie*

With its vivid yellow and red exterior making it a beacon for hungry diners, you can't miss this restaurant near the castle. Run by Irishman Adam Lyons and his Thai wife, Janya - whose family is steeped in the restaurant and food tradition – this is undoubtedly one of the best Thai restaurants in Ireland, and good value for money too. It is deservedly popular and reservations are strongly advised. Well worth a detour - you're in for a real treat here. *Seats 5. D daily; L Wed-Fri & Sun all day 1.30-10.30pm. Closed 24/25 Dec, Easter Sun. CC.* **Directions:** *Castle side of town, 100 metres from Seans Bar.*

The Left Bank Bistro

Fry Place Athlone Co Westmeath ✆ *090 649 4446 www.leftbankbistro.com*

Together with carefully sourced ingredients and snappy cooking, Annie McNamara and Mary McCullagh's elegantly informal, contemporary restaurant is a top choice for a meal in Athlone.The keenly priced menus offer a wide range of delicious-sounding dishes with a multicultural stamp - and for the quality of food and cooking, a meal here is always good value. Carefully selected small range of speciality products on sale too. *Seats 60. Open Tue-Sat from 10am; L&D. Closed Sun & Mon, bank hols & Christmas period. CC. Directions: Behind Athlone Castle, west side of the Shannon.*

The Locke Bar & Restaurant

St Peter's Port The Docks Athlone Co Westmeath ☎*090 649 4517*

Theatrically designed around the joint themes of church and river, this unusual quayside restaurant is full of character. Some tables in the first floor restaurant have river views but the whole interior is so full of interest, and staff are so friendly and willing, that other tables are almost equally appealing. Wide ranging menus are especially strong on the great midland meats and the early dinner offers good value. *Seats 90*. Open daily, 12-10. *Directions:* On the west bank of the Shannon, near Athlone Castle.

Radisson Blu Hotel Athlone

Northgate Street Athlone Co Westmeath ☎*090 644 2600 www.radissonblu.ie/hotel-athlone*

Magnificently located right on the river and bang in the middle of Athlone with a huge riverside deck overlooking the marina, this hotel has impressive public areas and great style. The usual Radisson attributes of contemporary chic and eco-awareness apply throughout the hotel and all rooms have excellent facilities. For those who like a town centre location, this would be hard to beat as a short break destination. *Rooms 124. Open all year. CC. Directions: Town centre, east side of the bridge.*

Sean's Bar

13 Main Street Athlone Co Westmeath ☎*090 649 2358*

West of the river, in the interesting old part of Athlone town near the Norman castle, this seriously historic bar lays claim to being the pub with the longest continuous use in Ireland, all owners since 900 AD are on record. Dimly lit, with a sloping floor (to allow receding flood waters to drain) mahogany bar, mirrored shelving and open fire, it's a legendary watering hole for Shannon boating folk. Food is restricted to sandwiches but they serve a great pint. *Closed 25 Dec & Good Fri. Directions: On the west quayside, just in front of the castle.*

Sheraton Athlone

Athlone Co Westmeath ☎*090 645 1000 www.sheratonathlonehotel.com*

While its leisure facilities and central location add appeal for all guests, this luxuriously appointed landmark hotel's key offering is exceptional conference, business and banqueting facilities. Views from upper floors take in the mighty Shannon and four surrounding counties (Westmeath, Roscommon, Longford and Offaly) as well as the town itself. *Rooms 167. Closed 25 Dec. CC. Directions: Adjoining town centre shopping centre.*

Thyme Restaurant

Custume Place Athlone Co Westmeath ✆*090 647 8850 www.thymerestaurant.ie*

'Delicious food at affordable prices' is the stated aim at this pleasing little town centre restaurant – and this they achieve very well. Owner-chef John Coffey sources ingredients with great care and ensures that everything travels as short a distance as possible. Most of the key ingredients on his imaginative, seasonally changing menus are from Athlone and the general midlands area and Kilmore Quay "Irish, sustainable and fresh" fish dishes are particularly interesting. Lovely food, and good value; the early dinner is a snip.

Seats 40. *D Mon-Sat, all day Sun 12-8. CC.* **Directions:** *Just off the main street, close to the bridge on the eastern side.*

Glasson Hotel & Golf Club

Athlone Area Glasson Athlone Co Westmeath ✆*090 648 5120 www.glassongolfhotel.ie*

Beautifully situated in an elevated position overlooking Lough Ree, the Reid family's impressive hotel has been developed around their fine old family home; although the golfing dimension has earned an international reputation as one of Ireland's premier inland courses, the hotel is equally geared to business guests and non golfers, and it is a lovely place to stay. **Rooms 65**. *Closed 25 Dec. CC.* **Directions:** *10km north of Athlone, off the N55 Cavan-Longford road.*

Lough Bishop House

Derrynagarra Collinstown Co Westmeath ✆*044 966 1313 www.loughbishophouse.com*

In a beautifully scenic area awash with lakes, gentle hills and rich farmland, Helen and Christopher Kelly offer a warm welcome and a genuine Irish family home experience on their organic farm, famed for its moiled cattle and Irish Draught horses. Everything is spotless and gleaming, and the very comfortable rooms are TV-free zones. Dinner offers excellent home-cooked food, some grown or reared on the farm, and there's home-baked bread, fresh fruit and apple juice from the orchard at breakfast. **Rooms 3** *(2 shower only). Residents' D at 7.30pm (book before noon). Cottage also available for self-catering or B&B (2 night min stay). No CC.* **Directions:** *Castlepollard R394, at Whitehall turn onto L5738, 3km on on right hand*

GLASSON

Originally built as an estate, the poet Goldsmith's "village of the roses" has old world charm, and (once you get away from the main Athlone-Cavan road) peacefulness. Glasson is surrounded by beautiful countryside on the shores of Lough Ree, where visitors can enjoy lakeshore or forest walks and anglers can take full advantage of some of Ireland's finest brown trout and pike fishing. Golfers will enjoy the Glasson Golf Club (090 6485120), whilst other activities available include pony trekking, cruises on the River Shannon or on Lough Ree. Historic buildings include an old schoolhouse built in 1844 and the local historical attractions include Athlone Castle (090 649 2912) and Fore Abbey (044 936 1780), which are the only Benedictine remains in Ireland, dating back to 630AD.

The Fatted Calf

Glasson Co Westmeath ✆*090 648 5208 www.thefattedcalf.ie*

Feargal O'Donnell and his wife, Fiona, chose well when they took over this pub in Goldsmith's pretty 'village of the roses'. Known for his commitment to seasonal and local foods, Feargal's enticing menus promise innovative modern Irish food in both the bar and restaurant, with suppliers of his carefully sourced ingredients proudly detailed on the menu. A timely combination of gastro-pub and contemporary fine dining in a family-friendly atmosphere - and with garden space for children to run around. *Seats 70 (outdoors, 40). L & D Tue-Sun. No food Mon (except bank hols). Closed Good Fri, 25 Dec. CC. **Directions:** Longford/Cavan exit from M6, 8km.*

Glasson Village Restaurant

Glasson Co Westmeath ✆*090 648 5001 www.glassonvillagerestaurant.ie*

Chef-proprietor Michael Brooks opened this restaurant in 1986, making his mark as a culinary pioneer in the area. The cooking is imaginative – traditional French meets modern Irish – and unusually for the area, fresh fish has always featured strongly. A true love of food, together with caring service under the direction of Michael's sister, Marie Brooks, and good value have earned a loyal following. *Seats 60. D Tue-Sat; L Sun only. Closed D Sun, all Mon, 3 weeks mid Oct, 3 days Christmas. CC. **Directions:** 8 km from Athlone on Longford/Cavan road (N55).*

Grogan's Pub

Glasson Co Westmeath ✆*090 648 5158*

Grogan's Pub is one of those proudly-run, traditional places with two little bars at the front (one with a welcome open fire in winter) and everything gleaming; it was established in 1750 and feels as if the fundamentals haven't changed too much since then. Wholesome food is served in the back bar and on Wednesday nights there's traditional music, when three generations of the same family play and visiting musicians are also welcome. *Food served Mon-Sat 12-9pm, Sun 2-5pm. Closed 25 Dec, Good Fri. **Directions:** Centre of village.*

Wineport Lodge

Glasson Co Westmeath ✆*090 643 9010 www.wineport.ie*

Ray Byrne and Jane English's lovely lakeside lodge styles itself 'Ireland's first wine hotel' and the accommodation - which offers thirty beautiful rooms (all with private balconies overlooking the lake) a hot tub and treatment rooms - is nothing less than stunning. Luxurious, romantic, beautiful, businesslike, this is a place of many moods: Wineport has everything you may expect an outstanding food experience to, where accomplished cooking and pleasing presentation make the most of the best local ingredients to make a meal here memorable. **Rooms 29** (2 shower only). Restaurant **seats 120** (outdoors, 50). D daily. L Sun only. Also Lounge Menu 12-9pm, daily. Closed 24-26 Dec. CC. **Directions:** Exit off the M6 at Athlone; fork left after 4km at the Dog & Duck; 1.5km, on the left.

KILBEGGAN

Kilbeggan is famous for its old distillery, which has returned to whiskey production after a long lapse, and is an interesting place to break a journey across the country. The Kilbeggan Distillery Experience (057 933 2134; www.kilbeggandistillery.com) is worth a visit, especially if you can combine it with an evening at the the 'very Irish experience' that is Kilbeggan Races (www.kilbegganraces.com). Walkers will enjoy The Westmeath Way walking route which stretches from Kilbeggan to Mulilngar (33km/21m) and includes some quiet towpath sections along the old canal.

 ### Kilbeggan Organic Foods

Ballard Organic Farm Kilbeggan Co Westmeath 📞*087 255 7679 www.kilbegganorganicfoods.com*

Fifth-generation farmer Pat Lalor runs this innovative organic farm. The main crop is oats, which they use to produce their own high quality porridge oats; outstanding for their texture and flavour, they're sold as Kilbeggan Organic Porridge. Ballard Organic Beef is a significant new enterprise currently being established and Ballard is an open farm, with facilities for visiting groups, with or without an agricultural background. Oats widely available from quality food stores. *Open Farm with Visitor Centre; groups of up to 45 by appointment, March-October.*

Old Kilbeggan Distillery

Kilbeggan Co Westmeath 📞*057 933 2134 www.kilbeggandistillery.com*

Established in 1757, the old Locke's Distillery has been restored and, after a 50 year closure, whiskey production recommenced in 2007.The Kilbeggan Distillery Experience is open to the public and is well worth a visit. Both guided and self-guided tours are available, with tastings. The Pantry restaurant offers refreshments on site and meals can be provided for groups by arrangement. *Open daily: Oct-Mar 10am-4pm, Apr-Sep 9-6. Closed Christmas-New Year.*

MULLINGAR

This thriving midlands town beside the Royal Canal is dominated by the cathedral, an imposing renaissance-style structure dedicated in 1939. Nearby Belvedere House and Gardens (044 934 9060) is a lovely place to spend a few hours, while a testing round of golf is available in Mullingar Golf Club (044 934 8366). Mullingar is also known for the neighbouring lakes, Lough Owel and Lough Ennell, which attract many anglers, while Lough Derravaragh is best known for its connection with the Irish legend of the Children of Lir. Having been turned into swans, the four children of King Lir spent three hundred years on Lough Derravaragh before moving to other locations around Ireland. It is also a great area for cycling. The weekly Farmers' Market (Sun 10.30- 2.30) is usually held at at Fairgreen, adjacent to Penneys, but the venue is subject to change.

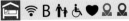 ### Annebrook House Hotel

Austin Friars Street Mullingar Co Westmeath 📞*044 935 3300 www.annebrook.ie*

Built around a beautiful old house, with the town park on the doorstep and the River Brosna flowing through the grounds, it's all distinctly fairytale for a town centre hotel. Bedrooms, in a new build, are comfortably furnished and impressive public rooms in the original house include the atmospheric Brook Restaurant. Popular for weddings and business, this friendly hotel is also an ideal destination for a weekend away. *Rooms 75. CC. Directions: On Main Street.*

  CR Tormey & Sons

15 Harbour Place Shopping Centre Mullingar Co Westmeath ☎044 934 5433 www.crtormeys.ie

These third generation farmers and family butchers are well known in the west and midlands, with shops in Mullingar, Tullamore and Galway. Recognised for high standards, combining tradition with innovation, they have achieved numerous awards for excellence – notably for their beef - and you will see them credited on many of the region's best menus. *Open Mon-Wed & Sat 8-6, Thu & Fri 8-8. Local delivery service. CC.*

  The Fish Market

6 Castle Street Mullingar Co Westmeath ☎044 933 0610

A former chef, George Stevens decided to leave the catering industry and go into the supply of quality food rather than cooking it. His fish shop attracts an enthusiastic clientele, keen to enjoy the wide variety of fresh fish and shellfish he stocks. *Open Tue-Sat. Closed Sun & Mon.*

  Gallery 29 Café

16 Oliver Plunkett St. Mullingar Co Westmeath ☎044 934 9449

Although only open three days a week, Ann and Emily Gray's smart premises is bright and welcoming and is a good place for any time of the day. The buzz of an open kitchen and the freshly cooked food on display draw people in. You'll find good soups, salads, a savoury tart of the day and tailor-made sandwiches as well as hot main courses. Outside catering, picnics and freshly made dishes for home freezing are also offered. *Seats 50. Open Thu-Sat 9am-6pm. Closed Sun-Wed, Christmas/New Year. No CC. Directions: Town centre.*

 Ilia A Coffee Experience

28 Oliver Plunkett Street Mullingar Co Westmeath ☎044 934 0300 www.ilia.ie

Julie Magan's delightful coffee house and informal restaurant in the centre of town caters for all the changing moods though the day, beginning with an extensive breakfast, then midday bites like home-made soup, panini, steak baguettes and more - including some of the tapas style dishes previously enjoyed at 'Ilia Tapas & More' (formerly on Dominick Street). Everything is deliciously fresh and wholesome, staff are charming and efficient, and all at reasonable prices. Takeaway is also available. *Seats 60. Open Mon-Sat 9am-6pm. Closed Sun, Christmas & bank hols. CC. Directions: Centre of town.*

 Mullingar Park Hotel

Dublin Road Mullingar Co Westmeath ☎044 933 7500 www.mullingarparkhotel.com

A spacious and friendly place with an unexpectedly pleasant outlook at the back, where there is a sheltered courtyard garden, this large hotel is has good business and leisure facilities, and offers a convenient journey break when travelling across the country. The Terrace Restaurant offers more than the usual hotel fare, and its well priced menus include interesting vegetarian choices. *Rooms 95. Closed 25-26 Dec. CC. Directions: Off the N4 - take exit no. 15.*

Oscars Restaurant

21 Oliver Plunkett Street Mullingar Co Westmeath ✆*044 934 4909*

Oscars enjoys enduring popularity locally, pleasing people of all ages with its lively atmosphere and mix of traditional and contemporary favourites at reasonable prices. This is beef country so expect great steaks, but there's much else besides, a range of classic favourites, pasta and pizzas – popular food, well executed. An affordable outing with something for everyone. *Seats 70*. *D daily, L Sun only. Closed 25/26 Dec, first 2 weeks Jan. MasterCard, Visa, Laser.*

Mary Lynch's Pub

Mullingar Area MacNead's Bridge Coralstown Nr. Mullingar Co Westmeath ✆*044 937 4501*

Tucked between the N4 and the Royal Canal, with a grandstand view of the new harbour from the back of the bar, John and Mary Moriarty's charming old-world pub is a short distance east of Mullingar. A blackboard menu offers traditional home-cooked dishes like fish pie, roast of the day and steak sandwiches. It's popular with locals, and a useful place for travellers to know about. Music at weekends. *Meals Mon and Wed-Sat 12-8, Tue 12-6. No food on Sun. CC. Directions: Exit 13 on N4, between the N4 and the canal.*

MULTYFARNHAM

Set in lovely unspoilt rolling countryside, this is a very attractive village with stone buildings and a pretty river. It is rich in history too, with a Franciscan monastery which was founded in 1268 and is still in use; today it is the site of one of the finest outdoor shrines in Ireland, with 14 life size Stations of the Cross on the monastery lawns, around the church and college. It is a lovely area for a short break and is close to Lough Derravaragh, with activities including horesriding, hill walking, boating, and fishing (with authorised permits) all nearby. Garden lovers staying in the area should make a point of visiting Tullynally Castle & Gardens (Castlepollard, 044 966 1159) especially in spring, as they are bulb specialists.

An Tintáin Restaurant

Main Street Multyfarnham Co Westmeath ✆*044 937 1411 www.antintain.com*

Set in a lovely and surprisingly little visited part of the country with lakes and rolling farmland, the pretty village of Multyfarnham is only a short detour off the N4. Niamh and Paul Murphy's attractive stone restaurant strikes a balance between comforting crowd-pleasers and more creative dishes, all prepared with a light touch and unexpected flourishes. Either way, the cooking is confident and well balanced - and servings are very generous. Well worth a stop when you're in the midlands. *Seats 70. Open Wed-Fri 4-9.30pm; Sat 12.30-9pm; Sun 12.30-7.45pm. Closed Mon & Tue. CC. Directions: At bottom of Main Street, beside bridge.*

Mornington House

Mornington Multyfarnham Co Westmeath ☎ *044 937 2191 www.mornington.ie*

Just a meadow's walk away from Lough Derravarragh where the mythical Children of Lir spent 300 years of their 900 year exile, Warwick and Anne O'Hara's gracious Victorian house has been in the O'Hara family home since 1858, and is still furnished with much of the original furniture and family portraits. Although centrally heated, log fires remain an essential feature, and the spacious bedrooms are well appointed, with old furniture but modern mattresses. Anne cooks proper breakfasts and country house dinners for residents, using fresh fruit and vegetables from the walled garden and local produce (Westmeath beef cooked in Guinness is a speciality). A tranquil and restorative place for a short break. **Rooms 4** *(1 with private bathroom, 1 shower only). Closed Nov-Mar. CC.* **Directions:** *Exit N4 for Castlepollard, take R1618 direction Multyfarnham.*

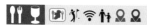

Weirs Bar & Restaurant

Multyfarnham Mullingar Co Westmeath ☎ *044 937 1111 www.weirsmultyfarnham.ie*

Pat and Una Weir's handsome stone pub and restaurant is an atmospheric place, especially the friendly front bar with its welcoming fire. Behind it is a restaurant serving home-cooked food, notably steaks (Angus sirloin, Hereford fillet), and the Weirs take pride in using as much local and organic produce as possible. A relaxed atmosphere, friendly service and good food – what more could you ask of a country pub? **Seats 60** *(outdoors, 8). Meals: Wed-Sat, 12.30-8.30; Sun, 12.30-8pm. No food served Mon (except bank hols) & Tue. Closed Good Fri, 25 Dec. CC.* **Directions:** *2km off N4 between Mullingar and Ballinalack.*

WEXFORD

The popular view of Wexford is beaches, sunshine and opera. The longest continuous beach in all Ireland runs along the county's east coast, an astonishing 27 kilometres from Cahore Point south to Raven Point, which marks the northern side of the entrance to Wexford town's shallow harbour. As for sunshine, while areas further north along the east coast may record marginally less rainfall, in the very maritime climate of the "Sunny Southeast" around Wexford, the clouds seem to clear more quickly, so the chances of seeing the elusive orb are much improved.

And opera.....? Well, the annual Wexford Opera Festival in October is a byword for entertaining eccentricity - as international enthusiasts put it, "we go to Wexford town to enjoy operas written by people we've never heard of, and we have ourselves a thoroughly good time."

Wexford itself is one of three substantial towns in the county, the other two being the market town of Enniscorthy, and the river port of New Ross. While much of the county is relatively low-lying, to the northwest it rises towards the handsome Blackstairs Mountains. There, the 793m peak of Mount Leinster may be just over the boundary in Carlow, but one of the most attractive little hill towns in all Ireland, Bunclody, is most definitely in Wexford.

In New Ross, the authentic re-creation of a 19th Century emigrant ship - the impressive Dunbrody - is proving to be a very effective focal point for the revival of the picturesque waterfront. It's a fitting place for the lovely River Barrow to meet ships in from sea in an area with strong historical links to President John F Kennedy - his great-grandparents sailed from New Ross to America on the original Dunbrody.

LOCAL ATTRACTIONS & INFORMATION

▸ **Abbey & Visitor Centre**
Dunbrody *051 388603*
▸ **Hook Head Lighthouse** Hook
Head *051 397055*

▸ **Castle Demesne &**
Agricultural Museum
Johnstown *053 42888*
▸ **Dunbrody Famine Ship**
New Ross *051 425239*

▸ **John F Kennedy Arboretum**
New Ross *051 388171*
▸ **John F Kennedy Homestead**
Dunganstown New Ross
051 388264

Carrigbyrne Cheese

Carrigbyrne House Adamstown *Enniscorthy Co Wexford* ✆053 924 0560 *www.carrigbyrne.ie*

Carrigbyrne Cheese is one of the most enduring success stories of the renaissance of artisan cheese making in Ireland. The main product, the camembert style Carrigbyrne St Killian, is one of Ireland's longest-established and most popular farmhouse cheeses. Easily recognisable by its smart hexagonal box (even when sold as an own-brand, eg M&S), this cheese has been made since 1982 by dairy farmers Patrick and Juliet Berridge on their Co Wexford dairy farm along with their other cheeses, St Brendans and Emerald Irish Brie. Widely distributed.

ARTHURSTOWN

This seaside village is a popular family holiday destination on the spectacular Hook Peninsula, home to many sandy coves, and historical sites such as Tintern Abbey (051 562650, open June to October), Dunbrody Abbey & Visitor Centre (051 388603, open May to September) and the Hook Lighthouse (051 397055/4, open all year). Tintern Abbey is a Cistercian Abbey set in a beautiful riverside woodland area alongside a small estuary, and Dunbrody Abbey dates back to 1210 AD, and is one of the most striking Cistercian ruins in the country. Visitors can take guided tours of Hook Head Lighthouse, which also dates back to the early 13th century and, although automated in 1996, is one of the oldest operational lighthouses in the world. Other local attractions include Ballyhack Castle (051 389 468) and Duncannon Fort (051 388 603).

Dunbrody House

Arthurstown Co Wexford ✆051 389 600 *www.dunbrodyhouse.com*

Celebrated chef Kevin Dundon and his wife Catherine's elegant Georgian manor is a tranquil and luxurious retreat set in parkland and gardens on the Hook Peninsula, just across the estuary from Waterford city. Public rooms and the spacious bedrooms are beautifully furnished and decorated, with all the comforts expected of such a fine house, while dining - whether formally in The Harvest Room or informally at Dundon's Champagne Seafood Bar & Terrace - is sure to be a treat. Converted outbuildings house what must be Ireland's most stylish cookery school, with a beautiful spa beside it. **Rooms 22**. *Harvest Room* **Seats 70** *(outdoors, 20). D Mon-Sat. L Sun only. Dundon's Champagne Seafood Bar Seats 20; food served daily 2-10pm. House closed 19-27 Dec. CC.* **Directions:** *N11 to Wexford, R733 from Wexford to Arthurstown.*

Glendine Country House

Arthurstown New Ross Co Wexford ✆051 389 500 *www.glendinehouse.com*

Ann and Tom Crosbie's large nineteenth century farmhouse is approached up a driveway off the main road to Arthurstown, and has magnificent views across the estuary from the main public rooms and all bedrooms. It is a comfortable and hospitable place to stay at a reasonable price and ideal for a family holiday, as there are sandy beaches nearby and an enclosed playground beside the house. The Crosbies take pride in giving their guests personal attention, a really good breakfast and lots of advice on local amenities and attractions. **Rooms 6**. *2 self-catering cottages are also available - details on application. Closed Nov-Jan. CC.* **Directions:** *From Wexford R733, on right before village.*

Marsh Mere Lodge

Arthurstown New Ross Co Wexford ✆ *051 389 186* www.marshmerelodge.com

The McNamaras' friendly almost-waterside bed and breakfast is beautifully located just outside Arthurstown, with lovely views toward the Hook Head lighthouse. With a well-kept cottage garden and a comfortably furnished veranda overlooking the bay, Marsh Mere complements other accommodation in the area and would make a relaxing base for a family break.Their own free range eggs feature in Maria's cooked-to-order breakfasts. *Rooms 4 (all shower only). Open all year. CC.*

 ### Ballycross Apple Farm

Bridgetown Co Wexford ✆ *053 913 5160* www.ballycross.com

The Von Englebrechtan family's farm produces a superb range of juices and visitors are encouraged – its beautiful stone courtyard and family-friendly activities make it a perfect weekend destination. Apples and juices take pride of place in the shop, but they also offer cider vinegar, apple chutney, honey and other speciality foods - and there's a gift shop upstairs. With coffee and freshly made waffles from the waffle bar too, it's a great day out. *Farm Shop open weekends in apple season (dates vary, late summer to spring); juices are well distributed and can be ordered online. CC. Directions: West of Rosslare, on the R376 (Wellington Bridge road).*

BUNCLODY

Situated seven miles from Enniscorthy, the picturesque town of Bunclody is set in wonderful rolling countryside on the edge of the Hall-Dare estate, with magnificent parkland and riverside walks along the River Slaney. Quietly located at the base of Mount Leinster, away from the bigger towns, with walking, fishing and a number of equestrian centres nearby which offer countryside treks for all standards, it is a place to enjoy the unspoilt countryside. The town is well known for the Eileen Aroon Festival during the months of July and August, and the wonderful Altamont Gardens (059 915 9444) are only a few miles away. Golfers will not have too far to travel to Enniscorthy Golf Club (053 923 3191), which is 18 holes, par 72 and is known for the high standard of its greens.

 ### Carlton Millrace Hotel

Carrigduff Bunclody Co Wexford ✆ *053 937 5100* www.millrace.ie

Ideally located for a break to explore this beautiful area, Bunclody is little more than an hour's drive from either Dublin or Rosslare. Many outdoor activities are available nearby and this large hotel offers good facilities. Despite its size, it's tucked quite neatly into a wooded site and does not spoil the village too much; however, its popularity for business and functions can show in wear and tear. *Rooms 72. Closed 22-26 Dec. CC. Directions: On the N80 between Carlow and Enniscorthy.*

  ### Sugar & Spice

Main Street Bunclody Co Wexford ✆ *053 937 6388*

Pat and Mary O'Neill's charming old world home bakery and 'foodhall' suits this delightful traditional village to a tee. They have a number of strings to their culinary bow, all with high quality and a wish to support the principle of artisan production as core values: the home bakery, an all day café - and the renowned O'Neills Dry Cure Bacon (see entry) which is Pat's other business. *Open Mon-Sat 8am-5.30pm (to 6pm Mon-Fri in summer).*

CAMPILE

The interest that will being many to this attractive village is Kilmokea Gardens (051 388109), which are situated on the joint estuary of the Nore and the Barrow and cover almost three hectares; originally started in 1947, they include walled gardens designed as a series of rooms around the house, and host a wide selection of rare and tender tress and shrubs in the very different lower garden. Other local attractions include Duncannon Fort (051 389454, open June to September), and Ballyhack Castle (051 389 468); within a short drive you will also find many other places of historical and cultural interest.

Kilmokea Country Manor

Great Island Campile Co Wexford ✆*051 388 109 www.kilmokea.com*

Mark and Emma Hewlett's peaceful and relaxing late Georgian country house is set in seven acres of Heritage Gardens which are a key attraction in the region and include formal walled gardens. The house is elegantly and comfortably furnished and the amenities offered to guests - including a tennis court, indoor swimming pool, gym and aromatherapy treatment rooms - are surprising for a rural hideaway. The lovely bedrooms have views over the gardens, and so does the Peacock Dining Room where meals that include home produce are served. *Rooms 6 (1 shower only) Self-catering also available. D daily (reservations required). Pink Teacup Café, 10-5 daily when gardens are open. Open weekends only 5 Nov-1 Feb. CC. Directions: Take R733 south from New Ross to Ballyhack, signposted for Kilmokea Gardens.*

Tinnock Farm Produce

Tinnock Campile Co Wexford ✆*087 220 3300*

Peggy Gaffney and John Murphy produce lamb, beef, free range eggs, buttermilk and homemade butter for direct sale. While the meats are excellent and very popular at the markets and for freezer orders, the homemade butter and buttermilk are more unusual - and well worth seeking out for a reminder of the flavour that dairy foods used to have. *Available from: Wexford farmers' markets and Dun Laoghaire Farmers' Market (Sun, 10-4pm).*

The Lobster Pot

Ballyfane Carne Co Wexford ✆*053 913 1110*

Friendly service, a relaxing atmosphere and carefully prepared fresh food promise an enjoyable visit to Ciaran and Anne Hearne's handsome country pub. Local seafood is the speciality, with daily deliveries ensuring fresh fish supplies. The catch dictates daily specials and simple but carefully prepared meals are served all day in the bar, along with an extensive evening menu - and good value too. Don't miss the house chowder. *Seats 100 (outdoors, 20). Bar menu all day Tue-Sun. D Tue-Sun. Families welcome during the day. Closed Mon except bank hols, 25 Dec, 1 Jan - 9 Feb. Good Fri. CC. Directions: 8 km south of Rosslare port.*

Birchwood House B&B

Ballyboggan Lower Castlebridge Co Wexford ℰ*053 915 9734 www.birchwoodbandb.com*

Situated in the lovely village of Castlebridge, Iris Sothern's relaxing and welcoming B&B is ideally located for visiting Wexford (only 10 minutes away), the wild life sanctuary and Curracloe beach. The house offers everything you could possibly need - but Iris's hospitality is perhaps best summed up by the memorable breakfast she cooks for guests. **Rooms 3**. *CC.*

DUNCANNON

This small seaside town and fishing port is famous for its excellent fresh fish and seafood and, with a beautiful blue flag beach, it is a popular family holiday destination. It is dominated by Duncannon Fort (051 389454, open June to September), a star shaped fort which was built in 1588 in expectation of an attack by the Spanish Armada. Cruises along the coast are available from the little harbour.

 **Aldridge Lodge**

Duncannon New Ross Co Wexford ℰ*051 389 116 www.aldridgelodge.com*

Billy Whitty and Joanne Harding have a well-earned following for the excellent food and warm hospitality at their restaurant with rooms overlooking the picturesque fishing village of Duncannon. Billy's fine modern Irish cooking showcases superb local produce, including crab and lobster supplied by his father and his sister's free range pork. A super destination, offering outstanding food. **Seats 32** *(outdoors, 12); reservations required. D Wed-Sun. L Sun. L available Wed-Sat for groups of 10+. Rooms 3 (2 shower only). Closed Mon & Tue, 24-28 Dec. CC.* **Directions:** *0.5km outside Duncannon, overlooking the beach on the Fethard-on-Sea road.*

 **Sqigl Restaurant & Roches Bar**

Quay Road Duncannon New Ross Co Wexford ℰ*051 389 188 www.rochesbar.com*

At Bob and Eileen Roche's fine traditional bar in the centre of Duncannon village, the bar food menu offers something for everyone, and if the weather is fine, you can enjoy it out in the beer garden. Their daughter Cindy Roche runs the appealing evening restaurant Sqigl, which offers a very attractive package with an emphasis on local produce, especially seafood. **Seats 36** *(outdoors, 12). D Tue-Sat (call to check, reservations advised). Bar food served daily, 12.30-6pm. Restaurant closed Sun (except bank hol Suns), Mon, off season (bar open all year), 24-27 Dec & 3-4 weeks in Jan. CC.* **Directions:** *R733 from Wexford & New Ross. Centre of village.*

ENNISCORTHY

This can be a pleasant place to stay or just to to break a journey - it's a good spot to stretch the legs while enjoying a riverside walk and there is a particularly good weekly Farmers' Market in the town (Abbey Square Carpark, Saturday 9am-2pm). Nearby, The Bay Garden (Camolin, 053 938 3349) is a series of contrasting gardens, each beautifully conceived and wonderfully planted, and well worth a visit.

  **Ballinkeele House**

Ballymurn Enniscorthy Co Wexford ℰ*053 913 8105 www.ballinkeele.ie*

Set in 350 acres of parkland, game-filled woods and farmland, this listed building has been the Maher family home since it was built in 1840 and, although grand, it's the centre of their working farm and has a hospitable and down-to-earth atmosphere. The large, comfortably furnished bedrooms have lovely countryside views and Margaret, who's a keen cook and a member of Euro-Toques, prepares 4-course dinners for guests. **Rooms 5** *(2 shower only); Residents Set D at 7.30 (book by 11am). Closed 30 Nov - 1 Feb. CC.* **Directions:** *From Wexford N11, north to Oilgate Village, turn right at signpost, follow to next signpost.*

 ### Regan Organic Produce

Dranagh Lane Caim Enniscorthy Co Wexford ☎*087 668 2461 www.reganorganics.com*

Regan's Organic Produce is a small mixed farm which has been certified by Organic Trust since 2006. Mary Regan produces oven-ready chickens, chicken portions and livers, ducks and turkeys, hen and duck eggs, pork roasts, sausages and seasonal vegetables. All are available from the farm shop, along with other locally produced items. Affordability is a priority and a box scheme also operates. Farm visits welcome by arrangement. To buy: Farm shop open anytime Mon-Sat, just phone ahead. Some products including chickens also at selected Farmers Markets, butchers and speciality stores in the South-East and Dublin. Pork also available in The Organic Supermarket, Blackrock. Farm visits by arrangement. Directions:About 6km west of Enniscorthy, off the N30 (see map on website).

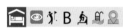 ### Riverside Park Hotel

The Promenade Enniscorthy Co Wexford ☎*054 37800 www.riversideparkhotel.com*

This modern riverside hotel contributes welcome amenities to the town and is well maintained. It's comfortably furnished in a moderate, contemporary style, and offers value breaks in a beautiful area, with fishing, golf and horse riding available locally. With a pleasant riverside path in a linear park beside the hotel, this can be a useful place to break a journey.

 ### Via Veneto

58 Weafer Street Enniscorthy Co Wexford ☎*053 923 6929 www.viaveneto.ie*

This authentic Italian restaurant, run by the highly regarded chef Paolo Fresilli, is buzzy and homely Italian in style. As well as the usual divisions - antipasti, pasta, main dishes, pizza - the menu offers an intriguing page of house specials for each course, including dishes that rarely feature on Irish/Italian menus. The locals have taken this place (which is very family friendly) to heart, so be sure to make a reservation. **Seats 72**; *L Fri only. D Wed-Mon. Closed Tue. CC.* **Directions:** *Enniscorthy centre, market square*

  ### Monart Destination Spa

Enniscorthy Area The Still Enniscorthy Co Wexford ☎*053 923 8999 www.monart.ie*

Arriving at Monart's imposing gates outside Enniscorthy, you get a sense that something quite special lies inside this private estate, which boasts miles of marked walks. Despite its striking design, the hotel and spa marry seamlessly with the wonderful old trees and clever landscaping. Rooms are spacious and access to the impressive thermal suite is complimentary for all guests. The Garden Lounge offers all day fare, becoming an intimate dining space by night. **Rooms 70**. *Restaurant* **seats 86**; *non residents welcome by reservation; L&D daily. Closed 18-27 Dec. CC.* **Directions:** *N11 from Dublin, then right on to N80, first left and follow the signs.*

O'Neills Dry Cure Bacon Co.

Bolinadrum Ferns Co Wexford ✆*053 923 3468 www.oneillfoods.ie*

Pat O'Neill's dry cured bacon is widely sought after in the South-East and no wonder. This excellent product is cured by hand for three weeks and, low in salt and phosphate-free, the difference is plain to see in the cooking - no white gunge and minimal shrinkage - and the taste. Look out for it on some very prestigious menus. Available from the factory (phone for details), Sugar & Spice in Bunclody, and specialist shops such as Ardkeen Quality Food Store in Waterford, Nolan's of Clontarf and Donnybrook Fair in Dublin. Full list on website.

 Horetown House

Foulksmills Co Wexford ✆*051 565 633 www.horetownhouse.ie*

Having been thoroughly renovated, the White family's 18th-century house offers a good level of comfort. Accommodation includes some suites, with Jacuzzi bath and sitting room, and all ten bedrooms are individually decorated. The Cellar restaurant offers both lunch and dinner but it's advisable to check, as meals, including dinner, may instead be served in a ground floor dining room overlooking the rural landscape. ***Rooms 10*** *(3 shower only). CC.* **Directions:** *In Taghmon take turn for Foulksmills, approx. 4km turn right immediately after bridge.*

GOREY

Conveniently situated midway between Dublin and Wexford, and now by-passed which makes it a much more enjoyable place to be, Gorey is an attractive town with many interesting old shop fronts and good shopping. It is handy to the many sandy beaches for which the area is famous, and close to the fishing village of Courtown, a popular family resort with an attractive harbour, where swimming and other water sports are available and walks in the surrounding countryside. Gorey has a vibrant cultural life and their Summer Theatre (www.GoreyTheatre.com) is among the many events taking place each year, with twice weekly performances at Gorey Little Theatre in July and August. Molumney Art Centre is open daily in summer. Numerous other activities available locally include championship standard golf, walking, watersports, horse riding and angling. For garden lovers, there is a Garden Festival in June, and the Ram House Gardens at Coolgreany (0402 37238) are a 'must visit'; The Ram family were responsible for the layout of Gorey, and the remains of Bishop Thomas Ram are buried in the Old Cemetery in the Market Square.

Ashdown Park Hotel

Gorey Co Wexford ✆*053 948 0500 www.ashdownparkhotel.com*

This hotel contributes much-needed amenities to the area, offering quality accommodation and providing facilities for conferences, weddings and other large functions. Modern bedrooms have all the expected conveniences, and the Ashdown Club provides an impressive health and leisure centre. An above-average carvery and light menu are available in the Ivy Bar – a useful place to break a journey. ***Rooms 79*** *(1 shower only). Closed 25 Dec. CC.* **Directions:** *Exit 22 off N11.*

The Cowhouse Cafe & Bistro

Tomsilla Courtown Road Gorey Co Wexford ✆*053 942 5666*

This former cowshed opposite the Greens Berry Farm Shop (and sharing its large car park) hasn't been over-gentrified, which adds to the charm. It now makes a quirky seasonal café, offering temptingly displayed home bakes and light meals all day in summer. On Friday and Saturday evenings in high season, it's transformed into a very popular casual bistro serving confident modern Irish cooking. BYO (corkage applies). *Seats 35 (+ several tables outdoors). Café daily in summer, 10-6; bistro weekends from mid June. CC. Directions: Located on Courtown Road, on the left hand side on the way into Green's Berry Farm.*

 ## Greens Berry Farm Shops

Ballinacolla Gorey Co Wexford ☎ *053 942 1783 www.greensberryfarm.ie*

From early May to September, the Tinnock Farm Shop is open (daily, 8.30-6), selling a wide range of fruits, fruit products and (in season) new potatoes. The Courtown Road Farm Shop, Tomsilla, opens for July and August (daily,10-6) and also offers a selection of locally produced cheese, honey, yoghurt, bacon, etc. and some wines - ideal when self-catering in the area, or when eating at The Cowhouse Bistro (unlicensed).

 ## The Kitchen @ Gorey

1-4 North Parade Gorey Co Wexford ☎ *053 948 0541 www.thekitchengorey.ie*

"Simple Rustic Seasonal" is the mission statement on the menu displayed outside the door of this spacious, informal and family-friendly cafe-restaurant. The ambience and long opening hours make it popular as a drop-in daytime place, evening meals have finesse, and (while you may have to ask to find this out) well-sourced ingredients are cooked with care. *Wed-Sat 12-9 (Fri & Sat to 10), Sun 12.30-9. Closed Mon & Tue. CC. Directions: Centre of Gorey.*

 ## La Baguette

4 Esmonde Street Gorey Co Wexford ☎ *086 192 3697 www.labaguettegorey.com*

French baker Didier Senecal describes his popular craft bakery and café in the centre of Gorey as "An Irish bakery with a French touch". Combining authenticity - and some specialised imported ingredients - with the best of local produce, it offers superb breads (everything from Irish soda bread to the sought-after sourdoughs), with a nice little lunch menu and a gorgeous array of patisserie and cakes. *Tue-Sat 9.30-5.30. Directions: On the main street.*

  ## Marlfield House

Courtown Road Gorey Co Wexford ☎ *053 942 1124 www.marlfieldhouse.com*

Often quoted as 'the luxury country house hotel par excellence', this impressive house outside Gorey was once the residence of the Earls of Courtown, and is now an elegant oasis of unashamed luxury offering outstanding hospitality and service, where guests are cosseted and pampered in sumptuous surroundings. Opened as a hotel in 1978 by Mary and Ray Bowe, their daughters, Margaret and Laura Bowe, now continue the family tradition of hospitality. Beautiful grounds include a fine kitchen garden that inspires proudly seasonal menus, while also giving pleasure to diners in the graceful restaurant. A visit here is always a treat. *Rooms 20. Restaurant seats 90 (outdoors 20). D daily; L Sun only. Light lunch served daily in Library, 12.30-5. Closed Jan & Feb. CC. Directions: Exit 23 N11, left at Courtown roundabout and follow signs.*

Partridges Artisan Café & Fine Food Shop

93/94 Main Street Gorey Co Wexford ☎ *053 948 4040 www.partridges.ie*

The café, at the back of a food shop selling artisan foods from Ireland and beyond, features simple, unpretentious dishes that allow the high quality of the ingredients to shine: good soups with home-baked bread, unusual pasta dishes, savoury tarts, flavoursome salads, an excellent farmhouse cheese and oatcake plate and an enticing selection of home-baked cakes and tarts. Wines by the glass. *Seats 48 (outdoors, 12); open all day Mon-Sat; D Sat only; L only Sun. Closed D Mon-Fri, Sun D. CC. Directions: Main Street Gorey town.*

 ### Seafield Golf & Spa Hotel

Gorey Area Ballymoney Gorey Co Wexford ☎ *053 942 4000 www.seafieldhotel.com*

Set in lush parkland adjacent to the Seafield Golf Club, this stylish hotel enjoys fine views of the Irish Sea. Its extensive facilities include an impressive spa and contemporary rooms, some with terraces. A popular business, conference and wedding venue, it's also a desirable destination for short breaks and - thanks to Executive Head Chef Malek Hamidouche's interesting and well executed menus - for dining too. The cooking has flair and, with its foundations in quality ingredients, including celebrated local foods, it offers real value too. *Rooms 265. Restaurant seats 110. CC. Directions: On coast north of Gorey, signed from N11.*

  ### Woodlands Country House

Gorey Area Killineirin Gorey Co Wexford ☎ *040 237 125 www.woodlandscountryhouse.com*

Easy to find and yet with a sense of seclusion, John and Philomena O'Sullivan's charming creeper-clad mid-19th country house between Inch and Gorey is ideal for a quiet break with woodlands, a river, a small lake and lots of seating areas to relax in. With antique furnishings, big log fires and good food too – a good breakfast is served, also tea or coffee and home made scones on arrival - it's a lovely place. *Rooms 6. Closed 1 Oct - 1 Apr. CC. Directions: 1.5km off the N11 north of Gorey.*

KILMORE QUAY

This picturesque fishing village is noted for its thatched cottages, as a base for sea angling and a popular place for family holidays. The area around Kilmore Quay has many unspoilt beaches which offer miles of the finest sand dunes in the south-east, and the nearby Saltee Islands are home to Ireland's largest bird sanctuary.

  ### Crazy Crab

Kilmore Quay Co Wexford ☎ *053 914 8848 www.crazycrab.ie*

Mairead and Mike Crowley have an honest formula for success at their contemporary harbourside café: simple, local food, skilfully cooked and served by friendly staff, plus good value. Everything is zinging fresh and very tasty, including home-baked breads, well-dressed salads and freshly made desserts, which are listed on a blackboard each day. Fish is the main attraction - try the Crazy Crab Seafood Platter for two - but there are other options too. *Summer Opening Times (from April 1st), Thu 5-8pm, Fri-Sun noon-8pm. Off-season call to check.* **Directions:** *Above Seaview Fish Shop, opposite play ground & car park.*

The Silver Fox Seafood Restaurant

Kilmore Quay Co Wexford 053 912 9888 *www.thesilverfox.ie*

A well known restaurant in Kilmore Quay since 1991, The Silver Fox has been owned by Shane Carroll and Gopal Kawander since 2006. Gopal is the head chef and, while his extensive menus offer something for everyone, his cooking of local fish include some interesting dishes with flavourings from South East Asia that set this restaurant apart. **Seats 60**. *Open daily, 12.30-9pm. Closed Feb. CC.* **Directions:** *20 min. drive from Rosslare ferry, Wexford Town and Ballyhack ferry.*

NEW ROSS

This old town on the estuary of the River Barrow has much of interest to the visitor - especially, of course, its key attraction, the recreation of the nineteenth century sailing ship the SS Dunbrody (South Quay, 051 425 239). The Kennedy Centre and Arboretum (051 388 171) just a few miles from the centre of New Ross are well worth a visit; you can picnic in the gardens or just stroll around many acres of parkland. New Ross is an ideal base for taking in a drive around the scenic Ring of Hook which features many historical sites including Dunbrody Abbey, Tintern Abbey and The Hook Lighthouse. The famous and reputedly haunted Loftus Hall is also located nearby. There are also many fine beaches and many other activities such as angling and charters, diving and snorkelling, canoeing, windsurfing, golf and river cruises (Galley River Cruises; 051 421723). Possible outings for garden lovers include Kilmokea Gardens (Campile, 051 388 109), with seven acres of Heritage Gardens. There is a Farmers' Market every Saturday (The Quay, 9-2).

Café Nutshell

In A Nutshell 8 South Street New Ross Co Wexford 051 422 777

Traditional country methods, handed-down recipes and a respect for fresh produce are at the heart of Philip and Patsy Rogers' shop and café, where everything is freshly made every day: breakfast and fresh bakes for elevenses; and soups, sandwiches, salads, quiche and classic platters for lunch. Check out the food to go too, which is of the same high standard as the food in the café. A little treasure. **Seats 50**; *Open Mon-Sat 9-5.30. Closed Sun, Bank Hols. CC.*

 ## Et Voilà French Bistro

Unit 2 8/9 Irishtown New Ross Co Wexford 051 421 307 *www.etvoilafrenchbistro.com*

Owner-chef Gilles Laforges's menus are displayed French-style outside his simple, smartly presented restaurant; you'll find classics, like snails in garlic butter, here and every dish seems appealing. As well as the excellent raw ingredients used, there is attention to detail in the cooking and additional small touches set it apart from anything else in the area. The fish cooking is excellent and it's refreshing to find such good vegetables. Good value too; a great find. **Seats 50** *(outdoors, 10). L&D Tue-Sun. Closed Mon, Bank Hols, 1 week Christmas, 1st week Jan. CC.* **Directions:** *Beside Pauline's Pub in Irishtown 5 minutes from New Ross centre.*

Greenpark

Creakan Lower New Ross Co Wexford ✆*051 421 028*

Anyone seeking the genuine experience of staying in a family home and enjoying the peace of the countryside will find it at John and Annette Kinsella's immaculate B&B. Bedrooms are compact but comfortable and breakfast, offering variations on the traditional Irish, is freshly cooked and generous. The gardens are sheltered, well planted and maintained, making a good spot for relaxing in summer. **Rooms 3**. *Closed 1 Nov - 1 May. No CC. **Directions:** Leave N25 at New Ross; onto R733, Greenpark is 4km on left. Well signed.*

Wexford Home Preserves

Unit 2a Block D Ind Bus Pk New Ross Co Wexford ✆*051 426 646 www.wexfordpreserves.ie*

Ellen O'Leary began making preserves in her kitchen in 1988 and, soon noticed for their great flavour, they found a ready market. When developing the business, she and her husband Sean kept using the old family recipes and the traditional open pan boiling method - and this, together with the famous Wexford fruit, is the secret of their success. Now nephew Tom and his wife Laura maintain the tradition, with their quality jams, marmalades and a Christmas range. Available from independent stores, some multiples and tourist attractions in the area.

Rathaspeck Manor

Rathaspeck Co Wexford ✆*053 914 1672 www.rathaspeckmanor.ie*

Surrounded by parkland and a Par 3 golf course (available to guests at very moderate cost), the Cuddihy family's handsome Georgian house is impressive, but it's a warm and welcoming family home that now offers very pleasing country house accommodation. A good breakfast features local produce, and Betty O'Kennedy-Cuddihy is happy to her offer her personal dinner recommendations to guests. **Directions:** *15 minutes drive South from Wexford Town.*

ROSSLARE & AREA

Ireland's Euro Port (ferry terminal, 053 916 1560) is also a seaside resort, with a magnificent beach and a 27 hole links golf course (053 913 2203). The Rosslare area is well placed for exploring the south east coast, and is within easy reach of Carne and Kilmore Quay. Local activities include golf, fishing, water sports and horse riding along miles of sandy beaches. Local attractions include Yola Farmstead Folk park (091 32610, open March to November), Our Lady's Island (053 913 1167), and Tacumskin Windmill.

Archways B&B

Rosslare Road Tagoat Rosslare Co Wexford ✆*053 915 8111 www.thearchways.ie*

Great food and genuine hospitality go hand in hand at Eileen and Chris Hadlington's smart modern B&B just outside Tagoat. The couple constantly find new ways to ensure a memorable stay for their guests and this includes exceptional food. Chris is an inspired chef and dinner for residents is a real treat: seasonal, local and home produced is the ethos, and it is a delicious one; his own rare breed pork may well be on the menu. It's the perfect place to overnight when arriving on the ferry and facing a long drive - and a snack can be arranged for late arrivals. Well worth seeking out. **Rooms 6** *(all shower only). Closed 26 Feb - 27 Mar. CC.* **Directions:** *Just off N25 main Rosslare Road.*

Kelly's Resort Hotel

Rosslare Strand Rosslare Co Wexford ✆*053 913 2114 www.kellys.ie*

With its special brand of relaxed professionalism, the Kelly family's renowned seaside hotel sums up all that is best about the sunny south-east for many regular visitors. Family ownership spans three centuries, so there's not a lot these hospitable people don't know about keeping guests happy. Its special qualities are so wide-ranging that it's hard to know where to begin. Take your pick, perhaps, from the beachside location, superb leisure and family facilities, the outstanding food served in two restaurants, the famous wine cellar, a stunning art collection... quite simply, this hotel has everything. **Rooms 118**. Beaches Restaurant **seats 270**. L&D daily. La Marine **seats 70**. L&D daily. Closed early Dec-mid Feb. CC. **Directions:** Beside Rosslare Strand beach.

WEXFORD

Located at the mouth of the River Slaney, 12 miles from Rosslare Euro port, Wexford is a lively cosmopolitan blend of historic and modern. Guided walking tours of the town are available to take visitors through its narrow meandering streets and old town walls which originate from early Celtic and Nordic heritage. Local attractions include the Irish National Heritage Park (053 912 0733, open all year), which allows visitors to experience 9000 years of Irish history in picturesque settings of woodland, riverbanks and historic Irish dwellings. The town offers many craft centres, art galleries and a weekly farmers' market (Fri 9-2).

Cistin Eile

80 South Main Street Wexford Co Wexford ✆*053 912 1616*

Proprietor-chef Warren Gillen has a well-earned following and is a great supporter of local and artisan producers. His short, interesting menus have a sense of place and promise modern Irish food with a rustic tone. Dishes are richly layered with flavours, yet this accomplished chef always enhances the delicious seasonal (and, often, less expensive) ingredients he has so carefully selected, and never seeks to overpower. Serving the best of contemporary Irish food at great value for money, this small restaurant merits wider recognition. **Seats 40**. L Mon–Sat; D Wed-Sat. Closed Sun, Mon D, Tue D, Bank Hols, 25-26 Dec, 1 Jan. CC. **Directions:** Main Street runs parallel to Crescent & Paul Quay.

Forde's Restaurant

Crescent Quay Wexford Co Wexford ✆*053 912 3832 www.wex.fordesrestaurant.com*

Happy customers and good lighting create a relaxed atmosphere at Liam Forde's informal restaurant overlooking the harbour. Known for reliability and seasonality, his varied menus offer value and - while there's an understandable leaning towards local seafood - there's something for everyone, including vegetarian (and vegan) options. Everything is made on the premises and Sunday lunch and the short dinner menu offer especially good value. **Seats 80**. D daily, L Sun *only. Closed 22-25 Dec. CC.* **Directions:** *On the quay front, opposite statue. [Also at Castlebridge (053 915 9767); open daily 12-9.30].*

 **Greenacres Bistro**

Greenacres Selskar Street Wexford Co Wexford ☎*053 912 3004 www.greenacres.ie*

Greenacres Bistro is in a complex that includes a wine shop, deli and an impressive modern art gallery. Wine buffs will relish the wine shop (2,500 bottles), private tasting room and fine wine vault. The bistro offers creative seasonally-aware cooking in a lovely atmosphere from breakfast onwards; cured meat and farmhouse cheese platters may appeal at lunchtime and a midweek 'Starter Selection Tasting Menu' is an interesting evening option, offered with or without matching wines. **Seats 60** *(outdoors, 25). Mon-Sat, 9-5; L & D daily. Closed 25/26 Dec, Good Fri. CC.* **Directions:** *Selskar Street runs into North Main Street.*

 Jacques Seafood Restaurant @ Sidetracks

Custom House Quay Wexford Co Wexford ☎*053 912 1666*

An unusual location for well known chef Jacques Carerra's latest venture: the daytime café Sidetracks, beside the town's unique quayside railway line, has operated in this building for several years. In the evenings it is now transformed into Jacques Seafood Restaurant and owner Fergie Keogh is front of house to welcome guests to a very professsional dining experience serving the best of local seafood (and some other popular choices). *Wed-Sat 6-9.30 pm. CC.*

  Kates Farm Shop

McQuillans Cross Clonard Wexford Co Wexford ☎*086 1727116*

You can't miss Kate and Ollie O'Mahony's shop with its colourful old farm cart and little mini-thatched 'gate posts' at the front. It's hugely successful thanks to their great selection of fresh local seasonal foods, plus carefully sourced fresh meats and poultry from the area and beyond, great home baking and a collection of other foods including foods for special dietary needs. Well worth a visit. *Open Mon-Sat, 9-6, Sun 10.30-5.30.* **Directions:** *Just outside Wexford Town (off N25); 200m from Whitford roundabout, on Duncannon New Line Road.*

 La Dolce Vita

6/7 Trimmers Lane Wexford Co Wexford ☎*053 917 0806*

In a quiet oasis just off Wexford's bustling North Main Street (look out for the big green, red and white canopy), Roberto Pons's popular daytime restaurant and deli offers seriously tempting food including a short takeaway menu. Favourites include homemade Italian bread with oil, risotto of the day, excellent salads, pasta dishes and some 'serious' dishes. Lovely desserts too. Arrive early for lunch or be prepared to wait. **Seats 45** *(outdoors, 20). Open Mon-Fri 9-5.30pm; Sat all day, 9am-9pm. Closed Sun, Bank Hols & 4 days Christmas. CC.*

 Maldron Hotel Wexford

Ballindinas Barntown Wexford Co Wexford
☎*053 917 2000 www.maldronhotels.com/hotel-wexford-home.html*

Just five minutes from Wexford Town this modern 3* hotel is useful to consider where value for money is the priority, offering good facilities and service to the budget-conscious family or business traveller. **Rooms 107.** **Directions:** *On N11, Dublin to Wexford.*

 **McMenamin's Townhouse**

6 Glena Terrace Spawell Road Wexford Co Wexford
✆ *053 914 6442 www.wexford-bedandbreakfast.com*

Seamus and Kay McMenamin's B&B has been one of the most highly regarded places to stay in this area for many years and their beautiful Victorian terrace house has everything you need to be comfortable away from home. The McMenamins' considerable local knowledge, together with a really good breakfast, gets you off to a good start and helps to make the most of every day. **Rooms 4** *(all shower only). Closed 20 Dec - 1 Mar. CC.* **Directions:** *Opposite county hall.*

 Nonna Rosa

106 South Main Street Wexford Co Wexford ✆ *053 917 4865 www.nonnarosa.ie*

Nonna Rosa has been one of Wexford's favourite Italian restaurants for some years and, although it has recently come under new management, this little piece of Italy continues to offer good, authentic Italian cooking. The range of menus offered includes all the classic Italian favourites in various combinations, but special features include the fact that so much is homemade. *Open Tue-Sat L12-3, D 5.30-11, Sun 1-10.30. Closed Mon.* **Directions:** *Town centre.*

  Pettitts SuperValu

St. Aidans Shopping Centre Wexford Co Wexford ✆ *053 912 4055 www.pettitts.ie*

Part of the SuperValu franchise, this store has a strong food management team who are particularly dedicated to improving the consumer's experience with seafood – a good range of fresh fish is on offer throughout the week. *Open 7 days.*

  Phelim Byrne Cookery Academy

Wexford Enterprise Centre Strandfield Business Park Kerlogue Rosslare Rd Wexford Co Wexford
✆ *053 918 4995 www.phelimbyrne.ie.*

Chef, Phelim Byrne, offers professional catering services and a cookery academy with a relaxed teaching style that is fun and informative. Classes designed to suit all levels of interest and experience cover popular themes from important basics, to international cuisines and ideas for quick dinners. Courses for group bookings (up to 12 students) can be tailored to suit the group.

 Riverbank House Hotel

The Bridge Wexford Co Wexford ✆ *053 912 3611 www.riverbankhousehotel.com*

Away from the bustle of town, this pleasant hotel is located just across the bridge. Rooms are on the small side, but comfortable, and overall there is a pleasingly personal style of hospitality and food service. An attractive Victorian-style bar and restaurant enjoy views of the river, and an adjacent conservatory area has character and interesting plants. **Rooms 23** *(14 shower only). Closed 25 Dec. CC.* **Directions:** *Directly across the bridge in Wexford town.*

 Rosemount House

Spawell Road Wexford Co Wexford ✆ *053 912 4609 www.wexfordbedandbreakfast.ie*

Carol and Tim Kelly's 18th century period residence is on a quiet road, within walking distance of the town centre. All the original features have been retained, allowing for bright, spacious and comfortable rooms, which are beautifully decorated and furnished with antique furniture throughout. A lovely place to stay. **Rooms 3** *(2 shower only). Closed 20 Dec - 5 Jan. CC.* **Directions:** *Follow N25 into town centre, on Spawell Road (signed).*

 ## Spice Indian Restaurant

Monck Street Wexford Co Wexford 053 912 2011 *www.spicerestaurant.net*

At Richard and Emma Lett's contemporary Indian restaurant above the Crown Bar, you'll find authentic cooking by a team of chefs from South India. Menus offer a combination of traditional Indian classics and more contemporary specialities, and are clearly defined into starters and 11 styles of main course. Delicious food, well-informed staff and great value sum up this restaurant. No wonder it's so popular. **Seats 60.** *Open nightly from 5.30pm (5pm Fri, Sat & Sun).* **Directions:** *Just off Custom House quay, west of Wexford bridge.*

 ## Talbot Hotel

On the Quay Wexford Co Wexford 053 912 2566 *www.talbotwexford.ie*

Dating back to 1905 and benefiting from a recent makeover, this popular hotel is well-located on the harbour-front yet convenient to the town centre - indeed, so many activities revolve around it that many would say the Talbot is the town centre. Rooms are pleasant and comfortable, and the basement leisure centre is unexpectedly full of character, confirming the feeling that the Talbot will always spring a few surprises. **Rooms 109.** *Closed 24-25 Dec. CC.* **Directions:** *On quay front.*

 ## Thomas Moore Tavern & Spires Restaurant

Cornmarket Wexford Co Wexford 053 917 4688 *www.thomasmooretavern.ie*

Now owned and run by the local Wright family, the Tavern claims to be Wexford's oldest pub. There's a choice of a casual bistro or a more formal evening in the splendid rooftop Spires Restaurant. Head chef Ryan Bell clearly relishes the quality of produce available in Co. Wexford and turns his hand with dexterity to dishes that combine rusticity and sophistication. *Food served: The Bistro - L&D daily. Spires Restaurant - D only, Thu-Sat (& Sun-Wed for private parties).* **Directions:** *Located on the Cornmarket in the heart of Wexford.*

 ## Westgate Design

22 North Main Street Wexford Co Wexford 053 912 3787 *www.westgatedesign.ie*

This bustling self-service café offers a wide-ranging menu with a wide choice of salads and good baking of delicious cakes and desserts. Good food at very reasonable prices is a winning combination for a daytime venue and this family friendly place is known for its generous portions. Take-away dishes are available and outside catering is also on offer for parties. **Seats 150;** *Open Mon-Sat, Food served 8.30am-5.30pm. Closed Sun, Bank Hols, 25/6 Dec. CC.* **Directions:** *Accessible from the main street or, through the lower level, at back.*

 ## Whites of Wexford

Abbey Street Wexford Co Wexford 053 912 2311 *www.whitesofwexford.ie*

Wexford's most famous hotel, which dates back to 1795, Whites underwent a total reconstruction in recent years. This now very large hotel has excellent facilities in all areas, including on-site leisure activities and pampering treatments and smart, contemporary guest rooms and suites that have all the bells and whistles. There's also a choice of bars and restaurants and extensive conference facilities. **Rooms 157**. *Closed 24-26 Dec. CC.* **Directions:** *Follow signs when leaving N25 or N11.*

Whitford House Hotel

New Line Road Wexford Co Wexford ✆ *053 914 3444 www.whitford.ie*

Probably the busiest hotel in the area, the Whitty family's hotel is a pleasant place to stay and there's always a buzz. Several grades of room are offered, and good facilities attract a wide clientele. It's a particularly appealing destination for family breaks. Self-catering accommodation is also available. **Rooms 36.** *Self catering accommodation is also available. Closed 24-28 Dec. CC.* **Directions:** *On N25 2km from Wexford Town (Rosslare direction).*

Ferrycarrig Hotel

Wexford Area Ferrycarrig Wexford Co Wexford ✆ *053 912 0999 www.ferrycarrighotel.ie*

This stylish, modern hotel overlooking the Slaney estuary has excellent amenities, including a superb health and fitness club, a bar with a large riverside deck, good food at the Courtyard Grill or fine dining at Reeds. Rooms are contemporary and comfortable, with views across the water. It's a very family-friendly and child-friendly hotel, especially in the summer. **Rooms 102.** *Restaurant* **seats 160**. *D daily. Bar food daily. CC.* **Directions:** *3km north of Wexford Town.*

Killiane Castle

Wexford Area Drinagh Wexford Co Wexford ✆ *053 915 8885 www.killianecastle.com*

Just a few miles from Wexford town, Kathleen and Jack Mernagh's magical farm B&B is the perfect place for stressed townies, especially with children in tow – a real castle, a 17th century house to stay in, and lots to do (including a driving range on site). The working farm allows visitors to see a modern dairy in action and their own hens supply the eggs for Kathleen's delicious breakfasts. It's ideal for an overnight on the way to or from Rosslare Harbour, although it's unlikely that you'll want to leave after just one night here. **Rooms 8** *(1 shower only). Self catering also available in 3 courtyard apartments. Closed 1 Nov-1 Mar. CC.* **Directions:** *Off N11 approx 7km from Wexford.*

Stable Diet

Wexford Town Main Street Wexford Co Wexford ✆ *053 913 1287 www.stablediet.com*

Katherine Carroll's bakery range has expanded considerably since she started. Production is at Yoletown but there's a smart little café and patisserie on Main Street in Wexford Town, where a changing menu is offered through the day and the full range of their excellent additive-free cakes, flapjacks and breakfast cereals is on sale, together with a newer range of dips, sauces and chutneys. Available nationwide from SuperValu, Centra, Superquinn and Dunnes Stores.

WICKLOW

Wicklow is a miracle. Although the booming presence of Dublin is right next door, this spectacularly lovely county is very much its own place, an away-from-it-all world of moorland and mountain, farmland and garden, forest and lake, seashore and river. It's all right there, just over the nearest hill, yet it all seems so gloriously different.

The people's sense of difference is easily understood, for even with today's traffic, it is only a short drive on notably handsome roads to transform your world from the crowded city streets right into the heart of some of the most beautiful scenery in all Ireland. Such scenery generates its own strong loyalties and sense of identity, and Wicklow folk are rightly and proudly a race apart. Drawing strength from their wonderful environment, they have a vigorous local life which keeps metropolitan blandness well at bay.

While being in a place so beautiful is almost sufficient reason for existence in itself, they're busy people too, with sheep farming and forestry and all sorts of light industries, while down in the workaday harbour of Arklow in the south of the county - a port with a long and splendid maritime history - they've been so successful in organising their own seagoing fleet of freighters that there are now more cargo ships registered in Arklow than any other Irish port.

LOCAL ATTRACTIONS & INFORMATION

▸ **Mount Usher Gardens**
Ashford *0404 40116*
▸ **Russborough House & Gardens** Blessington
045 865239
▸ **Kilruddery House & Gardens**
Bray *01 2863405*

▸ **National Sealife Centre** Bray
01 2866939
▸ **Dwyer McAllister Traditional Cottage** Derrynamuck
0404 45325
▸ **Powerscourt House & Gardens**
Enniskerry *01 2046000*

▸ **Glendalough Visitor Centre**
0404 45325
▸ **Avondale House** Rathdrum
0404 46111
▸ **Wicklow Historic Gaol**
Wicklow Town *0404 61599*

Christy's Bar & Lounge

38 Lr Main Street Arklow *Co Wicklow* 📞*0402 32145* *www.christysarklow.com*

Friendly staff are quick to welcome arriving customers to the Heffernan family's pleasant modernish pub in the heart of Arklow town. Comfortable and well run, it's popular with the local business community at lunchtime, and a reliable destination for visitors to the town, with a real fire, tasty and fairly priced food and good service. *Seats 100. Food served Sun-Fri 10.30am-10pm, Sat 10.30am-9pm. Live music Sat & Sun nights. Directions: On Main Street.*

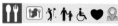 **The Park Restaurant**

Fenbyrne House Castlepark Arklow *Co Wicklow* 📞*0402 23894* *www.theparkrestaurant.ie*

Colin Byrne and Orla Killoran's smart contemporary restaurant attracts the eye, especially when the inviting outside seating area is set up in summer. Whether for a quick daytime bite or the full evening dining experience, there's a treat in store. Colin's mouth-watering menus have a sense of the locality and his simple yet deeply satisfying cooking style is based on classical training. Even a bowl of chowder with home-baked bread is worth a detour. *Seats 55. B & L Tue-Sat 10-12 & 12-6pm; D Thur-Sat; Sun L only. Closed Sun, Mon & 25-27th Dec. CC. Directions: In the town centre, opposite Garda station.*

 Wicklow Farmhouse Cheese

Curranstown Arklow *Co Wicklow* 📞*04029 1713;*

John Hempenstall makes the consistently excellent, gently flavoured and creamy Wicklow Blue Cheese on the family farm in South Wicklow, using pasteurised cows' milk and vegetarian rennet. Also made is a brie style cheese, Wicklow Baun, and mild cheddar style Wicklow Gold (plain and flavoured, including a Seaweed variety). The Hepenstalls also produce buttermilk and a catering brie, St Kevin Brie. *Available from some supermarkets, Sheridans, speciality foodshops and farmers' markets in the South-East.*

   Ballyknocken House & Cookery School

Gleanealy Ashford *Co Wicklow* 📞*0404 44627* *www.ballyknocken.com*

Perfectly placed for walking, playing golf, or exploring the area, Catherine Fulvio's charming Victorian farmhouse provides comfort, cosiness, home-cooked food and hospitality - and the option of classes at her well known cookery school. Antique-furnished bedrooms have very good beds and pretty bathrooms, and both the excellent breakfasts and her 4-course dinners showcase local produce. All this plus great picnics and a relaxing atmosphere keep guests coming back for more. *Rooms 7 (1 shower only). Residents D Tue & Thu-Sat, at 7.30. Lighter suppers also served midweek. Closed Mid Dec & Jan. CC. Directions: From Dublin turn right after Tougher Oil Petrol Station in Ashford. Continue for 5.5km.*

 The Garden Café @ Avoca

Mount Usher Gardens Ashford *Co Wicklow* 📞*0404 40205* *www.mount-usher-gardens.com*

In a low key shopping courtyard at the entrance to beautiful Mount Usher gardens, this pleasing café offers the fresh and delicious food that's the foundation of the Avoca reputation. Head chef Andrew Holmes commitment to using local and Irish artisan produce is reflected in menus that change with the seasons and showcase a wide range of local producers. There's also a small Avoca garden centre and shop/deli. Well worth a detour. *Seats 80 (outdoors, 35). Food served daily, 9.30am-5pm (to 5.30pm Sun). Closed 25/26 Dec. CC.* **Directions:** *Mount Usher gardens are in the centre of Ashford, just off the N11.*

 **Clone House**

Aughrim Co Wicklow ✆*0402 36121 www.clonehouse.com*

Nestled in the Wicklow hills in a tranquil and beautiful location, it's hard to believe the lively village life of Aughrim is just 4km down the road from Liam and Aine Ó Lorcáin's rural hideaway. Dating back to the 16th century, the sympathetically restored house provides modern comforts and the spacious bedrooms have large en-suite bathrooms. Aine's good food is a treat, and Liam looks after the front of house in fine style. ***Rooms 4*** *(1 shower only). Dinner - book previous day. Open all year. CC.* **Directions:** *Follow brown house signs from Aughrim or Woodenbridge.*

 **Avoca Handweavers**

Avoca Village Co Wicklow ✆*0402 35105 www.avoca.ie*

Ireland's oldest business (established in 1723), this is where the Pratt family's famous craft design company originated and where you can still see hand weavers at work. Today, with branches throughout the country, Avoca is known not only for its crafts, but also for their own ranges of clothing; restaurants with a well-earned reputation for imaginative, wholesome, home-cooked food; and delicious deli products and specialty foods to take home. ***Seats 75***. *Open all day (10-5) Mon-Sun. Closed 25-26 Dec. CC.* **Directions:** *Leave N11 at Rathnew and follow signs for Avoca.*

 **Grangecon Café**

Kilbride Road Blessington Co Wicklow ✆*045 857 892*

Wholesome aromas will draw you into Jenny and Richard Street's smashing café. The menu is fairly brief, but that's the beauty of it, allowing the cooking to be this good: everything on the menu is made on the premises, including the breads, pastries and ice cream. They also produce freshly cooked meals to take home on a busy day. While not cheap food - how could it be when the ingredients are of such high quality - it is extremely good value for money. We need more places like this. ***Seats 30***. *Open all day Mon-Wed, 9am-4pm; Thu-Sat, 9am-5pm. Closed Sun, Bank Hols & 25 Dec - 1 Jan. CC.* **Directions:** *Centre of Blessington village, just off main street (Kilbride turning).*

 Campo de' Fiori

1 Marlborough Terrace Strand Road Bray Co Wicklow ✆*01 276 4257 www.campodefiori.ie*

Marco Roccasalvo and Laura Chiavini's relaxed restaurant has a well-deserved following, merited by the authenticity of Marco's cooking, the choice of wine and the enticing atmosphere. Known for the exceptional quality of their carefully sourced meat, other wide-ranging choices include a varied selection of seafood and good pasta dishes for vegetarians. ***Seats 50***; *D daily; L Sat & Sun. Bank Hol Mon from 2pm. CC. Also at: Risto-Market, on Albert Avenue (around the corner).*

The Harbour Bar

1 Strand Road Bray Co. Wicklow ✆*01 286 2274 www.harbourbarbray.com*

Dating from the 1870s, and recently named as the best bar in the world by a popular international guide, the secret about this gem of a public house is well and truly out. Surprisingly perhaps, it remains its atmospheric self and no visit to Bray would be complete without calling in here for a pint. *Open Mon-Thu & Sun 4-11.30; Fri-Sat 4-12.30.* **Directions:** *Located across from the harbour at the north end of the promenade.*

 **Killruddery Estate**

Southern Cross Bray Co Wicklow ✆*01 286 3405 www.kilruddery.com*

Killruddery has been home to the Brabazon Family (Earls of Meath) since 1618. Designed on a large scale with a view to impressing visitors, the estate is a hive of activity and very accessible to the public. Reasons to visit include: the historic house itself and its beautiful gardens; farm produce supplied by Anthony Ardee (son of the 15th Earl of Meath), on sale at the weekly Farm Market; his wife Fionnuala Ardee's Tearoom, serving estate and local produce in a unique hexagonal former dairy - and the many events hosted at this remarkable venue. Not to be missed. *Opening Times: Summer (May to Sep) 9.30am-6pm daily (Thu to 10pm). Shoulder seasons (April and Oct) weekends only, 9.30am-6pm. Farm Market, every Saturday, 10am-4pm.(House open for tours daily Jul-Sep, 1-4pm).* **Directions:** *Off Southern Cross, between Bray and Greystones.*

 The Delgany

Glen Road Delgany Co Wicklow ✆*01 287 7102 www.thedelganygrocer.com*

Stylishly renovated, the former Delgany Inn houses several independent businesses operating jointly as The Delgany. Together, Firehouse Bakery (see entry for West Cork operation), Romany Stone Restaurant, The Delgany Grocer and The Bungalow florist and gift shop make an enticing go-to destination. Here you can shop for artisan breads and pastries, do your weekly shop at The Delgany Grocer, get some flowers or gifts at The Bungalow - and then enjoy a lovely informal meal upstairs in Romany Stone. A one-stop shop that betters the supermarket concept by a long mile, it's a great place to know about if you're visiting beautiful Co Wicklow or as a destination in its own right. *Romany Stone: Open all day Tue-Sun; also D Fri & Sat. Delgany Grocer: Tue-Sat 9-7, Sun 10-6. Firehouse Bakery: Tue-Sun 8-5.30.*

 Glenview Hotel

Glen O' The Downs Delgany Co Wicklow ✆*01 287 3399 www.glenviewhotel.com*

Famous for its views over the luxuriantly green and leafy Glen O'The Downs, this family-friendly hotel has all the advantages of a beautiful rural location, yet is close to Dublin. A popular wedding venue, it offers a wide range of facilities, including an excellent Health and Leisure Club and a conference centre. Special breaks offer good value. **Rooms 70**. Open all year. CC. **Directions:** *On N11, turn left 3km southbound of Kilmacanogue.*

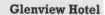 **Castleruddery Organic Farm**

Castleruddery Upper Donard Co Wicklow ✆*045 404 925*

Organically certified since 1989, Hilda Crampton and Dominic Quinn run one of the longest established organic farms in Ireland and have been an inspiration for many others, especially in the Wicklow area where there are now many organic holdings. They produce an exceptionally wide range of beautiful vegetables and herbs that are bursting with goodness and flavour, and also import carefully selected organic fruit and vegetables to provide all year supply. Farm Shop (Thu & Fri 9-6); also at Naas Farmers' Market (Sat 10-3).

ENNISKERRY

Nestling in a wooded hollow among the hills west of Bray, this pretty riverside village is close to the Powerscourt Demesne (01 204 6000, open all year). Nearby, the world-famous Powerscourt House and Gardens, built between 1731 and 1740, offers 47 acres of formal gardens, ornamental lakes, scenic walks and excellent views of Sugar Loaf Mountain. Other nearby attractions include the picturesque Glen of Dargle, and Coolakay House (01 286 2423), where there is an agricultural heritage display centre. The area is a favourite destination for walkers of all abilities, and golfers will enjoy the Powerscourt Golf Club (01 2046033) with a clubhouse in Georgian style, echoing Powerscourt House. Horse riding is on offer at Oakfield Equestrian Centre (01 282 9296), and anglers of all types are well catered for with the many local river, lake and sea fishing opportunities, with some excellent fly fishing for sea trout and sometimes salmon available at Tinnehinch Fishery (01 286 8652).

 Kennedy's of Enniskerry

Church Hill Enniskerry Co Wicklow ✆ *www.kennedysofenniskerry.com*

Pretty enough to make you stop and look, Santina and Andrew Kennedy's lovely speciality store and café is well worth a visit if only to buy a gorgeous Bretzel Bakery loaf (also used in the café). Once inside, it's tempting to browse and maybe have a bite - great home-made soups, salads and Santina's good home baking... Over 80% of their foods are produced in Ireland, and they also stock locally made crafts - if only Ireland's main visitor centres and tourist outlets could say the same. *Mon-Sat 9-6, Sun 10-3.* **Directions:** *Centre of village*

 Powerscourt Terrace Café

Powerscourt House Enniskerry Co Wicklow ✆ *01 204 6070 www.avoca.ie*

Overlooking the famous gardens and fountains of Powerscourt House, this appealing self-service restaurant is a delightfully relaxed space, with a large terrace. Everything is freshly made, using as many local ingredients as possible; expect the trademeark interesting salads, home-bakes, good pastries and excellent vegetarian dishes - many of which, such as oven-roasted vegetable and goat's cheese tart, have become specialities. **Seats 160** *(outdoors, 60). Open daily 9.30-5 (Sun 10-5.30). Closed 25-26 Dec. CC.* **Directions:** *3km from Enniskerry Village.*

 **The Ritz Carlton**

Powercourt Estate Enniskerry Co Wicklow ✆ *01 274 8888 www.ritzcarlton.com/powerscourt*

Scenically situated in the beautiful Wicklow Hills south of Dublin city, this deluxe hotel's palatial public areas make the most of the wonderful location, and accommodation is luxurious. Dining experiences range from afternoon tea or casual meals in The Pub bar or the foyer lounge area, to fine dining in Gordon Ramsay at Powerscourt. Excellent amenities include a leisure centre and destination spa, golf, and extensive conference/banqueting facilities. **Rooms 200. Seats 88** *(outdoors, 48); Restaurant L Sat/Sun only; D daily. Food served in the Sugar Loaf Lounge all day. Bar food also available from 4pm in McGills pub (open Wed-Sun). Open all year. CC.* **Directions:** *On Powerscourt Estate.*

Waterfall Farm Shop

Enniskerry Co Wicklow ☎*087 264 9537 www.waterfallfarm.ie*

Michael and Hannah Keegan have developed an interesting combination of enterprises to ensure viability for the Glencree Valley farm that has been in Michael's family for generations. "Quality, sustainability and seasonality" sum up the ethos of the lovely farm shop which showcases produce from the immediate area - including their own Lleyn lamb, which can be ordered in the shop - and other directly sourced Irish farm and artisan produce. They also offer camper van parking, and farm courses. Well worth a detour. Open Sat & Sun 10-5 (to 4 in winter). Weekday farm visits by arrangement only.

GLENDALOUGH

The Glen of the two lakes, Glendalough is a valley distinguished for its beauty and its historical and archaeological interest, notably the atmospheric monastic site established by St Kevin in the 6th century. The site includes the finest surviving example of a round tower in Ireland, a cathedral, St Kevin's Church and other stone churches dating back to the 8th and 12th centuries. There is a Visitor Centre (0404 45325, open all year) with an exhibition explaining the history of the site, and a market is sometimes held at Glendalough carpark, including arts, crafts and farmhouse produce. The Wicklow Mountains National Park (0404 45425) covers an area of 20,000 hectares, which includes the beautiful upper lake at Glendalough and most of the glaciated valley in which the lake is set. This is prime walking or driving country, and some of the most beautiful in Ireland - it is easy to see why Wicklow is known as 'Ireland's garden county.' The Wicklow Way is a popular route which covers 130km from Marlay Park in Dublin to Clonegal in County Carlow.

 The Conservatory

Glendalough Area The Old School House Laragh Glendalough Co Wicklow
☎*0404 45302 www.theconservatory.ie*

In a handsome old cut stone building, Lisa de la Haye's Conservatory Restaurant and Tea Rooms are wonderfully inviting and pretty as a picture. Varied menus are especially strong on bread making and pastry - eating here on a sunny summer day and enjoying the excellent home-cooked food and friendly service, it can be a hard place to leave. *Open Wed-Mon 10am-6pm & D Thu-Sun. Closed Tue.* **Directions:** *Just off centre of Laragh - off the Sallygap Road.*

 Glendalough Green

Glendalough Area Laragh Glendalough Co Wicklow ☎*0404 45151*

Clodagh Duff's shop/café looks humble enough from the outside but, once inside, you'll find a clever blend of foodie delights to cater for all customers. A simple but inviting café offers wholesome freshly made soups, hotpots and sandwiches alongside coffee, tea and freshly made cake and there's seating at the front for fine weather too. A very useful little place to know about. **Seats 16** *(outdoors, 14). Open daily, 8.30am-5pm (to 6pm Sun). Closed 25 Dec. CC.* **Directions:** *At the entrance to Laragh on the right side of the green.*

 **The Wicklow Heather**

Glendalough Area Laragh Glendalough Co Wicklow ☎*0404 45157 www.thewicklowheather.com*

Betty and John Kenny's inviting restaurant with accommodation in the heart of Laragh has been welcoming diners for over 40 years and, with consistently good locally sourced food and friendly and attentive staff, it is more popular than ever. It offers all day snacks and wide ranging lunch and evening menus, with a full bar - and a choice of dining outdoors, or in atmospheric rooms with unique historical interest (especially the Irish Writers' Room). Always buzzing with a happy blend of local families, couples and tourists, it offers something for everyone. *Seats 125 (outdoors, 40). Open daily L&D. Rooms 5 (all shower only). Closed 25 Dec. CC.* **Directions:** *Centre of Laragh Village.*

 **A Caviston**

1 Westview Church Road Greystones Co Wicklow ✆01 287 7637 www.acaviston.ie

The Caviston passion for all things piscine is very evident at this excellent café and deli in Greystones, run by Amy Caviston and her husband Shane Willis. The fish counter offers an astonishing array of the freshest produce, which is transformed into delicious dishes in the adjoining café; there are tempting non-fish dishes too, and half portions for children. Irish craft beers are the wine list's crowning glory, some featuring in innovative seafood & craft beer pairings. Another reason to visit this attractive seaside town. *Seats 66 (outdoors, 30). Open Mon-Sat, 9-5 (Mon from 10); D Thu-Sat 6-9.30 (early D 6-7). Sun brunch 10-4. Seafood & Irish craft beer pairings, 3-4pm daily. Closed bank hols; 1 week Christmas. CC.* **Directions:** *Top end of the town. Right from DART station, c. 300m.*

GREYSTONES

Quieter and more tranquil than its popular neighbour, Bray, Greystones is a fishing village which has become a commuter town for Dublin. Although it has grown significantly through the years and major harbour development has recently taken place, it still maintains its village atmosphere and the ambience of a small fishing harbour. There are magnificent views of Bray Head, Killiney, Dalkey Island and Howth to be admired from the cliff walk between Greystones and Bray. This long low coastline stretching south to Wicklow is bordered by the scenic Wicklow Mountains and the Sugar Loaf Mountain. Golfers will enjoy the 18 hole course at Greystones Golf Course (0287 4136).

 The Butlers Pantry

Burnaby Buildings Church Road Greystones Co Wicklow ✆01 201 0022 www.thebutlerspantry.ie

One of Eileen Bergin's small chain of classy convenience foodstores, the scale has grown since Eileen first started out cooking and selling everything herself, but the ethos remains the same ("Hand made delicious recipes from our kitchen to yours"). The philosophy of using fresh local and "free-from" ingredients produces great-tasting convenience foods - and is the secret of their success. *Open 7 days: Mon-Wed 9-7, Thu-Fri 9-8, Sat 9-7, Sun 9-6. Bank Hols 11-5.*

 Chakra by Jaipur

1st Floor Meridian Point Church Road Greystones Co Wicklow ✆01 201 7222 www.chakra.ie

This delightful sister to the other successful Jaipur restaurants in Dalkey, Dublin and Malahide (see entries) offers the same warmly attentive service and maintains Jaipur's crisp, modern, contemporary take on traditional Indian food with colourful, delicious dishes. There are numerous vegetarian choices and old favourites are served with splendid accompaniments. Unusually for an Indian restaurant, the dessert menu is also worth exploring and wines are carefully selected to match the food. *Seats 95. D daily & L Sun. Closed 25 Dec. CC.* **Directions:** *Just off main street in new shopping centre, 2 minutes from DART station.*

The Happy Pear

Church Road Greystones Co Wicklow ✆*01 287 3655 www.thehappypear.ie*

Twins David and Stephen Flynn run this cheerfully ethical vegetable shop, with smoothie bar and café - a lot for a vegetable shop, but the food is simple and tasty. The twins' younger brother Darragh runs their Living Foods sprout farm, where wheatgrass is the star. The Happy Pear may be small, it has a big heart - they even run their van on local rapeseed oil. *Seats 40 (outdoors, 30); Vegetarian; food served daily 9-5.30pm (from 10.30 Sun & bank hols). Online shop (orders over €50) CC.* **Directions:** *Main Street Greystones.*

The Hungry Monk

Church Road Greystones Co Wicklow ✆*01 287 5759 www.thehungrymonk.ie*

Wine buff Pat Keown and his wife Sylvie celebrated 25 years at this famously quirky restaurant in 2013. Pat is usually the host and his warmth and enthusiasm are undimmed. Fish is the the speciality in summer and game in winter, while the famous wine list is clearly a labour of love. Both in the restaurant and the ground floor Wine Bar & Bistro, great hospitality - from son Julian and his wife Samantha too - great wines and interesting, high quality and skilfully cooked food at affordable prices explain The Hungry Monk's lasting success. A place to treasure. *Restaurant Seats 35. D Thu-Sat 5.30-11, early D €23 (5.30-7, Thu-Sat); also à la carte. House wines from €21. Restaurant closed Sun-Wed. Bistro & Wine Bar:D Mon-Sat 5-11pm, Sun all day 12.30-9. Closed 24-26 Dec. CC.* **Directions:** *Centre of Greystones village near DART.*

Natures Gold

1 Killincarrig Road Greystones Co Wicklow ✆*01 287 6301 www.naturesgold.ie*

In business since 1977, Brod Kearan's ethically focused store is one of the oldest shops in Greystones - and one of Ireland's oldest health stores. They carry some excellent products, and a USP for foodies is the extra virgin olive oil; produced on their own chemilcal-free and pesticide-free olive farm near Barcelona, the olives are hand picked and cold pressed for top quality oil. *Open: Mon-Sat, 9-6. Closed Sun & bank hols.*

The Steak Shop

Trafalgar Road Greystones Co Wicklow ✆*01 255 7737*

A jaunty striped awning announces this traditional butchers, known especially for their steaks – 'Reared from our own farm and meats matured for at least 21 days,' says proprietor Barry King. They also sell other meats and quality poultry. Meat like it used to be. *Open Mon-Sat, 8-6.*

Summervilles of Greystones

1 Trafalgar Road Greystones Co Wicklow ✆*01 287 4228 www.summervillesofgreystones.com*

Since Niamh Tait and Katie Doyle took over Summervilles, there's a definite 'young' feel to the menu. Daily specials are displayed on a board on the counter while the large blackboard lists the regular dishes. Good home baking is hard to resist and everything is tasty, well presented and served by cheerful, well-trained staff who know the menu well. One of the most popular eating places in Greystones. **Seats 45** *(outdoors, 60). Open daily, 9am-5.30pm. Closed 25 Dec. CC.* **Directions:** *Right off Church Road, over bridge and on to Trafalgar Road.*

The Three Q's

Gweedore Church Road Greystones Co Wicklow 📞*01 287 5477 www.thethreeqs.com*

This small, stylish restaurant is run by three brothers, Brian, Paul and Colin Quinn, who bring together local foods and international inspiration to create innovative menus with real style. Wholesome daytime food is followed by creative dinner menus where the aromatic flavours of North Africa influence some dishes. Cooking from scratch in-house gives real flavour and there's welcome originality here. **Seats 30** *(outdoors, 8); food served daily 9.30am-10pm (Sun to 9pm). Closed Mon, Christmas week. CC.* **Directions:** *Main street Greystones, 100m from the Dart station.*

Janet's Country Fayre

Unit 13B Bullford Business Campus Kilcoole Co Wicklow
📞*01 201 8008 www.irishfoodproducer.ie*

Janet Drew produces an impressive range of 'free from' chutneys, relishes, sauces and marinades in her business unit at the edge of the Wicklow Mountains. Made in the traditional way in small batches and using ingredients that are natural, local whenever possible, and additive-free, 'taste, quality and goodness' are the qualities that sum up Janet's Country Fayre - and they are easily recognised by their distinctive handwritten labels, often on chunky square jars. Available from: Independent retailers and selected multiples.

Avoca, Kilmacanogue

Kilmacanogue Bray Co Wicklow 📞*01 286 7466 www.avoca.ie*

The flagship premises of Ireland's most famous group of craft shops, they have become equally popular for their wholesome, home-cooked food, which is based as much as possible on local and artisan produce. The style at Avoca is eclectic, and although they are especially well known for great baking and traditional dishes, their salads and vegetables are also legendary. Here, **The Fernhouse Café** offers an elegant option with table service, in addition to the familar self-service café and deli. *Self-service café* **seats 160** *(+outdoor dining, 100). Open daily, 9.30-5 (Sun 10-5). Fernhouse Café:* **Seats 100***; open 10am-5.30pm. Closed 25-26 Dec. CC.* **Directions:** *On N11 sign posted before Kilmacanogue Village.*

Barraderry Country House

Barraderry Kiltegan Co Wicklow 📞*059 647 3209 www.barraderrycountryhouse.com*

Olive and John Hobson's delightful Georgian house is in a quiet rural area close to the Wicklow Mountains. Big bedrooms with country views are beautifully furnished. Barraderry would make a good base for exploring counties Wicklow, Kildare, Carlow and Wexford and there's plenty to do nearby: golf, hunts and equestrian centres, three racecourses and walking in the lovely Wicklow Mountains. **Rooms 4** *(all shower only). Closed 15 Dec-15 Jan. CC.* **Directions:** *N81 Dublin-Baltinglass; R 747 to Kiltegan (7km).*

Organic Delights

Talbotstown Kiltegan Co Wicklow ☏*059 647 3193 www.organicdelights.ie*

Denis Healy is one of Ireland's most prominent suppliers of organic fruit and vegetables, both grown on the family farm in Wicklow and imported. A great supporter of farmers' markets, he was one of the founding stallholders at Dublin's Temple Bar Food Market. Orders can be collected at the many markets he attends and you can also buy direct. Delivery is possible in some areas.

The BrookLodge Hotel & Wells Spa

Macreddin Village Co Wicklow ☏*0402 36444 www.brooklodge.com*

Built on the site of a deserted village in a Wicklow valley, this extraordinary food, drink and leisure complex exists thanks to the vision of three brothers, Evan, Eoin and Bernard Doyle. The offering of this spacious and welcoming hotel is diverse, including 'green' conferences and events and a luxurious spa. The hotel and its main restaurant, The Strawberry Tree, have earned national recognition for their strong position on organic and wild food; memorable meals are good value, given the quality of the ingredients and the standard of cooking. An organic food market is held here on the first Sunday of the month (first and third in summer). *Rooms 86*. Restaurant *seats 90* (outdoors, 10). L Mon-Sat & D daily. Bar food daily, 12.30-9; La Taverna Armento, Italian D Thur-Sat & 1-6pm Sun. Open all year. CC. *Directions:* Signed from Aughrim.

Sweetbank Farm

Tiglin Newcastle Co Wicklow ☏*086 818 4162 www.sweetbankfarm.com*

Fourth generation farmers Debbie and David Johnston sell their beautiful hand-picked seasonal fruit through outlets such as Avoca, and their organic lamb can be ordered in half or whole boxes for collection from the farm. Courses and workshops are held at the farm - hens, and botanical paintings are two popular subjects.

The Buttery Café at Fishers

Newtownmountkennedy Co Wicklow ☏*01 281 2892 www.thebutterycafe.com*

Ballymaloe trained chef Claire O'Brien runs this very nice café in Fisher's renowned country-wear shop, offering wholesome fare such as homemade soups and freshly baked breads, generous pies - shepherds, cottage or fisherman's pie - honey baked ham on the bone, stuffed pancakes, quiches, salads and much else besides. The homemade desserts and cakes are particularly good and takeaway is available. A nice place to know about. *Seats 60* (outdoors, 20). Open Mon-Sat 10am-5pm; Sun & bank hols 1-5pm. Closed 25-27 Dec, Easter Sun. CC. *Directions: 2 mins off the N11 in Fishers Shop in the heart of Newtownmountkennedy.*

Druids Glen Resort

Newtownmountkennedy Co Wicklow ☏*01 287 0800 www.druidsglenresort.com*

This luxurious hotel and golf resort enjoys a stunning setting in the Garden of Ireland, between the mountains and sea. Spaciousness is a key feature of the hotel, from the extensive grounds to the suites and bedrooms and it offers excellent amenities. Always popular for conferences and events, families are also very well catered for. Contemporary cooking in Druids Brasserie has a pleasing emphasis on local produce, with some signature dishes created by TV chef Catherine Fulvio of nearby Ballyknocken House & Cookery School. ***Rooms 148****. Druid's Brasserie seats 75, B, L & D daily. Bar meals also available. CC. **Directions:** 36km south of Dublin on N11, at Newtownmountkennedy.*

Bates Restaurant

3 Market Street Market Square Rathdrum Co Wicklow ☏*040 429 988 www.batesrestaurant.com*

A long cottage with simply whitewashed interior, this attractive restaurant has lots of atmosphere and people travel long distances for its relaxed ambience and excellent food, made with simple, quality ingredients. Seasonal menus offer an appealing range of mainstream modern European dishes with an Italian accent, many of them featuring the excellent meats of the area. Good value too, including the wine list. ***Seats 46****. D Tue-Sun; L Sun only. Closed Mon, Bank Hols. CC. **Directions:** Near Cartoon Inn pub.*

Hunter's Hotel

Newrath Bridge Rathnew Co Wicklow ☏*0404 40106 www.hunters.ie*

Set in lovely gardens alongside the River Vartry, this much-loved hotel is one of Ireland's oldest coaching inns. It's run by fifth generation brothers, Richard and Tom Gelletlie, who offer old-fashioned comfort and food based on local and home-grown produce. There's a proper little bar and a traditional dining room overlooking the beautiful garden where their famous afternoon tea is served in summer. There's nowhere else in Ireland like it. ***Rooms 16*** *(1 shower only). Restaurant **seats 50**. L&D daily. Closed 3 days at Christmas. CC. **Directions:** Off N11 at Ashford or Rathnew.*

Roundwood Inn

Roundwood Co Wicklow ✆*01 281 8107*

Owners since 1980, Jurgen and Aine Schwalm have developed their own unique style at this atmospheric 17th-century inn. The ever-burning log fire in its enormous open fireplace is a welcome sight in the main bar food area, where their uniquely Irish-German food is served at sturdy wooden tables - Hungarian goulash, fresh crab bisque, Galway oysters and hearty meals, notably Wicklow venison and the delicious house variation on Irish stew, are all favourites. While slightly more formal, the restaurant style is similar. The food here has always had a special character and this, together with the place itself and its special brand of hospitality, has earned the inn an enviable reputation. *Restaurant seats 45. By reservation only. Bar meals 12-9.30 daily. Bar closed 25 Dec, Good Fri. Restaurant closed L Mon-Sat, D Sun-Thu. CC.* **Directions:** *N11, follow sign for Glendalough.*

Halpins Bridge Cafe

Bridge Street Wicklow Co Wicklow ✆*0404 32677 www.halpinscafe.com*

When Robert Doyle swapped his camera for a kitchen, photography's loss turned out to be a gain for Wicklow town, when his little café near the river opened in 2009 - and earned a loyal following in no time. Contemporary cooking offers regular café food and excellent daily specials too - shepherd's pie, goat's cheese tart, or maybe beef and Guinness stew, all served with three fresh salads. Wonderful homemade bread and cakes merit mention, also great staff and good value. Well worth knowing about when in the area. *Seats 36 (outdoors, 8). Open Mon-Fri 8.30-6, Sat 8-6 & Sun & bank hols 10-4. CC.* **Directions:** *Drive into town, take left fork at small railed monument, 75m down on left.*

Woodenbridge Hotel

Woodenbridge Vale of Avoca Arklow Co Wicklow ✆*0402 35146 www.woodenbridgehotel.com*

Possibly Ireland's oldest hotel (dating back to 1608), this popular wedding venue is also a good base for golf breaks, or to explore in this beautiful area. Cosy, with quirky charm, it offers refurbished bedrooms (many overlooking the golf course), and newer rooms (overlooking the River Aughrim). Wholesome fare is served in the lively bar and a formal restaurant. **Rooms 62.** CC. **Directions:** *N11 to Arklow; turn off - 7km.*

NORTHERN IRELAND

BELFAST

Belfast is much newer than Ireland's other cities. It was 1613 when it officially started to come to life at the head of Carrickfergus Bay beside the shallow River Lagan. The tiny settlement of beal feirste - the 'town at the mouth of the Farset or the sandspit' - hadn't even been named on maps until the late 15th Century. But Belfast proved to be the perfect greenfield site for rapid development as the Industrial Revolution got under way. Its rocketing growth began with linen manufacture in the 17th Century, and this was accelerated by the arrival of skilled Huguenot refugees after 1685. There was scope for ship-building on the shorelines in the valleymouth between the high peaks crowding in on the Antrim side on the northwest, and the Holywood Hills to the southeast, though the first shipyard of any significant size wasn't in being until 1791, when William and Hugh Ritchie opened for business.

The Lagan Valley gave convenient access to the rest of Ireland to encourage development of the port at the head of what was becoming known as Belfast Lough. Belfast took off in a big way, a focus for industrial ingenuity and manufacturing inventiveness, and a magnet for entrepreneurs and innovators from all of the north of Ireland, and the world beyond. Its population in 1600 had been less than 500, yet by 1700 it was 2,000, and by 1800 it was 25,000. The city's growth was prodigious, such that by the end of the 19th Century it could claim with justifiable pride to have the largest shipyard in the world, the largest ropeworks, the largest linen mills, the largest tobacco factory, and the largest heavy engineering works, all served by a greater mileage of quays than anywhere comparable. And it was ultimately a Victorian expansion - the population in 1851 was 87,062, but by 1901 it was 349,180 - the largest city in Ireland, with an exuberant new City Hall at its heart to express its fierce civic pride.

The City Hall may be on the grand scale, but it was nevertheless right at the heart of a very human town. Equally, while the gantries of the shipyards may have loomed overhead, they did so near the houses of the workers in a manner which somehow softened their sheer size. Admittedly this theme of giving great projects a human dimension seems to have been forgotten in the grand design and dominant location of the Government Building (completed 1932) at Stormont, east of the city. But back in the vibrant heart of Belfast, there is continuing entertainment and accessible interest in buildings as various as the Grand Opera House, St Anne's Cathedral, the Crown Liquor Saloon, Sinclair Seamen's Church, the Linenhall Library, Smithfield Market, and some of the impressive Victorian and Edwardian banking halls, while McHugh's pub on Queen's Square, and Tedford's Restaurant just round the corner on Donegall Quay, provide thoughtful reminders of the earlier more restrained style looking across the river to the modern developments of the Odyssey Arena and the Titanic Belfast exhibition centre, now one of Ireland's most popular tourist attractions.

Today, modern technologies and advanced engineering have displaced the old smokestack industries in the forefront of the city's work patterns, with the Harland & Wolff shipyard ceasing to build ships in March 2003. Shorts' aerospace factories are now the city's biggest employer, while parts of the former shipyard are being redeveloped as the Titanic Quarter in memory of the most famous ship built in Belfast.

The energy of former times has been channeled into impressive urban regeneration along the River Lagan. Here, the flagship building is the Waterfront Hall, a large concert venue which has won international praise. In the southern part of the city, Queen's University (founded 1845) is a beautifully balanced 1849 Lanyon building at the heart of a pleasant university district which includes the respected Ulster Museum & Art Gallery, while the university itself is particularly noted for its pioneering work in medicine and engineering.

There's a buzz to Belfast which is expressed in its cultural and warmly sociable life, and reflected in the internationally-minded innovative energy of its young chefs. But there is still much to it that speaks of a country town and port strongly rooted in land and sea, and it is all the better for that.

BELFAST - ST. GEORGE'S MARKET

Ireland's fastest changing city has a huge buzz about it. Food lovers visiting the city will of course want to go to St George's Market, which is one of Belfast's oldest attractions; since its refurbishment in 1997, the Friday (variety, including clothes, books and antiques) and Saturday (food and garden) markets held in this atmospheric Victorian building are among the most interesting things to visit in Belfast. The Saturday Market has won much acclaim, including a Supreme Award from the Irish Food Writers' Guild for Contribution to Food in Ireland; Portavogie fish, venison and pheasant in season, local beef and pork, local organic vegetables, herbs and fruit, and farmhouse cheeses are among the delicious things you'll find here. The Sunday Market (10-4) offers a combination of Friday and Saturday market attractions, with an emphasis on crafts.

  An Old Rectory

148 Malone Road Belfast Co Antrim BT9 5LH ☎ *028 90 66 7882 www.anoldrectory.co.uk*

Conveniently located near the King's Hall, Public Records Office, Lisburn Road and Queen's University, Mary Callan's lovely late Victorian house is a former Church of Ireland rectory. Every room has a desk and a sofa, magazines to browse and beverage trays including hot chocolate and soup sachets. A fridge on each landing contains iced water and fresh milk, and breakfast is made with organic produce where possible. **Rooms 5** *(2 shower only). Closed Christmas-New Year & Easter. No CC.*

  Arcadia Delicatessen

378 Lisburn Road Belfast Co Antrim BT9 6GL ☎ *028 9038 1779 www.arcadiadeli.co.uk*

The Brown family's long-established speciality food shop continues to do what it has always done, offering wines and some of the best local artisan foods (O'Doherty's Fermanagh black bacon, Clandeboye Estate Yoghurt, Causeway Cheeses, Bay Tree Relishes, Ditty's Oatcakes among them) alongside comparable products from abroad. Hampers for Christmas and other occasions are a speciality. *Open Mon-Sat 8.30-5.30. Closed Sun. Online shop.*

  Avoca Cafe Belfast

Arthur House 41 Arthur Street Belfast Co Antrim BT1 4GB ☎ *028 9027 9955 www.avoca.ie*

The style at Avoca is eclectic, and although they are especially well known for great baking and traditional dishes like beef and Guinness casserole, their salads and vegetables are also legendary. Quality ingredients-led menus follow the established formula here, with special strengths in breads and baking, along with a wide range of wholesome dishes. *Mon-Fri 9-4, Sat 9-5, Sun 12.30-5.*

 The Bar and Grill at James Street South

21 James Street South Belfast Co Antrim BT2 7GA
☎ *028 9560 0700 www.belfastbargrill.co.uk*

Niall McKenna, chef-proprietor of one of the city's top fine dining restaurants, James Street South, has brought a little bit of New York to Belfast with this other successful venture, a classy urban steakhouse. The menu is all about straightforward, gutsy dishes and steak, elevated to lofty, smoky heights thanks to the Josper charcoal grill and there's a small selection of salads, pasta and risotto too, and retro desserts like knickerbocker glory to finish. Belfast's top spot for a classy steak dinner. *Open daily, 12-9.30pm. CC*

The Barking Dog

33-35 Malone Road Belfast *Co Antrim BT9 6RU* ✆ *028 9066 1885* *www.barkingdogbelfast.com*

One of the restaurants in the successful Sam Spain and Tony O'Neill stable, The Barking Dog is handily located in the university area, near the Botanic Gardens - and it is just what the area needed. Chef Michael O'Connor offers a range of well-priced, carefully thought out menus for different times and occasions, from weekend brunch to bar food to a full evening menu, and well trained staff provide service to match the excellent, sometimes witty, food. A busy, popular place. **Seats 76** *(outdoors, 24). Open daily L&D. Closed 11-13 Jul, 24-26 Dec. CC.*

Beatrice Kennedy

44 University Road Belfast *Co Antrim BT7 1NJ* ✆ *028 9020 2290* *www.beatrice.kennedy.co.uk*

Named after the lady whose home it once was, proprietor-chef Jim McCarthy's restaurant has retained the authentic lived-in feeling of a private period residence. Jim's cooking is accomplished, ingredients are carefully sourced and the breads, desserts and ice creams are all homemade. The best thing about Beatrice Kennedy is that everything tastes as good as it looks. A delightful place. **Seats 80**. *D Tue-Sun; L Sun only. Closed Mon, 24-26 Dec. CC.*

Belfast Cookery School

53-54 Castle Street Belfast *Co Antrim BT1 1GH*
✆ *028 9023 4722* *www.belfastcookeryschool.com*

Right in the centre of Belfast, the city's first purpose built cookery school has state of the art equipment and a great team of tutors headed up by proprietor Andy Rea and Mourne Seafood Bar's head chef Wayne Carville. The 16 fully equipped cooking stations can be used by individuals or groups and the wide range of courses for all ages and skill levels includes popular themes like Dinner Party in 3 Hours - and (of course), a Seafood Master Class.

Benedict's Hotel Belfast

7-21 Bradbury Place Belfast *Co Antrim BT7 IRQ*
✆ *028 9059 1999* *www.benedictshotel.co.uk*

This reasonably priced city centre hotel in the heart of Belfast's 'Golden Mile' combines comfort and contemporary style with moderate prices. A wide range of attractions, including the Botanic Gardens, Queen's University, Queen's Film Theatre and Ulster Museum, are within a few minutes' walk. The comfortable beds invariably come in for special praise, also the warm and friendly staff. Fusion/modern Irish is the cooking style at the Bistro. **Rooms 32**. *Bistro L&D daily. Closed 24-25 Dec. CC.*

Bennetts on Belmont

4-6 Belmont Road Belfast *Co Antrim BT4 2AN* ✆ *028 9065 6590*

Good, fast and moderately priced food is the aim at this sister restaurant of Colleen Bennett's famous Holywood restaurant, Fontana. Informal ingredients-led dining in bright surroundings has always been the philosophy and it was the first to bring an element of style to this busy corner of Belfast. Zesty flavours, delicious desserts and great coffee. **Seats 60**. *Open daily 9am-9pm. CC.*

Café Conor

11A Stranmillis Road Belfast Co Antrim BT9 5AF 📞*028 9066 3266* *www.cafeconor.com*

Just across the road from the Ulster Museum, Manus McConn's unusual high-ceilinged room was originally the artist William Conor's studio. Open for breakfast and brunch, lunch, afternoon tea and dinner, this is a casual place with a distinctive style. Good coffee, home-baked scones and tasty informal meals make it popular with locals and a real find for those visiting the museum or nearby Botanic Gardens. **Seats 50**. *Open daily 9am-10pm (Fri & Sat to 11, Sun to 9). Closed July fortnight. CC.*

 Café Renoir

93/95 Botanic Avenue Belfast Co Antrim BT7 1JN 📞*028 9031 1300*

Lindsay and Karen Loney's restaurant has a great local following for its wholesome, homemade, European café food. They've earned respect for their support of local and organic produce as well as for good cooking with home flavour. The café begins early with a breakfast menu and is open until late at night and, although menus are wide ranging, home baking is a specialty. *Cafe/Bistro:* **Seats 100**. *8am-9.30pm (to 10.30pm Fri-Sun). Pizzeria: Seats 100. Open 5pm-'late'. *Also at: 5-7 Queen Street. Closed 25 Dec, 12 July. CC.*

 Cargoes Café

613 Lisburn Road Belfast Co Antrim BT9 7GT 📞*028 9066 5451* *www.cargoescafe.co.uk*

Produce for the deli side of the business at this long-established deli and café is meticulously sourced, and the same philosophy applies to the food served in the café. Although it changed hands in 2011, new owner Stephen Rogan clearly shares the philosophy that made Cargoes a much-loved destination for food lovers and he continues to provide great food together with friendly hands-on service. A great little place. **Seats 36** *(outdoors, 12). Open Mon-Thu 9-5, Fri & Sat 9-11, Sun 10-4. BYO. CC.*

 Chef Shop

29 Bruce Street Belfast Co Antrim BT2 7JD 📞*028 9032 9200* *www.thechefshop.net*

A specialist kitchenware shop offering unusual lines. Items not normally available to the general public can be bought online, with a trade rate offered to professionals. The Chef Shop is partnered with Belfast Cookery School (see entry), a purpose-built facility behind Mourne Seafood Bar. *Online sales (delivery in Ireland and the UK). CC.*

 CoCo

7-11 Linenhall Street Belfast Co Antrim BT2 8AA 📞*028 9031 1150* *www.cocobelfast.co.uk*

Assisted by his partner, Yvonne, and an excellent and well trained international staff, well-known chef Jason Moore runs a cool and keenly priced operation at this slightly funky venue. Excellent cooking, attractive presentation, attentive service and customer-friendly pricing make this a restaurant to return to. *[A newer sister operation, The Governor Rocks, in Donaghadee, Co Down, specialises in seafood.]* **Seats 90** *(outdoors, 10). L Mon-Fri; D Mon-Sat; Sun 12-4. Closed 24-25 Dec, 1 Jan. CC.*

Coppi

St Anne's Square Cathedral Quarter Belfast Co Antrim BT1 2LR
📞 *028 9031 1959 www.coppi.co.uk*

Another full-flavoured success story by Sam Spain and Tony O'Neill, whose restaurants are among the most popular in the city. An Italian take on the popular tapas concept, the speciality is cicchetti - small dishes traditionally served in Venetian bars - and other sharing plates; 'proper dinners' include fresh pasta dishes (try the one with guanciale) and superb Himalayan salt wall aged steaks from Hannan Meats in Moira. A great place to meet and eat. *Sun-Thu 12-11, Fri Sat 12 noon-1am.*

 The Crescent Townhouse

13 Lower Crescent Belfast Co Antrim BT7 1NR 📞 *028 9032 3349 www.crescenttownhouse.com*

This affordable boutique hotel is in an elegant 19th-century listed building on the corner of Botanic Avenue, just a short stroll from the city centre. Spacious accommodation includes suites and superior rooms with luxurious bathrooms, and all are comfortably furnished, with neat bathrooms. The popular Metro Brasserie offers well-sourced, often local, ingredients and accomplished cooking and has a following for its good value contemporary food and buzzy atmosphere. **Rooms 17** *(6 shower only).* **Seats 70**. *D daily, early value D midweek. L also at BarTwelve Mon-Sat. CC.*

 Crown Liquor Saloon

46 Great Victoria Street Belfast Co Antrim BT2 7 BA 📞 *02890 279 901*

Belfast's most famous pub was perhaps the greatest of all the Victorian gin palaces that once flourished in Britain's industrial cities and is now owned by the National Trust. A visit to one of its famous snugs for a pint and half a dozen oysters served on crushed ice, or a bowl of Irish stew, is a must. *Crown: bar food Mon-Sat 12-3. Flannigans: 11-9. Closed 25-26 Dec. CC.*

 Deanes at Queens

36-40 College Gardens Belfast Co Antrim BT 📞 *028 9038 2111 www.michaeldeane.co.uk*

One of the most attractive restaurants in the Deane empire - and in the area - this child-friendly all-day bar and grill has a large terrace and enjoys a lovely leafy location near the university and also handy to the Botanic Gardens and Ulster Museum. Impressive Head Chef Chris Fearon's menus include Deanes classics but he has also put his own stamp on the restaurant with his gutsy, flavoursome cooking style. Also a good venue for a private party. **Seats 140**. *Mon-Sat 12-9.45 (Mon & Tue to 8.45pm). Closed Sun.*

 Deanes Deli Bistro

44 Bedford Street Belfast Co Antrim BT2 7FF 📞 *028 9024 8800 www.michaeldeane.co.uk*

Just around the corner from Deanes Restaurant, this smashing all-day place serves great bistro food, given an extra twist by the sumptuous retail deli store next to the restaurant. The evening menu gears things up a bit, but is still very informal. There are loads of tempting things to take home from the deli, of course, including Deanes own label range. **Seats 80** *(outdoors, 10). Open Mon-Sat, 11.30-9pm (to 10pm Wed-Sat) L 12-3, D from 5.30. Closed Sun; 25 Dec; 12-13 Jul. CC.*

 **Deanes Restaurant & Seafood Bar**

36-40 Howard Street Belfast Co Antrim BT1 6PF
☎ *028 9033 1134 www.michaeldeane.co.uk*

Deservedly hailed as Northern Ireland's premier restaurant for many years, chef Michael Deane's Howard Street restaurant is a more relaxed place these days but it remains the benchmark by which others in the region are judged. Michael Deane and his team have spearheaded modern food in Belfast and continue to provide food of exceptional quality, both in the calm atmosphere of the exclusive first floor area The Circle and the ground floor restaurant, which continue to offer fine dining at its best, and also at the adjacent Seafood Bar, a popular bistro with its own entrance, a casual vibe and keen prices. An icon of excellence. *Seats 100*. *L&D Mon-Sat 12-3. Closed Sun; Bank Hols, 24-26 Dec, Jul 12-18. CC.*

  Equinox

32 Howard Street Belfast Co Antrim BT1 6PF ☎ *028 9023 0089 www.equinoxshop.com*

Kay Gilbert's stylish Equinox is not only a tempting homeware and gift shop but, atmospherically situated under an atrium roof, the café offers gourmet sandwiches, pasta, soups, brunch dishes and daily specials, all freshly cooked and based on carefully sourced ingredients. The home-baked patisserie is reason alone to stop at this popular spot. Simple, classy food cooked with care and a slightly decadent touch – 'cafe society' done the way it should be. *Open Mon-Sat, 9.30-5.30 (café to 4). Also food to go. Closed Sun CC.*

  Ewings Fishmongers

124 Shankill Rd Belfast Co Antrim BT13 2BD ☎ *028 9032 5534 www.ewingseafoods.com*

In business since 1911 and currently in the stewardship of one of Northern Ireland's most respected food suppliers, Walter Ewing, and his sons, Crawford and Warren. Ewing's is the fish supplier of choice for many of the region's top chefs, who appreciate the quality and freshness of their prime fish and shellfish as well as excellent cured and smoked fish. Their legendary smoked salmon, including their most famous line, Glenarm Organic Smoked Salmon, is available online. *Open Tue – Sat, 9am – 5pm. Closed Sun & Mon. Online shop.*

   **The Fitzwilliam Hotel Belfast**

1-3 Great Victoria Street Belfast Co Antrim BT2 7BQ
☎ *028 9044 2080 www.fitzwilliamhotelbelfast.com*

This smart hotel beside the Grand Opera House impresses from the outset and you'll find the trademark chic, modern-classic Fitzwilliam style and attention to detail throughout. Rooms have luxurious beds, sumptuous bathrooms and little extras - and corner rooms have windows on two sides overlooking the city. The stylish restaurant offers pleasing surroundings, good cooking and slick service at affordable prices, making this a popular dining destination for non residents. *Rooms 130*. *Restaurant seats 150*. *L Sun-Fri; D daily (to 9.30pm Sun). Bar food daily 11.30am-10pm. Hotel open all year. CC.*

Foodie Folk

121 Gilnahirk Road Belfast Co Antrim BT5 7QL ☎*028 90 796 761 www.foodiefolk.co.uk*

Mark Stone's forward-looking, mainly online shop, offers quality produce at supermarket prices, for delivery or collection; also open to personal shoppers six days a week (in-store café). Their range is mainly sourced within Ireland and includes some superior products, like Dexter beef, a good choice of poultry, including Silverhill duck, free-range chicken from Lissara Farm at Crossgar in Co. Down, a very good fresh fish range and Yellow Door breads. *Shop: Mon-Sat, 8-7. Café. Closed Sun. CC.*

 Ginger

7-8 Hope Street Belfast Co Antrim BT2 5EE ☎*028 9024 4421 www.gingerbistro.com*

At Simon 'Ginger' McCance's chic and cheerful bistro, local and carefully sourced ingredients have always been at the centre of this likeable chef's philosophy. Menus offer a good choice of vegetarian dishes alongside appealing meat dishes and the seafood that he likes to cook best. Offering great food and wine at affordable prices in a fun atmosphere, this is one of Belfast's most enduringly popular restaurants - and no wonder. *Seats 70. L&D Tue-Sat. Closed Sun, Mon L, Bank Hols; 4 days Jul, 4 days Christmas. CC.*

 Happy Angel

20 Belmont Road Belfast Co Antrim BT4 2AN www.happyangelbelfast.com

Happy Angel is the third restaurant to occupy this site in the ownership of Sam Spain and chef Tony O'Neill - originally the hugely popular Gourmet Burger Bank (GBB), then ACE, since spring 2013 it's taken the South East Asian route. A brief lunch menu of half a dozen popular Asian dishes (all at just £5) and an evening selection of mainly Thai favourites. A good team and quality ingredients are the points of difference - and Whitewater Brewery's Belfast Lager on draught. *Mon-Fri 12-3 & 5-10; Sat 12-11, Sun 12-10.*

 Hastings Europa Hotel

Great Victoria Street Belfast Co Antrim BT2 7AP ☎*028 9027 1066 www.hastingshotels.com*

Particularly striking when illuminated at night, this landmark city centre building is one of Northern Ireland's largest hotels. Service has always been outstanding and, following recent renovations and the addition of executive rooms, there is accommodation to match (with super-comfortable 'Cloud Beds' in all rooms). There's a constant buzz at the all-day brasserie and the lobby bar, and there's a quieter Gallery Lounge and a cocktail bar on the first floor. But this famous hotel's greatest assets are the function suites and, especially, its excellent staff. *Rooms 272 (85 shower only). Closed 24-25 Dec. CC.*

  Hilton Belfast

4 Lanyon Place Belfast Co Antrim BT1 3LP ☎*028 9027 7000 www.hilton.com/belfast*

The scale of this landmark hotel is grand, the style throughout is of contemporary, clean-lined elegance and it makes the best possible use of its waterside site on a rise beside the Waterfront Hall, with the Sonoma Restaurant and corner suites commanding exceptional views. All of the spacious rooms have blackout curtains and marbled bathrooms, and recreational facilities are also excellent. *Rooms 198. Open all year. CC.*

Holiday Inn Belfast

22 - 26 Ormeau Avenue Belfast Co Antrim BT2 8HS
☎ *028 9032 8511 www.belfast.holiday-inn.com*

Conveniently located near most of the main city centre attractions, this contemporary hotel has luxurious modern accommodation, with excellent business and leisure facilities. Bedrooms are designed with the business guest in mind – the decor is unfussy and warm, with comfort and relaxation to match its use as a work base. *Rooms 170.* Open all year. CC.

 Home

22 Wellington Place Belfast Co Antrim BT1 6GE ☎ *028 9023 4946 www.homepopup.com*

A semi-permanent pop-up, this one did move house once but owner-manager Stevie Haller (former front of house at the Mourne Seafood Bar) seems to have decided that Wellington Place is a good place to call Home. Quirky, with some of the local artwork and 'previously loved' furniture for sale, but not a place of style over substance: it's well managed and Ben Arnold's cooking is really brilliant. Highly recommended. *Mon-Sat from 10am for snacks. Restaurant: Mon 12-4, Tue-Thu 12-9.30, Fri Sat 12-4 & 5-10, Sun 1-9. D from 5pm.*

 Il Pirata

279-281 Newtownards Road Belfast Co Antrim BT4 3JF ☎ *0044 (0)28 90673421*

This venture by Sam Spain and chef Tony O'Neill is a far cry from the usual Italian offering of pizza and lasagne – Il Pirata is all about casual sociability. There's plenty of great-quality, rustic food for sharing, and the cooking reflects the Italian flare for simple combinations of quality ingredients, with a few curve balls to keep things interesting. Great value too – just the place for family and friends to meet around a table. No wonder it's so popular. *Open 12-10pm.* CC.

 James Street South

21 James Street South Belfast Co Antrim BT2 7GA
☎ *028 9043 4310 www.jamesstreetsouth.co.uk*

Just behind Belfast's City Hall, Niall and Joanne McKenna's bright and stylish restaurant conveys a welcoming sense of confidence. This gem of a restaurant has earned a loyal following for refined cooking which can be truly memorable - Niall's exuberant modern cooking is innovative, with seasonal and local produce very prevalent, and a harmonious balance of fresh flavours. Lunch and pre-theatre menus offer exceptional value, and the wine list is one of the best in town. *The Cookery School offers practical and demonstration classes. *Seats 70.* L&D Mon-Sat; closed Sun; 25-26 Dec, 1 Jan, 11-12 July. CC.

 The John Hewitt Bar & Restaurant

51 Donegall Street Belfast Co Antrim BT1 2FH ☎ *028 9023 3768 www.thejohnhewitt.com*

Owned by the adjacent Belfast Unemployed Resource Centre, established by the poet John Hewitt, discerning Belfast diners like the combination of traditional interior and good-quality, sassy modern food here. High-ceilinged, with a marble bar, a snug and an open fire, the preference is for conversation and civilised relaxation - perhaps over a glass of craft beer. It operates as a restaurant by day and there is live music most nights. *Seats 60.* Open daily; food served Mon-Thu 12-3pm; Fri-Sat, 3.30-6pm. Closed Sun, 25 Dec, Easter Mon. CC.

Jurys Inn Belfast

Fisherwick Place Great Victoria Street Belfast Co Antrim BT2 7AP
✆028 9053 3500 www.jurysinns.com

Located in the heart of the city, this well managed hotel offers comfortable accommodation in a central location at very reasonable prices. Rooms are well designed and regularly refurbished, with good amenities for a hotel in the budget class. High standards and good value, with secure parking nearby. **Rooms 190**. *Closed 24-26 Dec. CC.*

  Made in Belfast

Units 1 & 2 Wellington Buildings Wellington Street Belfast Co Antrim BT16ET
✆028 9024 6712 www.madeinbelfastni.com

Emma Bucknell's quirky, bohemian 'restolounge' has its feet firmly on the ground when it comes to food. There's a strong emphasis on local and sustainable ingredients and a bias towards retro food (a signature dish is a fish finger sandwich) and, while it might be expected to irritate, the place seems to please people of all ages and walks of life. Its central location and popularity give it a buzz at all times. *Open Mon-Wed 12-9.30, Thu 12-10, Fri & Sat 12-11, Sun 12-9.*

 Malmaison Hotel

34-38 Victoria Street Belfast Co Antrim BT1 3GH
✆028 9022 0200 www.malmaison-belfast.com

The stylish UK Malmaison group introduced a new wow factor to Belfast accommodation choices when they took over this hotel, which is in a beautiful building of historic interest. Accommodation is spacious, contemporary and luxurious, with all the technical gizmos you could possibly want. The Brasserie offers simple, quality fare and good breakfasts are smartly served here too. The bar, with an extensive cocktail menu, is an in-place at night. **Rooms 62**. *CC.*

 Malone Lodge Hotel

60 Eglantine Avenue Malone Road Belfast Co Antrim BT9 6DY
✆028 9038 8000 www.malonelodgehotel.com

This reasonably priced townhouse hotel near Queen's University is pleasantly located if you want to be in a quiet area, yet convenient to the city centre. Accommodation is comfortable and spacious, with all the facilities required by business guests, both in-room and in the hotel itself. It has recently undergone major refurbishment, with new rooms and facilities added, including a restaurant. **Rooms 51**. *Restaurant open for L&D daily (Sun all day from noon). 22 apartments also available. CC.*

  Maryville House & Tea Rooms

2 Maryville Park Belfast Co Antrim BT9 6LN ✆028 9068 1510 www.maryvillehouse.co.uk

Lindsay and Karen Loney restored this lovely old redbrick house and it has earned a name for attractive light lunches and lovely home baking; afternoon tea is a speciality. Guests lucky enough to be staying overnight will enjoy Victorian-style rooms and an excellent breakfast, served in the tea rooms. A special place that visitors to Belfast will be delighted to have found. *Tea Rooms daily 9am–3.45pm (outdoors, 10).* **Rooms 6**. *Closed 25 Dec, Easter Sun. CC.*

McHugh's Bar & Restaurant

29-31 Queen's Square Belfast Co Antrim BT1 3FG
028 9050 9999 www.mchughsbar.com

This remarkable pub near the Odyssey Arena is in one of Belfast's few remaining 18th century buildings; built in 1711, it is the city's oldest listed building. It has been renovated to retain its character while blending in a new café-bar and restaurant. It's worth a visit for its historical interest alone, and the modern food should also be enjoyable. *Seats 75. L Thu/Fri; D daily. Bar food 12-9 daily (to 8pm Sun). Closed 25 Dec, 1 Jan, 12/13 Jul. CC.*

The Merchant Hotel

35-39 Waring Street Belfast Co Antrim BT1 2DY
028 9023 4888 www.themerchanthotel.com

The grandeur of a larger-than-life Victorian banking building is a fit setting for Belfast's most dramatic and beautiful hotel. The lobby sets the tone for the whole hotel – luxurious, but not ostentatious – and the cocktail bar is beautiful. Each elegant, opulent bedroom and suite is named after a literary figure with Belfast associations. Everything at this hotel exudes indulgence. The house style in the aptly named Great Room Restaurant is upbeat classic and accomplished meals showcase local ingredients; a 9-course Tasting Menu offers good value, especially with matching wines and traditional Afternoon Tea is also a highlight. *Rooms 62 (2 shower only). Restaurant seats 65. L&D Mon-Sat, Sun, 12-9pm. Bar food also available. Closed 25 Dec. CC.*

Molly's Yard

1 College Green Mews Botanic Avenue Belfast Co Antrim BT7 1LW
028 9032 2600 www.mollysyard.co.uk

This atmospheric restaurant on two floors - informal ground floor bistro with a more elegant dining room above - is in the former stables of College Green House and there is nothing clichéd about it, giving an intriguing feeling that this place is a 'find'. Ciarán Steele, head chef since 2008, describes his focused food as 'a modern day take on Irish traditional cooking'; his seasonal menus showcase local produce, as does the bar - not surprisingly, as Molly's Yard is owned by Ireland's oldest independent brewery, Hilden Brewing Co, in nearby Lisburn. *Seats 40 (outdoors, 20). Food Mon-Sat 12-9pm (to 9.30pm Fri/Sat). Closed Sun, 25-26 Dec, 1 Jan. CC.*

Mourne Seafood Bar Belfast

34-36 Bank Street Belfast Co Antrim BT1 1HL 028 9024 8544 www.mourneseafood.com

This informal restaurant and fish shop owned by well known chef Andy Rae and business partner Bob McCoubrey of the original Mourne Seafood Bar in Dundrum, Co Down, has become a Belfast institution. Andy's passion for seafood is evident: he uses less popular local fish rather than trendy imports and, of course, mussels and oysters from their own shellfish beds in Carlingford. Everything is homemade and the menu changes daily according to the catch. They also have their own craft beer, Mourne Oyster Stout (made by Whitewater Brewery) and popup restaurant Home and Belfast Cookery School (see entries) are associated businesses. *Seats 75. Food: Mon-Thu 12-9.30, Fri & Sat 12-4 & 5-10.30, Sun 1-6. Closed Sun D; 24-26 Dec, 1 Jan, 17 Mar. CC.*

Northern Whig

2 Bridge Street Belfast Co Antrim BT1 1LU 📞 *028 9050 9888 www.thenorthernwhig.com*

Formerly home to the Northern Whig newspaper and convenient to the city's fashionable Cathedral Quarter, this is an impressive bar of grand proportions. It's popular with people of all ages and backgrounds, including the local business community, who come here for lunch and to relax after work. The cosmopolitan menus are based mainly on local ingredients and, with a decent wine list and excellent staff, it stands out in a city with many good eating places. *Open daily 10am-1.30am; bar food 12-9 (from 1pm Sun). CC.*

 Owen McMahon Butchers

3 Atlantic Avenue Belfast Co Antrim BT15 2HN 📞 *028 9074 3535 www.owenmcmahon.com*

Owen McMahon's shop is the only Elite Butchers Association member in Belfast. They sell meat, fish, poultry and fresh fruit and vegetables, but the specialities they are best known for are pork butchery (once a particular point of pride in Belfast, and indeed throughout Ireland). Their award-winning sausages, like steak and Guinness or steak and cracked pepper, are all excellent.

 **OX**

1 Oxford Street Belfast Co Antrim BT1 3LA www.oxbelfast.com

A new star is born at this relaxed Lagan-side restaurant. Stephen Toman and Alain Kerloc'h combine stylish modern ingredients-led food and impeccable service with a casual vibe. Describing itself simply as 'A restaurant with seasonal creativity', OX's short (and extremely reasonably priced) menu is a model of pared down promise and Stephen Toman's cooking is exquisite, with great attention to detail - a standard mirrored by seemingly laid-back, yet highly efficient service. A great team and a wonderful, affordable restaurant. *L Tue-Sat 12-2.45, D Tue-Sat 5.45-10. Closed Sun & Mon. CC.*

 The Potted Hen Bistro

11 Edward Street Saint Anne's Square Cathedral Quarter Belfast Co Antrim BT1 2LR 📞 *028 9023 4554 www.thepottedhen.co.uk*

A stylish younger sister of Dermot and Catherine Regan's highly regarded Newtownabbey restaurant, Oregano, The Potted Hen has made a lot of friends with its winning combination of a special setting and classy bistro food at good prices. Like Oregano, the food philosophy is focused firmly on using the freshest of ingredients in dishes that are imaginative yet allow the food itself to star; menus offer plenty of choice and the ambience is relaxing. *Mon-Sat, coffees from 10.30; L&D; Sun 12-9pm. CC.*

 Radisson Blu Hotel Belfast

The Gasworks 3 Cromac Place Ormeau Road Belfast Co Antrim BT7 2JB 📞 *028 9043 4065 www.radissonblu.co.uk/hotel-belfast*

You're in for a pleasant surprise upon entering this modern hotel: a highly original water feature has been created from the old 'grave dock' that was once a turning space for the boats coming up to the gasworks to deliver coal; it's worth a journey just to see it - the bar and the well regarded Filini Restaurant both overlook it. Friendly and helpful staff clearly take great pride in this hotel and accommodation is of the usual high Radisson standard. ***Rooms 120.*** *CC.*

Ramada Hotel Belfast

117 Milltown Road Shaws Bridge Belfast Co Antrim BT8 7XP
☎ *028 9092 3500 www.ramadabelfast.com*

The lovely location is the USP at this modern four star hotel; situated near Shaws Bridge, it enjoys a beautiful setting in the Lagan Valley Regional Park, overlooking the River Lagan. Bedrooms, which have all the facilities expected of a contemporary hotel, are decorated in a fairly neutral modern style and executive suites are available, intended mainly for business guests. Good leisure, conference and banqueting facilities. **Rooms 120**. *Open all year. CC.*

Ravenhill House

690 Ravenhill Road Belfast Co Antrim BT6 0BZ ☎ *028 9020 7444 www.ravenhillhouse.com*

The Nicholson family's late Victorian redbrick house has a sense of seclusion despite being on a busy road. Bedrooms are comfortable and stylish, but breakfast is sure to be a highlight. The Nicholsons buy all their fresh goods from local farmers and producers at the weekly St George's Market, and they make everything possible on the premises. An excellent, reasonably priced base for a stay in Belfast. **Rooms 5** *(3 shower only). Closed 2 weeks Christmas/New Year & 2 weeks in Jul. CC.*

Salt Bistro

Saint Anne's Square Belfast Co Antrim BT1 2LR ☎ *028 9023 8012 www.saltbistrobelfast.com*

Donal and Teresa Cooper, formerly of the much-missed little fine dining restaurant Brulées of Limerick, have fetched up in Belfast's exciting cultural quarter right beside the MAC (Metropolitan Arts Centre), where this less formal but equally polished operation is proving its worth. While offering predictable sounding food, it's the cooking that makes a difference - you can take the fine dining out of the menu, but you can't take the classical training out of the cook. Smart service, good wine list - and fair value too. *L&D Mon-Sat, Sun 12-6.*

Sawers Deli

College Street Unit 7 Fountain Centre Belfast Co Antrim BT1 1HF
☎ *028 9032 2021 www.sawersbelfast.com*

Purveyors of the finest local produce and speciality foods from around the world since the 1890s, this is a place to relish. Current owner Kieran Sloan combines support for local artisan producers with exotic and novelty items, which makes this an exciting place to visit. Renowned for cheeses and for fresh fish and shellfish, they also sell an extraordinary range of grocery products and deli items. *Open Mon-Sat 9-5.30.*

SD Bell & Co Ltd

516 Upper Newtownards Road Knock Belfast Co Antrim BT4 3HL
☎ *028 9047 1774 www.sdbellsteacoffee.com*

This legendary tea and coffee emporium dates back to 1887, and was an institution in Belfast's city centre until moving to these suburban premises in the 1970s. Headquarters, retail sales and the Leaf & Berry coffee bar/restaurant are now all located at Knock. Their premium teas and coffees are sold here, at St George's Market and at quality outlets throughout Northern Ireland. *Open Mon-Fri 8.30-5, Sat 8.30-2. Closed Sun except 'Leaf & Berry' café, open11-2.30 - Sun Jazz Brunch. Online shop.*

Shu

253 Lisburn Road Belfast Co Antrim BT9 7EN ☎028 9038 1655 www.shu-restaurant.com

Chef Brian McCann's enthusiasm for uncomplicated, quality food is unmistakable in the menus at Shu, which offer exceptional value and illustrates this chef's dedication to seasonal provenance. There's something to suit every taste and budget. With great food, service and atmosphere, Shu continues to provide the Belfast restaurant scene with a good-value, quality choice. It has been one of the city's most consistently popular dining destinations since opening, and that leading position is well deserved. *Seats 80. L&D Mon-Sat. Bar open Fri & Sat 7-1. Closed Sun, 24-26 Dec, 1 Jan, 11-13 Jul. CC.*

  Suki Tea

Unit 6 Twin Spires Business Park 155 Northumberland Street Belfast Co Antrim ☎028 9033 0938 www.suki-tea.com

This respected Northern Ireland-based tea company has an online shop selling a wide range of teas, including fruit and herbal teas, plus teapots and other accessories. Suki 'Belfast Brew' (a blend of the best leaves from the best Fairtrade tea gardens in Assam and Tanzania) is an ingredient in Ditty's of Castledawson's special Moist Irish Tea Cake - it is described by artisan baker Robert Ditty as 'smooth and bright yet strong and malty - a true ship builders' brew'.

 Sun Kee Restaurant

42-47 Donegall Pass Belfast Co Antrim BT7 1BS ☎028 9031 2016

The Lo family's famous city centre restaurant offers the classic, familiar Chinese dishes, but created in a style that doesn't panders to western tastes too much. They may also offer more unusual dishes, which can offer a genuine challenge to the jaded Western palate – be prepared to be adventurous. *Food daily, 12-10.30pm. CC.*

 Tedfords Restaurant

5 Donegall Quay Belfast Co Antrim BT1 3EF ☎028 9043 4000 www.tedfordsrestaurant.com

Alan and Sharon Fosters' quietly excellent seafood restaurant has a following for Alan's imaginative and carefully cooked food, yet it could be described as a hidden gem. Fish and seafood dishes are very much the speciality, but the meats and vegetarian options are equally creative. As it's close to the Waterfront Hall and Odyssey Arena, this is a good choice for a pre-theatre meal. *Seats 45; L Wed-Fri; D Tue-Sat. Closed Mon, July fortnight, 1 week Christmas. CC.*

  **Ten Square Hotel**

10 Donegall Square South Belfast Co Antrim BT1 5JD ☎028 9024 1001 www.tensquare.co.uk

This luxurious boutique hotel directly overlooking the historical City Hall is Belfast's coolest place to stay. The stylishly informal Grill Room, which occupies the whole of the ground floor, specialises in prime Irish steaks; it is one of Belfast's most popular restaurants and meeting places, which gives the hotel a great buzz. Attractively priced menus, cocktails and free evening entertainment make for an appealing package. *Rooms 22. Restaurant seats 120 (outdoors, 72). Open daily 12-10pm. CC.*

The Wellington Park Hotel

21 Malone Road Belfast Co Antrim BT9 6RU ✆*028 9038 1111* *www.wellingtonparkhotel.com*

Very conveniently located close to the University, the Mooney family's friendly hotel is a Belfast institution - the new-ish Wellie Bar & Grill reflects the affectionate local nickname for the hotel. It's a popular choice for business guests and as a conference venue, and also close to most of the city's cultural attractions. Although it is a little tired in places, the spacious foyer and public areas are comfortably furnished, as are the refurbished bedrooms, and it's a place where people feel welcome and at ease. **Rooms 75**. *Closed 24-26 Dec. CC.*

Yellow Door Deli & Patisserie

427 Lisburn Road Belfast Co Antrim BT9 7EY ✆*028 9038 1961* *www.yellowdoordeli.co.uk*

Simon Dougan is a key figure in the Northern Ireland food scene, known for his clear vision of simple, honest food and uncompromising standards. This Belfast branch of his renowned Portadown business reflects this philosophy. No additives or enhancers are used in any products - it is, as Simon says himself, " 'proper food' as it should be". *Open Mon-Sat 8am - 4.45pm.*

Zen

55-59 Adelaide Street Belfast Co Antrim BT2 8FE ✆*028 9023 2244* *www.zenbelfast.co.uk*

It would be interesting to know what the original owners of this 19th-century redbrick mill would make of its transformation by proprietor Eddie Fung into an ultra modern, stunningly cool Japanese restaurant. One of Belfast's most popular ethnic restaurants after a decade in business, Zen offers a unique dining experience and is especially known for the authenticity of their fresh sushi and sashimi. **Seats 170**. *Mon-Fri, L&D; Sat D only; Sun 1.30-10.30. Closed L Sat, 25 Dec, 12 July. CC.*

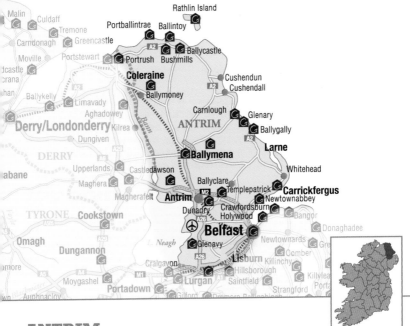

ANTRIM

With its boundaries naturally defined by the sea, the River Bann, the extensive lake of Lough Neagh, and the River Lagan, County Antrim has always had a strong sense of its own clearcut geographical identity. This is further emphasised by the extensive uplands of the Antrim Plateau, wonderful for the sense of space with the moorland rising to heights such as Trostan (551m) and the distinctive Slemish (438m), famed for its association with St Patrick.

The plateau eases westward to fertile valleys and bustling inland towns such as Ballymena, Antrim and Ballymoney, while the coastal towns ring the changes between the traditional resort of Portrush in the far north, the ferryport of Larne in the east, and historic Carrickfergus in the south.

In the spectacularly beautiful northeast of the county, the most rugged heights of the Plateau are softened by the nine Glens of Antrim, havens of beauty descending from the moorland down through small farms to hospitable villages clustered at the shoreline, and connected by the renowned Antrim Coast Road. Between these sheltered bays at the foot of the Glens, the sea cliffs of the headlands soar with remarkable rock formations which, on the North Coast, provide the setting for the Carrick-a-Rede rope bridge and the Giant's Causeway, a World Heritage site.

From the charming little port of Ballycastle, Northern Ireland's only inhabited offshore island of Rathlin is within easy reach by ferry, a mecca for ornithologists and perfect for days away from the pressures of mainstream life.

LOCAL ATTRACTIONS & INFORMATION

‣ **Carrick-a-Rede Rope Bridge**
Ballycastle *028 20 731582*
‣ **World's Oldest Distillery**
Bushmills *028 20 731521*
‣ **Carrickfergus Castle**
028 93 351273

‣ **Dunluce Castle Visitor Centre**
028 20 731938
‣ **Giants Causeway & Bushmills Railway**
028 20 741157

‣ **Irish Linen Centre & Lisburn Museum** Lisburn
028 92 663377
‣ **Patterson's Spade Mill**
Templepatrick
028 94 433619

The Red Door

14a Harbour Road Ballintoy Co Antrim BT546NA
028 2076 9048 / 0780 282 8908

Near the quaint little fishing harbour of Ballintoy and its iconic whitewashed church, Joan and Nigel Mc Garrity's little red-doored tea rooms has been such a hit since opening in 2012 that is has gradually developed into a small restaurant. Now with a drinks licence, they offer a short but tasty menu of locally sourced meals, toasted ciabattas and desserts, while still with the snacks and afternoon tea option. Right in the middle of the Causeway Coast, it's ideally placed for both locals and tourists. *Open all day; also occasional evenings in summer. CC.*

   **Whitepark House**

150 Whitepark Road Ballintoy Ballycastle Co Antrim BT54 6NH
028 2073 1482 www.whiteparkhouse.com

 A warm welcome from chatty and well-informed hosts Bob and Siobhán Isles awaits the lucky visitors to this pretty old house. Tucked away in a sylvan setting, well back from the road and with stunning views of Whitepark Bay, it has a path down to a beautiful beach just across the road. Stylish, cosy, luxuriously comfortable and with Bob's lovely gardens to enjoy in fine weather, it is an exceptional place to stay. Gorgeous food too, including immaculately presented afternoon tea on arrival as well as delicious breakfasts. A one off. **Rooms 3**. *Open all year. CC (5% surcharge).* **Directions:** *On Antrim coast road A2, 6m East of Bushmills*

BALLYCASTLE

Ballycastle, a friendly market town on the beautiful north-eastern corner of Co Antrim, has a museum (028 207 62942) on Castle Street which will be of interest to visitors who are curious about the folk and social history of the Glens of Antrim (open daily Jul-Aug, otherwise by arrangement; free entry), and a growing number of restaurants and bars. The famous local specialities 'Yellow Man' (a honeycomb toffee) is expecially associated with the Auld Lammas fair held in Ballycastle at the end of August, while it is on sale with other local foods including dulse (sea weed).

                                           Cellar Restaurant

11b The Diamond Ballycastle Co Antrim BT54 6AW
028 2076 3037 www.cellarballycastle.com

With an unusual barrel-vaulted roof and cosy snugs separated by traditional etched glass dividers, Chris McCauley's little restaurant just up the street from The House of McDonnell is highly atmospheric. Local lobster is a speciality on the daily specials menu, and fairly priced. Charming staff provide good service and, although the seating is a little cramped, a meal here should be very enjoyable. **Seats 46**. *Food served daily in Summer: Mon-Sat 12-10; Sun D only. 2-course early D Mon-Fri 5-7 £9.95 with glass of wine. Open at 5pm in winter. Closed Sun L & last Mon-Tue in August, 25-26 Dec, 1 Jan. CC.*

The House of McDonnell

71 Castle Street Ballycastle Co Antrim BT54 6AS
✆*028 2076 2975 houseofmcdonnell.blogspot.ie*

First opened in April 1766, this wonderful historic pub has been in the caring hands of Tom and Eileen O'Neill since 1979 and in Tom's mother's family for generations before that. Tom and Eileen delight in sharing the history of their long, narrow premises with its tiled floor and mahogany bar: it was once a traditional grocery-bar and is now a listed building. Traditional music Fri nights. *Usually open 11am-"late" at weekends, but only in the evenings midweek, although times might vary in winter. Check ahead.* **Directions:** *Town centre, near the Diamond.*

 Thyme & Co Café

5 Quay Rd Ballycastle Co Antrim BT54 76J ✆*028 2076 9851 www.thymeandco.co.uk*

With its welcoming, informal atmosphere, this is just the kind of place visitors to Ballycastle will be happy to find. Run by Tom and Eimear Mullin, who take great pride in doing the important things right, they've earned a following for the delicious homemade flavours of their food, which is based on locally sourced ingredients, and especially their home baking (including gluten-free). Also local crafts. *Tue-Sat 8.30am-4.30pm (Sun 10-3.30), sometimes open evenings. No CC.* **Directions:** *Centre of Ballycastle, beside park on A2 Quay Road.*

 Ballylagan Organic Farm

12 Ballylagan Road Straid Ballyclare Co Antrim BT39 9NF
✆*028 9332 2867 www.ballylagan.com*

No ordinary farm - Tom and Patricia Gilbert's farm, near Carrickfergus, was the first in Co Antrim to achieve organic certification from the Soil Association in the early '90s, and this was Northern Ireland's first organic farm outlet. The well stocked shop is well worth a visit and they have lovely accommodation too. A great place for a day out, or to stay. *Shop open Mon-Sat 10-5; tea shop last orders 4.30. Closed Sun.* **Rooms 4** *(3 shower only); B&B double £95; single £70. CC.* **Directions:** *From Carrickfergus, the Woodburn Road leads straight over the hill into Straid.*

 Oregano

29 Ballyrobert Road Ballyrobert Ballyclare Co Antrim BT39 9RY
✆*028 9084 0099 www.oreganorestaurant.co.uk*

A Victorian house in the village of Ballyrobert is the setting for this highly regarded rural restaurant run by Dermot and Catherine Reagan, whose passion for good food is evident from the moment you enter the contemporary dining room. Dermot transforms carefully sourced foods, including fish, duck, beef and venison, into delicious modern dishes and delightful service makes the good food served all the more enjoyable. Set menus offer especially good value. **Seats 60** *(outdoors, 6).Tue-Fri L&D; Sat D only; Sun all day 12-7pm. Closed Mon, 25-26 Dec, 1-2 Jan, 1 week around 12 Jul.*

 **Hastings Ballygally Castle Hotel**

Coast Road Ballygally Co Antrim BT40 2QZ ✆*028 2858 1066 www.hastingshotels.com*

This coastal hotel really has got a (very) old castle at the heart of it - and they've even got a ghost (you can visit her room at the top of the castle). Recent investment has improved standards, yet the hotel still has character; some of the older rooms are literally shaped by the castle itself and are quite romantic. Cosy wing chairs and open fires make welcoming lounge areas to relax in and the beach is just across the road. *Rooms 44*. *Open all year. CC.* **Directions:** *Situated on the coast road (A2) between Larne and Glenarm.*

 **Galgorm Resort & Spa**

136 Fenaghy Road Ballymena Co Antrim BT42 1EA ✆*028 2588 1001 www.galgorm.com*

Set amidst beautiful scenery, with the River Maine running through the grounds, this former gentleman's residence is one of Northern Ireland's best-known country house hotels. Following major redevelopment it retains its pleasant atmosphere but, now larger and more contemporary, it has taken its place among Ireland's leading hospitality players. Excellent facilities (including equestrian) are matched by outstanding food, notably in the River Room where accomplished chef Chris Bell's Taste of Antrim tasting menu is a memorable experience. *Rooms 75. Restaurant seats 40. D Wed-Sun. L Sun only. Bar food available daily 12-10pm. Hotel open all year. Restaurant closed L Mon-Sat; Mon, Tue. CC.* **Directions:** *From the Galgorm roundabout, take the third exit for Cullybackey (Fenaghy road). About 2 miles, on the left.*

 **Marlagh Lodge**

71 Moorfields Rd Ballymena Co Antrim BT42 3BU ✆*028 2563 1505 www.marlaghlodge.com*

Robert and Rachel Thompson restored early Victorian house now makes an unusual and comfortable haven for guests. The Lodge is a classic of its era, double fronted with spacious, with high-ceilinged reception rooms on either side of the entrance hall, and large, comfortably furnished bedrooms. Good food is at the heart of their ethos, and interesting dinners showcasing local produce are offered, as well as an excellent breakfast. *Rooms 3. Residents' D Mon-Sat, 8pm (book by noon); non-residents welcome on Fri-Sat by reservation. "Closed occasionally," and D Sun; ring ahead off-season. CC.* **Directions:** *On A36, 1/2m from Larne Road roundabout.*

BUSHMILLS & NORTH ANTRIM COAST

Located six miles east of Portrush, known for its distillery and for excellent fishing on the River Bush, Bushmills is an ideal spot from which to tour the north Antrim coast. The world famous Old Bushmills Distillery (028 2073 1521, open all year) is the world's oldest licensed whiskey distillery having received its licence to distil in 1608 and is devoted to the production of single malt Irish whiskey. The north Antrim coast has much of interest to offer but its biggest visitor attraction by far is the extraordinary geological feature, the Giants Causeway, a World Heritage Site with spectacular cliffs and headlands faced with basalt columns; there is also a nature reserve, and the Causeway Visitor Centre (028 2073 1855), which explains the geology of the area. Carrick-a-Rede rope bridge (028 2076 9839, open March to October) is another must-see, which has spanned the 60ft gap between the mainland and Carrick a Rede island for at least 200 years. The north Antrim coast is also home to one of Ireland's most spectacularly sited castles, 14th century Dunluce Castle (028 207 31938, open March to October), perched on a rock stack connected to the mainland by a wooden bridge.

Bushmills Inn

9 Dunluce Rd. Bushmills Co Antrim BT57 8QG ✆*028 2073 3000 www.bushmillsinn.com*

Originally a 19th-century coaching inn, the traditional tone of Alan Dunlop's famously interesting and well run hotel is set by the turf fire and country furniture in the hall and traditional public rooms, including an atmospheric gas-lit bar and unique circular library. Bedrooms have individuality, with new ones furnished in a cottage style that works well with the original building. Known for its wholesome food, pride in Irish ingredients is seen in A Taste of Ulster menus that offer traditional dishes with a modern twist. A great base for playing the famous golf courses of the area (Royal Portrush is just 5 miles away) or exploring this beautiful coastline. *Rooms 41. Restaurant seats 110 (outdoors, 32). L&D daily; Day Menu 12-6.00; (Sun: carvery from 12.30-2.30pm and day menu to 6pm). Bar food Sun only 12-4. House closed 24/25 Dec. CC.*

 ## The French Rooms

45 Main Streeet Bushmills Co Antrim BT57 8QA
📞 *028 2073 0033 www.thefrenchrooms.com*

Opened at Easter 2013 by experienced host Roy Bolton, this is a slice of French ambience, very tastfully designed and providing interesting French style food at very affordable prices in a relaxed Rural French setting. Easily the most elegant and stylish restaurant on the Causeway Coast, and affordable. *Open Wed-Sun.*

  ## Causeway Hotel

Bushmills Area 40 Causeway Road Co Antrim BT57 8SU
📞 *028 2073 1210 / 2073 1226 www.giants-causeway-hotel.com*

Located beside the entrance to the Giant's Causeway and the new interpretative centre, this well-known hotel was recently acquired by the National Trust and refurbished. Although quite modest, the location is exceptional, front rooms have stunning coastal views, the staff are very friendly and the prices are moderate considering it's within walking distance of a World Heritage Site. One to consider when visiting the beautiful north Antrim coast. *Rooms 28. Directions: On the Causeway Coastal Route, between Bushmills & Dunseverick. CC.*

  ## Tartine at The Distillers Arms

140 Main Street Bushmills Co Antrim BT57 8QE 📞 *028 2073 1044 www.distillersarms.com*

In a stylishly renovated 18th century building which was once the home of the distillery owners, Gary Stewart's atmospheric bar and restaurant is a lovely mixture of old and new. Open stonework and a fireplace lend rustic charm to the restaurant, where there is likely to be a focus on seafood, possibly including local lobster and crab, although other dishes - Tamworth rare breed pork, for example - are of equal interest, and the cooking is consistently pleasing.

 ## Londonderry Arms Hotel

20 Harbour Road Carnlough Co Antrim BT44 0EU 📞 *028 2888 5255 www.glensofantrim.com*

Originally a coaching inn, this traditional hotel was formerly owned by Sir Winston Churchill and has been in the caring hands of the O'Neill family since 1948. Many of the comfortably furnished bedrooms have sea views and this is a place where you can still get a proper Ulster high tea, as well as good home-made bar meals or a fireside afternoon tea in the old-fashioned lounge. A delightful place in a lovely village. *Rooms 35. Closed 24-25 Dec. CC. Directions: On the A2 Antrim coast road.*

Clarion Hotel

75 Belfast Road Carrickfergus Co Antrim BT38 8BX ✆ *028 9336 4556 www.clarioncarrick.com*

Conveniently located near Belfast airport and the scenic attractions of the Antrim coast, this modern hotel makes a comfortable base for business and leisure visitors. **Rooms 68**. *Open all year except Christmas. CC.* **Directions:** *Main coast road.*

 Ballyrobin Country Lodge

144 - 146 Ballyrobin Road Aldergrove Crumlin Co Antrim BT29 4EG ✆ *028 9442 2211 www.ballyrobin.com*

Literally 2 minutes' drive from Belfast International Airport and nestled between fields of barley, this small family-owned hotel has at its heart a restored 200-year-old country house. Both traditional and modern rooms are offered, and a restaurant serving interesting, fairly priced food featuring many of Northern Ireland's top producers. A unique combination of old-fashioned charm and contemporary style and efficiency. **Rooms 21**. *Restaurant Mon-Sat 12-9pm (to 10pm Fri & Sat); Sun 12-8.30pm. CC.* **Directions:** *Belfast International Airport - 2 minutes from the main terminal building.*

 Dunadry Hotel & Country Club

2 Islandreagh Drive Dunadry Co Antrim BT41 2HA ✆ *028 9443 4343 www.dunadry.com*

This famous riverside hotel near Belfast International Airport was formerly a mill and, at its best, combines the character of the old buildings with the comfort and efficiency of a modern hotel. Rooms vary; the best, overlooking gardens, are spacious and stylish. Meals, including breakfast, are served in the Linen Mill Restaurant or the Mill Race Bistro, which overlooks the river. The lovely setting makes it a popular wedding venue. **Rooms 83**. *Closed 24-26 Dec. CC.* **Directions:** *Near Belfast airport.*

GLENARM

Glenarm (in Irish: Gleann Airm, i.e. Glen of the Army) is a village on the North Channel coast and a popular port of call for sailors (visitors are welcome at the marina). The first of the Nine Glens of Antrim, Glenarm claims to be the oldest town in Ulster, having been granted a charter in the 12th Century. Glenarm Castle, ancestral home of the Earls of Antrim, offers much of interest including The Walled Garden (open 10-6 daily, May-Sep), and delightful Tea Rooms.

 Glenarm Castle Tea Rooms

2 Castle Lane Glenarm Co Antrim BT44 0BQ ✆ *028 2884 1203 www.glenarmcastle.com*

March-September, Mon-Sat 10-5, Sun 11-5.

Glenarm Castle, ancestral home of the McDonnell family, Earls of Antrim, offers much of interest including The Walled Garden (open 10-6 daily, Easter-Sep). The Castle itself is also open several times a year. The Tea Room is a charming setup in the old Mushroom House overlooking the kitchen garden; they offer tasty snacks, including many organic ingredients, and cream teas - it makes a lovely stopping off place when touring on the coast road. Gift shop. *Open: Mar-Sep, Mon-Sat 10-4.30, Sun 11-4.30.*

Glenarm Organic Salmon

8 Castle Demesne Glenarm Co Antrim BT44 0BD
☎028 2884 1691 www.glenarmorganicsalmon.com

Based in the historic village of Glenarm since 1989, the Northern Salmon Company produces high quality Glenarm Organic Salmon in the fast flowing sea water off the Antrim coast and is the only Atlantic salmon producer in the Irish Sea. The salmon of choice for many top chefs, Glenarm Organic Salmon has achieved widespread recognition in Ireland and is successfully exported to discerning customers abroad, who appreciate its superior flavour and texture - and also support responsible and sustainable aquaculture.

 Lily Johnstons Bar & Kitchen

22 Main Street Glenavy Co Antrim BT29 4LW ☎028 9442 2467 www.lilyjohnstons.com

Located in the heart of Glenavy village, chef Paul Masterson's attractive pub/restaurant's origins go back to the 17th century and an open fire provides a timeless welcome. Bistro-style menus offer something for everyone and the food is simplicity at its best: quality ingredients cooked with flair, served with pride and fairly priced. A good place to be. *Open Mon-Sat 11.30am-1am, Sun 12.30-midnight. Food served: Mon-Sat 11.30-9.30 (8.30 in winter), Sun 12.30-8.30. CC. **Directions:** In the heart of Glenavy village.*

  Country Kitchen Home Bakery

57-59 Sloan Street Lisburn Co Antrim BT27 5AG
☎028 9267 1730 www.countrykitchenlisburn.co.uk

Freshness is guaranteed at Chris and Audrey Ferguson's home bakery, where the day starts at 3am for second generation baker Chris, who gets in first to start baking the breads and sodas, cakes, pastries and savouries needed for the day's orders, as well as for their own bakery and restaurant. Traditional specialities include Belfast baps, soda farls and potato bread - and the Ulster Fry made in the restaurant next door. *Bakery open: Mon-Sat 8.30-5. Restaurant Mon-Sat 8.30-3.*

 Del Toro

19 Antrim St Lisburn Co Antrim BT28 1AU ☎028 9266 8755 www.deltoro.co.uk

Anton Campbell's popular steakhouse and grill bar attracts a mix of young and not so young who enjoy the relaxed ambience and appreciate the simple tasty food, friendly service and good value offered. Specialities include tapas-style starters, sharing platters, 28-day dry-aged steaks, burgers and ribs. Al fresco dining is available on The Terrace in summer. *Seats 75 (outdoors, 15). Open daily, noon-9.30pm (to 8.30pm Sun). Closed 25-26 Dec, 12-13 Jul. CC.*

  Hilden Brewing Company

Hilden Lisburn Co Antrim BT27 4TY ☎028 9266 0800

Hilden Brewery is Ireland's oldest craft brewery, run by the Scullion family in the former stables of historic Hilden House. The brewery is now managed by Seamus and Ann's son, Owen, and currently produces 11 draught beers and five bottled beers. You can sample the craft beers, both in and with food, at the adjacent Tap Room Restaurant and other outlets including their atmospheric Belfast restaurant Molly's Yard (see entry). Tours and off sales available. *Restaurant: L Tue-Sun 12-3, D Tue-Sat, 5.30-9.*

Tempted Irish Craft Cider

2 Agars Road Lisburn Co Antrim BT28 2TQ ✆ *028 9262 1219 www.temptedcider.com*

Davy Uprichard makes Tempted? Irish Craft Cider from a blend of Co. Armagh dessert and Bramley apples using traditional farmhouse methods to produce a lightly carbonated pure juice cider. The cider is made in a purpose-built cidery at his home outside Lisburn and the business now involves the whole family.

 Bayview Hotel

2 Bayhead Road Portballintrae Bushmills Co Antrim BT57 8RZ
✆ *028 2073 4100 www.bayviewhotelni.com*

Convenient to the Giant's Causeway and the Bushmills Distillery, this smartly-maintained seafront hotel in the attractive village of Portballintrae offers a tranquil and reasonably priced base for exploring the area. Rooms include some superior ones with magnificent sea views but all are comfortable, spacious. Good food is served in the cosy bar and restaurant, notably steaks and local seafood. **Rooms 25**. *Open all year.* **Directions:** *On the seafront.*

 Sweeney's Public House & Wine Bar

Seaport Avenue Portballintrae Co Antrim BT57 8SB ✆ *028 2073 2405*

Formerly a coaching stable for the Leslie estate, Seymour Sweeney's sympathetically restored bar and restaurant is one of the oldest surviving domestic buildings in this attractive village and listed as being of architectural and historic significance. It's a useful place to break a drive - although the food is a bit hit and miss, the ambience is always pleasing and the open fire can be a very welcome sight on a chilly day. **Seats 120** *(+50 outside). Open daily 11am-midnight L&D daily, 12-3 & 5-9 (Sun to 8.30). CC.*

PORTRUSH

Portrush is a popular seaside holiday resort, golfing destination and a good base for exploring the beautiful Antrim coast. The main attractions - Bushmills Distillery, the Giant's Causeway, Carrick-a Rede rope bridge - are all nearby. A golfer's heaven, the three main golf courses in the area are Royal Portrush (028 7082 2311), Portstewart (028 7083 2015) and Castlerock Golf Clubs (028 7084 8314).

   **Maddybenny Farmhouse**

Loguestown Road Portrush Coleraine Co Antrim BT52 2PT
✆ *028 7082 3394 www.maddybenny.com*

An exceptionally hospitable place to stay, the White family's Plantation-era farmhouse dates back pre-1650 and has since been extended many times. It is very comfortable and relaxed, with plenty of seating areas, indoor and outdoor games areas for children, and even an equestrian centre on site. The bedrooms are all en-suite, with all sorts of thoughtful extras, and Karen White's breakfasts are legendary, so allow plenty of time to start the day with one of her feasts. Six excellent self-catering cottages are also offered. *Rooms 3* *(all shower only). Closed 25-26 Dec. CC.* **Directions:** *Signposted off A29 Portrush/Coleraine road.*

 Ramore Restaurants

1 The Harbour Road Portrush Co Antrim BT56 8BN
☎ 028 7082 6969 www.ramorerestaurants.co.uk

The Ramore was once the leading light of cosmopolitan fine dining in Northern Ireland. Today, George and Jane McAlpin offer a different style of hospitality where quality goes hand-in-hand with value, but what is not the Ramore Complex remains one of the region's most popular dining destinations. The Ramore Wine Bar, Coast Restaurant (Italian style) and The Harbour Bar make up the Complex; cooking is as good as ever, and service is quick and attentive. *Ramore Wine Bar* **Seats 300**. *L & D daily (Sun, 5-9). Coast Restaurant D Wed-Sun. Coast Italiano* **Seats 90**; *D Mon-Sat (Sun 3-9.30). Harbour Bistro D Wed-Sun. Closed Mon, Tue, Bank Hols, 24-26 Dec. CC.* **Directions:** *At the harbour in Portrush.*

 **Royal Court Hotel**

233 Ballybogey Rd Portrush Co Antrim BT56 8NF ☎ 028 7082 2236 www.royalcourthotel.co.uk

Set in a spectacular clifftop location near the Giant's Causeway, this is the most desirable sea view hotel accommodation in the area. The decor is dated, but it's comfortable and spacious; the best rooms are on the sea side and have private balconies, and all may enjoy views from the dining room at breakfast. A good base for touring and close to a number of golf links, it is also a popular wedding venue. *Rooms 18. Closed 26 Dec. CC.*

RATHLIN ISLAND

This island off the north-east corner of County Antrim is accessible by ferry from Ballycastle (details from Ballycastle Tourist Information Office 028 207 62024). Popular with walkers and birdwatchers, it is a Special Area of Conservation and home to vast colonies of seabirds; the RSPB Rathlin Island Seabird Centre (028 2076 0062; open early Apr-end Aug), is at the West Lighthouse. A shop offers basics for campers and picnics for visitors.

 **The Manor House**

Rathlin Island Co Antrim BT54 6RT ☎ 028 2076 3964 www.rathlinmanorhouse.co.uk

Now owned by the National Trust, this handsome late Georgian gentleman's house overlooking Church Bay dates back to the 1760s and offers interesting accommodation and a simple evening meal for residents. Every bedroom has a sea view and, although there is currently no licensed restaurant or bar facility, nearby businesses fill the gap. *Rooms 11. Residents' D by arrangement. Unlicensed. Establishment closed mid Oct-end Apr. CC.* **Directions:** *Ferry from Ballycastle twice daily Oct-May, and four times a day in summer.*

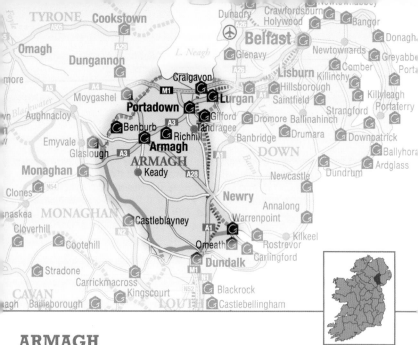

ARMAGH

Mention Armagh, and most people will think of apples and archbishops. In the more fertile northern part of the county, orchards are traditionally important in the local economy, with the lore of apple growing and their use a part of County Armagh life. And the pleasant cathedral city of Armagh itself is of course the ecclesiastical capital of all Ireland, and many a mitre is seen about it.

But in fact Armagh city's significance long pre-dates Christian times. Emhain Macha - Navan Fort- to the west of the town, was a royal stronghold and centre of civilisation more than 4,000 years ago. Marking the county's northern coastline, the inland freshwater sea of Lough Neagh provides sand for the construction industry, eels for gourmets, and recreational boating of all sorts. In times past, it was part of the route which brought coal to Dublin from the mines in Coalisland in Tyrone, the main link to the seaport of Newry being the canal from Portadown which, when opened in 1742, was in the forefront of canal technology.

That County Armagh was a leader in canal technology is only one of its many surprises. The discerning traveller will find much of interest, among the undulating farmland and orchards, the pretty villages, or the handsome uplands rising to Carrigatuke above Newtownhamilton, and on towards the fine peak of Slieve Gullion in the south of the county, down to Forkhill and Crossmaglen and the Gaelic football heartlands.

LOCAL ATTRACTIONS & INFORMATION

▸ **Planetarium** Armagh
  028 37 523689
▸ **Astronomical Observatory**
  Armagh *028 37 522928*
▸ **Palace Stables Heritage Centre** Armagh
  028 37 529629

▸ **St Patrick's Trian Visitor Centre** Armagh
  028 37 521801
▸ **Ti chulainn Cultural Centre**
  Forkhill (Slieve Gullion)
  028 30 888828

▸ **Discovery Centre** Oxford
  Island Lough Neagh
  028 38 322205
▸ **The Argory** (NT Mansion)
  Moy *028 87 784753*

ARMAGH CITY

Elegant Georgian buildings surround this city's impressive oval tree lined mall; turn any corner and you will see superb examples of Georgian terraced houses. Ireland's religious centre for 1,500 years and the seat of both Protestant and Catholic Archbishops, the city of Armagh predates Canterbury as a Christian religious site. Armagh was also the legendary seat of the Celtic Kings of Ulster. Local visitor attractions include the Armagh Cathedral, St Patrick's Anglican Church, the county museum (028 3752 3070, open all year), the Armagh Observatory (028 37 522928), and Palace Stables Heritage Centre (028 3752 1801, open all year) and the impressive Armagh Planetarium (028 3752 3689). Other places of interest in the area include the Navan Centre and Fort (028 3752 1801), which allows visitors to discover the archaeology and mythology of the area, or the Benburb Valley Heritage Centre (028 3754 9885, open March to September), which houses a former linen mill and collection of machinery used in linen making. Nearby Carnagh Forest (028 3755 1277) has many picturesque walking trails, with fishing lakes and an angler's inn.

 **Armagh City Hotel**

2 Friary Road Armagh Co Armagh BT60 4FR ☎028 3751 8888 www.armaghcityhotel.com

This functional hotel contributes welcome facilities to the area, and is home to Northern Ireland's largest hotel conference facility. Practical bedrooms should suit business guests, and there are pleasant landscaped gardens at the back. **Rooms 82.** *Closed 24-26 Dec. CC.*

 The Moody Boar

Palace Stables Palace Demesne Armagh Co Armagh BT60 4EL
☎028 3752 9678 www.themoodyboar.com

The picturesque Palace Stables Heritage Centre in Armagh city provides a great setting for Sean and Ramune Farnan's delicious food based on their holistic philosophy for 'sustainability, value, local produce and, most of all, flavour'. Original, unpretentious, tasty and fresh - and obviously cooked by one who loves food - a meal here is also very good value. We couldn't recommend it more highly. *Mon & Tue 10-4.30, Wed-Sat 10-9.30, Sun 12-8.30. CC.*

 Uluru

16-18 Market Street Armagh Co Armagh BT61 7BX ☎028 3751 8051 www.ulurubistro.com

Uluru claims to be Northern Ireland's only Australian restaurant and chef Dean Coppard, originally from Queensland, has created an adventurous menu which, with the exception of exotics, is based mainly on local and home grown produce. This popular restaurant has earned a reputation for good food using locally sourced seasonal produce served in an informal environment at reasonable prices. *L&D Tue-Sat 12-3pm & 5-late, Sun D only, 4-late. Closed Mon. CC.*

  Ballydougan Pottery Restaurant & Coffee Lounge

Bloomvale House 171 Plantation Road Gilford Craigavon Co Armagh BT63 5NN
☎028 3834 2201 www.ballydouganpottery.co.uk

With its traditional stonework and thatched roof, Ballydougan Pottery is a charming destination serving home-cooked food based on local produce and served on their own pottery. There's an excellent selection of scones, tray bakes, gateaux, pies, pavlovas, cheese and cakes, with heartier meals available at lunchtime, including vegetarian options. **Seats 125.** *Open Mon-Sat,*

9am-5pm (L 12-3pm). Shop; pottery classes. Closed Sun, 25 Dec - 2 Jan, 12/13 Jul, Easter Mon & Tue. CC. **Directions:** *Southeast of Craigavon on B3 Gilford Road (A50 end).*

Clanconnel Brewing Company

PO Box 316 Craigavon Co Armagh BT65 9AZ ✆*07711 626 770 www.clanconnelbrewing.com*

Clanconnel Brewing Company is Northern Ireland's newest microbrewery, committed to producing only natural, high-quality, handcrafted beers. They currently produce four beers: Weavers Gold, a blonde ale; McGrath's Irish Red, a traditional red ale; McGrath's Irish Black, a dry stout; and McGrath's Irish Blonde Ale.

Newforge House

58 Newforge Road Magheralin Craigavon Co Armagh BT67 0QL
✆*028 9261 1255 www.newforgehouse.com*

In the Mathers family for six generations, John and Louise Mathers's lovely Georgian country house is only a short drive from Belfast yet, set in mature trees, gardens and green fields, it feels like worlds away. Stylishly furnished throughout, it offers luxurious accommodation in individually decorated rooms with beautiful bathrooms. John's meals showcase local and organic produce and hens clucking around the orchard provide your breakfast eggs. It's a lovely spot for a short break and makes a perfect setting for special occasions. **Rooms 6** *(1 shower only). Dining Room* **seats 22**. *D daily 7-8.30 (to 9 Fri/Sat); Sun & Mon light dinner only. Closed 24 Dec - 8 Jan. CC.* **Directions:** *M1 from Belfast to Craigavon until junction for A3 to Moira; through Moira to Magheralin then turn left at Byrnes Pub (on the corner) onto Newforge Road and look out for signs.*

Mac's Armagh Cider

Leamhchoill Forest Road Forkhill Co Armagh BT35 9SA

Founded in 1995, Mac's Armagh Cider is the focal point of the Armagh 'revivalist' cider movement. Using only traditional cider techniques and local fruit, Mac's produces three ciders: Mac's Dry Cider, Mac's Sweet Cider and Mac's Lyte.

The Pot Belly Restaurant

59 Banbridge Road Tullylish Gilford Co Armagh BT63 6DL
✆*028 3883 1404 www.potbellyrestaurant.co.uk*

This charming rural restaurant in a converted linen mill is a hidden treasure. Fresh local produce, often free-range and organic (and named on the menu), is stylishly served from a tempting selection. Service is quick and efficient and staff are friendly, making for a relaxed and homely atmosphere and good value for money too - the lunch and early dinner menus are especially keenly priced. **Seats 90** *(outdoors, 20); open daily L&D. Closed 25 Dec. CC.* **Directions:** *Adjacent to Tullylish pottery outside the village of Gilford.*

John R Dowey

20 High Street Lurgan Co Armagh BT66 8AW ✆028 3832 2547 www.johnrdowey.co.uk

Established in 1936, butchers John Dowey and his son Simon now offer a successful balance of tradition and innovation – and have plenty of accolades to prove it. Known especially for traditional cuts of beef and prize-winning sausages, they make all their own butchery products and sell carefully selected deli products and speciality foods. Their popular coffee shop offers quality teas and coffees, some great home bakes and a light lunch menu. *Open Mon-Sat 8.30-5.30, Thu to 8.30. (Coffee shop closes 5pm). Closed Sun.*

PORTADOWN

The building of the canal from Newry to Lough Neagh in the 1730s brought wealth to Portadown, which grew with the linen industry and today has developed into a busy commercial centre. The town has a wide sloping main street and more than a dozen denominations have built churches and chapels in one small area. Local attractions include the Brackagh Moss Nature Reserve (028 3885 1102) which was originally a raised bog with a wide range of flora and fauna. Golfers will enjoy a round at Portadown Golf Course (028 3835 5356).

  ### Armagh Cider Company

Ballinteggart House Drumnasoo Road Portadown Co Armagh BT62 4EX ✆028 3833 4268 www.armaghcider.com

Armagh Cider Company is owned by fourth-generation apple growers Philip and Helen Troughton, whose family has been growing apples since 1898. They produce two ciders: Carsons Crisp Armagh Cider, a traditional cider, and Maddens Mellow Armagh Cider, a slightly sweeter cider. They also produce pure apple juice, a non-alcoholic apple punch and cider vinegar. *Hours: Mon-Fri 9-5.*

 ### Barnhill Apple Juice

23 Drumanphy Road Portadown Co Armagh BT62 1QX ✆028 3885 1190

Ken Redmond's family has been growing fruit at Barnhill Farm for over a century. Barnhill apple juice is a delicious blend of traditional varieties grown, harvested and pressed on the family farm, and the naturally cloudy apple juice is made directly from whole fruit, with no additives except, in the flavoured varieties, other whole fruit. Available direct from the farm and from St George's Market in Belfast, agricultural shows, craft fairs, farmers markets and selected shops.

  ### Mac Ivors Cider Co.

c/o MacNeice Fruit Ltd Ardress East Portadown Co Armagh BT62 1SQ ✆028 3885 1381 www.macivors.com

Mac Ivors is a handcrafted cider made from apples grown on a family orchard in Co. Armagh. Greg MacNeice has created two distinct ciders, Mac Ivors Medium and Mac Ivors Traditional Dry, using 100% fresh-pressed apples and cold-fermenting yeast to preserve the aroma. Check the website for a list of stockists throughout Ireland, both North and South.

Toby's Handcrafted Cider

Portadown Co Armagh BT62 1AJ 📞*079 7475 5554 www.TobysCider.co.uk*

Craig and Karen had been making cider for friends and family for years before they started to sell it to the public. Toby's Handcrafted Cider is made from apples grown within walking distance of the farm and is a completely natural product, with no artificial sweeteners, preservatives or concentrates used. A percentage from every bottle of Toby's Handcrafted Armagh Cider sold is donated to charity.

 Yellow Door Deli, Bakery & Café

74 Woodhouse Street Portadown Co Armagh BT62 1JL
📞*028 3835 3528 www.yellowdoordeli.co.uk*

Simon Dougan's Yellow door food is all local and homemade and his in-house bakery produces some of the finest bread in Northern Ireland. The deli also carries a selection of specialty foods, from Ireland and abroad; the wide range of in-house products supplies the shops and outside catering. Customers from all over the North home in on this smashing shop to top up with goodies and have a bite of lunch. *Café **seats 75**. Breakfast from 9am, L 12-2.45pm, otherwise food from deli all day until 5pm. Closed Mon, 12-13 Jul, 25-26 Dec, "some" Bank Hols. CC.*
Directions: *Off Main St. on left - only street on left as the traffic flows one way.*

  Forthill Farm

80 Ballymore Road Tandragee Co Armagh BT62 2JY 📞*028 3884 9754 www.forthillfarm.co.uk*

Visitors are welcome to Kenny and Jennifer Gracey's farm (phone to make sure somebody is available to show you around). Their rare breed pork (Gloucester Old Spot and Saddleback) and beef (Longhorn and Belted Galloway) are on sale at their farm shop. They are supporters of the Open Farm Weekend scheme, which aims to connect consumers with farmers, producers, processors and nature (www.openfarmweekend.com).

DOWN

County Down rings the changes in elegant style, from its affluent shoreline along Belfast Lough - the "Gold Coast" - through the rolling drumlin country which provides Strangford Lough's many islands, and on then past the uplands around Slieve Croob, with the view southward being increasingly dominated by the purple slopes of the Mountains of Mourne.

The Mournes soar to Northern Ireland's highest peak of Slieve Donard (850m), and provide excellent hill-walking and challenging climbing. When seen across Down's patchwork of prosperous farmland, however, they have a gentleness which is in keeping with the county's well-groomed style. In the same vein, Down is home to some of Ireland's finest gardens, notably Mount Stewart on the eastern shore of Strangford Lough, and Rowallane at Saintfield, while the selection of forest and country parks is also exceptional.

The coastline is much-indented, so much so that when measured in detail, County Down provides more than half of Northern Ireland's entire shoreline. Within it, the jewel of Strangford Lough is an unmatched attraction for naturalists and boat enthusiasts, while Portaferry has one of Ireland's longest-established saltwater aquariums in Exploris.

In the south of the county, the increasingly prosperous town of Newry on the river inland from Carlingford Lough is - with Lisburn in County Antrim - one of Ireland's two newest cities under a re-designation of 2003. Newry is responding with enthusiasm to its enhanced status, and the urban regeneration of this interesting canalside centre is intriguing to watch., while the Ship Canal down to the sea has been restored and was re-opened in 2006.

LOCAL ATTRACTIONS & INFORMATION

‣ **Castle Espie Wildfowl and Wetlands Centre**
Cultra
028 91 874146

‣ **Ulster Folk & Transport Museum** Cultra
028 90 428428

‣ **St Patrick Centre**
Downpatrick
028 44 619000

‣ **Hillsborough Castle Gardens**
Hillsborough
028 92 681300

‣ **Ballycopeland Windmill**
Millisle *028 91 861413*

‣ **Bronte Interpretive Centre**
Rathfriland *028 40 631152*

501

Curran's Bar & Seafood Steakhouse

83 Strangford Road Chapeltown Ardglass Co Down BT30 7SB
028 4484 1332 www.curransbar.net

Originally the Curran family home, this popular and atmospheric establishment dates back to 1791 and has earned a reputation as a food destination under the guidance of Paula Mahon. Seafood has always played a central role here, but there's also great steak - prime sirloin or fillet from local butchers - a daily roast dinner, homemade steak burger and much more. Children are also well catered for. *Seats 100 (outdoors, 44). Food 7 days, 12.30-9pm. Closed 25 Dec. CC. **Directions:** Main road between Ardglass (2 miles) and Strangford (6 miles).*

East Coast Seafoods

7-11 Killard Drive Ballyhornan Co Down BT30 7PN
028 4484 1196 www.eastcoastseafoods.co.uk

Since 1989 Marty Johnston's small family business near Ardglass has supplied seafood to leading chefs in the region. They are best known for local crab and smoked salmon, also langoustine ('scampi'/Dublin Bay prawns) and white fish landed at Ardglass; several of their smoked products have achieved Great Taste Awards recognition. Sometimes listed on menus as 'Marty Johnston' or 'Ballyhornan' without further explanation. Available from the premises in Ballyhornan; Makro, Belfast; www.buynifood.com.

The Bronte Steakhouse

69 Ballynafoy Road Banbridge Co Down BT32 5DN
028 4065 1338 www.brontesteakhouse.com

This attractive pub and restaurant is an ideal destination for anyone wishing to combine traditional dining in an informal setting with a little literary history. There's a wide range of popular, traditional dishes offered and many are based on locally sourced ingredients, but of course many people travel here especially for the steaks. *Mon-Thu 5.30-9pm; Fri & Sat 12-3 & 5.30-9; Sun 1-7.30pm. CC. **Directions:** 5 miles southeast of Banbridge off B3 Grovehill Road at Derrydrumuck.*

Greenbean Coffee Roasters

11 Townsend Street Banbridge Co Down BT32 3LF
028 4062 9096 www.greenbeanroasters.com

While top quality coffee is their specialty, renowned coffee roasters Deirdre and Pat Grant also offer unfussy, homely food, including breakfast and lunch specials like quiches, soups, salads, sandwiches and pastas as well as homemade desserts and sweet and savoury pastries. This reasonably priced gem is the perfect spot for a brunch, lunch, snack or caffeine hit. *Open Mon&Tue 9am-4pm; Wed-Sat 9am-5pm. Closed Sun.Online shop (trade and consumer). CC. **Directions:** Centre of Banbridge town.*

   Quails at the Gallery

200 Newry Road Banbridge Co Down BT32 3NB *028 4062 9667 www.quailsfinefoods.co.uk*

Everyone who visits the gallery praises the café and here you can enjoy a pleasant lunch here looking out through big glass walls into the sculpture garden. Operated by Joe Quail, who has a butcher's shop and café in the town, this excellent family-run food hall and deli serves breakfast and lunch as well as lots of scones, muffins, tray bakes and luscious desserts. **Seats 50**; Café Mon-Sat, 9-5; 11-5. Closed 25/6 Dec, 1 Jan, Easter Sun. Online shop. CC. **Directions:** Junction for Banbridge & Bridgewater Park (M1).

  Simply Deanes

Unit 1 The Outlet Bridgewater Park Banbridge Co Down BT32 4GJ
✆028 4062 7220 www.michaeldeane.co.uk

Useful to have in mind when travelling, this outpost of Michael Deane's Belfast empire is just outside Banbridge, at The Outlet discount designer centre ('the ultimate shopping destination'). A carefully constructed all-day menu and daily blackboard specials offer everything from snacks and salads to sandwiches to go. Open: 9.30am-5pm (to 8pm Thu). Closed Easter Sun, 25 Dec. CC. **Directions:** Well-signed on the main Dublin-Belfast road.

 **Windsor Bakery & Café**

36-38 Newry Street Banbridge Co Down BT32 3HA
✆028 4062 3666 www.thewindsorbakery.com

Craft bakers since 1957, the current master baker at this esteemed business, John Edwards, maintains the tradition of using the best ingredients for the homemade breads, cakes, buns and biscuits on sale in the shop and served in the café. An outside catering service is also offered. Open Mon-Sat, 7.30-5.30. Closed Sun.

BANGOR

A thriving shopping town and popular seaside resort easily accessible from Belfast, Bangor has a three mile seafront with extensive promenades, and a large municipal marina. Apart from water based activities such as sailing and fishing, it is garden lovers who are spoilt for choice in this area; Mountstewart House & Gardens (Newtownards, 028 4278 8387) is the big attraction, see tourist offices/NITB website for current list of gardens open. The treat for golfers, of course, is the famous seaside fairways of The Royal Belfast Golf Club (Craigavad, 028 9042 8165).

 **The Boathouse**

1a Seacliff Road Bangor Co Down BT20 5HA ✆028 9146 9253 www.theboathouseni.co.uk

Run by Dutch brothers Joery and Jasper Castel, who believe that good food (and wine) should be accessible to all regardless of budget, this restaurant reflects that philosophy and is full of character and charm. Menus also reflect chef Joery's upbringing in Holland and his respect for fresh, local produce, especially seafood. The emphasis is on great flavour and appealing combinations of colour and texture. You'll come away from a meal here licking your lips and wondering how soon you can get back. **Seats 38** (outdoors, 8). L&D Wed-Sat; Sun 1-9pm. Closed Mon & Tue. CC. **Directions:** On harbour front in Bangor.

Cairn Bay Lodge

278 Seacliff Road Bangor Co Down BT20 5HS ✆028 9146 7636 www.cairnbaylodge.com

An attractive, detached house overlooking Ballyholme Bay in Bangor and set in extensive gardens, Chris and Jenny Mullen's friendly guesthouse is a pleasant base in a desirable area of this popular seaside town. A large yet cosy house dating back to 1914, Cairn Bay Lodge is full of character and its numerous USPs include a lovely back garden, treatments, a little gift shop - and an excellent breakfast. **Rooms 7** *(all shower only). Closed 3 weeks in Feb. CC.* **Directions:** *Seacliff Road.*

  ## Clandeboye Estate Yoghurt

Bangor Co Down BT19 1RN 📞 *028 9185 2966* *www.clandeboye.co.uk*

Lady Dufferin is proud of her pedigree Holstein and Jersey cows, and so she should be, as it's the rich milk they produce that makes Northern Ireland's first artisan cows' milk yoghurt so special. Available in natural and Greek styles, which taste wonderful on their own or with fresh berries and can be used as a recipe ingredient, and in three delicious flavours, Toffee Caramel, Strawberry and Raspberry. Buy from estate dairy (beside Clandeboye Lodge Hotel); may also see milking here. Retailed throughout Northern Ireland.

  ## Corin Restaurant

119 High Street Bangor Co Down BT20 5BD 📞 *028 9122 7295* *www.corinrestaurant.co.uk*

Philip McCrea, the owner-chef of this appealing modern restaurant in the centre of Bangor, is a medical consultant in 'real life' with a busy practice in nearby Holywood, but inside that doctor of some thirty years there was a chef waiting to get out. And, following a three month stint at Dublin's Cooks Academy, the dream became reality. In spring 2013, Corin was born - and the accomplished modern French cooking, professionalism, relaxed ambience and fair prices made it an instant success. *D Wed-Sat, Sun reservations only.*

 ## Coyles Bistro

44 High Street Bangor Co Down BT20 5AZ 📞 *028 9127 0362* *www.coylesbistro.co.uk*

Just two minutes' walk from Bangor marina, this is a bustling, long-established bar and bistro serving skilfully prepared well-sourced food, often using organic ingredients. A good balance of generous, reasonably priced dishes is offered in a variety of styles, from upbeat traditional to international, including appealing vegetarian and low-fat options. *Restaurant D Tue-Sun; Bistro daily 11am-9pm. Music. CC.* **Directions:** *Two minutes walk from Bangor Marina.*

  ## David Burns Butchers

112 Abbey Street Bangor Co Down BT20 4JB 📞 *028 9127 0073* *www.burnsbutchers.co.uk*

Now run by Brian, son of the late David Burns, these popular family butchers take pride in offering the best local meats: beef matured for 4 to 5 weeks, 10-day matured Ards Peninsula lamb, prize sausages, dry-cured bacon, George's home-cooked ham and many other traditional and innovative prepared foods, including that Northern Ireland specialty, the vegetable roll. *Open Tue-Thu 7am-5pm, Fri 6am-7pm, Sat 6am-5pm. Closed Sun & Mon.* **Directions:** *Off the A2 - on the left as you come into Bangor from the dual carriageway from Belfast.*

  ## The Heatherlea

94-96 Main Street Bangor Co Down BT20 4AG 📞 *028 9112 3456* *www.theheatherlea.com*

Right on Bangor's main street, this inviting bakery, tea room/coffee shop, restaurant and deli is an institution in the town. Famous for its home baking, there's a wide selection of good things offered and also a hearty lunch. For those who don't have time to stop, there's plenty of choice at the takeaway bakery and deli counter, including local specialities – try the rich fruit loaf. *Mon-Sat 8.30am-5pm. Closed Sun. 25 & 26 Dec, 1 Jan, Easter Mon/Tue, May Day, 12/13 Jul.* **Directions:** *Centre of Bangor.*

 **Marine Court Hotel**

18-20 Quay Street Bangor Co Down BT20 5ED ☎028 9145 1100 www.marinecourthotel.net

Although it overlooks the marina views from this hotel are restricted, and good leisure facilities are its greatest asset. While a few bedrooms are on the front, most overlook (neatly maintained) service areas; however all are practical, with comfortable beds. But the bright first floor restaurant commands the best view, and this is where a good breakfast is served by delightful staff, starting the day on a high. **Rooms 51.** *Closed 25 Dec. CC.* **Directions:** *Harbour front.*

Primacy Meats Food Village

26a Primacy Road (off Balloo Road) Bangor Co Down BT19 7PQ ☎028 9127 0083 www.primacymeatsfoodvillage.co.uk

Originally a butchers providing a direct outlet for meats from the Bowman family's farm, this is now a busy one-stop farm shop offering local, seasonal vegetables, home bakery and ready meals as well as the meats that made their name. Their own-farm products are augmented by produce from other local farmers and artisan suppliers. There's also an all-day café and a gift shop. *Open Mon-Fri 8-5.30, Sat, 8-5. Coffee shop (B'fast 9.30-11.30, L 12-3,also snacks). Closed Sun.* **Directions:** *Behind Bloomfield SC (A2 S Circular Road), off Balloo Road.*

The Salty Dog Hotel & Bistro

10-12 Seacliff Road Bangor Co Down BT20 5EY ☎028 9127 0696 www.thesaltydoghotel.com

This small hotel is in a choice corner location overlooking Belfast Lough and Bangor Marina. Rooms vary, but most have sea views and it's a pleasant place to stay that's handy to the town but also within an easy waterside stroll of the attractive Ballyholme area. In the restaurant - where a very good breakfast is served - creative menus featuring local produce are offered throughout the day. A great casual dining destination. **Rooms 15.** *Restaurant* **seats 80** *(outdoors, 20). L&D daily. CC.* **Directions:** *Right along seafront in Bangor.*

Teddys

1 Castle Street Bangor Co Down BT20 4SO ☎028 9124 1130 www.teddysofbangor.com

Although a little off the beaten track, this friendly and reliable place is a hit with locals and visitors. Comprising a pub and wine bar as well as the contemporary restaurant, it's designed to offer something for everyone; local provenance is a priority and fish cooking is particularly good. Menus offered include an all-day à la carte with lunchtime specials and several imaginative vegetarian choices. *Open daily from noon, to 11pm Sun-Wed, 12 Thu, 1am Fri/Sat. CC.* **Directions:** *Castle Street is off the bottom of Main Street.*

Clandeboye Lodge Hotel

Bangor Area 10 Estate Road Clandeboye Bangor Co Down BT19 1UR ☎028 9185 2500 www.clandeboyelodge.com

Quietly set in woodland on the edge of the Clandeboye estate, this comfortable, modern hotel just outside Bangor offers a pleasing alternative to the town; it is a popular wedding venue and convenient to Belfast for business guests. The spacious, modern bedrooms have ample work space, and suites have whirlpool baths. Meals are served in the lobby bar and the adjoining Clanbrasserie restaurant - a pleasant place to eat after a long day, breakfast is also served here. *Rooms 43*. *Closed 24-26 Dec. CC.* **Directions:** *On outskirts of Bangor off A2.*

Anna's House

35 Lisbarnett Road Comber Newtownards Co Down BT23 6 AW
028 9754 1566 www.annashouse.com

Anna and Ken Johnson's charming house near Strangford Lough looks over their 10-acre wildfowl lake to the rolling north Down countryside and their own garden, developed over 30 years. Accommodation is simple and tastefully cottagey; two rooms have balconies and a splendid music room is available to all. Breakfast includes treats like organic porridge with Irish Mist and smoked salmon omelettes. *Rooms 4 (2 shower only). Closed Christmas & New Year. CC.* **Directions:** *A22 from Comber to Lisbane, follow the brown B&B signs.*

Mash Direct

81 Ballyrainey Road Comber Co Down BT23 5JU 028 918 78316 www.mashdirect.com

Mash Direct started out like many Irish food businesses: in a home kitchen. Martin and Tracy Hamilton, fifth-generation farmers, were looking for ways to add value to the crops they grew. Tracy started making champ and selling it at a local market and it took off to where they are today, with over 100 employees and their quick-serve mashed potato and vegetable products are sold throughout Ireland and abroad - and all from the factory located directly on their farm. An extraordinary success story.

The Old Post Office Tea Rooms & Gallery

191 Killinchy Road Lisbane Comber Co Down BT23 6AA
028 9754 3335 www.oldpostofficelisbane.co.uk

Here in the village of Lisbane, close to the shores of Strangford Lough, one of County Down's prettiest little treasures is to be found at the thatch-roofed Old Post Office, which dates back to the 1840's. Now home to Trevor and Alison Smylie's tea rooms and gift shop, breakfast, teas, coffees, light snacks, and a wholesome lunch are all served here, and a take-away service is available too. Trevor has years of experience as a baker and pastry chef in Australia and the U.K. under his belt, and his mouth watering scones, gateaux, pies and tarts are now enjoyed in these three atmospheric tea rooms, each with its own cosy peat fire. A delight. *Seats 70 (outdoors, 35). Open Mon-Sat 9am-4.30pm. Gift shop. Closed Sun & Bank Hols, 25-26 Dec, 1 Jan, Eater Mon. CC.* **Directions:** *Lisbane is south of Comber on A22.*

 **The Old Schoolhouse Inn**

100 Ballydrain Road Castle Espie Comber Co Down BT23 6EA
☎028 9754 1182 www.theoldschoolhouseinn.com

Near the shores of Strangford Lough, the Old Schoolhouse Inn is one of the North's hidden gems. Returning chef Will Brown brought back his considerable talent and a combination of classic and modern kitchen skills to transform this long established family business to a place of old school charm and vibrant contemporary cooking. Given the quality of the food, skilful cooking and attention to detail, it offers real value - and genuine hospitality from the well-trained staff in both restaurant and accommodation make it a memorable experience. *Restaurant **seats 85**. D Thu-Sat. **Rooms 8**. Self Catering also available. Open all year. CC.* **Directions:** *Well signed from Comber village - 3 miles south, 1 mile past Castle Espie on left.*

 **The Old Inn**

11-15 Main Street Crawfordsburn Co Down BT19 1JH ☎028 9185 3255 www.theoldinn.com

The pretty village setting of this famous and hospitable 16th century inn - the oldest in continuous use in all Ireland - belies its convenient location close to Belfast. A welcoming fire and friendly staff in the cosy reception area set the tone for the whole hotel, which is full of charm, very comfortable - and always well presented. It is a popular dining destination too, offering pleasing cooking at the comfortably smart Lewis Restaurant, named after author C. S. Lewis, and in The Parlour. *****Rooms 31**. Lewis **Seats 124** (outdoors, 50). The Sizzler' Mon-Fri 3-6. D Mon-Sat 7-9.30 (Sun 6-9): D for 2 incl wine £52.50, also à la carte. Sun L 12-3pm. Parlour Daytime Menu Mon-Sat 12-7pm (Sun 12-9). Closed 25 Dec. CC.* **Directions:** *Off A2 Belfast-Bangor, 6 miles after Holywood (exit B20 for Crawfordsburn).*

DONAGHADEE

A charming seaside town on the County Down coast, about five miles south east of Bangor and 18 miles from Belfast, Donaghadee is best known for its attractive little harbour and lighthouse. According to the Guinness Book of Records, Grace Neills (see entry) claims to be Ireland's oldest public house, opened in 1611 as the 'King's Arms'. The many places of interest to visit in the area include some wonderful gardens, notably Mountstewart House & Gardens (Newtownards, 028 4278 8387); a current list of gardens open is available from Tourist Information Offices. For golfers, the famous waterside fairways of the nearby Royal Belfast Golf Club (Craigavad, 028 9042 8165) beckon.

 The Governor Rocks

27 The Parade Donaghadee Co Down BT21 0HE
☎028 9188 4817 www.thegovernorrocks.com

An outpost of the well known Belfast city centre restaurant CoCo, Jason Moore's friendly shabby chic bistro offers great fish cooking at a great price. Very reasonable flat rates for most of the almost exclusively seafood starters and main courses make for happy punters, as does the BYO policy with modest corkage. Lobster is served matter-of-factly with garlic butter, salad and chips (half/whole, £12.50/21.50). A popular destination for seafood lovers. *Open L&D Mon-Sat, Sun 12-9.30. BYO (corkage £3 for wine, 50p for beer; off-licence nearby). No CC.*

Grace Neill's

33 High Street Donaghadee Co Down BT21 0AH ☎ *028 9188 4595 www.graceneills.com*

Dating back to 1611, Grace Neill's lays a fair claim to be one of the oldest inns in all of Ireland. The front bar is one of Ireland's best-loved pubs and would always be on the must-visit list for visitors to Donaghadee. There's also an informal restaurant at the back of the pub, serving easygoing food in a relaxed atmosphere. **Seats 80**. *L & D daily, Fri-Sun 12-9.30pm (12.30-8 Sun). Closed 25 Dec. CC.* **Directions:** *Centre of Donaghadee.*

Pier 36

36 The Parade Donaghadee Co Down BT21 0HE ☎ *028 9188 4466 www.pier36.co.uk*

A pub of character beside a picturesque harbour, the Waterworth family's lively, warmly traditional yet updated place has a welcoming fire in winter, a good buzz, friendly staff - and great food. Seafood lovers will enjoy treats like fresh Portavogie prawns, hand dived Copeland Island scallops and comforting Pier 36 fish pie - but their dry-aged locally reared beef, which is hung and butchered on site, makes it a meat lovers destination too. *Open: Sun-Thu 11.30am-11pm (Fri & Sat to 1am).* **Rooms 7** *(some shower only).*

Crossgar Foodservice

37A Farranfad Road Downpatrick Co Down BT30 8NH ☎ *028 4481 1500 www.crossgar.ie*

Wholesale suppliers well worth knowing about, and used by top chefs. As well as offering plenty of 'ordinary' products in their vast range (over 10,000 products), there are gems, especially in the Crossgar Provenance Collection, which includes dry-aged Dexter and Irish Moiled cattle in its beef range and local Lissara Farm free-range duck among the poultry. Look out for the Crossgar Provenance Collection on menus, it's a sure sign of a caring chef.

Denvirs

14 English Street Downpatrick Co Down BT30 6AB ☎ *028 4461 2012*

What a charmer this ancient place is. Established in 1642, it's a wonderful pub with two old bars and an interesting and genuinely old world, informal restaurant. Accommodation is offered in six simply furnished rooms, which most guests will see as charmingly updated. Good food and genuinely friendly service too. Go and see it – there can't be another place in Ireland quite like it. **Seats 40**. *Mon-Sat 12-8.15 (to 9.15 Fri/Sat), Sun 12-7.45pm. L daily & D Mon-Fri.* **Rooms 6**. *Closed 25 Dec. CC.* **Directions:** *On same street as Cathedral and Courthouse.*

Dunnanelly Country House

26 Rocks Chapel Road Crossgar Downpatrick Co Down BT30 9BA
☎ *077 1277 9085 www.dunnanellycountryhouse.com*

Idyllically set in gardens, fields and woodland, with views of the Mountains of Mourne to the south, this gorgeous house is just three miles from Downpatrick and would make a wonderful base for experiencing the St Patrick Story and exploring this beautiful county. Here Sally King, her husband and guests can enjoy all the benefits of a Georgian house with the comfort of mod cons too. The rooms are beautifully furnished with great attention to detail and every comfort you could wish for. The Kings also take pride in sourcing the best local products for breakfast, and Sally's jams are made with home-grown fruit. An absolute gem. **Rooms 3**. *Closed Christmas and occasionally at other times. CC.* **Directions:** *1/2 mile off A7 between Crossgar and Downpatrick.*

The Mill At Ballydugan

Drumcullen Road Ballydugan Downpatrick Co Down BT30 8HZ
℘028 4461 3654 www.ballyduganmill.com

Hidden away in rolling County Down countryside just outside Downpatrick, the site of this 18th century flour mill is very atmospheric: looking out onto ruined stone outbuildings, it is almost like being in a medieval castle courtyard. It is extremely popular as a wedding venue, but you don't have to be a wedding guest to use the simply furnished rooms, and rhe café and restaurant are open to non-residents. **Rooms 16** *(3 shower only). Restaurant* **seats 50**. *CC.* **Directions:** *Downpatrick enroute to Newcastle past race course take first right hand turn and follow road to the Mill.*

  Pheasants Hill Farm

37 Killyleagh Road Downpatrick Co Down BT30 9BL ℘028 4461 7246 www.pheasantshill.com

Janis and Alan Baily's home was a small Ulster farmstead for over 165 years until it was rebuilt in the mid-'90s - and is now a comfortable country house on a seven-acre organic small-holding within sight of the Mourne Mountains. They grow fruit using natural methods, rear the rare breed animals for which they are renowned and operate one of Norther Ireland's best farm shops. *Farm Shop open Mon-Sat 10-6. Also at St Georges Market, Belfast. Online shop. CC.* **Directions:** *On A22, 2.5m north of Downpatrick, 2.5m south of Killyleagh.*

  Abernethy Butter Company

Beechtree Farm 66 Ballynahinch Road Dromara Co Down BT25 2AL
℘028 9013 9357 www.abernethybuttercompany.com

Since turning their hand-churned butter making hobby into a business in 2005, and initially selling at markets, Will and Allison Abernethy's delicious and handsomely presented products are now in some prestigious shops (including Fortnum and Mason, in London) and many top restaurants. One of the great recent success stories of Northern Ireland's artisan food revival, the province's only handmade butter is churned in the traditional way and contains only locally sourced cream from grass-fed cows and a little salt. Available from: selected speciality stores and butchers; Donnybrook Fair branches Dublin; Firehouse Bakery, Delgany, Co Wicklow; Diva, Ballinspittle Co Cork. Online shop (fudge only).

  Boozeberries

62 The Belfry Dromore Co Down BT25 1TR ℘0778 011 7737 www.boozeberries.com

The brilliantly named Boozeberries fruit liqueur is very much like the familiar sloe gin that's been made from hedgerow fruits for generations. Berries are infused with Irish grain spirit in small batches and three flavours (blackcurrant, blueberry and wild cranberry). Versatile - drink on their own over ice or in cocktails, or as a cooking ingredient - and stylishly packed. A great gift idea. Available from Tesco, Superquinn, O'Briens and selected outlets.

DUNDRUM

Four miles north of Newcastle, Dundrum is noted for its 12th century castle (028 9181 1491) which boasts a circular keep with irregular curtain walls, surrounded by a rock cut fosse. Nearby is the Murlough National Nature Reserve (028 4375 1467), which covers an area of 698 acres, through which visitors can follow a path over sand dunes to Murlough Beach, one of the finest strands in the county.

The Buck's Head Inn

77 Main Street Dundrum Co Down BT33 0LU ☎*028 4375 1868*

Michael and Alison Crothers's appealing restaurant is one of the most popular destinations in the Mourne area for anyone who appreciates quality food. Alison sources local produce, especially seafood, and the well-balanced and interesting menus have a pleasing sense of place. The atmosphere is always relaxed and each intimate dining space has its own personality. Well worth planning a journey around. *Seats 80. L 12-2.30, High Tea 5-6, D 7-9 (Sun to 8.30). Closed Mon off-season (Oct-Apr); 25 Dec. CC.* **Directions:** *On the main Belfast-Newcastle road, approx 3 miles from Newcastle.*

The Carriage House

71 Main St. Dundrum Co Down BT33 0LU
☎*028 437 51635 www.carriagehousedundrum.com*

Everybody loves Maureen Griffith's B&B. It has great style and is furnished mainly with antiques, but she has an eye for unusual items and you will find interesting modern pieces amongst them. The three guest rooms include one away from the road at the back of the house, and all are quietly luxurious with beautiful bedding and delightful details. The garden is lovely too and Maureen is a terrific host, providing TLC and breakfasts to remember. *Rooms 3. No CC.* **Directions:** *The violet blue house next to The Bucks Head.*

Mourne Seafood Bar

10 Main Street Dundrum Co Down BT33 0LU ☎*028 4375 1377 www.mourneseafood.com*

Robert and Joanne McCoubrey's lively and informal seafood restaurant is the best bet for seafood in the Mourne area. In common with their Belfast sister restaurant, they specialise in fresh fish from the local ports and mussels, oysters and cockles from their own shellfish beds on Carlingford Lough. As they use local fish that is not under threat, their extensive menu changes according to what is caught - and they even have their own craft beer, Mourne Oyster Stout, to accompany it. *Seats 45 (outdoors, 20). Food daily, 12-9.30pm. Closed Mon & Tue in winter, 25 Dec. CC.* **Directions:** *Main street of village.*

Angus Farm Shop

42 Main Street Greyabbey Co Down BT22 2NG ☎*028 4278 8695 www.angusfarmshop.com*

Aberdeen Angus beef is the speciality at Noel Angus's esteemed butchers 'behind the yellow half door'. Committed to animal welfare and sustainable environmental practices, Noel's meats have exceptionally low food miles - just two in fact, from his farm on the shore of Strangford Lough to the shop. Other meats, including their own lamb, homemade sausages and burgers, are also stocked, along with carefully sourced pork, poultry and some other local produce. *Open Mon 8.30-12.30, Tue-Sat 8-5.30. Closed Sun.*

Harrisons of Greyabbey

35 Ballybryan Road Greyabbey Co Down BT22 2RB
☎*028 4278 8088 www.harrisonsofgreyabbey.co.uk*

With a farm shop offering some seriously good food shopping, a garden centre and gift shop to mosey around and a good restaurant with one of the best views of any on the island, the

COUNTY DOWN

Harrison family's scenically located one stop shop is the perfect destination for a day out. Enjoy a meal with a view, then take home some treats including meats by Angus Farm Shop (see entry) and freshly dug potatoes. *Shop: Mon-Sat 8-5.30. Restaurant Seats 105 (+ outdoor seating). Open Mon -Thu 9am-5pm, Fri 9am-8pm & Sat 9am-9pm. **Directions:** On the Ards Peninsula, c. 1 mile south of Greyabbey on A20.*

The Parson's Nose

48 Lisburn Street Hillsborough Co Down BT26 6AB
028 9268 3009 www.theparsonsnose.co.uk

Previously named after its original owner, The Marquis of Downshire, this charming 18th century pub and restaurant is a sister establishment to that great dining pub, Balloo House in Killinchy. Full of character and style - think old world with a modern twist - local meats and poultry are a highlight at this cosy venue. 'Honest Food and Ales' is the mantra, and it shows in their good food and drink, including a selection of local beers. **Seats 70**. *Food daily noon-9pm (to 9.30pm at weekends). Closed 25 Dec. CC. **Directions:** On right as you enter Hillsborough.*

The Plough Inn

3 The Square Hillsborough Co Down BT26 6AG
028 9268 2985 www.theploughhillsborough.co.uk

Established in 1752, this former coaching inn is owned by the Patterson family, who have built a reputation for hospitality and good food, especially seafood and great steaks. In a setting that combines old world charm with contemporary style, they manage to run several separate food operations successfully each day, some traditional and others less so, pleasing both casual daytime visitors including families, and more serious evening diners. Allow yourself time to have a good look around and get your bearings before settling down to eat. *Restaurant: L&D daily (all day Sun from 12 -8). Bar Retro Bistro:D Mon-Thu 5-9, Fri & Sat to 9.30, Sun 12-8.2/3 course early D 5-6.45 £12/15. Bar Retro Café: **Seats 150**; family friendly; food served all day, daily (D Fri & Sat only). Outdoor seating. Closed 25 Dec. CC. **Directions:** On village square.*

The Pheasant

Hillsborough Area 410 Upper Ballynahinch Road Annahilt Hillsborough Co Down BT26 6NR
028 9263 8056 www.the-pheasant-restaurant.co.uk

Everyone loves an old world pub, and at this welcoming cottagey bar and restaurant - sister to The Plough Inn nearby in Hillsborough and The Tannery in Moira - the Patterson family have earned a following for tasty food served at very reasonable prices. Everything is local and freshly prepared and even the most basic dishes are packed with flavour and well executed. All this plus good service and a children's play area makes it a good choice for a family outing. **Seats 90** *(outdoors, 40); bar food served all day daily. Closed 25-26 Dec; 12-13 Jul. CC. **Directions:** 4 miles from the A1 Hillsborough.*

HOLYWOOD

This prosperous satellite town of Belfast has plenty to offer the visitor including excellent restaurants, cafés along the busy main street and interesting historical sites including the 13th century clock tower and Holywood Motte; this is an earthen mound located off Brook Street in the centre of the town which was almost certainly a 12th century Norman motte. The nearby

Ulster Folk and Transport Museum (028 9042 8428, open all year) houses an impressive display of engines, coaches and is the home of the Irish railway collection. The folk section takes visitors on a journey around a typical 19th century Ulster town including farmhouses, a school and a corner shop. Golfers will enjoy a round at Royal Belfast Golf Course (028 9042 8165), which is reputedly one of the finest 18 hole parkland settings in the game, or there is also the option of Holywood Golf Course (028 9042 3135), established in 1904.

Bay Tree Coffee House & Restaurant

118 High Street Holywood Co Down BT18 9HW ✆ *028 9042 1419*

Since 1988, Sue Farmer's delightful restaurant and coffee house has been attracting customers from miles around. Great baking is a highlight, especially the famous cinnamon scones, which are a house specialty, and also lovely vegetarian dishes and organic salads, which you can enjoy outdoors in fine summer weather. Also food to go - and you can buy Sue's cookbook too. *Seats 55 (outdoors, 8).Open Mon-Sat 8-5 & Sun 10-3. D Fri only 5.30-9.30. Closed Christmas 4 days, Easter 3 days & 12 July 4 days. CC. Directions: Opposite the police station.*

Camphill Organic Farm Shop & Bakery

8 Shore Road Holywood Co Down BT18 9HX
✆ *028 9042 3203 www.camphillholywood.co.uk*

Run by the Holywood branch of the International Camphill Movement, this lovely shop stocks a wide range of organic products, including locally sourced fresh vegetables. Breads are all handmade. Gluten-free, dairy-free and sugar-free options are offered, and bakery products are also available in the café, where lunch is served as well as cakes, pies and other sweet indulgences. *Open Tue-Sun 9-5.30. Closed 10 days Christmas & Easter, 2nd & 3rd weeks July. CC. Directions: Holywood High Street towards Bangor, turn left at Maypole, on the left hand side.*

Enigma

2 Sullivan Place Holywood Co Down BT18 9JF
✆ *028 9042 6111 www.enigma-holywood.co.uk*

One of those useful places with long opening hours, this pleasing modern restaurant does a very nice breakfast at weekends, and appealing all-day and dinner menus offering a good choice of upbeat classics, including attractive vegetarian options. Dishes with eye appeal as well as flavour include lovely desserts - a luscious hot praline soufflé with berry compôte perhaps. *Seats 70. Open L&D daily. Closed 25/26 Dec. CC. Directions: Just off main Belfast-Bangor dual carriageway.*

Fontana Restaurant

61A High Street Holywood Co Down BT18 9AE ✆ *028 9080 9908*

A first-floor restaurant over a kitchen shop, Fontana is fresh and bright – perfectly in tune with proprietor-chef Colleen Bennett's zesty cooking style. Imaginative use of fresh seasonal produce is a striking feature: vegetables and salads are presented with panache and seafood is strongly represented. Offering accomplished cooking, stylishly simple presentation and clear flavours, a visit here is always a treat. *Seats 54 (outdoors, 12). L&D Tue-Sat (Sun brunch). Closed D Sun, all Mon, 25-26 Dec & 1 Jan. CC. Directions: Three doors from Maypole flag pole.*

Hastings Culloden Estate & Spa

Bangor Road Holywood Co Down BT18 0EX ✆*028 9042 1066 www.hastingshotels.com*

Formerly the official palace for the Bishops of Down, the region's premier hotel is romantically set in beautifully maintained gardens and woodland overlooking Belfast Lough and the Co. Antrim coastline; it is a lovely place to stay, with many of the sumptuous rooms and suites overlooking the lough, and makes an impressive wedding venue. The Culloden has always taken pride in the food served and its provenance: fine dining with a view in The Mitre Restaurant can be a memorable experience, while the 'Cultra Inn', in the grounds, offers an informal alternative. *Rooms 105. Restaurant **seats 110**. D daily; L Sun only. Open all year. CC. **Directions:** 6m from Belfast city centre on A2 towards Bangor.*

Helens Bay Organic Gardens

13 Seaview Terrace Holywood Co Down BT18 9DT
✆*028 9185 3122 www.helensbayorganicgardens.com*

Since 1991 the lucky people of North Down have been able to enjoy weekly deliveries of fresh seasonal organic produce from 'just up the road' thanks to John McCormick's 20 acre organic holding beside Belfast Lough. His fields and polytunnels supply a wide variety of vegetables, and other local organic farms extend the range - imports are only used when there is no local alternative available. The longevity of this affordable scheme proves that direct selling by delivery can really work.

Rayanne Country House

60 Demesne Road Holywood Co Down B18 9EX ✆*028 9042 5859 www.rayannehouse.com*

Near Holywood Golf Club and Redburn Country Park - and just 5 minutes from Belfast City Airport - second generation owners Conor and Bernie McClelland have built on this country house's long-standing reputation as a relaxing place, known for its friendly staff and excellent breakfasts. Some of the very comfortable bedrooms have views of Belfast Lough and all have thoughtful touches. Conor's cooking showcases local produce: the pièce de résistance is a 9-course Titanic Menu, which gives a fascinating insight into life on board. A great place to stay - and to dine. *Rooms 11 (4 shower only). D some nights, by reservation. Open all year. CC. **Directions:** Holywood to top of My Ladys Mile; turn right; 200 yards.*

Beech Hill Country House

Holywood Area 23 Ballymoney Road Craigantlet Holywood Co Down BT23 4TG
✆*028 9042 5892 www.beech-hill.net*

If you ever need somewhere really relaxing and peaceful to stay near Belfast, Victoria Brann's lovely Georgian-style house in the hills above Holywood is just the place. Rooms with lots of little extras look out over the rolling countryside and a delightful drawing room offers room to relax. Breakfast choices are delicious (often including fish) and Victoria is a very relaxed and engaging host. A lovely place to stay. *Rooms 3 (1 shower only). Open all year. Self-catering accommodation also offered. CC. **Directions:** A2 from Belfast; bypass Holywood; 1.5m from bridges at Ulster Folk Museum, turn right up Ballymoney Road signed Craigantlet - 1.5m on left.*

Mourne Seafood Cookery School

Nautilus Centre Rooney Road Kilkeel Co Down BT34 4AG
☎ 028 4176 2525 www.mourneseafoodcookeryschool.com

Overlooking Kilkeel Harbour, the home of Northern Ireland's largest fishing fleet, this state-of-the-art cookery school offers a range of cookery courses and demonstrations on local seafood. Just the place to learn more about what to look for when buying, handling and cooking seafood, it aims to be a fun, relaxed, learning experience for all levels, from the beginner to the more experienced cook. A wide range of non-seafood classes is also offered. *Centre open Mon–Sat 9-5 (closed 1-1.30 pm for lunch), closed Sun, also Sat off season (Nov-Easter). G*

  Whitewater Brewery

40 Tullyframe Road Kilkeel Co Down BT34 4RZ
☎ 028 4176 9449 www.whitewaterbrewery.com

Established in 1996 amidst the spectacular Mountains of Mourne, Whitewater Brewery is Northern Ireland's largest microbrewery. They produce a selection of cask beers, a lager in keg and many bottled beers, all of which are handcrafted in small batches. The brewery has its own gastropub, the White Horse Inn (see entry), located 30 miles from the brewery in Saintfield. Tours of the brewery are possible but must be booked in advance. Whitewater beers are widely available in Northern Ireland and also sold in the Republic.

 **Balloo House**

1 Comber Road Killinchy Co Down BT23 6PA ☎ 028 9754 1210 www.balloohouse.com

In 2004 when Ronan and Jennie Sweeney took over this famous old 19th century coaching inn, their ambition was to restore Balloo's reputation as one of the finest country dining pubs in Northern Ireland - and this they have achieved with spectacular success. The bistro is reliably good, but head chef Danny Millar is one of the region's culinary leaders and a well known advocate of local seasonal produce and the restaurant offers a memorable experience; menus showcase ingredients with style and every dish has a wow factor- and great flavour. Balloo's ever-growing reputation is well earned. *Downstairs bistro* **seats 80** *(outdoors, 12). Bistro: Food daily 12-9 (to 8.30pm on Sun, Mon). Restaurant* **seats 34**; *open D Tue-Sat. Closed 25 Dec. CC.* **Directions:** *At Balloo crossroads on main road from Comber to Killyleagh.*

Daft Eddys & Island Coffee Room

Sketrick Island Whiterock Killinchy Co Down BT23 6QB ☎ 028 9754 1615

Wholesome food, cheery staff and an exceptionally beautiful location make this island pub a popular casual dining destination. A comfortable old world bar leads into a cosy restaurant decorated with maritime memorabilia, where well-balanced menus offer plenty of choice, particularly local seafood. Window tables are at a premium. **Seats 80** *(outdoors, 100). Open L&D Mon-Fri; Sat & Sun 12.30-9 . CC.* **Directions:** *From Killinchy drive to shore and turn left for 1/2 mile - restaurant is on island over causeway.*

KILLYLEAGH

This charming village on the shores of Strangford Lough is best known for its fairytale castle, which is built in the style of a Loire valley chateau and believed to be the oldest inhabited castle in the country. For golfers, the championship course at Royal County Down (Newcastle,

028 4372 3314) is only a short drive away, and as with most of County Down, the main issue for garden lovers will be getting the time to see all of the wonderful gardens in the area, with Mountstewart House & Gardens (Newtownards, 028 4278 8387) being the star.

 ## Dufferin Coaching Inn

33 High Street Killyleagh Co Down BT30 9QF
028 4482 1134? www.dufferincoachinginn.com

Formerly a bank, Leontine Haines's Georgian house is a delightful place to stay close to the shores of Strangford Lough. The bedrooms vary according to their position in the building, but all are lovely. Breakfast showcases local foods like sausages and bacon from the family butcher and potato cakes and soda farls from the village bakery. At the back, under the beautiful old arch leading to the former coach house, an atmospheric venue is available for events. **Rooms 7**. Banqueting (150). **Directions:** *Right in the centre of Killyleagh.*

 ## Picnic

Killyleagh Co Down BT30 9QF 028 4482 8525

Katherine and John Dougherty's deli and café near the gates of Killyleagh Castle offer simple, delicious food to eat in or out. A constantly changing range of local and international stock is complemented by wholesome menus offering homemade soups, stews and casseroles, seasonal salads, charcuterie, artisan cheese boards and home-baked cakes. A must-visit when in Killyleagh. *Open Mon-Fri 7am-5pm, Sat 10-4. Closed Sun off season.* **Directions:** *Beside the castle in Killyleagh.*

  ## Glastry Farm Ice Cream

Glastry Farm 43 Manse Road Kircubbin Co Down BT22 1DR
078 0220 7838 www.glastryfarm.com

The Taylor family's Ards peninsula dairy farm dates back to 1856. Today, their pedigree herd converts lush pastures into top quality milk that's made into creamy 'free-from' ice cream daily, in their own creamery. Standout flavours in the extensive range (plus several sorbets) include Yellowman Honeycomb (inspired by the crunchy Co Antrim speciality), and Raspberry & Lavender (using lavender grown at Mount Stewart, nearby).

  ## Paul Arthurs Restaurant

62-66 Main Street Kircubbin Newtownards Co Down BT22 2SP
028 4273 8192 www.paularthurs.com

On the main street of his home town, Paul Arthur's attractive first floor restaurant exudes character and has a cheering fire on chilly days. Local produce features strongly, with more focus on meats than is usual, also seafood of course and game in season. The cooking is excellent and the same high standards apply in the casual Bella's Bistro and bar below, which has a large garden at the rear. Seven simply furnished en-suite bedrooms are offered too. **Seats 55** (outdoors, 20). L & D Tue-Sat. Closed Sun, Mon, 25 Dec & Jan. CC. **Directions:** *On main street, 1st floor, opposite supermarket.*

Hannan Meats & The Meat Merchant

9 Moira Industrial Estate Old Kilmore Road Moira Co Down BT67 0LZ
✆ *028 9261 9790 www.hannanmeats.com*

Peter Hannan's remarkable meat company is one of Ireland's most innovative, and renowned for the outstanding quality of its products - and its well-earned reputation is supported by many independent accolades. Now also producing under the Moyallon brand, established by quality food pioneer Jilly Dougan, the company won no less than 20 Great Taste Awards in 2012, including Supreme Champion, for a range of meat products. A seriously impressive Himalayan salt brick ageing chamber for their carefully selected beef is currently making waves; it produces meat with exceptional texture and flavour and is the largest of its type in the world. *Buy from The Meat Merchant at Hannan Meats: Mon-Wed 8.30 to 4, Thu & Fri 8.30-5, Sat 8.30-2. Online shop planned.*

McCartneys Of Moira

56-58 Main Street Moira Co Down BT67 0LQ
✆ *028 9261 1422 www.mccartneysofmoira.co.uk*

In the family for nearly one and a half centuries, George McCartney's shop is one of the oldest and best-loved butchery businesses in Northern Ireland. Renowned for their award-winning sausages (you'll see them on menus throughout the province) and the corned silverside beef made to George's grandfather's recipe that was Supreme Champion in the 2011 Great Taste Awards, this impressive business is committed to supporting local farmers and all meat is sourced within Northern Ireland. The more recently opened coffee shop and bistro has its specialities too, notably an all day breakfast which includes both soda bread and potato bread as well as a selection of the best breakfast meats you'll find anywhere. A place to treasure. *Butchery/deli open: Mon-Thu 8.30-5.30, Fri & Sat 8-5.30. Coffee shop/bistro, meals served Mon-Thu 8.30-4, Fri & Sat 8-4; drinks and snacks to 5pm. Closed Sun, 12-15 July incl.*

The Tannery

6 Chestnut Hill Road Moira Co Down BT67 0LW

Run by well known publicans, the Patterson family (The Plough, Hillsborough;The Pheasant, Annahilt), steaks and fresh, seasonal and local produce feature strongly here. The good cooking, good value and good service clearly please the mix of clientele: families, couples, the young and not so young. There's a nice atmosphere with lots of buzz in background. It's easy to see why this place is so popular. *Bistro L Mon-Fri, Sat 12-10pm, Sun carvery 12.30-3.30pm. Restaurant: Fri-Sat D. Bar snacks also available. CC.* **Directions:** *North of Moira on B106.*

NEWCASTLE

Approached from Dundrum, the resort town of Newcastle is spacious with a curved raised beach and sits in the shadow of the beautiful Mourne Mountains. The most distinctive building in the town is a 1960s Roman Catholic Church with a green copper parasol roof. Newcastle offers easy access to the Mourne Mountains, which include a large number of trails for hikers over this area of outstanding beauty. Tollymore Forest (028 4372 2428, open all year) is also a spectacular setting for walking whilst the Tollymore Mountain Centre (028 4372 2158) offers courses in rock climbing, canoeing and orienteering for the adventurous type. Golfers will enjoy the beautiful course at Royal County Down (028 4372 3314), set against the background of the Mourne Mountains, with a very high standard of greens that are swift and challenging. Annalong Corn Mill (028 3026 8877) is worth a visit, as guided tours are available around this 17th century corn mill which operated up until the 1960s, being one of Ulster's last working watermills.

Burrendale Hotel, Country Club & Spa

51 Castlewellan Road Newcastle Co Down BT33 0JY 028 4372 2599 *www.burrendale.com*

This friendly and well-managed hotel on the edge of the Mourne Mountains has a pleasingly remote atmosphere and spacious public areas, including the homely Cottage Bar with an open log fire. Well-appointed accommodation includes superior rooms and some suited to families, who appreciate the good leisure facilities. Head chef Ciaran Sansome and his team serve good locally sourced seasonal food in both The Cottage Kitchen and the evening restaurant, Vine. **Rooms 68.** *Open all year. CC.* **Directions:** *On A50 Castlewellan Road.*

The Cookie Jar Bakery

121 Main Street Newcastle Co Down BT33 0AE 028 4372 2427

Good baking is one of the most enjoyable things about Northern Irish cooking and small bakeries are benefiting from the revival of interest in artisan foods. The Herron family have run this craft bakery since 1965 and the current baker, James Herron, specialises in traditional breads - especially wheaten bread, and other handmade Irish breads and cakes. The Cookie Jar also invents some new ones from time to time, for special occasions and seasonal treats for example. *Open Mon-Sat 9-5.30. Also at: The Market Square, Kilkeel.*

Hastings Slieve Donard Resort & Spa

Downs Road Newcastle Co Down BT33 0AH 028 4372 1066 *www.hastingshotels.com*

This famous hotel stands beneath the Mourne Mountains in 6 acres of public grounds, adjacent to the beach and the Royal County Down Golf Links. The Victorian holiday hotel par excellence, the Slieve Donard first opened in 1897 and has been the leading place to stay in Newcastle ever since. It's the 'grand old lady' of the Hastings hotels, furnished to a high standard and known for its leisure amenities and short breaks. **Rooms 179.** *Open all year. CC.* **Directions:** *North end of Newcastle.*

The Corn Dolly Home Bakery

Jim & Anthony O'Keeffe 12 Marcus Square Newry Co Down BT34 1AE 028 3026 0524 *www.corndollyfoods.com*

Jim and Anthony O'Keeffe's traditional bakery is an institution in Newry and attracts shoppers from a wide area to purchase favourites from the tempting choice of quality breads, buns, cakes and savouries made here. You'll find the delicious traditional breads and cakes of the region - the wheaten loaves, soda farls, potato breads, fruit bracks and malt loaves that distinguish Northern Irish baking - but the range they offer is very wide. Caramel shortbread, porter cake and whiskey cake are particular treats. *Open: Mon-Sat, 8.30-5. Closed Sun.*

Bay Restaurant

Mount Stewart House & Gardens Portaferry Road Newtownards Co Down BT22 2AD
☎*028 4278 8387*
www.nationaltrust.org.uk/main/w-vh/w-visits/w-findaplace/w-mountstewart.htm

Mount Stewart is a gem in the National Trust's collection, but even if you don't want to visit the house or gardens, their Bay Restaurant is a popular destination in its own right. Locally sourced, seasonal produce is proudly showcased on menus and Head Chef Jason Carnduff and sous chef Glenn Swift's scones, cakes, tray bakes and hot lunchtime meals have homemade flavour. *Seats 60. Open 10-5 daily in summer; off season Mon-Fri 10-4, weekends 10-4. Menu may be limited to snacks on weekdays off season. Evening meals for groups only (book in advance).* **Directions:** *On East side of Strangford Lough on Belfast-Portaferry Road.*

 **Edenvale House**

130 Portaferry Road Newtownards Co Down BT22 2AH
☎*028 9181 4881 www.edenvalehouse.com*

Diane Whyte's charming Georgian house is set in 7 acres of garden and paddock, with views over Strangford Lough to the Mourne Mountains and a National Trust wildfowl reserve. Sensitively restored and modernised for the comfort of guests, Edenvale offers an exceptionally high standard of accommodation and hospitality. Guests are warmly welcomed and well fed, with excellent traditional breakfasts and afternoon tea with homemade scones. *Rooms 3 (1 shower only). Closed Christmas. CC.* **Directions:** *2m from Newtownards on A20 going towards Portaferry.*

 Homegrown

66B East Street Newtownards Co Down BT23 7DD ☎*028 9181 8318 www.homegrownni.com*

The White family's greengrocery and deli is keen to promote tasty vegetables from the surrounding area and local fruit such as Armagh apples. An online shop offers a wide range of mainly local fresh produce and and an extensive choice of deli products, including homemade items and some - such as Clandeboye yoghurt and Dunola Rapeseed Oil - that are produced fairly locally. Imports are offered too. *Open Mon 8-5.30, Tue-Thu 8.30-5.30, Fri & Sat 8-5.30.-Sat. Closed Sun. Online shop.*

 Knotts Bakery & Coffee Shop

49 High Street Newtownards Co Down BT23 7HS ☎*028 9181 9098 www.knottsbakery.co.uk*

Michael Knott's busy town centre bakery and restaurant is a hive of activity, with customers eager to buy specialities such as fruit loaves and cakes from the bakery or join the queue for tasty lunches. Although it is not a small bakery, the artisan ethos has been maintained; local produce is used and a surprising amount of the production work is done by hand. *Open Mon-Sat: 8.30-5.30. Restaurant L 12-2.30. Also at: Holywood, Co Down; Lisburn Road, Belfast.*

 McKees Country Store

28 Holywood Road Newtownards Co Down BT23 4TQ
☎*028 9182 1304 www.mckeesproduce.co.uk*

At this renowned family farm in the Craigantlet hills, third-generation farmer Colin McKee and his team sell their own farm produce (beef, pork and vegetables) and a range of other local produce. The country store is now a one-stop shop offering in-house bakery and deli products as well as dairy, groceries and frozen foods. Many of their products are also served in their popular daytime restaurant with views of Scrabo Tower and Strangford Lough. *Open Mon-Sat 8.30-5.30 (Restaurant Seats 130: 9-4.30). Online shop, free delivery locally; can also deliver to Republic and UK.*

 **Portaferry Hotel**

The Strand Portaferry Co Down BT22 1PE ✆*028 4272 8231 www.portaferryhotel.com*

This 18th-century waterfront terrace presents a neat, traditional exterior overlooking the lough towards the attractive village of Strangford, and the National Trust property, Castleward. Portaferry is one of Northern Ireland's most popular destinations for a short break or day out, and (although chefs are inclined to change) a meal here can be a highlight. The bar, a cosy sitting room and the restaurant all have an old-fashioned feeling to them and, while not luxurious, accommodation is comfortable. A lovely place with personality. **Rooms 14** *(2 shower only). Seats 65. L&D daily. Open all year except Christmas. CC.* **Directions:** *On Portaferry seafront.*

 The Quays

81 New Harbour Road Portavogie Co Down BT22 1EB
✆*028 4277 2225 www.quaysrestaurant.co.uk*

Francis Adair's cosy pub and restaurant is the kind of place where you can have a pint and a plate of simply cooked fresh seafood, with two of the best seasonings in the world: fresh sea air and the sight of moored fishing boats in the harbour as you eat. Their fish & chips with mushy peas is so popular that it's available in three sizes (plus a little one for kids) and there are plenty of other popular dishes offered too, including some for vegetarians. *Restaurant: L&D Mon–Fri, Sat & Sun all day 12-9pm (to 8pm Sun). Bar: Mon-Sat 11.30-11.30, Sun 12-10pm. CC.* **Directions:** *Overlooking the harbour.*

  Leggyowan Farm Cheese

94 Crossgar Road Saintfield Co Down BT24 7JQ ✆*028 9751 1433 www.leggyowanfarm.co.uk*

Brothers Adam, Ryan and Jason Kelly produce Northern Ireland's first blue goat cheese, using the milk of their own herd of goats. These small artisan producers have made the punchy Leggyowan Farm semi-soft blue cheese since 2010; it quickly became a familiar name and a semi-hard white cheese is now in production too. They also offer cartons of fresh pasteurised goats milk for sale, and produce a goat's milk soap.

  The White Horse Inn

49-53 Main Street Saintfield Co Down BT24 7AB
✆*028 9751 1143 www.whitehorsesaintfield.com*

Whitewater Brewing Company (see entry) owns this 200 year old coaching inn - which now makes a very pleasant bar and restaurant with a cosy ambience, and also a destination for craft beer enthusiasts. Like their beers, chef Billy Burns's food is sourced as locally as possible and something a bit different here is dishes that link with the brewery - brewer's bread roll with the soup, for example, and crisply beer-battered Kilkeel scampi or haddock & chips. *Bistro* **Seats 60:** *Mon-Thu 11.30-8, Fri-Sat 11.30-9, Sun 12-8. Bar: Mon-Sat 11.30-1am, Sun 12-10.* **Directions:** *Saintfield town centre.*

 **The Cuan Licensed Guest Inn**

6-10 The Square Strangford Village Co Down BT30 7ND
☎ *028 4488 1222 www.thecuan.com*

Over a century old, Peter and Caroline McErlean's immaculately maintained village inn has lots of character, with open fires, cosy lounges and a homely bar. Peter's seasonal menus have a strong emphasis on local provenance; summer menus, especially, major on seafood with the house Seafood Chowder and The Cuan's Seafood Platter (for two), among the specialities. The comfortable bedrooms have charm and include two family rooms; an ideal base for exploring this beautiful area. **Rooms 9** *(3 shower only). Food served daily to 8pm (Fri & Sat to 9pm, high season Sun to 8.30). Closed 25 Dec. CC.* **Directions:** *On the square, near the ferry.*

 **Restaurant 23 @ Balmoral Hotel**

13 Seaview Warrenpoint Co Down BT34 3NJ ☎ *028 4175 3222 www.restaurant23.com*

A smart room above the Balmoral Hotel now serves as a remarkable contemporary restaurant. owned by one of Northern Ireland's most highly-regarded chefs, Raymond McArdle, and his wife, Andrea. Enticing menus for varying occasions are based on carefully sourced, quality ingredients and designed to please all tastes. With such a talented chef in the kitchen, a relaxed ambience and good value, this stylish restaurant is a great asset to the area - and the view over Carlingford Lough is lovely. *L Wed-Sat, D Mon-Sat, Sun 12.30-8pm.* **Directions:** *on the seafront in Warrenpoint.*

 Sweet Pea Café

37 Rath Road Warrenpoint Co Down BT34 3RX ☎ *028 4175 3938 www.sweetpeacafe.co.uk*

In a pretty Victorian style house just beside the entrance to Annetts (fantastic) garden centre, and sharing its carpark, Nuala King's delightful café and weekend bistro has become a destination in itself. A daytime menu of homemade goodies offers a lovely breakfast, good soups and hot specials and great home baking, while change of style for the evening bistro allows the chef to flex his culinary muscles. A lovely spot. *Open: Mon-Thu 10-5.30, Fri & Say 10-9.30, Sun 12-6.* **Directions:** *At Annetts Garden Centre (well signed in the area).*

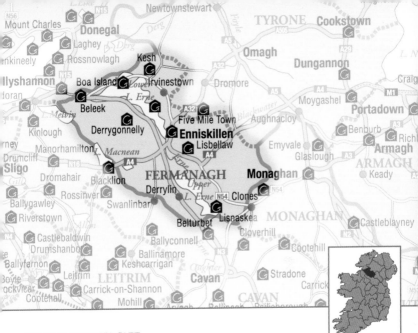

FERMANAGH

Ireland is a watery place of many lakes, rivers and canals. So it's quite an achievement to be the most watery county of all. Yet this is but one of Fermanagh's many claims to distinction. It is the only county in Ireland through which you can travel the complete distance between its furthest extremities entirely by boat.

Southeast of the historic county town of Enniskillen, Upper Lough Erne is a maze of small waterways meandering their way into Fermanagh from the Erne'e source in County Cavan. Northwest of characterful Enniskillen, the channels open out into the broad spread of Lower Lough Erne, a magnificent inland sea set off against the spectacular heights of the Cliffs of Magho. Through this broad lake, the River Erne progresses to the sea at Ballyshannon in Donegal by way of a rapid descent at Belleek in Fermanagh..

It's a stunningly beautiful county with much else of interest, including the Marble Arch caves, and the great houses of Castle Coole and Florence Court, the latter with its own forest park nestling under the rising heights of Cuilcagh (667m) - beyond it, the River Shannon emerges to begin its long journey south

For those who think lakes are for fishing rather than floating, in western Fermanagh the village of Garrison gives access to Lough Melvin, an angler's heaven which is noted particularly for its unique sub-species of salmon, the gillaroo. You just can't escape from water in this county, and Fermanagh is blessed as much of the rest of the world contemplates water shortages.

LOCAL ATTRACTIONS & INFORMATION

‣ **Porcelain and Explore Erne Exhibition** Belleek *028 68 659300*
‣ **Sheelin Lace Museum** Bellanaleck *028 66 348052*
‣ **Ardhowen Lakeside Theatre** Enniskillen *028 66 325440*

‣ **Castle Coole House & Parkland** Enniskillen *028 66 322690*
‣ **Waterways Ireland** Enniskillen *028 66 323004*
‣ **House and Garden** Florence Court *028 66 348249*

‣ **Marble Arch Caves** Florence Court *028 66 348855*
‣ **Castle Archdale Country Park** Kesh *028 68 621588*
‣ **Crom Castle** Newtownbutler *028 67 738174*

The Thatch

Belleek Co Fermanagh BT93 3SY ☎ *028 6865 8181*

This coffee shop is really special: a listed building dating back to the late 18th century, it's the only originally thatched building remaining in County Fermanagh and homemade food has been served here since the early 1900s. Today, you'll find homemade soups, sandwiches, hot specials, delicious baked goods and coffee. More unusually, you can also buy fishing tackle and hire a bike or even a holiday cottage here. *Open Mon-Sat. 9-5 (from 10 off-season). Closed Sun.* **Directions:** *On the main street.*

Inishmacsaint Brewing Company

Drumskimly Derrygonnelly Co Fermanagh BT93 ☎ *028 6864 1031*

Named after the nearby island of Inishmacsaint on Lower Lough Erne, Gordon Fallis's small, quirky brewery on a farm just outside the village of Derrygonnelly aims to brew beers that reflect the history and character of the local area. Having started off supplying just one local restaurant in Enniskillen, speciality and one-off brews are now in the pipeline as well as secret beer festivals for die-hard connoisseurs.

Blakes of the Hollow & Café Merlot

6 Church Street Enniskillen Co Fermanagh BT74 6JE ☎ *028 6632 0918*

One of the great classic pubs of Ireland, Blakes has been in the same family since 1887 and the classic Victorian front bar remains unchanged. But it's a large building and now, thanks to head chef Gerry Russell and front-of-house/wine man Johnny Donnelly, its atmospheric Café Merlot is a popular food destination, famed for creative modern cooking, a relaxed dining atmosphere and a great wine list. The formal restaurant No. 6 opens by reservation only. A must-visit when in Enniskillen. *Café Merlot (casual dining), L&D daily. No 6: D by reservation Fri-Sat 6-10; will open any day for parties 12+. Open all year. CC.* **Directions:** *Town centre.*

Dollakis Restaurant

2B Cross Street Enniskillen Co Fermanagh BT74 7DX ☎ *028 6634 2616 www.dollakis.co.uk*

This cheerfully cosmopolitan little restaurant is run by a terrific multinational team who have made it one of the area's favourite dining destinations. There's an obvious Greek influence in dishes like Dollakis pikilia platter, but there are also northern European dishes like gravadlaks and wiener schnitzel and plenty of others too. With tasty cooking, great service and very good value too, the popularity of this little place is well deserved. **Seats 40** *(outdoors, 4). Open Tue-Sat 10am-'late', L12-6, D 6-late (may open Sun & Mon in summer); 25/26 Dec, 1 Jan. CC.* **Directions:** *Town centre, down side of town hall.*

Franco's Restaurant

Queen Elizabeth Road Enniskillen Co Fermanagh BT74 7DY
☎ *028 6632 4424 www.francosrestaurant.co.uk*

If you want buzz, relaxed bustle and the best ambience in Enniskillen, this is the place. Informal meals, including pizzas, pastas and barbecues, seafood and more sophisticated dishes are the order of the day and it's all done with style, using quality ingredients including Mullaghmore lobster and local beef from renowned local suppliers Kettyle. Smart staff and reasonable prices keep this place busy, all the time. **Seats 140**. *Open daily, 12-10.30pm; open from 5pm Mon/Tue in Sept/Oct. Closed 25 Dec. CC.*

Frou Frou

37 Townhall Street Enniskillen Co Fermanagh BT74 7BD 📞 *028 6622 8479*

Renowned local baker and restaurateur Julie Snoddy runs this former draper's shop as a tea room and café. It boasts an impressive display of cakes, scones, tray bakes and giant meringues, and savoury favourites such as panini, toasties, quiches and sandwiches. Sunday Brunch is well worth knowing about, served from 11 am when few other places are open in the town. **Seats 30** *(outdoors, 10). Open Mon-Thu 8-6 , Fri 8-9, Sat & hols 8-6, Sun 11-6 in summer. Times may vary off season. CC.* **Directions:** *On the corner of Townhall Street and Regal Pass.*

 **Killyhevlin Hotel**

Killyhevlin Enniskillen Co Fermanagh BT74 6RW 📞 *028 6632 3481 www.killyhevlin.com*

This spacious four star hotel on the banks of the Erne suits business guests and would make a comfortable and relaxing base from which to explore this lovely area. Windows along the back offer wonderful views of the lake and the mountains. Gardens lead down to the hotel's own pontoon, and a fine leisure centre includes a spa, gym, pool, hot tub, hydrotherapy pool, sauna and steam room. Lakeshore self-catering chalets are also available. **Rooms 70**. *Closed 24-25 Dec. CC.* **Directions:** *On the A4 just south of Enniskillen.*

 Knockninny Country House & Marina

Knockinny Quay Derrylin Enniskillen Co Fermanagh BT92 9JU
📞 *028 6774 8590 www.knockninnyhouse.com*

Billed as "Lough Erne's original hotel", this attractive waterside property has recently been renovated and upgraded, making a lovely venue for weddings and other events, and an unusual place to stay and eat. The slightly quirky bedrooms have lovely lough views, and so does the Porter House Bistro. Drinks and light food are available in the bar all day, to enjoy beside an open fire on chilly days or outside overlooking the marina in fine weather. **Rooms 7** *(2 shower only) L&D Wed-Sun Easter-Sep, light refreshments all day.* **Directions:** *Take A509 south from Enniskillen for Derrylin.*

 Leslies Bakery

10 Church Street Enniskillen Co Fermanagh BT74 7EJ 📞 *028 6632 4902*

Leslie Wilkin's classic Northern Irish craft bakery and coffee shop is a popular spot, specialising in traditional wheaten bread, teabreads, cakes and buns. It's also a busy daytime cafe, serving tasty hot pies and lunch specials to hungry shoppers. *Open: Mon-Sat 8-5.30.*

Lough Erne Resort

Belleek Road Enniskillen Co Fermanagh BT93 7ED 📞 *028 6632 3230 www.lougherneresort.com*

Beautifully located in County Fermanagh's rolling lakelands, this is a world-class resort with two championship golf courses and an impressive spa - and the hotel had the distinction of being chosen as the venue for the G8 Summit in 2013. Accommodation is luxurious, with some rooms having lovely views across water, and it's a popular dining destination for non-residents. The Blaney Bar and Terrace Hall serve good bar food and Afternoon Tea, while the fine dining Catalina Restaurant allows Head Chef Noel McMeel to showcase local produce in style. Service at this well run hotel is attentive, warm and courteous. *Rooms 120. Catalina Restaurant: D nightly, L Sun; Bar & Drawing Room menus: 12-9.30 daily; Garden Hall Afternoon Tea: 2-5 daily.* **Directions:** *North of Enniskillen.*

O'Dohertys Butchers

Belmore Street Enniskillen Co Fermanagh BT74 6AA
✆*028 6632 2152 www.blackbacon.com*

A model Northern Ireland butchers shop, and home to Pat O'Doherty's famous Fermanagh Black Bacon, a local delicacy made from the meat of free range Saddleback pigs raised on nearby Inishcorkish Island. It's available in several versions 'like the oak-smoked one tastes 'like the bacon that used to be left up the chimney of the farmhouse to smoke'. O'Dohertys also stock a wide range of specialty meats, and their beef sausages, burgers and traditional black and white puddings attract praise too. *Open Mon-Sat, 8-6. Postal delivery service.*

Uno Restaurant & Cocktail Bar

17 Belmore Street Enniskillen Co Fermanagh BT74 6AA
✆*028 6634 2622 www.uno-restaurant.co.uk*

This popular bistro-style restaurant and wine bar pleases a wide range of customers with consistent cooking, friendly staff and an atmosphere of relaxed informality. Local produce features and wide-ranging menus offer everything from inexpensive pastas to modern classics like fillet steak with dauphinoise potato. There will be some interesting vegetarian options and plenty of seafood, usually on the daily specials. **Seats 147.** *D daily. Closed 24-26 Dec. CC.* **Directions:** *Access from main shopping centre.*

Westville Hotel

14-20 Tempo Road Enniskillen Co Fermanagh BT74 6HR
✆*028 6632 0333 www.westvillehotel.co.uk*

Hands-on owner-management is a plus at this modern hotel near the town centre. The setting is not picturesque, but the smart contemporary interior is well designed and the comfortable rooms have equal appeal to business and leisure guests. Head chef Gavin Cassidy, brother of the owner, Nicky Cassidy, has established a reputation for the Terrace Restaurant as a dining destination, backed up by very good service. **Rooms 30** *(2 suites). Restaurant* **seats 50+.** *CC.* **Directions:** *On A32, entering town from Belfast direction.*

Arch House

Enniskillen Area Tullyhona Florencecourt Enniskillen Co Fermanagh BT92 1DE
✆*028 6634 8452 www.archhouse.com*

Located near Marble Arch Caves and Florencecourt House, Rosemary Armstrong's eco-friendly farm guesthouse has four traditional en-suite bedrooms and a big comfortably furnished sitting room with lots of room for guests to relax. Good food is important at Arch House. Rosemary not only cooks meals for guests, but she does scone and bread-making demos in her kitchen and home produce is on sale in their own shop as well. A good place for a family stay. **Rooms 4.** *Open all year. CC.* **Directions:** *From Enniskillen A4 Sligo road for 2.5m, on to A32 Swanlinbar road, follow signs for Marble Arch Caves and turn right at posting for Florencecourt, 2m on.*

The Sheelin Brewery & Kitchen

Enniskillen Area 178b Derrylin Road Bellanaleck Enniskillen Co Fermanagh BT92 2BA
✆+44 (0) 77 31 595 422 www.sheelin.com

This charming place has been in the Cathcart family for three generations and is now run by George Cathcart and his wife Victoria as a craft brewery (The Sheelin Brewery) and café (The Sheelin Kitchen). The flagship brew is Sheelin Blonde Ale (tours by arrangement). In The Sheelin Kitchen, their homemade 'traditional Irish favourites with a cosmopolitan twist' use seasonal, local ingredients. Just the kind of place that visitors hope to find. *Seats 36 (outdoors, 12). Café open Mon-Wed 11-4, Thu-Fri 11-5, Sat 10-5, Sun 1-5. Closed 10 days at Christmas. CC. Directions: Centre of village, opposite petrol station.*

 Lough Erne Hotel

Main Street Kesh Co Fermanagh BT93 1TF ✆028 6863 1275 www.lougherhotel.eu

In an attractive location on the banks of the Glendurragh River, this pleasantly old-fashioned and friendly hotel in the centre of the little town has comfortable accommodation and is popular for fishing holidays. *Rooms 12. Closed 25 Dec. CC. Directions: Centre of Kesh.*

 **Lusty Beg Island**

Boa Island Kesh Co Fermanagh BT93 8AD ✆028 6863 3300 www.lustybegisland.com

The island is worth a visit if only to call into the pleasant waterside pub for a drink, a cup of tea or an informal bite. Accommodation is spread relatively inconspicuously around the wooded island in lodges, chalets and a motel. Visiting boats are welcome; phone ahead for details of barbecues and theme nights. *Rooms 40 (all shower only). Bar food available daily in summer, maybe weekends only off season Closed Christmas week. CC. Directions: Located off the main Kesh - Belleek Road A47.*

Manor House Country Hotel

Killadeas Co Fermanagh BT94 1NY ✆028 6862 2211 www.manor-house-hotel.com

Overlooking a marina, this impressive lakeside Victorian house makes a fine hotel, with furnishings and decor leaning towards the luxurious. Spacious accommodation includes romantic suites, and front rooms have stunning views - as does the Belleek Restaurant, where, in tune with the grand surroundings, quite classical food is served. A popular venue for conferences and weddings. *Rooms 81. Seats 65. L&D daily. Bar meals 12.30-9 pm daily. Open all year. CC. Directions: 7 miles from Enniskillen on the B82.*

 Tickety Moo

Moo HQ Oghill Farm Killadeas Co Fermanagh BT94 1RG
✆028 6862 8779 www.tickety-moo.com

The cleverly named Tickety Moo ice cream is made on the Grey family's innovative farm at Killadeas. Marcus is responsible for the pedigree Jersey cows - a robotic milking system allows milking on demand, and they have automatic groomers too and mattresses to lie on. Gareth is the ice cream man, converting their creamy milk into ice cream on site - about 18 tempting flavours and several sorbets too. Visitors are welcome to taste, buy and watch the milking. *Shop Open: March-end Sep; weekends off season, then 7 days a week in summer.*

Belle Isle Castle

Belle Isle Estate Lisbellaw Co Fermanagh BT94 5HG ✆*028 6638 7231 www.belle-isle.com*

Magically situated on an island on Upper Lough Erne, Belle Isle is part of the Duke of Abercorn's Estate and its impressive decor is by the renowned interior designer, David Hicks. In addition to the eight romantic bedrooms, guests have use of a magnificent drawing room and also the Grand Hall, complete with minstrels' gallery, where dinner is served – the perfect setting for an exclusive small wedding. For a naturally romantic venue, this would take some beating. **Rooms 8** *(1 shower only). Residents D daily, 8pm. Self-catering also offered. Open all year. CC.* **Directions:** *A4 to Lisbellaw - follow signs to Carrybridge.*

Belle Isle Cookery School

Lisbellaw Co Fermanagh BT94 5HG ✆*028 9581 0546 www.irishcookeryschool.com*

Located in the grounds of Belle Isle Castle (see entry), this purpose-built state-of-the-art cookery school opened in 2003 and was the first of its kind in Northern Ireland. Now run as an independent operation by Chef Joe Kelly, the school offers hands-on cookery courses and demonstration classes based on top quality seasonal produce and designed for all levels of cooking ability. It's a very personalised approach in a relaxed and informal atmosphere.

Kettyle Irish Foods

Manderwood Business Park Lisnaskea Co Fermanagh BT92 0FS
✆*028 6772 3777 www.kettyleirishfoods.com*

Maurice Kettyle's innovative food company, Kettyle Irish Foods, has developed out of their family farm and produces dry-aged beef, Lough Erne lamb, naturally reared Irish rose veal and chickens raised for flavour. The chickens follow a carefully planned programme of good husbandry, welfare and feeding and are genuinely free to roam outside in paddocks. The difference is clear: tender, fully-flavoured, succulent flesh - chicken like it used to be. Online shop. CC

Watermill Lodge

Kilmore Quay Lisnaskea Co Fermanagh BT92 0DT ✆*028 6772 4369*

Spectacularly situated on the shores of Lough Erne, this impressive restaurant with rooms is run by French chef Pascal Brissaud and his partner Valerie Smith and it's full of French character. Local produce includes vegetables from Pascal's garden, and lobster, scallops and Angus beef are among the specialities in cooking that's 'Irish with a French twist'. A visit to the Watermill will be memorable. **Seats 80.** *L&D daily (Sun 12-8.30pm);* **Rooms 7.** *Self catering accommodation also available. Restaurant closed Mon & Tue. CC.* **Directions:** *B127 from Lisnaskea south towards Tully, 3km.*

Pinsapo Restaurant

Main St Tempo Co Fermanagh BT94 3LW ✆*028 89 541 324 www.pinsaporestaurant.com*

Local girl Laura Armstrong and her husband José Manuel Mallo Varela's appealing restaurant bills itself as an 'Authentic Spanish Restaurant'. A first for Fermanagh, it attracts diners from a fair distance to enjoy the ambience and chef José's good cooking of regional Spanish dishes. The table is yours for the evening and menus - in Spanish, with English translation - offer a balance, with fish especially appealing. A genuine taste of Spain, not available elsewhere in the area. *Open Thu-Sun evenings 6 pm till late.*

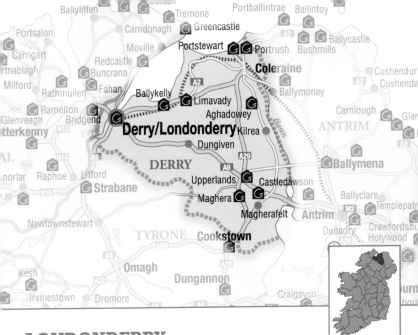

LONDONDERRY

When its boundaries were first defined for "modern" times, this was known as the County of Coleraine, named for the busy little port on the River Bann a few miles inland from the Atlantic coast. It was an area long favoured by settlers, for Mountsandel - on the salmon-rich Bann a mile south of Coleraine - is where the 9,000 year old traces of the site of some of the oldest-known houses in Ireland have been found.

The county was re-named after the City of Derry on the River Foyle became Londonderry in 1613, and it offers a fascinating variety of places and scenery, with large areas of fine farmland being punctuated by ranges of hills, while the rising slopes of the Sperrin Mountains dominate the County's southern boundary.

The lively seaport on the Foyle could reasonably claim to be the most senior of all Ireland's contemporary cities, as it can trace its origins directly back to a monastery of St Colmcille, otherwise Columba, founded in 546AD. Today, the historic city, its ancient walls matched by up-dated port facilities and a cheerfully restored urban heart, is moving into a vibrant future in which it thrives on the energy drawn from its natural position as the focal point of a larger catchment area which takes in much of Donegal County to the west in addition to County Londonderry to the east.

The area eastward of Lough Foyle is increasingly popular among discerning visitors, the Roe Valley through Dungiven and Limavady being particularly attractive, with the ferry between Magilligan Point and Greencastle in Donegal across the narrow entrance to Lough Foyle adding a welcome new dimension to the region's infrastructure.

LOCAL ATTRACTIONS & INFORMATION

▸ **Bellaghy Bawn** (Seamus Heaney centre) Bellaghy *028 79 386812*

▸ **Foyle Valley Railway Centre** Derry City *028 71 265234*

▸ **The Guildhall** Derry City *028 71 377335*

▸ **Millennium Forum Theatre** Derry City *028 71 264426*

▸ **Guy L Wilson Daffodil Garden** Coleraine *028 70 344141*

   **The Brown Trout Golf & Country Inn**

209 Agivey Road Aghadowey Co Londonderry BT51 4AD
📞 *028 7086 8209 www.browntroutinn.com*

Golf is a major attraction at the O'Hara family's lively country inn, but it is a pleasant and hospitable place for anyone to stay. While not especially luxurious, rooms arranged around the main courtyard are comfortable and accessible. The homely bar has an open fire and outside seating providing for all weathers; good home cooking, using fresh local ingredients, is served here and in the evening restaurant. Excellent self catering also offered. *Rooms 15*. Bar meals, *12-9.30 daily (to 10 in summer). Restaurant D only. Open all year. CC.* **Directions:** *Intersection of A54/B66, 7m south of Coleraine.*

                                             Greenhill House

24 Greenhill Road Aghadowey Coleraine Co Londonderry BT51 4EU
📞 *028 7086 8241 www.greenhill-house.co.uk*

Guests have been welcomed to the Hegarty family's Georgian farmhouse since 1980. In true Northern tradition, Elizabeth is a great baker and greets guests in the drawing room with afternoon tea - and her baking is also a highlight of the excellent breakfasts. Although not luxurious, bedrooms have many thoughtful touches that make them very comfortable. This lovely house and the way it is run demonstrate rural Irish hospitality at its best. *Rooms 4 (2 shower only). Closed Nov-Feb. CC.* **Directions:** *On B66 Greenhill Road off A29, 7m south of Coleraine, 3m north of Garvagh.*

                        Hunters at the Oven Door

34 Main Street Ballykelly Co Londonderry BT49 9HS 📞 *028 7776 6228*

Sean Hunter's third generation bakeries are a favourite destination for traditional foods and home baking (see Limavady; also at Coleraine). *Open Mon-Sat 8.30-5.30. Closed Sun.*

                                Ditty's Home Bakery

44 Main Street Castledawson Co Londonderry BT45 8AB
📞 *028 7946 8243 www.dittysbakery.com*

This shop and café is the home base for second generation artisan baker and real food campaigner Robert Ditty's famous range of traditional breads, oatcakes and the many other wonderful bakes that are Northern Ireland's pride and joy. The most famous products are the delicious Ditty's Irish Oat Biscuits and Shortbread, which are are distributed to speciality stores in Ireland and abroad. *Food Mon-Sat, 6.30am-5.30pm. Closed Sun.* **Directions:** *On Main Street.*

   **The Inn Castledawson**

47 Main Street Castledawson Co Londonderry BT45 8AA
📞 *028 7946 9777 www.theinncastledawson.com*

A place to stop for a bite in the welcoming bar or go for a full meal, Paula Sturges's delightful hotel and restaurant has the special ambience of a small boutique hotel that takes pride in its history. It offers well-priced menus showcasing quality produce (mainly local, some home grown) in skilfully prepared and presented dishes. Twelve chic contemporary bedrooms with river or courtyard views include a suite with its own riverside balcony. *Restaurant* **seats 80**. *Food Mon-Thu 12-7, Fri & Sat 12-5; Sun L 12-4.* **Rooms 12**. **Directions:** *On main street of Castledawson.*

Kittys of Coleraine

3 Church Lane Coleraine Co Londonderry BT52 1AG ✆*028 7034 2347*

A branch of Hunter's of Limavady, this renowned 4th generation family run bakery and coffee shop specialises in traditional Northern Irish products, baked fresh on the premises every morning. *Open Mon-Sat 9-5.30.*

Water Margin

The Boat House Hanover Place Coleraine Co Londonderry BT52 1EB ✆*028 7034 2222*

With its river views, plush bar and a luxuriously appointed dining room, this popular Chinese restaurant has all the ingredients for a special meal out. Extensive menus offer favourites like duck, sesame toast, sweet and sours and sizzling dishes, but more adventurous diners will find that this long established restaurant offers many unusual dishes too. *L & D Mon-Sat; Sun 12.30-10pm. CC.* **Directions:** *Above the boat club in Coleraine.*

LIMAVADY

An attractive Georgian town in the leafy Roe Valley, a few miles east of Derry city, the main focus of interest for visitors is the beautiful Roe Valley Country Park.

Antoinettes Café

17a Market Street Limavady Co Londonderry BT49 0AB ✆*028 7772 9194*

A daytime successor to Neil and Louise Gibson's well known restaurant Preference Brasserie in nearby Portstewart. Antoinettes may be more informal, but you will find the same attention to quality in the appealing range of casual food offered for breakfast and lunch, as well as snacks throughout the day. *Mon-Sat: 8.30am-5pm. Closed Sun. CC.* **Directions:** *On Market Square car park, behind Lidl.*

Hunters

53-55 Main Street Limavady Co Londonderry BT49 0EP ✆*028 7776 2665*

The late Norman Hunter was a household name in Northern Ireland, synonymous with quality local meats, and his son Ian now runs this excellent butcher and deli with equal dedication. Carefully sourced meat is all Northern Irish and mainly from local farms, and the quality speaks for itself. Other things to look out for include great dry-cured bacon, home-cooked meats and Irish cheeses. *Open Mon-Sat 9-5.30.*

Hunters Bakery & Café

5 -11 Market Street Limavady Co Londonderry BT49 0AB ✆*028 6632 4902*

In business since 1920, the Hunter family's renowned bakery specialises in traditional Northern Irish products, especially traditional wheaten breads and scones, made from scratch and baked fresh on the premises every morning. You can try some of them in the old fashioned coffee shop, which is especially famous for the quality of the cakes. *Open Mon-Sat 8.30-5.30. Cafe* **seats 120**.

Lime Tree Restaurant

60 Catherine Street Limavady Co Londonderry BT49 9DB
028 7776 4300 www.limetreerest.com

Loyal customers come from far and wide for the pleasure of dining at Stanley and Maria Matthews' long-established restaurant on the handsome, wide main street of this attractive town. And no wonder, as Stanley is a fine chef and Maria is a welcoming and solicitous hostess. Stanley's ingredients are carefully sourced, many of them local, and his menus are generous, with a classical base that he works on to give popular dishes a new twist. Good cooking and good value go hand in hand with warm hospitality here. **Seats 30**. L Thu & Fri. D Wed-Sat. Closed Sun-Tue, 25 Dec, 12 Jul. CC. **Directions:** On the outskirts of town, main Derry-Limavady road.

  Mullans Organic Farm

84 Ringsend Road Limavady Co Londonderry BT49 0QJ
028 777 64940 www.mullansorganicfarm.com

Since gaining full organic status in 2000, the Mullan family's traditional beef and sheep hill farm has diversified and now produces Aberdeen Angus beef and hill lamb (assorted breeds), poultry (chicken, ducks and geese) and eggs. Their produce is available from several small retailers but main sales are at St. George's Saturday Market in Belfast. Visitors are also welcome to call to the farm to buy produce on Fridays (advisable to ring ahead). Self-catering accommodation is also available.

  **Roe Park Resort**

40 Drumrane Road Roe Park Limavady Co Londonderry BT47 2AH
028 7772 2222 www.roeparkresort.com

Set in rolling countryside, this imposing hotel outside Limavady dates back to the eighteenth century and has a pleasing air of relaxed luxury. It is a popular conference venue, with excellent leisure facilities for all to enjoy, and spacious bedrooms overlooking the golf course or a courtyard garden. Formal dining is available in Greens Restaurant or a more relaxed style in the Coach House Brasserie. **Rooms 118**. Greens Restaurant: **Seats 80** D daily L Sun only. Informal L&D available daily. Open all year. CC.

LONDONDERRY / DERRY CITY

Standing on a hill beside the Foyle estuary this historic city dates back to 546 AD; designated UK City of Culture in 2013, it has a modern attitude and is wonderfully compact with a whole host of attractions contained within the city walls. The city contains an array of historic buildings, excellent restaurants, lively pubs, theatres such as the Millennium Forum Theatre (028 264426) and great shopping including a craft village in the city centre. Local attractions include the award winning Tower Museum (028 7137 2411, open all year), which gives visitors a wonderful insight into the city's history, the Foyle Valley Railway Centre (028 71 265234), the Harbour Museum (028 71 377331), and St Columb's Cathedral (028 71 267

313). The famous walls of the city offer visitors one of the finest and best preserved of all the town fortifications in Ireland, a walk along these historic walls is a must for any visitor, with scenic views across the River Foyle to be enjoyed. The city's well known Guildhall (028 7137 7335) built in neo-gothic style houses various artefacts and acts as a civil and cultural centre for Derry. Local activities include an 18 hole championship golf course at the City of Derry Golf Club (028 7143 6369), and anglers will enjoy the Foyle river system famous for its salmon or a trip to the Oaks Trout Fishery (028 8224 4932), a 15 acre spring fed lake with a healthy stock of rainbow trout. The nearby Ness Wood Country Park is a beautiful spot for walking, offering 50 hectares of mixed woodland and includes a spectacular waterfall.

  Beech Hill Country House Hotel

32 Ardmore Road Londonderry Co Londonderry BT47 3QP
☎ 028 7134 9279 www.beech-hill.com

Beautifully set in 42 acres of peaceful woodland, waterfalls and gardens, this charming hotel dates back to 1729 and has retained many period details. Proprietor Patsy O'Kane is a caring hostess and the comfortable rooms feature her ever-growing collection of antiques. US Marines had their headquarters here in World War II and a small museum of the US Marine Friendship Association is of special interest. Modern classic cooking with a strong Irish twist is served in the very attractive Ardmore Restaurant, overlooking gardens. A popular wedding venue and a lovely place to stay. **Rooms 30** *(10 shower only). Restaurant* **seats 100***. L&D daily. Closed 24-25 Dec. CC.* **Directions:** *Main Londonderry road A6.*

Browns Restaurant & Champagne Lounge

1-2 Bonds Hill Londonderry Co Londonderry BT47 6DW
☎ 028 7134 5180 www.brownsrestaurant.com

The city's most highly-regarded restaurant over two decades, Browns is now in an exciting new phase in the ownership of Ian Orr. A leading chef who is renowned for his dedication to fresh, seasonal produce and support of local suppliers, he cooks with a deft hand and a light touch. Some of the finest cooking in the land is on offer here, and very reasonably priced – visitors keen to experience the best that this fulsome area has to offer will not be disappointed, and the Tasting Menu in particular is highly recommended. A must-visit when in Derry. *L Tue-Fri & Sun; D Tue-Sat. Closed Sun D & Mon. CC. [Also at: Browns Bistro Culmore (at the 'Magnet' bar); Browns in Town, Strand Road (just open at time of going to press, fine dining; 028 71362889).* **Directions:** *In a cul-de-sac opposite the old Waterside railway station.*

City Hotel

Queens Quay Londonderry Co Londonderry BT48 7AS ☎ 028 7136 5800 www.gshotels.com

Centrally situated and overlooking the River Foyle, this modern hotel is bright and contemporary and would make an equally attractive base for a leisure visit or for business. Well-located close to the old city, business districts and main shopping areas, it also has free private parking for guests and on-site leisure facilities. **Rooms 145***. CC.*

Custom House Restaurant & Wine Bar

Custom House Street Queens Quay Londonderry Co Londonderry BT48 7AS
📞028 7137 3366 www.customhouserestaurant.com

Located in a luxuriously converted listed building with a sense of fun, The Custom House kitchen elevates familiar dishes with style and turns out bold, uncomplicated plates of succulent food with big flavours. Friendly, well-trained staff make a major contribution to the dining experience, providing service to match the food and the setting. A great place for a stylish night out, or as a special business or wedding venue. *Seats 110. Lunch Mon-Sat, D Mon-Thur, Sun 1-9pm. Closed 25 Dec. CC.*

 Encore Brasserie

Millenium Forum Complex Newmarket Street Londonderry Co Londonderry BT48 6EB
📞028 7137 2492

This appealing brasserie in the centre of the Millennium Forum offers interesting, fairly priced food and a well-chosen wine list. As well as pre-theatre meals, it's good for business lunches and its location between the city's two main shopping centres widens the appeal, especially as children are very well catered for. *Seats 70. Open daily L&D when there is a show on, otherwise open L&D Wed-Sat. Closed Sun-Tue when there is no show on, 24-26 Dec, 1 Jan. CC.*

 Exchange Restaurant & Wine Bar

Queens Quay Londonderry Co Londonderry BT48 7AY 📞028 7127 3990

Although seriously modern, Mark Caithness's popular restaurant is a friendly and welcoming place that appeals to all age groups and their colourful, fresh-flavoured food suits the surroundings perfectly. They seem to have a winning formula here as prices are reasonable, ingredients are sourced locally as far as possible and the cooking hits the mark. One of Derry's favourite restaurants and deservedly so. *Seats 120. L Mon-Sat; D daily. No reservations. Closed 25 Dec. CC.*

 Fitzroys Restaurant

2-4 Bridge Street 3 Carlisle Road Londonderry Co Londonderry BT48 6JZ
📞028 7126 6211 www.fitzroysrestaurant.com

This large, modern restaurant beside the Foyle Shopping Centre is on two floors and very handy for shoppers, visitors or pre- and post-theatre meals. Their central philosophy is to provide good-quality, reasonably priced food in enjoyably informal surroundings. A conveniently located, family-friendly restaurant, this is one of the city's most consistent restaurants and offers great value - no wonder it is also one of the most popular. *Seats 80. Open daily, L&D, Sun 1-8pm. Closed 25 Dec. CC.*

 **Hastings Everglades Hotel**

Prehen Road Londonderry Co Londonderry BT47 2NH
📞028 7132 1066 www.hastingshotels.com

Set on the banks of the River Foyle, close to the airport and convenient to the city, this modern, quietly situated hotel is well located for business and pleasure, including golf. The bedrooms are well maintained and, although beds are only standard double, otherwise very comfortable and with good amenities. A pleasant place to stay, with friendly staff. *Rooms 64. Open all year. CC.*

 ## The Merchants House

16 Queen Street Londonderry Co Londonderry BT48 7DB
☏ *028 7126 9691 www.thesaddlershouse.com*

Joan and Peter Pyne's Georgian-style 1867 townhouse offers an interesting alternative to hotel accommodation and is popular with cultural visitors to the city. The rooms vary in size, position within the building and outlook, but are well appointed and a good breakfast features local foods. Offering an authentic experience, this listed building is conveniently located, full of charm and reasonably priced. *Rooms 8 (shower only; some shred facilities). Closed Jan & Feb. CC.*

 ## Ramada Da Vinci's Hotel

15 Culmore Road Londonderry Co Londonderry BT48 8JB
☏ *028 7127 9111 www.davincishotel.com*

This very popular hotel is about a mile from the city centre; it has private car parking and there is a pleasant riverside walkway into the city from the hotel. *Rooms 65 (1 shower only). Closed 24-25 Dec. CC.*

 ## Tower Hotel Derry

Off The Diamond Londonderry Co Londonderry BT48 6HL
☏ *028 7137 1000 www.towerhotelderry.com*

This attractive hotel has the distinction of being the only one to have been built inside the city walls. Accommodation and facilities suit both leisure and business visitors (one floor is designated executive); the bistro appeals to non-residents as well as hotel guests and a fitness suite has a great view across the city. Limited underground parking (not bookable except disabled). *Rooms 90. Closed 24-27 Dec. CC.*

 ## Waterfoot Hotel

Caw Roundabout Waterside Londonderry Co Londonderry BT47 6TB
☏ *028 7134 5500 www.waterfoothotel.com*

Located in the Waterside area, just beside the beautiful new Foyle Bridge, this glamorous younger sister to the city's popular Da Vinci Hotel is only a short drive into the city and convenient to many visitor attractions, golf and wonderful scenery in both County Derry and nearby Donegal. Accommodation is smart and contemporary and the Waterfoot offers spacious conference and banqueting facilities. *Rooms 44. CC.*

 ## McKees Butchers

78 Main Street Maghera Co Londonderry BT46 5AF ☏ *028 7964 2559 www.mckeespies.com*

Established in 1898 by owner George McKee's grandfather, these family butchers have always had a great reputation for their meats but the business became an early example of diversification in the 1980's, when George's sister Iris started making magnificent homemade pies to sell in the shop. Today, McKees still sells great meat and offers a full range of family butchery services - but, thanks to Iris, the name is now synonymous with quality pies. *Open Mon-Fri 8-7, Sat 8-6. Closed Sun. Parking.*

Church Street Restaurant

23 Church Street Magherafelt Co Londonderry BT45 6AP
📞 *028 7932 8083 www.churchstreetrestaurant.co.uk*

Just across the road from Laurel Villa (see entry), highly regarded chef Roly Graham's restaurant opened in 2012 and set the bar high from the outset, with seasonally-led menus changing daily and an emphasis on quality ingredients from local suppliers. Fish and seafood features strongly among a varied offering, also very good beef. Friendly and attentive staff, together with attention to detail and assured cooking at attractive prices, make this a deservedly popular destination. *Wed & Thu 5-9pm, Fri & Sat: 5-10pm, Sun 12-8pm. CC.*

Ditty's Home Bakery & Coffee Shop

33 Rainey Street Magherafelt Co Londonderry BT45 5AA
📞 *028 7963 3944 www.dittysbakery.com*

A sister to Ditty's of Castledawson (see entry), renowned for their excellent home baking. Helen, wife of famous artisan baker Robert Ditty, runs the Magherafelt bakery and shop, offering their famous range of home-bakes. The café is in the bakery, mainly serving baked treats to have with a tea or coffee, although several hot dishes are also served every day. **Seats 20.** *Mon-Sat all 6.30am-5.30pm, closed Sun.* **Directions:** *Centre of Magherafelt.*

Gardiners G2

7 Garden Street Magherafelt Co Londonderry BT45 5DD
📞 *028 7930 0333 www.gardiners.net*

Sean and Helen Owens have run this impressive restaurant since 1999 and, although the premises has seen changes, their stated aim - to bring quality local food and service to the people of the area – has never wavered. Committed supporters of local produce and suppliers, they offer quality food through accessible menus that offer creative variations of popular dishes - and some unusual specialities too. A great neighbourhood restaurant and a good night out. **Seats 90.** *D Wed-Sun, L Sun only. Closed Mon, Tue, 25-26 Dec, 12-13 Jul. CC.* **Directions:** *To diamond in Magherafelt, down Rainey St., first right into Garden St.*

JC Stewarts

1 Union Road Magherafelt Co Londonderry BT45 5DF
📞 *028 7930 2930 www.jcstewart.co.uk*

"If it is a quality product, grown, reared or produced in this area then JC Stewart Foodhall wants to stock it." This means "... local meat, local bacon, ham and dairy products, together with bread from a dozen local bakeries..." And you'll find many familiar local specialities on the shelves, like McKee's pies from Maghera and Ditty's of Castledawson famous oatcakes, alongside their own home made products. This was Northern Ireland's first self-service supermarket and it remains one of the best. *Open: Mon-Wed 8-7, Thu & Fri 8-9, Sat 8-6. Closed Sun.*

Laurel Villa

60 Church Street Magherafelt Co Londonderry BT45 6AW
☎ 028 7930 1459 www.laurel-villa.com

Gerardine and Eugene Kielt's supremely comfortable Victorian townhouse exudes charm and instils a sense of curiosity within the many guests who travel here from far and wide to experience their hospitality and the unique cultural experience they offer. They host a permanent exhibition of the poet Seamus Heaney, who was born nearby; Eugene conducts heritage and cultural tours, and special poetry reading evenings and events are held, some with Seamus Heaney present. Delicious breakfasts featuring local produce have freshly baked wheaten bread among the treats. An absolute gem. *Rooms 4. CC. Directions: Church Street is on the main Castledawson Road (A31).*

Moss Brook Farm

6 Durnascallon Lane Desertmartin Magherafelt Co Londonderry BT45 5LZ
☎ 028 7963 3454 www.mossbrookfarm.weebly.com

Trevor Barclay's Moss Brook Farm pigs are pedigree Landrace, born and bred on the farm, and the delicious meat boiling bacon, dry-cured rashers, and mild-cured gammon they provide is sold at the farm, and at St. George's Saturday Market in Belfast. They cook up their rashers, sausages and burgers there, to serve in lovely big crusty Belfast baps - and there's the Moss-Hog Spit Roast too, which they also offer for special events. Well worth a visit. Sold at the farm, and at St. George's Saturday Market in Belfast (9-2, right beside the fish).

PORTSTEWART

This seaside resort town includes a small sheltered harbour, with attractive houses along the promenade and a beautiful three mile strand stretching to the mouth of the Bann River. The strand at Portstewart is the main attraction for visitors and offers excellent surf fishing for bass. Other local attractions include Agherton Old Church (028 7083 3277), Portstewart's original church dating from the 1300s and the Flowerfield Arts Centre (028 7083 1400), which is a venue for arts and crafts courses, and also houses exhibitions and provides art lectures. The nearby Mussenden Temple and gardens (028 70 848728) at Downhill, owned by the National Trust is well worth a visit, and was originally built as a library by the Earl Bishop of Derry. The golf enthusiast will enjoy a round at the 18 hole championship links course at Portstewart Golf Club (028 7083 2015), which provides magnificent views of the Atlantic and Donegal.

Cromore Halt Inn

158 Station Road Portstewart Co Londonderry BT55 7PU ☎ 028 7083 6888 www.cromore.com

This friendly, family-owned guesthouse and restaurant, managed by Niall and Kate O'Boyle, is a good base for business or leisure. The rooms are furnished in an uncluttered, modern style and have all the expected facilities. The restaurant is open for lunch and dinner every day and has earned a reputation in the locality for quality, value and good service. *Rooms 12. Restaurant: L&D daily. Closed 24-26 Dec. CC. Directions: on left as you enter Portstewart.*

 **Strand House**

105 Strand Road Portstewart Co Londonderry BT55 7LZ
☎028 7083 1000 www.strandguesthouse.com

Tom and Ernestine McKeever's spacious family-run B&B in Portstewart offers a stylish alternative to hotel accommodation on the Causeway Coast. Big windows take advantage of the sea views across to Greencastle in Donegal and uncluttered bedrooms have bathrooms with shower/Jacuzzi baths. Homemade scones are served when guests arrive and a very good breakfast includes freshly squeezed orange juice and organic porridge. *Rooms 7 (3 shower only). Closed mid Dec-mid Jan. CC.* **Directions:** *On Strand Road (from first road coming from Strand & Golf Course).*

 Strandeen B&B

63 Strand Road Portstewart Co Londonderry BT55 7LU ☎028 7083 3159 www.strandeen.com

Rooms at Debbie Blaney's friendly B&B overlooking Portstewart Strand have all the details that make for a really comfortable stay, and a welcoming big sitting room has comfy seating, picture windows over the bay and a real fire. Debbie is a can-do host who obviously enjoys spoiling her guests with afternoon tea in the sitting room and a good Northern Irish breakfast. Picnic lunches can also be arranged. *Rooms 3 (all shower only). Open all year. CC.* **Directions:** *0.5m from Portstewart Main street.*

 **Ardtara Country House**

8 Gorteade Road Upperlands Maghera Co Londonderry BT46 5SA
☎028 7964 4490 www.ardtara.com

Former home to the Clark linen milling family, Ardtara is now an elegantly decorated Victorian country house and manager Valerie Ferson gives it a genuinely hospitable atmosphere. Guest rooms are luxuriously furnished in period style. Informal meals are offered in the bar and conservatory and dinner is served in the former snooker room, which features an original skylight and hunting frieze. An excellent base for exploring this beautiful and unspoilt area. *Rooms 9 (1 shower only). Restaurant seats 80. L Sun, D Daily. CC.* **Directions:** *M2 from from Belfast to A6. A29 to Maghera. B75 to Kilrea.*

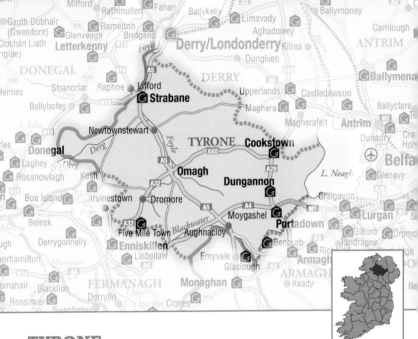

TYRONE

Tyrone is Northern Ireland's largest county, so it is something of a surprise for the traveller to discover that its geography appears to be dominated by a range of mountains of modest height, and nearly half of these peaks seem to be in the neighbouring county of Londonderry.

Yet such is the case with Tyrone and the Sperrins. The village of Sperrin itself towards the head of Glenelly may be in Tyrone, but the highest peak of Sawel (678 m), which looms over it, is on the county boundary. But much of the county is upland territory and moorland, giving the impression that the Sperrins are even more extensive than is really the case.

In such a land, the lower country and the fertile valleys gleam like jewels, and there's often a vivid impression of a living - and indeed, prosperity - being wrested from a demanding environment. It's a character-forming sort of place, so it's perhaps understandable that it was the ancestral homeland of a remarkable number of early American Presidents, and this connection is commemorated in the Ulster American Folk Park a few miles north of the county town of Omagh.

Forest parks abound, while attractive towns like Castlederg and Dungannon, as well as villages in the uplands and along the charming Clogher Valley, provide entertainment and hospitality for visitors refreshed by the wide open spaces of the moorlands and the mountains.

LOCAL ATTRACTIONS & INFORMATION

▸ **Benburb Castle and Valley Park** Benburb
028 37 548241

▸ **Clogher Valley Rural Centre** Clogher *028 85 548872*

▸ **Wellbrook Beetling Mill (Corkhill)** Cookstown
028 86 748210

▸ **Sperrin Heritage Centre** Cranagh (Glenelly)
028 81 648142

▸ **Tyrone Crystal** Dungannon *028 87 725335*

▸ **Clogher Valley Railway Exhibition** Fivemiletown
028 89 521409

▸ **Ulster-American Folk Park** Omagh *028 82 243292*

▸ **President Wilson Ancestral Home** Strabane
028 71 3844

Suitor Gallery Tea Room

17 Grange Road Ballygawley Co Tyrone BT70 2LP ☎*028 8556 8653 www.suitorgallery.com*

Despite its location beside Ballygawley Roundabout, a converted barn in a small orchard provides an attractively rustic setting for this long-established business. It is an excellent gift shop - way above the average, lots of gift ideas including lovely things for children - and also a teashop, serving teas, coffees, snacks and lunches. Everything is home made and tasty - what a good little place this is. *Open Tue-Sat 9.30-5.30. (L to 2.55). Online shop. CC.*

Cloughbane Farm

160 Tanderagee Road Pomeroy Dungannon Co Tyrone BT70 3HS
☎*028 8775 8246 www.cloughbanefarm.com*

Fourth generation farmers, the Robinson family focus on beef (Aberdeen Angus/Limousin cross heifers), lamb (Texel cross) and free-range egg production on their 185 acre farm. Since being introduced to direct sales when the local farmers' market started in 2002, they have never looked back. This is one of Northern Ireland's biggest and best organised farm shops, selling their own produce and that of hand picked local farmers who can live up to their telling slogan, 'Taste You Can Trust'. Also other products, including their own prepared meals. *Shop open: Mon-Fri 8.30-6, Sat 8-5. Closed Sun. Extended hours pre-Christmas. Online shop.*

 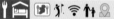

Grange Lodge

7 Grange Road Dungannon Co Tyrone BT71 7EJ
☎*028 8778 4212 www.grangelodgecountryhouse.com*

Ralph and Norah Brown's renowned Georgian retreat offers comfort, true family hospitality and good food. The house is furnished with antiques and family pieces throughout and bedrooms are exceptionally comfortable and thoughtful in detail. Norah, a Rick Stein 'food hero', is well known for her home cooking and provides delicious residents' dinners and outstanding breakfasts, so allow time to indulge. Cookery classes offered too. **Rooms 5** *(3 shower only). Residents D Mon-Sat, 7.30pm, by arrangement. Closed 15 Dec-1 Feb. CC.* **Directions:** *1 mile from M1 junction 15. On A29 to Armagh, follow "Grange Lodge" signs.*

Stangmore Town House

24 Killyman Road Dungannon Co Tyrone BT71 6DH
☎*028 8772 5600 www.stangmoretownhouse.com*

Anne and Andy Brace's conveniently central property offers very comfortable accommodation, great hospitality and immaculate housekeeping. Rooms are bright and and spacious, and there's a relaxing sitting room for guests' use. Their breakfasts are renowned but their USP is the restaurant, where Andy - a committed environmentalist and a health-conscious chef - offers dinners based on the best of local produce. **Rooms 5** *(1 shower only). Restaurant* **Seats 50**. *D daily by reservation, L groups only, closed Sun; house closed 1 week Jul & Christmas. CC.*

The Brewer's House

Dungannon Area 73 Castlecaulfied Road Donaghmore Dungannon Co Tyrone BT70 3HB
☎*028 8776 1932 www.thebrewershouse.com*

Ciaran and Vicki McCausland's 18th century hostelry offers perfect pub food – straightforward, hearty plates served by friendly staff. No formal supplier list (and imports like the ubiquitous tiger prawn feature), but Brian McMonagle's interesting menus include great local produce like Lough Neagh eel, Lissara chicken and Cloughbane beef. Expect confidently simple, well cooked and attractively presented food, with Sunday lunch a triumph and tender Crossgar Old Spot pork with crispy crackling taking pride of place. Well worth a visit. *Seats 100. Open Thu & Fri12-9, Sat 12-10, Sun 12-8.30. Closed Mon-Wed.*

Fivemiletown Creamery

14 Ballylurgan Road Fivemiletown Co Tyrone ✆*028 8952 1209 www.fivemiletown.com*

Situated in the lush Clogher Valley, Fivemiletown Creamery is a long-established cheese producer. Unusually, these highly regarded producers are now better known for the cheese brands they have bought in recent years than for their own lines - Boilié goats cheeses, for example and, since 2012, the four cheeses in the Causeway Cheese Company range - Castlequarter, Ballyknock, Ballybradden and Coolkeeran.

Deli on the Green

The Linen Green Moygashel Co Tyrone BT71 7HB
✆*028 8775 1775 www.deliontthegreen.com*

Besides a classy deli, this popular spot offers café-style seating for coffee and snacks, and a stylish bistro. A member of both Taste of Ulster and Flavour of Tyrone, the seasonal, frequently changed menus reflect proprietor Claire Murray's commitment to profiling quality local produce and no GM foods are used. *Seats 45. Mon-Sat 8.30-5.30pm, D Thu-Sat. Closed Sun. CC.*

The Loft @ The Linen Green

Moygashel Co Tyrone BT71 7HB ✆*028 8775 3761 www.theloftcoffeebar.com*

Developed on the site of a former textile mill, the Linen Green discount designer outlet and retail park complex retains an historic feel. Upstairs in the main building, The Loft café is an attractive pitstop run by Claire Murray (of Deli on the Green) with high ceilings, lots of light and some memorabilia from Moygashel's days as a textile mill. *Open Mon-Sat, 9am-5pm. Closed Sun. Directions: Just off main Belfast road, follow signs to Moygashel.*

Oysters Restaurant

37 Patrick Street Strabane Co Tyrone BT82 8DQ ✆*028 7138 2690 www.oystersrestaurant.co.uk*

Owned by Kevin and Caroline Clarke, Strabane's leading restaurant is an attractive building near the courthouse and the town theatre, with pretty hanging baskets to welcome arriving guests, and menus displayed on either side of the front door. As a Taste of Ulster member, menus reflect the availability of local foods, such as 28-day hung Northern Ireland beef, game in winter, and seasonal vegetables. Delicious Glastry Farm Ice Cream is offered alongside the homemade desserts, and the cheeseboard offers a selection from nearby Fivemiletown Creamery. Expect confidently contemporary cooking and stylish presentation, sometimes with quirky details. *Food served all day, 7 days, 12-9.30pm. Closed 25/26 Dec. CC. Directions: Near the court house.*

JOURNEY PLANNER - WITH SUGGESTED PLACES FOR A BREAK...

ⓔ – EAT   ⓓ – DRINK   ⓢ – STAY

Dublin - Belfast

Travel Time (approx): 2 Hours

Distance: 168 km (104 miles)

Roads: M1 / N1 / A1 / M1

DUBLIN → BELFAST

25% 50% 75%

	Town	County	Road	Km from Dublin	Km from Road	Category
1	Malahide	Dublin	M1	12	5	ⓔ ⓓ ⓢ
	Swords	Dublin	M1	12	3	ⓔ ⓓ ⓢ
2	Skerries	Dublin	M1	16	16	ⓔ ⓓ ⓢ
3	Bettystown	Meath	M1	35	11	ⓢ
4	Drogheda	Louth	M1	45	4	ⓔ ⓓ ⓢ
	Termonfeckin	Louth	M1	45	13	ⓔ
5	Slane	Louth	M1	45	12	ⓔ ⓓ ⓢ
	Clogherhead	Louth	M1	61	13	ⓔ
6	Ardee	Louth	M1	65	9	ⓔ ⓓ
7	Annagassan	Louth	M1	70	6	ⓔ ⓓ
8	Blackrock	Louth	M1	78	7	ⓔ ⓓ ⓢ
9	Dundalk	Louth	M1	90	2	ⓔ ⓓ ⓢ
10	Warrenpoint	Down	A1	103	13	ⓔ
	Rostrevor	Down	A1	103	15	ⓔ
	Newry	Down	A1	103	3	ⓔ ⓓ
11	Banbridge	Down	A1	125	3	ⓔ ⓓ
	P/down/Cragiavon	Armagh	A1	125	20	ⓔ ⓓ ⓢ
12	Moira/Magheralin	Armagh	A1	150	14	ⓔ ⓓ ⓢ
	Hillsborough	Down	A1	150	3	ⓔ ⓓ
	Lisburn	Antrim	M1	150	3	ⓔ

JOURNEY PLANNER - WITH SUGGESTED PLACES FOR A BREAK...

⊖ – EAT   Ⓓ – DRINK   Ⓢ – STAY

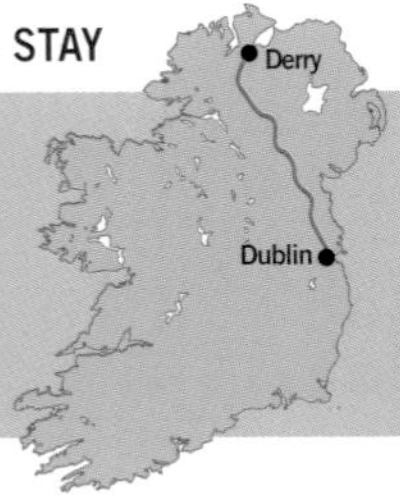

Dublin - Derry

Travel Time (approx):
3.5 Hours

Distance:
230 km (145 miles)

Roads:
M2 / N2 / A5

DUBLIN → ──────────── DERRY

25% | 50% | 75% |

❶ ❷ ❸ ❹ ❺   ❻❼   ❽   ❾

	Town	County	Road	Km from Dublin	Km from Road	Category
1	Ashbourne	Meath	M2	19	2	⊖ Ⓢ
2	Navan	Meath	N2	50	13	⊖ Ⓓ Ⓢ
3	Slane	Meath	N2	50	0	⊖ Ⓓ Ⓢ
4	Collon	Louth	N2	57	0	⊖
5	Ardee	Louth	N2	68	0	⊖ Ⓓ
5	Carrickmacross	Monaghan	N2	85	2	⊖ Ⓓ Ⓢ

	Town	County	Road	Km from Dublin	Km from Road	Category
6	Monaghan	Monaghan	N2	124	2	⊖ Ⓓ Ⓢ
	Clones	Monaghan	N2	124	21	Ⓢ
7	Glaslough	Monaghan	N2	126	8	⊖ Ⓢ
8	Dungannon	Tyrone	A5	154	20	Ⓢ
	Moygashel	Tyrone	A5	154	20	⊖
9	Strabane	Tyrone	A5	208	2	⊖

JOURNEY PLANNER - WITH SUGGESTED PLACES FOR A BREAK...

ⓔ – EAT   ⓓ – DRINK   ⓢ – STAY

Dublin - Donegal

Travel Time (approx):
3.25 Hours

Distance:
231 km (143 miles)

Roads:
M3 / N3 / A509 / A46 / N3 / N15

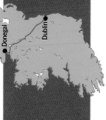

DUBLIN ➞ ❶ ❷   ❸❹ ❺   ❻ ❼   ❽   ❾ ❿⓫ ⓬ ⓭ ⓮ **DONEGAL**

25%   50%   75%

	Town	County	Road	Km from Dublin	Km from Road	Category
1	Dunboyne	Meath	M3	18	3	ⓔ ⓓ ⓢ
2	Kilmessan	Meath	M3	28	13	ⓢ
3	Tara	Meath	M3	41	3	ⓓ
4	Navan	Meath	M3	46	6	ⓔ ⓓ ⓢ
5	Athboy	Meath	M3	51	14	ⓔ ⓢ
6	Kells	Meath	M3	65	2	ⓔ
7	Virginia	Cavan	N3	84	1	ⓔ ⓓ ⓢ
	Mount Nugent	Cavan	N3	85	18	ⓢ
	Bailieborough	Cavan	N3	85	13	ⓔ
8	Cavan	Cavan	N3	112	2	ⓔ ⓓ ⓢ
9	Cloverhill	Cavan	N3	120	4	ⓔ ⓓ ⓢ
10	Belturbet	Cavan	N3	129	0	ⓔ ⓓ ⓢ
11	Ballyconnell	Cavan	N3	130	10	ⓔ ⓓ ⓢ
12	Blacklion	Cavan	A509	161	16	ⓔ ⓓ ⓢ
	Enniskillen	Fermanagh	A509	161	3	ⓔ ⓓ ⓢ
13	Belleek	Fermanagh	A46	201	1	ⓔ
14	Ballyshannon	Donegal	N3	208	0	ⓔ ⓓ
	Rossnowlagh	Donegal	N15	210	8	ⓔ ⓓ ⓢ

JOURNEY PLANNER - WITH SUGGESTED PLACES FOR A BREAK...   🕒 – EAT   🍷 – DRINK   🛏 – STAY

Dublin - Sligo

Travel Time (approx):
3 Hours

Distance:
207 km (130 miles)

Roads:
M4 / N4

DUBLIN → 25% | 50% | 75% → SLIGO

	Town	County	Road	Km from Dublin	Km from Road	Category
1	Lucan	Dublin	N4	13	2	🕒 🛏
2	Leixlip	Dublin	N4	15	2	🕒 🛏
	Celbridge	Kildare	N4	15	5	🕒
3	Clane	Kildare	M4	23	12	🕒
	Maynooth	Kildare	M4	23	2	🕒 🍷 🛏
	Straffan	Kildare	M4	23	6	🕒 🛏
4	Enfield	Kildare	M4	41	3	🛏
5	MoyValley	Kildare	M4	42	6	🕒 🍷 🛏
6	Mullingar	Westmeath	N4	76	3	🕒 🍷 🛏
7	Multyfarnham	Westmeath	N4	86	3	🕒 🍷 🛏
8	Granard	Longford	N4	105	12	🛏
9	Longford	Longford	N4	118	2	🕒 🍷 🛏

	Town	County	Road	Km from Dublin	Km from Road	Category
10	Rooskey	Leitrim	N4	131	3	🛏
11	Drumshanbo	Leitrim	N4	146	17	🛏
	Leitrim	Leitrim	N4	146	10	🕒 🍷
12	Jamestown	Leitrim	N4	149	1	🕒
13	Carrick on Shannon	Leitrim	N4	153	0	🕒 🍷 🛏
	Keshcarrigan	Leitrim	N4	153	15	🕒
14	Knockvicar	Roscommon	N4	160	5	🕒 🍷
	Cootehall	Roscommon	N4	160	4	🕒 🍷
15	Castlebaldwin	Sligo	N4	182	0	🕒 🍷 🛏
16	Riverstown	Sligo	N4	186	4	🛏
17	Collooney	Sligo	N4	196	0	🛏
	Ballygawley	Sligo	N4	196	3	🕒 🛏

SLIGO

Dublin - Westport

Travel Time (approx):
3.5 Hours

Distance:
271 km (168 miles)

Roads:
N4 / M4 / N5

DUBLIN ❶ ❷ ❸ ❹ ❺ 25% 50% ❻ ❼ 75% WESTPORT ❽ ❾

	Town	County	Road	Km from Dublin	Km from Road	Category
1	Lucan	Dublin	N4	13	2	☺ ⓢ
	Leixlip	Dublin	N4	15	2	☺ ⓢ
	Celbridge	Kildare	N4	15	5	☺
2	Clane	Kildare	M4	23	12	☺
	Maynooth	Kildare	M4	23	2	☺ ⓓ ⓢ
	Straffan	Kildare	M4	23	6	☺ ⓢ
3	Enfield	Kildare	M4	41	3	ⓢ
	MoyValley	Kildare	M4	42	6	☺ ⓓ ⓢ

	Town	County	Road	Km from Dublin	Km from Road	Category
4	Mullingar	Westmeath	N4	76	3	☺ ⓓ ⓢ
5	Multyfarnham	Westmeath	N4	86	3	☺ ⓓ ⓢ
	Granard	Longford	N4	105	12	ⓢ
6	Longford	Longford	N4	118	2	☺ ⓓ ⓢ
7	Tarmonbarry	Roscommon	N5	129	0	☺ ⓓ
8	Turlough	Mayo	N5	243	5	☺
9	Castlebar	Mayo	N5	254	1	☺ ⓓ ⓢ

Dublin - Galway

⊖ – EAT   ⊕ – DRINK   Ⓢ – STAY

Travel Time (approx): 2.5 Hours

Distance: 207 km (129 miles)

Roads: M4 / N6

DUBLIN → → → 25% → → 50% → → 75% → → GALWAY

#	Town	County	Road	Km from Dublin	Km from Road	Category
1	Lucan	Dublin	N4	13	2	⊖Ⓢ
2	Leixlip	Dublin	N4	15	2	⊖Ⓢ
	Celbridge	Kildare	N4	15	5	⊖
3	Clane	Kildare	M4	23	12	⊖
	Maynooth	Kildare	M4	23	2	⊖⊕Ⓢ
	Straffan	Kildare	M4	23	6	⊖Ⓢ
4	Enfield	Kildare	M4	41	3	Ⓢ
5	MoyValley	Kildare	M4	42	6	⊖⊕Ⓢ
6	Kilbeggan	Westmeath	M6	89	1	⊖
	Tullamore	Offaly	M6	89	12	⊖⊕Ⓢ

#	Town	County	Road	Km from Dublin	Km from Road	Category
7	Moate	Westmeath	M6	103	3	Ⓢ
8	Glasson	Westmeath	M6	117	8	⊖⊕Ⓢ
	Athlone	Westmeath	M6	117	6	⊖⊕Ⓢ
9	Shannonbridge	Offaly/Roscommon	M6	145	11	⊖⊕
10	Ballinasloe	Galway	M6	149	3	⊖⊕Ⓢ
11	Athenry	Galway	M6	185	3	⊖⊕
	Craughwell	Galway	M6	185	9	⊖Ⓢ
12	Clarinbridge	Galway	M6	197	8	⊖

JOURNEY PLANNER - WITH SUGGESTED PLACES FOR A BREAK...

☺ – EAT   🥤 – DRINK   Ⓢ – STAY

Dublin - Limerick - Killarney

Travel Time (approx):
4.5 Hours

Distance:
303 km (189 miles)

Roads:
N7 / M7 / N21 / N23

25% | 50% | 75%

DUBLIN → .... → **KILLARNEY**

	Town	County	Road	Km from Dublin	Km from Road	Category
1	Red Cow R/about	Dublin	N7	8	0	Ⓢ
2	Newlands Cross	Dublin	N7	10	0	Ⓢ
	Liffey Valley	Dublin	N7	10	0	☺ Ⓢ
3	Saggart	Dublin	N7	15	1	Ⓢ
4	Naas	Kildare	N7	28	3	☺ 🥤 Ⓢ
5	Newbridge	Kildare	M7	45	3	Ⓢ
6	Killenard	Laois	M7	58	11	☺ Ⓢ
7	Portlaoise	Laois	M7	87	1	☺ 🥤 Ⓢ
	Ballyfin	Laois	M7	87	3	Ⓢ
	Mountrath	Laois	M7	87	10	Ⓢ

	Town	County	Road	Km from Dublin	Km from Road	Category
8	Roscrea	Tipperary	M7	126	5	☺
9	Nenagh	Tipperary	M7	152	4	☺ 🥤 Ⓢ
	Garrykennedy	Tipperary	M7	152	11	☺ 🥤 Ⓢ
10	Dromineer	Tipperary	M7	158	12	☺ 🥤
11	**LIMERICK**	Limerick	M7	191	6	☺ 🥤 Ⓢ
12	Adare	Limerick	N21	210	0	☺ 🥤 Ⓢ
	Ballingarry	Limerick	N21	210	12	☺ Ⓢ
13	Listowel	Kerry	N21	255	16	☺ Ⓢ
14	Tralee	Kerry	N21	274	18	☺ 🥤 Ⓢ

JOURNEY PLANNER - WITH SUGGESTED PLACES FOR A BREAK...

ⓔ – EAT   ⓓ – DRINK   ⓢ – STAY

Dublin - Cork

Travel Time (approx):
3 Hours

Distance:
253 km (165 miles)

Roads:
N7 / M7 / N8

DUBLIN ➡ ➡ ➡ ➡ ➡ ➡ CORK

① ② ③ ④ ⑤ ⑥ ⑦ ⑧ ⑨ ⑩ ⑪ ⑫ ⑬ ⑭

25% | 50% | 75%

	Town	County	Road	Km from Dublin	Km from Road	Category
1	Red Cow R/about	Dublin	N7	8	0	ⓢ
2	Newlands Cross	Dublin	N7	10	0	ⓢ
3	Liffey Valley	Dublin	N7	10	0	ⓔ ⓢ
4	Saggart	Dublin	N7	15	1	ⓢ
5	Naas	Kildare	N7	28	3	ⓔ ⓓ ⓢ
6	Newbridge	Kildare	M7	45	3	ⓢ
7	Killenard	Laois	M7	58	11	ⓔ ⓢ
7	Portlaoise	Laois	M7	87	1	ⓔ ⓓ ⓢ
	Ballyfin	Laois	M7	87	3	ⓢ

	Town	County	Road	Km from Dublin	Km from Road	Category
8	Abbeyleix	Laois	M8	110	10	ⓔ ⓓ ⓢ
8	Durrow	Laois	M8	110	10	ⓔ ⓢ
9	Thurles	Tipperary	M8	138	9	ⓔ ⓢ
10	Cashel	Tipperary	M8	162	3	ⓔ ⓓ ⓢ
11	Clonmel	Tipperary	M8	173	16	ⓔ ⓓ ⓢ
12	Clogheen	Tipperary	M8	181	11	ⓔ ⓢ
13	Mitchelstown	Cork	M8	198	6	ⓔ
14	Fermoy	Cork	M8	214	2	ⓔ ⓢ

JOURNEY PLANNER - WITH SUGGESTED PLACES FOR A BREAK...

🍴 – EAT   🍷 – DRINK   🛏 – STAY

Dublin – Kilkenny – Waterford

Travel Time (approx):
2 Hours

Distance:
164 km (102 miles)

Roads:
N7 / M7 / M9 / N9

DUBLIN ←————————————————————————————→ WATERFORD

25% | 50% | 75% |

❶ ❷ ❸   ❹   ❺   ❻ ❼   ❽ ❾ ❿   ⓫   ⓬

	Town	County	Road	Km from Dublin	Km from Road	Category
1	Red Cow R/about	Dublin	N7	8	0	🛏
2	Newlands Cross	Dublin	N7	10	0	🛏
	Liffey Valley	Dublin	N7	10	0	🍴 🛏
3	Saggart	Dublin	N7	15	1	🛏
4	Naas	Kildare	N7	28	3	🍴 🍷 🛏
5	Ballymore Eustace	Kildare	M9	46	13	🍴 🛏
	Dunlavin	Wicklow	M9	47	13	🍴 🍷 🛏
6	Castledermot	Kildare	M9	74	3	🛏
	Athy	Kildare	M9	62	11	🍴 🍷 🛏
7	Carlow	Carlow	M9	80	8	🍴 🍷 🛏

	Town	County	Road	Km from Dublin	Km from Road	Category
8	Leighlinbridge	Carlow	M9	93	4	🍴 🍷 🛏
9	Bagenalstown	Carlow	M9	105	8	🛏
	Borris	Carlow	M9	105	20	🍴 🍷 🛏
	Maddoxtown*	Kilkenny	M9*	105	10	🛏
10	**KILKENNY CITY***	Kilkenny	M9*	114	10	🍴 🍷 🛏
11	Inistioge	Kilkenny	M9	133	18	🍴
	Thomastown	Kilkenny	M9	133	10	🍴 🛏
12	New Ross	Wexford	M9	148	20	🍴

* Turn on to N10 for Kilkenny

JOURNEY PLANNER - WITH SUGGESTED PLACES FOR A BREAK...

☻ – EAT   🍸 – DRINK   Ⓢ – STAY

Dublin - Wexford

Travel Time (approx):
2.15 Hours

Distance:
147 km (92 miles)

Roads:
N7 / M7 / M9 / N9

DUBLIN ← --- **1 2** --- **3 4** --- **5 6** 25% --- **7** --- **8** 50% --- **9** --- **10** 75% --- **11** → WEXFORD

	Town	County	Road	Km from Dublin	Km from Road	Category
1	Enniskerry	Wicklow	N11	29	6	☻ 🍸 Ⓢ
2	Kilmacanogue	Wicklow	N11	30	2	☻
3	Greystones	Wicklow	N11	37	4	☻ 🍸
	Delgany	Wicklow	N11	37	2	Ⓢ
4	Ntwnmtkennedy	Wicklow	N11	40	2	☻ Ⓢ
5	Ashford	Wicklow	M11	48	2	☻ Ⓢ
6	Rathnew	Wicklow	M11	52	6	☻ Ⓢ

	Town	County	Road	Km from Dublin	Km from Road	Category
	Rathdrum	Wicklow	M11	52	20	Ⓢ
7	Avoca	Wicklow	N11	63	11	☻
	Woodenbridge	Wicklow	N11	63	14	Ⓢ
8	Arklow	Wicklow	N11	74	4	☻
9	Gorey	Wexford	M11	90	5	☻ 🍸 Ⓢ
10	Bunclody	Wexford	N11	112	17	☻ Ⓢ
11	Enniscorthy	Wexford	N11	124	0	☻ 🍸 Ⓢ

INDEX

'Enjoy' at White Gables, Moycullen 245
101 Talbot Restaurant, Dublin 1 7
1826 Adare, Adare 331
777 Restaurant, Dublin 2 12
A Caviston Greystones 467
A Slice of Heaven Kilkenny 303
A Taste of Days Gone By Newport 360
Abbey Blue Cheese, Ballycolla 314
Abbey Hotel & Leisure Centre,
  Roscommon 391
Abbey Tavern, Howth 81
Abbeyglen Castle Hotel, Clifden 236
ABBEYLEIX 312
Abbeyville House, Fermoy 170
Aberdeen Lodge, Dublin 4 44
Abernethy Butter Co., Dromara 509
Absolute Hotel, Limerick 324
ACHILL ISLAND 349
Actons Hotel, Kinsale 176
Adare Farm Adare 331
Adare Manor Adare 331
ADARE 331
Aghadoe Heights Hotel, Killarney 273
Aherne's Youghal 196
Aillwee Cave, Ballyvaughan 108
Aine Hand Made Chocolates,
  Stradone Village 106
Al Mezza, Athlone 437
Aldridge Lodge, Duncannon 449
Alexander Hotel, Dublin 2 12
Ali's Fish Shop, Barna 235
Alix Gardners Cookery School, D4 45
Allo's, Listowel 282
Amicus, Cork 129
An Caife Bia Sláinte, Co Sligo 322
An Cupán Caifé, Mountshannon 124
An Cupan Tae, Galway 215
An Dún, Aran Islands 230
An Fear Gorta, Ballyvaughan 108
An Fulacht Fia, Ballyvaughan 108
An Grianan, Termonfeckin 347
An Old Rectory, Belfast 474

An Port Mór, Westport 362
An Sugan, Clonakilty 162
An Tintáin, Multyfarnham 443
Ananda, The, Dublin 16 68
Andersons Creperie, Dublin 9 64
Andersons Food Hall, Dublin 65
Andy's Bar, Monaghan 379
Anglers Rest, The, Dublin 15 67
Anglers Return, The, Roundstone 251
Angus Farm Shop, Greyabbey 510
Aniar Restaurant, Galway 215
Anna's House, Comber 506
Annaharvey Farm, Tullamore 387
Annebrook House Hotel, Mullingar 441
Antica Venezia, Dublin 6 54
Antoinettes Café, Limavady 529
Antonio's Ristorante & Pizzeria 147
Antons, Galway 215
Apple Farm, The, Cahir 405
Aqua Restaurant, Howth 81
Aran View House Hotel, Doolin 111
Arbutus Breads 129
Arbutus Hotel, Killarney 274
Arcadia Delicatessen, Belfast 474
Arch Bistro, The, Dublin 14 66
Arch House nr Enniskillen 524
Archways B&B, Rosslare 455
Ard Bia, Galway 216
Ard na Breátha, Donegal 203
Ard na Sidhe Hotel, Caragh Lake 257
Ardagh Hotel, Clifden 237
Ardawn House, Galway 216
ARDEE 338
Ardeen, Ramelton 211
Ardilaun Hotel, Galway 216
Ardkeen Quality Food, Waterford 430
ARDMORE 420
Ardmore Country House, Kinnitty 384
Ardmore House Hotel, Westport 362
Ardrahan Dairy Products, Kanturk 175
Ardsallagh Cheese, Carrigtwohill 159
Ardtara Country House, Upperlands 536

Ariel House, Dublin 4 45
Armagh Cider Co., Portadown 499
Armagh City Hotel 497
ARMAGH 497
Arnold's Hotel, Dunfanaghy 204
Aroma, Donegal 203
Arthur Mayne's Pharmacy 130
ARTHURSTOWN 446
Arundels by the Pier, Ahakista 144
Asador, Dublin 4 45
ASHBOURNE 368
Ashdown Park Hotel, Gorey 451
Ashes Bar & Restaurant, Dingle 260
Ashes Butchers, Annascaul 253
Ashford Castle, Cong 357
Ashlee Lodge, Blarney 157
Ashley Park House, Nenagh 414
Ashling Hotel, Dublin 8 61
Asian Tea House, Galway 216
Athenaeum Hotel, Waterford 430
ATHLONE 437
Athlumney Manor, Navan 373
Aubergine Gallery Café, Longford 336
Avenue Café, Maynooth 294
Avoca Cafe, Belfast 474
Avoca Cafe, Rathcoole 90
Avoca Café, Dublin 2 13
Avoca Handweavers, Avoca 463
Avoca, Kilmacanogue 469
Avoca Handweavers, Kenmare 273
Avoca, Letterfrack 244
Avoca, Malahide 86
Azur, Limerick 324
Azzurro at The Ship, Dunmore East 426

Baan Thai, Dublin 4 45
Badger & Dodo, Fermoy 170
Bailey, The, Dublin 2 13
Baileys Hotel, Cashel 407
Baking Academy
  of Ireland, The, Dublin 20 72
Baldwins Ice Cream, Knockanore 428
Ballaghtobin, Callan, 300
Ballinacurra House, Kinsale 180
Ballinalacken Castle, Doolin 111
Ballinderry Park, nr Ballinasloe 234

Ballinkeele House, Enniscorthy 449
Ballinwillin House, Mitchelstown 188
Balloo House, Killinchy 514
Ballybrado Ltd, Cahir 405
BALLYCASTLE 353
BALLYCASTLE 488
Ballycotton Seafood, Midleton 184
Ballycross Apple Farm, Bridgetown 447
Ballyderrin House, Tullow 100
Ballydougan Pottery
  & Restaurant, Craigavon 497
Ballyduff House, Thomastown 309
Ballyfin House, Ballyfin, 314
Ballygarry House Hotel, Tralee 284
Ballyhoura Mountain Mushrooms 148
Ballykealey Manor Hotel, Ballon 95
Ballykine House, Clonbur 239
Ballyknocken House
  & Cookery School, Ashford 462
Ballylagan Organic Farm, Ballyclare 489
Ballylickey House, Ballylickey 148
Ballyliffin Lodge, Ballyliffin 199
BALLYMACARBRY 421
Ballymaloe Cookery School 186
Ballymaloe Country Relish 186
Ballymaloe House, Shanagarry 186
Ballymaloe Shop Café, Shanagarry 187
Ballymascanlon House Hotel 345
Ballymore Inn, Ballymore Eustace 289
Ballynahinch Castle Hotel, Recess 249
Ballyrafter Country House Hotel,
  Lismore 428
Ballyrobin Country Lodge, Crumlin 492
Ballysax Organic Chicken, Curragh 291
Ballyseede Castle, Tralee 284
Ballyvolane House, Fermoy Area 171
Ballywarren Country House, Cong 358
Bambury's Guesthouse, Dingle 260
BANAGHER 381
Bang Restaurant, Dublin 2 13
BANGOR 503
Bar and Grill at James Street,
  South Belfast 474
Bar Italia IFSC, Dublin 1 7
Bar Italia, Dublin 1 7
Bar One Gastro Pub, Castlebar 355

Bar Pintxo, Dublin 2 — 13
Barberstown Castle, Straffan — 298
Barking Dog, Belfast — 475
Barn Restaurant, The, Glanmire — 173
Barnabrow Country House, Cork — 187
Barnhill Apple Juice, Portadown — 499
Barraderry Country House, Kiltegan — 469
Barrons Bakery & Coffee Shop, Cappoquin — 422
Barrowville Townhouse, Carlow — 97
Barrtra Seafood Restaurant, Lahinch — 121
Barry's Tea, Cork — 130
Basilico Restaurant, Oranmore — 246
Bates Restaurant, Rathdrum — 471
Bay Lough Cheese, Clogheen — 408
Bay Restaurant, Newtownards — 518
Bay Tree, Holywood — 512
Bay Tree Restaurant, Carlingford — 339
Bayview Hotel, Ballycotton — 146
Bayview Hotel, Portballintrae — 494
Beach Bar/Aughris House — 394
Beach Guesthouse, Dunmore East — 426
Beach House, Buncrana — 201
Beacon Hotel, The, Dublin 18 — 70
Beal Organic Cheese, Listowel — 282
Bear, Dublin 2 — 13
Beatrice Kennedy, Belfast — 475
Beaufield Mews Restaurant — 92
Beaufort Bar & Restaurant — 279
Beaufort House, Carlingford — 339
Becketts Hotel, Leixlip — 293
Becketts, Waterford — 431
Bective, The, Kells — 371
Beech Hill Country House — 513
Beech Hill House Hotel, L'Derry — 531
Beechlawn Organic Farm, Galway — 233
Beehive, The, Achill Keel — 349
Befani's, Clonmel — 409
Béile le Chéile, Dingle — 260
Belfast Cookery School — 475
BELFAST — 473
Bella Cuba Restaurant, Dublin 4 — 45
Bellagio, Dublin 6W — 58
Belle Isle Castle, Lisbellaw — 526
Belle Isle Cookery School, — 526
Belle's Kitchen / Salt n Batter — 212

Belleek Castle, Ballina — 351
Bellinter House, Navan — 374
Bellissimo, Waterford — 431
BELMULLET — 354
Belvedere House, Carlingford — 339
Belvelly Smokehouse, Cobh — 165
Benedict's Hotel, Belfast — 475
Bennetts on Belmont, Belfast — 475
Berfranks, Waterford — 431
Berkeley Lodge, Adare — 331
Berman & Wallace, Dublin 4 — 46
Berry Lodge, Miltown Malbay — 124
Bervie, Achill — 350
Beshoffs the Market, Howth — 81
Best Western Plus Academy Plaza Hotel, Dublin 1 — 7
Bewley's Café, Dublin 2 — 13
Bewleys Hotel, Dublin 4 — 46
Bewleys Hotel Leopardstown — 70
Bewleys Hotel, Newlands X — 72
Bijou Bistro, Dublin 6 — 54
Birchwood House B&B, Wexford — 449
BIRR — 382
Bison Bar, Dublin 2 — 14
Bistro One, Dublin 18 — 70
Bite, Dublin 2 — 14
BJ Crowe Quality Meats, Cavan — 104
Black Oak, Miltown Malbay — 124
Black Pig Winebar & Café, Kinsale — 176
Blackberry Café, Leenane — 243
Blackberry Café, Thomastown — 309
Blackboard Bistro, The, Dublin 2 — 14
Blackstairs Eco Trails, Killedmond — 99
Blairs Inn, Blarney — 157
Blairscove House, Durrus — 169
Blakes Hotel & Spa, Dublin 4 — 46
Blakes of the Hollow — 522
Blanchville House, Maddoxtown — 308
Blarney Castle Hotel — 157
Blas by Cafe Noir, Limerick — 324
Blazing Salads, Dublin 2 — 14
Blindgate House, Kinsale — 176
Bloom Brasserie, Dublin 2 — 14
Blue Apron, Tullamore — 385
Blue Bar, The, Skerries — 90
Blue Bicycle Tea Rooms, Newport — 360

Blue Haven Hotel, The, Kinsale — 176
Bluebell Falls Goat Cheese, Ennis — 114
Bo Bristle Brewing Co., Banagher — 381
Boardwalk Bar & Grill, The, Cork — 130
Boathouse Bistro, Kenmare — 267
Boathouse Seafood
  & Grill, The, Oranmore — 246
Boathouse, The, Bangor — 503
Bobby Byrnes's Bar, Limerick — 325
Bodéga! Waterford — 431
Bon Appetit, Malahide — 86
Boojum, Dublin 1 — 7
Boozeberries, Dromore — 509
Bosun, The, Monkstown — 189
Boulabane Ice Cream, Roscrea — 415
Box Tree, The, Dublin 18 — 70
Boyne Valley Goats Cheese, Slane — 376
Brady Family Ham, Naas — 295
Brake, The, Blackrock — 338
Brambles Cafe & Deli, Birr — 382
Bramley Lodge, Carrigtwohill — 159
Brandon Hotel, Tralee — 284
Brass Monkey, The, Howth — 82
Brasserie 15, Carlow — 97
Brasserie Le Pont, Dublin 2 — 15
Brasserie Mark Anderson, Killaloe — 119
Brasserie Sixty6, Dublin 2 — 15
Brazen Head, Dublin 8 — 61
Breadcrumb, The, Kenmare — 268
Breaking Eggs, Recess — 249
Brehon, The, Killarney — 274
Brennans, Bundor — 201
Brennans Lane, Ballina — 351
Bretzel Bakery, Dublin 8 — 61
Brewer's House, nr Dungannon — 538
Brian Boru, The, Dublin 9 — 65
Bricín, Killarney — 274
Bridge Bar & Bistro, Dublin 2 — 15
Bridge House Hotel, Tullamore — 386
Brigit's Garden Café, nr Oughterard — 248
Brioche ce Soir, Dublin 2 — 15
Broadhaven Bay Hotel, Belmullet, — 354
Broadmeadow Country House,
  Ashbourne — 368
Brocka-on-the-Water Restaurant,
  Ballinderry — 405

Bronte Steakhouse, Banbridge — 502
Brook Lane Hotel, Kenmare — 268
Brook Manor Lodge, Tralee — 284
Brookhaven House, Waterville — 287
BrookLodge, Macreddin — 470
Brooks Hotel, Dublin 2 — 15
Brown Bear Restaurant, Naas — 295
Brown Envelope Seed Co, Co Cork — 193
Brown Hound Bakery, Drogheda — 342
Brown Trout, Aghadowey — 528
Brownes, Dublin 4 — 46
Browns Restaurant, Londonderry — 531
Bru Bar Bistro, Drogheda — 342
Bruckless House, Bruckless — 200
Bruno's Restaurant, Knockvicar — 390
Buck's Head Inn, Dundrum — 510
Builín Blasta Café, Spiddal — 251
Bull and Castle, Dublin 2 — 16
BUNCLODY — 447
Bunnyconnellan, Crosshaven — 168
Bunratty Cookery School, Bunratty — 110
Bunratty Manor Hotel, Bunratty — 110
Burkes Farm Ice Cream, Navan — 374
Burlington Hotel, Dublin 4 — 46
Burns Butchers, Sneem — 283
Burren Fine Wine & Food,
  Ballyvaughan — 108
Burren Free Range Pork, Kilfenora — 117
Burren Perfumery Tea Rooms — 111
Burren Smokehouse, The,
  Lisdoonvarna — 123
Burrendale Hotel, Newcastle — 517
Bush Hotel, Carrick-on-Shannon — 319
Bushe's Bar, Baltimore — 150
Bushmills Inn, Bushmills — 490
BUSHMILLS — 490
Buswells Hotel, Dublin 2 — 16
Butcher Grill, The, Dublin 6 — 54
Butler Arms Hotel, Waterville — 287
Butler House, Kilkenny — 303
Butlers Chocolate Café, Dublin 2 — 16
Butlers Chocolate Experience,
  Dublin 17 — 69
Butlers Pantry, Greystones — 467
Butlers Pantry, The, Blackrock — 74
Butlers Town House, Dublin 4 — 46

Buttermarket Café, The, Kilrush 121
Fishers, Newtownmountkennedy 470
Byrnes Restaurant, Ennistymon 116

C R Tormey, Galway 217
C.R. Tormeys Butchers, Tullamore, 386
Cabra Castle Hotel, Kingscourt 106
Cafe @ Ballyseedy, Carrigtwohill 160
Cafe Bar H, Dublin 2 16
Café Conor, Belfast 476
Café en Seine, Dublin 2 16
Café Gusto, Cork 130
Café Hans, Cashel 407
Café Mao Chatham Row, Dublin 2 17
Café Mao, Dublin 16 68
Café Mao, Dun Laoghaire 78
Café Noir @ Glór, Ennis 114
Cafe Noir, Limerick 325
Café Nutshell, New Ross 454
Café Paradiso, Cork 130
Café Renoir, Belfast 476
Café Rua, Castlebar 355
Café Sol, Kilkenny 304
Caherbeg Free Range, Rosscarbery 190
Cahernane House Hotel 274
Cairbre House, Dungarvan 423
Cairn Bay Lodge, Bangor 503
Cake Café, The, Dublin 8 61
Cake Stand, The, Newcastle 89
Cakes & Co, Blackrock, Co Dublin 74
Callaghans Butchers, Ardee 338
Camden Court Hotel, Dublin 2 17
Camden Kitchen, Dublin 8 61
Campagne, Kilkenny 304
Camphill Farm Shop
  & Bakery, Holywood 512
CAMPILE 448
Campo de' Fiori, Bray 463
Canal Bank Café, Dublin 4 47
Canal View, Keshcarrigan 321
Cannaboe Confectionery 318
Cape Greko, Malahide 86
Carbery Cottage, Durrus 169
Cargoes Café, Belfast 476
Carlingford House, Carlingford 339
CARLINGFORD 338

Carlow Brewing Co., Bagenalstown 95
Carlow Farmhouse Cheese, Fenagh 99
Carlton Atlantic, Westport 362
Carlton Hotel Blanchardstown 67
Carlton Hotel, Dublin Airport 77
Carlton Kinsale Hotel, Kinsale 176
Carlton Millrace Hotel, Bunclody 447
Carlton Shearwater, Ballinasloe 234
Carluccio's Caffe, Dublin 2 17
Carraig Fhada Seaweed, Easky 395
Carriage House, Dundrum 510
CARRICK ON SHANNON 318
CARRICK ON SUIR 406
Carrig House, Caragh Lake 258
Carrigaline Court Hotel 158
Carrigaline Farmhouse Cheese 158
Carrigbyrne Cheese, Adamstown 446
Carrowholly Cheese, Westport 366
Carrygerry Country House,
  Newmarket-on-Fergus 126
Carton House Hotel, Maynooth 294
Casa Pasta, Howth 82
Casey's of Baltimore, Baltimor 150
Casey's of Glandore 172
Casey's Hotel, Glengarriff 173
Cashel Blue & Crozier Blue, Fethard 411
Cashel House Hotel, Cashel 235
Cashel Palace Hotel, Tipperary 407
CASHEL 406
Castle Café, The, Cork 131
Castle Country House, Millstreet 429
Castle Dargan Hotel, Ballygawley 394
Castle Durrow, Durrow 314
Castle Grove House, Letterkenny 208
Castle Hotel, Macroom 181
Castle Murray House, Dunkineely 206
CASTLEBAR 355
Castlecoote House, Castlecoote 389
Castlefarm, Athy 289
Castleknock Hotel, Dublin 15 67
Castlemartyr Resort, Castlemartyr 160
Castlemine Farm, Roscommon 391
Castleruddery Organic Farm Donard 464
Castletroy Park Hotel, Limerick 325
Castlewood House, Dingle 261
Causeway Hotel, nr Bushmills 491

Cavan Crystal Hotel, Cavan ... 104
Cavistons, Dun Laoghaire ... 78
Cedar Tree, The, Dublin 2, ... 17
Cellar Restaurant, Ballycastle ... 488
Celtic Ross Hotel, Rosscarbery ... 191
Celtic Whiskey Shop, Dublin 2 ... 17
Central Fish Market, Bantry ... 154
Chakra by Jaipur, Greystones ... 467
Chapel Steps, Bandon ... 152
Chapter One Restaurant, Dublin 1 ... 7
Charlie Mac's, Fermoy ... 171
Chart House, The, Dingle ... 261
Cheese Pantry, The, Dublin 9 ... 65
Chef Shop, Belfast ... 476
Cherry Tree Restaurant, Killaloe ... 119
Chestnut, The, Birr ... 382
Chez Emily, The Ward ... 93
Chez Hans, Cashel ... 407
Chez Max, Dublin 2 ... 17
Chez Pierre, Kilkenny ... 304
Chili Club, Dublin 2 ... 18
China Sichuan Restaurant, Dublin 18 ... 71
Chocolate Boutique, Ashbourne ... 368
Chocolate Garden, The, Tullow ... 100
Chocolate Shop, The, Cork ... 131
Chocolate Shop, The, Doolin ... 112
ChocOneill, Aughnacliffe ... 336
Chop House, The, Dublin 4 ... 47
Christmas Made Easy ... 378
Christy's Bar & Lounge, Arklow ... 462
Church Street, Magherafelt ... 534
Cill Rialaig Café, Ballinskelligs ... 253
Cillín Hill, Kilkenny ... 304
Cinnamon Cottage, Cork ... 131
Cinnamon Garden, Ashbourne ... 368
Cistin Eile, Wexford ... 456
City Hotel, Londonderry ... 531
Clanconnel Brewing Company, Craigavon ... 498
Clandeboye Estate Yoghurt, Bangor ... 504
Clandeboye Lodge Hotel, Bangor ... 505
Clanwood Farm, Cloghan ... 384
Clare Island Organic Salmon ... 356
Clare Jam Company, Doolin ... 112
Claregalway Hotel ... 236

Clarence Hotel & Tea Room Restaurant, Dublin 2 ... 18
Clarion Hotel, Carrickfergus ... 492
Clarion Hotel, Cork Cork ... 131
Clarion Hotel, Dublin Airport ... 77
Clarion Hotel, Dublin IFSC, Dublin 1 ... 8
Clarion Hotel, Limerick ... 325
Clarion Hotel, Sligo ... 397
Clarkes Fresh Fruit, Stamullen ... 376
Clarkes Salmon, Ballina ... 351
Clarkes Seafood Delicatessen, Westport ... 362
Clayton Hotel, Galway ... 228
Clevery Mill, Castlebaldwin ... 394
Clifden Station House Hotel ... 237
Cliff House Hotel, Ardmore ... 420
Cliff Town House, The, Dublin 2 ... 18
CLOGHERHEAD ... 341
Clonalis House, Castlerea ... 389
Clone House, Aughrim, ... 463
CLONEE/DUNBOYNE ... 370
CLONMEL ... 409
Clonmore Goats Cheese, Charleville ... 162
Clontarf Castle Hotel, Dublin 3 ... 42
CLONTARF/FAIRVIEW ... 42
Cloudberry Bakery, Castlemine ... 259
Cloughbane Farm, Dungannon ... 538
Cloughjordan Wood-fired Bakery ... 411
Club Brasserie, The, Cork ... 131
Clynes Bros, Dublin 4 ... 47
Coach Lane Restaurant, Sligo ... 397
CoCo, Belfast ... 476
Cocoa Atelier, Dublin 2 ... 18
Coffee Dock, Bundoran ... 201
Comeragh Mountain Lamb ... 428
CONG ... 357
Connemara Abalone, Barna ... 235
Connemara Coast Hotel, Furbo ... 228
Connemara Hamper, Clifden ... 237
Connemara Hill Lamb ... 239
Connemara Smokehouse ... 234
Conrad Dublin & Alex Restaurant, Dublin 2 ... 18
Conservatory, The, Laragh ... 466
Conyngham Arms Hotel, Slane ... 375
Cookie Jar Bakery, Newcastle ... 517

Cookies of Character, Dunmanway 168
Cooks Academy Cookery School,
Dublin 2 19
Coolanowle Country House 98
Coolattin Cheddar, Tullow 100
Coolbawn Quay, Nenagh 414
Coolclogher House, Killarney 274
Coolea Cheese, Macroom 181
Cooleeney Cheese, Thurles 417
Coolfin Gardens Organic Bakery 381
Coolnagrower Organic Produce, Birr 383
Coopershill Irish Venison,
Riverstown 396
Coopershill House, Riverstown 396
Copper & Spice, Limerick 326
Copper Hen, Fenor 427
Coppi, Belfast 477
Coppinger Row, Dublin 2 19
Corin Restaurant, Bangor 504
Cork International Airport Hotel 129
Corleggy Cheese, Belturbet 103
Corn Dolly Home Bakery, Newry 517
Corner Bakery, Dublin 6 55
Cornstore at Home, Limerick 326
Cornstore Winebar & Grill, Cork 132
Cornstore Winebar & Restaurant,
Limerick 326
Cornucopia, Dublin 2 19
Corrib House, Galway 217
Corrib Wave, Oughterard 246
Corthna Lodge, Schull 192
Cosgroves, Sligo 398
Cottage Coffee Shop, Achill 349
Cottage Restaurant, Jamestown 321
Country Choice, Nenagh 412
Country Kitchen Bakery, Lisburn 493
Country Market, The, Howth 82
Country Store, The, Dungarvan 423
Coursetown Country House, Athy 289
Courthouse Restaurant, C'macross 378
Courthouse Restaurant, Kinlough 322
Courtyard Bar and Grill, Kilkenny 304
Courtyard Hotel, The, Leixlip 293
Courtyard Kitchen, Carrick 319
Cove, The, Dunfanaghy area 205
Cowhouse Cafe & Bistro, Gorey 451

Coyles Bistro, Bangor 504
Coynes Bar, Kilkerrin 241
CR Tormey & Sons, Mullingar 442
Crackpots Restaurant, Kinsale 177
Crag Cave, Castleisland 259
Cramers Grove Ice Cream, Kilkenny 304
Cratloe Hills Sheeps' Cheese 111
Crawford Gallery Café, Cork 132
Crazy Crab, Kilmore Quay 453
Creagh House, Doneraile 168
Crescent Townhouse, The, Belfast 477
Crinnaghtaun Juice, Cappoquin 422
Crockets on the Quay, Ballina 351
Croke Park Hotel, The, Dublin 3 42
Cromleach Lodge Hotel 395
Cromore Halt Inn, Portstewart 535
Cronin's Pub, Crosshaven 167
Crookhaven Inn, The, Crookhaven 167
Crossgar Foodservice, Downpatrick 508
Crossogue Preserves, Thurles 417
Crottys, Kilrush 121
Crowes Farm, Dundrum, 411
Crown Liquor Saloon, Belfast 477
Crowne Plaza Blanchardstown, The,
Dublin 15 67
Crowne Plaza, Dublin Airport 77
Crowne Plaza, Dundalk 345
Cryan's Hotel 319
Cuan Licensed Guest Inn, Strangford 520
Cucina, Kinsale 177
Cucina Italiana, Killarney 275
Cuinneog Dairy Products, Castlebar 356
Cullinan's, Doolin 112
Cupan Tae, Kenmare 268
Curragower Seafood Bar, Limerick 326
Curran's Bar & Seafood Steakhouse,
Ardglass 502
Currarevagh House, Oughterard 247
Custom House Restaurant, L'Derry 532

D Hotel, Drogheda 343
D.P. Connolly, Abbeyleix 313
D'Vine, Drogheda 343
Da Roberta, Galway 217
Da Tang Noodle House, Galway 217
Dada, Dublin 2 19

Daft Eddys, Killinchy	514
Dail Bar, The, Galway	218
Dalkey Food Company, The, Dalkey	75
DALKEY	75
Dalton's, Kinsale	177
Damson Diner, Dublin 2	19
Dan Ahern Organic Chickens	184
Dan Lowrey's Tavern, Cork	132
Daniel Finnegan, Dalkey	75
Danny Minnie's Restaurant, Annagry	198
Darwins, Dublin 2	20
Davenport Hotel, Dublin 2	20
David Burns Butchers, Bangor	504
Davis's Restaurant & Yeats Tavern, Drumcliff	395
Davy Byrnes, Dublin 2	20
Dax Restaurant & Dax Café Bar, D2	20
De Barra Lodge, Rosscarbery	191
Deanes at Queens, Belfast	477
Deanes Deli Bistro, Belfast	477
Deanes Restaurant & Seafood Bar	478
Deasy's Harbour Bar, Clonakilty	165
Del Toro, Lisburn	493
Delgany, The, Delgany	464
Deli on the Green, Moygashel	539
Delicious, Carrigaline	158
Delicious, Cork	132
Delphi Lodge, Leenane	243
Delphi Mountain Resort & Spa	243
Denvirs, Downpatrick	508
Derg Inn, The, Terryglass	416
Derrycamma Farm Rapeseed Oil	341
Derryclare Restaurant, Clifden	237
Derrymore Farmhouse, Claremorris	357
Derrynane Hotel, Caherdaniel	256
Derryvilla Blueberries, Portarlington	385
Devour Bakery, Ballinrobe	353
Devoys Organic Farm, Rosscarbery	191
Diamond Hill House, Waterford	432
Diamond Rocks Cafe, Kilkee	117
Diep Le Shaker, Dublin 2	20
Dillinger's, Dublin 6	55
Dingle Benners Hotel, Dingle	261
Dingle Brewing Company, Dingle	261
Dingle Peninsula Cheese	258
Dingle Skellig Hotel, Dingle	261
Dingle Whiskey Distillery, Dingle	262
Ditty's Home Bakery, Castledawson	528
Ditty's Home Bakery, Magherafelt	534
Diva Boutique Bakery, Café & Deli	145
Dobbins Wine Bistro, Dublin 2	21
Doheny & Nesbitt, Dublin 2	21
Dollakis Restaurant, Enniskillen	522
Dolphin Hotel, Inishbofin	241
Domini & Peaches Kemp at The Restaurant, Dublin 2	21
DONAGHADEE	507
Donegal Brewing Company	200
Donegal Cookery School, Donegal	203
Donegal Rapeseed Oil, Raphoe	212
Doneraile Court Tea Rooms	168
Donnelly Fresh Foods	91
Donnelly's of Barna	228
Doonmore Hotel, Inishbofin	241
Dorans on the Pier, Howth	82
Dovinia Chocolates, Dingle,	266
Downhill House Hotel, Ballina	351
Downstairs Restaurant, Dublin 3	43
Doyle's Seafood Restaurant, Dingle,	262
DROGHEDA	342
Drombeg Premium Irish Spirit	195
Dromoland Castle, Newmarket-on-Fergus	126
Druids Glen, Newtownmountkennedy	471
Dualla House, Cashel	408
DUBLIN 18	70
DUBLIN 8	61
Dublin Cookery School, Blackrock	74
Dublin Wine Rooms, Dublin 1	8
Duchess Tea Rooms Bandon	152
Dufferin Coaching Inn, Killyleagh	515
DUN LAOGHAIRE	78
Dunadry Hotel, Dunadry	492
Dunany Organic Flour, Drogheda,	344
Dunboyne Castle Hotel	370
Dunbrody House, Arthurstown	446
DUNCANNON	449
DUNDALK	345
DUNDRUM	509
DUNDRUM	68
DUNGANNON	538
Dungarvan Brewing Company	423

DUNGARVAN	423
Dunloe, The, Killarney	280
Dunmore Country School, Durrow	315
DUNMORE EAST	425
Dunmore House Hotel, Clonakilty	162
Dunnanelly House, Downpatrick	508
Dunne & Crescenzi, Dublin 2	21
Dunne & Crescenzi, Dublin 4	47
Dunraven Arms Hotel, Adare	332
Durrus Farmhouse Cheese	154
Durty Nelly's, Bunratty	110
Dylan Hotel Dublin, Dublin 4	48
Dyson's Restaurant, Portumna	248
Eagle House, Dun Laoghaire	79
Eala Bhan, Sligo	398
Earls Court House, Killarney	275
Earls Kitchen, Navan	373
East Coast Seafood, Naas	295
East Coast Seafoods, Ballyhornan,	502
Eastern Seaboard Bar	
& Grill Drogheda	343
Eat @ Massimo, Galway	218
Eatery 120, Dublin 6	55
Eatzen Chinese, Ashbourne	368
Eccles Hotel, Glengarriff	173
Eden Bar & Grill, Dublin 2	21
Eden Deli Café, Edenderry	384
Edenvale House, Newtownards	518
Edward Twomey, Clonakilty	163
Egans House, Dublin 9	65
Egans Ocean Fresh, Skerries	90
Eight Degrees Brewing	189
EIGHT, Bar & Restaurant, Galway	218
Eithna's by the Sea, Mullaghmore	396
Elbow Lane Craft Beer, Cork	132
Electric, Cork	133
Elephant & Castle, Dublin 2	22
Ella, Howth	82
ely bar & brasserie, Dublin 1	8
ely gastrobar, Dublin 2	22
ely winebar, Dublin 2	22
Embassy Wine Bar & Grill, Sligo	398
Emlaghmore Lodge, Ballyconneely	234
Emmas Cafe & Deli, Birr	382
Encore Brasserie, Londonderry	532
ENFIELD	370
Enigma, Holywood	512
Ennis Butchers, Dublin 8	62
Ennis Gourmet Store, Ennis,	114
Enniscoe House, Ballina	353
ENNISCORTHY	449
ENNISKERRY	465
Eno Bar Grill & Pizza, Dundalk	345
Enoteca delle Lnghe, Dublin 1	8
Enoteca Torino, Dublin 8	62
EPICUREAN FOOD HALL, Dublin 1	8
Equinox, Belfast	478
Essence Bistro, Swords	92
Et Voila French Bistro, New Ross	454
Europe Hotel & Resort, Killarney	280
Eves Chocolate Shop, Cork	133
Ewings Fishmongers, Belfast	478
Exchange Restaurant, Londonderry	532
Exchequer, The, Dublin 2	22
Fabiolas Patisserie, Doolin	112
Fabios, Sligo Town	401
Fade Street Social, Dublin 2	22
Fairhill House Hotel, Clonbur	239
Fairways Bar & Orchard Restaurant,	
Nenagh	415
Fairyhouse Food & Wine School	374
Faithlegg House Hotel, Waterford	435
Fallon & Byrne, Dublin 2	23
Fallons of Kilcullen, Kilcullen	292
Farm Factory Direct, Tullamore	386
Farm, The, Dublin 2	23
Farmgate Café, Cork	133
Farmgate, Midleton	184
Fatted Calf, The, Glasson	440
Fenns Quay Restaurant	134
Fenton's of Dingle	262
Fergus View, Corofin	111
Fermoy Natural Cheese	171
Ferndale, Achill	350
Fernhill House Hotel, Clonakilty	163
Ferrycarrig Hotel, Wexford	460
Fiacrí House Restaurant	
& Cookery School, Roscrea	416
Fields SuperValu, Skibbereen	194
Filligans, Glenties	206

Finders Inn, Oysterhaven	190
Finíns, Midleton	184
Finn's Table, Kinsale	177
Finns Bar & Restaurant, Tuam	251
Finnstown House Hotel, Lucan	85
Fire, Dublin 2	23
Firehouse Bakery, Heir Island	195
Fish Kitchen, Bantry	154
Fish Market, The, Mullingar	442
Fish Shop, The, Union Hall	195
Fisherman, The, Galway	218
Fishermans Catch, Clogherhead	342
Fishermans Thatched Inn, B'brittas	314
Fishy Fishy, Kinsale,	177
Fitzgeralds Woodlands Hotel	332
Fitzpatrick Castle Hotel, Killiney,	85
Fitzpatrick's Bar, Dundalk	346
Fitzroys Restaurant, Londonderry	532
Fitzwilliam Hotel, Belfast	478
Fitzwilliam Hotel, Dublin 2	23
Fitzwilton Hotel Waterford	435
Fivemiletown Creamery	539
Flahavans Oats, Kilmacthomas	427
Flanagans On The Lake, Killaloe	119
Flappers Restaurant, Tulla	127
Flemings Restaurant, Cork	134
Flemingstown House, Kilmallock	334
Flynns Bar & Restaurant, Banagher	381
Folláin Teo, Ballyvourney	149
Fontana Restaurant, Holywood	512
Food For Thought, Carlingford	339
Food Heaven, Ennis	114
Food Room, The Dublin 3	43
Food Store, The, Claremorris	356
Foodie Folk, Belfast	479
Foods of Athenry, Athenry	232
FoodWare Store, Malahide	87
Foodworks Café, Kilkenny	305
Forde's Restaurant, Wexford	456
Forge Restaurant, Ballon	96
Forge, The, Carnaross	369
Forge, The, Moycullen	245
Forthill Farm, Tandragee	500
Fortview House, Goleen	174
Fota Island Resort, Cobh	165
Fothergills Deli, Dublin 6	55
Four Seasons Hotel, Dublin 4	48
FOXFORD	358
Foxmount House, Waterford	432
Foyles Hotel, Clifden	237
Franciscan Well Brewery & Pub	134
Franco's Restaurant, Enniskillen	522
Franzini O'Briens, Trim	376
Freddy's Bistro, Limerick	327
French Paradox, Dublin 4	48
French Rooms, Bushmills	491
French Table, Limerick	327
Fresco, Cork	134
Fresh Good Food Market, Dublin 7	58
Frewin, Ramelton,	211
Friar's Lodge, Kinsale	178
Friendly Farmer, The, Athenry	233
Front Door, The, Galway	218
Frou Frou, Enniskillen	523
Fruit Hill Farm, Bantry	154
Fuchsia House, Ardee	338
Furama Restaurant, Dublin 4	48
Fureys Bar, Moyvalley	294
G Hotel, The, Galway	219
G's Gourmet Jams, Abbeyleix	313
Gables Restaurant, The, Dublin 18	71
Gaby's Seafood Rest., Killarney	275
Galgorm Resort & Spa, Ballymena	490
Gallagher's Seafood Rest., Bunratty	110
Gallan Mor, Durrus	169
Gallery 29 Café, Mullingar	442
Gallery Café Restaurant, Gort	240
Gallic Kitchen, Abbeyleix	313
Gallo & Galetti	134
Galway Bay, Brewery	219
Galway Bay Hotel	219
Galway Hooker, Roscommon	391
Gannet Fishmongers, Galway	219
Garden Café @ Avoca, Ashford	462
Garden Café, The, Dingle	262
Gardiners G2, Magherafelt	534
Gateway Café & Brasserie, Durrus	170
Gathabawn Ice Cream, Kilkenny	303
Gaughans, Ballina	352
Gaultier Lodge, nr Dunmore East	427
George Hotel, Limerick	327

Georges Fish Shop, Dun Laoghaire 79
Georges Patisserie, Slane 375
German Butcher Shop, Killarney 275
Ghan House, Carlingford 340
Gibson Hotel, The, Dublin 1 8
Gilberts, Cobh 166
Ginger, Belfast 479
Gingergirl, Limerick 327
Gingerman, The, Waterford 432
Glandore Inn, Glandore 172
Glasha, Ballymacarbry 421
Glasrai & Goodies, Gowran 302
Glasshouse Hotel, Sligo 398
Glasshouse Restaurant, Limerick 327
Glasson Hotel & Golf, nr Athlone 439
Glasson Village Restaurant 440
GLASSON 439
Glastry Farm Ice Cream, Kircubbin 515
Glebe Brethan, Dunleer 346
Glebe Country House, Kinsale 180
Glebe House Gardens, Baltimore 150
Gleeson's Townhouse, Roscommon 391
Glen House, Clonmany 199
Glen House, Kilbrittain 175
Glenarm Castle Tea Rooms 492
Glenarm Organic Salmon, Glenarm 493
GLENARM 492
Glendalough Green, Laragh 466
GLENDALOUGH 466
Glendine House, Arthurstown 446
Glenilen Farm Dairy, Drimoleague 168
Glenisk Organic Dairy 387
Glenlo Abbey Hotel, Galway 228
Glenogra House, Dublin 4 49
Glenview Hotel, Delgany 464
Glenview House, Ballinamore 318
Glenwood House, Carrigaline 158
Gleveagh Castle Tearooms 207
Global Village, The, Dingle 262
Glyde Farm, Castlebellingham 341
Glyde Inn, Annagassan 338
Goat Street Cafe, The, Dingle 263
Goatsbridge Trout, Thomastown 310
Good Fish Company, Carrigaline 159
Good Herdsman Organic Meats 405
Good Things Café, Durrus 170

Good World Chines, Dublin 2 23
Goosers, Killaloe, Co Clare 119
GOREY 451
Gorman's Clifftop House, Dingle 265
Gortnadiha Lodge, Dungarvan 425
Gotham Café, Dublin 2 24
Gougane Barra Hotel 174
Gourmet Food Parlour, Swords 92
Gourmet Food Parlour, Ballyboughal 73
Gourmet Food Parlour, D.Laoghaire 79
Gourmet Food Parlour, Malahide 87
Gourmet Parlour, Sligo 399
Gourmet Store, Kilkenny 305
Gourmet Tart Co, Galway City 219
Gourmet Tart Company, Galway 220
Governor Rocks, The, Donaghadee 507
Goya's, Galway 220
Grace Neill's, Donaghadee 508
GRAIGUENAMANAGH 302
Granary Café, Waterford 432
Grand Canal Hotel, Dublin 4 49
Grand Hotel, Malahide 87
Grand Hotel, Tralee 285
Grand Hotel, Tramore 429
Grange Lodge, Dungannon 538
Grangecon Café, Blessington 463
Granville Hotel, Waterford 432
Granville's Bar & Restaurant, Macroom 181
Gray's Guest House, Achill 349
Green 19, Dublin 2 24
Green Apron, The, Ballingarry 333
Green Hen, Dublin 2 24
Green Man, The, Dunfanaghy 205
Green Saffron Spices, Midleton 184
Greenacres Bistro, Wexford 457
Greenbean Coffee, Banbridge 502
Greenes Restaurant, Maynooth 294
Greenhill House, Aghadowey 528
Greenhills Hotel, Limerick 328
GreenHouse, The, Dublin 2 24
Greenmount House, Dingle 263
Greenpark, New Ross 455
Greens Berry Farm Shops, Gorey 452
Gregans Castle Hotel, Ballyvaughan 109
Gresham Metropole Hotel
  & Leisure Centre, Cork 135

Gresham, The, Dublin 1	9
Griffins Bakery	220
Grogan's Pub, Glasson	440
Grove House, Schull	192
Gubbeen Farmhouse Products	192
Gweedore Court Hotel, An Chuirt	207
Gwens Chocolates, Schull	192
Hadji Bey, Newbridge	297
Half Door, The, Dingle	263
Halpins Bridge Cafe, Wicklow	472
Hamptons Grill, Limerick	328
Hanged Mans, Newbridge	297
Hanley at the Bar, Dublin 7	59
Hannan Meats &	
The Meat Merchant, Moira	516
Hanora's Cottage, Ballymacarbry	421
Happy Angel, Belfast	479
Happy Heart Rapeseed Oil	311
Happy Pear, Greystones	468
Harbour Bar, Bray	464
Harbour Hotel, Galway	220
Harbour House, Castlegregory	258
Harbour Master's House, Banagher	381
Hargadons, Sligo	399
Harkins Bistro, Dromod	320
Harlequin, Waterford	433
Harrington Hall, Dublin 2	24
Harrisons of Greyabbey	510
Harry's Bridgend	200
Hartes Bar & Grill, Kildare	292
Hartley's, Dun Laoghaire	79
Harts Coffee Shop, Clonakilty	163
Harty-Costello, Ballybunion	254
Harvest Kitchen, Naas	295
Harvey Nichol's First Floor Restaurant	68
Harvey's Point Hotel, Lough Eske	210
Hastings Ballygally Castle Hotel	489
Hastings Culloden Estate, Holywood	513
Hastings Europa Hotel, Belfast	479
Hastings Everglades Hotel, L'Derry	532
Hastings Slieve Donard, Newcastle	517
Hatch & Sons, Dublin 2	25
Hayes' Bar, Glandore	172
Hayfield Manor Hotel, Cork	135
Headfort Arms Hotel, Kells	371
Healys Honey, Cork	144
Heatherlea, The, Bangor	504
Heatons House, Dingle	263
Heffernans Fine Foods, Ballina	352
Hegarty's Cheddar, White Church	195
Helena Chocolates, Castlebar	355
Helens Bay Organic Gardens	513
Hemmingways, Dublin 3	43
Henry Downes, Waterford	433
Herb Garden, The, Naul	89
Herbert Park Hotel, Dublin 4	49
Herbstreet, Dublin 2	25
Heritage Resort, Killenard	315
Heron's Cove, The, Goleen	174
Heron's Rest B&B, Galway	220
Herring Gull, The, Ballycotton	146
Hickeys Bakery & Café, Clonmel	409
Hickeys Bakery, Waterford	433
Hickeys Farm Shop, Ardee	338
Hicks of Dalkey, Dalkey	75
Highbank Organic Orchards	301
Highlands Hotel, Glenties	206
Hilden Brewing Company, Lisburn	493
Hill House, Cashel	408
Hillcrest House, Ahakista	144
Hillgrove Hotel, Monaghan	379
Hilton, Belfast	479
Hilton Dublin Airport Hotel	77
Hilton Dublin Kilmainham	62
Hilton Dublin, Dublin 2	25
Hilton Park, Clones	378
Hodson Bay Hotel, Athlone	437
Holiday Inn Belfast	480
Hollywell Country House,	
Carrick-on-Shannon	319
HOLYWOOD	511
Home, Belfast	480
Homegrown, Newtownards	518
Honest2Goodness, Dublin 11	66
Horetown House, Foulksmills	451
Horseshoe, The, Kenmare	268
Hot Stove Restaurant, The, Dublin 1	9
Hotel Isaacs & Greenes Restaurant	135
Hotel Kilkenny Kilkenny	305
Hotel Meyrick, Galway	221
Hotel Minella, Clonmel	409

Hotel Westport	363
House Café, Cork	135
House Hotel, The, Galway	221
House of McDonnell, Ballycastle	489
House, The Howth	82
Hudson's Pantry, Louisburgh	359
Hudsons, Ballydehob	147
Hugh Maguire Butchers, Ashbourne	369
Hugo's, Dublin 2	25
Hungry Monk Café, Cong	358
Hungry Monk, Greystones	468
Hunter's Hotel, Rathnew	471
Hunters at the Oven Door	528
Hunters Bakery & Cafe	529
Hunters, Limavady	529
Huntsman Inn, Galway	221
Hylands Burren Hotel, Ballyvaughan	109
Ice House Hotel, The, Ballina	352
Idaho.Café, Cork	135
Iggy's Bar, Kincasslagh	208
Il Folletto,Galway	221
Il Fornaio, Dublin 5	54
Il Pirata, Belfast	480
Il Posto, Dublin 2	25
Il Primo Restaurant, Dublin 2	26
Il Valentino Continental Bakery, D2	26
Il Vicolo, Galway	222
Ilia A Coffee Experience, Mullingar	442
IMI Residence, Dublin 16	69
Imperial Hotel, Cork	136
Inch House Black Pudding, Thurles	418
Inch House Country House, Thurles	418
Inchydoney Island Lodge & Spa	163
Indie Dhaba, Dublin 2	26
Indie Spice Naas, Naas	295
Indie Spice Sandymount, Dublin 4	49
Indie Spice, Swords	92
Inis Meáin Restaurant	
& Suites, Aran Islands	230
Inish Beg House Cookery School,	
Baltimore	150
Inishbofin House Hotel	
& Marine Spa, Inishbofin	241
Inishmacsaint Brewing Co,	522
Inn @ Ballilogue Clochan, Inistioge	303
Inn at Dromoland, Co Clare	126
Inn, Castledawson	528
Innishannon House Hotel	174
International Bar, Dublin 2	26
International Fishing Ctre, Belturbet	103
Irish Atlantic Sea Salt	161
Irish Piemontese Beef, Thurles	418
Irish Seed Savers Association	126
Isaacs Restaurant, Cork	136
Isabels, Dublin 2	26
Iskeroon, Caherdaniel	257
Island Cottage, Heir Island	151
itsa@IMMA, Dublin 8	62
Itsa4 Café, Dublin 4	49
Ivans Oyster Bar & Grill	83
Ivyleigh House, Portlaoise	316
J Hick & Sons, Dun Laoghaire	79
J L Fitzsimons Fresh Fish , D12	66
J.J.Hough, Banagher	381
Jack McCarthy Butchers, Kanturk	175
Jack's Coastguard , Killorglin	281
Jackson's Hotel, Ballybofey	198
Jacobs On The Mall, Cork	136
Jacques Restaurant, Cork	136
Jacques Seafood Restaurant	
@ Sidetracks, Wexford	457
Jaipur Restaurant, Malahide	87
Jaipur Restaurant Ongar, Dublin 15	67
Jaipur Restaurant, Dalkey	75
Jaipur, Dublin 2	26
Jam, Castleisland	259
Jam Cork, Ballycurreen	147
Jam, Kenmare	269
Jam, Killarney	275
James Ashe, Camp	257
James Street South, Belfast	480
James Whelan Butchers, Clonmel	409
Jameson Experience, Midleton	185
Jamie's Italian, Dublin 16	69
Jamie's Restaurant, Tullamore	386
Jane Russell's Sausages, Kilcullen	292
Janet's Country Fayre, Kilcoole	469
Jarrow Café, Castlecomer	301
JC Stewarts, Magherafelt	534
Jerry Kennedy Butchers, Dingle	263

Jim Edwards, Kinsale 178
Jim Flavin Butchers, Limerick 328
Jo'Burger, Dublin 6, 55
John David Power Butchers 424
John Downey & Son, Dublin 6 55
John Hewitt, The, Belfast 480
John J. Burke & Sons, Clonbur 239
John Kavanagh (Grave Diggers) D9 65
John Mulligan, Dublin 2 27
John R Dowey, Lurgan 499
John Rs Home Bakery, Listowel 282
Johnnie Fox's Pub, Glencullen 81
Johnny Morgans Fish, Dundalk 345
Johnstown House Hotel, Enfield 371
Joyces Supermarket, Galway 222
Juniors, Dublin 4 49
Junos Café, Dublin 8 62
Jurys Custom House Inn, Dublin 1 9
Jurys Inn, Belfast 481
Jurys Inn Christchurch, Dublin 8 63
Jurys Inn, Galway 222
Jurys Inn Parnell Street, Dublin 1 9
Just Cooking, Killarney 276

K C Blakes, Galway 222
K Club, Straffan 298
Kai Cafe & Restaurant, Galway 222
Kajjal, Malahide 87
Kalbos Café, Skibbereen 194
Kate Browne's Pub, Ardfert 253
Kate McCormack & Sons, Westport 363
Kates Farm Shop, Wexford 457
Kates Kitchen, Sligo 399
Kathleen Noonan Pork & Bacon 136
Kathleens Country House, Killarney 276
Kay O'Connell Fishmongers, Cork 137
Keadeen Hotel, Newbridge 297
Kealys Seafood Bar, Greencastle 207
Kee's Hotel, Ballybofey 199
Keelings, St Margarets 91
Keenans, Tarmonbarry 392
Kehoe's, Dublin 2 27
Kells Wholemeal, Bennettsbridge 300
KELLS 371
Kelly Galway Oysters, Kilcolgan 241
Kelly's of Newport 361
Kelly's Resort Hotel, Rosslare 456
Kellys Bar & Lounge, Galway 223
Kenmare Select Smoked Salmon 268
Kennedy's of Enniskerry 465
Kennedys Food Store & Bistro, D3 43
Keogh's Bar & Restaurant, Kinvara 242
Keogh's Potatoes, Oldtown 89
Keoghs Model Bakery, Callan 300
Keshk Cafe, Dublin 4 50
Kettyle Irish Food, Lisnaskea 526
Kiernans SuperValu, Dublin 6 56
Kilbawn House, Dungarvan 301
Kilbeg Dairies, Kells 372
KILBEGGAN 441
Kilbeggan Organic Foods 441
Kilbrogan House, Bandon 152
Kilcooly's Country House, B'bunion 254
Kilgraney House, Bagenalstown 95
Kilkenny Café, Shanagarry 187
Kilkenny Design Centre, Kilkenny 305
Kilkenny Hibernian Hotel 305
Kilkenny Ormonde Hotel 306
Kilkenny River Court Hotel 306
KILKENNY 303
Kilkenny, Dublin 2 27
Kilkieran Cottage Restaurant,
  Carrick-on-Suir 406
Killarney Lodge, Killarney 276
Killarney Park Hotel 276
Killarney Plaza Hotel, 276
Killarney Royal Hotel 277
Killashee House Hotel & Villa Spa 296
Killeen Cheese, Portumna 248
Killeen House Hotel, Killarney 277
Killiane Castle, Wexford Area 460
Killorglin Cheese, Killorglin 280
Killruddery Estate, Bray 464
Killyhevlin Hotel, Enniskillen 523
KILLYLEAGH 514
KILMALLOCK 334
Kilmaneen Farmhouse, Clonmel 410
Kilmokea Manor Campile 448
KILMORE QUAY 453
Kilmurvey House, Aran Islands 230
Kilronan Castle, Ballyfarnon 389
Kilshanny Cheese, Lahinch 121

Kimchi Restaurant
@ The Hop House, Dublin 1 — 9
Kin Khao Thai, Athlone — 437
Kinara Kitchen, Dublin 6 — 56
Kinara Restaurant, Dublin 3 — 43
King Sitric & East — 83
Kingdom Food & Wine, Tralee — 285
Kingfisher Bistro, Carlingford — 340
Kingfisher Lodge Ballina, Killaloe — 119
Kinnegar Brewing, Rathmullan — 212
Kinnitty Castle Hotel, Kinnitty — 385
Kinvara Smoked Salmon, Kinvara — 242
Kirks Seafood, Castleblayney — 378
Kirwan's Lane, Galway — 223
Kirwans Fish Cart, Drogheda — 343
Kish Fish, Dublin 7 — 59
Kitchen @ Gorey, The, Gorey — 452
Kitchen Complements, Dublin 2 — 27
Kitchen in the Castle, Howth — 83
Kitchen Restaurant, Drogheda — 343
Kites Restaurant, Dublin 4 — 50
Kitty Kellys, Killybegs — 208
Kittys of Coleraine, Coleraine — 529
Knightsbrook Hotel & Golf, Trim — 376
Knightstown Coffee Valentia Is. — 286
Knockalara Cheese, Cappoquin — 422
Knockanore Cheese, Knockanre — 428
Knockdrinna Cheese, Stoneyford — 309
Knockeven House, Cobh — 166
Knockninny House & Marina — 523
Knockranny House Hotel, Westport — 363
Knocktullera Farm Produce, Newmarket — 189
Knotts Bakery & Coffee Shop — 518
Konkan Indian Restaurant, Dublin 8 — 63
Kooky Dough, Dublin 7 — 59
Kylemore Abbey, Letterfrack — 244
Kylenoe House, Terryglass — 417

L Mulligan Grocer, Dublin 7 — 59
L'Arco Restaurant, Ballyvaughan — 109
L'Atitude 51, Cork — 137
L'Atmosphère, Waterford — 433
L'Ecrivain, Dublin 2 — 27
L'Gueuleton, Dublin 2 — 28
L'Officina by Dunne
& Crescenzi Kildare — 292

L'Officina by Dunne & Crescenzi,
Dublin 16 — 69
La Baguette, Gorey — 452
La Banca, Lucan — 86
La Bigoudenne, Fermoy — 171
La Bohème, Waterford, — 434
La Boulangerie Francaise, Swords — 93
La Cave Wine Bar
& Restaurant, Dublin 2 — 28
La Cucina, Limerick, — 328
La Dolce Vita, Wexford — 457
La Fantasia, Letterkenny — 209
La Jolie Brise, Baltimore — 150
La Mère Zou, Dublin 2 — 28
La Palma on the Mall, Waterford — 434
La Péniche, Dublin 4 — 50
La Reserve, Dublin 6 — 56
La Rouge Wine & Grill, Dublin 18 — 71
La Touche Organics, Cappoquin — 422
Lake Hotel Killarney, Killarney — 277
Lakeside Hotel, Killaloe — 120
Lancaster Lodge, Cork — 137
Landmark Hotel, The,
Carrick-on-Shannon — 319
Langton House Hotel, Kilkenny — 306
Laragh House, Kilkenny — 306
Larder, The, Dublin 2 — 28
Larkins, Garrykennedy — 412
Las Tapas de Lola, Dublin 2 — 28
Laurel Villa, Magherafelt — 535
Lautrecs, Kilkenny — 306
Lavistown House, Kilkenny — 307
Lawlors Butchers, Dublin 6 — 56
Le Bon Crubeen, Dublin 1 — 10
Le Fournil, Sligo — 399
Le Fournil, Donegal — 204
Le Petit Parisien, Dublin 2 — 29
Left Bank Bistro, The, Athlone — 437
Leggyowan Cheese, Saintfield — 519
Leixlip House Hotel, Leixlip — 293
Lemon Leaf Café, Kinsale — 178
Lemon Tree Café, Dunmore East — 426
Lemon Tree, Letterkenny — 209
Lennons @ VISUAL, Carlow — 98
Lennox Café Bistro, Dublin 8 — 63
Leonard's, Lahardane — 359

Les Frères Jacques, Dublin 2 — 29
Les Gourmandises Restaurant — 137
Leslies Bakery, Enniskillen — 523
Letts Craft Butchers, Newcastle — 89
Levis' Bar, Ballydehob — 147
Liam O'Riain's, Killaloe — 120
Liberty Grill, Cork — 137
Lilliput Stores, Dublin 7 — 59
Lily Finnegans, Carlingford — 341
Lily Johnstons, Glenavy — 493
LIMAVADY — 529
Lime Tree Restaurant, Kenmare — 269
Lime Tree Restaurant, Limavady — 530
Limerick Strand Hotel, Limerick — 328
LIMERICK — 323
Linnalla Ice Cream, New Quay — 125
Linnanes Lobster Bar, New Quay — 125
Lisdonagh House, Headford — 240
Lisloughrey Lodge, Cong — 358
LISMORE — 428
Liss Ard Estate, Skibbereen — 194
Listons, Dublin 2 — 29
Listowel Arms Hotel, Listowel — 282
Little Cheese Shop, Dingle — 264
Little Irish Apple Co, Piltown — 309
Little Strand, Clogherhead — 342
Llewellyns Orchard, Lusk — 86
Lobster Pot, Burtonport — 202
Lobster Pot, Carne — 448
Lobster Pot, The, Dublin 4 — 50
Locke Bar & Restaurant, Athlone — 438
Locks Brasserie, Dublin 8 — 63
Lodge at Castle Leslie, Glaslough — 379
Lodge at Doonbeg — 113
Lodge, The, Kenmare — 269
Loft @ The Linen Green, Moygashel — 539
Loft Café Birr — 382
Loft Restaurant, Navan — 373
LONDONDERRY / DERRY CITY — 530
Londonderry Arms, Carnlough — 491
Long Dock, The Carrigaholt — 110
Long Hall Bar, Dublin 2 — 29
LONGFORD — 335
Longford Arms Hotel — 336
Longueville House Cider, Mallow — 183
Longueville House, Mallow — 183

Lord Bagenal Hotel, Leighlinbridge — 99
Lord Baker's, Dingle — 264
Lord Edward, The, Dublin 8 — 63
Lord Kenmare's Restaurant — 277
Lorge Chocolates, Kenmare — 269
Lorum Old Rectory, Bagenalstown — 95
Lough Allen Hotel, Drumshanbo — 321
Lough Bishop House, Collinstown — 439
Lough Boora Farm, Tullamore — 386
Lough Derg Chocolates, Nenagh — 413
Lough Erne Hotel, Kesh — 525
Lough Erne Resort, Enniskillen — 523
Lough Inagh Lodge, Recess — 249
Lough Key House, Boyle — 389
Lough Rynn Castle Hotel, Mohill — 322
Loughcarrig House, Midleton — 185
Louis Mulcahy Pottery Café, Dingle — 260
Lovin Catering, Dublin 8 — 64
Lusty Beg Island, Kesh — 525
Lyons Cafe, Sligo — 400
Lyrath Estate Hotel, Kilkenny — 307

M O'Shea, Borris — 96
M. J. Henry, Cootehall — 390
M&D Bakery, Waterford — 434
Mabel Crawford's Bistro, Glanmire — 173
Mac Ivors Cider Co., Portadown — 499
Mac's Armagh Cider, Forkhill — 498
MacCarthy's, Castletownbere — 161
MacNean House & Restaurant — 104
Macroom Oatmeal Mills, Macroom — 182
Maddybenny Farmhouse, Portrush — 494
Made in Belfast, Belfast — 481
Magees Bistro, Carlingford — 341
Mainistir House, Aran Islands — 230
Maldron Hotel Cardiff Lane, D2 — 29
Maldron Hotel, Cork — 138
Maldron Hotel, Galway — 229
Maldron Hotel, Wexford — 457
Malin Hotel, Malin — 211
Mallmore Country House, Clifden — 237
Malmaison Hotel, Belfast — 481
Malone Lodge Hotel, Belfast — 481
Malones Fruit Farm, Ballon — 96
Malt House Restaurant, Galway — 223
Malthouse Granary, The, Clonakilty — 164

Malton, The, Killarney 277
Man Friday, Kinsale 178
Man Of Aran Cottages, Aran Is. 231
Man of Aran Fudge, Ballivor 369
Mangos Restaurant, Westport 364
Mannings Emporium, Ballylickey 154
Manor House Hotel, Killadeas 525
Manor House, Rathlin Island 495
Maples House Hotel, Dublin 9 65
Marble City Bar, Kilkenny 307
Marco Pierre White Steakhouse
  and Grill, Dublin 2 29
Marine Court Hotel, Bangor 505
Marine Hotel Sutton 85
Marine, The, Glandore 72
Maritime Hotel, Bantry 155
Marker Hotel, The, Dublin 2 30
Market Bar & Tapas, The, Dublin 2 30
Market Kitchen, Ballina 352
Market Lane Restaurant & Bar 138
Market Place Brasserie,
  Newcastle West 334
Market Street Restaurant, Tramore 430
Markree Castle, Collooney 395
Marlagh Lodge, Ballymena 490
Marlenes Chocolates, Westport 364
Marlfield House, Gorey 452
Marsh Mere Lodge, Arthurstown 447
Martin Divilly, Galway 223
Martines Restaurant, Galway 224
Martinstown House, Curragh 291
Mary Ann's Bar
  & Restaurant, Castletownshend 161
Mary Annes Tea Rooms, Tralee 285
Mary Kathryns Deli, Kildare 293
Mary Lynch's Pub, Mullingar 443
Mary's Bakery, Ballycastle 354
Maryborough Hotel, Cork 138
Maryville House & Tea Rooms 481
Mash Direct, Comber 506
Matt Molloy's Bar, Westport 364
Matt the Thresher, Dublin 2 30
Maudlins House Hotel, Naas 296
Max's Wine Bar, Kinsale 178
Maxwells Bistro, Galway 224
McAllister's Fishmonger, Lucan 85

McCambridges of Galway 224
McCartneys Of Moira 516
McConnells Fish, Dublin 24 72
McCormack's at The Andrew
  Stone Gallery, Westport 364
McDaids, The, Dublin 2 30
McDonaghs Seafood House, Galway 224
McEvoys, Abbeyleix 313
McEvoys Farm Shop, Termonfeckin 347
McGeoughs Connemara
  Fine Foods, Oughterard 247
McGettigan & Sons, Donegal 204
McGrory's of Culdaff 202
McHugh's Bar, Belfast 482
McHughs Wine & Dine, Dublin 5 54
McKees Butchers, Maghera 533
McKees Country Store, Newt'nards 518
McKeown's Bar & Lounge, Dundalk 345
McMenamin's Townhouse 458
Meadowlands Hotel, Tralee 285
Meadowsweet Apiaries, Ballinahown 379
Meat Centre, The, Cork 138
Mella's Fudge, Clonakilty 164
Melody's Nire View Bar, 421
Merchant Hotel, The, Belfast 482
Merchants House, Londonderry 533
Merrion Hall, Dublin 4 50
Merrion Hotel, The, Dublin 2 30
Merry Ploughboy, The, Dublin 16 69
Mespil Hotel, Dublin 4 50
Metalman Brewing Company 434
Michael McGrath Butcher, Lismore 429
Michael's Food & Wine, Mt Merrion 89
Micheal O'Loughlin Butchers 329
Michie Sushi, Dublin 6 56
Midleton Park Hotel 185
Milano, The, Dublin 2 31
Milesian Restaurant, Castlegregory 258
Mill At Ballydugan, Downpatrick 509
Mill Restaurant, The, Dunfanaghy 205
Milleens, Beara 156
Mills Inn, Macroom 182
Mimosa Wine & Tapas Bar, Carlow 98
Mint Leaf, The, Dunboyne 370
Miss Courtney's Tea Rooms 278
Miss Crumpets, Adare 332

Mitchel House, Thurles	418
Mitchell & Son, Dublin 1	10
Mitchell's Restaurant, Clifden	238
Mitsuba, Dublin 1	10
Mobarnane House, Fethard	412
Molly's Yard, Belfast	482
Moloughney's, Dublin 3	43
Monaincha House & Health Spa	415
Monart Spa, Enniscorthy	450
Mont Clare Hotel, The, Dublin 2	31
Montenotte Hotel, The, Cork	138
Montmartre, Sligo	400
Montys of Kathmandu, The, Dublin 2	31
Moody Boar, Armagh	497
Mooreen House, Dublin 22	72
Moorings, The, Dungarvan	424
Moorings, The, Portmagee	282
Moran's Oyster Cottage, Kilcolgan	242
Morgan Hotel, The, Dublin 2	31
Morgans Fine Fish, Omeath	347
Mornington House, Multyfarnham	444
Morrison Hotel, The, Dublin 1	10
Morrissey's, Abbeyleix	313
Morrissey's Seafood Bar & Grill, Doonbeg	113
Mortell's, Limerick	329
Mortons of Galway, Galway	225
Mortons, Dublin 6	57
Moss Brook Farm, Magherafelt	535
Mossfield Farm, Birr	384
Mossies at Ulusker House, Beara	157
Motte Restaurant, Inistioge	302
Mount Callan Farmhouse Cheese, Ennistymon	116
Mount Falcon Estate, Ballina	353
Mount Juliet, Thomastown	310
Mount Vernon, New Quay	125
Mount Wolseley Hotel, Tullow	101
Mountshannon Hotel	125
Mourne Seafood Bar, Belfast	482
Mourne Seafood Bar Dundrum	510
Mourne Seafood Cookery School	514
Moy House, Lahinch	122
Moyvalley Estate, Moyvalley	294
Muckross Park Hotel, Killarney	280
Mulberry Garden, Dublin 4	51
Mulberrys Restaurant, Barna	229
Mulcahy's, Kenmare	269
Mullans Organic Farm, Limavady	530
Mullichain Café, St Mullins	100
MULLINGAR	441
Mullingar Park Hotel, Mullingar	442
Mulloys, Howth	83
Mulranny Park Hotel, Mulranny	360
MULRANNY	359
MULTYFARNHAM	443
Mulvarra House, St Mullins	100
Murphy Blacks, Kilkee	117
Murphy Fisheries, Inistioge	302
Murphy's Butchers, Tullow	101
Murphys Ice Cream & Café, Dingle	264
Murphys Ice Cream, Killarney	278
Murphys Ice Cream, Dublin 2	31
Muskerry Arms, Blarney	157
Mustard Seed at Echo Lodge	333
Muxnaw Lodge, Kenmare	270
MV Cill Airne , River Bar & Bistro, Dublin 1	10
Nancy's Bar, Ardara	198
Nash 19 Restaurant, Cork	138
Natasha's Living Foods, Dublin 12	66
Natures Gold, Greystones	468
Naughton's Bar, Kilkee	118
NAVAN	372
Neary's, Dublin 2	31
NEDE, The, Dublin 2	32
NENAGH	412
Nevins Newfield Inn, Mulranny	360
NEW ROSS	454
NEWCASTLE	516
Newforge House, Craigavon	498
Newgrange Gold Premium Irish Seed Oils, Slane	375
Newmans, Schull	193
Newpark Hotel, Kilkenny	307
Newpark House, Ennis	115
Newport House, Newport	361
NEWPORT	360
Newtown House Youghal	196
Nicholas Mosse, Bennettsbridge	300
Nick's Fish, Ashbourne	369

Nick's Fish, Newbridge 297
Nick's Seafood Rest., Killorglin 281
Nickys Plaice, Howth 84
Nirvana, Ballyshannon 200
No 57 Gourmet Kitchen, Macroom 182
No. 1 Pery Square Hotel, Limerick 329
Nolans Butchers, Kilcullen 292
Nolans Supermarket, Dublin 3 44
Nonna Rosa, Wexford 458
Northern Whig, Belfast 483
Nude Food, Dungarvan 424
Number 31, Dublin 2 32
Number 35, Kenmare 270
Number Fifty Five, Dingle 264
Nuremore Hotel, Carrickmacross 378
Nurney House Produce, Carbury 290

O'Briens Farm Shop, Cahir 406
O'Callaghan-Walshe, Rosscarbery 191
O'Callaghan's, Mitchelstown 189
O'Cathain Iasc Teo Fish, Dingle 264
O'Conaills Chocolates, Cork 139
O'Connell's, Tara Area 376
O'Connells Restaurant
  in Donnybrook, Dublin 4 51
O'Connor's Restaurant, Bantry 155
Ó'Crualaoí Butchers, Ballincollig 144
Ó'Crualaoí Butchers
  & Delicatessen, Carrigaline 159
O'Dohertys Butchers, Enniskillen 524
O'Donnell's Crisps, Clonmel 410
O'Donoghue's, Dublin 2 32
O'Donohue's Bakery, Tullamore 387
O'Donovan's, Midleton 185
O'Flynns Butchers, Cork 139
O'Grady's on the Pier, Barna 229
O'Keeffe's, Kilcock 291
O'Keeffe's of Clonakilty 164
O'Keeffes Shop, Cork 139
O'Leary's, Cootehill 105
O'Loclainn, Ballyvaughan 110
O'Looney's Bar, Lahinch 122
O'Neill's, Butlerstown 158
O'Neill's Pub & Townhouse, D2 32
O'Neills - The Point Bar 255
O'Neills Dry Cure Bacon Co 451

O'Shaughnessy's, Glin 334
O'Sullivan's Butchers, Sneem 283
O'Sullivans Bar, Crookhaven 167
O'Toole Master Butchers, Dublin 6W 58
O'Dowds, Roundstone 250
Oak Room Bistro, Cavan 104
Oakwood Arms Hotel, Shannon 127
Oar House, The, Howth 84
Oarsman, Carrick-on-Shannon 320
Oceanpath Seafood, Howth 84
Octopussys Seafood Tapas, Howth 84
Odessa Lounge & Grill, Dublin 2 32
Okra Green, Howth 84
Old Arch Bar & Bistro, Claremorris 356
Old Bank House, Bruff 333
Old Bank Town House, The, Kinsale 179
Old Barracks Bakery, Athenry 233
Old Boro, The, Swords 93
Old Cable House, The, Waterville 287
Old Convent Gourmet
  Hideaway, Clogheen 408
Old Fort, Shannonbridge 392
Old Ground Hotel, Ennis 115
Old Imperial Hotel, Youghal 196
Old Inn, Crawfordsburn 507
Old Jameson Distillery, Dublin 7 60
Old Kilbeggan Distillery, Kilbeggan 441
Old Pier, The, Dingle 266
Old Post Office, Comber 506
Old Presbytery, The, Kinsale 179
Old Schoolhouse Inn, Comber 507
Old Schoolhouse, Swords 93
Olde Castle & Red Hugh's, Donegal 203
Olde Glen Bar, The, Carrigart 202
Olde Post Inn, Cloverhill 105
Oldfarm, Nenagh 413
Oldtown Hill Bakehouse, Tullaroan 311
Olesyas Wine Bar, Dublin 2 33
Olive, Skerries 90
Omega Direct, Clonmel 410
On The Pigs Back, Cork 139
On The Wild Side, Castlegregory 259
One Pico Restaurant, Dublin 2 33
Oregano, Ballyclare 489
Organic Centre, Rossinver 322
Organic Delights Kiltegan 470

Organic Store, Birr	383
Organic Supermarket, Blackrock, Co Dublin	74
Organico Cafe Shop Bakery, Bantry	155
ORSO Kitchen & Bar, Cork	140
Oscars Restaurant, Mullingar	443
Oscars Seafood Bistro, Galway	225
Osta Café & Wine Bar, Sligo	400
Ostan Gweedore, Bunbeg	200
Ostan Inis Meain, Aran Islands	231
Out of the Blue, Dingle	265
Ouzos, Dalkey	75
Ouzos Bar & Grill, Blackrock	74
Owen McMahon Butchers, Belfast	483
OX Belfast	483
Oyster Tavern, The, Tralee	286
Oystercatcher Bistro, Carlingford	341
Oystercatcher Lodge, Carlingford	341
Oysters Restaurant, Cork	140
Oysters Restaurant, Strabane	539
P F McCarthys, Kenmare	270
P. McCormack, Dun Laoghaire	79
Packie's, Kenmare	270
Palace Bar, The, Dublin 2	33
Pandora Bell, Ballysimon	333
Panem, Dublin 1,	10
Pantry & Corkscrew, Westport	365
Pantry, The, Nenagh	413
Pantry, The , Midleton	185
Pantry, The, Kilkee	118
Paris Bakery & Pastry, Dublin 1	10
Park Hotel Kenmare, Kenmare	271
Park House Hotel, Galway	225
Park Inn by Radisson, Cork Airport	129
Park Restaurant, The, Arklow	462
Parknasilla Resort, Sneem	283
Parson's Nose, The, Hillsborough	511
Partridges Artisan Café & Fine Food Shop, Gorey	453
Pat Shortt's Bar, Castlemartyr	160
Patisserie de Pascal	202
Patrick & Mary Walsh's Vegetables	187
Paul Arthurs Restaurant, Kircubbin	515
Pavilion/Earthly Delights Cafe	140
Pavilion, The, Limerick	329
Pax House, Dingle	265
Pay As You Please, Killarney	278
Pearl Brasserie, Dublin 2	33
Péarla na Mara, Oranmore	246
Pembroke Hotel, Kilkenny	307
Pembroke Townhouse, Dublin 4	51
Peperina Garden Bistro, Dublin 6	57
Peploe's Wine Bistro, Dublin 2	34
Pepper Mill, The, Nenagh	413
Pepper Pot, The, Dublin 2	34
Pepperstack Bistro at Rosies Bar Lr Aghada	187
Perryville House, Kinsale	179
Pettitts SuperValu, Wexford	458
Pheasant, nr Hillsborough	511
Pheasants Hill Farm, Downpatrick	509
Phelim Byrne Cookery Academy, Wexford	458
Phoenix Café, The, Dublin 8	64
Phoenix, The, Tralee	286
Pichet, Dublin 2	34
Picnic, Killyleagh	515
Pielows Restaurant, Dublin 18	71
Pier 36, Donaghadee	508
Pier Head Restaurant, Kinvara	242
Pier House Guest House, Aran Is.	231
Pig's Ear, The, Dublin 2	34
Pilgrim's Rest, Rosscarbery	191
Pillo Hotel, Ashbourne	369
Pink Elephant, Kilbrittain	175
PinkGinger, Dublin 4	51
Pinocchio Restaurant, Dublin 6	57
Pinsapo Restaurant	526
PJ O'Hares, Carlingford	341
Plan B, Dublin 7	60
Plough Inn, Hillsborough	511
Poachers Inn, The, Bandon	153
Polo D Restaurant, Ballyconnell	103
Pontoon Bridge Hotel, Foxford	358
Port House, The, Dublin 2	34
PORTADOWN	499
Portaferry Hotel, Portaferry	519
Porterhouse North, Dublin 9	66
Porterhouse, The, Dublin 2	35
Portfinn Lodge, Leenane	243
Portlaoise Heritage Hotel, Portlaoise	316

PORTLAOISE — 315
Portmarnock Hotel & Golf Links — 89
PORTRUSH — 494
PORTSTEWART — 535
Pot Belly Restaurant, Gilford — 498
Potted Hen Bistro, Belfast — 483
Powerscourt Terrace Café — 465
Powersfield House, Dungarvan — 424
Primacy Meats Food Village — 505
Purple Heather, Kenmare — 271
Purple, Tarmonbarry — 392
Purty Kitchen, The, Monkstown — 88
Putóg de Róiste, Ballyvourney — 149

QC's, Cahirciveen — 255
Quails at the Gallery, Banbridge — 502
Quality Hotel, Clonakilty — 164
Quality Sea Veg, Burtonport — 202
Quarry Restaurant, Cahirciveen — 255
Quarrymount Free Range Meats — 384
Quay Co-op, Cork — 140
Quay Cottage Restaurant, Westport — 365
Quay Food Company, Kinsale — 179
Quay House, The, Clifden — 238
Quays, The, Portavogie — 519
Quealy's Café Bar, Dungarvan — 424
Queen of Tarts, The, Dublin 2 — 35
Queen's Bar & Restaurant, Dalkey — 76
Quigleys, Nenagh — 414
Quinlan's Kerry Fish, Caherciveen — 256
Quinlans Seafood Bar, Killarney — 278

Rachels Garden Café, Leighlinbridge — 99
Radharc An Chlair, Aran Islands — 231
Radisson Blu Farnham Estate, Cavan — 105
Radisson Blu Hotel & Spa, Cork — 140
Radisson Blu Hotel & Spa, Limerick — 330
Radisson Blu Hotel & Spa, Sligo — 401
Radisson Blu Hotel, Athlone — 438
Radisson Blu Hotel, Belfast — 483
Radisson Blu Hotel, Dublin Airport — 78
Radisson Blu Hotel, Letterkenny — 209
Radisson Blu Royal Hotel, Dublin 8 — 64
Radisson Blu St Helen's Hotel, D4 — 51
Raftery's Bar, Craughwell — 240
Ragazzi, Dalkey — 76

Raheen Woods Hotel, Athenry — 233
Railway Lodge, Oughterard — 247
Ramada Da Vinci's Hotel, L'Derry — 533
Ramada Hotel Belfast, Belfast — 484
Ramore Restaurants, Portrush — 495
Randles Hotel, Killarney — 278
Rasam, Dun Laoghaire — 80
Rathaspeck Manor, Rathaspeck — 455
RATHLIN ISLAND — 495
Rathmullan House, Rathmullan — 212
Rathsallagh House, Dunlavin — 291
Rathwood, Tullow — 101
Rattlebag Café, Carlow — 98
Ravenhill House, Belfast — 484
RAW Restaurant, Galway — 226
Ray Collier, Howth — 85
Rayanne Country House, Holywood — 513
Raymond's Restaurant, Midleton — 186
Real Olive Company, The, Cork — 140
Red Bank, Skerries — 91
Red Cliff Lodge, Spanish Point — 127
Red Door Restaurant, Fahan — 206
Red Door Tea Room, Ballintoy — 488
Redcastle Hotel, Moville — 211
Regan Organic, Enniscorthy — 450
Rene Cusack Fish, Ennis — 115
Rene Cusack Fish, Limerick — 330
Renvyle House Hotel, Renvyle — 250
Residence - Restaurant
  Forty One, Dublin 2 — 35
Restaurant 23, Warrenpoint — 520
Restaurant at Donnybrook Fair, D4 — 52
Restaurant Number Thirty Two — 346
Restaurant Patrick Guilbaud, D2 — 35
Restaurant Ten Fourteen, Dublin 3 — 44
Revive Café, Galway — 226
Rezidor Park Inn, Shannon — 127
Rhu-Gorse, Lough Eske — 210
Richmond House, Cappoquin — 422
Richy's Restaurant
  & The R Café, Clonakilty — 164
Rigbys, Dublin 4 — 52
Rigneys Farm, Kilcornan — 334
Ring of Kerry Quality Lamb — 256
Rising Tide, The, Glounthaune — 174
Ristorante Rinuccini, Kilkenny — 308

Ristorante Terrazzo Italia, Dublin 2	36
Ritz Carlton Powerscourt	465
River Bistro, Limerick	330
River House, Cahir	406
River Lee Hotel, The, Cork	141
Riverbank House Hotel, Wexford	458
Riverbank Restaurant, Dromohair	321
Riversdale Farm Guesthouse, Ballinamore	318
Riverside Bistro, Doolin	112
Riverside Cafe, The, Skibbereen	194
Riverside Park, Hotel	450
Roadford House Restaurant, Doolin	112
Roadside Tavern, The, Lisdoonvarna	123
Roberts Cove Inn, Carrigaline area	159
Roberts of Dalkey	76
Rochestown Park Hotel, Cork	141
Rock Lobster, Dublin 4	52
Roe Park Resort, Limavady	530
Roganstown Hotel, Swords	93
Rolf's, Baltimore	151
Roly's Bistro, Cafe & Bakery, D4	52
Romanos, Dublin 1	11
Rory Conner Knives, Bantry	155
Rory O'Connell Cookery School,	146
Rosapenna Hotel & Golf, Downings	204
ROSCREA	415
Rose Garden, Kenmare	271
Rosemount House, Wexford	458
Rosleague Manor Hotel, Letterfrack	244
Rosquil House, Kilkenny	308
Ross Lake House Hotel, Oughterard	248
Ross, The, Killarney	279
ROSSES POINT	397
ROSSLARE & AREA	455
Rossnaree, Slane	375
Roundstone House Hotel & Vaughan's Restaurant	250
Roundwood House, Mountrath	315
Roundwood Inn, Roundwood	472
Rowan Tree Cafe Bar, Ennis	115
Royal Court Hotel, Portrush	495
Royal Marine Hotel, Dun Laoghaire	80
Rua Cafe & Deli, Castlebar	356
Russell Gallery, The, New Quay	125
Russell Restaurant, Navan	373
Rustic Stone, The, Dublin 2	36
Ryan's Bar, Navan	373
Ryan's Farm, Kells Area	372
Ryan's of Parkgate Street, Dublin 8	64
Ryeland House Cookery School	301
Saagar Indian Restaurant, Dublin 2	36
Saba, Dublin 2	36
Sage, Westport	365
Sage Café, Limerick	330
Sage Restaurant, Midleton	186
Salamanca, Dublin 2	37
Sallyport House, Kenmare	271
Salt Bistro, Belfast	484
Salt Café, Monkstown	88
Salty Dog Hotel & Bistro, Bangor	505
San Lorenzos, Dublin 2	37
Sand House Hotel, Rossnowlagh	213
Sandymount Hotel, Dublin 4	53
Sandymount House, Abbeyleix	313
Sarah Baker Cookery School	411
Saratoga Lodge, Templemore	416
Sargasso, Letterkenny	209
Savoy Hotel, Limerick	331
Sawers Deli, Belfast	484
Scallys SuperValu, Clonakilty	165
Scholars Townhouse Hotel	344
Schoolhouse Hotel, Dublin 4	53
Scullery, The Nenagh	415
SD Bell & Co Ltd, Belfast	484
Sea Mist House, Clifden	238
Sea Shore Farm House, Kenmare	271
Seabank Bistro, Malahide	88
Seafield Hotel, nr Gorey	453
Seafood Centre, The, Galway	226
Seagrass, Dublin 2	37
Sean Tierney, Clonmel	410
Sean's Bar, Athlone	438
Seapoint Fish & Grill, Monkstown	88
Seaview House Hotel, Ballylickey	148
Secret Garden Centre, Newmarket	190
Select Stores, Dalkey	76
Seven Horseshoes, Belturbet	104
Seven, Dublin 7	60
Seymour Organic Farm, Borrisokane	405
Seymour's Fine Foods, Bandon	153

Sha-Roe Bistro, Clonegal	98
Shamrat Restaurant, Carrick-on-Shannon	320
Shanagarry Smoked Salmon	188
Shanahan's on the Green, Dublin 2	37
Sheebeen, The, Westport	365
Sheedys Hotel & Restaurant, Lisdoonvarna	123
Sheelin Brewery & Kitchen	525
Sheen Falls Lodge, Kenmare	272
Shelbourne Dublin, The, Dublin 2	37
Shelburne Lodge, Kenmare	272
Shells Bakery Cafe, Strandhill	402
Sheraton, Athlone	438
Sheridans Cheesemongers, Carnaross	370
Sheridans Cheesemongers, Galway	226
Sheridans Cheesemongers, Dublin 2	38
Sherwood Park House, Ballon	96
Shu, Belfast	485
Siam Thai Restaurant, Malahide	88
Side Door, The, Cavan	105
Silk Road Café, Dublin 2	38
Silver Fox Restaurant, Kilmore Quay	454
Silver Hills Foods, Emyvale	379
Silver Restaurant, Newbridge	298
Simply Deanes, Banbridge	503
Sion Hill House & Gardens, Waterford	434
SiRocco's Restaurant, Tullamore	387
Skeaghanore West Cork Duck, Ballydehob	147
Skelligs Chocolate, Ballinskellig	254
Skinflint, Dublin 2	38
Skipper, The, Dingle	266
SLANE	374
Slice @ The Model, Sligo	400
Slieve Aughty Centre, Loughrea	245
Slieve Russell Hotel, Ballyconnell	103
Sligo Park Hotel, Sligo	401
SLIGO	397
Smoke House, The, Killarney	279
Smugglers Creek Inn, Rossnowlagh	213
Smugglers Inn, The Waterville	287
Snug, The Bantry	155
SoHo Dublin 2, Dublin 2	38
Sol Bistro, Thomastown	310
Sol Rio, Westport	365
Sol y Sombra, Killorglin	281
Solaris Botanicals, Galway	226
Solis Lough Eske Hotel	210
Sonairte National Ecology Centre, Laytown	372
Soulful Bistro, Dublin 7	60
Soup Dragon, Dublin 1	11
Source Sligo	401
South Aran House & Fisherman's Restaurant Aran Is.	231
South Pole Inn, Annascaul	253
Spa Seafoods & Café, Tralee	285
Spaniard Inn, The, Kinsale	179
Spearman, The, Cashel	408
Spice Indian Restaurant, Wexford	459
Spillanes, Castlegregory	259
Spinnaker Bar, Dunmore East	426
Spinning Wheel, The, Ballincollig	145
Spirit Store, Dundalk	346
Springfort Hall Hotel, Mallow	183
Sqigl Restaurant & Roches Bar, Duncannon	449
St Johns House, Lecarrow	390
St Kyrans Country House & Restaurant, Virginia	106
St Tola Organic Goat Cheese, Inagh	117
Stable Diet, Wexford Town	460
Stables Emporium & Tearoom, Birr	383
Stag's Head, The, Dublin 2	38
Stangmore Townhouse, Dungannon	538
Stanley House, Schull	193
Star Anise, Cork	141
Starfish Cafe & Bistro, Dunfanaghy	205
Station House Hotel, Kilmessan	372
Stauntons on the Green, Dublin 2	39
Steak Shop, The, Greystones	468
Steam Café, Clifden	238
Stella Maris Hotel, Ballycastle	354
Stella Maris Hotel, Kilkee	118
Step House Hotel, The, Borris	97
Stephen Pearce Pottery, Shanagarry	188
Stephen's Green Hotel, Dublin 2	39
Steps of Rome, Dublin 2	39
Stillorgan Park Hotel, Stillorgan	92
Stockwell Artisan Foods, Drogheda	344
Stone Cutters Kitchen, Doolin	113

Stonehouse Restaurant, Clonmel	410
Stonewell Irish Craft Cider, Kinsale	180
Stoop Your Head, Skerries	91
Stradbally Fayre, Stradbally	316
Strand House, Portstewart	536
Strand House Bar, Strandhill	402
Strand Inn, Dunmore East	427
Strand Restaurant	
& Guesthouse, Kilkee	118
Strandeen B&B, Portstewart	536
Strandfield House, Dundalk	346
Strandhill Lodge & Suites	402
Strawberry Field, Kenmare	273
Stuffed Olive, The Bantry	156
Sugar & Spice, Bunclody	447
Suir Inn, The, Cheekpoint	423
Suitor Gallery, Ballygawley	538
Suki Tea, Belfast	485
Summerhouse, The, Lismore	429
Summervilles of Greystones	468
Sun Kee, Belfast	485
Sunville House, Ballycotton	146
Superquinn, Lucan	85
Sussex, The, Dublin 4	53
Swans Chinese, Kilkenny	308
Sweeney's, Portballintrae	494
Sweet Pea Café, Warrenpoint	520
Sweetbank Farm, Newcastle	470
T. Staunton, Lecanvey	359
Table, Cork	141
Tahilla Cove Country House, Sneem	283
Talbot Hotel, Belmullet	354
Talbot Hotel, Wexford	459
Tankard, The, Fenit	267
Tankardstown House, Slane	375
Tannery, Moira	516
Tannery Cookery School	425
Tannery, The, Dungarvan	425
Tara Hotel, Killybegs	208
Tartine at The Distillers, Bushmills	491
Tartine Organic Bakery, Swords	93
Taste, Castletownbere	161
Taste a Memory Foods, Ballincollig	145
Taste Matter, Loughrea	245
Tasty Tart, Termonfeckin	347
Tattie Hoaker, The, Roscommon	391
Tavern Bar & Restaurant, Murrisk	366
Tea Room, The, Bantry	156
Teach an Tae Tea Rooms, Aran Is.	232
Teach de Broc, Ballybunion	255
Teach Nan Phaidai, Aran Islands	232
Ted Browne (seafood), Dingle	265
Teddys, Bangor	505
Tedfords Restaurant, Belfast	485
Teltown House, Navan	374
Temple Bar Hotel, Dublin 2	39
Temple Gate Hotel, Ennis	115
Temple House, Ballymote	394
Tempted Irish Craft Cider, Lisburn	494
Ten Square Hotel, Belfast	485
Tenors Grill Room, Naas	296
TERMONFECKIN	347
Terra Madre, Dublin 1	11
Terroirs, Dublin 4	53
Thady Inn, Farnanes	170
Thai House Restaurant, Dalkey	76
Thatch Bar & Restaurant, Birr	383
Thatch, The, Belleek	522
The Bay Leaf, Turlough	357
The Dining Room	
at La Stampa, Dublin 2	39
The Islanders Rest, Sherkin	152
The Lovely Food Co, Dublin 6W	58
Thomas Fletcher, Naas	296
Thomas Moore Tavern, Wexford	459
Thomas's, Dublin 18	71
THOMASTOWN	309
Thornton's Restaurant, Dublin 2	39
Three Q's, Greystones	469
Thyme & Co Café, Ballycastle	489
Thyme Out, Dalkey	76
Thyme Restaurant, Athlone	439
Tibors Bistro, Dublin 3	44
Tickety Moo, Killadeas	525
Tiernan Brothers, Foxford	359
Tig Bhric, Dingle	266
Tig Congaile, Aran Islands	232
Tigh Fitz, Aran Islands	232
Tigh Neachtain	
& Artisan Restaurant, Galway	227
Tin Pub, The, Ahakista	144

Tinnock Farm Produce, Campile 448
Tir na Nog, Sligo 401
Toby's Handcrafted Cider 500
Toddies at The Bulman 181
Tom Crean Fish & Wine, Kenmare 272
Tom Durcan, Cork 142
Tom Kearneys Butchers, Waterford 435
Tom Sheridans, Galway 227
Toners, Dublin 2 40
Tonic, Blackrock, Co Dublin 74
Toons Bridge Dairy, Macroom 182
Torc Café & Foodhall, Longford 336
Toscana, Dublin 2 40
Tower Hotel Derry, Londonderry 533
Tower Hotel Waterford 435
Tower Winebar & Grill, Drogheda 344
Town Hall Café, Ennis 115
Town Kildare Street, Dublin 2 40
Townsend House, Birr 383
Trá Bán Restaurant, Strandhill 402
Traders Coffee House, Drogheda 344
Travelodge, Cork 129
Travelodge, Dublin Airport 78
Travelodge, Galway 227
Trax Brasserie, Naas 296
Trean House, Tremone 213
Treyvaud's Restaurant, Killarney 279
TriBeCa, Dublin 6 57
Tribes, Dun Laoghaire 80
Trident Hotel, Kinsale 180
TRIM 376
Trinity Capital Hotel, Dublin 2 40
Trinity Lodge, Dublin 2 40
Triple House Restaurant, T'feckin 347
Triskel Cheese, Portlaw 429
Trocadero Restaurant, Dublin 2 40
Trouble Brewing, Allenwood 289
Truffle Fairy, The, Thomastown 310
Truffle Pig Fine Foods, Kenmare 272
Tullamore Court Hotel, Tullamore 387
TULLAMORE 385
Tulsi, Ennis 116
Tuscany Bistro, Annacotty 332
Tuscany Bistro, Killaloe 120
Twelfth Lock, The, Dublin 15 68
Twelve Hotel, The, Barna 229

Uluru, Armagh 497
Ummera Smokehouse, Timoleague 195
Úna's Pies, Ballincollig 145
Unglerts Bakery, Ennistymon 116
Unicorn Restaurant, Dublin 2 41
Uno Restaurant & Cocktail Bar 524
Upstairs @ McCambridges 227
Urru, Bandon 153

Valentia Island Farm Ice Cream 286
Vanilla Pod Restaurant, Kells 371
Vasco, Fanore 116
Vaughan Lodge, Lahinch 122
Vaughans Anchor Inn, Liscannor 122
Venison, Coopershill, Riverstown 396
Venue Bar & Restaurant, The,
   Strandhill 403
Vermilion, Dublin 6W 58
Via Veneto, Enniscorthy 450
Victoria Hall, Carrick-on-Shannon 320
Vie de Chateaux, Naas 297
Vienna Woods Hotel 173
Viewmount House, Longford 336
Vikki's, Cork 142
Village at Lyons, Celbridge 290
Village Tavern, The, Shannonbridge 385
Vintage Kitchen, The , Dublin 2 41
Virginia's Guesthouse, Kenmare 272
Vittos Restaurant, Carrick 320
Vogelaars Apple Farm 427
Vsughans, Kilfenora 117

Wagamama, Cork 142
Wagamama, Dublin 2 41
Walter Raleigh Hotel, Youghal 196
Walton Court Café, Oysterhaven 190
Wandesforde House, Castlecomer 301
Water Margin, Coleraine 529
Waterfall Farm Shop, Enniskerry 466
Waterfoot Hotel, Londonderry 533
Waterford Castle Hotel 435
WATERFORD 430
Waterfront, The, Rosses Point 397
Waterfront, The, Baltimore 151
Waterloo House, Dublin 4 53
Watermill Lodge, Lisnaskea 526

WatersEdge Hotel, Cobh — 166
Waterside, Graiguenamanagh — 302
Waterside House Hotel, Donabate — 77
Weafer & Cooper, Dun Laoghaire — 80
Weirs, Multyfarnham — 444
Wellington Park Hotel, Belfast — 486
West Cork Gourmet Store, Ballydehob — 148
West Cork Hotel, Skibbereen — 194
West Cork Salamis, Schull — 193
West End Bar & Restaurant, Fenit — 267
West End House, Killarney — 279
West Kerry Brewery — 266
Westbury Hotel, The, Dublin 2 — 41
Westcove Farm Shop, Castlecove — 258
Westgate Design, Wexford — 459
Westgrove Hotel, Clane — 290
Westin Dublin, The, Dublin 2 — 41
Westlodge Hotel, The Bantry — 156
Westport Plaza Hotel, Westport — 366
Westport Woods Hotel, Westport — 366
WESTPORT — 361
Westville Hotel, Enniskillen — 524
Westwood, The, Galway — 228
Wexford Home Preserves — 455
WEXFORD — 456
White Cottages, The, Skerries — 91
White Gables Restaurant — 245
White Gypsy, Templemore — 416
White Horse Inn, Saintfield — 519
White Horses Restaurant, Ardmore — 420
White Tea at Brian S Nolan, Dun Laoghaire — 81
Whitefriar Grill, Dublin 2 — 42
Whitepark House, Ballintoy — 488
Whites of Wexford — 459
Whitewater Brewery, Kilkeel — 514

Whitford House Hotel, Wexford — 460
Wicklow Cheese, Arklow — 462
Wicklow Heather, The, Laragh — 466
Wild Geese Restaurant, Adare — 332
Wild Goose Grill, The, Dublin 6 — 57
Wild Honey Inn, Lisdoonvarna — 124
Wilde Irish Chocolates, Tuamgraney — 127
Wildside Catering, Shanagarry — 188
Willie Scannell, Ballycotton — 146
Winding Stair, The Dublin 1 — 11
Windsor Bakery & Café, Banbridge — 503
Winehouse, The Tuam — 251
Wineport Lodge Glasson — 440
WJ Kavanagh's, Dublin 1 — 12
Woodcock Smokery — 161
Wooden Spoon, The, Killaloe — 120
Woodenbridge Hotel — 472
Woodford, The, Cork — 142
Woodhill House, Ardara — 198
Woodlands Country House, Gorey — 453
Woodside Farm, Midleton Area — 188
Wrights of Marino, Dublin 3 — 44
Wynns Hotel, Dublin 1 — 12

Yamamori Noodles, Dublin 2 — 42
Yawl Bay Seafoods Ltd — 196
Yellow Door, Belfast — 486
Yellow Door Deli, Bakery & Café, Portadown — 500
Yellow Pepper, Letterkenny — 209
Yew Tree, The Lecarrow — 390

Zen, Belfast — 486
Zest, Clane — 290
Zetland Country House, Cashel — 236
Zuni, Kilkenny — 308